Parties and Elections in America

Parties and Elections in America

The Electoral Process

Fifth Edition

L. Sandy Maisel and Mark D. Brewer

ROWMAN & LITTLEFIELD PUBLISHERS, INC.
Lanham • Boulder • New York • Toronto • Plymouth, UK

ROWMAN & LITTLEFIELD PUBLISHERS, INC.

Published in the United States of America
by Rowman & Littlefield Publishers, Inc.
A wholly owned subsidiary of The Rowman & Littlefield Publishing Group, Inc.
4501 Forbes Boulevard, Suite 200, Lanham, Maryland 20706
www.rowmanlittlefield.com

Estover Road, Plymouth PL6 7PY, United Kingdom

British Library Cataloguing in Publication Information Available

Library of Congress Cataloging-in-Publication Data

Maisel, Louis Sandy, 1945–
    Parties and elections in America : the electoral process / L. Sandy Maisel and Mark D. Brewer.—5th ed.
      p. cm.
    Includes bibliographical references and index.
    ISBN-13: 978-0-7425-4764-3 (pbk. : alk. paper)
    ISBN-10: 0-7425-4764-7 (pbk. : alk. paper)
    1. Elections—United States. 2. Political campaigns—United States. 3. Political parties—United States. I. Brewer, Mark D. II. Title.
JK1965.M35 2008
324.973—dc22

2007028848

Printed in the United States of America

⊗ ™ The paper used in this publication meets the minimum requirements of American National Standard for Information Sciences—Permanence of Paper for Printed Library Materials, ANSI/NISO Z39.48-1992.

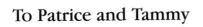

To Patrice and Tammy

Contents

Figures, Tables, and Boxes

FIGURES

TABLES

BOXES

Preface

You don't have to unwind at the end of the day with C-SPAN or spend your nights dreaming of conversations with Tim Russert to be excited about American politics these days. The Supreme Court–decided 2000 presidential election, which we discussed in the preface to the previous edition of this book, was followed by the highly polarized and hotly contested presidential election of 2004 and 2006 midterm elections that generated much more attention than is normal for off-year contests. As we write the preface for the fifth edition in June 2007, the 2008 presidential race is already well under way, off to the earliest start ever. And not only is it under way, people are already paying attention.

Who can blame them? There are certainly a large number of compelling storylines among the 2008 hopefuls. Can Senator Hillary Clinton become the first woman to garner a major party's presidential nomination? Can she become the first female president? Can Senator Barack Obama become the first African American to do the same? Will former vice president Al Gore, more popular than ever due to his Oscar-winning documentary *An Inconvenient Truth*, decide to enter the race late? The dramatics are by no means the province of Democrats alone. On the Republican side many wonder how his membership in the Church of Jesus Christ of Latter-day Saints will affect the candidacy of former Massachusetts governor Mitt Romney. Can "America's Mayor," Rudy Giuliani, become the first American president of Italian heritage? And what about former Tennessee senator and actor Fred Thompson? Can he follow in the footsteps of Ronald Reagan and go from actor to president? For candidates of both parties, the issue of the ongoing war in Iraq looms in the background, demanding attention.

The 2008 election season promises to be a tense affair. In the chapters ahead we hope to give students the tools to analyze the upcoming elections, from nomination to voting day. The election of 2008 provides us with the unique opportunity to study the two major parties during a period of relative parity in the electorate: How will the Democratic and Republican parties organize to maximize voter turnout and electoral success in 2008? How important are the parties during this election cycle to the candidates running for office? How important is party label to the voters heading to the polls this November? What role will the parties play in governing in the 110th Congress? What about the media and campaign finance in 2008? This book aims to provide students with the theoretical tools and historical background to answer these questions and more.

Chapter 1 is a conceptual introduction to the study of political parties and elections: parties are defined, and their role in the electoral process is made clear. Chapter 2 recognizes that modern political parties are a distinctly American invention. Since the founding of our nation, politicians have taken an ambivalent position on the American party system, playing a role in its development while bemoaning its existence. This chapter explains the evolution of today's Democratic and Republican parties in terms of six distinct party systems in American political history. We examine how each system has contributed to the development of modern party organizations—their institutions, structure, and norms.

But just who participates in the parties, in the elections, and in the American political system? Chapter 3 examines who votes and who does not, and who participates in political activities beyond casting a ballot on election day. In this chapter we look at motives and incentives for political participation, providing a detailed examination and careful review of the voluminous professional literature on voting behavior. Chapter 4 expands our understanding of political participation to organized groups and the extent to which they influence the voting behavior of their members. Political observers, from Tocqueville to V. O. Key, have commented that Americans congenitally tend to join groups and that they often relate to the electoral process as members of their groups. It could even be argued that some interest groups fit our definition of *political party* almost as well as the Democratic and Republican parties do and indeed better than some minor parties. Organized group behavior has long had an impact on American politics—a phenomenon perhaps more important today than at any other time in our history, as groups vie for influence over policy outcomes in 2008, from immigration to health care, in a world where money continues to flow freely into political life.

In the twenty-first century, no one doubts the importance of money in electoral politics. Campaign financing is such an important topic that an entire chapter has been devoted to exploring the current situation. Chapter 5 examines the evolution of campaign finance reforms, from the 1970s to the seven-year battle to pass

McCain-Feingold and the Bipartisan Campaign Reform Act of 2002 and its aftermath. Data are presented that summarize the costs of maintaining our democracy. In addition, we examine the sources to which politicians turn for campaign funding, with particular emphasis on political action committees.

Chapters 6, 7, 8, and 9 examine nominations and election campaigns in the United States, with the former two dealing with gubernatorial, senatorial, congressional, and state and local elections, and with the latter two, the presidential election. Chapter 6 begins with a discussion of common views on the nominating process and then examines how reality differs from these views. We also explore the development of the direct primary as a means of securing partisan nominations, the variety of primaries that exists in various jurisdictions, and the politics of securing party nominations.

Chapter 7 examines general election campaigns below the presidential level. The conventional wisdom holds that politics has changed dramatically as the age of television and computers has evolved. The argument presented in this chapter is that "new politics" is very much in evidence in some campaigns but that the "old politics," the politics of personal contact and detailed organization, remains essential for many local politicians. In addition, the chapter explores the role of third parties, more specifically, what factors determine whether third parties are likely to have an influence in elections.

The American presidential nomination process is so complex that it is often misunderstood in the national media. In chapter 8, we explain changes to the nomination process and review recent presidential contests and the strategic considerations that determine how such contests were fought. We consider conflicting viewpoints on the role of national party conventions, the ultimate spectacle in American politics: Are they important elements of the electoral process or, as their critics would argue, useless vestiges from a bygone era, no longer worthy of serious consideration?

When many Americans think of election campaigns, they focus on the general election of the president. Chapter 9 considers how such an election is organized, what the recent strategies were (and what tactics were used for implementing those strategies), and what impact the campaigns ultimately had. While the topic would seem to be a familiar one, many of the nuances of presidential campaigns are obscure except to the most practiced observer.

Chapter 10 highlights another distinct aspect of the electoral process: the impact of the media—both paid and unpaid—on American elections. Constraints on the ways in which newspapers and television cover politics explain some of such media's apparent shortcomings. The controversy over negative advertising comprises an important aspect of the discussion of paid media, as does the use and possible misuse of issue advocacy advertising.

Chapter 11 examines the role of parties in government. The American political system is not a parliamentary one; it is not structured to encourage strong and responsible party governance. Instead, the American democracy is one of checks and balances in which separate institutions share legislative power. Parties are clearly the most dominant organizing element in Congress, but their leaders are constrained in how much they can control policy outcomes. Members of Congress owe their seats to their constituents, not to party leadership. This chapter explores congressional constraints to partisan governance, within and across both the House and the Senate, and the impact such constraints have on policies in the 110th Congress.

Finally, in chapter 12, we return to the themes raised in the introductory chapter: How well does the electoral process function? What role do parties play in the modern American democracy, and how does that differ from their traditional function? What institutions have replaced parties in functional terms? What are the consequences for our political system of candidate-oriented campaigns? . . . of increased political action committee influence? . . . of public financing? . . . of the recently passed campaign finance reform? What does this view of the electoral process imply about the link between (1) parties as the organizing structure of elections and (2) parties as the organizing structure of our governmental institutions? Can and should this process be reformed?

NEW TO THE FIFTH EDITION

The most important change to the new edition of this book is the addition of a new coauthor. We share a passion for teaching and a commitment to scholarship, and we hope that this book reflects both. Our goals for this text are threefold: first, to give students the tools to analyze the political world around them, empowering them to be political pundits in their own right; second, to get students to see that the outcomes of the electoral battles being waged in 2008 affect their lives—whether the contests are between the Democratic and Republican parties or between candidates and challengers at any other level of government; third, and most important, to get students excited about politics. Of course, we do not expect you to wait by your mailbox in the freezing rain for the next issue of *Congressional Quarterly Weekly Report,* nor do we anticipate that you will change your Friday night plans to watch Gwen Ifell's *Washington Week.* Rather, we simply hope you will be an interested, informed, and educated participant in, and analyst of, our exciting electoral process.

Understanding modern politics means understanding political history—today's parties and electoral processes did not emerge full grown. This new edition reflects our continuing emphasis on the foundations of our modern political system by providing a historical context where appropriate throughout the text. We have also extensively revised the chapters on campaign finance (chapter 5), the media (chapter 10), and party governance (chapter 11), owing to the important changes occurring in each area. Other chapters have been revised and updated, but the changes are less significant than in those mentioned here.

Acknowledgments

In preparing this fifth edition of this text, Sandy Maisel wants to start by acknowledging the contributions and friendship of Kara Buckley, his collaborator on the most recent iterations. He also thanks Mark Brewer for joining him on this enterprise and for his incredible efforts at bringing this edition in on time. And Brewer thanks Maisel for inviting him to join in this project.

We have had the opportunity to reflect on the comments of those who used the first four editions and to see how those have worked in various classrooms. Maisel has also edited four editions of an anthology designed for a course on parties and elections (Maisel 2002 is the most recent version) and to discuss topics for inclusion in works of this type with a wide range of scholars in political science and closely related fields.

We are also indebted to all of the colleagues with whom we have discussed our mutual concerns about how to teach political parties and elections for their advice on improving this work. The addition of a separate chapter in this text on the role of the media and the expansion of a number of other points are directly attributable to comments and reactions of friends in this profession. We want to begin by thanking all of those who have aided this work in that way.

Similarly, this book has benefited from the comments of those for whom it is intended, student readers. Sandy Maisel is grateful to generation after generation of Colby students—and to those students he has taught at the University of Melbourne, at Monash University, at Harvard, and at Stanford. One of the real joys of teaching is to have the opportunity to test one's ideas on the palette of relatively unpainted young minds and to learn from the ways in which the colors are reflected. For more than three decades Maisel has tested his ideas about elections and politics on Colby students. Their insights have helped to shape and refine those ideas; their reactions have led to a better understanding of what works and what does not work in a teaching environment, of how complex ideas can be effectively communicated, of how concern and enthusiasm can be transmitted to those who will carry the political banners in the years ahead. Brewer feels the same way about the students he has had the opportunity to work with, first at Colby and now at the University of Maine. For Brewer one of the biggest rewards of teaching is witnessing his students' passion during campaigns and elections. In a very real sense this book is written for students and because of students; any success it enjoys as a teaching tool is a direct result of what has been learned from them.

This edition, like previous ones, has benefited from research assistance from particular students. Much of the work of students cited in earlier editions is still in evidence in this work. For the fifth edition, Sarah Whitfield was Maisel's principal research assistant. He is also indebted to Andrea Berchowitz, Brooke McNally, Abe Summers, and Claire Walsh for helping to update material throughout the text. Kate Gould was Brewer's research assistant, and she did a wonderful job in a tight time frame.

As one finishes work on a text, one almost automatically thinks back to those who have influenced the book's development in less specific ways. We feel fortunate to be part of a very special community, the community of scholars, in this case the specific community of scholars of American politics. Our work has been influenced over the years by conversations with and encouragement from literally scores of fellow political scientists. We want to mention specifically those close friends and colleagues who have influenced our professional development—John Bibby, Dave Brady, Chuck Bullock, Joe Cooper, Linda Fowler, Paul Herrnson, Chuck Jones, Ruth Jones, Suzanne Mettler, the late Warren Miller, Eric Petersen, Ron Rapoport, Walt Stone, and Jeff Stonecash among others—and those who have led and contributed to three groups in which we have been active and from which we have gained a great deal: the Political Organizations and Parties, the Legislative Studies, and the Religion and Politics organized sections of the American Political Science Association. Much of the material in this book is derived from the ideas and research of the colleagues and friends who have seen the importance of sharing ideas, working together, and growing as a cooperating community of scholars. We feel fortunate to work in a profession that so clearly sees growth as a community to be a critical common goal.

This book would not be possible were it not for the efforts of Niels Aaboe, who took on this project from our original editor, Jennifer Knerr, to whom a great debt is still owed. Niels has a firm belief in the importance of good scholarship and relating that scholarship in a way that works in the classroom. He has worked with us to assure that this book meets those standards. We are most grateful to him for both his talents as an editor and his friendship. We also want to thank the others at Rowman & Littlefield who have worked on this book: Asa Johnson, Niels's highly capable assistant; Alden Perkins, a most efficient production editor; and Scott Jerard, a superb copyeditor who has not only saved us from many errors but worked hard to improve our prose.

Finally, we want to thank our family and friends—who support us in all that we do. Mark would like to thank in particular his daughter, Megan, and son, Jack, for understanding why Daddy had to stay late at work. This book is dedicated to Sandy's wife, Patrice Franko, and Mark's wife, Tammy Tetreault Brewer. Only authors know how important support from a spouse is as one struggles to finish a work such as this. We are both grateful that our spouses have been patient and supportive of our efforts.

L. Sandy Maisel and Mark D. Brewer

CHAPTER 1

Elections and Political Parties

Balloons and confetti fall from the ceiling of the United Center in Chicago as Bill Clinton completes his speech accepting the Democratic Party's nomination to run for reelection as president of the United States, August 29, 1996. While they have certainly changed over time, political parties and elections remain central to America's representative democracy.

Let's begin by talking about the electoral careers of four contemporary political figures, members of the U.S. Senate. Massachusetts's senior senator, Democrat Edward M. "Ted" Kennedy, was first elected to the Senate in 1962 in a special election to fill the remaining years of the term for the seat left vacant when his brother, John F. Kennedy, was elected president. Ted Kennedy won election to a full term in 1964 and has won reelection seven times since then. Only once in that time did he poll less than 60 percent of the vote; his highest total was nearly 75 percent.

Arlen Specter, a Republican senator from Pennsylvania since 1980, was first elected after having lost his party's primaries for senator in 1976 and governor in 1978. Specter made his reputation as an elected Republican district attorney in Democratic Philadelphia, but he had difficulty transferring that reputation to a statewide electorate. When he won the nomination in 1980, his margin of victory was only 3 percent over the former state Republican chairman. Specter won the general election by 2 percent. He has continued to win, though his margin of victory in 1992 was only 3 percent, as he became a target of feminists angry over his treatment of Anita Hill during the confirmation hearings of Supreme Court Justice Clarence Thomas. Specter is viewed as a moderate Republican willing to challenge President Bush on many issues, a characteristic which has angered many conservative Republicans over the years. He faced a tough primary challenge from former House member Pat Toomey in 2004, which he won 51 percent to 49 percent, with the support of the Bush White House. Specter then dramatically outspent his Democratic opponent in the general election ($21.6 million to $4.6 million) and won 53 percent to 42 percent.

In 1986 Alabamans elected Richard C. Shelby to the Senate. Shelby, a Democratic congressman from Birmingham, defeated one-termer Jeremiah Denton, who in 1980 had been the first Republican elected to the Senate from Alabama since the passage of the Seventeenth Amendment to the U.S. Constitution, calling for the direct election of senators.[1] After having beaten an incumbent in a very close election, Shelby went on to win reelection in 1992 by a margin of almost two to one. In 1994, after Republicans won partisan control of the Senate, Shelby announced his intention to switch from the Democratic to the Republican party, a move welcomed by the Republicans because it strengthened their thin majority. He won reelection as a Republican handily in 1998 (63 percent to 37 percent), and improved on his margin in 2004 (68 percent to 32 percent).

Finally, Dianne Feinstein (D-Calif.) took a more circuitous route to the Senate. As president of the San Francisco board of supervisors, Feinstein succeeded to the position of mayor (which she had twice sought and lost) when the incumbent, George Moscone, was assassinated in 1978. Elected and reelected in her own right in 1979 and 1983 but ineligible to seek a third full term in 1987, Feinstein left city government and ran for governor of California in 1990, winning the Democratic primary and barely losing the general election to Republican Pete Wilson. To assume the governorship, Wilson had to vacate his seat in the Senate. He appointed a little-known Republican, John Seymour, to replace him; Feinstein immediately declared her candidacy to fill the remaining two years of Wilson's term. In 1992 she defeated Wilson's appointee quite easily, polling nearly 60 percent of the vote. Most political observers felt that she would have an easy contest in 1994 as she sought to win a full six-year term. But that was not to be. In 1994 she was opposed by Republican congressman Michael Huffington, who became a serious contender because of his willingness to spend millions of his own dollars to win the seat. Feinstein prevailed by 2 percent in an election in which she spent nearly $15 million; her opponent spent twice as much as she did. California Democrats hoped that Feinstein would seek their state's governorship again in 1998, but she elected to remain in the Senate, in part at least because multimillionaire Al Checchi entered the Democratic primary and thereby raised the specter of another exorbitantly expensive campaign.[2] Feinstein won reelection to the Senate in 2000 by a margin of nearly 20 percentage points, and then again in 2006 with an edge of 25 percentage points.

These cases are presented as instructive places to begin an examination of elections and political parties in the United States. Four senators followed four very different routes to power and have had four very different careers. Kennedy essentially followed a family tradition, winning his first election largely on the power of his family name. Despite personal scandal, he has maintained a prominent place in his state's and the nation's political arena. Residing in a state dominated by his political party, he has been able to thwart even serious opponents with little difficulty. Specter won a difficult primary in his own party, after making his reputation as something of a maverick in local politics. A moderate Republican in a closely divided state, he has navigated a difficult course, trying not to offend his copartisans while at the same time attracting enough Democrats to win general elections. Even after twenty-six years in the Senate he is not safe from electoral defeat. Richard Shelby changed with a changing political environment. As Republicans came to power in the once solidly Democratic South, Shelby judged that his politics were more in line with the rising power than with those whose power was fading. Finally, Dianne Feinstein came to prominence by being in the right place at the right time. In a two-party state, she has won and lost, has contested for office, and has chosen to forgo contests in the process, building a personal following that makes her one of the state's most popular figures.

LEGITIMACY

Acceptance of the right of public officials to hold office and to promulgate policies because of the means by which they were chosen.

POLITICAL CULTURE

Norms, expectations, and values concerning political life in a particular polity or region.

Under the American system of government, elections are used to ensure popular support and **legitimacy** for those who make governmental decisions. In his classic study *The Theory and Practice of Modern Government,* Herman Finer (1949) summarizes this connection between democracy and elections: "The real question . . . is not whether the government deigns to take notice of popular criticisms and votes, but whether it can be voted out of office or forced by some machinery or procedures to change its policy, above all against its own will" (219).

The examples cited here illustrate that the process is a most complex one. To even begin to understand American politics, one must know something about the political history and **political culture** not only of the nation but also of various regions. One must understand the kinds of choices that individuals make and the political contexts in which they make them. One must look at the role of political parties, individual voters, policy issues, and money. And one must always remember that politics is not only about power but also about personalities; the importance of how different people react to situations should never be underestimated. For many, those personalities are what make politics so interesting, but their role must be understood in terms of the process in which they participate.

I. AN EXAMINATION OF ELECTIONS IN THE UNITED STATES

The contest for office is the machinery used by Americans to change policy and to change those who govern, often against their will. And the American electoral process is clearly different from that in other countries. A number of aspects distinguish how we use this machinery from how other countries do so. First, Americans are expected to go to the polls more frequently and to vote for more officeholders. Table 1.1 shows the elections in which citizens of Bangor, Maine, were asked to vote from 2003–2007. In some of these elections, citizens were asked to vote for local, state, and federal offices, in addition to referenda questions. Critics of American democracy complain about low turnout rates for our elections, but they rarely note how often we are asked to vote. The implication of this difference between the American system and those in most other countries is worth contemplating.

Second, our elections are held at regular intervals, regardless of the flow of world events, and are never changed because of particular national crises. President Bush did not have the luxury that, say, former British prime minister Tony Blair had, to call for a reaffirming election at a time when his popularity was high in 2002, nor could

Table 1.1   Elections Held in Bangor, Maine, 2003–2007

2003	June	Special municipal election, slot machines
	June	Referendum election
	November	Referendum election
2004	June	Primary and referendum election
	November	General and referendum election
2005	November	Referendum election
2006	June	Primary election
	November	General and referendum election
2007	June	Special municipal election, school committee
	June	Referendum election
	November	Referendum election

Source: Data provided by State of Maine Department of the Secretary of State and Office of the City Clerk, Bangor, Maine.

he postpone the regularly scheduled 2004 election as opposition to the war in Iraq was on the rise. Our presidential elections are held on the first Tuesday after the first Monday in November of every fourth year, without exceptions. Period! No exceptions! For example, President Franklin D. Roosevelt won reelection twice during World War II, once on the eve of our entry into the war and once as the push to victory neared completion; the dates of American elections are never changed because of particular national crises.

Third, the terms of various offices in our system are not all the same; thus, though elections are held at regular intervals, exactly which offices are contested in any particular election varies, not only from election to election but also from state to state and locality to locality for the same election. All members of the U.S. House of Representatives are up for election every two years; only one-third of Senate seats (plus special elections to fill vacancies) are contested in any one national election.[3] The president is elected for a four-year term, as are most governors. Some governors, however, are elected for two-year terms, and most of the four-year gubernatorial terms do not end when the president's term ends. The complexity is accentuated by state legislatures and local offices. Table 1.2 summarizes the terms of office and election cycles for state governors and legislators.

Fourth, the rules in different states and for different offices vary significantly. The Constitution specifies that states have the right to control the times and places of elections, even national elections, except for instances in which special provisions apply. The states also control most aspects of their own political systems, again with a few exceptions, as, for exámple, the "one man–one vote" provision imposed on drawing district lines through a Supreme Court inter-

Table 1.2   Terms of State Offices and Election Cycles (in years)

	Governor	Expiration	Senator	Representative
Ala.	4	Jan 2011	4	4
Alaska	4	Jan 2011	4	2
Ariz.	4	Jan 2011	2	2
Ark.	4	Jan 2011	4	2
Calif.	4	Jan 2011	4	2
Colo.	4	Jan 2011	4	2
Conn.	4	Jan 2011	2	2
Del.	4	Jan 2009	4	2
Fla.	4	Jan 2011	4	2
Ga.	4	Jan 2011	2	2
Hawaii	4	Jan 2011	4	2
Idaho	4	Jan 2009	2	2
Ill.	4	Jan 2011	4	2
Ind.	4	Jan 2011	4	2
Iowa	4	Jan 2011	4	2
Kans.	4	Jan 2011	4	2
Ky.	4	Dec 2011	4	2
La.	4	Jan 2008	4	4
Maine	4	Jan 2011	2	2
Md.	4	Jan 2011	4	4
Mass.	4	Jan 2011	2	2
Mich.	4	Jan 2011	4	2
Minn.	4	Jan 2011	4	2
Miss.	4	Jan 2008	4	4
Mo.	4	Jan 2011	4	2
Mont.	4	Jan 2009	4	2
Neb.	4	Jan 2011	4	—ᵃ
Nev.	4	Jan 2011	4	2
N.H.	2	Jan 2009	2	2
N.J.	4	Jan 2010	4	2
N.Mex.	4	Jan 2011	4	2
N.Y.	4	Jan 2011	2	2
N.C.	4	Jan 2009	2	2
N.Dak.	4	Dec 2008	4	2
Ohio	4	Jan 2011	4	2
Okla.	4	Jan 2011	4	2
Ore.	4	Jan 2011	4	2
Pa.	4	Jan 2011	4	2
R.I.	4	Jan 2011	2	2
S.C.	4	Jan 2011	4	2
S.Dak.	4	Jan 2011	4	2
Tenn.	4	Jan 2011	4	2
Tex.	4	Jan 2011	4	2
Utah	4	Jan 2009	4	2
Vt.	2	Jan 2009	2	2
Va.	4	Jan 2010	4	2
Wash.	4	Jan 2009	4	2
W.Va.	4	Jan 2009	4	2
Wisc.	4	Jan 2009	4	2
Wyo.	4	Jan 2011	4	2

Source: Almanac of American Politics, Secretaries of State.
ᵃUnicameral.

pretation of the **equal protection clause** of the Constitution.[4] One recent controversy that illustrates this point relates to **legislative term limits.** In an effort to limit the power of entrenched incumbents, a number of states have imposed limitations on the number of terms their state legislators can serve in office.[5] States that have imposed such limitations and the variation among states in how this concept has been implemented are shown in table 1.3. Of course, most states (though not all) restrict their governors to two terms, paralleling the federal example of the president.

In some states it has been possible to run for more than one office in the same election. Joseph Lieberman (then a Democrat, now an independent) was reelected to the Senate from Connecticut on the same day in 2000 that he lost the election to be vice president of the United States as the running mate of Al Gore; Lloyd Bentsen, Michael Dukakis's running mate, had had the same experience in 1988.[6] In Pennsylvania, one has been able to run for the party nomination of more than one office on the same day. At the opposite extreme, in Hawaii, a state officeholder must resign if he or she seeks another office. Vacancies in some offices are filled through an automatic succession. On the national level the vice

EQUAL PROTECTION CLAUSE

The phrase in section 1 of the Fourteenth Amendment to the U.S. Constitution that guarantees that no state may deny any person within its jurisdiction the "equal protection of the laws."

LEGISLATIVE TERM LIMITS

Fixed limitations on the number of terms of office that members of a legislature may serve.

Table 1.3   Term-Limited States

State	Enacted	House		Senate	
		Limit	Effective	Limit	Effective
Ariz.	1992	8	2000	8	2000
Ark.	1992	6	1998	8	2000
Calif.	1990	6	1996	8	1998
Colo.	1990	8	1998	8	1998
Fla.	1992	8	2000	8	2000
La.	1995	12	2007	12	2007
Maine	1993	8	1996	8	1996
Mich.	1992	6	1998	8	2002
Mo.[a]	1992	8	2002	8	2002
Mont.	1992	8	2000	8	2000
Neb.	2000	n/a	n/a	8	2006
Nev.[b]	1996	12	2010	12	2010
Ohio	1992	8	2000	8	2000
Okla.	1990	12	2004	12	2004
S.Dak.	1992	8	2000	8	2000

Source: National Conference of State Legislatures (www.ncsl.org).

Note: In six states (Idaho, Massachusetts, Oregon, Utah, Washington, and Wyoming), term limits have been repealed.

[a] Due to special elections, term limits were effective in 2000 for eight current members of the House and one senator in 1998.

[b] The Nevada Legislative Council and attorney general have ruled that Nevada's term limits cannot be applied to those legislators elected in the same year term limits were passed (1996). They first apply to persons elected in 1998.

president becomes president upon the death, resignation, or declared disability of the president. Other vacancies are filled by appointment; governors appoint senators to fill vacant seats until the next general election. Still other offices, such as U.S. representative, can only be filled by election and remain vacant until a special election can be held if an incumbent dies, resigns, or is removed from office.

Generally speaking, well-known state laws and party rules structure most contests for office, but we will constantly reassess that situation. We will also ask whether the role that party plays is a good one or a bad one and will be concerned with what standards should be used to answer that question. This text also assumes that the electoral contest provides a mechanism for expressing **popular support** or disapproval and for granting legitimacy, as Finer posited. We will ask whether or not we are satisfied with how this part of our democracy is working.

POPULAR SUPPORT

Public approval of the officials running the government and, by implication, of the policies they are pursuing.

Recall that Jeremiah Denton, the Republican predecessor of Senator Shelby (discussed earlier), was the first Republican ever to be popularly elected to the Senate from Alabama. In fact, most of the Democratic senators who preceded Senator Denton won with over 80 percent of the popular vote. In what sense, then, could it be said that political parties structured that contest for office? There was no contest for office, at least not in the general election. What possible interpretation could be given to those senators' mandates to govern? We will ask this question over and over again. How well does our system work? And, to the extent that we are not happy with its functioning, what can be done to make it more effective?

One important feature of contemporary politics is that intense partisan competition does not exist everywhere in the country. In 2006, thirty-six winners in the House of Representatives ran completely unopposed in the general election and another seventy-five faced opponents who spent no money. These numbers are not atypical. When 111 House races offer no real choice, how can the public express popular support in these "contests" for office?

We should also note what happened when Democrat Shelby switched to the Republican party in 1994. If party membership is important in elections, as we have posited it is, shouldn't switching parties be anathema for elected officials? On the contrary, the Republicans embraced Shelby and gave him a position in their party's seniority as if he had been a Republican since he was first elected to the Senate. What does Shelby's experience say about the role of party? While party switching is not an everyday occurrence, it has happened a number of times throughout American history. Even former president Ronald Reagan was once a Democrat and an active member of the quintessentially liberal Americans for Democratic Action. Thus, ample evidence exists for the proposition that the most basic assumptions about the role of party, and even the role of elections themselves require careful study.

It is our goal to examine the process through which **partisan elections** are contested in the United States.[7] While the examples adduced here call into question certain basic assumptions about the role of political parties, it would be naive to ignore the role that parties historically have played in American elections and continue to play.

This text addresses a tension as it emphasizes the role of political parties as well as the more broadly defined electoral process. Partisan elections are, by definition, elections contested by nominees of political parties. For much of our nation's history, the parties dominated the contest for office (see Silbey 1998, 2002). Citizens typically supported candidates of one party or the other with great loyalty. In order to understand elections in the contemporary contexts, we must understand this background.

Thus, this text looks at the history and development of the role played by parties in structuring American elections. It also looks at the current role of parties in the contest for office. However, in the chapters to follow, we will also explore ways in which other groups may now be playing the role that parties once played and, if so, with what impact. That is, parties have played and continue to play an important role in elections. But parties do not constitute the sum total of the electoral process.

The clear theme of this book is that the contest for office is the most crucial element to be examined. Political parties play an important role in that process, but only one role. It is not possible to understand the contest for office without understanding parties. But merely understanding how parties function does not tell the student much about how elections are fought. Our goal is to reach that latter understanding.

II. THE ROLE OF ELECTIONS IN DEMOCRATIC THEORY

Scholars are fond of pointing out that modern political parties are an American invention even though such parties are never mentioned in the Constitution. In *Federalist* 10 (1787) Madison warns of the mischief of faction, reasoning that many groups must be allowed to flourish so that no one group becomes too powerful. Such was the concept of "party" at the time the Constitution was drafted.

The Founding Fathers, moreover, defined democracy in a somewhat limited way: the masses were not to be trusted with political power. Thus, while the House of Representatives was to be popularly elected (certainly a necessity, given the history of our Revolution and its most famous slogan, "Taxation without representation

---

PARTISAN ELECTIONS

Elections in which those on the ballot are identified by their political party affiliation; by contrast, in nonpartisan elections no designation appears next to a candidate's name.

is tyranny!"), the Senate was indirectly elected by state legislatures, and the president was even more indirectly elected through the cumbersome mechanism of the electoral college.

A. Modes of Elections

1. Direct Elections

What general principles guided these rules for contesting offices? For direct representation in the House of Representatives, two were primary: districts with small populations so that the voters could "know" their representatives and frequent elections so that citizens had the opportunity to express their views on how the government was working. The Founding Fathers would have been appalled by twentieth-century recommendations to extend congressional terms to four years. They envisioned an intimate connection between a congressman and his constituents. He would be one of them, one who was just like his neighbors and thus best suited to serve them. He would do his duty and return home to be replaced by another. If he became too headstrong in support of his own alien ideas, frequent elections would guarantee that the violation of trust would not go on too long.

2. Indirect Elections

The other elected officials of the federal government were chosen through a filtering process. Only the "best of the best" were supposed to make the grade and be chosen to represent the interest of the people. Only those who really understood what was best for the masses would be chosen to serve in the Senate. Further, the elaborate mechanism for choosing the president can be understood best if one realizes that all those at the Constitutional Convention assumed that the towering figure of his time, the "father" of the new nation, George Washington, would be the first president. The mechanism was designed to pick the "right" leader, that is, someone like Washington.

B. Implications for Representation

1. Representatives' Perspectives

However, this system of elected representatives—or any other system yet devised—faces an inherent conflict. On the one hand, elected representatives should accurately represent the views of the people who choose them. On the other hand, they must have enough freedom to act on what they determine to be in the best interest of the people. One need not long debate the merits of the two theories of representation implied by these statements to see that a conflict exists. The American solution to this problem has been to give representatives a good deal of freedom to act, but to hold elections frequently in order to keep them accountable for their actions. One of the basic questions raised in this text is, How does that system work?

2. The Public's Perspective and the Role of Parties in Representation

Democratic theory also requires a citizenry that has the ability to convert its views on the issues of the day—certainly the pressing, salient issues—into public policy. Frequent elections do not serve their intended purpose if the electorate is not given a choice nor if, after that choice is expressed, public policy does not reflect that preference.

The role that political parties have traditionally played in this context has been to structure the contest for office so that elections can perform their role most effectively. One of the key questions facing the American polity concerns how effectively that role is played (Brady, Bullock, and Maisel 1988; Brady and Stewart 1986). Pomper (1972) and Fishel (1977), among others, have demonstrated that the Republican and Democratic parties differ from each other on major policy questions. But the links among differing party platforms, elections, and subsequent public policies are less clear in the American system than they are in parliamentary democracies.

V. O. Key Jr. (1964) highlights the important distinctions among **party in the electorate, party organization**, and **party in government**. The term "party in the electorate" refers to voters who generally align themselves with a particular party, the party's supporters at the polls. "Party organization" is the formal structure of the party, the elite that leads the party in election campaigns. Finally, "party in government" is composed of the individuals who serve in the government as a result of having run on a party label or having been appointed by someone who ran on a party label.

This text is mainly concerned with party in the electorate (i.e., the extent to which party determines how citizens vote) and with party organization (i.e., how political parties are structured as institutions), but we cannot ignore the governmental context either. We elect members of Congress in individual districts and stress their electoral independence, but we should not forget that these individual representatives often consider the position of their party when deciding how to vote once in office.

For many years *Congressional Quarterly* has reported **party unity scores** for members of Congress each year. A **party unity vote** is one on which a majority of one party votes together against a majority of the other party. A member's party unity score is the

PARTY IN THE ELECTORATE

Those who support a political party at the polls—the loyal followers.

PARTY ORGANIZATION

The formal structure of a political party's professional and volunteer workers.

PARTY IN GOVERNMENT

Members of a political party who are serving in an official capacity in the government.

PARTY UNITY SCORES

The percentage of time a legislator votes with his or her party on those votes on which a majority of one party votes against a majority of the other party.

PARTY UNITY VOTE

A vote in a legislature in which a majority of one party votes in opposition to a majority in the other party.

percentage of time he or she votes with his or her party on those votes. During the Clinton administration, more than half of the votes in each session in each house of the Congress were party unity votes. And in each case the average party unity score for members of each party exceeded 80 percent. The same general pattern has followed during the Bush years. This period of extremely high party unity covers periods in which each party has been in the majority. Thus it seems clear that party affiliation is far from unimportant as a **linkage** between citizens as they cast their votes and policies that are eventually adopted. (See chapter 11.)

LINKAGE

That which connects one actor or set of actors in a polity with others.

Similarly, the extent to which recent presidents have imposed partisan tests on their principal appointees is without precedent. Presidents Reagan, George H. W. Bush, Clinton, and George W. Bush all replaced party recruiters with their own White House personnel offices, but those selected for important positions have almost all been members of the president's party (Mackenzie 1990, 1998, 2002). Thus, while the takeover of the national government by committed conservatives hailed as the **Reagan revolution** in 1980 might not have changed the role of government as completely as its perpetrators might have hoped; while Clinton's recapturing of the White House for the Democrats might not have reversed all trends started in the previous twelve years of Republican rule; and while George W. Bush's winning the White House while the Republicans controlled the Congress did not presage as many policy changes as his supporters would have liked, each of those elections did lead to significant changes in who populated the government. Just as surely they led to changes in the philosophy of governing espoused by those in appointive as well as elective office. For our purposes, the importance of those appointments is also that they demonstrate another link between elections and subsequent government policies.

REAGAN REVOLUTION

Changes in policy direction, reversing liberal policies with conservative alternatives, thought to follow from the election of President Reagan in 1980.

That political parties would serve as the linkage mechanism between electorate and governing officials was not envisioned by the Founding Fathers; in fact, it has evolved quite slowly (see chapter 2). Historically, the effectiveness of parties as the bridge between citizens and those they elect to govern has not been judged with universal acclaim, nor has that role remained constant in the face of a changing political environment. In order to understand this role, we must more carefully define what is meant by "political party" in the American political context.

III. DEFINITIONS OF "POLITICAL PARTY" AND "PARTY SYSTEMS"

French political scientist Maurice Duverger (1951, 62ff.), in a classic study entitled *Political Parties*, drew an important sociological distinction between **cadre parties** and **mass membership parties**. Duverger starts with a definition of *party member* in the European setting, one that most Americans would find restrictive. For Duverger "the concept 'member' of a party coincides with that of adherent. . . . The latter is distinguished from the 'supporter,' who declares his agreement with the doctrines of the party and sometimes lends it his support but who remains outside its organization and the community it forms" (62). Cadre parties, then, have relatively few members; mass membership parties tend to have a large number of dues-paying supporters.

However, Duverger's distinction is broader than that. Cadre parties (most conservative European parties fit into this mold) are organizations whose primary goal is to obtain electoral success. They are subordinate to leaders in government and are basically inactive between elections. Not only are there not many members, but the staffs of these organizations are also small.

Mass membership parties, at the opposite extreme, are ideological and educational organizations. Their goal is to convince the working class of the desirability of their point of view and thus to change the system radically. To succeed, they must maintain a large, permanent, continuously active professional organization. When mass membership parties gain control over the government, the party organization maintains an influence unimagined in the case of cadre parties. Socialist parties in Europe meet most of Duverger's criteria for mass membership parties.

Duverger's definition is really a distinction among types of political parties. He never does arrive at a concise definition of what constitutes a political party, though he identifies a number of important considerations—membership, level of activity, type of activity, type of leadership, relationship to the government. On the other hand, several scholars studying American parties have attempted to define exactly what constitutes a political party:

> We may define "political party" generally as the articulate organization of society's active political agents, those who are concerned with the control of governmental power and who compete for popular support with another group or groups holding divergent views. (Sigmund Neumann 1956, 396)

> A political party is a team of men seeking to control the governing apparatus by gaining office in a duly constituted election. (Anthony Downs 1957, 25)

> Pat definitions may simplify discussion but they do not necessarily promote understanding. A search for the fundamental nature of party is complicated by the fact that "party" is a work of many meanings. . . . The nature of parties must be sought through an

CADRE PARTIES

Parties dominated by politically elite groups of activists.

MASS MEMBERSHIP PARTIES

Political parties characterized by large memberships that determine party direction; tend to have ideological positions and play an educational role in the system; concern is with governing more than electing.

appreciation of their role in the process of governance. (V. O. Key Jr. 1964, 200)

Any group, however loosely organized, seeking to elect governmental office-holders under a given label. (Leon D. Epstein 1967, 9)

A party is any political group that presents at elections, and is capable of placing through elections, candidates for public office. (Giovanni Sartori 1976, 64)

The major American political parties exist, as do other political organizations, to organize large numbers of individuals behind attempts to influence the selection of public officials and the decisions these officials subsequently make in office. . . . The differences between parties and other political organizations are often slender. (Frank J. Sorauf 1980, 17)

A number of themes emerge from this group of definitions. First, as Sartori claims, a minimal definition of contesting for office emerges. Second, as Neumann, Downs, and Epstein state, some type of organization is assumed. Third, as Key and Sorauf imply, "party" is a multidimensional term. Defining "party" too narrowly excludes organizations that ought to be included. Defining "party" too broadly takes in organizations that would be excluded by general consensus. The student almost has to fall back on the classic test, "If it looks like a duck, swims like a duck, flies like a duck, and quacks like a duck." Thus the Republican party is a party; the AFL-CIO, despite the fact that it does many of the same things, is not.

THIRD PARTIES

Political parties that enter into electoral contests without having a realistic chance of winning an election; at times these parties do affect the outcome of the contest between the two major parties.

For most purposes this definition is sufficient, but for others, often very important ones, it is not. For instance, when John Anderson ran for president as an independent, or **third-party** candidate, in 1980, the Federal Election Commission (FEC) had to rule on whether John Anderson's "party" in the 1980 presidential election constituted a party in any meaningful sense.[8] The FEC ruled that it did, thus making Anderson eligible for federal campaign financing in 1984.[9] The FEC ruled similarly on Ross Perot's "party" in the 1992 presidential election, even though the party under whose label he ran in 1996, the Reform party, did not exist in 1992. What definition is appropriate in that context?

This text adopts a fairly restrictive definition of *political parties*. Political parties are organizations, however loosely organized, that (1) have, for a period of time, run candidates for public office; (2) have earned the support of a significant following in the electorate for those candidates because of their allegiance to the organization; and (3) must be taken into account by other similar competing organizations. Did Anderson's party meet this definition in 1980? Remember it disappeared by 1984. It did not meet the definition, then, because it did not meet the test of time. Did Perot's Reform party meet the definition?

This definition also implies acceptance of the concept of **party systems**, at least in its simplified form.[10] In democracies, if parties are to contest for public office, they must take into account others who are also competing for office. William N. Chambers (1975, 6) defines a party system as "a pattern of interaction in which two or more political parties compete for office or power in government and for the support of the electorate, and must therefore take one another into account in their behavior in government and in election contests."

Party systems are characterized on two different axes. First, they are distinguished by the number of parties competing. Second, they are distinguished by the intensity of competition. The American national party system is generally classified as a **competitive two-party system**. The Democratic and Republican parties compete with each other for national offices; each has a chance of winning. Minor parties may be on the ballot from time to time, but they neither persist nor have a chance of winning. In the 1992 presidential election (and to a lesser extent in the 1996 campaign) Ross Perot's third party threatened the hegemony of the Democratic and Republican parties. But in the final analysis his effort to undermine the two-party system fell short (Bibby and Maisel 1998, 2003; Rapoport and Stone 2005). Thus our national system remains the competitive two-party system it has been since the election of 1828, though the parties have changed during that period.[11]

Tables 1.4, 1.5, and 1.6 show a number of different measures of national electoral competition in this century. The pattern is clear: Democrats compete with Republicans for control of our national government. Other parties can and do contest for federal offices, but real competition is restricted to two parties. It is in this sense of structuring the contest for national power that the role of parties in the electoral process must be evaluated.

For all that, it is very misleading to look only at national politics. American politics is perhaps most notably characterized by its **decentralization**; local and state politics are not totally controlled by national forces. An observer cannot stop after saying that the American party system is a competitive two-party system. At the very least, one must look at the fifty separate state party systems. For most of the twentieth century all of the South was solidly Democratic; now state legislatures in the South are virtually evenly divided between the two parties, even though the South is solidly Republican at the federal level. Similarly, much of the nation's heart-

PARTY SYSTEMS

Electoral arrangements in which two or more parties compete for support of the electorate and control of the government and take each other into account as they set various electoral and governing strategies.

COMPETITIVE TWO-PARTY SYSTEM

A system dominated by the two main political parties, Republicans and Democrats.

DECENTRALIZATION

Power and decision making are removed from the most central locus in a political system and spread to regional and local officials.

Table 1.4   Two-Party Competition in Twentieth- and Twenty-first-Century
Presidential Elections

	Percentage of Popular Vote	
	Democratic	Republican
1900	45.5	51.7
1904	37.6	56.4
1908	43.0	51.6
1912	41.8	23.2
1916	49.2	46.1
1920	34.2	60.3
1924	28.8	54.1
1928	40.8	58.2
1932	57.4	39.6
1936	60.8	36.5
1940	54.7	44.8
1944	53.4	45.9
1948	49.5	45.1
1952	44.4	55.1
1956	42.0	57.4
1960	49.8	49.5
1964	61.0	38.5
1968	42.7	43.2
1972	37.5	60.7
1976	50.1	48.0
1980	41.0	50.7
1984	40.6	58.8
1988	45.6	53.4
1992	43.0	37.4
1996	49.2	40.7
2000	48.4	47.9
2004	48.3	50.7

Source: Vital Statistics on American Politics (Stanley and Niemi 2006a).
Note: Percentages are of total vote; other parties not shown.

land has long favored Republicans. While presidential politics may
be hotly contested at the national level, Kansas has had two Republican senators in every Congress since 1939. At the other extreme,
the Massachusetts state legislature has been under Democratic control for more than four decades. Thus the domination of a single
party within certain states can be veiled by a claim that we have a
competitive two-party system nationally. Similarly, changes in national politics can reflect either trends across the entire nation in
one direction or asymmetrical offsetting trends in a number of directions in a number of states or regions (Brunell and Grofman
1998). The reality is that in some instances we have fifty-one party
systems—one federal system, and fifty state systems.

IV. POLITICIANS VIEW THE PARTY SYSTEM

This text is not intended to be a workbook. However, if one home-work exercise were to be assigned, it would be to have each reader call his or her state representative and ask, "What is the dimension of the party system that I should examine in order to understand the role that party plays in structuring your own electoral contest?" Merely posing the question should be sufficient to demonstrate how ludicrous it is. While it is important to understand "the role of party," "structuring the contest for office," and "party systems" in order to analyze elections in America, these abstract terms are not in the working vocabulary of most politicians. Therefore this text regularly steps back from the analytical world of the student of poli-tics to the practical world of the politician.

In that regard, it is important to understand that politicians only rarely look beyond the next election. Elections serve as their link to the people in a very concrete way. If the people vote for them, they are in office; if the people vote for someone else, they are out. The questions that politicians ask relate to what they must do in order to ensure their continuation in office or their advancement to the next office.

Important questions immediately arise. Are elections in America an effective way for the citizenry to control politicians? That is, do politicians lose because of the dissatisfaction of their constituents? This question can be answered empirically by looking at incumbent losses and the reasons for them, at the knowledge that constituents have of their officeholders' position, and at major swings in the for-tunes of the two parties (see Jacobson 1980; Maisel and Cooper 1981; Stokes and Miller 1962; Sundquist 1983).

However, equally important is how politicians think the elec-toral process works. Do politicians change their positions because they fear electoral reprisals? The late senator Henry Jackson (D-Wash., 1952–1983), sometimes referred to as the senator from Boe-ing (because the aircraft manufacturer is located in Washington State and Jackson saw it as part of his job to represent the interests of the thousands of his constituents who were Boeing employees), early in his Senate career explained the apparent contradiction be-tween his "liberal" views on social and economic policies and his "conservative" views of defense matters. Jackson contended, "I have to be a senator before I can be a statesman." His winning per-centages in four reelection campaigns for the Senate were 72 per-cent, 82 percent, 72 percent, and 69 percent; consequently, his fear of electoral reprisal might have been slightly exaggerated. But it was real nonetheless.

Anyone who has worked closely with an elected officeholder

Table 1.5　Two-Party Competition in the Twentieth- and Twenty-first-Century Senate

	Cong	Seats Occupied by Party		
		Dem	Rep	Other
1899–1901	56th	26	53	8
1901–1903	57th	31	55	—
1903–1905	58th	33	57	—
1905–1907	59th	33	57	—
1907–1909	60th	31	61	—
1909–1911	61st	32	61	—
1911–1913	62d	41	51	—
1913–1915	63d	51	44	1
1915–1917	64th	56	40	—
1917–1919	65th	53	42	—
1919–1921	66th	47	49	—
1921–1923	67th	37	59	2
1923–1925	68th	43	51	1
1925–1927	69th	39	56	—
1927–1929	70th	46	49	1
1929–1931	71st	39	56	1
1931–1933	72d	47	48	1
1933–1935	73d	60	35	2
1935–1937	74th	69	25	4
1937–1939	75th	76	16	4
1939–1941	76th	69	23	2
1941–1943	77th	66	28	1
1943–1945	78th	58	37	1
1945–1947	79th	56	38	—
1947–1949	80th	45	15	—
1949–1951	81st	54	42	—
1951–1953	82d	49	47	1
1953–1955	83d	47	48	1
1955–1957	84th	48	47	—
1957–1959	85th	49	47	—

(continued)

facing another election knows that nearly all such officeholders consider public opinion very important.[12] Politicians panic if their margin of victory goes down from one election to the next; they fret over the effects on their popularity of votes on controversial, salient issues. Study after study has emphasized how safe most incumbent legislators are from electoral defeat, in both the Congress and in the state legislatures (Herrnson 1998a, 2000; Jewell 1984; Jacobson 1992, 1996, 2001; Holbrook and Tidmarch 1991; Weber, Tucker, and Brace 1991). Although few incumbents are thrown out by constituents because of their stand on public policy issues, elections do work as a means of public control because politicians act as if they

Table 1.5   (Continued)

	Cong	Seats Occupied by Party		
		Dem	Rep	Other
1959–1961	86th	64	34	—
1961–1963	87th	65	35	—
1963–1965	88th	67	33	—
1965–1967	89th	68	32	—
1967–1969	90th	64	36	—
1969–1971	91st	57	43	—
1971–1973	92d	54	44	2
1973–1975	93d	56	42	2
1975–1977	94th	60	37	2
1977–1979	95th	61	38	1
1979–1981	96th	58	41	1
1981–1983	97th	46	53	1
1983–1985	98th	45	55	—
1985–1987	99th	47	53	—
1987–1989	100th	55	45	—
1989–1991	101st	55	45	—
1991–1993	102d	56	44	—
1993–1995	103d	57	43	—
1995–1997	104th	47	53	—
1997–1999	105th	45	55	—
1999–2001	106th	45	55	—
2001–2003	107th	50	50	—
2003–2005	108th	48	51	1
2005–2007	109th	44	55	1
2007–2009	110th	49	48	2

Source: Vital Statistics on American Politics (Stanley and Niemi 2006a); Data for the 110th
Congress compiled by authors.
Note: The two independents in the 110th Congress caucus with the Democrats, giving
control of the Senate to the Democrats. Figures for 110th Congress accurate as of June 6,
2007.

might be thrown out by the voters if they do not heed perceived
voter opinion. In this case, a politician's perception of reality is
more important than reality itself.

Similarly, just as it is important to understand how politicians
view elections, it is important to know how they view party. In this
case, the answer is very simple: it all depends.

Politicians may not understand abstract notions of party system
and electoral environment, but they certainly do understand what
the party—whether it is defined as the label or the formal organization—means for their election or reelection chances. In all but a
very few cases, office seekers need a major party nomination in
order to get on the ballot and stand any chance for success. However, that generalization is perhaps the only one that can be made.[13]

Table 1.6 Two-Party Competition in the Twentieth- and Twenty-first-Century
House of Representatives

		Seats Occupied by Party		
	Cong	Dem	Rep	Other
1899–1901	56th	163	185	9
1901–1903	57th	151	197	9
1903–1905	58th	178	208	—
1905–1907	59th	136	250	—
1907–1909	60th	164	222	—
1909–1911	61st	172	219	—
1911–1913	62d	228	161	1
1913–1915	63d	291	127	17
1915–1917	64th	230	196	9
1917–1919	65th	216	210	6
1919–1921	66th	190	240	3
1921–1923	67th	131	301	1
1923–1925	68th	205	225	5
1925–1927	69th	183	247	4
1927–1929	70th	195	237	3
1929–1931	71st	167	267	1
1931–1933	72d	220	214	1
1933–1935	73d	310	117	5
1935–1937	74th	319	103	10
1937–1939	75th	331	891	3
1939–1941	76th	261	164	4
1941–1943	77th	268	162	5
1943–1945	78th	218	208	4
1945–1947	79th	242	190	2
1947–1949	80th	188	245	1
1949–1951	81st	263	171	1
1951–1953	82d	234	199	1
1953–1955	83d	211	221	1
1955–1957	84th	232	203	—

(continued)

Beyond a means of access to the ballot and perhaps some legitimacy in the eyes of the voters, major party designation means different things to different politicians. The key variables are the office being sought and the strength of the party, in terms of both organizational resources and voter identification, in the particular district.

Thus in many major cities, such as Chicago or Philadelphia, the Democratic primary is tantamount to election; candidates worry a great deal about party in those cases. On the other hand, in many other cities, candidates know that their nomination is no guarantee of election. Furthermore, the help that the candidates can expect from party organization in terms of financial support or other campaign services varies widely.

Similarly, campaigns for state legislature vary widely from area

Table 1.6 (Continued)

		Seats Occupied by Party		
	Cong	*Dem*	*Rep*	*Other*
1957–1959	85th	233	200	—
1959–1961	86th	283	153	—
1961–1963	87th	263	174	—
1963–1965	88th	258	177	—
1965–1967	89th	295	140	—
1967–1969	90th	247	187	—
1969–1971	91st	243	192	1
1971–1973	92d	254	180	—
1973–1975	93d	239	192	—
1975–1977	94th	291	144	—
1977–1979	95th	292	143	—
1979–1981	96th	273	159	—
1981–1983	97th	243	192	—
1983–1985	98th	267	168	—
1985–1987	99th	252	182	—
1987–1989	100th	258	177	—
1989–1991	101st	259	174	—
1991–1993	102d	267	167	1
1993–1995	103d	258	176	1
1995–1997	104th	204	230	1
1997–1999	105th	207	227	1
1999–2001	106th	211	223	1
2001–2003	107th	212	221	2
2003–2005	108th	205	229	1
2005–2007	109th	202	230	1
2007–2009	110th	232	201	0

Source: Vital Statistics on American Politics (Stanley and Niemi 2006a); Data for the 110th Congress compiled by authors.
Note: Figures for 110th Congress accurate as of June 6, 2007.

to area. In Massachusetts in 2006 twenty-seven of the forty seats in the state senate were won without any major party opposition (68 percent); 128 out of 160 house members won election with no major party opponent (80 percent). On the other hand in Pennsylvania in 2006, only seven of the twenty-five state senate seats up in that cycle were won without major party opposition (28 percent), while the figure for the lower chamber was 66 out of 203 (33 percent).

The role of party in funding legislative campaigns also varies significantly (Gierzynski 1992). In Maine organized parties rarely have enough strength to help state legislative candidates significantly; however, in states such as Minnesota (or in some areas in other states, such as Cook County in Illinois) party organizations practically run the campaign for candidates.

Congressional elections engender another set of problems. Congressional districts only occasionally share boundaries with other political units. Most American political organizations are based on the county as the organizing unit. In some states congressional districts span more than one county. Some of those counties may have strong parties, some weak; some may be heavily Republican, some competitive, some heavily Democratic. But in other states or areas within states, several congressional districts may be found in the same county. Only rarely is a U.S. congressman a key figure as a party leader; Rahm Emanuel (D-Ill.) distinguishes himself as one example. Similarly, party leaders do not generally play key roles in many congressional campaigns. But one cannot overgeneralize; certainly members of Congress as different as Louise Slaughter (D-N.Y.), Howard Berman (D-Calif.), Mark Souder (R-Ind.), and Bill Shuster (R-Pa.) would never deny the importance that party organization has played in their electoral careers.

Statewide party influence differs widely as well. Party nomination is often decisive in states where one party tends to dominate, though as the recent successful gubernatorial campaigns of William Weld and Mitt Romney in Massachusetts demonstrate, in no state is it impossible for the candidate of the weaker party to win. However, some of the strongest one-party states have the weakest party organizations; this was particularly true in the South when Democrats had total domination but were often split internally. It remains true in areas dominated by one party as different as Nebraska and Massachusetts. Thus candidates in those states must form their own organization and draw on their own resources in order to capture first the party nomination and subsequently the office they seek. On the other hand, party nomination guarantees considerable support in some of the more competitive states such as Illinois or New York due to the strength of the party organizations at work.

Finally, in the battle for the White House, only the two major party candidates really have a chance to win. Whether party organization is of any help to a candidate before the nominating convention varies with incumbency and intraparty competition. Bill Clinton, who as president had no challenger in his own party in 1996, was able to use the Democratic party apparatus to smooth his path through the nominating process and the convention; the same was true for President George W. Bush and the 2004 nomination. But President Bush's father, President George H. W. Bush, as a president with a challenger in his own party in 1992, or Mike Dukakis, as a nonincumbent dealing with defeated rivals who were not fully behind his candidacy even at the time of the 1988 Democratic National Convention, had to deal with party organizations that played more neutral roles. And both party organizations will have to be extremely careful to maintain neutrality during the prenomination phase of the wide-open 2008 presidential race.

Whatever the case prior to the nomination, merely winning the presidential nomination of either major party guarantees the successful candidate access to the ballot in nearly every state[14] and financial support through federal funding. Access to additional resources for the party nominee used to vary significantly from state to state, but recent national party fund-raising efforts and reinvigorated state party organizations and regulations have reduced that variation.

What role do politicians see party playing in the elections? Again, it all depends. The biggest mistake a political analyst can make in writing about elections is to overgeneralize. We must distinguish election from election by constituency and by geography. Campaigns for local office are, for example, different from those for congressional or statewide offices. And no other election compares to a race for the presidency.

Those who are tremendously successful at one level often find that they fail miserably at another. Consider the experience of Democrat Wilbur Mills (Ark., U.S. House of Representatives, 1939–1977), the once powerful chairman of the House Ways and Means Committee, whose presidential campaign in 1972 was all but ignored by the voters; of Republican (but former Democrat) John Connally, a former governor of Texas and secretary of the treasury, who spent more money to win fewer delegates to a nominating convention than anyone would have thought possible; of former Republican senator Howard Baker of Tennessee, who felt that a leadership position in the Senate would aid a bid for the Republican presidential nomination. Baker discovered that his duties in Washington left him too little time to campaign and that the voters were not in the least interested in the important role he played in senatorial debates, only in whether he cared enough to trudge through the snows of New Hampshire in that state's media-dominated primary election.

Demonstrating the lesson he learned, Baker declined to seek reelection to the Senate in 1984 in order to run for the presidency in 1988, a race he eventually passed up when he was asked to serve as White House chief of staff under Ronald Reagan. Or consider Bob Dole (R-Kans.). Senator Dole, perhaps the most respected Republican legislator of his generation, desperately wanted to be president. He ran unsuccessfully for vice president as Gerald Ford's running mate in 1976; he campaigned for his party's nomination and lost in 1988. He finally won the Republican nomination in 1996 and resigned his seat in the Senate, and thus his position as majority leader, to concentrate on his presidential bid. And he lost badly. Senator Dole never came to understand why the qualities that made him a successful candidate in rural Kansas and a respected leader in the Senate did not translate into presidential politics. (See chapter 10.)

The list of congressmen and congresswomen seeking to move to the Senate or of state legislators seeking to move to the House and failing repeatedly would fill volumes. Likewise, no modern mayor of the city of New York has ever successfully sought higher office, a lesson that must give Rudolph Giuliani, the immensely popular and politically ambitious Republican former mayor of the city, some pause.

In much the same way, campaigns in the East are different from those in the Midwest, and each of these is different from campaigns in the South or the Far West. Significant variations exist among geographic areas within these regions. The history of a particular area—particularly its political history—must always be taken into account. As noted here, the single most salient feature of the American political system is its decentralized nature. Unfortunately for the social scientist, much more is lost in accumulating what should be kept separate than is gained by trying to generalize about a series of diverse experiences.

For a political analyst to state at the outset of a text that generalizations about the electoral process might prove imprecise seems blasphemous, but the key point is that practicing politicians do not base their judgments on such academic generalizations. They base them on instincts, often faulty ones, about individual situations in particular circumstances. It might be argued that politicians are foolish to do so, but that does not change the reality. All too often politicians and political scientists seem to be operating in different worlds. But one thing that perhaps both groups can agree on is that electoral politics in the United States, at least at the federal level and in most cases at the state level too, is partisan politics. The role that parties and partisanship play certainly varies by time and circumstance, but party always matters somehow. The overwhelming majority of candidates for federal and state office run as partisans in a partisan context, which can either assist or constrict (or both) them, depending on circumstances.

WEBSITES

www.google.com/Top/Society/Politics/: An index of links to political websites, arranged by category.

www.yahoo.com/Government/Politics/Elections: An extensive site of links to election websites. Contains listings for the 2008 election, for international elections, and for commercial products. Also, links to elections by region, to election archives, and to voter information.

www.vote-smart.org: Project Vote Smart home page, with information on and links to a vast array of information dealing with parties, campaigns, and elections.

www.govspot.com: Links to a wide array of information on politics, including many on parties and elections in the United States.

CHAPTER

American Political Parties and Party Organization

A classic New England fall setting marks Election Day in Hopkinton, New Hampshire, November 2, 2004. Election Day is the culmination of a long process, one in which political party organizations continue to play key roles.

I. THE DEVELOPMENT OF AMERICAN POLITICAL PARTIES

Modern political parties are a distinctly American invention. They did not appear fully formed; rather, they evolved slowly, the product of experimentation and innovation by the leaders of the nation's new form of government, at the end of the eighteenth and beginning of the nineteenth centuries. The first of the American parties, the **Federalist party**, was shaped largely by Alexander Hamilton, George Washington's treasury secretary. It was Hamilton's controversial economic proposals and his efforts to cultivate support for the administration's program in Congress that essentially gave rise to the first legislative party. Ironically, Hamilton is often credited with drafting Washington's Farewell Address, the theme of which was to warn of the *dangers* of party:

> In contemplating the causes which may disturb our Union, it occurs as a matter of serious concern, that any ground should have been furnished for characterizing party by *geographical discriminations*. . . . To the efficacy and permanency of your Union, a Government of the whole is indispensable. . . . Let me now take a more comprehensive view, and warn you in the most solemn manner against the baneful effects of the spirit of party. (Sparks 1840, 221–24)

Likewise, James Madison, in *Federalist* 10, warned his contemporaries of **factions**, by nature "adverse to the rights of other citizens, and to the permanent and aggregate interest of the community." Yet it was Madison who pressured a reluctant Thomas Jefferson to join him in organizing an opposition party to Hamilton's Federalists. Jefferson's Democratic-Republicans formed as a reaction to the rising tide of Federalist policies gaining support in Congress, policies that favored New England merchants and manufacturers at the expense of Southern and Western farmers and tradesmen.

Why did these early political leaders, virtually all of whom took pride in their stand against parties, play such critical roles in creating them? Clearly, Washington, Hamilton, Madison, and Jefferson recognized the negative power of factions—the Constitution, which Madison, Washington, and Hamilton all played large roles in drafting and getting ratified, never explicitly mentions parties, but its structure reflects its authors' fears. The very blueprint for the American political system is deliberate in its separation of powers and in its system of checks and balances. These early American political leaders were all too aware of the European experience with parties, and hoped to avoid a similar situation in their new nation. The antipartisan feelings of many of the founders were reinforced by the

FEDERALIST PARTY

One of the first American political parties, composed of the followers of George Washington and the architect of his administration's policies, Alexander Hamilton.

FACTIONS

Divisions within the population, forming at first over economic interests, that were the precursors of American political parties.

troubles during the French Revolution, when factions divided the French citizenry and when parties formed on the basis of economic self-interest and organized in opposition to the common good. But if the existence of parties in the new American democracy could not be prevented, then at least their influence would be controlled.

Eighteenth-century European political philosophy reflects this tension between parties as negative factions and parties as legitimate and necessary governing coalitions. In 1732, the political philosopher and English democratic conservative Lord Bolingbroke wrote of the difficulty in distinguishing between faction and party—or, in other words, between party in the negative sense and party in the positive sense: "Governing by party . . . must always end in government of a faction. . . . Party is a political evil, and faction is the worst of all parties" (Bolingbroke [1841] 1976, 401; Sartori 1976, 6, 30). The British political philosopher David Hume was not as anti-party as Bolingbroke, though on factions he was very hard: "Factions subvert government, render laws impotent, and beget the fiercest animosities among men of the same nation" (Hume 1976, 58; Sartori 1976, 7, 31). Not a party advocate by any means, Hume nonetheless accepted parties as coalitions that formed naturally in free governments.

Observations made by British statesman Edmund Burke went beyond the denouncement or resigned acceptance of parties in a democracy. In 1770 he defined party as "a body of men united, for promoting by their joint endeavors the national interest, upon some particular principle in which they are all agreed" (1976, 425–26). Parties are not divisive but rather advance the national interest; they are *for* the common good, not the subversion of it. In essence, Burke proposed that parties play a role in doing the work of governing within an established set of rules. Burke's definition of party was unique largely because he was describing a political entity that *could* in fact exist but did not exist at that time (Sartori 1976, 10).

Thus, while most political leaders in the early years were loath to endorse the concept of political parties, they did recognize the need to organize those who shared their views in order to succeed with this new form of government. In their efforts to make American democracy work, they invented the political institution that suited their needs: the party. But if this gestation had difficulty coming to term, then the birth itself was outright dangerous.

This chapter describes that birth as well as the development of American political parties and their organization within the framework of the five (arguably six) party systems in American political history. Each of these eras is marked by a new national issue/set of issues or crisis that polarizes the party elite; divides the electorate; increases turnout at the polls; and, in some cases, fuels the rise of third parties. The electoral eras are sometimes separated by **critical**

CRITICAL ELECTION

An election in which there is a sharp alteration of pre-existing cleavages within the electorate.

elections, a term first used by political scientist V. O. Key Jr. to describe elections in which "there occurs a sharp and durable electoral cleavage between the parties" (Key 1955). In other instances, the transition between electoral eras occurs more gradually, as "the rise and fall of parties may to some degree be the consequence of trends that perhaps persist over decades and elections may mark only steps in a more or less continuous creation of new loyalties and decay of old." Key termed this type of change **secular realignment** (Key 1959).[1] But regardless of whether change is dramatic or gradual, as the major parties adopt distinct positions in response to the divisive national issue or set of issues, the groups that support each party oftentimes reorganize, or "realign," along the new **line of cleavage**. Thus, by examining the evolution of American parties from their inception to modernity in terms of distinct party systems, we can explain how and why party coalitions have shifted over time and how American parties respond to change.[2]

A. The First Party System

One commonly held view about the founding of American political parties is that they were born of the battle over the ratification of the Constitution—the Federalists versus the anti-Federalists, or the Rats versus the anti-Rats. Surely the new nation was divided over ratification, but, as Washington said in addressing the First Congress, "The fight over the Constitution is over." Instead, it was the economic program of the first administration that drew new and polarizing battle lines that encouraged and in fact necessitated party organization. Although the first session of the First Congress went smoothly as the mechanics of governing were worked out, by the time Alexander Hamilton presented his economic agenda to the second session of that Congress, President Washington's "honeymoon" period was clearly over.

Hamilton felt that the strength of the new government would depend on its ability to demonstrate economic stability. Thus, the keystone of his program, which Washington adopted, was full funding of the entire federal debt and the assumption of all state debts by the national government. Others disagreed. On the question of funding, Madison and his followers felt that only notes held by original lenders, the true patriots, should be fully paid off. Notes held by speculators should only be repaid in part so that individuals did not profit from the war effort. Simply and rationally put: regarding the assumption of each state's debt, those from states that stood to gain, supported; those who stood to lose, opposed. These two issues—funding and assumption—led to a new line of division, a line that paralleled the political and theoretical divide on how one stood on the expansion of the central government.

SECULAR
REALIGNMENT

Long-term, gradual shift in the partisan attachments of groups of voters that eventually results in a new party system.

LINE OF
CLEAVAGE

Dividing line that separates supporters of one party from those of another.

Whereas the fight over the Constitution pitted large states against small states, economic issues presented to Congress in 1790 divided the nation along sectional lines. Broadly speaking, the North was for Hamilton's funding plan; the South opposed it. Similarly, the North was for assumption of state debts, but the South opposed it. The other major issues of Hamilton's economic program—the charter of the Bank of the United States and the imposition of an excise tax—crystallized and invigorated public opinion and hardened the new lines of division.

Parties, in the sense of permanent entities with well-developed organizational bases, had certainly not yet formed; however, the national issues of funding and assumption marked the start of enduring new divisions. Leaders in Washington's administration were uncertain about how to deal with these political differences. The overriding factor for most was success of the new government. A close second was personal loyalty to Washington, who, it is said, reigned more than ruled. The first president allowed his cabinet secretaries considerable autonomy, intervening only when they disagreed. Hamilton aggressively took the initiative and gained Washington's support for his program of economic growth. Adams, who disliked Hamilton personally and opposed some of his programs (feeling, for instance, that banks helped only the moneyed class), went along for the good of the nation. Jefferson also believed that his hands were tied: despite his strong objection to Hamilton's program, he remained in the cabinet until 1793, demonstrating his intense loyalty to Washington.

These divisions carried over into Congress, reaching new heights with the debate over ratification of the Jay Treaty with Great Britain. Hamilton, the Anglophile, led the Federalist party in support of the treaty that Ambassador Jay had consummated, a treaty that leaders such as Madison and the Francophile Jefferson denounced as a complete concession to the British. The Senate ratified the treaty before the opposition had time to focus its efforts, but the battle waged on in the House over appropriations to fund the economic compromise with Great Britain. The battle over the Jay Treaty marked the first—and perhaps only—time in our history in which an issue of foreign policy divided the legislature strictly on party lines. Those who opposed the administration realized that they had to organize their supporters if their vision of a new American society was to be fulfilled; to defeat the Federalist policies, they had to recruit candidates for Congress. Thomas Jefferson, overcoming his sense of loyalty to Washington and his fear of dividing the nation, assumed the leadership of the opposition, the **Jeffersonian (or Democratic) Republican party**.

Thus marked the rise of two-party competition, from the inside out—that is, from the halls of Congress to the limited electorate,

JEFFERSONIAN (OR DEMOCRATIC) REPUBLICANS

The party of Thomas Jefferson that formed around opposition to many of the policies proposed by Alexander Hamilton.

limited by low suffrage, by a relatively small and remote national government, and by the difficulty of information dissemination to voters. Given that presidents and senators were not popularly elected, the Federalists and Democratic-Republicans had to extend their efforts to the states to woo potential presidential electors and to recruit state legislators who were supportive of their respective parties' national candidates. It was largely the legislative leaders who met, planned strategy, and sought and decided upon candidates. The **congressional caucus** came to be the scene of partisan maneuvering.

1. The Elections of 1796 and 1800

Two elections were particularly important in the development of the first American parties. In 1796 John Adams defeated Thomas Jefferson to succeed George Washington, who had stepped down, declining to seek a third term. Washington's action provided for orderly succession in a way virtually unknown until that time; in other words, Washington established the important two-term precedent, which has been violated only once in American history and is now written into the Constitution. While partisan ties were strong enough to carry Adams into the presidency, the votes for vice president were widely scattered. By virtue of the electoral system of the time, second-place finisher Jefferson became vice president. Jefferson agreed to serve under Adams, who thus accepted the legitimacy of his political opposition.

Four years later the two leaders would run against each other again. In 1800 the Federalists chose President Adams to seek reelection against the Democratic-Republican's choice, Vice President Jefferson. By this time, partisan allegiance was much more firmly established. Jefferson and his running mate, Aaron Burr of New York, each received seventy-three **electoral votes**. Adams and his vice presidential nominee, Charles Cotesworth Pinckney of South Carolina, received sixty-five and sixty-four votes, respectively. Because Jefferson's copartisans each cast their two electoral votes for both of the party's candidates, the election ended in a tie and went to the Federalist-controlled House of Representatives. Rumors of possible Federalist action to prevent Jefferson's election were rife: Hamilton devised a strategy to secure concessions from Jefferson, and Adams met with Jefferson for the same purpose. The House meanwhile cast thirty-five inconclusive ballots. Finally, after several desperate Federalist caucuses, Thomas Jefferson was elected the third president of the new democracy (see Chambers 1963, 162–69).

The new governmental system had thus demonstrated remarkable stability: the House had ratified as the new president the man

---

CONGRESSIONAL CAUCUS

The meeting of all members of Congress affiliated with one party; used during the early period to nominate candidates for president.

ELECTORAL VOTE

The votes cast by electors in the indirect system used for choosing the president of the United States; each state is allotted a number of electors equivalent to the number of representatives in Congress plus the number of senators; states determine how the electors will be selected; the winner is the candidate with a majority of the electoral votes.

the nation had elected, despite the fact that he epitomized the political opposition. The peaceful transfer of power from Adams to Jefferson marked a most critical step in legitimating the new system of government and the role of opposition parties within that government.

The election of 1800 marked the high point of partisan conflict during these early years. The Federalist party soon became a New England sectional party, promoting policies too conservative to appeal to the greater electorate. More specifically, the Federalists' denouncement of Congress's declaration of war against Britain in 1812 further diminished their party's credibility in government and among the national electorate. Never able to develop the national following that the Jeffersonians enjoyed, they became politically irrelevant. The Democratic-Republicans dominated the political scene for twenty-four years, without serious opposition during the administrations of Jefferson, Madison, and Monroe. Gone was the intense party competition in Congress; gone was the party competition for electoral support.[3] With the virtual collapse of the Federalist party, the first American party system essentially collapsed.

While the elimination of a major party may seem incredible from today's perspective, we must remember that parties were weak and fragile in the early years of the nineteenth century. Partisan loyalties were not well established; political leaders themselves shifted frequently. In his inaugural address in 1800, Jefferson reflected not on the acrimony of the presidential campaign but on the commonalities shared by the two parties: "Every difference of opinion is not a difference of principle. We have called by different names brethren of the same principle. We are all Republicans, we are all Federalists" (Blum et al. 1993, 176). By the end of the first party system, Jefferson's figure of speech was a matter of reality, with the eclipse of the Federalist party.

Even in Jefferson's administration, few legislators identified themselves according to party. James Young's (1966) renowned study of early American party politics demonstrates that boardinghouse ties—the congressional "fraternities" in which members lived in Washington, essentially social units that formed primarily along regional lines—were as strong as party and that President Jefferson's personal appeals through carefully planned dinners were necessary to gain supporters for his legislation. Coalitions were built from the center out, not from the grass roots into the political arena. Consequently, when the Federalists adopted unpopular policies, they failed to respond to popular protest and quickly lost support. No stable organization saved them from their decline.

Finally, the patrician politicians of the Federalist party had few incentives to save their national party. They viewed themselves as political amateurs, content to return to their prosperous farms and businesses once their service was over. The first "professional" politicians did emerge in this era—lawyers such as Aaron Burr and the first clerk of the House, John Beckley—but these men were thought to be morally inferior to such "true" leaders as Washington, Adams, and Hamilton.

2. Contributions of the First Party System

The most important contributions of the first party system were the invention of the modern political party and the provision of an orderly means of settling political disputes and legitimating the victory of the winner. Instead of being antigovernment, parties became integral to government. In other words, parties became the mechanism through which it was possible to legitimately oppose the policies and leaders of the government without seeming to oppose the form of government itself. The first American parties were, in fact, the kind of parties that Burke had hypothesized as possible some thirty years earlier.

Parties as political institutions developed as enduring organizations during this period.[4] The first party system grew from the center out, the parties at first being elite associations without **grassroots** support. The Democratic-Republican party began with an opposition to administration policy; then legislators realized that they had to find a means to induce the election of like-minded colleagues if their policy preferences were to be adopted. (For other interpretations of this period in the history of American political parties, see Binkley 1963.) The Democratic-Republicans began to develop a party structure based on the congressional caucus, and they began to recruit candidates for all offices. To secure the election of these candidates, the parties had to develop popular followings; and to do so, they had to enlist party workers, that is, adherents who would carry their cause to eligible voters. In sum, American politics was born at this time. During this relatively short period, the groundwork was laid on which subsequent politicians were to build.

GRASS ROOTS

The rank-and-file voters or party members.

B. The Second Party System

Parties thrive on tension and conflict; they cannot grow if they are electorally irrelevant. Thus, the Federalists faded, the last of their presidential nominees readily defeated by Monroe in 1816. With the dissolution of the Federalist party, legislators in Congress were essentially nominal members of the Democratic-Republican party. With little opposition to speak of, Monroe was reelected in 1820, his two terms so lacking in party conflict that the pundits deemed it the "era of good feelings." But the lack of another party to compete with in the electoral arena did not mean a lack of conflict within the dominant party (Courser 2007). Party competition would emerge again from within the ranks of the Democratic-Republicans, as co-partisans competed for the presidency.

Campaigning for the 1824 presidential election began shortly after Monroe's reelection in 1820. Today's political analysts may complain about the length of presidential campaigns and the number of candidates vying for the party nomination, but long campaigns and large presidential candidate pools are not a strictly modern phenomenon. John C. Calhoun, the secretary of war, declared himself a candidate in 1821. Within the next two years, the names of Secretary of State John Quincy Adams; Secretary of the Treasury William H. Crawford; Speaker of the House Henry Clay; and the hero of the battle of New Orleans, General Andrew Jackson, had all been put forward by their supporters.

Crawford might well have been the front-runner, but he suffered a paralyzing stroke in the fall of 1823 and had to stop campaigning. Calhoun withdrew when he was promised the vice presidential nomination by both Adams and Jackson. In the election itself, Jackson led both the **popular vote** (in the eighteen states in which electors were chosen by popular vote) and the electoral vote, but he lacked the majority of the electoral vote needed to gain election. Once again, as had been the case in 1800, the election was thrown to the House of Representatives, where each state's delegation cast one vote.

The House had to choose among the top three finishers—Jackson, with ninety-nine electoral votes; Adams, with eighty-four; and Crawford, with forty-one. Clay, whose power came from the House, had been eliminated by finishing fourth, with thirty-seven electoral votes; but his allies in the House guaranteed him influence. After careful consideration, Clay threw his support behind Adams, who was then chosen by the congressional caucus. When the new president subsequently made Clay his secretary of state, cries of **"corrupt bargain"** were heard throughout the land. No clear evidence of such a trade-off exists, but the "coincidence" of events permanently scarred Clay's reputation. The results also angered Jackson, who felt he had been deprived of what was rightly his.

The election of 1824 created a violent split in the Jeffersonian Republican party, between the backers of Adams (the National Republicans) and those of Jackson (the Democratic-Republicans). Jackson's men organized furiously, and the personal competition increased national interest in politics. By 1828 all but two of the twenty-four states selected their electors by popular vote. The popular vote in 1828 more than tripled that of 1824; thus, Andrew Jackson had his revenge. He defeated the **King Caucus** (as the congressional caucus came to be known) and the elite rule with a

POPULAR VOTE

An election in which the winner is decided by the number of citizens casting their votes directly for particular candidates.

"CORRUPT BARGAIN"

The claim that Henry Clay threw his support in the House of Representatives in the 1824 presidential election to John Quincy Adams, thereby ensuring Adams's election, in exchange for Clay's appointment as secretary of state.

KING CAUCUS

The domination of the nominating process by the legislative caucus.

populist "revolution." More important, Jackson's election marked the beginning of a series of maneuvers that were to solidify the shape of American politics from that date onward.

Jackson's victory in 1828 put a premium on party organization to mobilize voters. The successful grassroots organization by Jackson's supporters was due much in part to the leadership of Martin Van Buren. Often referred to as the "father of parties," Van Buren was the chief architect of the first American mass party and the chief defender of the **patronage system** that supported it. True believers in the adage "to the victors belong the spoils," Jacksonian Democrats doled out jobs and government contracts as rewards for party loyalty, securing a dependable and motivated voting base in the electorate. Supported by a loyal following, Jackson readily won reelection in 1832, having been renominated by his party at the first **national party convention**, with Van Buren on the ticket as vice president. The establishment of the national convention for the purpose of nominating presidential candidates was a deliberate reform to democratize the selection process, by stripping nomination power away from Congress and the King Caucus and giving it to the party rank and file.

As Jacksonian Democrats continued to build support, a new opposition party led by Henry Clay and Daniel Webster, the **Whigs**, was formed to oppose Jackson. The traditional view is either that the Whig party represented the prosperous classes or that the split echoed ethnic heritage, but such easy answers do not explain why New Hampshire was heavily Democratic and why Vermont was heavily Whig or why adjacent areas in New York State often differed in partisan allegiance. The simple truth is that the Whigs united those who opposed Jackson. "Old Hickory" had honed the **spoils system** to a fine point, rewarding legions of friends who helped him politically. Those who lost jobs (or sought and did not get jobs) became "King Andrew's" enemies and joined the political opposition.

By the election of 1836, competition between the Democrats (as the Jeffersonian or Democratic-Republicans came to be called) and the Whigs was intense, and this level of competition lasted into the 1850s. The Whigs learned much from the Democrats, mimicking their mobilization efforts as well as their electioneering style, and even "out-Jacksoning the Jacksonians" in 1840 by nominating a war hero for president—William Henry Harrison, victor against a coalition of Native Americans in the Battle of Tippecanoe and victor against the British in the Battle of the Thames.

The acrimonious presidential campaign of 1840, between Harrison and Van Buren, was run by a new breed of professional politicians; by the mid-nineteenth century, skilled politicians had raised the practice of their profession to an art. Political rhetoric incited

PATRONAGE SYSTEM

An incentive-and-reward system through which those loyal to, and working for, a political party benefit materially when that party wins elections and holds office.

NATIONAL PARTY CONVENTION

A means of nominating presidential candidates by delegates from each state; replaced the congressional caucus as part of democratizing reforms of the Jacksonian era.

WHIGS

Political party that succeeded the Federalists and competed with the Democratic-Republicans through much of the pre–Civil War period.

SPOILS SYSTEM

Reward system under which the spoils of victory, that is, patronage, went to the party workers from the winning party, at the expense of workers for the losing party.

the people; parades stoked their emotions; and catchy slogans, such as the Whigs' "Tippecanoe and Tyler Too" and "Van, Van Is a Used Up Man," simplified their views. Bringing out the vote meant bringing politics to the "common man." Strong party organization on both sides yielded a record number of voters at the polls: 78 percent of adult white males voted in the 1840 presidential election, up from the record set previously by Jackson (the 56 percent turnout in 1828 was more than double the 1824 percentage). Politics had emerged as the true national pastime, and the spoils system retained its place as a powerful tool in the arsenal of nineteenth-century party warfare. Once in office, even the Whigs, who criticized the Democrats' use of patronage as corrupt, proved to be as adept as their counterparts in utilizing the spoils of success to their maximum electoral advantage (Blum et al. 1993, 231, 252–53). Indeed, those who view the current intensity of partisan conflict and competition in American politics as unique would be well served by an examination of this time period.

By the 1850s, it was clear that the leaders of the two major parties could no longer sidestep an inevitable political time bomb: the slavery issue. The slavery question had been a latent source of political conflict within the parties since the Missouri Compromise of 1820, which attempted to "resolve" the intense debate within Congress over the spread of slavery into the new territories. Recognizing the balance between the Union's eleven slave states and eleven free states (a balance that was difficult to change in the evenly apportioned senate), the compromise allowed for Missouri to be admitted as a slave state whereas Maine would gain admission as a free state. In all other territories above latitude 36° 30' north, slavery would be "forever prohibited." Not only did the new law fail to resolve the issue, but it also solidified the growing sectional division in Congress between the Northern and Southern wings of the two parties.

By the 1850s the slavery issue was front and center, igniting the passions of citizens and politicians throughout the country. With the outbreak of war with Mexico in 1846 and the debate over the Wilmot Proviso to prevent slavery in any newly acquired territory, the proslavery and antislavery divisions raged on in the House and Senate. While the Compromise of 1850 secured the admission of California as a free state and abolished the use of the District of Columbia as a depot in the interstate slave trade, it also opened the door to slavery in the New Mexico and Utah territories by granting popular sovereignty on the issue. Neither of the two major parties was willing (or able) to take a definitive stand on slavery, fearing that the inevitable alienation of one wing of their party would result in electoral losses. Yet slavery would prove too difficult an issue for political leaders to straddle. By the election of 1852, the Whig party was in shambles, with the "cotton" Whigs of the South bent on preserving slavery for their economic survival and with the "conscience" Whigs of the North bent on eliminating it. In their last election as a national party, the Whigs received a majority of the votes in only one state.

While the major parties tried to skirt the most crucial question of the 1850s, other parties—that is, third parties in a two-party system—were willing to stand (or fall) on slavery alone. One of the important roles that nonmajor parties play in two-party systems is that of raising and debating the controversial issues of the day (Bibby and Maisel 1998; Sundquist 1983). New parties—first the **Liberty party**, then the **Free Soil party**—brought the slavery issue to the political forefront. Each of these antislavery factions drew significant numbers of votes in presidential elections and thereby elected their supporters to Congress and the state legislatures. The shape of the political system was changing (see figures 2.1 and 2.2).

A coalition of antislavery parties united in opposition to the Kansas-Nebraska Act of 1854, which overturned limits on the expansion of slavery into the new territories. The **Republican party** thus emerged out of this coalition.[5] In 1856 the new Republican party held its first national nominating convention. The nominee, General John C. Fremont, called for the admission of Kansas to the Union as a free state and advocated a policy that upheld congressional authority over slavery in the territories. The Republican party was a sectional party from the start. Drawing on "conscience Whigs," antislavery Democrats, old Free Soilers, and some former "Know-Nothings," (nickname of the nativist anti-Catholic American Party) Fremont got nearly 40 percent of the vote in 1856 (a majority in the North), but he was not even on the ballot in most of the Southern states.

But four years later, the Republicans would take the presidency. Gone were the Whigs, and divided were the Democrats—the North-

LIBERTY PARTY

One of the pre–Civil War parties that brought the issue of slavery into the forefront of the nation's political agenda.

FREE SOIL PARTY

Another of the pre–Civil War parties that focused on the issue of slavery.

REPUBLICAN PARTY

The political party, formed in 1854, that emerged as the major alternative to the Democrats on the issue of the spread of slavery and has remained one of the two parties dominating American politics since that time.

Figure 2.1 Party Division Prior to Realignment on Slavery Issue

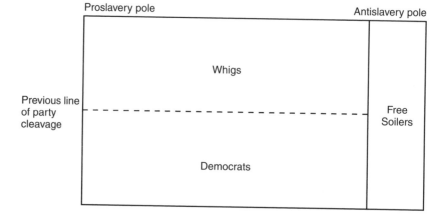

Figure 2.2 Stress on Party System Caused by Slavery Issue

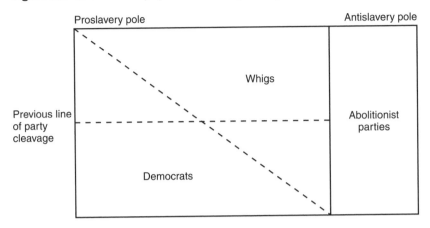

ern and Southern wings each nominated their own presidential candidates. In the election of 1860, Abraham Lincoln, only the second Republican candidate to seek the presidency, defeated Democrat Stephen A. Douglas as well as Southern Democrat candidate John C. Breckinridge and the Constitutional Union party's John Bell, thereby realigning the electorate and ushering in the third party system. Figure 2.3 depicts the **realignment** at the time of the Civil War. For the only time in American political history, a major party was supplanted by a third party, a new party that served virtually no "apprenticeship" but immediately achieved major party status.

The Civil War, of course, meant much more than a change in the party system. The entire political system was threatened, and it nearly collapsed. What emerged was a badly torn nation, divided on the issue of slavery—an issue that was resolved by bloodshed, not political debate. The politics of the post–Civil War period reflected the split of the nation and a whole new way of resolving conflict.

REALIGNMENTS

Fundamental changes in the party system signaled by a new line of cleavage and significant shifting of individuals' party identification.

Figure 2.3 Party System after Realignment on Slavery

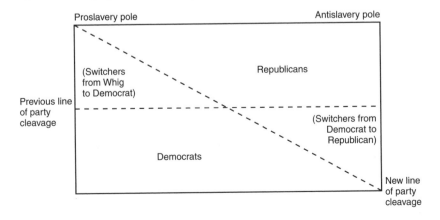

I. Innovations of the Second Party Period

The key innovation of the second party system was the development of an elaborate, complex, and decentralized party organization. Parties began to organize followers and workers at the local, grassroots level, establishing autonomous local units to see to the business of elections. National conventions drew on these local units, emphasizing citizen participation. By the 1830s, politics involved true two-party competition in every region—in fact, in every state except, perhaps, South Carolina. Unlike the first party system in which policy differences were front and center, the electoral aspects of party were critical in this second party system.

The changing attitude toward politics was accompanied by equally significant changes in the law, changes that encouraged the spread of popular participation. Presidential electors came to be chosen by popular vote, with a whole slate of electors running at large in each state. As the Constitution leaves the method of choosing electors to the states (Article 2, Section 1), state politicians soon realized it was to their state's advantage if the winner received all the electoral votes, not just a share. Thus, the "winner-take-all" system was born, and it is still in place in every state except Maine and Nebraska. In addition, the need for a closer link between representatives in Washington and their constituents back home was recognized and actuated by district elections (as opposed to at-large elections) as early as the Jacksonian period, and it was eventually written into law as part of the reapportionment legislation following the Census Act of 1840.

Similarly, the populace began to participate in other elections during this time. More and more governors, previously selected by state legislatures, were now popularly elected. Many local officials, heretofore appointed, had to stand for election. All federal, state, and local elections were conducted according to new democratic rules designed to encourage increased participation. Some of these new election procedures were basic, such as the provision of printed ballots by the state. Some seem only logical, such as holding all elections on the same day and drawing small voting districts (to decrease unneeded and difficult travel). Taken together, these regularized procedures had an enormous impact. Although change came slowly during the second party period, the long-term effect was profound. By 1850, the basic features of the American political system were not unlike those in place today.

C. The Third Party System

The contributions of the second party system—party organization and popular participation—became the foundation for the next.

The third party system roughly coincided with the "Gilded Age of parties" (Dobson 1972; Keller 1977; McCormick 1986; Silbey 1994), the period following the Civil War to the mid-1890s, when political parties achieved unprecedented levels of power and organization. It remains the most competitive period in American history, characterized by intense electoral competition in districts across the country and popular votes in presidential elections so extremely close that pundits of the day called it "the era of no decision." Political historians argue that this competitive atmosphere put a premium on party organization (Silbey 1994; Jensen 1971; Keller 1977). Winning marginal elections required discipline, coordination, and energy; thus, the parties organized and mobilized like "armies drawn up for combat" (Burnham 1970, 72). As a result, this period had the highest turnout of any in American history; from 1868 to 1892, almost 80 percent of all eligible voters showed up at the polls for presidential elections (Silbey 1994, 219), although certainly these figures are inflated somewhat by various forms of election fraud (Rusk 1970, 1974). During the 1870s and 1880s, American political parties became more finely tuned and more fully developed vote-mobilizing institutions than ever before (Silbey 1994, 221–22; Brady, Buckley, and Rivers 2000).

While the nation as a whole was very competitive, rare was the state that was not dominated by one party or the other. For example, consider the instances when Republican James Garfield won the election of 1880 and when Democrat Grover Cleveland won the election of 1884; in each case, with a popular plurality of less than 1 percent, the winning candidate had at least a 10 percent margin of victory in more than half the states. The Republicans would have dominated this period more convincingly had not a series of seemingly unrelated events hurt Republican political fortunes—namely, the economic depression in 1873, the scandals of the Grant administration, a decline in agricultural production in 1884, and the depression of the 1890s. The Democrats, after Reconstruction, made political gains in the South, where resentment by whites toward Republican domination of their region after the Civil War was high and when Southern blacks were prohibited from active participation in politics by the notorious Jim Crow laws. The Democrats won some political skirmishes, but the Republicans were the well-financed and powerful party of the captains of American capitalism. Both national parties were captured by the industrialists, but it was the Republicans that sponsored governmental programs favoring industrial growth and westward expansion.

In addition to being a time of rapid industrialization, the last quarter of the nineteenth century was also a period of significant immigration. Newly arrived immigrants would play an important role in the development of the most significant political innovation

POLITICAL
MACHINE

A group that controls the
activities of a political
party.

MATERIAL
INCENTIVES

Tangible rewards for work
well done.

PATRONAGE

Jobs or other material incentives given to party campaign workers after a successful election.

of this period: the urban **political machine**. In many ways, it is logical that political machines grew up during an era dominated by business growth. As Banfield and Wilson argue, the party organiza- tion of this period was essentially "a business organization in a par- ticular field of business—getting votes and winning elections" (1963, 115).

Each machine was organized as a structured hierarchy: a domi- nant leader, the political boss, ward leaders beholden to the boss, precinct captains beholden to their ward leader, and those who worked the streets beholden to those organizing the precinct. The glue that held these machines together was **material incentives**, tangible rewards for work well done (and the withdrawal of those rewards if the work was not done). **Patronage** jobs were the reward for electoral success. Aid—to the newly arrived immigrant, the un- employed, or the underemployed—ensured loyalty to the machine. The political system proved an effective means for immigrants to assimilate themselves into American society. The political machine provided jobs, lodging, extra groceries, and a means of socialization for new groups of citizens. In return, the immigrant groups pro- vided votes for the machine. Historian Richard Hofstadter went so far as to characterize this third party system as being fueled by these rewards for loyalty: "The parties of the period after the post–Civil War were based on patronage, not principle; they divided over the spoils, not issues. Although American political parties are never cel- ebrated for having sharp differences of principle, the great age of the spoilsmen was notable for elevating crass hunger for office to the level of a common credo" (Hofstadter 1948, 169; Brady, Buck- ley, and Rivers 2000). Material rewards secured loyalty and main- tained discipline among the ranks, both of which were necessary to win closely fought elections.

Perhaps the classic example of an urban political machine dur- ing this era was Tammany Hall, the Democratic New York City ma- chine and its notorious ringleader, Boss William Marcy Tweed. Box 2.1 explains the electoral success of the Tammany machine through the astute and frank insights of one of their own, George Washing- ton Plunkitt, ward boss of the Fifteenth Assembly District in New York.

The importance of patronage, material goods, and constituent services in securing party loyalty to the machine is clear; as Plunkitt acknowledges, "you can't keep an organization together without patronage. Men ain't in politics for nothin'" (Riordon 1995, 37). It is important to note, however, that machines' success was built on more than just patronage. Machines emphasized politics of per- sonal contact, and often provided a welcoming place for newly ar- riving immigrants in an otherwise hostile society (see Handlin 1951; Merton 1957).

Box 2.1
HOLDIN' YOUR DISTRICT MACHINE-STYLE:
LESSONS FROM A TAMMANY TITAN

"Who reads speeches, nowadays, anyhow? It's bad enough to listen to them. You ain't goin' to gain any votes by stuffin' the letter boxes with campaign documents. Like as not you'll lose votes for there's nothin' a man hates more than to hear the letter carrier ring his bell and go to the letter box expectin' to find a letter he was lookin' for, and find only a lot of printed politics. I met a man this very mornin' who told me he voted the Democratic State ticket last year just because the Republicans kept crammin' his letter box with campaign documents.

What tells in holdin' your grip on your district is to go right down among the poor families and help them in the different ways they need help. I've got a regular system for this. If there's a fire in Ninth, Tenth, or Eleventh Avenue, for example, any hour of the day or night, I'm usually there with some of my election district captains as soon as the fire engines. If a family is burned out I don't ask whether they are Republicans or Democrats, and I don't refer them to the Charity Organization Society, which would investigate their case in a month or two and decide they were worthy of help about the time they are dead from starvation. I just get quarters for them, buy clothes for them if their clothes were burned up, and fix them up till they get things runnin' again. It's philanthropy, but it's politics, too—mighty good politics. Who can tell how many votes one of these fires brings me? The poor are the most grateful people in the world, and, let me tell you, they have more friends in their neighborhoods than the rich have in theirs. . . . The consequence is that the poor look up to George W. Plunkitt as a father, come to him in trouble—and don't forget him on election day.

Another thing, I can always get a job for a deservin' man. I make it a point to keep on the track of jobs, and it seldom happens that I don't have a few up my sleeve ready for use. I know every big employer in the district and in the whole city, for that matter, and they ain't in the habit of sayin' no to me when I ask them for a job.

And the children—the little roses of the district! Do I forget them? Oh, no! They know me, every one of them, and they know that a sight of Uncle George and candy means the same thing. Some of them are the best kind of vote-getters. I'll tell you a case. Last year a little Eleventh Avenue rosebud, whose father is a Republican, caught hold of his whiskers on election day and said she wouldn't let go till he'd promise to vote for me. And she didn't."

Source: William L. Riordon, *Plunkitt of Tammany Hall: A Series of Very Plain Talks on Very Practical Politics* (1995), 27–28.

"THAT'S WHAT'S THE MATTER."

BOSS TWEED. " As long as I count the Votes, what are you going to do about it ? say ?"

A different type of patronage fueled the predominantly Republican state party machines—financial support from business interests. The state and regional machines were frequently run by a U.S. senator, and, as a consequence, the Senate of the 1880s resembled a "sort of federation of state bosses" (Dobson 1972, 33). For example, in return for party contributions (and personal gifts of new corporate shares), Pennsylvania Republican senators Simon Cameron and Matt Quay advocated high tariffs in Congress, prevented industry strikes, and kept local and state authorities out of the affairs of business (Dobson 1972, 25; Reichley 1992, 143–45; Brady, Buckley, and Rivers 2000).

The machine bosses—Democratic and Republican, urban and state—directed the party activity, reinforced partisanship, and knew how to mobilize the masses and win elections. "Part skilled, part professional, part tribal chieftain, the boss flourished in a time when a complex industrial society outstripped the instruments of governance" (Keller 1977, 541–42; Brady, Buckley, and Rivers 2000).

Not only did the Gilded Age parties control patronage jobs, but they were the gatekeepers to elected offices as well. During this period, the parties controlled the nominating procedures for all elected offices—that is, a candidate could not get on the ballot without the backing of a party. Parties printed and distributed their own ballots, and, in most states, the parties listed their candidates for national, state, and local elections all on one ballot. Such a system encouraged straight party voting, making it difficult for voters to cross party lines and split their tickets. The different appearance of the party-printed ballots (strategically varied in color and size) made it easy for party workers to spot both loyalists and defectors as they stood in line to cast their votes (Brady, Buckley, and Rivers 2000).

In the Gilded Age of parties, the bosses dominated politics, and the industrialists dominated society. As immigrants found jobs in the expanding factories, their employment symbolized a period of transition in American life, from an agricultural economy to an urban industrial economy. The political system reflected this shift.

But not everyone was satisfied. With the rapid industrialization of the country and the domination of politics and government by the business community, the farmers of the Midwest discovered that they were the consistent losers. As neither major party took up their cause, they soon set out on their own, forming a series of organizations to challenge the existing power structure. The Granger movement spread rapidly in the 1870s, founding a range of cooperatives (from buying and selling grain, to banking and manufacturing) to stop business interests from reaping profits at the expense of farming communities. By the 1880s the Farmers' Alliance emerged as the most powerful of the farmers' organizations to succeed the Grange as a strident voice of agrarian discontent. By the 1890 election, the pressure of the alliance was felt by Democratic candidates across the West and South as they were called upon to "stand up and be measured" against the yardstick of agrarian demands (Blum et al. 1993, 522–23). Finally, the Populists took the frustrations of the farmers into the political realm, their new party raising concerns that threatened the continuation of the existing two-party system. These groups signaled splits that were to lead to a significant change in the context of American partisan politics.

D. The Fourth Party System

Before 1896 both parties favored industrialization, and both parties sought to appeal to urban populations. Things changed, however, in 1896. First, the Democratic party had to carry the burden of the 1893 economic panic during the Cleveland administration, which led to a huge Republican landslide in the congressional election of 1894: Republicans gained 132 seats and completely controlled twenty-four state delegations. Second, the Democratic party became associated with a charismatic leader who attacked business interests, called for softer money and a silver standard, and appealed to the farmers of the nation in a way that alienated urban workers. None could deny the powerful rhetoric of quasi-Populist Democrat William Jennings Bryan:

> The great cities rest upon our broad and fertile prairies. Burn down your cities and leave our farms, and your cities will spring

up again as if by magic; but destroy our farms, and the grass will grow in the streets of every city in the country. (from Bryan's "Cross of Gold" speech ["You shall not press down upon the brow of labor this crown of thorns. You shall not crucify mankind upon a cross of gold."] quoted in Hofstadter 1955, 34)

But many doubted the economic effectiveness of the cause. The campaign of Republican William McKinley—led by perhaps the first modern campaign manager (Marcus A. Hanna) and financed by the nation's industrial leaders—was efficient and effective. Bryan was portrayed as a radical enemy of urban workers. Virtually all the cities came into the Republican fold. The new issue that divided the nation, the silver standard versus the gold standard, caused new regional splits—West versus East, rural areas versus urban—and the Democrats had defined for themselves a losing coalition.

The election of 1896 shifted the line of cleavage between the two major parties, from old Civil War allegiances, which had weakened and led to more intense competition by the 1890s, to economic issues of gold versus silver. Urban, Northern areas were thus aligned against rural, Southern and Western areas. Even though the majority party remained the same, a new party system was in place. The issues that separated the parties and the allegiances of large groups of voters had changed dramatically. The 1896 election determined a new course for American politics, setting a pattern that would see the Democrats as the minority party for years to come.

REALIGNING ELECTIONS

Elections in which the lines of cleavage on which the electorate is divided shift, resulting often, but not always, in a new majority party. See CONVERTING ELECTIONS (p. 457).

The **realigning election** of 1896 signaled the end to the "era of no decision." The Republicans would hold the White House for sixteen consecutive years and for twenty-eight of the next thirty-six years. Although Democrat Woodrow Wilson won the presidency in 1912 and 1916, the electoral coalitions did not change: the Republicans remained the majority party. Wilson won the 1912 election because Teddy Roosevelt split the Republican vote, running on his own third-party ticket, that of the Progressive Bull Moose party. Wilson barely won again in 1916, as many old Progressives marched back to the Republicans. By 1920 the Republican coalition had regained prominence.

With the realignment of the electorate after 1896, Republicans dominated the North and Midwest while Democrats maintained a stronghold in the Southern states and border states. The regional dominance of each party eliminated much of the marginal districts of the Gilded Age (Schattschneider 1956, 1960; Burnham 1965; Price 1971). The decline in competition between the two major parties would take its toll on party organization; that is, no longer were the tightly run, vote-mobilizing institutions of the Gilded Age needed to win (Brady, Buckley, and Rivers 2000).

I. The Era of Reform

Party organization was dealt another blow by the antimachine movements, which were gaining speed at the end of the third party system and which reached their peak in the forth. The most notable reform movements to target the "graft and corruption" of the powerful party machines were the Populists and, after their defeat in the 1896 election, those of the Progressive movement. The antiparty battle cry of the Populists is captured in the preamble of their platform:

> Corruption dominates the ballot box, the legislatures, the Congress, and touches even the ermine of the bench. The people are demoralized. Most of the states have been compelled to isolate the voters at the polling-places to prevent universal intimidation or bribery. . . . We have witnessed for more than a quarter of a century the struggles of the two great political parties for power and plunder. (quoted in Fink 1983, 182).

Popular momentum for the first of the antimachine reforms was provided by Charles J. Guiteau, the deranged, disappointed office seeker who shot President Garfield. His crime and Garfield's death focused popular criticism on the spoils system and indirectly created the **civil service system**. The Pendleton Civil Service Reform Act of 1883 was the first step in the decline of the urban machines, depriving them of their very lifeblood: patronage jobs. The new restriction on patronage positions and the eventual replacement of the spoils system with a merit-based system for government jobs meant voters had less incentive to work for, or remain loyal to, the party machines.

Progressive reforms in the electoral arena had more immediate impacts. The first was the **Australian ballot**, a state-printed ballot cast in secret and listing all candidates for a particular position (not one party's candidates for all positions). The new ballot, adopted in all but two states from 1889 to 1891, enabled **split-ticket voting** and reduced voter intimidation at the polls. The second Progressive reform to reduce the powerful hold of the Gilded Age parties over the electoral arena was the adoption of **direct primary elections**. The mandated primary, which most states instituted from 1905 to 1910, stripped the parties of a critical source of power: control over nominations. Candidates no longer needed the party nod to get on the ballot (Brady, Buckley, and Rivers 2000). In addition, many cities at this time introduced **nonpartisan elections**, in which party names do not even appear on the ballots, further reducing the stronghold of parties at the local level.

These Progressive reforms sapped the strength of the parties by limiting their resources (the "spoils" of nineteenth-century politics)

CIVIL SERVICE SYSTEM

The system of filling government positions through tests of merit rather than allegiance to a political party, instituted in the United States after the assassination of President Garfield.

AUSTRALIAN BALLOT

The form of secret ballot that came into use in the United States during the Progressive Era.

SPLIT-TICKET VOTING

Casting votes for candidates of more than one party in the same election—for example, voting for the Democratic candidate for president and the Republican candidate for the U.S. House.

DIRECT PRIMARY ELECTION

A preliminary election where delegates or nominees are chosen directly by voters.

NONPARTISAN ELECTION

Elections that are determined without reference to a candidate's party affilianiton.

and by restricting their control over nominations and elections. Other reforms of the Progressive Era that were primarily aimed at reining in the powerful corporate interests of the industrial revolution also had a long-term impact on the American political system. For example, in a revolt aimed primarily at politicians who represented the interests of the formidable Southern Pacific Railroad, California governor Hiram Johnson and the new state legislative majority in 1911 passed twenty-three amendments to the California state constitution. Aptly nicknamed by political historians as the "Camelot of California Progressivism," Johnson, with the support of his colleagues, empowered the populace with such electoral ammunition as the **initiative**, the **referendum**, and the **recall**—the last of which would enable voters to remove the governor of California from office ninety-two years later (Schrag 2003).

Lastly, the **Seventeenth Amendment**, adopted in 1913, would further rein in the power of the parties. With the mandated direct election of U.S. senators, no longer would the choice of a state's senators be left to the state legislature and, ostensibly, to the dominant state party.

Thus, the fourth party system was marked by declining party competition after the election of 1896 and by rising Progressive reforms. Given the new rules of the game, American political parties would never again attain such levels of organizational strength and electoral control as they had achieved in the latter half of the nineteenth century (Brady, Buckley, and Rivers 2000).

E. The Fifth Party System

The regional dominance of the major parties and the economic and social groups that supported each since 1896—rural interests for the Democrats, industry and business interests for the Republicans—remained in place for over thirty years. The context of electoral battles shifted during the Progressive Era, but the line of cleavage dividing the parties did not. However, the stock market crash in 1929 and the Great Depression changed everything, shattering the allegiances of the fourth party system and recasting the shape of electoral coalitions for decades to come.

In simplest terms, the American public blamed the Great Depression on Republican president Herbert Hoover and his party. In 1932, Franklin Roosevelt gave hope to the millions who had been hurt by the Depression; they responded by giving their allegiance to the Democratic party. In perhaps the perfect example of a critical election, FDR swept into office with 57 percent of the popular vote and carried the Electoral College 472 to 59. In addition to the traditionally Democratic Southerners, the **New Deal coalition** that brought Roosevelt to office and whose support ensured Democratic

---

INITIATIVE

The process through which citizens can bring a proposed law to a vote by the electorate without legislative approval.

REFERENDUM

An election in which the citizens are asked to vote directly on passage of a piece of legislation.

RECALL

A procedure through which citizens by petition can call for a vote on removing an elected official from office before the end of his or her term.

SEVENTEENTH AMENDMENT

The amendment to the U.S. Constitution that calls for the direct election of U.S. senators; prior to its adoption in 1913, senators had been appointed by state legislatures.

NEW DEAL COALITION

A diverse collection of groups of voters who supported the U.S. Democratic party from 1932 until 1964, making it the majority party at that time.

electoral dominance for the next thirty years were urban workers, minorities (African Americans, ethnic Americans, Jews), and farmers—all of whom were attracted to the increased role of the federal government through the New Deal's public works, prounion legislation, social welfare programs, and farm supports. Throughout the New Deal era, the two major parties were aligned roughly along class lines: the Democratic party supported the working class and the poor; the Republicans represented business interests and the more affluent.

Political scientist Robert Axelrod (1972, 11–12) defines the new coalitions more carefully,[6] maintaining that a group's contribution to a political coalition is a product of three factors: the size of the group, the percentage of the group that turns out to vote, and the loyalty of the group's members to a political party. The interplay of these factors is crucial. For instance, African Americans (those outside of the South) were loyal to the Democratic party during the New Deal (and remain so); but because they represented a small percentage of the population (approximately 10 percent) and because many African Americans either chose not to vote or were prevented from doing so by Jim Crow laws (average turnout of under 25 percent), they did not make up a significant component of the New Deal coalition.

According to Axelrod, the groups contributing most to the New Deal coalition were Roman Catholics as well as union members and their families (each accounting for approximately two in five Democratic voters). Catholic support gained momentum in the 1928 presidential election, when the Democratic party nominated Al Smith, the first Catholic to attain a major party's presidential nomination. Solidifying Catholic support for the Democrats were FDR's promise to repeal prohibition (a policy considered anti-immigrant) as well as the Republican's Know-Nothing past. What solidified union support for the Democratic party were the extensive works programs under the New Deal and the commitment of Roosevelt to the Wagner Labor Relations Act of 1935—or labor's "bill of rights," which established the right to organize, outlawed unfair labor practices, and provided guarantees for collective bargaining.

Significant but smaller contributions to the New Deal coalition were made by the poor (defined as those with relative annual incomes of $3,000), by residents of the twelve largest metropolitan areas, and by Southerners and African Americans (Axelrod 1972, 14). With the exception of the poor and large-city residents, each of these groups was significantly more loyal to the Democratic party during the New Deal than the country as a whole.

What is significant is that although Axelrod was able to sort out members of a Republican coalition—nonunion members, nonpoor, whites, Protestants, residents of smaller cities and rural areas—

none of these groups was much more loyal to the Republican party than the nation as a whole (Axelrod 1972, 18). That is, the Republicans attracted voters disaffected by the Democratic party, but those disaffected were so few as to constitute only a losing coalition during the period of the New Deal and its immediate aftermath.

The division as outlined here defined the cleavage in the American political system for an unprecedented period of time. Most analysts believe that a description of electoral coalitions accurate to the mid-1930s would have been similarly accurate into the 1960s. Even though the Republicans won Congress in 1946, and despite President Eisenhower's defeat of Democrat Adlai Stevenson in both 1952 and 1956, these elections were seen as deviations—Eisenhower's success was more a result of a war hero's popularity than it was an electoral shift to the GOP. The majority of Americans still owed allegiance to the Democratic party, and the issues dividing the electorate were still the New Deal issues. For more than three decades the political agenda would be defined primarily by the same question: Does the federal government have a responsibility to serve as the employer of last resort, intervene actively in the economy, and help those who are unable to help themselves?

While this question remains an important one today, it has been joined by new questions having to do with issues of race (Carmines and Stimson 1989) and, more recently, culture (Brewer and Stonecash 2007; Layman 2001, Leege et al. 2002). As these new issues assumed their place on the national agenda, the New Deal coalition began to show signs of strain.

F. A Sixth Party System?

Political journalists and political scientists have spent a substantial amount of time and effort debating if and when the fifth party system ended (see, e.g., Brunell and Grofman 1998; Ladd 1978, 1991; Silbey 1991; Burnham 1991; Aldrich and Niemi 1990). The best answer seems to be that no one critical election can be isolated as a point to define a critical realignment; instead, the American political system has been undergoing a gradual transformation (Abramowitz and Saunders 1998; Burnham 1991; Ladd 1978, 1991; Ladd and Hadley 1975; Silbey 1991). If 1932 was the quintessential example of Key's theory of critical realignment, then perhaps the period from the late 1960s through the present is exactly what Key had in mind in his theory of secular realignment (Stonecash 2006). Although there is still debate in the field as to whether we are in a sixth party system, scholars do agree that there has been significant change in American electoral politics since the 1960s. Four changes are particularly important to understanding the contemporary electoral universe in the United States: the realignment of the South into a

Republican bastion, the emergence of cultural issues as important factors in elections, the development of a close division between the parties, and the decline and resurgence of partisanship.

1. Realignment of the South

The first noticeable tension in the New Deal electoral coalition was provided by the South (see Aistrup 1996; Alt 1994; Brunell and Grofman 1998; Bullock 1988). Abundant evidence exists that a realignment has happened in the South since the 1960s (Abramson, Aldrich, and Rohde 1998, 2007; Abramowitz and Saunders 1998; Black and Black 2002; Miller 1998; Frymer 1994; Glaser 1996; Jacobson 1996; Mattei and Niemi 1991). But the irreconcilable regional and ideological division within the ranks of the Democratic party that would result in the Southern abdication to the GOP had deep historical, social, and economic roots. Slavery, the Civil War, and Reconstruction not only pitted "the party of Lincoln" against Democrats but region against region: within the Democratic party, these were difficult historical obstacles to overcome.[7] The prominent issues of the 1960s—civil rights and the Vietnam War—further drove the wedge in the Democratic party between conservative Southerners and their more liberal copartisans in the North. The result would be the loss of the South to the Republicans.

The divides between the Northern and Southern wings of the Democratic party were evident even in the early years of the New Deal. What electoral coalitions brought together in the New Deal era, policy coalitions drove apart. In 1938, a group of conservative Southern Democrats voted with Republicans to block passage of Roosevelt's Fair Labor Standards Act. The act would have increased union membership and equalized wages, stripping the South of its major economic advantage over the North: cheap labor. Thus was born the Conservative Coalition, a dominant force in Congress from 1938 to 1965. Conservative Democrats (nearly all Southerners during the New Deal period) continued to vote with Republicans against a majority of the rest of the Democrats on a range of social issues, stopping (or seriously watering down) the passage of Medicare, civil rights, and fair housing legislation; increases in government management of the economy; and welfare policies such as food stamps and Aid to Families with Dependent Children (Brady and Buckley 2002).

But the primary issue that would initially force conservative Southern Democrats into the Republican party was race (Carmines and Stimson 1989). The presidential election of 1948 can be seen as a precursor of this shift. In that campaign, Southern Democrats walked out of their party's national convention in protest over the party platform on civil rights; conservative South Carolina governor

Strom Thurmond, then a Democrat, ran for president under the label of the States' Rights party (the segregationist "Dixiecrats") throughout the South, and he won enough states to garner thirty-nine electoral votes. At the presidential level, the South never returned to the Democratic party as a monolithic bloc. But for state and local offices, Democratic loyalties remained strong for two more decades.

The realignment of the South that began in the 1960s was precipitated by certain critical events: the lunch counter sit-ins that began in Greensboro, North Carolina, in 1960; the freedom rides in 1961; the forced integration of the state universities of Mississippi in 1962 and of Alabama in 1963; the protests in Birmingham, Alabama, and other Southern cities; Martin Luther King's march on Washington, which was the stage for his powerful "I Have a Dream" speech in 1963; and the march from Selma to Montgomery, Alabama, in 1965. Responses by political leaders to those events included passage of the **Civil Rights Act of 1964**, which prohibited discrimination in employment and in public accommodations and which penalized educational systems that discriminated against minorities. Also of great impact was the **Voting Rights Act of 1965**, which protected the voting rights of blacks by outlawing literacy tests and other methods of keeping blacks from voting (Weisbrot 1990). These events accelerated a redefinition of voting allegiances among Southern voters. Black voters registered and turned out to vote in numbers never before seen (see chapter 3). White voters began to look for conservative Republican alternatives. While they initially had difficulty finding such Republican options below the presidential level because the GOP as an organization was so moribund throughout the South that it ran few credible candidates for any office, this eventually changed as the Republican "farm team" developed and grew. Over time conservative Republican options were available up and down the ballot all through the South (Black and Black 2002).

It is important to note that while the issues surrounding race were of critical importance to change in the South, Southern realignment to the GOP was not based solely on race alone. Class too played a significant role. Until relatively recently, the South was the economic backwater of the United States. Most Southerners—black and white—were poor. However, as Key (1949) notes, class conflict stifled the dominance of issues surrounding race. If one was white, one was a Democrat, end of story. As the South began to develop economically after World War II, questions of class began to assume new importance in the region. As early as the 1950s, more affluent white Southerners began to vote Republican in presidential elections. As the region grew more prosperous, Americans from other parts of the country began moving south, and some of them

CIVIL RIGHTS ACT OF 1964

An important piece of legislation, passed as a tribute to President Kennedy after his assassination, that included among its major provisions equal access to public accommodations without regard to race.

VOTING RIGHTS ACT OF 1965

Critical piece of civil rights legislation that permitted the federal government to impose federal registrars on voting districts in which a minority of black citizens were registered to vote.

brought Republican partisanship with them. By the 1960s class concerns, along with race, were clearly moving wealthier Southerners toward the GOP. This trend has continued ever since, and the South now exhibits patterns of class and partisanship similar to those that exist in the rest of the nation (Shafer and Johnston 2006; Stonecash 2000; Stonecash et al. 2003). The rise of cultural issues has also been important to the South's move into the Republican coalition. More will be said on this below.

The shift in Southern alignment is clear in the presidential elections of 1964 and 1968. The only Southern state to cast its electoral votes for the Democratic nominee in 1968 was Texas. Four years earlier, all electoral votes of conservative Republican senator Barry Goldwater came from Southern states. What appeared to be a rising trend in Southern support for GOP candidates had yet to manifest itself at the congressional, state, or local level—at the time of the 1964 election, no Republicans were serving as governor in a Southern state; none was elected to the U.S. Senate; and only 17 of 106 representatives elected to the House of Representatives from the South were Republicans. The Republican state legislator in the South was a rare breed indeed (Bullock and Brady 1983).

By 1996, however, the picture had radically changed. The Republican party was flourishing throughout the South: after the 1996 election, eight of the eleven Southern governors were Republicans; eight of the ten senators up for reelection from the South in that year were also Republicans, and all were reelected; and of the 125 Southerners elected to the House in that election, 71 were Republicans. Republican strength in state legislatures throughout the South reached new post-Reconstruction peaks. That pattern has continued, even with some relatively large Democratic gains in 2006. After the 2006 elections, the Republicans hold six of eleven Southern governorships; seventeen of twenty-two Southern Senate seats; and 76 of the 130 Southern House seats (the total having expanded as a result of reapportionment following the 2000 census). Given these figures, along with Southern patterns in presidential voting, it is difficult to argue that the South has not realigned and that this realignment has not affected national politics.

2. The Rise of Cultural Issues

As noted above, one of the engines driving Southern realignment has been the rise to prominence of cultural issues like abortion and gay rights. From the New Deal through the early 1960s economic issues and class concerns were the primary source of cleavage in the American party system. But by the late 1960s, this had begun to change. In a series of cases beginning in the 1950s, the Supreme Court gradually relaxed prohibitions on pornographic material. In the early 1960s, the Court banned prayer and Bible reading in public schools. The late 1960s saw the second wave of the feminist movement in the United States, along with the full flowering of the counterculture and the sexual revolution. Increasingly, social conservatives became concerned about the direction American society was headed in. Then in 1973 the Court produced the biggest factor in the chain of events that thrust social issues onto the political agenda, declaring abortion legal throughout the United States in *Roe* v. *Wade*.

After *Roe* American electoral politics changed, and this change is still being felt today. Initially, the parties took somewhat ambiguous stands on the new hot-button cultural issues, unsure of where they stood. By the 1980s, however, each party had determined its stands and made them clear for all to see. The Republicans, due in no small part to Ronald Reagan, declared themselves consistently conservative on cultural issues. The Democrats delineated themselves as liberal on these same issues. American voters noticed, and responded. Since the 1980s, cultural issues have become much more important in which party an individual chooses to identify with and which parties' candidates he or she votes for on election day. It is not that these issues have replaced class concerns, but rather that cultural issues have joined class issues in shaping electoral outcomes (for more, see Brewer and Stonecash 2007; Edsall 2006; Frank 2004; Hunter 1991; Layman 2001; Leege et al. 2002)

3. The Parties and the Closely Divided American Electorate

Today one often hears the United States referred to as a "50/50 nation." What does that mean? It means that in terms of politics, the American electorate is almost evenly divided between the two major political parties. There is a certain amount of truth to this description. It is certainly the case that neither party holds a commanding edge over the other—measures of partisanship in the electorate regularly show almost parity between the Democrats and Republicans, the presidential elections of 2000 and 2004 were decided by slim margins, and in 2006 the Democrats retook control of Congress by a slight margin from the Republicans who had been in charge with an almost equally slim majority.

What does this mean for American politics? At the very least it means that it will be very difficult for either party to attain the dominance that the Democrats held during the New Deal era or that the Republicans possessed after 1896, at least barring some dramatic event. It also means that elections will be more closely fought, as control of government could hinge on a handful of races in any given election. We saw this in 2006, and likely will again in 2008. Under conditions like these, partisan political conflict becomes more pervasive and intense, and tensions rise accordingly. It is as if the parties have battled to a tough and bitter draw. Neither side is willing to concede any advantage to the other, and each side is relentless in its respective search for such advantage. While there is considerable debate as to whether this current divide is deep or shallow (Abramowitz and Saunders 2005; Fiorina et al. 2006), there is little doubt that the divide is real (Brewer and Stonecash 2007).

4. The Decline and Resurgence of Partisanship

There is one final phenomenon that has marked the last thirty to forty years of American politics, one that is perhaps more important than any other. That is the decline and resurgence of partisanship in the United States. During the 1970s and 1980s it was common place to read works that basically amounted to the obituaries of American political parties (e.g., Broder 1971; Crotty 1984). Parties no longer structured the electorate, they no longer served as issue shortcuts for voters, they no longer activated and mobilized voters on election day, and they were no longer relevant to candidates for or holders of public office. Elections now, it was argued, are all about individual candidates, personalities, and, perhaps if we were lucky, issues (Beck 1984; Nie et al. 1979; Shea 1999; Wattenberg 1998).

Perhaps these views held some validity for a time, particularly in the 1970s as the American polity (including its parties) recovered from the Vietnam era and Watergate and struggled to find its footing. But views of parties as in decline or somehow losing relevance have no place in contemporary American politics. Wherever they may have been a few years ago, political parties are certainly back now. While the parties do not control nominations as they did during the late nineteenth and early twentieth centuries, the presence and power of parties and partisanship is ubiquitous in the United States of the early twenty-first century. Partisanship structures individual vote choice today at levels not seen since the 1950s. Split-ticket voting is decreasing, and the number of strong partisans in on the rise (Bartels 2000; Hetherington 2001; Stonecash 2006). Partisanship extends across a broader range of issue areas than at any time since the advent of modern survey data (Brewer 2005; Layman and Carsey 2002a, 2002b). The levels of intraparty unity and interparty conflict in Congress are higher than at any time since the nineteenth century, and have been now for a number of years (Rohde 1991; Sinclair 2006; Stonecash et al. 2003). Put simply, parties matter.

II. THE MODERN PARTY ORGANIZATION

The modern American party is no longer one that controls its candidates, no longer the sole keeper of the keys to nomination and ballot access, and no longer the only route to political office and electoral success. In the modern political system it is the constituents, not the parties, who hire and fire candidates. Thus, the Democratic and Republican national parties have had to adapt to this new political environment or risk obsolescence. Overcoming their collective action problem—how to influence individual voting behavior to win elections and implement party policy—required incentives for candidates to commit to the Democratic or Republican label. Parties had to make themselves of use to their candidates—a task that demanded well-funded, well-staffed, and well-coordinated party organization to provide candidates with a gamut of services, from campaign assistance to vote mobilization. Thus, in the latest American party system, a new type of party has emerged. The Democratic and Republican parties are no longer parties in control of their candidates; rather, they have evolved into parties in service to their candidates (Aldrich 1995, 273), and that service is provided from the local level on up. Interestingly, as these services have become more crucial to electoral success, the parties have regained a good deal of the importance that they may have lost from the 1950s through the 1970s. Parties are once again key players in American elections.

A. Local and County Organizations

Organizing party workers, energizing local support, and mobilizing voters to get to the booths are certainly not new to the latest party system. Recall Tammany Hall and the Gilded Age machines, the quintessential local political organizations, and their bosses, the masters of grassroots politics. Lest one think the topic of **local party organization** dry, just think of the infamous Boss Tweed or of Frank Hague of Jersey City, New Jersey, and the four O'Connell brothers of Albany, New York, dominant bosses for most of the first half of the last century; or James Michael Curley of Boston, the engaging rogue on whom Edwin O'Connor patterned *The Last Hurrah*; or Tom Pendergast of Kansas City, Missouri, the local boss who started the career of President Harry Truman. Ed Crump of Memphis, Tennessee; Anton Cermak, Pat Nash, and Richard Daley, of Chicago, Illinois; the list goes on and on. Even after the reforms of the Progressive Era sapped the strength of the urban party machines and weakened party organization in general, some **political bosses** and their local organizations managed to thrive as late as World War II (Mayhew 1986). Their stories are the stuff of legend, their seventy-five-year life span marking a time of colorful, if corrupt, politics in America (Banfield and Wilson 1963; Bridges 1984; Erie 1988; Rakove 1975; Riordan 1963; Steinberg 1972; Tolchin and Tolchin 1971; Wilson 1973).

LOCAL PARTY ORGANIZATIONS

The level of party organization, composed of precinct and ward leaders, that is geographically closest to the voters; in age of strong parties such organizations were cemented together by material incentives controlled by powerful leaders.

POLITICAL BOSSES

Derogatory characterization of the leaders of local party organizations.

But even at their height, organized machine politics did not dominate all of American politics—their operating prowess was not standard procedure across the United States. Political machines existed in approximately two-thirds of the largest American cities during at least a part of this period, but they did not all exist at the same time, nor did they maintain the same level of dominance.[8] And surely, by the last quarter of the twentieth century, traditional political machines had been changed by new moralities and reforms and by new styles of politics and political communications.

Gone are the days when local party organizations relied on material incentives—goods, services, patronage jobs—to cement support in the community. In the days of the classic political machine, precinct leaders were deeply involved in politics—their livelihood dependent on delivering votes for the party. Precinct committees were active and vibrant; precinct clubhouses served as neighborhood social centers; and politics was integral to the lives of those who worked for the government—their very jobs dependent on the outcome of elections. Today precinct captains remain active and committed in only a few urban centers with strong party organizations, most notably in Chicago but to a lesser extent in other cities (see Banfield and Wilson 1963; Gosnell 1939; Tolchin and Tolchin 1971).

Theoretically, the Democratic and Republican parties are organized in each of the roughly 190,000 precincts in the United States. But in practice, a wide variety is the norm—searching for the phone numbers of the Democratic and Republican precinct committees across the United States would prove to be an exercise in futility. Oftentimes, only one party has a precinct committee, and even then, it would be a bonus to have an interested contact person willing to act as a precinct committee chair. But this apparent lack of a comprehensive party structure at the precinct level—the level at which parties are geographically the closest to the electorate—can provide opportunities for influence as well. For example, in the 1980s and into the 1990s, the Christian right motivated their members to show up for local precinct committee meetings in their areas and to attend the nominating caucuses to promote conservative candidates. This grassroots strategy eventually led to conservative control of local Republican party organizations in states such as Texas and Minnesota and has continued to provide a critical base of electoral support for GOP candidates (see Rozell and Wilcox 1995; Green et al. 2006).

The county, however, is the more consistent organizational presence for the Democrats and Republicans at the local level. Each party is organized to some credible degree in most of the three thousand counties across the United States. Large enough for a "critical mass" of politicians to form, county committees tend to have formal rules and officers and are often much more politically active than precinct and ward committees. County committees (and their chairs) are usually elected by meetings of the party faithful—the precinct committee members or, in large urban areas, the ward committees. Elected county committee members are in large part self-selected, with real competition a rarity; they are mostly volunteers. There was a point in the 1970s and 1980s where the vast majority of county organizations were weak, and in many areas that is still the case. However, more and more county organizations are beginning to actively raise money and hire at least some professional staff.

County organization remains an important building block in the overall party structure: many officials are elected at this level; what few patronage jobs remain in the nation are often county jobs; and state legislative districts often fall within county lines. The most active and "professional" county organizations work year-round, building local organizations, recruiting desirable (or discouraging undesirable) candidates, and raising money. But during campaign season, activity heats up in counties for both parties across the nation. The county organizations help register voters, work on get-out-the-vote drives, and coordinate field campaigns for all the candidates running within their jurisdiction, focusing on candidates for local office or on local candidates for state office.

How important are these locally driven activities in the age of modern campaigns, with polling, television, the Internet, and relatively little grassroots campaigning? Many local races are far from "new style" campaigns; often candidates cannot afford the cost of modern campaigning. Local candidates remain dependent on labor-intensive efforts, still heavily reliant on the foot soldiers of American politics—the organizational volunteers at the precinct and county levels. In addition, a good deal of evidence suggests that strong local party organizations do indeed contribute to larger numbers of votes for the national party (Bibby and Holbrook 1996; Frendeis, Gibson, and Vertz 1990; Gibson 1991). Strong county-level organizations can coordinate the various campaigns in an area and thus recruit "better" candidates—functions that the Republican and Democratic national parties have seen as important enough to fund, especially in presidential election years, when each party invests millions of dollars in local and county organizations. Frendeis and colleagues (1990) demonstrate that the ability of a local party organization to recruit candidates is indicative of its strength—the more full the slate on election day, the more likely the county has an actively functioning party organization. When this **recruitment** function is added to the more traditional grassroots roles that party organization plays, the total impact of a strong local party organization on vote totals—while not overwhelming—is still significant.

RECRUITMENT

Effort by party officials to find candidates to run for various offices.

For a local party organization to be successful, it must have a solid base. Grassroots politics is about people, and people need incentives to participate. Without the material incentives most often connected with strong local party machines of the past, fewer and fewer people are becoming involved in local politics. But reversing this trend, energizing activists, and recruiting volunteers require resources, not the least of which is money. Increasingly, local party organizations are getting their hands on this money.

B. State Party Organizations

The storied past of the incentive-based, patronage-fueled party "machine" was not limited to the cities or to local party organization. Many notorious and powerful state-run party machines dominated the politics of the Gilded Age, into the Progressive Era as well. Generally, the "machine" of the dominant party in a state was headed by one of its two U.S. senators, as the prevailing tradition of the day, **senatorial courtesy**, granted majority party senators control of most federal patronage in their home state. Put simply, the practice of senatorial courtesy meant that if a senator in the president's party objected to an appointment, the other senators would refuse to confirm the prospective appointee. The existence of this potential veto thus made it possible for senators to determine who in their state would get federal appointments, providing the necessary material incentives to cement a strong state party organization. Furthermore, senators had their own self-interested incentives for utilizing patronage to build and maintain strong state party organizations and for supporting candidates of their party to the state legislature. Until the passage of the Seventeenth Amendment to the U.S. Constitution (passed in 1912 and ratified in 1913 as part of the Progressive agenda), U.S. senators were appointed by state legislatures, not elected by the people. Their own reelection was dependent on maintaining their party's majority status back home.

Some of these senator-bosses were as powerful and almost as legendary as the notorious urban machine leaders: Republicans Boies Penrose, Simon Cameron, and Matt Quay, all of Pennsylvania; Republican Thomas Platt of New York; Republican Stephen B. Elkins of West Virginia; Democrat Arthur Pue Gorman of Maryland; and Democrat Thomas Martin of Virginia. The power of state organizations seemed to wane after World War I, but some notable exceptions persisted: the Democratic machine founded by Huey Long and continued by his heirs in Louisiana; Eugene Talmadge's Democratic organization in Georgia; and the Republican organization headed by J. Henry Roraback and the Democratic organization controlled by John M. Bailey, both of Connecticut.

For a period of time, however, state party organizations seemed

SENATORIAL COURTESY

The right of any U.S. senator to veto (and as a practical matter to approve) any appointee from that senator's state if the appointment requires senatorial confirmation.

ready to disappear not only from public view but also from any place of significance in the political process (Key 1956). State party committees were largely shadow organizations, their only possible function being to serve the will and the cause of a few elected politicians. In the last quarter century, however, in terms of their role in the political system and the interest of political analysts, state-level organizations have made a remarkable comeback (Cotter et al. 1984, 1989; Huckshorn 1976).

I. The Structure of the State Party

Today, state party central committees operate for both parties in each of the fifty states, and the means of choosing committee members is set by state law. In twenty-seven states, the law mandates that state committee members be chosen by local-level committee members or by delegates to state, congressional district, or county conventions. In fourteen other states, the law mandates that the parties determine their own selection process. In the remaining nine states, the law grants voters the right to choose state committee members in primary elections. All of these means of selection are significant. Those who favor strong party organizations, such as the bipartisan Committee for Party Renewal (Epstein 1991; Mileur 1991), believe that the state should interfere as little as possible with the internal workings of political parties. The further the member selection process is removed from the public—though not from public view or accountability—the more likely it is that party leaders will maintain a firm hold on state committee operations, the most important of which are electing the state party chair and supporting the initiatives of the headquarters staff.[9]

Effective state party chairs not only lead the state committee—defining its tasks and setting its goals—but they also act as the linchpin between the grassroots party and the national party. Each state party chair coordinates state, county, and local organizations, directing an increasingly complex and electorally involved state headquarters—the engine of the success or failure of the state party organization. Surely, state party machines of the pre–World War I period had headquarters and workers on a payroll; but for many years, from the administration of Franklin Roosevelt through that of Dwight Eisenhower, little was known about what went on in state headquarters.

The rejuvenation of state headquarters seems to have begun in the early 1960s—ironically at the same time that the candidate-directed campaign replaced the traditional, party-directed one. At that time, only a few state chairs occupied full-time paid positions. By 1990, however, nearly every state party was administered by either a full-time paid chair or a full-time paid executive director, or both. Whereas once the headquarters of the state committee "traveled" from city to city as the hometown of the state chair changed, now virtually all state committees are housed in permanent headquarters, almost always in the state capital. Some of the headquarters contain the most up-to-date campaign technology, allowing for sophisticated campaigning for candidates for state and local office (Appleton and Ward 1997; Reichley 1992; Bibby 1990, 1998; Sabato 1988).

Concomitant with this strengthened presence has come a sizable increase in the budgets for state headquarters. The Party Transformation Study revealed that the average budget for state parties rose nearly five times (to nearly $300,000 annually) between 1961 and 1979. By 1984, the average had risen to nearly $350,000, with the largest state budgets reaching $2.5 million and with only a quarter of the party committees operating with budgets of less than $100,000. Impressive as these increases are, they have been dwarfed in recent years by the shear amount of money that state party organizations are now raising. According to the Institute on Money in State Politics, the one hundred state party committees (fifty for each party) raised $457.6 million in 2000, and followed that with $571.6 million in 2002. In 2004, even after losing access to millions in soft money contributions from the national parties (see chapter 5), the state party committees still pulled in an impressive $296.7 million. The California Republican Committee alone raised $26.7 million (Barber 2005). If one adds the state party legislative committees to the mix, the total raised by state party organizations rises to $411.2 million for 2004 (Institute on Money in State Politics 2005).

Clearly, state parties now have significant resources at their disposal.

2. The Role of the State Party

Professionally staffed with increased budgets and a permanent headquarters, the modern state party organization is a service-oriented entity continually engaged in building the state party and in supporting candidates for local and state offices. Not only do the state organizations raise funds to meet their own budget projections, but the state parties also directly support their candidates through individual contributions, a factor that can make all the difference in campaigns with smaller expenditures (such as that of a state representative). The state party organizations actively recruit[10] (and even **decruit**) candidates for local and state offices to ensure the strongest party candidate in the general election. Endorsement by a strong and effective party organization can have a great deal of impact because primaries are typically characterized by low voter turnout. State parties are continually at work to increase turnout in

DECRUITMENT

The effort of party officials to discourage an individual from seeking a particular party nomination.

both primary and general elections, identifying potential supporters and registering new voters well in advance of election day. They conduct public opinion polls to identify issues important to state and local residents, and they get out the word to the rank and file through newsletters and communiqués. Last but certainly not least, the state party organizations exercise their influence on the national party by selecting delegates to national nominating conventions. (For elaboration on these activities see Huckshorn 1991, 1061–63.)

State party organizations have grown and developed in recent decades, in part because of an infusion of funds and influence from the national level. At the same time, state organizations stand as a cogent reminder of an organization's ability to adapt to a changing environment (Maisel 1998; Bibby 1998). Three decades ago, candidates could safely ignore most state party organizations if they were interested in running for office. Analysts could be ignorant of the functioning of the state party and miss little of what was important in a state's politics. Neither is true today.

C. Party Organization at the National Level

In 1964 Cotter and Hennessey called their important study of the two **national committees** *Politics without Power.* Their title aptly caught the significance of what transpired at the two national committee offices. Politics was everywhere; politicians were everywhere; intrigue was everywhere. But no one cared. The national committees had no resources, they had no influence, and they had no power. Nearly three decades later, Paul Herrnson (1990, 41) wrote that "national party organizations in the United States are now financially secure, institutionally stable, and highly influential." Virtually every aspect of party organization has been transformed in recent years, but in no case is this change more apparent than in the national party organizations, the major components of which are the **Democratic National Committee (DNC)** and the **Republican National Committee (RNC)**, the pinnacle of the party hierarchy, and the so-called **Hill committees**, the congressional and senatorial campaign committees of the two major parties.

1. The National Committees

The Democratic National Committee has existed continuously since 1848; the Republican National Committee, since 1856. Each was structured as a means of coordinating national election campaigns. (For an exhaustive history of the national committees and their chairs, see Goldman 1990, in addition to Cotter and Hennessy 1964.) Formation of the national committees was an important step in changing the parties from loose and totally autonomous confederations of state party activists to more federalized organizations

---

NATIONAL COMMITTEES

The pinnacle of the national party organizations, comprised of delegates from the states and from groups important to the political parties.

DEMOCRATIC NATIONAL COMMITTEE (DNC)

The ruling body for the Democratic party between national conventions.

REPUBLICAN NATIONAL COMMITTEE (RNC)

The highest-ranking body in the Republican party, though party rules restrict its power in ways in which the DNC cannot.

HILL COMMITTEES

The name applied to the four party committees, one for each party in each house, charged with aiding candidates for Congress.

with a unified purpose (Herrnson 1990, 41–42). For the first century of their existence, the two national committees were involved principally with presidential elections. Only in recent decades have their roles expanded.

Although each party's national committee is composed of representatives from the various states, the Republican National Committee (RNC) follows a principle of equality among the states in determining membership. The RNC is composed of three representatives from each state: a national committeeman, a national committeewoman, and the state party chair.[11] The Democratic National Committee (DNC), however, begins with state representation—a national committeeman, a national committeewoman, the state chair, and the highest-ranking officer of the opposite gender from each state—and expands from there. Two hundred additional members are apportioned among the states according to a formula weighing population and Democratic vote in the last presidential election. Others are added ex officio because of positions they hold—the officers of the DNC (who need not otherwise qualify as members); three governors, including the chair of the Democratic Governors' Association; the party leaders in the House and Senate and an additional member of each body; representatives of the Young Democrats and the National Federation of Democratic Women; representatives of Democratic mayors, county officials, and state legislators; and up to twenty other at-large members to accommodate groups still underrepresented. The DNC in 2004 totaled 440 members. Because each committee is too large and unwieldy to work as an efficiently functioning body, each meets only twice a year. Thus, it is the RNC's executive council and the DNC's executive committee that serve as the actual decision-making organizations.[12]

RNC chair Mike Duncan and DNC chair Howard Dean each have substantial influence among respective copartisans. They are in some instances the spokespersons for their parties and, in the case of the "in-party chair," spokespersons for the president on party matters. For the Republicans, the chair and the cochair (one man, one woman) are elected by the full RNC in January of each odd-numbered year for a two-year term, a full-time paid employee of the committee (currently the RNC also has a general chairman in the person of Senator Mel Martinez [Fla.]). During the Reagan and Bush administrations, chairs were "nominated" by the presidents and anointed by the RNC. After the Republicans lost the White House in 1992, they turned to Haley Barbour as their new chair. A longtime party official from Mississippi, Barbour was one of those credited with the rejuvenation of the GOP in the South. A prodigious fundraiser, Barbour spent much of his two-year term criticizing President Clinton and working with Republican leaders in Congress, most notably, playing a critical leadership role in the 1994 House Republican revolution. Barbour did not seek a third term as chair in 1997 and was replaced by Jim Nicholson, who had served for a decade on the RNC representing Colorado. Whereas Barbour's selection had been without opposition, Nicholson emerged from an eight-person field, a clear demonstration that the office is one prized by party leaders.

Typically less precise, the Democratic party rules call for a chair, five vice chairs, a secretary, a treasurer, and "other appropriate officers." The "old tradition" allows for the successful Democratic presidential candidate to name the DNC chair, but competition is more open when Republicans win the White House. After the party's debacle in the 1994 congressional elections, the position of party leader was transformed: the general DNC chair became the public face of the party whereas the **national chair** administered the party apparatus. Each of these was the clear choice of the White House. The decision to split leadership between a visible public official and a more nuts-and-bolts-oriented party leader represents a new pattern for the party.

For professional politicians, the national committee chair—the most important position for setting and coordinating the electoral strategy of the party—is a position of status and career value. Because of its high visibility within the party rank and file and because of its importance to the electoral careers of fellow copartisans in, and aspiring to, Congress and the White House, serving as the national committee chair can be not only a rational, hierarchical career move to the pinnacle of the party organization but also a stepping-stone to those aspiring to elected federal and state positions. For example, Haley Barbour followed his successful stint as GOP chairman by becoming governor of Mississippi. Many believe that current DNC chair Howard Dean so actively sought the post, at least in part, with an eye on another future run for elected office.

But the high visibility and responsibility of the position also mean that the party faithful and the pundits alike point their fingers first and foremost at the national party chair when the party suffers at the polls. The position of national party chair can be a lightning rod in times of electoral loss. For example, then DNC chair Terry McAuliffe took much of the heat for the historic midterm Democratic losses in the 2002 election, blamed for the lack of cohesive party strategy to defeat the GOP and to prevent unified Republican control of Congress and the White House.

2. The "Hill Committees"

Composed of House incumbents, the **National Republican Congressional Committee (NRCC)** and the **Democratic Congres-**

NATIONAL CHAIRS

The heads of the national committees, charged with the day-to-day functioning of the national parties.

NATIONAL REPUBLICAN CONGRESSIONAL COMMITTEE (NRCC)

The Republicans' party committee that is charged with raising money for and aiding in the campaigns of candidates for the House of Representatives.

sional **Campaign Committee (DCCC, or "D triple C")** have been in existence since the end of the Civil War, growing out of members' typical insecurity concerning the majority status of their party. The Hill committees of the Senate are the **National Republican Senatorial Committee (NRSC)** and the **Democratic Senatorial Campaign Committee (DSCC)**, both created by Senate party leaders after the passage of the Seventeenth Amendment. During most of their existence, however, the Hill committees were of little consequence. They did not have access to the resources—specifically grassroots organization and volunteers—that were critical to winning campaigns. As campaigns moved into the electronic media age and candidates began to take more responsibility for directing their own campaigns, the most important resource became money, not party workers. The Hill committees have proven very adept at raising money, and thus have become far more important players in recent years (Dwyer and Kolodny 2006; Kolodny 1998).

3. The National Parties Respond

At the dawn of the modern electoral era, parties as significant contributors to electoral politics appeared to be a threatened species. With candidates taking greater responsibility for directing their own campaigns and the use of "wholesale" techniques of reaching voters (radio, television, and computer-generated mailings) rather than the "retail" techniques of traditional parties (personal relationships and loyalty), the Democratic and Republican party organizations appeared to be heading toward obsolescence. Instead of becoming the dinosaurs of American politics, however, the parties responded to change, adopting a new role in an evolving political reality (Aldrich 1995; Maisel 1990c, 1998).

The initial impetus for organizational change in the Democratic party was the 1968 party convention. From riots outside to fighting within, it was clear that the party was unraveling. After the election of President Nixon, the Democrats undertook a period of intense **party reform** with the goal of making the party more open, more representative, and more democratic. To achieve this goal, the party became more centralized, with reform commissions operating out of national headquarters and stipulating rules that governed state and local party procedures (for assessments of these reforms, see Polsby 1983; Polsby and Wildavsky 1996; Wayne 1996).

For the Republicans, the catalyst for change was the Watergate debacle, the disastrous 1974 congressional elections, and Jimmy Carter's defeat of Gerald Ford in the 1976 presidential election. One veteran GOP operative explained this turning point in the party's organization as such: "You almost have to roll over and be dead before you can revive. We had to do new things because we had

DEMOCRATIC CONGRESSIONAL CAMPAIGN COMMITTEE (DCCC, OR "D TRIPLE C")

The Democrats' party committee that is charged with raising money for and aiding in the campaigns of candidates for the House of Representatives.

NATIONAL REPUBLICAN SENATORIAL COMMITTEE (NRSC)

The Republican party committee that is charged with raising money for and aiding in the campaigns of candidates for the U.S. Senate.

DEMOCRATIC SENATORIAL CAMPAIGN COMMITTEE (DSCC)

The Democratic party committee that is charged with raising money for and aiding in the campaigns of candidates for the U.S. Senate.

PARTY REFORMS

The efforts to change the rules and proceedings of the political parties to make them more democratic and responsive to the citizenry.

PARTY RENEWAL

The effort to change the way in which political parties operate so that they can play a more important role in the electoral process.

one foot in the grave" (Clymer 2003a). Former Tennessee senator William Brock, an advocate of **party renewal**, won the election to head the Republican National Committee in 1977. At approximately the same time, two other strong party advocates—Representative Guy Vander Jagt of Michigan and Senator Robert Packwood of Oregon—were chosen to head the NRCC and the NRSC, respectively. These three leaders saw it as their mission to build their organizations into effective campaign support for Republican candidates, focusing on party building for the long haul—the results of which GOP candidates are reaping the benefits of today.

First and foremost, a rigorous program for building the party's financial base was developed. The Republican party's finances increased dramatically after Brock, Vander Jagt, and Packwood took command—notably, through direct mail fund-raising, which provided a reliable and steady flow of checks to the party, however small the donation. With a sound financial base, the Republicans moved all their national organizations into a party-owned national headquarters and hired a sophisticated staff to serve the campaign needs of Republicans throughout the nation.

The RNC's long-term electoral strategy was to groom candidates at the local and state level to ensure the depth of the GOP candidate pool in future elections. Fostering this GOP "farm team" placed a premium on candidate recruitment for local offices and state legislatures. Campaign training schools were established, and local liaisons put in place. The GOP national committees worked with regions and states, appointing policy directors, organizational consultants, and fund-raising advisers to fan out across the country. Computer services were made available for all party candidates to assist, for instance, with compliance with campaign finance regulations, research on public opinion, compilation of voting lists, and analyses of opponents' records. In short, the RNC provided a full-service campaign consulting organization for Republican candidates (see Herrnson 1990, 1998b).

The Republicans did not stop there. The RNC and their two Hill committees developed truly awesome fund-raising capabilities so that they could support Republican candidates for federal office to the full extent permitted by law. The NRCC and the NRSC entered into "agency agreements" with state party organizations, empowering the national offices to pay the state parties' share of campaign contributions and coordinated expenditures in House and Senate races (Herrnson 1988, 1990, 1998b; Jacobson 1985a).

In the starkest terms, the Democrats were caught napping—and they fell far behind in their fund-raising and organizational efforts. While their party's initial reforms may have conformed to a philosophical need to democratize the party, greater organizational change and party renewal would be essential for the DNC and the

Democratic Hill committees to begin to support Democratic candidates in ways even remotely similar to the Republican model. As with the Republican party, the impetus for Democratic party reorganization was massive electoral defeat. The 1980 election saw President Carter's landslide loss to Ronald Reagan, the loss of the Democratic majority in the Senate for the first time since 1954, and the loss of thirty-four House seats (half the margin the Democrats held before the election).

Charles Manatt, a longtime Democratic activist and fund-raiser, was elected chair of the DNC after the 1980 debacle. At the same time, the enterprising and ambitious Representative Tony Coelho of California took over the DCCC (Herrnson 1988; Jackson 1988). And in rapid succession, two senators committed to party building: Lloyd Bentsen of Texas and George Mitchell of Maine were elected to chair the DSCC. Although the Democratic national party was still organizationally behind its GOP counterpart, party efforts finally began to pay off. Task forces of consultants were established to aid Democrats in about a third of the states—double that number by 1988—with the same kinds of services the Republicans were supplying throughout the nation. The Democrats even moved all their organizations into a new party-owned building, complete with an impressive media studio. But catch-up is a difficult game to play, and for many years the Democrats were simply unable to match Republican efforts in terms either of supplying services or of helping candidates and parties with significant infusions of funds (Herrnson 1998b). To paraphrase George Washington Plunkitt of Tammany Hall, the Republicans saw their opportunities first and they took them, and the Democrats have been swimming upstream ever since. However, the Democrats are closer now than they have been since the rejuvenation of the national party organizations began in the 1970s (more will be said on this in chapter 5).

Both parties have used knowledge and experience gained at the national level to improve state and local organization. While the national Democratic party has imposed rules on its local party units—that is, "sticks" to compel action—the Republicans have refused to do so. However, the Republican party has used money and services as financial inducements to entice its state and local units to professionalize their operations, "carrots" also used by the Democrats but in much smaller amounts. Thus, though in different ways, the "nationalization" of party organization goes on in both parties, affected more by the recognition of the sources of funds and of expertise than by philosophical concerns. The parties have adjusted to new situations, realizing that they are primarily electoral institutions and that they have had to find a means to make their contribution significant to those running for office. They have successfully done so, and the parties are once again key actors in the drama of American elections.

III. POLITICIANS VIEW PARTY ORGANIZATION

"Getting out the vote—(GOTV)" has traditionally been the forte of one party in particular—the Democrats. By November 2002, it became clear that vote mobilization was no longer a cornered market. When a Republican National Committee study of the 1998 and 2000 elections revealed Democratic candidates consistently gaining ground from union vote drives in the final hours before the polls closed, the GOP created its own turnout machine to counter the Democratic advantage. The 72-Hour Task Force—spearheaded by the RNC, with White House GOP strategist Karl Rove—sent fifteen hundred operatives across the country with one mission: to mobilize Republican voters, especially those who tended to avoid voting in nonpresidential election years (such as evangelical Christians). Supervisors and their field operatives recruited volunteers—from churches to rotary clubs—to make phone calls and canvass neighborhoods. Volunteers were bused from safe GOP districts to neighboring ones in need of assistance—a program credited to future majority House leader Tom Delay. Tested in governors' races in 2001, the task force was deployed in over thirty states to help GOP candidates beat their challengers in the 2002 midterm elections (Halbfinger 2002; Clymer and Rosenbaum 2002).

In Georgia, the new vote-mobilizing arm of the RNC proved a formidable one. Led by GOP state party chair Ralph Reed, a proven master of grassroots politics after years as head of the Christian Coalition, the 72-Hour Task Force was put in place well in advance of election day. In the summer of 2002, Reed deployed three thousand volunteers and five hundred paid workers to knock on 150,000 doors in six hundred target areas across Georgia. President Bush's visit three days before the election signaled the final push for GOP votes. After the president's pep rally for Republican senate and gubernatorial challengers Saxby Chambliss and Sonny Perdue, five hundred volunteers boarded buses to canvass thirty thousand GOP homes in just five hours. The results were record breaking, with the organizational prowess of the task force undeniable. For the first time since Reconstruction, the Republican party won the governorship and held a majority in the state senate. Even the Democratic Speaker and senate majority leader in the state house were defeated. As Reed explained, "The story of 2002 is not that Democrats stayed home. . . . It was that Republicans came to the polls in historic numbers" (Halbfinger 2002).

Thus the "story of 2002" is really one about the modern American party and its adaptability. Even in this age of candidate-centered elections and personal-vote bases, the Republican National Committee (and Karl Rove) emerged as the MVP of the 2002 midterms, while the DNC and Democratic house leader Richard Gephardt were held accountable for Democratic defeat at the polls. In other words, Republican victories and Democratic losses in Georgia were less about individual candidates and more about the power of party organizations in determining the outcome of the elections. Much of the decline in competitive races across the nation in the post-1960s electoral era, primarily owing to the incumbency advantage and the personal vote, negated the need for strong party organization to get out the vote for candidates. But in areas where party competition is heightened, parties offer invaluable services to their candidates, which can be the difference between victory and defeat. The critical role of the parties and their GOTV efforts was on display once again in 2004 as many attributed President Bush's reelection to the yet again superior seventy-two-hour strategy of the GOP (especially in the critical state of Ohio) (Edsall and Grimaldi 2004) and 2006 as the Democrats, with a big assist from organized labor, responded to the recent Republican edge with an impressive effort of their own (Balz and VandeHei 2006; Greenhouse 2006).

The American party may not be on a historical trajectory from development to dominance to decline to disappearance, as some political historians have argued.[13] An electoral system where candidates are prominent and take active roles in directing their own campaigns need not be void of strong and relevant party organizations. The strength of the modern-day parties rests not in the controls they wield over their candidates but in the services they can provide them. In today's closely divided polity, those services are sometimes the difference between election night celebration and a sleepless night wondering what could have been.

WEBSITES

www.democrats.org: The official website of the Democratic party.
www.rnc.org: The official website of the Republican party.
www.politics1.com: Directory of (and links to) third parties in the United States.
www.lib.umich.edu/govdocs/polisci.html: Go to "United States Politics and Elections" for extensive information.

CHAPTER 3

Voting and Other Forms of Political Participation

Young people demonstrate at a Republican rally featuring Vice President Dick Cheney at Allegheny College in Meadville, Pennsylvania, in 2004. Both parties, but especially the Democrats, placed a high premium on turning out the youth vote in 2004.

If you travel abroad and talk to your hosts about American elections, the most often-heard complaint about our system of government is that so few citizens turn out to vote. In the 2004 presidential elections only about 55 percent of those of voting age bothered to go to the polls. In the 2006 congressional elections, slightly more than one-third voted. Citizens of "less developed" democracies—ironically, those countries with voter turnout of over 75 percent—ask incredulously, "How can you say the United States is a model we should follow when so few bother to take part in your democratic processes?"

When you think about the razor-thin margin by which President Bush carried Florida and thus won the presidency in 2000, think about how many Floridians did not even bother to vote. The 2000 election showed everyone that the question of "Who votes and who does not?" is more than just a question of how one evaluates American democracy: it is often crucial to who wins.

Extremely close races are not all that rare. In Connecticut's Second Congressional District in 2006, Democrat Joe Courtney won by an eighty-three-vote margin over incumbent Republican Rob Simmons. The issue is not just how many turn out to vote but which voters go to the polls. Simmons was left to wonder whether the Senate race in Connecticut—a race in which incumbent Senator Joe Lieberman lost his party's primary but then ran and won in the general election as an independent—led some Republicans to stay home. The Republican Senate candidate won the lowest percentage of votes for any major party candidate in Connecticut history. A stronger candidate might have brought more Republicans to the polls, saving Simmons's seat.

In the closest Senate races in 2006, Democratic challengers Jim Webb in Virginia and Jon Tester in Montana beat incumbent Republicans George Allen and Conrad Burns by 0.4 percent out of nearly 2.4 million votes cast and 0.9 percent out of nearly half a million, respectively.[1]

Voting is only one aspect of political participation, albeit the only type of activity in which most citizens participate (see Verba, Scholzman, and Brady 1995). It is perfectly legitimate to question whether other forms of participation are more important than voting or whether any participation at all is better than none. This chapter begins with an examination of voting, exploring the expansion of the **franchise** and the exercise of the right to vote. Then we turn to the question of how people decide for whom they will vote, a complex question that political scientists have worked on for decades. Finally we look at other forms of political participation, activities that require more commitment by citizens and are therefore the choice of fewer Americans. We also raise questions about nontraditional forms of participation, some of which are viewed as acceptable in other nations but not ours.

FRANCHISE

The right to vote.

I. WHO VOTES; WHO DOESN'T

The discussion of voting in America can be broken down into two separate topics: who is eligible to vote and who exercises the franchise.

A. Expansion of the Franchise

In 1789, only white males who owned property, about one in thirty Americans, were generally eligible to vote (Bone and Ranney 1976, 35). Today, legal limitations keep very few citizens from voting. The history of this aspect of electoral reform in America has been one of continuous expansion of the franchise. This history has four phases: increase in white male eligibility, enfranchisement of black citizens, enfranchisement of women, and enfranchisement of those between the ages of eighteen and twenty-one. More recently, reformers have turned from asking who is eligible to vote to asking what impediments keep those who are eligible to vote from actually exercising that constitutionally mandated right.

1. Property Requirements

The first step in expanding the franchise involved eliminating the property requirement for white males, namely, by replacing it with the requirement that only taxpayers could vote. This reform happened on a state-by-state basis, starting before the ratification of the Constitution, when Vermont granted universal male suffrage in 1777 and when South Carolina substituted a taxpayer requirement for a property-holding requirement, in 1778. The property qualification finally disappeared when Virginia eliminated it in 1850.

A taxpayer requirement persisted for some years, often being fulfilled with the payment of a nominal **poll tax.** The poll tax, employed mainly in the South to keep blacks from voting, affected poor whites as well. By the 1960s all but five states had eliminated even nominal poll taxes. Those remaining taxes were rendered void for national elections with the ratification of the **Twenty-fourth Amendment,** in 1964; two years later, the Supreme Court held poll taxes to be unconstitutional in any election (*Harper v. Virginia State Board of Elections,* 383 U.S. 663, 1966).

2. Black Suffrage

The **Fifteenth Amendment** to the Constitution, ratified in 1870, was the culmination of a number of post–Civil War steps toward granting black males the right to vote. That amendment forbade states from denying or abridging the right to vote based on "race, color, or previous condition of servitude."

POLL TAX

A tax paid by each person as he or she exercised the right to vote; the tax weighed especially heavily on poorer citizens, as marginal dollars meant more to them.

TWENTY-FOURTH AMENDMENT

The amendment to the U.S. Constitution that prohibited the use of the poll tax or any other tax as a requirement for voting.

FIFTEENTH AMENDMENT

Amendment to the U.S. Constitution that explicitly states that individuals could not be denied the right to vote based on "race, color, or previous condition of servitude."

However, that seemingly broad prohibition did not end the problem of racial discrimination in voting. Post-Reconstruction Southern legislators were extremely inventive in creating ways to prevent, or at least discourage, blacks from voting. These legal limitations, the so-called **Jim Crow laws**, included literacy tests, tests on interpreting the Constitution, **"whites only" primaries**, poll taxes, and **residency requirements**. Social and economic pressures as well as administrative decisions, such as locating polling places in remote areas or in areas that had been the site of black lynchings, further restricted black voting. The black vote was more apparent than real in most Southern states during the first half of the twentieth century. In 1960, fewer than 10 percent of the African American citizens of Mississippi were registered to vote.

The first important attack against Southern restrictions on black voting was the landmark Supreme Court decision in *Smith v. Allwright,* 321 U.S. 649 (1944). Southern states had established in law that political parties were private organizations that could decide their own membership, including a provision excluding blacks. Democratic primaries were then activities of "whites only" private groups. Since the Republican party was weak throughout the South, receiving the Democratic party nomination in the primary was tantamount to election. Thus, Southern states effectively eliminated blacks from the political process. In *Smith v. Allwright,* the Court ruled that the primaries were part of one electoral process, during which the exclusion of blacks would violate the Fifteenth Amendment. The "whites only" primary was thus ruled unconstitutional.

Black enfranchisement was an important goal of the civil rights movement of the 1950s and 1960s (see Weisbrot 1990; McClain and Stewart 1995, 1999, 2002, 2006). The Civil Rights Act of 1957 created the Civil Rights Commission, empowered it to investigate voting rights violations, and gave the U.S. attorney general the power to seek court relief from voting rights violations through the injunction process. In 1960 the federal courts were empowered to appoint referees to help blacks register in areas in which discrimination had been found.

But as table 3.1 shows, such efforts had little effect on black suffrage in many states. Many states used literacy tests or tests on the Constitution to keep blacks from the polls. Local officials exercised a good deal of leeway in administering these tests. The Voting Rights Act of 1965 addressed this problem head-on, suspending literacy tests, a provision upheld by the Supreme Court in *Oregon v. Mitchell*, 400 U.S. 112 (1970), and empowering federal registrars to replace local or state officials in areas in which fewer than half of those eligible had registered and voted in 1964 (in a total of seven states). That act, which has been renewed and expanded ever since,

JIM CROW LAWS

Laws designed to restrict the activities of former slaves in the South; included provisions that kept black citizens from voting.

"WHITES ONLY" PRIMARIES

An example of a Jim Crow law by which Southern Democratic parties established themselves as private organizations open only to whites and then nominated candidates for office in elections normally not contested by Republicans, thus effectively denying black citizens the right to vote.

RESIDENCY REQUIREMENTS

Requirement that a citizen live in a community for a specified period of time before becoming eligible to vote.

Table 3.1 Black Voter Registration in Southern States

State	1960	1964	1969	1970	1971	1976	1980	1982	1984	1986	1992	1994	1996	1998	2000	2002	2004
Ala.	13.7	19.3	61.3	66.0	54.7	58.4	55.8	69.7	71.4	68.9	71.8	66.3	69.2	74.3	72.0	67.6	72.9
Ark.	38.0	40.4	77.9	82.3	80.9	94.0	57.2	63.9	71.2	57.9	62.4	56.0	65.8	51.8	60.0	62	63.7
Fla.	39.4	51.2	67.0	55.3	53.2	61.1	58.3	59.7	57.3	58.2	54.7	47.7	53.1	50.4	52.7	47.9	52.6
Ga.	29.3	27.4	30.4	57.2	64.2	74.8	48.6	50.4	58.0	52.8	53.9	57.6	64.6	64.1	66.3	61.6	64.2
La.	31.1	31.6	60.8	57.4	58.9	63.0	60.7	61.1	74.8	60.6	82.3	65.7	71.9	69.5	73.5	73.5	71.1
Miss.	5.2	6.7	66.5	71.0	59.4	60.7	62.3	64.2	85.6	70.8	78.5	69.9	67.4	71.3	73.7	67.9	76.1
N.C.	39.1	46.8	53.7	51.3	49.8	54.8	51.3	50.9	59.5	58.4	64.0	53.1	65.5	57.4	62.9	58.2	70.4
S.C.	13.7	37.3	54.6	56.1	49.2	56.5	53.7	53.9	62.2	52.5	62.0	59.0	64.3	68.0	68.6	68.3	71.1
Tenn.	59.1	69.5	92.1	71.6	65.6	66.4	64.0	66.1	78.5	65.3	77.4	70.0	65.7	64.8	64.9	54.1	63.9
Tex.	35.5	~	73.1	72.6	68.2	65.0	56.0	49.5	65.3	68.0	63.5	58.5	63.2	62.1	69.5	65.1	68.4
Va.	23.1	35.5	64.8	57.0	52.0	54.7	53.2	49.5	62.1	56.2	64.5	51.1	64.0	53.6	58.0	47.5	57.4
Average	29.7	33.2	63.8	63.4	59.6	64.5	56.5	58.1	67.8	60.9	66.8	59.5	65.0	62.48	65.66	61.25	66.53

Source: U.S. Bureau of the Census, *Statistical Abstract of the United States: 1982–1983.* Data for 1984 taken from "Population Characteristics," *Current Population Reports,* series P-20, no. 397, issued January 1985. Note that the figures for 1964 and 1969 are based on the recorded voting age population for 1960. Other data collected by Voter Education Project, Inc., Atlanta, Ga. 1992 data taken from "Voting and Registration in the Election of November 1992," *Current Population Reports,* series P-20, no. 471, issued Sept. 1993. 1994–2004 data collected from U.S. Bureau of Census, www.census.gov.

Note: All figures are percentages of the eligible, voting age population. Florida, Louisiana, North Carolina, South Carolina, and Georgia since 1980 have kept records of voter registration by race. The other states' figures are based on estimates by state officials.

most recently for twenty-five years in 2006, has been credited with causing the dramatic impact on black registration.

The 1970 extension of the Voting Rights Act also dealt with the question of residency requirements, frequently used by local officials to keep mobile populations from voting—namely, blacks in the South and others such as young people. The 1970 Voting Rights Act set thirty days as the maximum residency requirement permissible for presidential elections. In *Dunn v. Blumstein,* 405 U.S. 330 (1972), the Supreme Court ruled that the thirty-day residency limit should be used for all elections.

Legal restrictions on black voting have been all but eliminated, through a long series of constitutional amendments, congressional actions, and Supreme Court decisions. The path to this goal has been long, but legal limitations on black suffrage no longer keep black Americans out of polling places in the South or anywhere else in this country.

3. Women's Suffrage

In the early years of the abolition movement, the call for women's suffrage was closely linked to cries for black freedom and black voting rights. However, male leaders of the abolition movement soon found it in their interest to separate the two causes (for a full history of the struggle for women's suffrage, see Catt and Shuler 1969). While not abandoning their participation in the movement to free those who were enslaved, women came together in the famous conference at Seneca Falls, New York, in 1848 to assert their own rights. From that point until the successful adoption of the **Nineteenth Amendment,** in 1920, women **suffragists** waged a valiant, prolonged, often brilliant, and frequently frustrating battle to win the right to vote.

NINETEENTH AMENDMENT

Amendment to the U.S. Constitution granting women the right to vote in all elections.

SUFFRAGISTS

The group of political leaders, mostly women, who campaigned for more than six decades at state and federal levels to gain the right to vote for women.

Women were first given the right to vote on school questions, presumably because these matters were closely related to "female" duties (Key 1964, 614). In 1869, while still a territory, Wyoming had granted women the right to vote on all matters, in recognition of the equal role women played on the frontier. Wyoming's constitution included women's suffrage when the territory applied for admission to the Union. Congress first rejected this expansion of the franchise but ultimately relented, admitting Wyoming in 1890 as the first state with universal female suffrage. Other Western states followed Wyoming's lead, but the progress was slow and often frustrating.

The suffrage movement had to fight on a state-by-state basis while pursuing a national strategy. A variety of tactics were used. In states in which women had the right to vote, they pressured congressmen and senators to push for a national amendment. When the Democratic party proved recalcitrant, women demonstrated their power by organizing a campaign against all Democratic congressmen in suffrage states and were credited with defeating a great number.

Faced with this power, the parties began to listen. By 1916 women's suffrage was included in both party platforms, though some suffragists still wanted state action. In 1917 women turned to more militant actions, picketing the White House and delivering petitions to the president. Some were jailed; others replaced them. Those in jail demonstrated for the cause of prison reform; some engaged in hunger strikes. When female prisoners were force-fed, the press had a field day. More women came to Washington, and the jails became increasingly crowded. The effect of the pressure was telling.

The women's suffrage amendment passed the House in the second session of the Sixty-fifth Congress, but it failed to achieve the two-thirds vote necessary in the Senate. More women came to Washington, more picketed, more were jailed, and more hunger strikes ensued. Finally President Wilson was won over to the cause. When the Republican-controlled House repassed the measure in 1919, Wilson pressured his fellow Democrats in the Senate to enact women's suffrage. At long last, in August 1920, the Nineteenth Amendment was ratified by the requisite three-quarters of the states, and women won the right to vote in all elections. No further legal barriers could be used to prevent women from voting.

This abbreviated description of the battle for women's suffrage points to a number of important conclusions. First, the tactics of the suffragists deserve much more attention than they are traditionally given. The suffragists' ability to gain their end, without the stimulus of a cataclysmic event like the Civil War or the benefit of the threat of electoral reprisal in most states, is a tribute to the skills of the women as politicians—skills seldom recognized by American scholars.

Second, political participation is most often defined as voting. The suffragists demonstrated that less-traditional political participation (e.g., the hunger strike) can be equally effective in the American polity.

Third, the contrast with black suffrage is instructive. Black men won the right to vote through a constitutional amendment that forbade certain disenfranchisements by the states, but many states found ways around that amendment, restricting black suffrage for nearly a century. Women won their right to vote first on a state-by-state basis, after decades of struggle at the national level; yet, once that battle was won, no further legal impediments stood in women's way. However, social pressures did keep women from voting in numbers equal to men for many years; the difference between legal eligibility and actual voting requires further examination.

4. Lowering the Voting Age

As is the case with other eligibility standards for voting, the age at which a citizen can exercise his or her right to vote is determined by the constitution and laws of the state in which that citizen resides. For much of American history, twenty-one was the traditional voting age. During World War II, when eighteen-year-olds were conscripted into military service, many people believed that the voting age should be lowered to eighteen. In 1943 Georgia lowered its voting age to eighteen, but no other state followed suit. President Eisenhower expressed support for eighteen-year-old voters during his first term, but only Kentucky amended its constitution to effect that change. When Alaska and Hawaii were admitted to the Union in the late 1950s, their constitutions called for voting ages of nineteen and twenty, respectively.

TWENTY-SIXTH AMENDMENT

Amendment to the U.S. Constitution setting eighteen as the minimum age for voting.

No further changes ensued until the Vietnam War. Once again, the cries were heard: "old men send young men to die in foreign wars" and "old enough to die but not old enough to vote." In response to this agitation and to the general public dissatisfaction with the war in Vietnam, one provision of the Voting Rights Act of 1970 made eighteen-year-olds eligible to vote in all national, state, and local elections. In *Oregon v. Mitchell,* however, the Supreme Court struck down this provision, asserting that Congress could not constitutionally take such actions for state and local elections. As a response to this ruling, Congress passed—and the requisite thirty-seven states ratified—the **Twenty-sixth Amendment** to the Constitution, making eighteen the minimum voting age for all elections and expanding the electorate more than it had been expanded by any action other than the Nineteenth Amendment.

5. Additional Regulations: Residency and Registration

With few exceptions, the potential voting population in the United States today includes all citizens over eighteen years of age. Even citizens who had once been prevented from voting because of their inability to read and understand English can now vote; the 1975 extension of the Voting Rights Act requires bilingual ballots in areas of the country with large non-English-speaking populations. A Native American tribe with no written language is even permitted to vote orally.

The other major barrier to voting involves the mobility of the American electorate. The 1970 Voting Rights Act extension established a maximum of thirty days as a residency requirement; it also established uniform state standards for absentee voting. But even this law did not answer all of the questions regarding who should be eligible to vote.

Voting participation is actually a function of three factors: eligibility requirements; registration laws, that is, how one gets one's name on the voting roster; and the decision to vote, turnout on election day. Table 3.2 shows how each of these factors affects the number who actually vote. Turnout is usually expressed as a percentage of the voting age population—that is, those who have reached the age of eighteen in a given area who actually vote. But, as the table demonstrates, many of those who do not vote do not do so because they have never registered.

The debate over ease or difficulty of registration has been long and heated. Robert Erikson (1981) has demonstrated that the biggest reason citizens do not vote is that they are not registered. A number of other studies have examined the relationship between registration laws and the number of people registered (Teixera 1992, 23–38; Timpone 1998; Powell 1986; Squire, Wolfinger, and Glass 1987; Wolfinger and Rosenstone 1980).

States vary significantly in their registration procedures.

Four states—Maine, Minnesota, Oregon, and Wisconsin—have allowed so-called instant registration for many years: citizens may register to vote up to and on the day of an election. Critics believe that this procedure could lead to voter fraud, but no evidence of efforts to subvert the system has been uncovered in states that use it. And registration in those states has increased.

In 1993, the Congress passed and President Clinton signed the so-called **Motor Voter Bill,** an effort to address the registration issue on the national level. The bill had been debated for some years and, in fact, passed Congress but was vetoed by President Bush a year earlier. The Motor Voter Bill requires states to allow citizens to register to vote when applying for a driver's license, to permit mail-

MOTOR VOTER BILL

Legislation to increase the number of citizens who are registered to vote by expanding the availability of registration possibilities.

Table 3.2 Registered Voters and Percentage of Voter Turnout, 1988–2004

Year	Voting Age Population (VAP) (in millions)	Percentage of VAP Reporting They Registered	Percentage of VAP Reporting They Voted	Turnout as a Percentage of Reported Registered Voters
1988	178.1	66.6	57.4	86.2
1990	182.1	62.2	45.0	72.3
1992	185.7	68.2	61.3	89.9
1994	190.3	62.0	44.6	71.9
1996	193.7	65.9	54.2	82.2
1998	198.2	62.1	41.9	67.5
2000	202.6	63.9	54.7	85.5
2002	210.4	60.9	42.36	69.4
2004	215.7	65.9	58.3	88.5

Source: 1988–1998 Statistical Abstract of the United States 1999; 2000–2004 data from www.census.gov.

in registration, and to provide registration forms at certain public assistance agencies. Passage of this law has led to continued assessment of the impact of easier registration laws on voting turnout (see Knack 1995).

The debate on voter registration laws continues today. On the one hand, the issue poses a normative question about public policy: Shouldn't a democracy encourage its citizens to vote? Shouldn't all restrictions on voting be eliminated? On the other hand, the question is a pragmatic one: Is there evidence that restrictive voter registration laws significantly decrease participation? Do those whose names are added to the rolls by eased registration requirements necessarily turn out to vote? (See Bennett 1990; Bennett and Resnick 1991; Cassel and Luskin 1988; Gans 1990; Hill 2006; Jackman 1987; McDonald and Popkin 2001; Piven and Cloward 1988, 1989, 1990, 2000; Powell 1986; Rosenstone and Wolfinger 1978; Squire, Wolfinger, and Glass 1987; Teixeira 1987; Wolfinger and Hoffman 2001; Wolfinger and Rosenstone 1980.)[2]

But the issue is also a political one. Surely Republicans and Democrats did not split on the motor vehicle registration bill because of differing views on the questions raised here; and surely the cost of this procedure for registering voters was not enough to cause such a complete partisan division. Further, the issue was not one of big federal government telling the states what to do—though each of these arguments was made. The crucial question was the political one: If people were encouraged to register and they turned out to vote, for whom would they cast their ballots? Democrats and Republicans alike believed that more of these newly registered voters would vote Democratic; thus, each party dug in its heels and fought hard for its position on this seemingly innocuous change in electoral law.

B. Decline in Voter Participation

Figure 3.1 shows the historical pattern of low voter turnout in the United States. Turnout declined for more than three decades before showing slight increases in the most recent elections.

Neither the decline nor recent increases have been precipitous. The pattern of low turnout relative to other nations has been persistent. States vary tremendously in their turnout rates. In the 2004 election, six states had turnout rates greater than two-thirds of the voting age population (led by Minnesota, at 73.0 percent); at the other extreme, four states had turnout rates less than 50 percent of the voting age population (with Hawaii below 45 percent). If the United States has become "one big country," with state and regional differences blurred because of our mobile population and our reliance on a national media for setting so many standards, why do states vary to the degree that they do?

Figure 3.1 Turnout in National Elections, 1930–2004

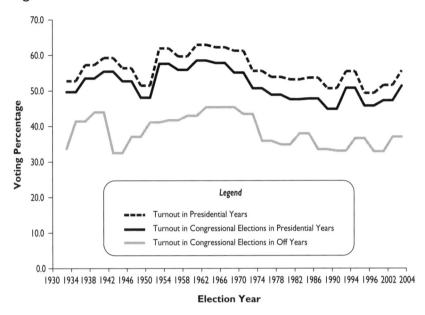

Source: Vital Statistics on Congress, 2002–2004; Federal Election Commission.

The rather simple reason is that the degree of nationalization has been overstated. The populations of the fifty states vary in all sorts of ways, some of which have implications for voting turnout. In addition, state election laws vary, and these too impact voting turnout rates. We explore some of these factors in the paragraphs that follow.

1. Voting by Blacks

Examine figure 3.2. These data demonstrate the impact of the registration and voter turnout efforts aimed at black voters, such as the one led by the Reverend Jesse Jackson and Operation PUSH (People United to Serve Humanity) in the mid-1980s and renewed efforts in recent years. The gap in turnout between blacks and whites decreased significantly in those periods.

Hispanics are the fastest-growing group in the United States today; however, the Hispanic turnout is even lower than the black turnout, and the gap between Hispanic turnout and that of other racial groups has not decreased significantly. The barriers to effective Hispanic participation, including language and education level, remain serious obstacles; but in certain geographic areas, such as border districts in Texas and California, Hispanic voters have become powerful forces (McClain and Stewart 1995, 1999, 2002, 2006).

Figure 3.2 Voter Turnout by Race, 1964–2004

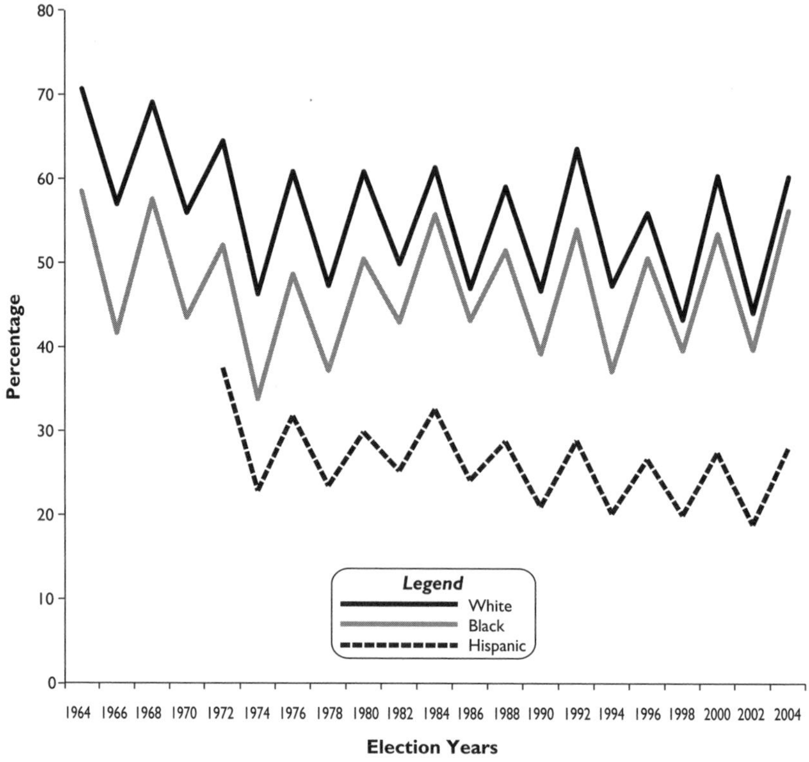

Source: U.S. Census Bureau.

2. Voting by Young Voters

For many years political scientists have known that the youngest voters vote in the smallest proportion (see figure 3.3; Timpone 1998, 145–58; Miller and Shanks 1996; Wolfinger and Rosenstone 1980, 37; Converse and Niemi 1971; Campbell et al. 1960). Since the passage of the Twenty-sixth Amendment, the young have constituted an increased portion of the total electorate; therefore, their unwillingness to vote contributes increasingly to the overall decline in voter turnout.

Some controversy in the professional literature concerns this trend. Basing their findings on data from the late 1970s and early 1980s, some scholars have suggested that voters who came of political age in an era during which political activity was not an expected norm would not increase their participation rate with age, as had been the case in the past (Tarrance 1978, 12). The "negative" trend in overall voter participation, which was evident in the late 1970s, was attributed to a replacement of the age cohort that reached voting age before the New Deal, one with a consistently high turnout rate, with a cohort that first voted after the Great Society administra-

Figure 3.3 Voter Turnout by Age, 1964–2004

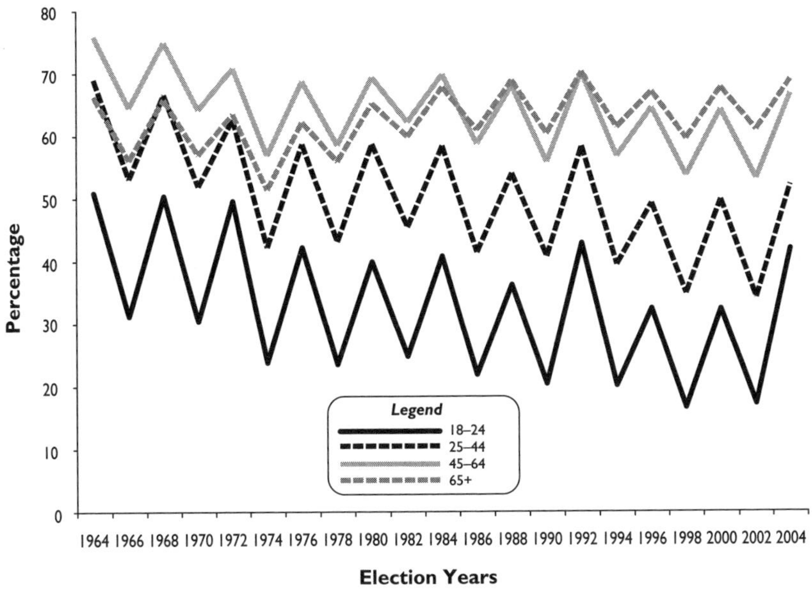

Source: U.S. Census Bureau.

tion of Lyndon Johnson, a group discouraged by the politics of their time (Miller 1992; Teixeira 1987). The fear was that this younger cohort of voters would never increase in participation rates as had the generation before them.

However, the pattern of youthful voters participating in numbers much lower than their elders continued for many years. As each cohort has aged, their participation rate has increased (Miller and Shanks 1996). With an increase in age expectancy and with older Americans constituting a larger share of the population as the baby boomer generation ages, the oldest segment of the population has become the most overrepresented. To the extent that they share opinions on the issues of the day, their views might well also be overrepresented by those whom they elect.

In the most recent elections, the gap between youth voters and older cohorts has shrunk slightly, with campaigns making a concerted effort to appeal to the youngest eligible voters through different media, e.g., MTV and blogs, and with specific issue appeals.

3. Voting by Women

Turnout among women was quite low in the years immediately after enfranchisement; however, the number of female voters steadily increased until it leveled off by 1972, at a turnout level only slightly below that of men (see figure 3.4).

The rejuvenation of women's political awareness, spurred by

Figure 3.4 Voter Turnout by Gender, 1964–2004

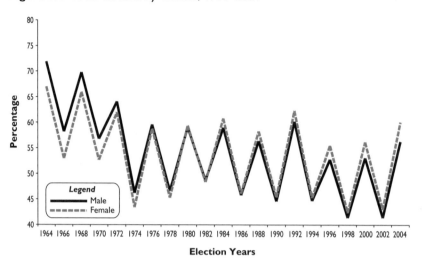

Source: U.S. Census Bureau.

the women's movement in the 1970s, led to another increase in participation, and turnout rates of women voters have exceeded the rates for men in every national election since 1980. Because more women than men are eligible to vote, women now constitute a majority of the electorate. Women in the South participate in politics less than women in other regions because of regional cultural norms; therefore, it is clear that women in other regions now participate in significantly higher percentages than men in those areas (Pomper 1975, 88).

Politicians understand this phenomenon. In the 1996 election, political strategists explored how issue after issue would appeal to the so-called soccer moms, a subgroup never before seriously considered. In the post-9/11 world, women's concern for personal security—their own and that of their families—has led to directed appeals during campaigns. Similar strategies will undoubtedly mark future campaign efforts. Nevertheless, we must go beyond mere demographic characteristics in distinguishing voters from nonvoters.

4. What Distinguishes Voters from Nonvoters?

For more than three decades social scientists have been examining the American electorate in some depth. Despite a variety of research techniques, scholars have come to a remarkable consensus on what distinguishes voters from nonvoters. None of these conclusions is surprising, but some of the more important ones should be noted.

First, voting is a function of the "rules of the game." If it is easier to vote and if fewer roadblocks are put in the voter's way, more people vote. Thus, the expansion of the franchise, the easing of registration requirements, and the continued efforts to open the doors to black and Hispanic voters have increased the number of individuals voting (Campbell et al. 1960; Hill 2006; Milbrath and Goel 1977, chap. 5; Piven and Cloward 2000).

Again, state experiences demonstrate this point. One claim is that requiring citizens to go to a voting booth during set hours on election day decreases turnout and unfairly disadvantages some citizens. Proposals have been floated to have twenty-four-hour voting days and to make election day a national holiday (or to hold elections on Sundays, when fewer people are at work). These proposals have been rejected for a variety of reasons, including expense and legitimate questions of whether they would have the desired impact.[3] However, state experiments have demonstrated that changing election procedures can increase turnout.

In Texas, since 1991, citizens have been permitted to cast ballots in their local polling place on election day or at any time from seventeen days prior to the election up until four days before at a designated site in their community. Votes are not tallied until the polls close on election day, but citizens are given many more options about when to cast their vote. Nearly a third of the votes cast in recent Texas elections have been cast prior to the election, and counties with a higher proportion of the early-cast vote have had significantly higher total voter participation (Stein and Garcia-Monet 1997, 657–71). In the 2006 election, twenty-three states offered the opportunity for early voting; twenty-six states (including nineteen of those with early voting) allow for absentee voting, with no reason necessary for requesting an absentee ballot.

In Oregon, state officials began experimenting with mail ballots for certain elections as early as 1987 and have now moved to mail ballots for all elections. Citizens can vote from their own home; they can review material carefully before they vote. Turnout has clearly increased. While this voting technique causes considerable difficulty for campaign strategists (see chapter 7), the goal of increased turnout has evidently been achieved (Southwell and Burchett 1997, 53–57).

Second, social position distinguishes voters from nonvoters. "Citizens of higher social and economic status participate more in politics. This generalization . . . holds true whether one uses level of education, income, or occupation to measure social status" (Verba and Nie 1972, 125; see also, Berelson, Lazarsfeld, and McPhee 1954; Campbell et al. 1960; Dahl 1961; Lane 1959; Milbrath and Goel 1977). Wolfinger and Rosenstone have refined this commonplace notion by isolating the effect of the various components of a voter's socioeconomic status. They conclude that "even after controlling for all other variables, education has a very powerful independent effect on the likelihood of voting" (Wolfinger and Rosenstone 1980, 24). Education has the greatest effect on those with low-income or low-status jobs, but it has a continuing effect at all levels, a finding attributed to the increased information made available to more educated voters, their ease of acquiring more information, and their decline in anxiety because of greater political knowledge (Wolfinger and Rosenstone 1980, 18–22).

Third, certain attitudes about politics distinguish voters from nonvoters. Those who have the strongest feelings toward one political party or the other are much more likely to vote than those without such intense partisan affiliation, though the size of this gap has varied without discernible pattern. We also know that people who are more interested in politics tend to vote more frequently than those who are less interested. Partisans tend to be more interested than nonpartisans and hence vote in higher percentages. Even in the 1992 and 1996 presidential elections, when third-party candidate Ross Perot attracted attention with his rhetoric decrying major party politicians, self-proclaimed independents voted at a lower rate than Republicans or Democrats.

We also know that certain elections, such as those with compelling candidates (e.g., Kennedy versus Nixon in 1960) or those in which the outcome is in doubt (e.g., 2000), stimulate increased turnout; others seem to depress turnout—for example, the seemingly predetermined presidential election of 1996, between one flawed candidate and one boring candidate (Berelson, Lazarfeld, and McPhee 1954; Campbell et al. 1960; Hill and Luttbeg 1980, chap. 3; Milbrath and Goel 1977, chap. 3; Verba and Nie 1972).

So far the discussion has focused on turnout in presidential elections. As noted in table 1.1, Americans are asked to go to the polls frequently. Turnout is much lower for elections that do not include a presidential race. Congressional elections are held every two years, whereas presidential elections take place every four years; thus, half of the congressional elections take place in off-presidential years (e.g., 2002, 2006). Turnout in these years is typically under 40 percent and has always been lower than that in adjacent presidential election years.[4]

In addition to partisanship, socioeconomic status, and interest in a campaign, researchers have found that voters are distinguished from nonvoters by the number of political stimuli to which they are exposed. We would expect those most interested in politics to receive the most political communication and, in fact, to seek out such contacts. This expectation is particularly apt for those highly involved with political parties. Both of these expectations are supported by a good deal of evidence. Similarly, those less interested would doubtless not go out of their way to look for political information.

Yet we do not always control the information we receive, and

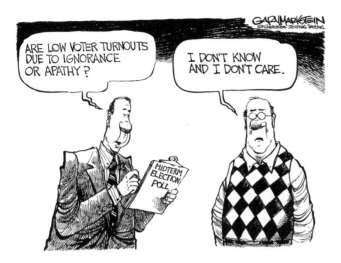

campaign managers know that those who receive more information vote more frequently. Therefore, one of their goals is to bombard citizens with political messages, trying to penetrate the defenses of those who seek to avoid politics. Why? The more people are reminded about politics, the more they are reminded of their civic duty to vote—and the more they are reminded of their civic duty to vote, the more they feel guilty about not voting. Thus, one clear campaign strategy is to work hard to stimulate the participation of those most likely to support one's cause. If people are not interested in politics, the office seeker must stimulate that interest among his or her likely supporters, must appeal to their sense of civic duty, and must turn nonvoters into voters (Almond and Verba 1965; Berelson, Lazarsfeld, and McPhee 1954; Campbell et al. 1960; Lazarsfeld, Berelson, and Gaudet 1944; Milbrath and Goel 1977, chap. 2).

Finally, in a number of different ways, scholars have demonstrated that those who are more knowledgeable about politics participate in greater numbers than those who are less knowledgeable. Furthermore, those who tend to vote for either ideological or issue-based reasons vote in higher proportions than those who vote more on image or emotions. Certainly, many of these factors are interrelated, but the clear implication of these data is that frequent voters are becoming more knowledgeable and are distinguishing themselves more from nonvoters who are less informed (Gant and Luttbeg, 1991, chap. 2; Hill 2006).

II. Voters in Presidential Elections

We turn now from the question of "Who votes?" to the questions of "For whom do they vote?" and "Why?" How many times have you heard someone say, "I am not a Republican or a Democrat; I vote for the person." What exactly does that mean?

When you ask friends about their choice for a certain office, say, whether they supported President Bush for reelection or how they decide to vote for any particular candidate, how do they normally respond? Do they begin elaborate discussions of different candidates' stands on different issues? Do they talk of one issue that is most important to them? Do they talk about party only? Or do they talk about a candidate's personal characteristics? How do they decide?

The individual voter is, after all, the basic building block of the political world. We really want to know how each individual votes, but we cannot know this factor for every one of the millions of people who vote, and so we often group individuals together and look at their voting patterns.

Too often students of political science are aware of what the current professional literature says but are ignorant of earlier writings that laid the groundwork for current studies. Much is lost by ignoring the work of scholars writing a generation ago, especially in the study of voting behavior. Moreover, it is always beneficial for students to see how a discipline progresses; in political science, this progression, from the work of one group of scholars to the next, from one generation of scholars to the work of their students and even their students' students, is evident in a brief overview of what is known about voting behavior.

A. Models of Voting Behavior: *The American Voter*

Few books have dominated an area of study in the way that *The American Voter* (Campbell et al. 1960) has influenced the study of electoral behavior, for a period of five decades. Angus Campbell, Philip Converse, Warren Miller, and Donald Stokes, the authors of this classic study, were not the first to study voting behavior in depth. They owed and acknowledged a debt to earlier students of voting behavior in local communities, particularly to Bernard Berelson, Paul Lazarsfeld, and their associates at Columbia University (Berelson, Lazarsfeld, and McPhee 1954; Lazarsfeld, Berelson, and Gaudet 1944), who had earlier hypothesized that social characteristics determine political preference. What they focused on was two questions that had held the attention of a good segment of the research community: First, who decides to vote, and who opts not to participate in this way? Second, once a citizen has decided that he or she will vote, how does that citizen decide for whom to cast a ballot?

The authors of *The American Voter* and their colleagues at the University of Michigan Survey Research Center refined the national survey as a research instrument for social scientists, and they presented their findings in such a clear and coherent way that their work essentially became the model against which all others compared their results. All students of electoral behavior need to be aware of its conclusions.

Oversimplification in presenting the findings of *The American Voter* risks masking the sophistication and richness of the analysis. However, as with many such classics, what people believe Campbell and his associates said is in many ways more important than what they actually did say. It is, after all, this oversimplified view of *The American Voter*—and not a detailed, careful analysis—that has determined the influence of this book. With this caveat, we will attempt to summarize the book's conclusions.

Campbell and his associates were engaged in a study of the psychological and sociological determinants of voting behavior. They looked to the end of what they called a **funnel of causality**: at the narrow end of the funnel was the **variable** they sought to understand, the individual's vote (figure 3.5). Leading into the funnel were factors that caused the individual to vote or not and, if that individual did vote, to vote for a certain candidate; these factors—for example, socioeconomic status, parents' partisan leanings—were deemed to be the determinants of voting behavior. But there were intermediate steps along the way. The authors of *The American Voter* studied, first, how voters perceived parties, candidates, and issues, and, second, why they perceived them as they did.

Their first conclusion was that voter perception is a mixture of cognition and evaluation, of perception and affect. How the voter perceives politics is a mixture of what that voter chooses to know

FUNNEL OF CAUSALITY

Symbolic depiction of discussion of why Americans vote as they do.

VARIABLE

The measure used to capture the variation in observations of a concept one is interested in studying.

Figure 3.5. Funnel of Causality

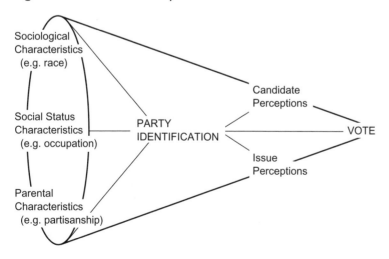

Source: Authors, derived from *The American Voter.*

and how that voter feels about a political situation. The average voter is concerned about politics, but not all *that* concerned. While the average American does vote, he or she does not think about politics a great deal, does not become involved in many other political acts, and does not spend a good deal of time keeping informed about politics.

A number of conclusions follow from this finding. First, the average American has an extremely unsophisticated view of politics. Campbell and his associates note the inability of the voter to view politics in abstract terms, to develop a coherent **ideology**. Rather than make judgments based on a sophisticated view of the issues, voters view candidates as representatives of the two major parties; the parties in turn are viewed as feeling certain ways on issues and toward certain groups in society. Whether these views are accurate, the voters use their perceptions in making decisions by fitting or ordering their view of politics to the outlines of the perceptions. Because most people do not care much about politics, it is fairly easy to manipulate their views.

According to *The American Voter* model, most Americans have developed a strong, long-term commitment to one or the other of the major political parties, and this commitment is a most significant guide to voting behavior. How is this tie to a political party developed? Campbell and his associates conclude that the individual's home is the most important source of partisan affiliation. The two most influential factors seem to be the parents' partisanship and their level of political activity. If both parents are strongly involved with one party, the children are likely to follow the same course. If the parents' **party identification** is not the same or if the commitment of the respondent's parents to politics is not strong, then the likelihood of the children affiliating with one of the parties declines commensurably.

Other elements also influence the choice of party, particularly when parental pressure is not strong. Among these influences are other important **socializing elements of American society**—the school, the work group, the church. Once partisan affiliation is confirmed, it is quite difficult to change; however, factors such as marriage, increased education, changes in job, social status, and neighborhood can each have an impact. More significantly, cataclysmic events such as the Great Depression can affect the partisan political affiliation of entire generations.

Most important to remember is what this view says about the role that the voter plays in democratic theory. This is essentially a pessimistic view of the American electorate's ability to control its own destiny. Voters are not capable of making decisions based on a rational consideration of issues. To cast "issue-oriented" votes, the

IDEOLOGY

A coherent set of beliefs that structure one's thinking about political issues.

PARTY IDENTIFICATION

Self-assessment of a person's allegiance to one or the other of the major political parties.

SOCIALIZING ELEMENTS OF AMERICAN SOCIETY

Institutions that teach those in a social grouping its norms, expectations, values, ideas, and so on.

citizen must have an opinion on an issue (or "cognize" the issue, per *The American Voter*), must have knowledge of current governmental policy on the issue, must have some information about the competing party's position on the question, and then must feel strongly enough to vote according to the perceived differences between the parties on that issue.

According to Campbell and associates, voters meet none of these criteria. Rather, partisanship is determined by socializing instruments in society. Voters follow partisan cues for voting. When they stray from these partisan predilections, it is not because of opinions on issues but because of appeals based on the personality or media image of the particular candidate or because of a particularly compelling short-range issue—such as a scandal or the appeal of a demagogue.

Looking further into *The American Voter,* one reads that **independents**, those without a strong partisan affiliation, tend to be those least involved in politics, least interested, and least committed. Independents are the voters most likely to be swayed by emotional appeals, by charismatic candidates. Given that the Democrats' lead in voter allegiance constituted less than a majority in the 1950s, at the time this study was done, these least attractive voters—in terms of a democratic model—are often the ones who determine election results.

Not a very optimistic picture. Remember, this summary is an exaggeration of what Campbell and his associates actually wrote. After analyzing the American electorate in great depth, they did not set out to paint such a bleak picture. Rather, they seemed to predicate standards for performance that the electorate, taken as a whole, was unable to meet. Campbell and his coauthors asked for an electorate that was able to order complex political issues, one that was able to make voting decisions based on comparative stands on particular issues, and one that demonstrated qualities such that elections were in fact viewable as **mandates** for the policies proposed by opposing candidates.

They found instead an uninvolved, unconcerned, unsophisticated electorate, voters making decisions based largely on partisan affiliations, which in turn were handed down from generation to generation. This partisanship was, in the first place, often based on issues that were perhaps no longer relevant, an oversimplification that led citizens to view American political dialogue in often unrealistic ways. The element of this electorate that usually held the balance of power between the two parties was the group that met the tests of "good" citizens least well; that was most responsive to emotional appeals; and that was least well informed, least concerned, and least involved.

INDEPENDENTS

Those who do not identify with one major party or the other.

MANDATES

Instructions or directions from the electorate to adopt certain policy alternatives based on what the electorate meant to say in an election.

B. Critics of *The American Voter* Model

Just as it is important for students of political science to know the foundations for current research, so too is it important for them to realize that even basic understandings of significant aspects of American political behavior can and do change over time. The fact that "revealed wisdom" of political analysis is overhauled is not a negative comment on those who have explicated the original model; rather, it is a testament to the progressive way in which we learn, drawing on and going further than those who preceded us.

The views presented in *The American Voter* were not accepted without controversy. Two schools of criticism stand out. V. O. Key Jr. and others maintained that Campbell and his associates placed too heavy a burden on the American electorate and that the view presented was far more negative than the actual situation warranted. The second group claimed that the heavy reliance on data from the 1950s led the authors to draw certain conclusions about the electorate that would not hold true over longer periods of time, even when applying the same theories to data gathered in the same manner. The two schools are discussed in turn.

I. Criticism by V. O. Key Jr. and His Followers

V. O. Key Jr. was perhaps political science's consummate believer in American democracy. While not refuting the data presented by Campbell and his associates, Key insisted that an expert could reinterpret those data and still arrive at the conclusion that the American electorate was a responsible and trustworthy body. Key's slim volume *The Responsible Electorate,* published posthumously with the assistance of Milton Cummings, is dedicated to the theme that the "voters are not fools" (Key 1966, 7).

Rather than divide the population by partisan affiliation, awareness of issues, concern over politics, and ability to conceptualize ideology, Key used survey data to categorize citizens according to how they voted in sets of elections. Looking at presidential elections, Key characterized those who vote for the same political party in two consecutive elections as **standpatters**; those who voted for one party in one election and the other party in the subsequent election as **switchers**; and those who voted in one election after not having voted in the preceding one as "in-and-outers," or "new voters" (see table 3.3).

Key then examined the behavior of voters in each of these categories, trying to determine if their behavior could be understood as rational. Most of the voters in any election are standpatters, those who vote the same way in at least two consecutive elections. However, these voters are rarely numerous enough to determine a winner. The next largest group is the new voters. These voters tend

STANDPATTERS

V. O. Key Jr.'s term for those voters who support the candidate of the same party for two consecutive elections.

SWITCHERS

V. O. Key Jr.'s term for those voters who vote for the candidate of one major party in one election and the candidate of the other party in the next election.

Table 3.3   How V.O. Key Would Have Characterized Voters after the 2004 Election (major party supporters only)

		2000 Presidential Vote		
		Gore	Bush	Did Not Vote
2004	*Kerry*	standpatter	switcher	new voter/in-and-outer
Presidential	*Bush*	switcher	standpatter	new voter/in-and-outer
Vote	*Did Not Vote*	in-and-outer	in-and-outer	_____

Source: Authors, derived from *The Responsible Electorate* (Key 1966).

to side heavily with the winner. In the time Key studied, switchers constituted between 13 and 20 percent of the electorate.

Key's findings about the relative positions of the two parties was important, particularly given the conclusion offered in *The American Voter,* about party affiliation and its determining effect on vote. Key discovered some shifting between elections, even though most voters maintain stable party allegiance. Although the maintenance of the relative strength of the two parties between elections implied that a static situation existed, the supposed immobility was in fact the net result of a dynamic flow.

> A series of maintaining elections occurs only in consequence of a complex process of interaction between government and populace in which old friends are sustained, old enemies are converted into new friends, old friends become even bitter opponents, and new voters are attracted to the cause. (Key 1966, 30)

Key further maintained that membership in certain cultural, economic, and social groups was an important factor in deciding how an American voted, again as Campbell and his associates maintained but not in an irrational or predeterministic way. Group pressure or group membership becomes important only for issues affecting that particular group. The fact that a voter is a member of a racial group or a religious group only affects that person's vote if and when that person believes that his or her racial or religious affiliation has an impact on how one distinguishes among candidates. This kind of analysis is significant in viewing the high percentage of blacks who vote Democratic or the Catholic voters' switch to Kennedy in 1960.

Perhaps Key's preeminent conclusion was that the most admirable, most rational voters were the switchers. He maintained that individuals switch because of the way that they perceive the government as treating them in the intervening period between elections. If they are happy with what the incumbent has done, regardless of whether they voted against him in the past, they will support him in the next election. In a parallel way, supporters of an incumbent in one election will turn against him—and, more important, against a subsequent nominee of his party—if those voters are unhappy with the effects of policies adopted during the intervening four years.

Similarly, Key maintained that standpatters are rational voters. Those voters who support the same party in consecutive elections do so either because they like what their party's winner has done or because they dislike what their party's competition has done. "Like" and "dislike" in this context are defined according to how those policies affect the individual in the areas that are of most concern to him or her.

Key's view of the new voters was not so sanguine. He viewed these two subcategories as distinct: one, first-time voters, and, two, "in-and-outers," who vote in one election but not in the next. New voters tend to go along with the tide. Nonregular voters are similar to the independents described in *The American Voter*: uninformed, unconcerned, and uninvolved. This group that tends toward trendiness is not the group that ultimately determines the winner in elections. Key maintained that the switchers play this role in American politics.

Two other conclusions follow from Key's analysis. First, he explicitly rejected the cult of personality. One need not have been a charismatic figure like Franklin Roosevelt to convince the Republican voters of 1928 to vote Democratic in 1932. Voters switched because of how they felt about the policies of the Hoover administration.

The other conclusion that follows from Key's analysis has served to structure much of the debate over voting behavior in the last three decades. Key (1966, xii) maintains that voters respond to the past, not the future. He draws an explicit distinction between **prospective (future) voting** and **retrospective (past) voting**.

Modern scholars are quick to criticize Key's methods, particularly his reliance on recall data (voters' remembering their past actions). However, few underestimate his instinctive knowledge of politics and the important questions to be examined. Key's influence persists more than five decades after his death.

The American Voter maintained that voters fail to vote prospectively because they are not well enough informed or concerned.

Key claimed that evaluation is the most important element in rational voting. Key's responsible voters evaluate what has happened in the past four years and make judgments. They are concerned with results only, not with policy promises. They do not give mandates; rather, they respond to results of past performance. To vote rationally in this context, one does not need to understand issues thoroughly, recall where the party stands on those issues, and know precisely what the government has been doing. A rational voter only needs to know if "the shoe is pinching" and, if so, who is causing it to pinch. According to Key, this much easier test is also a perfectly appropriate test.

Scholars have expanded on Key's concept of retrospective vot-

PROSPECTIVE (FUTURE) VOTING

Casting a vote based on what the voter thinks candidates for office are likely to do after the election.

RETROSPECTIVE (PAST) VOTING

Casting a vote based on the records that candidates have built prior to the time of an election.

ing. Drawing on the theoretical writing of Anthony Downs (1957), Morris Fiorina has developed a carefully crafted conceptual model of individual voting behavior (Fiorina 1977b, 1981; see also, Franklin 1984; Franklin and Jackson 1983; Jackson 1975). Fiorina claims that the electorate makes rational choices. Citizens vote retrospectively because doing so is patently more manageable. Human beings simply find it easier to get information about what has gone on in the past than to evaluate what may happen in the future. Retrospective information, in fact, is acquired without effort. Furthermore, it is much more reliable than evaluative projections. Who, as a rational actor, believes politicians' promises?

For retrospective voting to be rational, voting citizens must see some tie between candidates and parties; they must understand that parties are consistent on the issues that most affect them. Thus, in this context, a vote for Al Gore in 2000 was a rational vote if one believes that voters favored Bill Clinton's policies and linked Gore with those policies.

An extension of this logic also holds that it is perfectly rational for a citizen to vote for a presidential candidate of one party and a congressional candidate of the other—if one does not want policy to move too far toward one party's view or if one was satisfied with the policies produced by divided government (Fiorina 1996).

2. Criticism from Successors in the Michigan School

The second line of criticism for *The American Voter* came from scholars at the Survey Research Center, who sought to explain changes they noticed in voter behavior while analyzing the series of **National Election Studies (NES)** subsequent to the ones on which *The American Voter* is based. Many articles published in the 1970s provided new interpretations of the American electorate's behavior (Brody and Page 1972; Miller 1978; Miller and Miller 1977; A. Miller et al. 1976), but it was left to another group of scholars, using National Election Studies data from the 1960s and 1970s, to question some of the basic findings of *The American Voter.*

In *The Changing American Voter*, Norman Nie, Sidney Verba, and John Petrocik explicitly acknowledged their debt to the authors of the earlier classic work by dedicating it to Campbell, Converse, Miller, and Stokes, "on whose coattails we ride." In calling the paradigm laid out in *The American Voter* into question, the authors of *The Changing American Voter* stated that such criticism "does not imply criticism of the paradigm makers" (1979, 8).

However, they most definitely did call the conclusions into question.

The basic criticism was that the model constructed by the au-

NATIONAL ELECTION STUDIES (NES)

Series of studies of the American electorate carried out over the last half century under the direction of a national board of scholars by the Survey Research Center at the University of Michigan.

thors of *The American Voter* was based largely on the NES's 1956 survey and that the year 1956, a time of placidity in American politics, was hardly a baseline on which to construct a sound hypothesis. The task of *The Changing American Voter* was "to separate the time-bound from the timeless in political attitudes" (7). Which characteristics of voting behavior are indeed truly timeless? Which are time bound and therefore in need of reinterpretation? Posing that question demonstrates how knowledge accrues.

The major findings of *The Changing American Voter* began with an electorate much less committed to party than the earlier work described. Evidence was found in a rise in the number of independent voters, in a decline in strong partisans, in increased dissatisfaction with the two major parties, and in an increase in ticket splitting. Nie and his associates found that voters use two kinds of measures in presidential voting: first, the personal characteristics of the candidates; second—and this is the one emphasized—the issues.

Parties as institutions had weakened in the time since *The American Voter* was published. With Walter Burnham (1970), they argued that this weakness may well represent a long-term trend. Whatever the length of the trend, its significance was clear. Parties as organizations were feebler. Citizens might not oppose parties, but their commitment to parties was wavering; therefore, parties were less relevant to electoral behavior.

The authors of *The Changing American Voter* went further. They argued that the new independent voters fall into two groups. One group is the same as those Campbell and his associates identified nearly twenty years earlier; the other group, quite different. While the original group of independents constituted the least involved, least concerned, and least informed voters, Nie and colleagues found that the new group to be well informed, concerned about politics, involved in every way, people who charge the two major parties with irrelevance but take politics seriously and choose a candidate based on their perception of the candidate's stand on issues (see also Miller and Wattenberg 1985; Wattenberg 1984, 1986, 1990, 1994). Thus, these authors claimed that the way in which Americans decide how to vote has changed because the times have changed. Issues have become more important in people's lives.

What issues? The new and important issues of the day, a new set of issues that distinguish this time from the 1950s. War and peace in Vietnam, lifestyle, and race relations were important concerns for the American electorate of the late 1960s and early 1970s. Voters formed coherent political ideologies based on these issues; they could vote on issue preference.

Nie, Verba, and Petrocik claimed that these issues have not led to a realignment because parties are so weak and inconsistent in policy that retrospective voting is impossible. The individual candidates are more independent of party; they run on the basis of their own characteristics and programs, not as representatives of continuing party institutions. Thus, electoral choice can no longer be retrospective. Voters are less able to vote on the basis of past performance because the candidate cannot be held responsible for what others in his party have done while in office—unless, of course, the incumbent is the candidate (Nie, Verba, and Petrocik 1979, 346–47).

How does one know that the elections of 1974, 1968, and 1972, those on which *The Changing American Voter* is based, are not as atypical in terms of their being elections determined by highly salient issues as 1956 was atypical in terms of being a low-saliency election?

According to Nie, Verba, and Petrocik, the election of 1964 was the one that best defined the parties in terms of issues. This election was perhaps the most ideological of the late twentieth century. Senator Barry Goldwater (Ariz.), the Republican candidate, was referred to as "Mr. Conservative" by friend and foe alike.

During the election of 1968, the nation was torn apart by the Vietnam War. Try as he might, Hubert Humphrey, the Democratic candidate, could not separate himself from Lyndon Johnson, whom he had served with utmost loyalty as vice president. Johnson was generally perceived to be the architect of our military involvement in Vietnam.

Finally, the election of 1972 was the one in which the Democrats chose an extremist candidate, perhaps more in appearance than reality but certainly in the perception of the voting public. Senator George McGovern (S.Dak.) was viewed as the candidate of "acid, amnesty, and abortion." That the McGovern election was tainted on the Republican side by Watergate and dirty tricks and that McGovern was not so far to the left as he was often depicted does not negate how easy it was for the public to see this election in ideological terms as well.

When the authors of *The Changing American Voter* enlarged their book to include the 1976 election, they began to see a trend that called some of their findings into question. They assumed that the 1976 election would be different, as it was an election that pitted two centrist candidates as opponents: Gerald Ford, the Republican incumbent who had succeeded to the presidency when Richard Nixon resigned amidst the Watergate scandal, and former Georgia governor Jimmy Carter. But some of the differences turned out to deserve further analysis. This was particularly true of the voters' tendency to move away from voting without reference to a candidate's partisan affiliation and back to their previous allegiance, to candidates of one political party (see table 3.4). Again, we are left asking which of the findings are timeless and which are time bound.

At this point it might be worthwhile to recall Nie, Verba, and Petrocik's rejection of Key's retrospective voting. Two phrases stand out in our words: "Insofar as this is the case" and "unless, of course, the incumbent is the candidate." A third phrase might have been necessary: "If the electorate sees that the candidates are rejecting party." The evidence really is not clear on these issues (Wattenberg 1984, 1986, 1990, 1994, 1996). The electorate seems to be linking candidates of the same party, whether the candidates want to be linked or not. In the 1968 election, Hubert Humphrey did all he could to separate himself from Lyndon Johnson but failed. Al Gore tried to separate himself from the personal aspects of the Clinton presidency while tying himself to the economic progress made under Clinton; the public seemed to view his connection differently. Of course, often one of the candidates is the incumbent, as Ronald Reagan was in 1984, George H. W. Bush in 1992, Bill Clinton in 1996, and George W. Bush in 2004. That link is all that is necessary for retrospective voting at the presidential level to be possible.

Political scientists can become overly involved in their own struggles over methods. The controversy over how one decides if the American public votes prospectively or retrospectively, over how much issues matter, over what circumstances are important, and over whose interpretation of the same data is correct may well be one such parochial involvement. At times it may be appropriate to reject the most sophisticated research methodology and go with one's instincts, to use the old Studs Terkel method—sit down in an Irish pub and ask people how they decided. If an analyst had done that for the 1980 election, the answer should have been clear: Ronald Reagan had his finger on the pulse of the people. He asked them one question—or, rather, he asked them to ask themselves one question:

> Next Tuesday is election day. Next Tuesday all of you will go to the polls; you'll stand there in the polling place and make a decision. I think when you make that decision, it might be well if you would ask yourself, are you better off than you were 4 years ago? Is it easier for you to go and buy things in the stores than it was 4 years ago? Is there more or less unemployment in the country than there was 4 years ago? Is America as respected throughout the world as it was? Do we feel that our security is as safe, that we're as strong as we were 4 years ago? And if you answer all of those questions yes, why then I think your choice is very obvious as to who you'll vote for. If you don't agree, if you don't think that this course that we've been on for the last 4 years is what you would like to see us follow for the next 4, then I could suggest another choice that you have. (Carter 1982, 250–51)

Table 3.4   Party Identification, 1952–2004

Identification	1952	1956	1960	1964	1968	1972	1976	1980	1984	1988	1992	1996	1998	2000	2002	2004
Strong Dem.	22	21	20	27	20	15	15	18	17	17	18	18	19	19	16	16
Weak Dem.	25	23	25	25	25	26	25	23	20	18	18	19	18	15	17	16
Ind. Dem.	10	6	6	9	10	11	12	11	11	12	14	14	14	15	15	17
Ind. Ind.	6	9	10	8	11	13	15	13	11	11	12	9	11	12	8	10
Ind. Rep.	7	8	7	6	9	10	10	10	12	13	12	12	11	13	13	12
Weak Rep.	14	14	14	14	15	13	14	14	15	14	14	15	16	12	16	12
Strong Rep.	14	15	16	11	10	10	9	9	12	14	11	12	10	12	14	16
Apolitical	3	4	2	1	1	1	1	2	2	2	1	1	2	1	1	0

Source: National Election Studies.

C. Presidential Voting Reviewed

Where does this review leave the question of how Americans decide for whom to vote? Certainly the professional social science community is not of one mind. Parts of the model developed by Campbell, Converse, Miller, and Stokes have been rejected; other parts remain intact. Portions of the criticism of Nie, Verba, and Petrocik have been accepted; other portions might well need reexamination. The theory of retrospective voting, propounded by V. O. Key Jr. as a defense of the American electorate against the implied view of *The American Voter* and amplified by Morris Fiorina and others, has attracted some strong adherents.

In a magisterial book, *The New American Voter*, Warren Miller and Merrill Shanks revisit the entire question of determinants in individual voting behavior (Miller and Shanks 1996; see also Miller 1991). While we cannot review the findings of this entire book, Miller and Shanks reaffirm the importance of party identification in determining voters' choices. They claim that the much-discussed dealignment of the American electorate misrepresents the actual situation. According to the Miller and Shanks analysis, younger voters entering the electorate are not aligning with either party, but voters in older-age cohorts have maintained their party identification, with certain caveats regarding Southern white voters.

What is impressive about *The New American Voter* is the extent to which it draws scholars back to a reexamination of a fundamental set of questions: Who votes, and who does not? How do voters decide for whom they will vote?

The link between party identification and voting/rationality of voters has consumed political scientists' attention for decades. Human behavior is complex and difficult to comprehend. No clear consensus has emerged, as research controversies abound (see Gant and Luttbeg 1991, 29–82; Niemi and Weisberg 1993, 2001). The necessity of examining the context of each particular election is absolutely clear (see Miller and Wattenberg 1985). In the final analysis, it is important to supplement scientific examinations with common sense, with the knowledge of politics, and with a feel for people—not just numbers.

To this point, we have considered only presidential voting. Only the president and vice president run in elections that have a visibility approaching that discussed in the literature reviewed to this point. How do voters decide in cases different from those at the presidential level?

III. VOTERS IN CONGRESSIONAL AND SENATORIAL ELECTIONS

Almost all the research into American voting behavior has focused on presidential voting. In 1958, and again in 1978, studies were done of the electorate and how they voted in congressional and senatorial elections during a nonpresidential year. In other years, questions have been asked about congressional elections, but the total amount of research is much less than that on presidential elections.

The most often cited analyses of the data generated by the 1958 study of congressional voters describe an electorate not very concerned or knowledgeable about congressional politics (Miller and Stokes 1963; Stokes and Miller 1962). Nearly half the respondents replied that they had neither read nor heard anything about either candidate. For every one respondent that knew something about the challenger, more than two knew something about the incumbent, but few had any sense of how their representative stood on issues. With so little knowledge, voters relied heavily on party affiliation to determine their congressional choice. This view of electoral behavior is consistent with the *American Voter* model, only more so.

The 1978 study produced a wealth of literature on congressional elections that reevaluates the Stokes and Miller view (see Abramowitz 1981; Hinckley 1981; Jacobson 1980; Maisel and Cooper 1981; Mann and Wolfinger 1980). The most noticeable change is that most voters have an increased awareness of congressional candidates. Depending on the measure used, voters are able to express an opinion on over 90 percent of the incumbent candidates and on nearly half the challengers.

For some years, scholars had noted that an extremely high percentage of congressional leaders who were seeking reelection were in fact reelected (see, e.g., Fiorina 1978; Mayhew 1974a, 1974b). The 1978 data afford scholars the opportunity to explore the reasons for this phenomenon. What they find is that partisanship has been replaced by incumbency as the key voting cue. Further, voters support incumbents because they have more positive information about them, resulting in large part from the incumbents' skillful use of the resources available through their offices.

Some of the data are particularly striking. Nearly 90 percent of the respondents report having had some contact with their congressmen; almost a quarter had personally met their representatives; and almost three-quarters had received mail from their representative in Washington. These associations, all structured by the incumbent and virtually all positive in content, build a favorable image that is all but impossible to overcome. Typically, challengers are not known at all; voters do not choose between two candidates on equal footing but between one who is well known and positively viewed and another who has to fight to be viewed at all. These findings hold for the 2004 election—and even for the 2006 election in which control of the House switched hands but over 90% of the incumbents running for reelection did so successfully—as much as they did nearly three decades earlier. The electoral success of the incumbents should not be surprising. (See figure 3.6.)

Just as scholars are interested in incumbent advantages in House elections, they are also interested in why incumbent U.S. senators are frequently defeated. The data from 1978, again data that has not changed greatly in the ensuing years, show that senatorial incumbents do not have the advantages over their challengers that House incumbents have. Senatorial challengers are more well known, and they contact voters more frequently. Incumbents also cannot "control" all their contacts with constituents as well as members of Congress can. Senators are more frequently covered by the news media in situations they cannot control; in most states, their jobs make them more prominent politicians. Most senators cannot build the personal relationships with constituents that representatives in the House can because of the size of their constituency. That combination—the "balanced" image building, the challengers who start out with better name recognition, and the challengers' ability to spend money to become even more widely known—has significantly reduced the advantage of the incumbent in Senate races. The variation in the number of incumbents winning reelection demonstrates that other factors are clearly at work in these elections (see figure 3.7).

Some of you reading this analysis of how citizens vote in congressional and senatorial elections might well be asking: How can this analysis explain 1994, when the Republicans took over Congress by running on the Contract with America or 2006, when the

Figure 3.6 Electoral Success of House Incumbents, 1946–2006

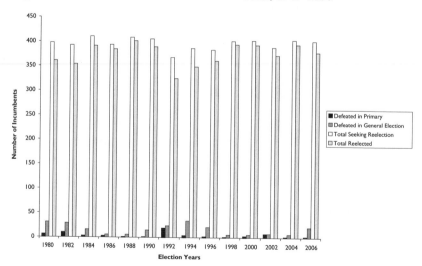

Source: Ornstein, Mann, and Malbin 2002; 2002: *CQ Weekly* (11/9/2002); 2004: *Vital Statistics on American Politics*; 2006: CNN.com; *Cook Political Report.*

Figure 3.7 Incumbents Defeated in Senate Elections, 1946–2006

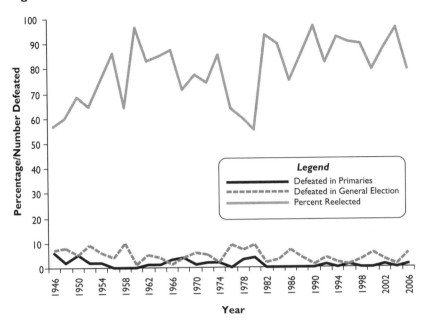

Source: 1946–2004: Stanley and Niemi 2006a; 2006: compiled by authors.
Note: One incumbent defeated in a primary in 2006 was then Democratic senator Joseph Lieberman (Conn.), who went on to win reelection running as an independent.

Democrats regained control, running against the war in Iraq? The short answer to that question is that the theories of voting behavior still hold.

Those elections were not "normal" elections. In each case the party out of power, in both the Congress and the White House, took advantage of widespread public dissatisfaction and blamed the "ins." Normal election momentum turned into what analysts described as an electoral tsunami, with all close elections going to the Republicans in 1994 and the Democrats in 2006. Virtually all open seats—and there were many, particularly in 1994—went to the out party. The incumbent return rates were higher than those for most recent elections; but they only seem low because of the extraordinarily high rates in the other years.

Finally, the case of 2006 essentially proves the rule. In essence this was an issue-oriented election in the districts that were closely contested. But the two parties competed effectively against each other in only about 15 percent of all House seats. In the others, the normal pattern was evident. In the few highly competitive seats, voters focused on the national issues of the day; most voters in the other districts voted for the incumbent knowing little of the challenger.

The Democrats in the 110th Congress—like the Republicans in

the 104th—argued that they had a mandate to change policy. In each case, the new majority in the House passed promised legislation very quickly. But neither election returned huge majorities. Each new majority faced a president of the opposite party. And the normal pattern of incremental policy change followed. The Republicans' proposing a Contract with America in 1994 and Democratic opposition to the war in Iraq in 2006 are examples of successful campaign tactics, but their impact on the midterm elections do not call into question previous theories of how the electorate determines for whom it will vote in congressional elections (Jacobson 1996).

What of electoral behavior in elections for statewide offices or local offices? Until recently, political scientists have not produced systematic studies of elections at these levels (see Cox and Morgensten 1993, 1995; Garand 1991; Gierzynski and Breaux 1991; Jewell and Breaux 1991; Weber, Tucker, and Brace 1991). However, some conclusions are inescapable. Races for governor, for instance, feature voting behavior parallel to that for senator. Governors are well known, but so are their opponents. Their accomplishments in office are examined in detail in the press. Gubernatorial opponents spend a good deal of money portraying the negative parts of incumbents' records. Voters decide based on these appeals—on party, image, and record. Figure 3.8 shows the electoral success of incumbent governors seeking reelection in the last three decades.

State legislators and others running in smaller constituencies face an electoral environment similar to that of members of Congress, with one notable exception—districts in many states are small enough that a significant percentage of the voters know their legisla-

Figure 3.8 Electoral Successes of Incumbent Governors, 1980–2006

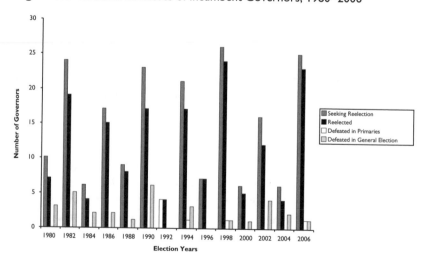

Source: *Vital Statistics on American Politics* 2005–2006; CNN.com; America Votes 21.

tor on a personal basis. When this is the case, particularly in the smaller states, partisanship and issues become less important; however, when the personal relationship does not exist, partisanship and name familiarity again dominate (Garand 1991; Weber, Tucker, and Brace 1991).

IV. VOTING BEHAVIOR THEORY REVISITED

The picture that emerges of the American electorate is not a clear one. As table 3.4 shows, a bare majority of Americans identify with one major party or the other; movement toward more independents and fewer party identifiers, particularly fewer with strong party identification, is evident. Questions have arisen about the strength of party allegiance and about the significance of that strength (see Converse and Pierce 1987 for a discussion of means of measuring partisanship; Miller 1998; Mattei and Niemi 1991; Finkel and Scarrow 1985).

The research community has been watching elections for signs of a new partisan realignment for decades. After the 1988 presidential election, Warren Miller (1990, 110–15) described a two-stage realignment:

> My analysis of the 1988 elections thus supports the thesis that a significant first phase of the 1980–1988 realignment occurred between 1980 and 1984 among the less experienced and less sophisticated voters who responded to Reagan's personal leadership with an increase in Republicanism. A smaller but perhaps more meaningful second phase then occurred between 1984 and 1988, particularly among the older and better-educated voters who ultimately responded favorably to the Reagan administration's emphasis on conservatism. (Miller 1990, 114; see also Miller 1991; Shanks and Miller 1989, 1990)

But those conclusions did not go unchallenged. In the 1990s, scholars had continued to debate such topics as the extent to which the most recent realignment was regional, rather than national, in scope (Black and Black 1987); the question of whether voters' identification with party is different at the national and state levels (Hadley 1985; Niemi, Wright, and Powell 1987); the group composition of the two parties and its significance (Stanley, Bianco, and Niemi 1986; Stanley and Niemi 2006b); and the extent to which dealignment is merely a reflection of "unrealized partisanship" (Carmines, McIver, and Stimson 1987) or the degree to which the apparent dealignment is in fact a reflection of the nonalignment of the newest voters (Miller and. Shanks 1996).

Two concerns drive this research: how do citizens make voting decisions and what is happening to the American electorate as a whole. Some have begun to ask whether the realignment paradigm is no longer appropriate and whether another should replace it, perhaps one based on divided government as the defining feature of American electoral behavior at the turn of the century (Fiorina 1996).

How one views the role of *party* in the electoral decisions reached by voters in the modern context depends on what theory one espouses. Parties are still important to many; the Democrats advantage in party identification over the Republicans has narrowed and, at times, even disappeared. We also know that many people eschew party allegiance, identify with neither party, and vote based on other cues.

What else enters into that decision? When issues seem to play a crucial role in election races or when the parties clearly differentiate themselves on ideological grounds, issues and ideology can have a large impact on voting behavior. The authors of *The Changing American Voter* explicitly illustrate such an impact.

However, voters do not care about the details of issues; they are more concerned about their overall well-being and how politicians—in their role as government officials—have contributed to that well-being. Voting based on the evaluation of an incumbent's performance, rather than promises of future action, is the most common explanation of the Reagan and Bush victories in 1980, 1984, and 1988 (Pomper 1981a, 97); the Clinton victories in 1992 and 1996 (Arterton 1993; Quirk and Dalager 1993; Elshtain and Beem 1997); and the George W. Bush win in 2004 (Abramson, Aldrich, and Rohde 2005; Nelson 2005). According to this school of thought, the electorate in 2000 was evaluating two aspects of President Clinton's performance as they decided whether to support his vice president, Al Gore—his personal behavior and the performance of the government over which he presided—and they reached conflicting judgments.

One school of thought claims that voters are casting rational, considered votes when they choose to support a presidential candidate of one party and a congressional or senatorial candidate of the other. These scholars say that voters want to hedge their bets. They might favor one candidate for president, but he or she might be a little too liberal than they really want; they will thus temper their vote by choosing a congressional candidate who is more conservative, to keep the president from going too far (Fiorina 1996; Jacobson 1996).

Given what we know about the level of information citizens have concerning their representatives in Washington or the issues of the day, it is difficult to imagine citizens sitting down and thinking in this way; but perhaps it is not too difficult to imagine them doing so intuitively. If they believe the government has gone too far in one direction or not far enough in another, they can cast their vote accordingly.

Even this retrospective evaluative voting is not always in evidence. Below the presidential (and perhaps senatorial and gubernatorial) level, citizens know little of incumbents' records or the issues with which they are concerned. They might blame Congress for the mess the country is in (Fenno 1972), or they might not have much faith in government and politicians in general, but they rarely blame their own representatives. Voters know these local politicians, view them positively, and frequently reelect the ones who seek reelection. Voters distinguish between the individual they know and trust and the impersonal institution—far removed from their daily lives—that is allegedly causing trouble.

V. PARTICIPATION IN POLITICS IN AMERICA

Voting is the most prominent form of political participation, but it is far from the only form. Social science research into political participation has consistently emphasized voting, since it can be measured easily. Official returns show how many go to the polls; census data provide a demographic breakdown of the electorate; and survey research reveals something about the voters' opinions, attitudes, motivations, backgrounds, affiliations, and other such characteristics.[5]

Finding out about other activities involves carefully identifying them, grouping them, and then analyzing them. Few are dichotomous variables. An individual either votes or not. But what about talking about politics? Or trying to tell others how to vote? If a woman casually complains to a friend that the charges of sexual impropriety by Arnold Schwarzenegger offend her, is that discussing politics? How should we measure that activity against a long discussion of President Bush's policy on Iraq? Should an individual who gives $25 to a friend running for school board be grouped with an individual who gives $1,000 to each of ten congressional candidates, by listing both as "those who contribute to campaigns"?

Finding out about political "passivists" is also difficult. Probably half the nonvoters in this country tell survey analysts that they vote. Who are they? Why don't they vote? Why do they lie about it? If it is not easy to ascertain what low voter turnout means for the American system, it is even more difficult to evaluate political behavior that is nonconventional or even illegal. How many individuals who have been involved in burning abortion clinics would discuss their reasons for doing so in response to a scholar's open-ended questions?

Thus, our knowledge about political participation is not as extensive as we would like, but we still do know a good deal. The most extensive research on this subject is found in an important study by Sidney Verba, Kay Lehman Schlozman, and Henry Brady (1995). What they studied was the political and voluntary activities of a large sample of American citizens. We can only highlight some of the findings of this monumental study.

Social and economic resources influence not only the ways in which citizens participate in political and other voluntary organizations but also the extent to which they participate. The views of those who are active in these types of organizations are not representative of the views of inactive minority group members, whether examined by race or ethnicity. Furthermore, activity in politics is more skewed by demographic and socioeconomic factors than activity in either religious or community organizations. The implication of these conclusions is stated in the title of the book *Voice and Equality;* that is, those who are not equal in other ways are not heard equally through participation in voluntary groups in our society, particularly not in political activities.

Earlier studies found that it is possible to break the American electorate's political behavior down into certain modes of participation (Verba and Nie 1972; Milbrath and Goel 1977). Citizens were classified as either *active, passive but supportive,* or *inactive.* The active group includes those who are identified as party and campaign workers, those who are community activists, those who frequently contact officials about particular problems, and those who are involved in a communications network that discusses political matters (a group identified only by Milbrath).

Not many Americans fit into these groups ranging from about 4 percent, who contact officials about particular problems, to 20 percent, who are community activists, to over 30 percent, who engage in some form of campaign activity, such as contributing money, wearing a button, or putting a bumper sticker on their car. Although most of these "active" individuals also vote, voting is a separate style of participation.

By far the largest group consists of those identified as passive supporters—individuals who pay taxes, who rise and sing the national anthem at ball games, but whose active involvement in politics is limited to voting. Large numbers of Americans support the system, at least passively—nearly everyone stands for the flag, and over 90 percent pay the taxes they owe. More than three in five Americans claim to vote regularly; the number who actually vote is less than that, but voting occasionally is not viewed as an onerous task by most Americans.

The group of citizens defined as inactive, or apathetic, is the smallest group, constituting less than a quarter of the population. We know little about why they are not involved. We do know that they are uninterested, uninformed, and alienated from the system. Nevertheless, these individuals who engage in no political activity are supportive of the system and patriotic enough to fly the flag on the Fourth of July. They cheered for the American women when they won the soccer World Cup, and they grieved for the victims in New York, Washington, and Pennsylvania on September 11, 2001. If these citizens maintain their love of country, even though they do not participate in politics, perhaps their apathy really does not hurt the political system.

This group can be compared with those unconventional activists labeled "protesters."[6] Milbrath and Goel (1977, 14–19) gather into this category those who would "protest vigorously if the government does something morally wrong (26 percent)," "refuse to obey laws (16 percent)," "attend protest meetings (6 percent)," "join a public street demonstration (3 percent)," and "riot if necessary (2 percent)." These findings should be viewed as tentative because they were derived from one city at a time of considerable urban unrest (1968), but they also reinforce the conclusion drawn here, because protesters, by and large, participate in all forms of political activity. They did not withdraw from politics and thus "[voted] with their feet." They were active in politics and saw protesting as an extension of their activity.[7]

One could look at the American experience through a slightly different lens, however. Protesting against the government—that is, trying to "redress grievances" through nontraditional means—has a long history in this country. After all, what were our nation's founders, if not violent protestors against the British? The nonviolent protests of the civil rights movement led to the Civil Rights Act of 1964 and the Voting Rights Act of 1965. Student protesters on college campuses throughout the land were instrumental in changing the nation's policy in regard to the Vietnam War. And students today continue to protest in hopes of changing environmental policies and economic policies affecting developing nations.

Although the number of citizens involved in protests of these types is typically small, especially compared with the number who vote, the impact of their actions has at times been far reaching. Critics of the American political system say that our politics are ineffective because, to use an analogy from football, everything happens between the forty-yard lines. When people want to change a situation drastically, they have to act in a totally different way. These means are nontraditional and are not much discussed in books on elections and the electoral process. But shouldn't we be concerned about a system that often fails to address such important problems in a way that defuses these kinds of protests? Does the need to protest signal a failure in the electoral system?

Are there signs that the system is not working for a significant group of citizens today? Susan Tolchin, in a book entitled *The Angry American* (1999), presents evidence that the electorate is angry. Others disagree, citing reelection rates for incumbents as a sign that voters at least are not discontent. How many of you live in states with active militia movements? The militia movements generally are composed of Americans who are extremely unhappy with the system, with the intrusion of government into their lives, with the loss of independence and individual freedom. Some have taken their protests to an extreme, arming themselves and resisting all forms of government intervention.

Are these protestors so far outside the mainstream that they should be ignored? Congress does not think so. The Senate Judiciary Committee held hearings on the 1992 shoot-out at Ruby Ridge, Idaho, and heard testimony from militia leaders. Critics in Congress believed these hearings to be inappropriate because they lent credibility to those at the fringe of American politics, who might well want to change the system so drastically as to bring it down. Do you think that makes them so anathema that they should be ignored? Might ignoring them play into their hands? How should our system treat those who hold extreme views and choose to participate in the most nontraditional ways? This question has confounded elected officials throughout our nation's first two centuries.

Consider Operation Rescue, a small group headed by Randall Terry. Its members firmly believe that abortion is murder, and they are dedicated to closing down abortion clinics. Their moral position is that other citizens' rights are less important than an unborn fetus's right to life. Of course, the rights of other citizens, those who believe that the decision to abort a fetus should be made primarily by the woman carrying that fetus, are abrogated by the actions of Operation Rescue.

When rights clash, the government generally intervenes. But what level of protesting at abortion clinics is permissible? Most would agree that marching outside a clinic is a permissible exercise of First Amendment free speech rights. What about blocking clinic entrances? Some might claim that preventing abortions is so important that restricting other people's freedom of access, requiring intervention by local police to open the doors, is a legitimate action. Others would disagree.

What about bombing an empty clinic? That would shut it down without hurting anyone.

What about bombing a clinic that is open? Some people might be hurt, but abortion protesters might find that price acceptable for ending abortion.

What about shooting a physician who performs abortions? Is that level of violence permissible? Most people would draw a line well short of this type of violence. But clearly others disagree, and it is important to understand that their actions, while not considered traditional political participation, are participation of an important kind that cannot be ignored.

Is it possible to draw a profile of political participation among Americans? First, most Americans only engage in voting, not in any other political activity. In any given election, 30 to 80 percent of the electorate does not vote, but these nonvoters do not make up a stable group. Over three-quarters of all American citizens consider themselves regular voters.

Beyond voting, political participation falls way off. Only one in ten Americans either belongs to a political club or an organization or contributes money to political campaigns; only a slightly larger number ever wear a button or display a sticker; and only one in four tries to convince others to vote for specific candidates.

Other modes of behavior have been distinguished from those that some believe are in political decline (Putnam 2000). Nearly a third of all Americans are involved in community activities, and many more make certain they are involved in communicating about politics. A much smaller number contact public officials about their personal problems with the government, regardless of their level of participation. Furthermore, some evidence points to the thesis that a small group of people are actively involved in political life in an unconventional way—that is, they are people willing to protest (and even riot, if necessary) to accomplish their political ends. These protesters do not view their activity as illegitimate but as the ultimate expression of their patriotism.

Finally, a small but relevant number of Americans are inactive and apathetic. They rarely even vote; however, they remain patriotic citizens. It appears that they truly are unconcerned yet not turned against the system.

VI. POLITICIANS VIEW POLITICAL PARTICIPATION

A county chairman, along with his friend, walked up the stairs and into the first meeting of the county committee after the state convention. The chairman had been something of a hero at that convention, defending a gay rights plank against an attack from the religious right. This meeting would be a mere formality; he would be reelected, discuss plans for the upcoming election year, and adjourn the meeting in time to catch the last few innings of the Red Sox game. As he opened the door into the meeting room packed with people, he turned to his friend and said, "We're in for a long evening."

"What do you mean? Who are these people?"

"I don't know, but they sure didn't get elected to the county committee to come to vote for me." The about-to-be-ex-county-chairman had learned an important political lesson.

For practicing politicians, the most important part of citizen political participation is predictability. If only 50 percent turn out to vote, no one is bothered, as long as it is always more or less the same 50 percent. If attendance at county committee meetings is sparse, the chairman breathes easily as long as he knows who will be there. If a few people complain when an officeholder takes a controversial stand, she will not get upset—if that reaction was expected. But the unpredictable reaction—the large turnout, the new faces, the massive protests—doesn't just worry politicians. Unpredictable participation gives politicians nightmares.

The county chairman mentioned here lost because he took a stand that caused people who had never been concerned before to take an interest in party politics. When he saw a sea of unfamiliar faces, he knew only too well why they were there. His opponents took advantage of the meeting to get rid of an unacceptable "radical."

The same scenario is repeated often. Voter turnout, particularly in primary elections, is difficult for politicians to predict accurately. Figure 3.9 shows the turnout in Iowa presidential caucuses from 1968 to 2004. A campaign manager looking at the data up to 1976 and planning for the 1980 caucuses would know how many votes his or her candidate needed to win. Using sophisticated techniques

Figure 3.9 Estimated Turnout in Iowa Democratic Caucuses, 1968–2004

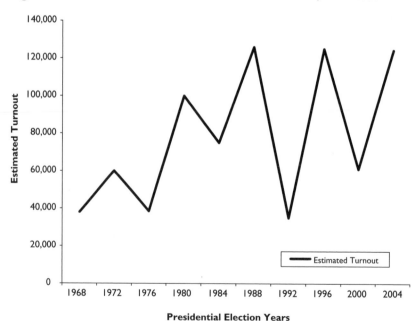

Source: Iowa Democratic Party.

for identifying supporters and getting them to the polls, such a manager could judge quite accurately how the candidate would do on the eve of the caucuses. Then he or she would be faced with the 1980 turnout: two-and-a-half times that of four years earlier. The campaign manager throws out all previous assumptions. Who can judge who these new participants are and how they will react?

In 2004 Howard Dean and John Kerry spent much more money than the other candidates, by raising their own money rather than relying on public matching funds (see chapter 5). Their entire premise was that they could change political behavior by "encouraging" more voters to attend the caucuses. Many came to the caucuses, but not all of them voted as Dean and Kerry hoped.

How then have practicing politicians viewed the changes in the electorate presented earlier in this chapter? First and foremost, they view it as unfamiliar terrain that they have to cross. When the electorate has expanded, politicians have dealt with that expansion, making appeals to new voters as they have seen fit. Those who have predicted accurately how the new voters would react have prospered, such as the Southern politicians who have softened their formerly racist rhetoric. Those who have guessed wrong have lost, often badly—such as George McGovern, who assumed that masses of young voters against the war in Vietnam would rush to the polls in 1972. Others learn for the next electoral round. For instance, today's politicians are faced with an expanding Hispanic electorate, and they are faced with an electorate divided on social issues. How do they appeal to those voters? The Democrats in 2007 are striving to capture the center. Republican leaders are remaining true to their conservative base. Some will strike a responsive chord and succeed; others will not be so fortunate—or prescient.

Politicians look upon the American electorate as consumers. They, the politicians, are the products that have to be sold, and they are sold in any way that is effective in getting the most people to vote for a candidate.

An oft-stated theoretical argument is that politicians seek only a plurality of the votes while making as few commitments and concessions as possible to guarantee a winning coalition. This argument badly misreads politicians. Politicians fear losing; they do not fear commitments or concessions. Officeholders never feel secure; they have too much to lose if they are wrong. Consequently, in setting electoral strategy, they seek to generate maximum support, not merely to win.

It is also evident to most politicians that an individualized sales approach is the most effective. As one member of Congress put it, "I love going door-to-door. When I talk to someone in their living room, and when they say they'll support me, *I know* I have their vote. No question about it."

Door-to-door campaigning, the one-on-one sale of self, has proven successful in campaign after campaign. The New Hampshire presidential primary is based on the premise that candidates will go from little town to little town and meet all of the people—and relatively unknown candidates, such as Jimmy Carter in 1976, have won by doing just that. Many members of Congress, many senators, and even governors have followed a similar strategy, some walking the length and breadth of their district or state; however, the publicity that initially accompanied such walks and added to their effectiveness as a campaign technique has lessened considerably, as campaign "walks" have become commonplace.

But consider the problems of bringing one's campaigning to individual voters. The average congressional district has approximately 650,000 citizens. Maybe 450,000 of those are potential voters, who live in 200,000 households. If a candidate spent twenty minutes in each living room, assuming everyone was home and that no time was needed between stops, that candidate would have to have put in nearly fifty-five hundred twelve-hour campaign days. Candidates accomplishing 1 percent of such a schedule in a two-year cycle feel that they have developed the common touch. Even with surrogates and volunteers, the enormity of "personal" effort becomes apparent, and the effort must be multiplied many times over for senatorial, gubernatorial, or presidential campaigns. Campaigning for individual votes might well work in local elections, and it is used to good effect for some offices in larger districts; but most politicians must use other means to approach the electorate.

Rather than see voters as individuals, politicians tend to see them as members of groups to whom appeals can be made. Once the decision has been made to group individuals, a number of options are open, some of which can complement one another; some others, however, seem to preclude possible strategies.

RELIGIOUS RIGHT

Group that believes that adherence to certain moral principles constitutes an important aspect of political life.

One of the most influential groups in the Republican party today is the so-called **religious right** (see Wilcox 1996, 2000). This group of citizens, defined in various ways, agrees that certain moral principles they share should be important in political decision making (see chapter 4). Among the issues most important to this group are banning gay marriages, outlawing abortion, and permitting prayer in schools. In some areas of the country, those who adhere to these principles and believe that they are the most important issues on the political agenda constitute a majority of the Republican party. If Republican candidates appeal directly to these voters, they might well be hindering their chances of winning over other voters for whom Republican stances on economic issues are more important.

In seeking the Republican presidential nomination in 1996, magazine publisher Malcolm "Steve" Forbes stressed his economic platform, calling for replacement of the Internal Revenue Service code with a flat tax. He tried to avoid the litmus test issues on the religious right's social agenda. He fared poorly in Republican primaries in states dominated by this group. After 1996 Forbes made a determined effort to appeal to the religious right, clearly acknowledging that his 1996 strategy had failed. What he could not know, however, was whether his new approach would alienate the economically conservative but socially moderate voters who had favored him earlier.

In 2006, many Republicans consciously appealed for the support of those hurt by waves of illegal immigrants in states such as California, Texas, and Florida. They called for stricter immigration laws, increased use of the border patrol, and denial of benefits to those who entered the country illegally and to their children. Although some voters responded to these appeals, Hispanic voters reacted negatively. An appeal to one group precluded an appeal to another.

Democratic candidates face similar dilemmas. An appeal to the least advantaged elements in society might alienate Democrats who believe that the welfare system has run amuck or that government is too inefficient. Democrats taking a strong pro-choice position on abortion, a position favored by a majority in their party, might alienate anti-abortion proponents whose votes they will need in the general election.

Each candidate must define his or her constituency by grouping the potential electorate in ways that are meaningful to his or her campaign. Some groupings preclude others; it is not possible to appeal to both the religious right and to activist women's groups. Other strategies are less limiting; a candidate can appeal to the elderly on social security or health care issues without ruling out ardent environmentalists.

But politicians can also look at their constituency as a whole and break it down into groups of people who are concerned with particular issues. Which groups seemed to favor President Bush in 2000 and 2004? In 2000 candidate Bush talked of being a "compassionate conservative" and someone with a strong moral sense. He sidestepped the issue of his conservatism and tied Vice President Gore to the questionable personal moral code of President Clinton. In 2004, Bush, as incumbent president, emphasized that he was a decisive leader, needed at a time of danger symbolized by the constant reference to a post-9/11 world. In his reelection campaign he portrayed his opponent, a decorated war veteran, as wishy-washy and indecisive.

A second strategic approach groups voters by geographic region, not by interests or similar categorizations. Candidates for statewide office in Massachusetts look at how their campaign is doing in Boston—and then the rest of the state. In New York, they look at New York City, the suburbs, and upstate; in Illinois, at Chicago and downstate; in Colorado, at Denver and at those areas on the western slopes of the continental divide and at the arid plains on the eastern slopes; in California, at liberal Northern California versus conservative Southern California. In some congressional districts, the geographic distinctions are almost as pronounced. Connecticut's Fifth District is divided between poor mill towns and affluent bedroom suburbs of New York City. California's Forty-fifth District includes not only Palm Springs and other wealthy suburbs of Los Angeles but also lush farmlands and nearly unirrigatable desert. When politicians in any of these areas campaign, they are acutely aware of their geographic surroundings.

Note the distinction. In this case the politicians are appealing to those who live in a certain area because politicians assume that citizens relate to others in that area. This strategy is quite different from that appealing to groups based on shared issue concerns. But in a broader sense, the theory is the same. Electoral strategies do not normally involve appeals to individuals. Individuals vote, but candidates appeal to them in groups, groups defined by the candidates and their strategists according to their strengths and perceptions of what will work. The larger the constituency, the more this is the case.

Tip O'Neill (D-Mass., 1953–1987; Speaker of the House 1977–1987) has been quoted as saying, "All politics is local." Politicians still believe Tip, decades after his death. Many started out as local politicians, and they know the effectiveness of one-on-one campaigns. Their goal is to make national or statewide politics local by defining smaller groups into which voters fall and then seeking to appeal to these groups. Many techniques are available for these appeals—mass media directed at a certain audience, targeted mailings, the Internet, speeches to certain groups. But in the end, the political strategy is the same: make an appeal, in any way possible, to the largest number of people so that it will seem personal to each voter. Campaigners sell the product by figuring out what the voters want to buy.

Whereas political scientists seek to explain voting behavior with some degree of precision, politicians—with the souls of artists, not scientists—try to mold the electorate into the shape they want. The skills of both the scientist and the artist deserve attention.

WEBSITES

www.census.gov: The U.S. Census Bureau provides information not only on population statistics but also on citizen responses to a detailed survey regarding political participation and other areas of interest.

www.electionstudies.org: The National Election Studies (NES), conducted by the Center for Political Studies of the Institute for Social Research at the University of Michigan, has polled the American electorate for decades. Data are available from surveys maintained by the Inter-university Consortium for Political and Social Research.

www.ropercenter.uconn.edu: The Roper Center for Public Opinion Research holds the largest library of public opinion data in the world. Much of this data is available online, as are its publications *America at the Polls* and *Public Perspective*.

www.pollingreport.com: An independent, nonpartisan resource on contemporary public opinion.

www.people-press.org: The Pew Research Center for the People and the Press is an independent public opinion research organization that includes as one of its focuses contemporary views of the American electorate.

CHAPTER 4

Organized Groups in the Political Process

AFL-CIO member and election volunteer John Michalec mans a phone bank at the AFL-CIO's Michigan headquarters in Lansing, Michigan, November 2, 2006. Michalec and other volunteers are working the phones encouraging fellow union members to vote on Election Day. Organized groups have assumed critical roles in the American electoral process, providing information and voting cues to their members, campaign resources to political parties and candidates for office, and extensive efforts aimed at getting out the vote on Election Day.

Think about yourself and the others in your class. In what ways are you the same? In what ways are you different? Many campuses have had long discussions of diversity in recent years. Is your class a diverse group or a homogeneous group? What do those terms mean to you? How do you think these questions relate to politics?

A recent National Election Study survey from the Survey Research Center at the University of Michigan asked a series of questions about groups, including the following:

> There's been some talk these days about different social classes. Most people say they belong either to the MIDDLE CLASS or the WORKING CLASS. Do you think of yourself as belonging to one of these classes?
>
> In addition to being an American, what do you consider your main ethnic group or nationality group?

The question "How would you rate the following groups?" was followed by a list: labor unions, feminists, civil rights leaders, people on welfare, women, conservatives, poor people, Catholics, big business, blacks, evangelical groups active in politics, the federal government in Washington, liberals. Obviously, the designers of this question believe that Americans respond to political messages by filtering those messages through reactions that they have as members of a group. But aren't there really different types of groups?

A similar perspective marked the analysis of candidate appeal by journalists during the prenomination phase of the 2008 presidential elections. How will women respond to Hillary Clinton? Would African Americans more heavily support Clinton or Barack Obama? Could any Democratic candidate appeal to religious voters? And speaking of religious voters, could any of the GOP front-runners—Rudy Giuliani, John McCain, and Mitt Romney—gain their support, or would these religious voters turn to another Republican option, such as actor and former Tennessee senator Fred Thompson?

If you are a careful reader, you probably are troubled by the conceptual inconsistency in applying the concept "group." The groups cited in the National Election Study (NES) questions were different kinds of groups—social groups, ethnic groups, racial groups, ideological groups, occupational groups, and others. Not only are these groups not mutually exclusive (e.g., one could certainly be a black teacher who is a union member), but they are also generically different. The first NES questions seek to find out how the respondent perceives himself or herself. The questions allow for more than one answer and then probe for primary **self-identification**. In analyzing the influence of groups on the electoral process, however, a researcher must distinguish among types of groups and the effect these groups have on politics.

SELF-IDENTIFICATION

Responses that individuals give about their own sense of who they are or to what groups they belong.

Americans, like citizens of many other nations, divide themselves "automatically" into certain types of groups. The electorate can be divided by race (blacks, whites, Hispanics, Asians, etc.), by religion (mainline Protestants, evangelical Protestants, Catholics, Jews, Muslims, etc.), by age (the elderly, the middle-aged, young adults, etc.), by sexual orientation (gay, straight, etc.), or by occupation (farmers, teachers, construction workers, lawyers, etc.). Other similar groupings could be added to this list. As mentioned in chapter 3, politicians often treat the electorate as a collection of such groups, appealing to voters to react through their **group consciousness**. In this regard it is important to find out which groups with which voters principally self-identify (as the survey asks) and how candidates will appeal to their rivals' social groups—as journalists wondered in trying to predict the races for the 2008 presidential nominations.

But what commentators have noted for centuries as a distinguishing characteristic of the American populace is not the ability to identify with demographic, occupational, or social groups but rather a long-lived tendency to join organized groups. Until very recent times, analysts, from the authors of the *Federalist* papers through V. O. Key Jr., have focused their attention on the impact of organized groups on the policymaking process, not the electoral process. In the last edition of his classic text *Politics, Parties, and Pressure Groups*, published in 1964, Key wrote:

> A striking feature of American politics is the extent to which political parties are supplemented by private associations formed to influence public policy. These organizations, commonly called **pressure groups**, promote their interests by attempting to influence government rather than by nominating candidates and seeking responsibility for the management of government. Such groups, while they may call themselves non-political, are engaged in politics; in the main theirs is a politics of policy. (18)

Key (1964, 19) acknowledges that "pressure groups may campaign for party candidates and may even become, in fact if not in form, allied with one or the other of the parties." However, the emphasis in his five chapters on pressure groups is most decidedly on how these organizations seek to effect policy changes *after* elections have been held.

Within a decade of Key's death in 1963, even much less perceptive observers of American politics had come to realize that the role of interest groups (the term "pressure groups" has been all but dropped because of its pejorative connotation) has been drastically altered. Although they continue to play an important role in all aspects of the policymaking process, organized interest groups acting

GROUP CONSCIOUSNESS

Concept that certain attitudes and opinions are adopted because they reflect the views of those in a group with which one associates.

PRESSURE GROUPS

Descriptive name by which interest groups were known in the past.

as organizations, not merely associations with which voters identify, now play a central role in the electoral process as well. (See, e.g., Berry and Wilcox 2007; Cigler and Loomis 1995, 2007; Herrnson et al. 1998, 2005; Schlozman and Tierney 1986; Wright 1996) When Democratic candidates challenging first-year Republicans in the 1996 election were dubbed as "the tools of organized labor," the appellation stemmed from endorsement and support by organizations *as* organizations, not because individual voters who were members of those groups supported them.

This chapter focuses on the role of organized groups in the electoral process. Two aspects of this role will be examined separately: (1) the ways in which these organizations enter into the campaigns of various candidates and (2) the effectiveness of these groups in controlling their members' votes. As you read these sections you should be asking yourself about what role you think groups should be playing in the process. What were once referred to as "pressure groups" have become "interest groups." But political journalists talk all the time about the pressure put on politicians by those groups whose support they seek. Is that good or bad in your view? What is the relationship between interest groups and political parties? The Democrats are often viewed as the party of the labor unions, and the Republicans as the party of big business. What do those connections entail? How often do parties and interest groups work together? When are they at odds? Before turning to these questions, however, we need an explicit understanding of types of groups to be examined.

I. ORGANIZED GROUPS IN AMERICAN POLITICS

Table 4.1 lists a sampling of organized groups in the United States today. Organized groups cover a wide array of interests, from those concerned with more general topics, like the AFL-CIO, to those concerned with very specific subjects, like the National Rifle Association. They come in a variety of sizes, from a few hundred members, like the National Football League Players' Association, to tens of millions, like the American Association of Retired People (AARP). They engage in a variety of activities, from sponsoring agricultural fairs like 4-H Clubs to sponsoring presidential candidate debates like the League of Women Voters. Only some of these groups are involved in the political process as groups, though members of virtually every group are involved in politics and any group can become involved in politics if it wishes to do so.

A. Political and Nonpolitical Associations

Americans form associations for various reasons: camaraderie, education, charitable work, economic advancement (Walker 1983;

Table 4.1   Types of Organizations and Examples of Associations

Health and Medical	Aerospace Medical Association
	American Board of Allergy and Immumology
	American Council on Pharmaceutical Education
	International Association for Accidental and
	Traffic Medicine
	March of Dimes Birth Defects Foundation
	National Council on the Aging
	Society of Behavioral Medicine
Religious	American Zionist Movement
	Christian Coalition of America
	Fellowship of Concerned Churchmen
	Interfaith Alliance
	International Conference of Police Chaplains
	National Association of Church Personnel
	Administrators
	United States Conference of Catholic Bishops
Cultural	American Bridge Association
	Association of Aviation and Space Museums
	Authors Guild
	Business Committee for the Arts
	Friends of the American Museum in Britain
	United States Chess Federation
	Virgil Society
Scientific, Engineering, and Technical	American Board of Clinical Chemistry
	American Political Science Association
	American Society of Landscape Architects
	Herb Society of America
	Musser International Turfgrass Foundation
	Roller Bearing Engineers Committee
	Stonehenge Study Group

Source: Encyclopedia of Associations.

Verba, Schlozman, and Brady 1995). Some of these groups have an obvious stake in the political process. For example, the National Federation of Independent Businesses clearly is concerned with legislation affecting small business establishments. Some of these organizations were formed for political purposes, the liberal Americans for Democratic Action standing as one such group. Other groups were formed for purposes unrelated to politics, but they became politically involved as the government began to involve itself in matters relating to that group's purpose. For most of its first hundred years, the American Medical Association (AMA) tried to stay out of organized politics. But for the last fifty years or so, the AMA has monitored national legislative action and has frequently lobbied and campaigned to protect its perceived interest. Finally, some groups have stayed above the political fray, despite the expanding role of government. Phi Beta Kappa, the academic honor society formed in the year of our Revolution, has never entered the political realm in over two hundred years and remains removed from politics today.

As the leaders of an organization see that their group's interest is affected by governmental action, they must make an important decision regarding whether they would like to play a more active political role. The decision of whether to become involved in politics—through either the policymaking process or the electoral process, or both—is a significant one for an organization. Politicization may make fund-raising more difficult for other groups. However, if they stay out of politics, the group's members may decide that the group has become irrelevant to the issues around which it has formed; this perception may erode the group's membership and support as well.

If they decide to become politically involved, they take on a new status. If they decide to lobby the Congress for legislation, they must register as a **lobbying** organization. If they decide to support candidates for office, they must form a separate **political action committee**. This is not an easy decision for a number of reasons. For instance, organizations that have been granted tax-exempt status by the Internal Revenue Service may well lose that status.

At times these decisions are easy for leaders to make; at other times they are not. Environmental groups are an interesting example. In the early years of its existence, the only political activities engaged in by the Sierra Club involved efforts to create more national parks. In the late 1960s, however, as environmental concerns heightened, the club became involved with lobbying on more issues. In 1975, for the first time, the Sierra Club opened a Washington office in order to focus its political efforts. It began to use paid advertising to extend its message of environmental concern to a wider audience. Because the Sierra Club spent more than 10 percent of its revenues for political purposes, the Internal Revenue Service revoked its status as a tax-exempt foundation.

Obviously, the leadership of the Sierra Club was aware of the implications of the decision to expand its political activities. The Audubon Society, an organization with a similar perspective, has decided to forgo this approach and has remained a foundation exempt from federal taxes and eligible for tax-deductible contributions.

B. Politically Active Groups

Our concern is with groups (or individuals representing groups) that have decided to become involved politically. The number of

LOBBYING

Taking actions to persuade legislators or those in government to pursue policies favored by one's group.

POLITICAL ACTION COMMITTEES

Organizations that receive contributions from fifty or more individuals and contribute money to at least ten candidates for federal office; often, but not always, affiliated with lobbying organizations.

such groups is staggering: over twenty-two thousand individuals were listed in a recent directory of Washington lobbyists. Over sixteen hundred political action committees contributed to candidates in the 1978 congressional elections; more than four thousand had registered with the Federal Election Commission by the end of 1988, a number more or less maintained since that time (see table 4.2). In the face of these awesome numbers, we should look carefully at the rationale behind the formation of such a farrago of interest groups.

1. Economic or Noneconomic Interests

One way to analyze interest groups is on the basis of their membership. If the members are motivated by *primarily* economic interests, they can be distinguished from other groups whose members have fewer (or at least less obvious) immediate tangible concerns.

A preponderance of the groups active today exists in order to defend their members' economic interests. Why do people find this economic defense so crucial? As the American economy diversified, our citizens increasingly felt that they needed to band together with people of similar interests to defend themselves against those who seemed to be more powerful. Thus farmers' cooperatives and labor organizing began at various times in the 1800s. As these groups diversified further—and thus developed separate interests—more groups were formed. At present, groups with very specific interests have registered themselves with the Federal Election Commission. For example, groups that are active politically include the Florida Tomato Exchange Committee for Responsive Government, the Missouri Soybean Association, and the Ice Cream, Milk, and Cheese Political Action Committee.[1]

The number of economic interest groups also increased rapidly when the federal government became more and more involved in regulating the daily life of most Americans. As government played an increasingly intrusive role in regulating economic matters, greater numbers of Americans came together to advance or defend those interests. Similarly, as the American economy became more and more diversified, the associations became more and more specialized. Many Americans have strong feelings about the overall tax rates in the country, but one group, called the "Beer Drinkers of America," lobbies specifically to keep Congress from raising the alcohol tax. The group is made up mostly of friends and family of brewery owners and employees. They also have a wide representation of regular citizens, though, who like beer and feel strongly that a higher tax should not be imposed on an item that gives them pleasure.

Examples of economic interest groups abound. Some are quite

Table 4.2 Growth of Political Action Committees, 1974–2006

	Corporate	Labor	Trade/ Membership/ Health	Nonconnected	Cooperative	Corporation w/o Stock	Total	Contributions to Congressional Candidates
1974[a]	89	201	318	—	—	—	608	$ 12.5 million
1976[a]	433	224	489	—	—	—	1,146	22.6
1978	785	217	453	162	12	24	1,653	34.1
1980	1,206	297	576	374	42	56	2,551	60.2
1982	1,469	380	649	723	47	103	3,371	87.6
1984	1,682	394	698	1,053	52	130	4,009	113.0
1986	1,744	384	745	1,077	56	151	4,157	139.8
1988	1,816	354	786	1,115	59	138	4,268	159.2
1990	1,795	346	774	1,062	59	136	4,172	159.1
1992	1,735	347	770	1,145	56	142	4,195	188.9
1994	1,660	333	792	980	53	136	3,954	189.6
1996	1,642	332	838	1,103	41	123	4,079	217.8
1998	1,567	321	821	935	39	115	3,798[b]	219.9
2000	1,545	317	860	1,026	41	118	3,907	259.8
2002	1,528	320	975	1,055	39	110	4,027	282.0
2004	1,622	306	900	1,223	34	99	4,184	289.1
2006	1,621	283	935	1,233	40	105	4,217[cd]	N/A[e]

Source: Data from Federal Election Commission.

[a] These numbers represent all other PACs; no further characterization is available.

[b] During the first six months of 1997, 227 PACs were administratively terminated because of inactivity.

[c] During the second six months of 2005, 189 PACs were administratively terminated because of inactivity.

[d] 2006 figures as of July 1, 2006.

[e] 2006 contributions data not available at time of publication.

well known, such as the United Auto Workers or the National Association of Manufacturers. Others are considerably more obscure, like the Coalition for Common Sense in Government Procurement or the Joint Labor Management Committee of the Retail Food Industry.

Noneconomic groups, sometimes called **public interest groups**, pursue goals that their members view as good for the entire society, even if those goals do not serve the economic interest of one particular segment of society. The individual most closely associated with the formation of public interest groups is **Ralph Nader**. He first made his reputation by crusading against General Motors for producing unsafe automobiles (Nader 1965). He was instrumental in forming a cadre of public interest groups concerned with consumer issues, government reform, health care, and other issues. Currently active "Naderite" organizations include Public Citizen, Congress Watch, Critical Mass, Public Citizen Litigation Group, Tax Reform Research Group, Health Research Group, and various state and local public interest research groups (PIRGs).

Others associate public interest groups with Common Cause, an organization of nearly a quarter-million members formed by former health, education, and welfare secretary John Gardner in 1970 (McFarland 1984). Common Cause bills itself as the "citizens' lobby" and concentrates heavily on issues of government reform.

However, many other groups—some older, some younger; some larger, some smaller; some more effective, some less effective—have formed around noneconomic issues and remain active in politics today. These include the environmental groups mentioned earlier, civil rights organizations, ideological groups of the left and the right, religious groups, groups interested in government reform, and many more. Their impact on public policy and on elections is often just as great as that made by their economic counterparts.

Although the distinction between economic and noneconomic groups is a useful one, it should not be overemphasized. The line can become blurred and can change over time. The organized women's groups that formed around the issue of suffrage are a good example. Suffrage, once achieved, gave way to certain other rights, culminating in the unsuccessful drive for ratification of the Equal Rights Amendment (ERA). Along the way, however, women's economic rights were recognized as being as clearly involved as their other rights. One important goal of the women's movement became "equal pay for equal work." The goal was symbolized by the "59 cents" button, signifying that women earned only fifty-nine cents for every dollar a man earned. Although equal pay is now mandated by law, "equal pay for comparable work" has remained a goal of the

**PUBLIC
INTEREST
GROUPS**
Organizations that lobby the government and work for a political agenda that is not defined by economic or other narrowly defined interests.

RALPH NADER
Consumer advocate who has pressured government for reform agenda since the 1960s.

women's movement. The economic concerns of organizations like the National Organization for Women (NOW) have spread to include the allegedly discriminatory practices of the insurance industry, compensatory pay for past discrimination, and many other important issues. NOW is not primarily an economic interest group, but it cannot ignore women's economic concerns.

2. Multipurpose or Single-Purpose Groups

SINGLE-PURPOSE GROUPS

Interest groups that concentrate their efforts on one particular issue.

MULTIPURPOSE GROUPS

Interest groups that reflect the views on a variety of issues on which their members express concern.

The discussion of the women's movement raises another possibility for categorizing groups active today. Some groups—**single-purpose groups**—are organized for a single purpose; others—**multipurpose groups**—lobby on a whole range of issues of interest to their membership. The size of each division depends on how narrowly or widely the term "single interest" is defined. Again, some examples are self-evident; others, however, cannot be so clearly defined.

During the first two decades of the last century, the Congressional Committee of the National American Women's Suffrage Association was organized for the sole purpose of achieving women's right to vote. Similarly, today's Pro-Life Association and NARAL Pro-Choice America (previously the National Abortion Rights Action League) are associations whose purpose relates to only one issue—the existence or nonexistence of a woman's right to choose. On the other hand, groups such as NOW, the League of Women Voters, and the American Association of University Women are concerned with a whole array of women's issues.

The distinction between single-purpose and multipurpose organizations has important implications for the effectiveness of these groups. When Nancy Keenan, the leader of NARAL, speaks on the question of abortion, she speaks authoritatively for the approximately five hundred thousand dues-paying members of her group. They joined the group, combining their financial investment often with a personal investment of time, because they feel a strong commitment to one side of the issue of abortion. No one can question the firmness of their stand on this issue.

On the other hand, if Nancy Jackson, the leader of the Business and Professional Women's (BPW) Foundation of America, were to speak on the same question, despite the fact that she "represents" that group's members (thirty thousand members in two thousand local organizations), her audience could certainly question the commitment of her members to a strong stand on this particular issue. BPW's views are not self-evident. The same questions regarding commitment are also important in trying to determine how important membership in a group is to the members' other political activities.

3. Federal or National Groups

A distinction like the one made above differentiates **federal groups** from **national groups**. National organizations are ones in which members, be they individuals or groups, belong directly to the national organizations. The National Association of Manufacturers is a national organization to which various corporations belong individually. Decisions in these organizations are made directly, with the leaders of the national organization responsible (in ways that are often difficult to define) to their members (see Eismeier and Pollock 1984).

Federal organizations are ones whose national organization is a joining together of state or local organizations, each of which is itself autonomous or semiautonomous. The AFL-CIO is the obvious example of such a group, but it is only one of many that could be given. In organizations of this type, lines of authority are much less distinct. If the various constituent units split on a particular issue, how can the federal leadership speak authoritatively, particularly if the local units are permitted to retain their autonomy? Thus federal organizations may spend a good deal of time on internal politics, assuring that stands taken in Washington do not cause problems out in Pocatello.

The same distinction between national and federal organizations affects the input they make to the electoral process. When the Grocery Manufacturers of America, a national organization, decides to back a candidate for U.S. Senate in Illinois, it is clear that the organization has spoken. However, before the Americans for Democratic Action decides to take a similar stand, the leadership in Washington has to consult with the local Illinois affiliate. The problems of federal organizations multiply when the autonomous members disagree. The power of such a group is diminished when politicians perceive that it does not speak for "all."

FEDERAL GROUPS

Interest groups whose structure reflects a decentralized organization with local, state, or regional units contributing policy views to the federal unit.

NATIONAL GROUPS

Interest groups whose structure is centralized, without powerful local, state, or regional component units.

II. ELECTORAL ACTIVITIES OF ORGANIZED GROUPS

The purpose of drawing the distinctions noted above relates to the varying impact that groups have on the electoral process. The groups became involved in electoral politics in the first place in order to effect changes in public policy. For many years "interest group" or "pressure group" was used as a synonym for "lobbyist." The primary means used by these groups was lobbying legislators and, to a lesser extent, administrators (Key 1964, chaps. 2–6). Only *after* the lobbying role was firmly established did organized interest groups become involved in the electoral process in a meaningful way. Today it is not far from the truth to assert that most people who think of interest groups assume that they are synonymous with political action committees. Although this connection is not absolute, the role of interest groups in campaigning has indeed become prominent.

Even as their role has expanded, however, it is distinct from the role played by political parties. Parties run candidates for office and seek control in order to organize the governing process. The parties stand for certain principles, but they use these principles chiefly as a means to attract adherents. Interest groups, contrarily, became involved in the electoral arena *only* to forward their policy preferences. Put simply, instead of taking positions to attract followers, they support candidates who support their positions—or oppose candidates who do not favor their positions. This last point is important. Political parties field candidates in order to *win* positions; interest groups at times support one candidate simply to bring about the defeat of another.

In the 1996 congressional election, for example, the AFL-CIO, the main arm of organized labor, opposed a group of freshman Republicans who had taken stands opposed by labor in the 104th Congress. The AFL-CIO was against these incumbents; the quality of the challengers in these districts was almost completely inconsequential, though their views on the key issues were not. Political parties, conversely, would not be so concerned with policy positions as they would be with a partisan label.

How do interest groups affect the electoral arena? In the following section, which deals with the group's impact on the voting behavior of group members, we will examine the activities through which these groups seek to have an impact in the broadly defined political environment. (See Wolpe and Levine 1996, 48–54; Wright 1996; and Schlozman and Tierney 1986, 200–20.)

A. Working within the Party

Most interest groups attempt to maintain some degree of bipartisanship because they do not want to alienate, in either party, public officials who favor their policy preferences. However, remaining "above" the partisan battle does not mean removing themselves wholly from the internal operations of both parties. Traditionally, interest groups have attempted to effect changes in the two party platforms.

It has already been noted that the suffragists defined platform support for the women's vote as one of their goals earlier in the last century. Similarly, those favoring passage of the Equal Rights Amendment fought to have it included in both parties' platforms. Republicans first expressed support for the ERA when they were seeking to build opposition to four-term president Franklin Roosevelt. One of the most interesting aspects of the 1980 Republican Convention was the successful effort by anti-ERA groups to keep support for that amendment out of the GOP platform. Similarly, the Pro-Life Impact Committee was successful in having an anti-abortion plank inserted into that platform. In both cases, the debate before the Republican Platform Committee was structured by interest groups (Malbin 1981, 100–110).

Many groups have been actively involved in the platform-writing process. Before most recent conventions, each party has held a series of platform hearings. The stated goal has been to reach out for the opinions of rank-and-file Republicans and Democrats. To a great extent the effect was to reach out for the views of organized groups. The groups send their leaders to testify; they prepare their own "miniplatforms," and they "lobby" with members of the platform committee. The most involved groups even campaign, often successfully, to have their followers made members of platform committees. Certainly this has been the case with the religious right, which has been most successful at capturing control over Republican delegations in states with permeable delegate selection rules, rules that make it relatively easy for those not normally involved with a political party to take part in its work (Usher 1998). Although debate continues over the importance of platforms in the policy-making process (see Pomper with Lederman 1980, chap. 8; Wayne 1988, 147–51), interest group leaders unquestionably see the platform as one place in which they can have an impact.

In the 1998 election cycle, anti-abortion forces went one step further in trying to influence the Republican party. Instead of seeking to have their position inserted in party platforms, they attempted to make adherence to their position a sine qua non for receiving campaign funding support from the national Republican party, essentially applying a litmus test that GOP candidates had to pass in order to receive support. The effort, put forth at a Republican National Committee (RNC) meeting by committee members from states with strong religious right delegations, was narrowly defeated after the intercession of RNC chair Jim Nicholson, who argued that he did not want to exclude candidates from the party who would be potentially strong in some regions. This example also demonstrates the sometimes conflicting needs of interest groups and of parties. Parties certainly want the support of members of important interest groups (and party leaders court the leaders of various groups who are thought to be influential in gaining that support), but at the same time, the parties do not want to be captured by the interest groups. Party leaders must look to a broader audience with a wider range of views than is true of group leaders.

While groups try to maintain ties in both parties, no one doubts that many groups are closer to one party than the other. The more feminist-oriented women's groups—NOW, NARAL, ERAmerica—certainly feel more at home in Democratic party circles than they do in Republican circles. The same can generally be said for black organizations. While these groups maintain contact with Republicans and attempt to influence the positions of Republican party candidates, they have been more successful with the Democrats. And, of course, the opposite can be said for groups such as the Christian Coalition or the National Federation of Independent Businessmen, whose allies are mostly Republicans.

The relationship between organized labor and the Democratic party brings this tie to the extreme. While labor has traditionally been close to the Democratic party, labor's loyalty was strained at the 1972 National Convention when the AFL-CIO—as well as many other groups traditionally part of the New Deal coalition—felt excluded. After its overwhelming electoral defeat in 1972, the Democratic party needed once more to appeal especially to labor. Party chairman Robert Strauss appointed a new Commission on Delegate Selection and Party Structure, to be chaired by United Auto Workers president Leonard Woodcock. Five other prominent labor leaders were appointed to the panel. When Woodcock resigned, claiming he did not have time to devote to the task, the leadership fell to the vice chair, Barbara Mikulski, then a little-known Baltimore city councilwoman. Mikulski, appointed as a representative of ethnics and women, proved to be a feisty and outspoken chair. Labor received less than it wanted from the Mikulski Commission, but a foot was back in the Democrats' door (Crotty 1983; see chapter 8).

Labor has continued its active involvement in the Democratic party. When the Democratic National Committee was elected in 1980, party leaders felt that too few of the members were labor leaders. Consequently, the chair of the DNC used fifteen of his twenty-five at-large appointments to name union officials to the party's ruling body. In addition, four of these union leaders were appointed to the Executive Committee of the DNC, the most important decision-making group.

To cement its ties with the Democratic party further, organized labor formed an advisory committee to help with party fund-raising and strategy setting immediately before the 1982 elections. Union-represented groups have contributed substantially to the DNC each year since. As a final step in reasserting its role in the Democratic party, and in order to guarantee an impact on the internal workings of the party, the AFL-CIO Executive Committee decided that labor leaders would gather in advance of the 1984 presidential primaries to endorse the candidate they felt should be supported as the opponent of President Reagan. They tapped Walter Mondale and then faced the test of delivering their members' votes in the subsequent primaries and caucuses. A divergence of opinion between union leaders and their membership is a fairly recent phenomenon that reduces the influence of labor leaders in today's politics. Regardless of the impact of this endorsement, its intent was clear.

Organized labor was saying that union members had a home in the Democratic party. And one way they intended to effect the public policy changes they desired was through a continuing influence over the internal operations of the party. In 1988 labor leaders backed away from a preprimary endorsement of a presidential candidate, but again many labor leaders were active in candidate organizations. As the 1992 nomination approached, with few Democrats out front looking to be tapped (see chapter 8), labor leaders played a more low-key role. However, even early in the process they made it known that they stood ready as a group to support New York governor Mario Cuomo should he decide to advance his candidacy. When Cuomo opted out, labor did not come down strongly in any one camp. However, it remained a force in the party by assuring that each potential nominee had labor leaders among their top supporters.

Labor leaders have also been important in the internal functioning of many state and local Democratic organizations. They have played key roles as Democrats plotted strategies for congressional and senatorial elections. And, as noted earlier, they took the lead in the effort to recapture the House of Representatives after the Republican takeover in 1994. They did this not only through financial contributions, but through working with Democratic strategists in planning attacks on the freshman Republicans seeking reelection throughout the nation.

The extent and openness of organized labor's commitment to the Democrats is unique. At the same time, women and minorities, despite the fact that both groups were also given positions of privilege within the Democratic party, still maintain ties with the Republicans. The National Women's Political Caucus has cochairs of different parties, for instance. Attempting to bring influence to bear on internal party matters is clearly one technique that interest groups use to reach their goals.

B. Group Ratings

Increasingly, organized groups are "rating" representatives and senators in terms of the degree to which they support or oppose legislation favored by those groups. These ratings, which usually range from zero (no support) to one hundred (total support), are computed by the groups after they select the issues most important to them (Fowler 1982).

Group ratings differ in terms of which issues are chosen (those deemed appropriate to the group's concern), how many votes are chosen (all or only the most important on the selected issues), and how scores are computed (how absentee or proxy votes are counted). For example, the Chamber of Commerce of the United States constructs an index of how members vote on a series of issues on which they take a position and communicates that position to members in advance of a vote (Gugliotta 1998). Other groups choose issues after the session is over and rate members without regard to whether the group's position was known in advance. Whatever means are chosen, the ratings are identical in intent: they identify friends and enemies of the groups for the group members to see and for others interested in the group's opinions to weigh in judging incumbents.

Some of the ratings are more prominent than others. *The Almanac of American Politics* and *Politics in America,* two widely circulated books that give basic information on every representative and senator, list how various groups rate the officeholders. *The Almanac of American Politics* uses ten different group ratings, whereas *Politics in America* restricts itself to four. Two of the more widely used scores are attempts to rate legislators ideologically across a range of issues. Americans for Democratic Action uses a series of votes—on both domestic and foreign policy issues—which it asserts are litmus tests for liberals. In 2006, twelve senators and thirty members of the House scored a perfect one hundred (all liberal votes). The number of members with perfect ADA ratings has been increasing in recent years.

At the other ideological extreme, the American Conservative Union (ACU) uses a sophisticated system to show how frequently members of Congress vote "for safeguarding the God-given rights of the individual" (Malbin 1981, 126), that is, to determine how conservative legislators are, according to the ACU's definition. Unsurprisingly, those who score high on the ADA scale frequently score low on the ACU scale, though the two scales are not exact opposites because of different issues chosen and different ways of handling absences. In 2006 the ACU gave perfect scores to five senators and eight members of the House. These totals are much lower than those in the recent past, and most likely represent a one-year aberration based on the inclusion of a few specific votes where the vast majority of members voted contrary to the ACU's position in the 2006 scores (e.g., a vote on embryonic stem cell research in the Senate and a vote on a very spartan budget alternative in the House). The general pattern indicates that both houses of Congress have more members willing to be categorized at ideologically extreme positions.

Similarly, those who do well on the AFL-CIO Committee on Political Education (COPE) rating often do not do well on ratings published by the Chamber of Commerce of the United States. Each of these groups, as well as the more than a dozen others that issue ratings, try to inform voters on how legislators stand on issues of particular relevance to group member sympathizers.

The exploding number of ratings can confuse even the most sophisticated political observer. Groups often change their method of computing an incumbent's scores, making comparisons over time difficult. Frequently two groups representing variant elements of the same "constituency" define important issues differently, leading to different ratings of incumbents. This dissimilarity has been the case in recent years with the National Tax-Limitation Committee and the National Taxpayers Union. The National Tax-Limitation Committee seeks to limit government spending and taxation by campaigning for federal and state constitutional amendments designed for those purposes. Taking a different approach, the National Taxpayers Union wants to limit taxes through specific cuts, not a constitutional restriction.

The ratings of incumbents often have direct electoral implications. Although few citizens, and not even most members of the involved groups, monitor these group ratings closely, many interest groups weigh them heavily in determining whom to help financially in upcoming campaigns. In addition, groups take particular care to identify those on the "extreme" as special friends or enemies, of whom members should be aware.

Since the 1970s one group, the League of Conservation Voters (LCV), each election year has identified the twelve "worst" members of Congress according to their rating on environmental concerns. The group dubs these representatives the "dirty dozen" and targets them for defeat. Of fifty-two incumbents given the label over the course of the five elections ending with the election of 1978, twenty-five were defeated in the same year they were targeted, giving increased credibility the power of this group (*Congressional Quarterly Weekly Report* 1981, 510). Since the 1980s, the LCV has combined its legislative rating with a compilation of how much political action committee money incumbent candidates had accepted in the previous election cycle from PACs representing corporations it dubbed the "filthy five"; the LCV list has included senators and nonincumbents in more recent rankings.

Besides wishing to avoid being dubbed one of the twelve "worst" legislators on environmental issues, incumbents want to avoid being targeted for defeat by this particular group. In 2006 the LCV actually expanded its list to a baker's dozen (fifteen if you count Tom DeLay and Bob Ney, who were replaced on the list after deciding not to seek reelection), directing their efforts at seven incumbent representatives and four senators seeking reelection, at one member of the House seeking a seat in the Senate, and, for the first time ever, at a member of the House seeking the governor's office in his state. Nine of these thirteen—Rep. Bob Beauprez (R-Colo., gubernatorial election), Rep. J. D. Hayworth (R-Ariz.), Rep. Richard Pombo (R-Calif.), Rep. Charles Taylor (R-N.C.), Sen. Jim Talent (R-Mo.), Sen. Conrad Burns (R-Mont.), Sen. Rick Santorum (R-Pa.), Sen. George Allen (R-Va.), and Rep. Katherine Harris (R-Fla., Senate election)—were defeated on election day. Clearly, the rating systems perform an important function for the politically involved interest groups and, by implication, for legislators as well.

C. Political Action Committees

Although some politicians complain about the impact of group activity on the political parties themselves, and many think that the various rating systems portray them unfairly, neither approach has had the influence or has caused the controversy of groups participating in the electoral process through political action committees.

The financing of campaigns is considered at length in chapter 5, but a short history of the rise of political action committees is appropriate at this point (see Alexander and Haggerty 1981, chaps. 1–4; Epstein 1980; Magleby and Nelson 1990; Sorauf 1988, chap. 2). The year 1974 was critical in terms of changes in campaign finance laws affecting groups. Before that year (or, more accurately, before 1971, when the Federal Election Campaign Act was passed, even though that year's provision did not affect groups), the difference between legality and reality was extreme.

The financing of federal elections was governed by a series of outmoded and largely ignored laws—the 1907 Tillman Act, which prohibited corporate contributions; the 1925 Corrupt Practices Campaign Act, which set limits on expenditures in House ($2,500 to $5,000) and Senate ($10,000 to $25,000) campaigns but not on presidential campaigns; the 1939 and 1940 Hatch Acts, which put limits on contributions and involvement of federal employees; and the 1944 Smith-Connally and 1947 Taft-Hartley Acts, which prohibited labor unions from contributing directly to campaigns. The most significant aspects of these laws were the ease and impunity with which they were ignored (Epstein 1980; Sorauf 1988, 28–33).

Candidates set up multiple committees to avoid the campaign spending limits. Corporations were notorious for giving election-year "bonuses," which were then passed on by obedient executives to deserving candidates. According to a *Congressional Quarterly* study of corporate executive giving in 1968, these contributions may have totaled millions of dollars (*Congressional Quarterly Weekly Report* 1971, 35). Labor unions set up committees on political education (COPE) that were used to solicit "voluntary" contributions from union members, funds that were then used to "educate" members about the issues of the day and the candidates most deserving of support. COPE sought to "interest" members in the political process through registration drives, get-out-the-vote drives, and poll watching. COPE activities were also worth millions of dollars, largely to Democrats.

The reality of campaign financing as America entered the decade of the 1970s revealed a picture of significantly increasing expenditures, corporate influence, and union activity, all sidestepping the intent, if not the letter, of the law, and all far removed from public view. The Federal Election Campaign Act (FECA) of 1971 marked the first step in reforming these practices. The major provisions of this act put a limit on media expenditures, deemed to be the major source of drastically escalating campaign costs. The FECA called for disclosing the source of campaign contributions, identifying them by occupation and business as well as by name and address. The theory was that disclosure was the best means of control (Corrado 1991a).

The 1974 amendments to the FECA of 1971 have led to a tremendous change in the role played by organized interest groups. The 1974 amendments limited individual contributions to $1,000 per campaign but permitted the establishment of political action committees, which could contribute up to $5,000 in each campaign. The amendments specifically allowed corporations or unions to use money for the "establishment, administration, and solicitation of contributions to a separate, segregated fund" (*Congressional Quarterly Report* 1982, 43). The weight carried by this action was made all the more clear when, in a 1975 case involving Sun Oil Company, the Federal Election Commission ruled that corporations could use general treasury funds to establish political action committees. This ruling was opposed by organized labor, since the AFL-CIO foresaw the rapid expansion of corporate PACs (Epstein 1980). Table 4.2 (p. 126) shows that union fears had a firm foundation.

Organized labor unions formed PACs shortly after they were legalized; the number peaked at 394 in 1984 and has declined somewhat since that time. Similarly, trade, membership, and health associations—the organized interest groups with which we are concerned—saw the opportunity quickly. While we can list many more PACs in this category than in the labor category, their growth also slowed after the early 1980s, though nearly seventy new PACs in this category were added between 1992 and 1996, the first substantial growth in more than a decade. Corporate PACs, to the contrary, are another phenomenon. From the time of the SUNPAC decision in 1975 until the election of 1988, the number of corporate PACs expanded more than twentyfold, though the peak seems to have been reached. In absolute numbers, there are approximately five times as many corporate PACs as labor PACs, and twice as many as PACs representing trade associations, membership groups, or health associations.

Why do we discuss corporate PACs in a chapter on organized group activity? The answer should be evident. To a large extent corporate PACs are an extension of trade association PACs. Each PAC is limited in the amount it can contribute to any one campaign. However, corporate members of trade associations can form their own PACs and then give as separate entities, thus becoming the functional equivalents of interest groups (Schlozman and Tierney 1986, 9–12).

Table 4.3 lists the ten largest PACs in the 2003–2004 election cycle in terms of dollar contributions made to candidates. Six of the ten are membership or trade associations, three are labor PACs, and one is a corporate PAC. However, while only one corporate PAC made the top ten, taken cumulatively, their power seems evident. In the 2003–2004 election cycle, corporate PACs contributed over $104.3 million to House and Senate candidates, according to Federal Election Commission records. Membership and trade association PACs contributed a total of $78.2 million. Labor PACs contributed $50.3 million.

Another type of political action committee is the so-called independent, or nonconnected, PAC. These PACs do not grow out of a parent organization but are formed for specifically political purposes. The prototype of this form of organization is the National Conservative Political Action Committee (NCPAC). These PACs can contribute to individual campaigns, and they also take advantage of a provision in the Federal Election Campaign Act that maintains that PACs can make independent political expenditures as long as they are not coordinated with a particular candidate. The Supreme Court in *Buckley v. Valeo,* 424 U.S. 1 (1976), the suit that challenged the constitutionality of the Federal Election Campaign Act, had ruled

Table 4.3   Top Ten PACs in Contributions to Federal Candidates, 2003–2004

	PAC	Contributions
1	National Association of Realtors	$3,771,083
2	National Automobile Dealers Association	$2,584,800
3	International Brotherhood of Electrical Workers	$2,304,600
4	National Beer Wholesalers Association	$2,289,000
5	Laborers' International Union	$2,249,000
6	National Association of Home Builders	$2,221,500
7	Association of Trial Lawyers	$2,170,499
8	United Parcel Service	$2,139,929
9	American Medical Association	$2,077,899
10	United Auto Workers	$2,065,200

Source: Federal Election Commission.

that limitations on such independent expenditures was an abridgment of the freedom of speech. In 1976 the FECA was amended to correct this constitutional fault; nonconnected PACs were first registered with the FEC in 1978; today more than sixteen hundred such PACs register and contribute to federal campaigns.

Using sophisticated direct mail techniques, independent PACs have raised a substantial amount of money. As early as the 1981–1982 election cycle, NCPAC raised over $7 million. By the 1995–1996 cycle, the amount spent by nonconnected PACs had reached $22 million; in the 2001–2002 election cycle, the amount rose to $165.7 million; and in 2003–2004, the total amount spent by nonconnected PACs was $255.2 million. This increase is dramatic (much more will be said on campaign finance in the next chapter). How was this money spent? On whose behalf? It was spent as the directors of the fund wished, on behalf of or against any candidates they chose. As John T. Dolan, head of NCPAC said, "I am responsible to absolutely no one." NCPAC and other nonconnected PACs have run extensive campaigns *against* particular candidates. At times they have advertised against certain incumbents well before the surfacing of an opponent. In 1980 NCPAC's use of this technique was deemed successful in contributing to the defeat of liberal senators Birch Bayh (D-Ind.), John Culver (D-Iowa), Frank Church (D-Idaho), and George McGovern (D-S.Dak.). NCPAC was a feared opponent and an actor others sought to emulate as well. Now independent PACs cover the entire political spectrum.

The success or failure of specific interest groups does not alter the two most important basic questions about independent PACs: (1) unlike labor unions, trade associations, or even corporations, these groups represent leaders who are not held accountable in any way to their constituency and (2) these groups influence elections in ways that are by their very nature not connected with the candidates who are running but are very influential. Let's deal with these two points separately.

First, these PACs have no members per se. Individuals are contributors; they can fail to contribute again. But talented fund-raisers will tell you that there is no dearth of small contributors, which raises the key defense for independent PACs and political action committees generally and relates to participation in politics, by individuals and individuals acting as groups. A salient goal of campaign reform has always been to increase the number of small contributors. The objective is to get "big money" out of politics. PACs do indeed increase the number of small contributions. These contributors know the causes they are supporting. But do PACs get the big money out of politics? That conclusion is more doubtful. For years Common Cause and other reform-minded interest groups have waged a vigorous (but so far unsuccessful) campaign against PACs.

Those who oppose the ability of PACs to contribute to campaigns, at least without further restrictions, argue that PACs hinder the political process by giving undue influence to powerful groups. PAC defenders argue that these organizations get individuals involved—just as has always been desired. To a large extent one's stand on this debate depends on where one sits. If you sit in Congress as a recipient of PAC money, you are unlikely to oppose PACs. But if you are a challenger on the outside—or one who is not likely to receive PAC money—PACs look much more evil.

Second, these groups use independent expenditures to influence elections. Figure 4.1 depicts the amount of money spent on congressional and senatorial campaigns through independent expenditures in the last twenty years. Readers should note that not all independent expenditures come from PACs. Even casual observers of American politics noticed the "spike" that is represented by expenditures in the 1995–1996 election cycle. First organized labor and then interest groups representing more conservative causes, such as the National Federation of Independent Business, spent millions of dollars in attempts to influence congressional campaigns. They did so by targeting individual representatives and attacking their records, often pointedly and sometimes (some would claim) unfairly. The result was the creation of a negative impression of the candidates under attack; their opponents, however, did not bear responsibility for the attacks. NCPAC's successful technique of twenty years ago has been used by other PACs—labor, association, and corporate, and nonconnected PACs, and more recently by 527 and 501(c) groups (more on these groups in chapter 5) and the parties themselves. Many observers believed that the extent of these expenditures in 1995 to 1996 fundamentally altered the political process in a deleterious way; the continued high levels of spending, particularly in the presidential campaign of 2000, did nothing to lessen that concern. The Bipartisan Campaign Reform Act of 2003

Figure 4.1 Independent Expenditures in Congressional Elections, 1978–2004

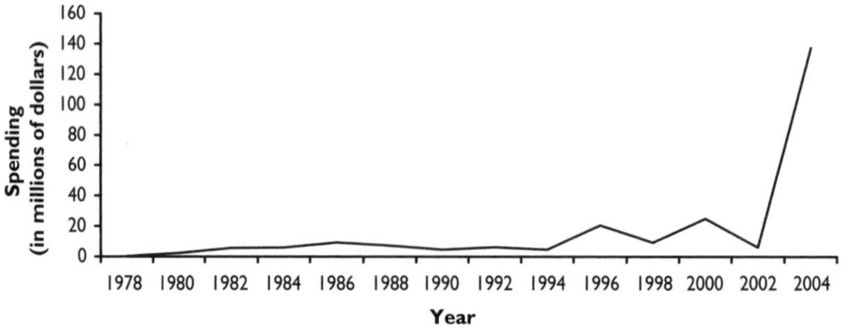

Source: Federal Election Commission. Data for 2004 reported in Patterson (2006).

(more on this in the next chapter) aimed to address this concern, but the large jump in independent expenditures in 2004 (the first election after reform) seems to indicate failure on this front.

The proliferation of PACs and the ever-increasing amounts of money that they contribute have caused many to question the consequences of campaign finance reforms. These issues are discussed at length in chapter 5.

III. INTEREST GROUPS' INFLUENCE ON THEIR MEMBERS

As stated above, interest groups try to affect the electoral process in two distinct ways. In addition to attempting to influence the ways in which candidates and parties present themselves, and the ways in which those campaigns are perceived by the electorate at large, interest groups try to influence the voting behavior of their own members.

Leaders of interest groups try to exert this influence for two distinct reasons. The simplest, most direct reason is that they believe their choice of candidates is the best for those sharing their interest; it is logical to try to convince others that Senator X is *their* candidate. A less direct reason is that the influence of interest group leaders with political figures varies with the extent to which politicians feel that the group leaders have influence with their members. That influence is demonstrated in two ways—getting members to give money to a campaign and convincing members to support a candidate with their votes.

In this context we should separate interest groups in a way distinct from those already mentioned. Some interest groups—referred to as trade associations earlier—are actually confederations of other *organizations,* most frequently corporations. The leaders of these parent groups can speak to the leaders of their member groups; they can convince lesser officials to support candidates with their dollars, but in fact few votes are involved. This type of association is, however, not unimportant. In fact, the unanimity of corporate PAC support for candidates who are also favored by their trade associations is a testimony to the effectiveness of this kind of network. However, the influence of this partnership is different from that of a union leader who claims to speak for tens of thousands of his members. In the latter case, politicians are increasingly distrustful of the effectiveness of these spokespeople. It is important, therefore, for interest group leaders to demonstrate that they can distinctly influence their members.

How is this influence achieved? Interest groups use a number of techniques to persuade their members to support the candidates their leaders have identified. One technique has already been identified: the group rating. Interest group leaders make certain that their members know the politician who supported them in the past and the one who did not. They clearly identify friends and enemies for their members. But few citizens follow politics closely enough to keep up on group ratings. These ratings can be used as evidence for identifying friends and enemies, but persuasion must come about through other means.

A second technique is producing a newsletter. Various groups use newsletters of varying levels of sophistication. The express purpose of communicating with group members through a newsletter is educational. The staff of an interest group wants the members to know what and how much they have been doing for the group, how various issues affect the group's interests, and which political officials have been helpful in their efforts to support favorable legislation or oppose that which is harmful. Using this technique, interest group leaders frequently try to counter the "generalizing" effects of the mass media. The popular media give a general audience a particular view of a political issue and/or a political leader. Through interest group mailings, interest group leaders try to teach their members that they are a specific segment of the public and that issues and leaders affect them in a *particular* way.

Specialized approaches to a particular audience distinguish other techniques used by group leaders as well. Many groups use direct mail and/or telephone campaigns to inform their members about specific pending issues in which they have a stake. Similarly, they make certain that their members know when the leaders feel that they have a pressing interest in a particular candidate, when one of their favorites is in trouble, or when they have an opportunity to beat one of their enemies.

Groups vary tremendously in terms of their effectiveness in reaching members. Some groups, like realtors, have a reputation of reaching members with persuasive messages in a very short time. Some labor union leaders, on the other hand, seem to be increasingly far removed from the opinions of the rank and file. Certainly during the Reagan years the leaders were more liberal and more clearly tied to the Democratic party than were their members; much of this disparity has been reduced because of confrontations between the Gingrich-led Republican-controlled Congress and labor leaders during the 104th and 105th Congresses.

In the last few years, more and more groups have concentrated their efforts on educating their members. Labor unions began to use cable television as a means of reaching their constituencies in the 1980s; other groups soon followed suit. Teleconferencing has become a common means of bringing group leaders in Washington into touch with their constituents across the nation. The Internet marks the latest phase of the communications revolution to attract widespread interest group attention (Berry 1997; Patterson 1990; Coval 1984).

The effectiveness of interest groups in influencing the political opinion of their members has frequently been explored by political scientists. Nearly five decades ago, David B. Truman published his seminal interpretation of American politics based largely on group influence. Truman's book *The Governmental Process* (1951) dealt with much more than the influence of organized groups. Truman's explanation of competing group influences is as persuasive today as it was when first presented.

Imagine the predicament of a certain hypothetical citizen: a Catholic woman who is a union member and an ardent hunter, along with her husband. Many years ago they joined the National Rifle Association (NRA) and have become active members. Their children have learned about gun safety at NRA workshops. She is faced with a choice in a congressional election between a Democrat who is very much a union supporter but a firm advocate of gun control, and his Republican opponent, a woman who is supported by the local business community for her economic stands and backed by the NRA because she opposes any further restrictions on handgun ownership. Our hypothetical voter is urged by her union leaders to support the Democrat; her economic interest seems to lie in that direction and, after all, good union members *should* vote for pro-labor Democrats. But she is torn. Her NRA friends are for the Republican because of the contrast between that candidate's stand on gun-related issues and the Democrat's hard-line approach, which they see as a step toward taking their guns away. She is puzzled and confused. Clearly, neither the union leader nor the NRA leader can speak authoritatively as her representative.

The issue gets even more complicated. Let us suppose that our hypothetical voter has become something of a feminist as a reaction to the way women are treated in the workplace; in fact, she has become active in certain women's organizations. Her deep religious beliefs lead her to oppose abortion. Her feminist friends urge her to look at the predicament in which many working women, facing unwanted pregnancies, find themselves. She is frankly not certain about her own feelings on the abortion issue. The Democratic candidate is also a Catholic and states quite frankly that he is morally opposed to abortion. She agrees. The Republican candidate says that women often find themselves in untenable situations, that abortion is a terrible alternative, but it is one that many women need. Our hypothetical voter agrees with that assessment as well.

Truman presents exemplary cases of competing group demands, and his book demonstrates that group membership does not always determine a voter's choice on election day. Our hypothetical voter's dilemma reflects these competing influences. The position in which she finds herself, although exaggerated, is typical of many real situations. Her quandary shows us how difficult it is for group leaders to claim that they can speak for all the members of their association.

One case stands out, however, in which group membership seems to be a determining factor. Let us assume that our female Catholic union member is not just interested in women's issues but is a member of the National Abortion Rights Action League. She has had an unwanted pregnancy and has gone through the painful process of examining her own beliefs. She has emerged from this examination with the firm view that a woman must be able to control her own body, that her religious doctrine must be put aside in this instance, and that it is wrong for others to let their moral convictions dictate her actions. She did not arrive at these decisions lightly. The process that led to her decision was the most difficult she ever had to undertake. Further, she had to back up her conviction with action, undergoing an abortion, a step she had always been taught was against the law of God. In reaching the decision that an abortion was right for her, she also reached the very strong conclusion that no one should dictate what another may do. After all, anyone who asserted the right to make those decisions for all in society was directly calling into question the very process and the very decision in which she had been so intimately involved.

For this voter, only the candidates' stand on the abortion issue mattered. If the Democrat was pro-choice and the Republican was for restricting a woman's right to have an abortion, our hypothetical voter would have cast her vote for the Democrat. If the candidates held the opposite opinions, her vote would have changed accordingly.

The interest group leaders who are most effective at claiming to represent their members' views and the leaders who are most effective at convincing their members how to vote are the leaders of single-issue groups whose members care more about that one issue than any other. These groups are few and far between. In recent years, in some geographic areas, the groups representing the two sides of the abortion question or the gun control issue have been in that situation. In close elections, those who vote on the basis of only one issue may in fact determine the result. Certainly it is in the interest of the group leaders to make it appear that they and their members can tip the balance. Single-interest groups seem to be most effective in multicandidate primary fields (Maisel 1986). However, in closely contested elections, no candidate can ignore the appeal of these groups with impunity.

IV. POLITICIANS VIEW INTEREST GROUPS

In a very real sense, interest group leaders are politicians. They try to influence who is elected to office, attempt to affect policy outcomes, and deal with other politicians in striving for these goals. But they themselves do not seek office and do not vote on policy outcomes; the effectiveness of their advocacy for the interests they represent depends on how they are perceived by elected and appointed government officials.

Let's look at some poignant examples from the not-too-distant past. In the 1996 congressional elections, labor, business, and environmental groups spent more than $100 million in excess of what candidates had spent on campaign expenses (including the money candidates received from political action committees). Most of this money was spent on so-called **issue advocacy advertisements**, advertisements that are permitted because the group expressing its view is exercising its First Amendment right of free speech and thus cannot be restricted.

Labor began this barrage in 1996, aiming its attack at Republican freshman congressmen, most of whom had backed the Contract with America and other legislation opposed by labor. How did politicians respond? In two ways. First, those under attack found allies to counter these attacks. Pro-Republican groups responded by defending some of their allies under attack. The level of rhetoric escalated throughout the land. But, second, many of those under attack responded by softening their records, by looking for some votes they could use to counter the attacks on their records. They did this because they did not want to be deemed as anti-labor or anti-environment. No politician wants to be painted with a broad brush as controlled by one group or another.

Undeniably, politicians respond to organized interests. The 108th Congress saw a continuation of a battle between two powerful organized groups, the National Association of Realtors and the American Bankers Association. The issue is one over which few Americans lose sleep: Should banks be allowed to sell and manage real estate? But it is the most important issue on the legislative agenda for real estate agents and one in which bankers have a keen interest.

In 1999, for the first time, Congress passed legislation allowing banks to sell insurance and securities; a year later, they asked to be able to expand their business to real estate. While the insurance and securities lobbies had not responded quickly to a threat to their share of their respective markets in 1999, the realtors, one of the most powerful groups in Washington, did in 2000. How powerful are the realtors? Look back at table 4.3; they are right at the top of the list. And real estate agents live in every congressional district in the country. Their business is to know people and to talk to them. In short, no incumbent wants local realtors united in favor of a challenger. But the bankers are big-time players as well. Banking interests, all together, gave over $20 million in the 2001–2002 election season, about three-fifths of it to Republicans.

ISSUE ADVOCACY ADVERTISEMENTS

Advertisements in which the sponsor's primary interest is in forwarding an issue position, not supporting a particular candidate; money spent in this way is unregulated as long as it is separate and distinct from candidate efforts.

So who won? In the most recent battle, the realtors got a rider attached to a huge appropriations bill, prohibiting banks from selling or managing real estate for the next year. But the battle is not over. Despite the fact that more than half of the House and a quarter of the Senate have cosponsored legislation that would make that ban permanent, the legislation is held up in the Financial Services Committee, by supporters of the banking industry. The battle will go on; politicians will keep listening; and the political action committee will keep supporting its friends and punishing its enemies (Rosenbaum 2003).

It is not always easy for politicians to know how to view interest groups. Consider the National Rifle Association as an example. The NRA has approximately three million members and chapters in every congressional district in every state. The organization's overall expenditure, including funds for lobbying Congress, is approximately $120 million annually. In the 2002 election cycle, the NRA spent more than $10 million in direct campaign contributions, independent expenditures, and voter mobilization—the largest election effort in the group's history. They are adamantly opposed to any form of gun control and state publicly that their members will punish those who favor gun control.

But will they? Do all NRA members really feel that every citizen has a right to own an automatic pistol? Will all NRA members vote against a Congress member who favors handgun registration laws? Especially after the devastation at Columbine High School? Or the fear imposed on the nation's capital by a sniper killing innocent people seemingly at random? The simple answer is that politicians do not know. Politicians must get a feel for their district and have a sense of their constituents' feelings. Interest group leaders try to "educate" politicians about the allegiance of their followers, but in the final analysis, it is the elected officials who must know their own districts or suffer the consequences.

One more example can demonstrate how interest group leaders at times misrepresent the views of their members. In 1988, Congress passed and President Reagan signed into law the Medicare Catastrophic Coverage Act. Congress had acted after the AARP, which claims to be the nation's largest interest group representing senior citizens, lobbied long and hard for the legislation. The new policy extended supplemental health insurance benefits for catastrophic illnesses, paying for that coverage with a surtax on middle- and upper-income senior citizens. When legislators returned to their districts after the law was implemented and those affected saw the increase in their taxes, those very same senior citizens who were supposed to be the beneficiaries of the policy—and on whose behalf the AARP claimed to speak—were in an uproar. Protests were so vociferous that Congress repealed the program in 1989. One lesson

clearly learned by members of Congress was that the AARP might be the largest senior citizens' lobby, but its leaders certainly did not speak for their members (Daley and Worthington 1989; McKibben 1989).

In the final analysis the question of how politicians view interest groups and their leaders becomes a question of how effective these leaders are at representing the views of their members. It is clear that the more specialized a group is, the more accurately its leadership can reflect members' views; but such groups are often quite small. As groups become larger and larger, their leaders claim to reflect the views of more and more voters. However, politicians have come to realize that these large groups often have diverse memberships and that people join for various reasons. Many of the AARP's millions become members to obtain the discounts the organization has negotiated from merchants to entice new members to join. The leadership does not necessarily reflect their political views. For politicians, the need is to weigh influence when deciding how to respond to interest group demands.

WEBSITES

www.aflcio.org: The AFL-CIO is the umbrella organization for many labor unions in the country. It has been active in political campaigns through its Committee on Political Education and its active PAC contributing.

www.nfib.com: The National Association of Independent Businesses is an advocacy group for small and independent businesses. It has actively campaigned in recent election cycles.

www.fec.gov: The Federal Election Commission website provides historical and contemporary information on political action committees and their contributions to federal candidates.

www.nra.org: The National Rifle Association is the largest progun interest group in the country.

www.handguncontrol.org: Handgun Control is an organization dedicated to limiting the availability of handguns, through legislative initiatives and educational campaigns.

CHAPTER 5

Campaign Finance

Representative Marty Meehan, D-Mass. (left), Senator John McCain, R-Ariz., and Senator Russ Feingold, D-Wis. (right), descend the steps of the Supreme Court, September 8, 2003, following arguments in a challenge to their cosponsored Bipartisan Campaign Reform Act (BCRA). Three months later, the Justices ruled in their favor: the key provisions of McCain-Feingold—the ban on soft money contributions and the limits on negative attack ads—were declared constitutional. Some of these limits have since been eliminated by the Court. Two rounds of national elections—2004 and 2006—have since been held under the new rules and restrictions established by BCRA, and the implications of this legislation are still unfolding.

BIPARTISAN CAMPAIGN REFORM ACT (BCRA), OR MCCAIN-FEINGOLD

Bipartisan campaign finance legislation proposed and debated in the last congresses of the 1990s and finally passed in 2002.

HARD MONEY

Political money that is raised and spent under federal guidelines monitored by the Federal Election Commission.

FEDERAL ELECTION COMMISSION (FEC)

The regulatory body charged with implementing the Federal Election Campaign Act.

SOFT MONEY

Money raised for political purposes that is outside of the constraints specified under the Federal Election Campaign Act, unregulated money not to be used directly for federal campaigns.

What one issue could possibly unite leaders of the National Rifle Association and the California Democratic Party; the Sierra Club and the National Republican Committee; Americans for Civil Liberties Union and the National Right to Life Association; organized labor and the Chamber of Commerce? What bill could be so powerful that it brings together all of these ideologically opposed interest groups to fight shoulder to shoulder against its passage? The answer: the **Bipartisan Campaign Reform Act (BCRA)**, known simply as **McCain-Feingold**.

No wonder the McCain-Feingold bill took seven years to reach its final passage in 2002—seven long, arduous, and often disappointing years for its supporters. Even with the money spent on federal campaigns rising exponentially (reaching a record-breaking $1 billion spent by congressional candidates alone in the 2000 election) and even with the polls consistently showing the American public in support of reforming the system, the victory of McCain-Feingold was more of a surprise than an inevitability—and it wasn't just because of the powerful coalition of interest groups that rallied to protect the status quo. The new law aimed to completely overhaul a campaign finance system that supported incumbents and party organizations as well.

Under the "old" system—in place since the post-Watergate reform era—two types of money funded campaigns in the United States. The first, **"hard" money,** is money raised by candidates and parties and spent on their own campaigns. Regulated by the **Federal Election Commission (FEC)**, hard money contributions are capped and all candidates and parties must disclose their donor lists. The second type of money, **"soft" money**, is money not regulated by the FEC. It is collected by the parties (pre-BCRA) from corporations, labor unions, and wealthy individuals who write checks of $100,000 or more for "party-building activities"—that is, activities that run the gamut, from public education to vote mobilization.

The leaders of the campaign finance reform movement in the Senate, Senators John McCain (R-Ariz.) and Russell Feingold (D-Wisc.), focused their attack on the latter type of campaign funds. In merely six years—from 1994 to 2000—the total amount of soft money raised by the Democratic and Republican parties had risen nearly fivefold, from $102 million to $495 million. Both political parties took in nearly twice as much in soft money in the 2000 election cycle as they had four years earlier. Unrestricted by caps on contributions, both parties were raising exorbitant amounts of soft money with little evidence of (and little incentive for) a leveling off of the skyrocketing totals.

But the issue was not merely the amount of soft money raised—albeit staggering by any measure—but how parties were spending it. Reformers pointed to the fact that soft money was not being used for its intended purpose, that is, for getting out the vote and for voter registration drives. Rather, soft money was being used to fund **issue advocacy** commercials, thinly disguised attack ads (and some not so thinly disguised) for or against federal candidates (Polsby 2002). The following is one such "issue ad":

> Senate candidate Winston Bryant's budget as attorney general increased 71 percent. Bryant has taken taxpayer-funded junkets to the Virgin Islands, Alaska and Arizona. And spent about $100,000 on new furniture. . . . Winston Bryant: government waste, political junkets, soft on crime. (quoted in Waxman 2002)

According to a Supreme Court ruling, as long as the magic words "elect," "defeat," "vote for," or "vote against" did not appear in the commercial, the ad was not within the reach of the FEC. In fact such a commercial (more specifically, the money spent on it) was a form of free speech, steadfastly protected by the U.S. Constitution.

Corporations and labor unions have long been banned from directly influencing the outcomes of federal elections. Supreme Court Justice David Souter explains the reasoning for the century-old ban: "In barring corporate earnings from conversion into political 'war chests' the ban was and is intended to prevent corruption or the appearance of corruption" (quoted in Greenhouse 2003). Reformers argued that under the guise of soft money contributions, these very interests—corporations and unions, as well as wealthy individuals—were financing final-hour negative attack ads on specific candidates; their money, in effect, directly influenced who won and who lost federal elections. Thus, supporters of McCain-Feingold aimed to ban both parties from raising soft money altogether, forcing them to rely instead on the tightly regulated hard money donations, while curbing the use and content of issue advocacy commercials.

Regardless of the type of money raised by candidates and parties, it is clear that the amount of money spent on campaigns in the United States has grown exponentially. In 1952, political scientist Herbert Alexander calculated that approximately $140 million was spent on political campaigns nationwide (Alexander and Bauer 1991). In 2004, $4.27 billion was spent on campaigns for federal office alone, with an additional unknown amount spent on state and local races across the nation. And this total spending is growing rapidly; the 2004 figure cited above represents an almost $500 million increase from the previous presidential election cycle in 2000 (Patterson 2006). The amounts spent on some individual races are enough to move even the most laissez-faire observer to raise an eyebrow—for example, the $69.1 million spent on the Corzine-

ISSUE ADVOCACY

Constitutionally protected advertisements that advocate a particular position on an issue of the day; thought to abuse the spirit of law by implying support for or against a particular candidate.

Franks Senate race in New Jersey or the $11.1 million spent on the Schiff–Rogan congressional race in California (both in 2000, both records). It is easy to see why McCain, Feingold, and millions of other Americans were concerned about campaign finance.

But what exactly do the dramatic general rise and specific examples of seemingly out-of-control spending imply? Does the rising cost of campaigns necessarily distort election outcomes in the direction of moneyed interests? Does undue influence accrue to those who give large sums of money to successful politicians' campaigns? In other words, how do the escalation in campaign costs and the politicians' search for sources of money affect the government? Do spending limits help or hinder American democracy, and more specifically, what impact do they have on free speech? These are the basic questions in the ongoing debate over the role of money in federal elections and the ones to which we turn in this chapter.[1]

The Bipartisan Campaign Reform Act is not an endpoint in the struggle over campaign finance reform in the United States but rather one step in a continuing, uncertain, and relatively fluid process. In fact, by the time this book hits shelves it is almost guaranteed that something we have written in this chapter will be outdated. Every new reform comes with its own promise and problems. As Democratic presidential candidates vied for their party's nomination in the fall of 2003 and into the 2004 primary season, they did so under uncertain conditions. BCRA rewrote the rules governing their campaigns—so much so that many candidates, as well their staff and campaign managers, attended their respective party's so-called McCain-Feingold School to get up to speed on the new regulations. More important, candidates were unclear as to whether the ban on soft money would sustain court challenges to its constitutionality. Even supporters of McCain-Feingold were unsure as to how the Supreme Court would rule on specific provisions in the new law, in place the day after the congressional midterm elections in November 2002. Candidates and their parties would have to abide by the new regulations forbidding them to solicit and accept soft money contributions, all the while wondering whether the Supreme Court would pull the rug out from under McCain-Feingold during the height of the 2004 campaign season.

Having heard arguments for and against specific provisions of McCain-Feingold in September 2003, the Supreme Court issued its landmark ruling on December 10, 2003, to the surprise of opponents and supporters alike. The soft money ban would be upheld; the 2004 campaign season would chart new grounds. The 2002 midterm elections were the last ones conducted under the old rules, essentially the "last call at the bar" for the parties in their drive to collect soft money before McCain-Feingold kicked in (in the twenty days before the election, the RNC collected $8.4 million, the

DNC $15.2 million) (Seelye and Mitchell 2002; Keller 2003). The 2004 and 2006 elections—both conducted under BCRA—have demonstrated both how significant the reforms of McCain-Feingold are, and how adept political actors of all stripes are in quickly and effectively adapting to change.

I. THE LONG HISTORY OF CAMPAIGN FINANCE REFORM

The McCain-Feingold battle cry to reduce the power of money in American politics is not a new one. In fact, it resonates back over the past century. Since the days of Teddy Roosevelt, there has been a national consensus that corporate contributions have no place in our federal election system. In 1907, Roosevelt signed into law the **Tillman Act**, banning campaign contributions from corporations and banks to those running in federal elections. The law was intended to cut the ties between special interests and politics by curbing the influence of corporate money on the outcome of federal elections. Roosevelt's efforts were a response to the success that Republican boss Mark Hanna had in soliciting campaign money in the 1896 election—hundreds of thousands of dollars—directly from such corporations as Standard Oil (Keller 2003). However, corporations remained active in financing political activity through indirect means—most notably, election year "bonuses" to executives, which often found their way quickly to the appropriate campaign coffers— and through visible and generous contributions by well-known corporate presidents and chief executive officers.

TILLMAN ACT

Early twentieth-century legislation designed to curb political abuse by corporations.

The first actual restrictions on spending were imposed under the aptly named **Federal Corrupt Practices Act of 1925**, the principal means for regulating campaign financing for almost fifty years. The 1925 act called for disclosure of receipts and expenditures by candidates for the House and the Senate and by political committees that sought to influence federal elections in more than one state. (The law was silent, however, on the campaign activities of presidential and vice presidential candidates.) But the act could be circumvented by simply establishing a large number of committees in support of a particular candidate; multiple committees made it nearly impossible to find out who was giving how much to a candidate and how much was being spent on behalf of a candidacy.

FEDERAL CORRUPT PRACTICES ACT OF 1925

The campaign finance act in place prior to the reforms of the 1970s; honored more in breach than practice.

The first limit on the amount an individual could donate to a candidate was established in the **Hatch Act of 1940**, which also prohibited political activities by certain federal employees. The cap was meaningless, however, because the law was interpreted to allow contributions to a number of different committees all supporting the same candidate. With nobody to enforce the early regulations—no one was ever even prosecuted under the Federal

HATCH ACT

Legislation aimed at preventing political abuse of and by federal employees.

Corrupt Practices Act—campaign finance regulations held little weight for politicians and parties and held little public attention.

This would all change in the 1960s, with the rise of costly media-dependent campaigns and candidates taking more responsibility in conducting and financing their own campaigns. Once campaigning entered the television age, the first impetus for reform came from President Kennedy. Sensitized to the issue by claims that his father had "bought" the Democratic nomination for him, Kennedy appointed a bipartisan Commission on Campaign Costs, which was charged with examining ways to both reduce the costs of presidential campaigns and finance necessary costs. The commission's recommendations, which were endorsed by Kennedy and his two immediate predecessors, Presidents Truman and Eisenhower, set the agenda for future reformers, though few of the recommendations were immediately enacted (President's Commission on Campaign Costs 1962). (For histories of campaign finance and reform efforts before 1970, see Corrado et al. 2005, chap. 2; Heard 1960; Mutch 1988, chaps. 1–2; Overacker 1932; Sorauf 1988, 16–34; for a more journalistic account, see Thayer 1973.)

A. The Climate for Reform

Concern over the cost of campaigns and the impact of media advertising reached a crescendo after the gubernatorial elections of 1966. Two of those elections stand out. First, in Pennsylvania, millionaire Milton Shapp, an ambitious man with no previous political experience, decided that he wanted to be governor. He hired media consultant Joseph Napolitan to design an advertising campaign to sell "Shapp for governor" to the Pennsylvania voters. Napolitan spent millions of dollars to help Shapp win the Democratic nomination, though he lost the general election (Agranoff 1976, 9). In the next election, however, Shapp, again spending his own money quite heavily, became Pennsylvania's chief executive.

In neighboring New York State, incumbent governor Nelson Rockefeller was thought to be out of favor with his constituents as the 1966 election approached. He mounted a successful multimillion-dollar campaign to win reelection, relying heavily on paid media to transform the Rockefeller image and the public perception of his tenure as governor. Other examples abound. Politics seemed to be leaving the realm of political parties and entering the suites of advertising executives. The impression was that those who could afford extravagant media campaigns won the privilege of governing.

After Richard Nixon outspent Hubert Humphrey by two to one in the 1968 presidential election, the problems of campaign financing were given renewed attention. The election presented the nation with a "new" Nixon, carefully packaged to rectify an unfavorable image that had emerged from the former vice president's first two decades in public life—a phenomenon not lost on Joe McGinniss, in his chronicle of Nixon's transformation and electoral success entitled *The Selling of the President 1968* (1969)—borrowing from the well-known series of books by Theodore White (*The Making of the President* 1961, 1965).

Despite a general dissatisfaction among the populace with the system in existence, reform would not come easily. As has been oft stated, the rules of the game are not neutral—a truism particularly applicable to campaign finance laws where members of Congress must legislate the rules that govern their own reelection campaigns. In this case, reform gains momentum when change is in members' best electoral interests. Thus, it was the congressional Democrats that pushed for reform in the early 1970s. The Democratic party was heavily in debt after its defeat in 1968, and Democrats had much to gain in closing the gap with such reforms as **public financing** of presidential elections.

B. The Federal Election Campaign Act of 1971 and Efforts at Amendment

In 1971 Congress passed two significant pieces of legislation.[2] The more comprehensive piece of legislation, the **Federal Election Campaign Act (FECA)**, attacked three perceived problems. First, it dealt with the problem of extremely wealthy candidates "buying" their own elections by limiting the amount of money a candidate and the candidate's family could spend to win federal office. Second, it dealt with the "Madison Avenue approach" to politics by placing a limit on media expenditures. And, third, it dealt with the sources and uses of campaign funds by tightening the requirements for disclosure of receipts and of expenditures by candidates for federal office (Corrado 1991a; Corrado et al. 2005; Sorauf 1988).[3] For the next thirty years, meaningful disclosure of campaign expenditures and receipts, as well as the impact of media advertising and the influence of personal wealth, would remain front and center for reformers.

The second piece of reform legislation to pass in 1971 was the **Revenue Act**. This law encouraged small contributions to political campaigns by allowing a tax credit or (alternatively) a tax deduction for limited contributions to campaigns. In addition, the Revenue Act provided for a **tax checkoff** to subsidize future presidential campaigns. The tax checkoff has been used for the Presidential Campaign Fund, which has been used to fund presidential campaigns since 1976.[4]

The 1972 election was the first to be regulated under the new FECA provisions, and with considerable understatement one can

PUBLIC FINANCING

Any of the various schemes used to fund state or federal campaigns with taxpayer dollars.

FEDERAL ELECTION CAMPAIGN ACT (FECA)

Reform act passed in 1971, amended significantly in 1974 and in less important ways thereafter, that sets the rules for funding federal elections.

REVENUE ACT

The 1971 law that encouraged small contributions to political campaigns through tax incentives.

TAX CHECKOFF

The means through which citizens can contribute money to support the public funding of campaigns.

conclude that the 1972 experience was not one that would convince reformers that all was in order. When Richard Nixon's reelection campaign spent over $60 million, more than twice the amount spent on his 1968 campaign, analysts began to focus serious attention on the fact that the costs of campaigns were escalating out of sight. The unethical and illegal practices of the Committee to Reelect the President (and, to a lesser degree, some of the Democratic campaigns in 1972) have been well documented, not only by the General Accounting Office (GAO) but also by two special prosecutors (Archibald Cox and Leon Jaworski); by the Senate Select Committee on Presidential Campaign Activities (the Ervin Committee); by the House Committee on the Judiciary, as it considered impeachment proceedings in the summer of 1974; and by journalists and scholars too numerous to list.

1974 AMENDMENTS TO THE FECA

The significant changes to the 1971 FECA that structure most of campaign finance law today.

Suffice it to say that Congress passed the **1974 amendments to the FECA** (over President Nixon's veto) in response to the first election under the FECA and to the increased urgency that many felt after Watergate.

The 1974 act totally revised the 1971 FECA, fundamentally changing the ways in which all federal campaigns were funded for the next thirty years (Corrado 1991b; Corrado et al. 2005; Sorauf 1988). Presidential elections (including the prenomination phase) were to be publicly financed, at least in part. Candidates who accepted public financing also had to accept a cap on their total spending, so as to halt the runaway inflation on the cost of running for president. While the cap on media spending for congressional elections that was imposed in 1971 was lifted, much stricter limits were placed on

1. *individual contributions:* $1,000 to any campaign—primary, runoff, or general—in a single election, with a total cap of $25,000 to all campaigns in any one year; and

2. *PAC contributions:* $5,000 to any campaign in a single election but with no cumulative limitation.

Additionally, reporting and disclosure requirements were improved. Even the amount that an individual could spend on electoral activities independent of an organized campaign was limited. Finally, an independent, bipartisan Federal Election Commission (FEC) was established to oversee the reporting and enforcement requirements.

C. *Buckley v. Valeo*, 424 U.S. 1 (1976) and Its Impact

Shortly after the 1974 amendments became effective, a curious coalition of liberals and conservatives (not so dissimilar to the "strange bedfellows" that challenged McCain-Feingold in 2003) joined in a lawsuit challenging the constitutionality of the FECA. The law was attacked because it allegedly limited free speech and discriminated against presidential candidates of minor parties. The judicial branch of the government was asked to define the line between the guaranteed rights to free speech and free association and the obligation of the polity to protect the integrity of elections.

In the landmark case **Buckley v. Valeo** (424 U.S. 1, 1976), the Supreme Court ruled that some aspects of the 1974 act were unconstitutional while other provisions, deemed separable, were permitted to stand. The Court permitted the disclosure requirements and campaign contribution limits to remain in place; recall Justice Souter's argument on the necessity of preventing "corruption or the appearance of corruption." But with regard to the question of free speech, the Court held that limits on campaign spending, on **independent expenditures**, and on the amounts individuals could contribute to their own campaigns restrained the interchange of ideas necessary to bring about social change and were therefore unconstitutional. The spending limits were constitutional, however, if presidential candidates accepted **public funding** (Gottlieb 1985, 1991; Lowenstein 1991a). The Court also struck down the way in which the FEC was appointed, requiring that all appointments be made by the president with the advice and consent of the Senate, essentially ruling the existing FEC unconstitutional.

Buckley v. Valeo was handed down in January 1976, right in the middle of the 1976 presidential campaign. The decision effectively closed down the FEC for four months; it wasn't until May 11 that President Ford and Congress "fixed" the problems with the FEC to comply with the Supreme Court ruling. In the meantime, there was no commission to provide the much-needed matching funds to the major parties' presidential candidates, funds they had been counting on to finance their campaigns. Jimmy Carter was the only Democratic contender able to secure loans from a sympathetic bank until the matching funds were available. Meanwhile, his rivals for the Democratic nomination were broke by the time the primaries were held in Michigan and Pennsylvania, two states critical to Carter's success (Clymer 2003b). While the election of 2000 may have been the first time the Supreme Court was accused of "electing a president," the Supreme Court's ruling in *Buckley v. Valeo* in 1976 played an unexpected role in the nomination of soon-to-be president Jimmy Carter.

When the FECA was eventually revised and passed by May 1976, the new amendments reflected the recent Supreme Court decision, including reconstitution of the Federal Election Commission, caps on contributions, public disclosure of all donations above $200, partial public financing for presidential primaries, and complete

BUCKLEY v. VALEO

Supreme Court decision overturning certain aspects of the 1974 Amendments to the FECA that remains the ruling precedent for challenges to reform in campaign finance laws today.

INDEPENDENT EXPENDITURES

Money spent during an election year that is not coordinated with or controlled by a candidate's campaign.

PUBLIC FUNDING

Paying for an election campaign with money raised from taxpayers and distributed by the government.

public financing for presidential elections for candidates who voluntarily accepted campaign spending limits. (Notably missing from the final version was any provision for public funding of congressional elections.) But the amendments didn't stop there. In 1979, concerned that FECA was stifling grassroots politics at the state and local level, Congress amended the act to permit state and local parties to solicit unlimited contributions for "party-building" activities. In addition, state and local party committees were allowed to contribute volunteer time to individual campaigns so that the traditional role of local party organizations in federal elections was not lost in the rush to reform (on the role of campaign finance legislation in the revival of political parties, see Adamany 1984; Aoki and Rom 1985; and Jacobson 1985b, 1985–1986).

But when one venue is closed, another will open: "money in politics is like water"—it finds its way through the cracks. The major unintended consequence of the new FECA limits on contributions was the proliferation of political action committees (PACs), which were free to raise and spend as much money as possible in the name of "party building." As a result, soft money grew exponentially. From the 1980s on, there was much talk of an overhaul to the system by both parties and by both chambers of Congress, but little action ever came of it—proposals fell victim to Senate filibusters, presidential vetoes, and conference committees that either failed to deliver or, in some cases, never met.

Clearly, incumbency presented a formidable obstacle to reform. For example, President Clinton included campaign finance reform as an important part of his platform when he sought the presidency in 1992. During the first Congress of his administration, both the House and Senate passed separate versions of campaign finance legislation that dealt with voluntary spending limits and restrictions on PAC contributions and soft money. But the "Democratic majority allowed the legislation to languish until the final days of the 103rd Congress, when Senate Republicans used a filibuster to block a conference with the House" (*Congressional Quarterly Almanac* 2001, 64; *Congressional Quarterly Almanac* 1994, 32). It would take more than a presidential priority to motivate a majority of members to overhaul a campaign finance system that contributed to their electoral advantage over their challengers.

II. The Seven-Year Battle for McCain-Feingold

The "seven-year odyssey" of McCain-Feingold—beginning in 1995 and culminating in the Bipartisan Campaign Reform Act of 2002—highlights the formidable obstacles not only to campaign finance reform but to any sweeping reform before Congress that aims to significantly shift policy away from the status quo. In considering the long road to its passage, the question may not be why McCain-Feingold took so long but, rather, how did it overcome such formidable obstacles—what finally motivated members of Congress to pass the first sweeping reform to campaign finance laws in thirty years? (This section draws from *Congressional Quarterly Weekly Report*, March 23, 2002.)

Senators John McCain and Russ Feingold first introduced their campaign finance bill in 1995, with the major goals of banning soft money, restricting "issue advocacy ad" contributions to PACs, and granting free television time to candidates willing to limit spending. Supporters argued the bill would put an end to the corrupting influence of big money contributions in American politics. Opponents, led by Senator Mitch McConnell (R-Ky.), chair of the National Republican Senatorial Committee and so-called Darth Vader of campaign finance reform, argued McCain-Feingold would infringe on free speech, weaken political parties, and give more power to outside special interests operating independent of candidates and parties. McConnell and his fellow Senate Republicans successfully filibustered the first version of McCain-Feingold; it never came up for a vote in the 104th Senate.

In the 104th House, however, Representatives Christopher Shays (R-Conn.) and Martin Meehan (D-Mass.) introduced the companion legislation to McCain-Feingold, aptly named Shays-Meehan. The Republican leadership, having just taken control over the House in the 1994 election, proposed its own campaign finance reform package, a bill that would have made it more difficult for unions to raise money for their political action committees and would have restricted the amount of money a candidate could raise from outside his or her district or state. These provisions were seen as detrimental to Democratic candidates and were opposed by enough Republicans that the bill was not passed. Neither the GOP plan nor Shays-Meehan could garner a majority in the 104th House.

The election of 1996, however, provided greater momentum for change. Five months before the 1996 presidential and congressional elections, the Supreme Court ruled that parties could spend unlimited amounts to promote positions on issues so long as they did not coordinate directly with candidates—that is, so long as they were "independent" of candidates (*Colorado Republican Federal Campaign Committee v. FEC*, 518 U.S. 604, 1996). Taking advantage of the Court's decision, parties raised record-breaking amounts of soft money in 1996: $260 million, three times the amount raised in 1992—money widely used for individual campaigns.

After the much-publicized excesses in fund-raising techniques during the 1996 elections—including reports of major donors sleeping in the Lincoln bedroom, allegations of foreign money being donated to the DNC, and photographs of Vice President Al Gore accepting "gifts" at a Buddhist temple—campaign finance reform was given new impetus during the 105th Congress (1997–1998). Public pressure was clearly mounting for some congressional attention to be devoted to the problem. The Clinton White House, reeling under charges that the president's 1996 campaign had violated the spirit if not the letter of the existing law, supported the Bipartisan Campaign Reform Bill.

In the spring of 1998, GOP leaders in the House tried to block Shays-Meehan from getting to the floor, but the cosponsors gathered enough votes for a **discharge petition**, and Speaker Gingrich was forced to put the bill on the floor, conceding to an up-or-down vote on campaign finance reform. In August, a significantly watered-down version of Shays-Meehan passed the House, 252–179, its major accomplishment to ban soft money and redefine **express advocacy**.

But the "victory" in the House for the forces of reform was empty because the Senate took no action. Majority Leader Lott allowed Senate consideration, knowing a GOP **filibuster** would prevail. Proponents could not garner the sixty votes needed to invoke **cloture**, despite numerous efforts to rewrite the bill to make it palatable to more senators—such as lowering (not eliminating) PAC contributions, offering incentives for candidates who voluntarily limit spending, and drawing the line between spending to promote candidates and spending to promote issues.

Reformers started the process over in the 106th Congress. Shays and Meehan forced another vote on their reform bill in 1999, on the same bill as the one that passed the year before, and once again the bill passed. But for the third consecutive Congress, McCain-Feingold was blocked by a GOP-led filibuster in the Senate. In October 1999, a cloture motion to break the filibuster failed, essentially killing the legislation yet again.

By 2000, however, the climate for reform had changed. Senator John McCain's presidential bid in 2000 brought greater attention and urgency to the campaign finance reform movement by making his bill the centerpiece of his national campaign. Turnover in the Senate after the 2000 election favored an overhaul. Six Republican senators who had voted against bringing McCain-Feingold up for a vote on the floor in 1999 were replaced by Democrats, all of whom favored the bill. One other proreform Republican, Senator Lincoln Chaffee (R.I.), replaced his father, who had voted against cloture. In addition, five GOP senators, led by Thad Cochran (Miss.) changed their position. When the reformers agreed to raise the limits on hard money (the type of funds Republicans had proven more adept at raising than Democrats), Republicans found greater incentives to support McCain-Feingold. Under the final plan, individual

DISCHARGE PETITION

A legislative devise by which a majority of a legislature can remove a bill from consideration by a committee that is delaying that bill and bring it directly to the floor for a vote.

EXPRESS ADVOCACY

Advertisements taking a position on issues or controversies, a constitutionally protected right.

FILIBUSTER

The procedure in the U.S. Senate through which a senator or group of senators can maintain the floor and thus prevent passage of a piece of legislation, thereby talking a bill to death; often used as a delaying tactic in the modern Senate.

CLOTURE

The procedure through which a filibuster can be broken, requiring sixty votes in the modern Senate.

donors could contribute twice as much to senators, lifting the $1,000 cap in 1974 to $2,000 under McCain-Feingold. Democrats began to express doubts about banning soft money because they had become heavily dependent on this kind of fund-raising in order to be competitive with Republicans. A ban on soft money, coupled with an increase in hard money limits, could clearly play into the hands of Republicans. But after rallying around the bill in their own reelection campaigns as well as on the floor of Congress, Democrats could not turn around and vote against McCain-Feingold when it finally had a chance at passage.

With new votes on his side, McCain was able to force Republican Senate majority leader Trent Lott to bring his bill up for debate. Lott, who had long maneuvered to keep the bill off the floor, agreed to clear the calendar for two weeks of debate. But the Senate leader was not going to give in on procedure, assigning the bill an open amendment process, in which a new amendment was debated and voted on every three hours. However, supporter solidarity paid off, as each of the amendments designed to poison the bill was defeated and the leading alternative bill failed to garner enough votes. McCain-Feingold finally passed the Senate, 59–41, on April 2, 2001.

All eyes turned to the House. Although the companion bill to McCain-Feingold had passed in the House in the two previous Congresses, passage in the 107th was far from a sure thing. The biggest deterrent against success in the House was the fact that it had passed in the Senate. In 1998 and 1999, representatives, namely House Democrats, could go on record as being proreform—signing discharge petitions and voting for Shays-Meehan—knowing full well the bill would be filibustered in the Senate. But when a soft money ban became a potential reality, many House black and Hispanic caucus members indicated that they might split with the party and vote against Shays-Meehan. They argued that soft money was critical to get-out-the-vote drives and voter registration in their districts, pointing to the fact that it was more difficult to raise hard money in poorer and more rural communities. The House Republican alternative, they pointed out, just restricted but did not ban soft money. In response to their concerns and to those of the many Democrats who worried about a soft money ban as the 2002 midterms approached, Shays and Meehan changed their bill to include one of the provisions that had already passed the Senate—state and local parties would be allowed to spend some soft money on vote mobilization and registration.

In July 2001, aiming to keep the House legislation as close to the Senate version as possible, to prevent the final bill from being killed or rewritten in conference, Shays and Meehan requested that changes to their bill be voted on in one bloc, a so-called **manager's amendment**. Such an amendment would allow the fourteen

MANAGER'S AMENDMENT

An amendment to a pending piece of legislation presented by the legislators who are orchestrating the passage of the bill through the House or Senate.

changes to Shays-Meehan to be bundled into one vote, bringing their bill in line with the reform legislation passed in the Senate. But the Rules Committee, controlled by GOP leadership, rejected Shays and Meehan's request, assigning instead a rule that would put each of the fourteen changes to a floor vote. The decision infuriated proponents, who accused the Speaker and the Rules Committee of rigging the procedure to ensure defeat of the bill. Speaker Hastert offered to compromise on the rule, but conservatives in his caucus would not hear of it: if Shays-Meehan was to reach the floor under a GOP-controlled Congress, the caucus demanded it would do so in pieces.

When Hastert ordered a routine procedural vote on the rule—without a rule, there can be no vote—supporters of Shays-Meehan were put in a precarious position. Knowing the fourteen changes to Shays-Meehan would not survive separate votes, supporters of campaign finance reform voted against bringing their bill to the floor. The resulting defeat of the rule was an embarrassment for the Republican leadership. For the first time in his tenure as Speaker, Hastert lost on a rules vote—usually a party line vote from which members rarely deviate. Burned once, Hastert refused to bring the bill back to the floor. Supporters were left with one final option: a discharge petition—218 signatures from members could force the bill to the floor for a vote. Although the tragic events of September 11, 2001, put campaign finance reform low on the congressional priority list, by December 2001, when the session of the 107th Congress adjourned, four more House members had stepped up to sign the petition, almost enough votes to circumvent the Speaker and get Shays-Meehan to the House floor.

In February 2002, in an attempt to fracture the growing coalition of Democrats and Republicans who supported Shays-Meehan, House leaders put forth their own rival bill. The GOP leaders, long opposed to a ban on soft money—they argue it infringes on free speech, intrudes on states' rights to regulate elections, and disadvantages Republicans in need of soft money to counter organized labor's get-out-the-vote drives for Democratic candidates—proposed even *more* stringent reforms than those advocated in Shays-Meehan. Their strategy was simple: the GOP alternative would provide political cover for Republicans who wanted to be on record as voting for reform while at the same time effectively killing Shays-Meehan; a stricter bill would never make it through the Senate. Supporters of Shays-Meehan would be on record as voting against tougher reforms while GOP moderates would be on record as voting against big money.

But the supporters of the Bipartisan Campaign Reform Bill had an unpredictable ally in the winter of 2002—the Enron Corporation. The Enron bankruptcy scandal essentially provided the final push to passage (Foerstel 2002a). When the company's collapse exposed $3.6 million dollars in soft money contributions to both parties since 1990, the media frenzy only added to the pressure for real reform. Supporters of McCain-Feingold and its companion, Shays-Meehan, could not have asked for a better example to promote their cause in Congress, as stories of Enron's corporate contributions potentially buying political influence and disproportionate access to lawmakers flooded the media.

On February 14, 2002, after a marathon debate of seventeen hours and after defeating two rival bills and weathering ten attempts by Republicans to change the bill—major changes would necessitate a conference committee—forty-one Republicans voted with a majority of Democrats to pass Shays-Meehan, 240–189. One month later, on March 20, the Senate passed the final version of the bill, 60–40, as reformers retained their filibuster-proof margin.

In the end, the White House decided not to fight the reform. President Bush had opposed the bill during the 2000 campaign; but after the Enron scandal, he clearly needed to counter the fact that he was one of the biggest recipients of the corporation's contributions. Campaign finance reform was clearly a winning issue in the national electorate and would do much for his own reformer image. Despite objections of GOP leaders and conservatives in the House Republican Study Group, President Bush signed into law the Bipartisan Campaign Reform Act of 2002.

The seven-year odyssey to final passage was over. Members of Congress had voted for what many political observers believed to be the impossible—they had voted to change the very system that had elected them. To the American public the solution seemed an obvious one: reform the system before campaign spending spiraled out of control. But few in Washington actually expected the system to be changed, let alone overhauled. Soft money was invaluable in the House and Senate, where majorities were held by slim margins and where parties were perpetually fighting to take or maintain control of each chamber from election to election.

The fight, however, was far from over, as opponents moved from the congressional arena to the courts. The staunchest opponent to the new law, Senator McConnell (along with dozens of groups across the ideological spectrum), vowed to fight its constitutionality, specifically its infringement on First Amendment rights to free speech. Knowing the inevitability of a court challenge, sponsors included a provision in the new law that provided for an expedited judicial review process, ensuring a hearing by the Supreme Court. The cosponsors were careful to make sure the bill's provisions were severable—if one section was held to be unconstitutional, the rest of the bill could still stay in place. The critical question before the

Court in 2003 remained whether the Bipartisan Campaign Reform Act curbed corruption or violated the right to free speech.

On December 10, 2003, the Supreme Court answered that question. In a narrow five–four decision on *McConnell v. the Federal Elections Commission*, the court ruled that BCRA's ban on soft money contributions to political parties and candidates does not violate rights delineated in the U.S. Constitution. Writing for the majority, Justices John Paul Stevens and Sandra Day O'Connor spoke directly to the corrosive nature of soft money:

> Just as troubling to a functioning democracy as classic *quid pro quo* corruption is the danger that officeholders will decide issues not on the merits or the desires of their constituencies but according to the wishes of those who have made large financial contributions. . . . The best means of prevention is to identify and remove the temptation. The evidence set forth . . . convincingly demonstrates that soft-money contributions to political parties carry with them just such a temptation. (*Congressional Quarterly Weekly Report* 2003, 3078)

McConnell v. the FEC is clearly the most important Supreme Court case on campaign finance reform since *Buckley v. Valeo* in 1976. The Supreme Court's decision to uphold the core provisions in McCain-Feingold—the ban on soft money and the restrictions on political ads by outside groups—will greatly determine the role of money in congressional and presidential campaigns from 2004 on. The extent to which the new law eliminates "corruption or the appearance of corruption" remains to be seen. As the final paragraph of the majority opinion recognizes: "Money, like water, will always find an outlet." While the supporters of campaign finance reform celebrated their Supreme Court victory, Senator McConnell was quick to warn: "Soft money is not gone, it has just changed its address" (Cochran 2003b, 3076). Indeed, the Court has already reversed itself on one key component of BCRA. As we were going to press with this fifth edition, the Court essentially declared the ban on the groups using a candidate's name in issue advocacy ads thirty days before a primary election or sixty days before a general election unconstitutional. Writing for the majority in a closely divided five-four decision, Chief Justice John Roberts stated: "Discussion of issues cannot be suppressed simply because the issues may also be pertinent in an election. Where the First Amendment is implicated, the tie goes to the speaker, not the censor," (*Federal Election Commission v. Wisconsin Right to Life, Inc.* 551 U.S. __ (2007).

III. THE COSTS OF DEMOCRACY AND WHO PAYS FOR IT

To determine the actual and potential consequences of the new campaign finance law, it is necessary to take a more detailed look at the

Box 5.1
UNDERSTANDING THE BIPARTISAN CAMPAIGN REFORM ACT OF 2002

Soft Money
- For national parties, banned—cannot accept or spend it.
- For state parties, limited—can accept up to $10,000 per donor per year, to be spent specifically on voter registration and get-out-the-vote drives for federal elections.

Hard Money
- For each candidate per campaign, individual contribution limit raised from $1,000 to $2,000.
- Individual contribution limit to national parties increased from $20,000 to $25,000 per year.
- Individual aggregate annual limit raised to a total of $95,000, including contributions to candidate campaigns, parties, and PACs.[1]
- PAC limit to each candidate for each election is $5,000.
- PAC limit to each party for each election cycle is $15,000.
- No limit on total PAC giving.

"Millionaire's Amendment"
- Allows for additional increases in hard money contributions to candidates running against wealthy opponents who spend large amounts of their own money.

Advertisements Referring to a Federal Candidate
- Advertisement by unions, corporations, or nonprofit organizations that refer to a federal candidate, reach his or her electorate, and run within sixty days of a general election or thirty days of a primary must be paid for with regulated hard money through PACs. This regulation was designed to control thinly disguised political advertisements previously permitted under the concept of issue advocacy, if they are run during the period immediately before federal elections.[2]

1. BCRA also indexed these individual limits to inflation. The limits for the 2007–2008 election cycle are $2,300 per candidate, per campaign; $28,500 per year to the national parties; and $108,200 for the individual aggregate limit per cycle.
2. As we were going to press with this fifth edition, the Supreme Court ruled this component of BCRA unconstitutional in *Federal Election Commission v. Wisconsin Right to Life, Inc.* 551 U.S. ___ (2007).

actual costs of American democracy—that is, how much money is raised and spent by parties and candidates, and where the money is coming from. In the following section, we first explore the price tag of federal, state, and local elections over the past thirty years. What patterns in campaign expenditures have developed in response to previous regulations? Then we look at the sources of campaign funds, more specifically at the contributions of individuals, political action committees, and political parties, as well as the controversial roles of soft money and public funding in American elections.

A. The Costs

As we have discussed, concern over the rising costs of campaigns first manifested themselves at the presidential level, particularly after the elections of 1968 and 1972. Figure 5.1 shows the rapid rise in the costs incurred directly by presidential candidates during the general election phase of the campaign and the disparity that existed between the two major parties before 1976, the first election in which costs were contained through the use of public funds.[5] But even as steep as the increase shown in figure 5.1 is, in many ways it dramatically underrepresents the true amount of money that is spent on presidential campaigns today. The totals in figure 5.1 only include funds spent directly by the candidates' campaigns during the general election. If one also considers the money spent by the campaigns during the nomination phase, and some additional independent expenditures by the parties, the figure for the 2004 presidential campaign rises to $1.23 billion, a figure that itself is an increase from $671 million in 2000. And even these sums are under-

Figure 5.1 Total Campaign Spending in Presidential Years, 1952–2004

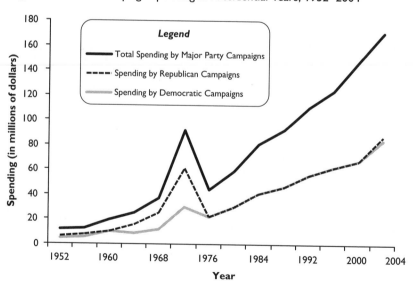

Source: Federal Election Commission.
Note: Major party candidates only.

estimates because they do not include all money spent by interest groups, 527 groups, and other party expenditures (Patterson 2006).

Although the percentage of funds spent on radio and television advertising jumped from approximately 33 percent, in 1952, to 50 percent, in 1968 (Alexander 1976a, 28), not all of the increased spending was due to television advertising. In 1972, partly as a response to criticism of the 1968 campaign, the Nixon strategy called for spending far less on television and far more on other forms of campaigning. The radio and television budget of the 1972 Nixon reelection campaign was only $54.3 million, compared with the $51.2 million spent on electronic media during his 1968 effort. Nixon as president used free media (to be discussed more fully in chapter 10) expertly, emphasizing his service in office and permitting a campaign strategy by other means—direct mail.

One response to the 1972 campaign was the passage of public financing for the 1976 presidential election. Reflecting this change in policy are the elections after 1976, in which the two parties spend the same amount each year (see figure 5.1). But those who financed campaigns in the past had to look elsewhere to spend their money to influence the political process. One of the results of this reallocation of political resources is the pattern of House and Senate campaign spending, as revealed in figures 5.2(a and b) and 5.3(a and b), respectively.

No matter how these data are read, the pattern is clear: increasingly large sums were being spent to finance campaigns. In 1974, the mean expenditure for all candidates for the House of Representatives was over $53,000; in 1990, it was close to $325,000; in 2004, it reached approximately $773,000. The gap between incumbents

Figure 5.2a Mean House Campaign Expenditures, by Party

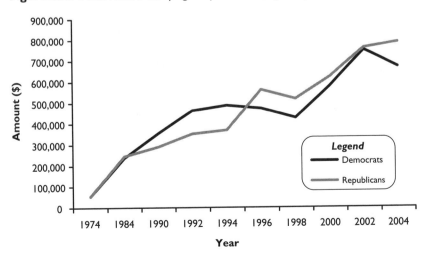

Source: Federal Election Commission. Data for 2002 and 2004 provided by Gary Jacobson. We thank him for sharing with us.

Note: These figures exclude uncontested races.

Figure 5.2b Mean House Campaign Expenditures, by Candidate Status

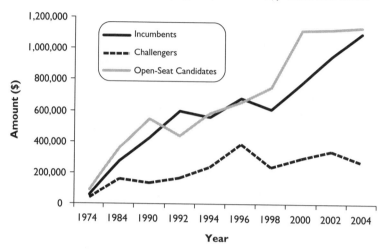

Source: Federal Election Commission. Data for 2002 and 2004 provided by Gary Jacobson. We thank him for sharing with us.
Note: These figures exclude uncontested races.

and challengers widened as well.[6] The mean expenditure for incumbents rose from approximately $57,000 to $422,000 to $1,000,000, for the same years; and for challengers, from $40,000 to $134,000 to $322,000. For open seats, the mean expenditure rose from about $90,000 to $543,000 to $1.2 million.

In the Senate, the mean expenditure for all candidates went from approximately $437,000, in 1974; to $2.6 million, in 1990; to $5.4 million, in 2004. For incumbents the mean expenditure sur-

Figure 5.3a Mean Senate Campaign Expenditures, by Party

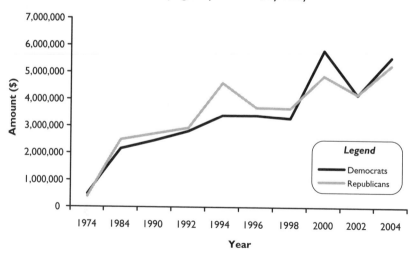

Source: Federal Election Commission.
Note: These figures exclude uncontested races.

Figure 5.3b. Mean Senate Campaign Expenditures, by Candidate Status

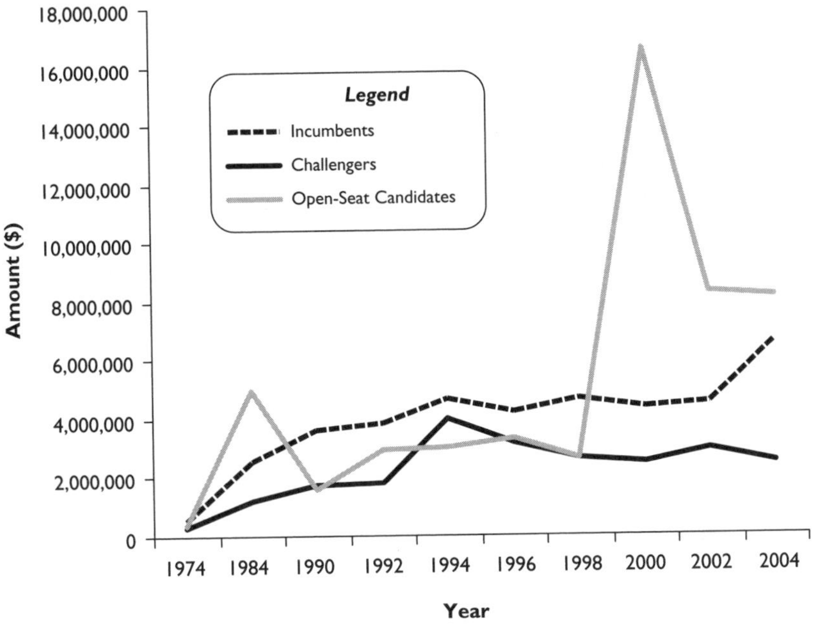

Source: Federal Election Commission.
Note: These figures exclude uncontested races.

passed $6.6 million, in 2004; for challengers, the mean was still a daunting $2.4 million. The mean expenditure in the open-seat races was $8.4 million. Because only one-third of the Senate is up for reelection in every election year, year-by-year comparisons can be misleading—especially open-seat data—as the same states do not necessarily have open seats. However, when examining figure 5.3b, if one focuses on elections separated by six years (e.g., 1998 and 2004), when the same seats were contested (though recognizing that different seats were open), one can see the extent to which campaign expenditures have continued to rise, with overall expenditures rising 50 percent between each set of elections.[7]

In 1974, only ten candidates for the House of Representatives spent over $250,000 on their campaigns, and none spent over $500,000. In 1990, the average incumbent spent nearly $400,000, and forty spent over $1 million each. By 2004 the average incumbent spent $1.1 million; and the candidate who ranked fiftieth in amount spent on an election campaign, Patrick Kennedy (D-R.I.), spent $2.2 million.

The million-dollar campaign for the Senate was the exception in 1974; that amount was only spent in expensive campaigns in large states. But by 1982 even candidates in a small, financially conservative state such as Maine contemplated million-dollar expenditures. By 1990, twenty-seven of the thirty-two incumbents seeking reelection spent at least $1 million. In 2004 all twenty-six incumbents, sixteen of the seventeen candidates in open-seat races, and twelve challengers to incumbents all spent more than $1 million. By every possible means, candidates were raising and spending money. Politicians and the public expressed a good deal of concern about what it meant to spend these huge sums in attaining public office. Concern was expressed about the amounts being spent, regardless of where the money came from.

Despite the limitations of the data available, those who study state and local elections have concluded that the same escalating campaign costs seen at the federal level are present at state and local levels. In 1980, Herbert Alexander of the Citizens' Research Foundation estimated that $265 million was spent on state elections and $200 million on local elections (Alexander 1984, 104). A decade later he estimated that $540 million was spent on state elections and $365 million on local elections, an amount that constituted 45 percent of the total spent on all elections in 1990 (Alexander and Bauer 1991, 3).[8] After the 1996 campaigns, Alexander's estimates rose to $650 million for state elections and $425 million for local elections, just under 25 percent of the total amount spent. It should be remembered that more state and local elections are held in non-presidential years than in presidential election years and, further, that some of these elections (e.g., New Jersey's or Virginia's) are held in odd-numbered years.

Ruth Jones (1984) and Anthony Gierzynski and David Breaux (1991) found significant increases in spending by candidates as well as significant variance across states in the years after the first campaign finance reform act. Michael Malbin and Thomas Gais, in their study of spending in state house races from 1982 to 1992, found that "after controlling for inflation, total campaign expenditures in Kansas House elections grew by 66 percent . . . in Kentucky House elections by 45 percent . . . in Oregon House elections by 225 percent . . . and in Maine Senate elections by 292 percent over the same period" (1998, 15). More recent data on spending on state and especially local elections are hard to come by, but it is certain that spending on these elections has increased significantly from the late 1990s. According to the Institute on Money in State Politics (2004, 2005), $2.1 billion was spent on elections for state offices in 2002, and $1.8 billion was spent in 2004.

B. Sources of Campaign Funds

While some people have a vaguely uneasy sense that campaigns in America cost too much, many more people are concerned about where the money for campaigns comes from and what strings, if any, are attached to political contributions. This type of concern led to the laws that prohibit individuals from contributing large sums of money to specific campaigns. The presumption is that these individuals do not act charitably but rather contribute huge sums in reward for past action and in hope of some later benefit. Although little empirical evidence supports the assumption of a link between contribution and payoff, the general perception—if not the reality—is that few people give something for nothing. In the sections that follow, we examine the five primary sources of money and the questions that accompany each funding base.

Although the Federal Election Commission has changed the ways in which it categorizes the sources of campaign contributions to federal campaigns, we can nonetheless discuss relative contributions with some historical perspective—for both congressional and presidential elections. Generally, campaign funds come from the following sources: the candidate, individuals, political action committees, political parties, and public financing—the last of which is only available to presidential candidates and some state and local candidates.

As shown in table 5.1, the majority of contributions to House and Senate candidates come from individuals (for more on individual donors to congressional campaigns, see Francia et al. 2003). Although the amount that candidates contributed to their own campaigns was not reported in the early 1970s, House candidates tended to give just under 10 percent in the earlier period and much less more recently. There is wide variation, however, with some candidates financing much of their own campaigns and with others contributing relatively little (Wilcox 1988).

The same variations hold for Senate candidates, but because so few Senate elections are held in each election year, no pattern emerges. For instance, when John Heinz (R, 1973–1991) spent a large amount of his own money to win the Pennsylvania Senate seat in 1976, his expenditures raised the average for all Senate races in that year. The same would hold true of races in New Jersey in 2000 (John Corzine) or North Carolina in 2002 (Erskine Bowles) or Nebraska in 2006 (Pete Ricketts). Blair Hull spent almost $29 million of his own money to lose the Democratic nomination to Barack Obama in 2004. When the amount that individuals donate to their own campaigns is estimated, it is clear that well over half the money spent in congressional campaigns comes from contributions from other individuals, the amounts of which were first limited by the FECA in 1974.

One conclusion that can be drawn from table 5.1 is that restricting and disclosing contributions by individuals has solved most of the problem about the source of campaign funds in congressional races. However, further study of these data clouds that relatively optimistic view. Two patterns have emerged since 1974. The clearest pattern is that the role of PACs has increased at a rapid pace. Jacobson (1985b, 40) has determined that the increase in PAC contributions from 1980 to 1982 was over 200 percent for House and

Table 5.1   General Election Funding Sources for Congressional Candidates, 1974, 1984, 1994–2004

	Raised[a]	PACs	Party[b]	Individuals	Self[c]	Other
			Percentage Distribution			
House						
1974						
All candidates[d]	$45.7	17	4	79	—	—
Democrats	23.9	22	1	77	—	—
Republicans	21.7	10	7	83	—	—
1984						
All candidates	$203.8	36	7	47	6	5
Democrats	107.2	41	3	44	6	6
Republicans	96.6	30	11	49	6	5
1994						
All candidates	$371.3	34	5	49	8	4
Democrats	196.7	43	5	43	5	4
Republicans	174.6	24	6	56	11	3
1996						
All candidates	$460.7	25	5	52	10	8
Democrats	211.5	29	4	44	12	11
Republicans	249.2	21	6	58	9	6
1998						
All candidates	$425.7	36	3	53	6	2
Democrats	195.2	38	3	51	6	4
Republicans	230.5	34	3	54	6	4
2000						
All candidates	$542.4	35	n.a.	53	7	0
Democrats	268.3	36	n.a.	50	8	0
Republicans	274.1	34	n.a.	55	6	0
2002						
All candidates	$548.6	36	n.a.	49	9	0
Democrats	270.0	36	n.a.	46	12	0
Republicans	278.1	36	n.a.	52	7	n.a.
2004						
All candidates	622.6	36	n.a.	56	5	0
Democrats	279.8	35	n.a.	57	5	n.a.
Republicans	342.8	36	n.a.	55	4	n.a.
Senate						
1974						
All candidates	$27.8	11	6	83	—	—
Democrats	16.2	13	2	85	—	—
Republicans	11.6	7	13	80	—	—

(continued)

Table 5.1   (Continued)

	Raised[a]	PACs	Party[b]	Individuals	Self[c]	Other
				Percentage Distribution		
1984						
All candidates	$157.7	18	6	61	10	4
Democrats	73.1	18	6	56	16	4
Republicans	84.6	18	6	65	5	4
1994						
All candidates	$291.7	15	8	54	19	4
Democrats	124.9	18	10	55	12	5
Republicans	166.7	13	6	53	24	4
1996						
All candidates	$242.0	16	9	59	8	5
Democrats	116.2	12	8	59	16	5
Republicans	125.8	20	9	59	8	4
1998						
All candidates	$247.1	19	7	62	11	0
Democrats	116.7	17	8	63	10	0
Republicans	130.5	21	7	61	13	0
2000						
All candidates	$371.3	14	n.a.	55	25	0
Democrats	205.0	9	n.a.	41	44	0
Republicans	166.3	20	n.a.	73	2	0
2002						
All candidates	$288.7	20	n.a.	65	8	0
Democrats	137.8	17	n.a.	69	8	0
Republicans	150.9	22	n.a.	62	8	0
2004						
All candidates	$373.9	16	n.a.	72	0	n.a.
Democrats	194.8	14	n.a.	77	3	0
Republicans	179.1	19	n.a.	67	0	n.a.

Source: 1974–1994 data from Ornstein et al. (1998) Table 3-9; 1996, 1998, 2000, and 2004 data based on FEC sources.

[a] Amount raised by candidates, including party expenditures on behalf of candidates (in millions).

[b] Including contributions and expenditures.

[c] Includes candidates' contributions to selves and unrepaid loans.

[d] For all years, includes major party candidates only.

Note: The FEC did not report candidates' contributions to selves and unrepaid loans separately in 1974, and thus for this year these sources of funding are included in the "Individuals" category. The figures reported by the FEC do not add to 100 in some years.

Source: 1974 data from Ornstein et al. (1992), table 3-5; 1984–1996 data from Ornstein et al. (1998), table 3-9; 1998–2004 data from Federal Election Commission.

Senate races. By 1988, PACs were contributing between 33 and 40 percent of the money given to House campaigns, and their contribution level has stabilized at that level. More interesting, perhaps, is the fact the PACs continue to contribute nearly half the money raised by House incumbents. Thus, the fact that more contributions come from individuals than PACs does not allay the fears of those concerned about group influence.

In addition, the role of political party organizations has changed drastically over recent years (see chapter 2). The data in table 5.1 only consider party contributions made directly to candidate campaigns. In 1982 and again in 1984, the Republican party spent a significant amount of money on behalf of congressional candidates independent of their campaign committees. In 1982 the Republican National Committee spent more than $200,000 on behalf of sixteen Senate candidates; the Democrats spent that much for only one candidate. Direct spending on behalf of candidates, particularly by the Republican party (but also by the Democrats), has increased, while direct contributions by the parties to candidates have not been rising as rapidly in recent years.

The sources of presidential campaign funding is a somewhat murkier and also a more fluid picture. Before FECA and its later reforms, not much was known about where presidential campaigns got their money, although many had heard stories of Richard Nixon and money stuffed into brown paper bags. This of course was one of the concerns that FECA was designed to address. The public financing component of the 1970s reforms was also meant to "level the playing field" in presidential elections: each campaign was supposed to spend the same amount of money; each candidate received the same federal grant; and each national committee was allowed to spend the same amount of money directly on each campaign. And while some would argue that public financing did equalize things to a certain degree, the total amounts spent by presidential campaigns have varied considerably since the inception of the program.

During the 1980s, the major source of this variation was independent expenditures. Nearly $13 million in independent expenditures was spent on behalf of the Reagan–Bush campaign compared to only $1.7 million on behalf of Carter–Mondale. In 1984 the total spent by independent groups exceeded $17 million, with the bulk of it spent on behalf of the Reagan–Bush ticket. When the Supreme Court ruled that these expenditures could not be limited, it formalized a new, unregulated source of funding for the two major party candidates' presidential campaigns (*Federal Election Committee v. National Conservative Political Action Committee,* 470 U.S. 480, 1985). However, despite fears that the sums spent independently could skyrocket—and that they would cause an imbalance between the campaigns—the amount actually spent in 1988 declined to about $10 million, though the Republicans did hold a three-to-one advantage (Alexander and Bauer 1991, 82–85).

From 1992–2000, the major source of variation—and the major factor in the escalation of the total costs of presidential campaigns— was soft money. In 1992, the Republicans raised nearly $50 million in soft money, compared to $36.3 million for the Democrats. In 1996, total soft money receipts reached $263.5 million, with the

Republicans having an advantage of approximately $20 million over the Democrats. The amount raised in the 2000 campaign was nearly double that total, with the two parties' shares about equal. With the BCRA's ban on soft money, many were interested to see what the 2004 presidential election would produce in terms of equity in spending. The answer, once again, was an uneven playing field, although in this case a field that tilted in favor of Democratic candidate John Kerry. The Kerry campaign outspent the Bush campaign in the general election by a little over $100 million dollars. Most of this difference was accounted for by spending on behalf of Kerry by the Democratic party and interest groups (including 527 groups) in the form of independent expenditures (Corrado 2006b). It is likely that the 2004 presidential election will be the last of this contemporary public financing era (more will be said on this at the end of this chapter), so the race for each campaign to outraise and outspend the other will only intensify in upcoming years.

1. Individual Contributions

Although early reformers focused their attention on large contributions by individuals, that concern has been tempered in the last decade, at least if one looks only at hard money (there is still a good deal of concern about large soft money contributions by wealthy individuals, as we will discuss below). If the campaign finance reforms of the 1970s have been successful in any one area, it has been in curbing significant hard money contributions by wealthy individuals and thus limiting the alleged abuse caused by such huge donations. Gone are situations, as in 1972, when Stewart R. Mott contributed nearly a half-million dollars to various Democratic presidential candidates in the prenomination phase of the campaign and over $800,000 to all campaigns in that year; or, in that same year, when fifty-one multimillionaires contributed a total of over $6 million to political campaigns, with more than $5.5 million to Republican candidates.

With the advent of the campaign finance reforms, the amount that individuals could give to a single campaign was set at $1,000, and the total amount that they could contribute to all campaigns was restricted (with the exception of contributions to their own campaigns and independent expenditures). The clear result of this change has been that large, individual contributions play a smaller role in politics, and smaller contributions play a larger role.[9]

A second implication of this change has been that candidates have had to work at developing a broader base of smaller contributors to fill their campaign coffers. Candidates have had to develop new techniques for raising money. The Goldwater campaign of 1964 and the George Wallace campaign of 1968 demonstrated the power of direct mail as a tool for raising large amounts of money (and for cementing the allegiance of a massive number of voters). The techniques used in those campaigns have been emulated and improved on by all politicians in the ensuing decades. In the most recent election cycles, presidential candidates John McCain and (especially) Howard Dean have demonstrated the effectiveness of the Internet for raising money. Many congressional, senatorial, and gubernatorial candidates hope to copy these success stories.

The more ominous implication of the move away from reliance on large, individual contributions is that candidates have looked elsewhere for funds, particularly to political action committees.

2. Political Action Committees

If large contributions from individuals are not so threatening as they were thought to be before the reforms of the 1970s, contributions from political action committees are more so. In fact, it can be argued that the evils of PACs, for those who see such evils, are direct consequences of the reform movement; and as a consequence of recent experience, PAC reform has been highest on the agenda of campaign finance reformers.

Much has been written about PACs, so it is important to understand clearly what is meant by a political action committee. As is not atypical when one scrutinizes commonly used terms, one finds that the term *political action committee* does not appear in the statutes of the federal government. However, the statutes do refer to *political committees,* which are distinct from either *party committees* or *candidate committees.* A political committee, according to the U.S. Code (26 U.S.C. 9001[9]) is "any committee, association, or organization (whether or not incorporated) which accepts contributions or makes expenditures for the purpose of influencing, or attempting to influence, the nomination or election of one or more individuals to Federal, State, or local elective public office."

MULTI-CANDIDATE POLITICAL COMMITTEE

Committee that supports more than one candidate for a federal office.

The U.S. Code further defines **multicandidate political committee** as "a political committee which has been registered . . . for a period of not less than 6 months, which has received contributions from more than 50 persons, and, except for any State political party organization, has made contributions to 5 or more candidates for Federal office" (4 U.S.C. 441 [a]).

SEPARATE SEGREGATED FUND

The way in which a corporation or other entity must maintain a distinction between corporate funds and money raised and spent for political purposes.

Finally, political action committees, as we normally think of them, are separate from their parent or sponsoring organization (if there is one). Campaign finance legislation has long prohibited direct political contributions by labor unions or corporations; however, provisions have been made for establishing a **separate segregated fund** for political purposes. The law specifies how money for this fund may and may not be raised. Political action committees with parent organizations, then, are the committees set up to administer these "separate segregated funds" (Sorauf 1984, chap. 1; 1991). The acronym PAC is thus commonly used to refer to a nonparty, noncandidate committee that funds more than one candidate and may or may not be affiliated with an established corporation, union, or interest group (Sabato 1985).

The Federal Election Commission identifies four major types of political action committees: labor, corporation, trade/membership/health, and nonconnected.[10] The first three types identified can be defined as multicandidate political committees that are administering campaign funds that have been raised from, but kept separate and segregated from, a parent organization—be that a labor union; a corporation; or a trade, membership, or health organization (such as the American Bankers Association or the American Medical Association). The nonconnected PACs tend to be ideological multicandidate political committees that have come together for specific political purposes and that do not draw on an established parent organization.

While their prominence is a recent phenomenon, political committees have been on the American political scene for some time. From the 1940s, until its merger with the American Federation of Labor (AFL) in 1955, the Congress of Industrial Organizations (CIO) operated a separate fund to receive and dispense voluntary contributions from labor unionists to political campaigns. The AFL-CIO Committee on Political Education (COPE), established after the 1955 merger, has been described as "the model for virtually all political action committees" (Epstein 1980, 100). In the late 1950s and early 1960s, some of the larger membership and trade professional organizations, such as the American Realtors and the American Medical Association, formed political committees (Alexander 1979b, 559–66; Sorauf 1984, 33).

However, the factors that have caused most concern are the increase in the number of PACs, especially in the decade following the passage of the FECA of 1974 and the increase in the magnitude of the role PACs play, as measured in the dollars they contribute. The FECA amendments of 1974 put a more stringent limit on individual contributions than on contributions by multicandidate political committees. This followed naturally from the fact that reformers were more concerned about huge contributions by individuals than by group contributions.

The 1974 amendments also lifted the restriction that had prohibited government contractors from setting up separate segregated political committees. The public financing of presidential elections, effective for the 1976 election, led PACs to switch their emphasis from presidential to congressional campaigns. But, because the viability of PACs under the FECA was initially unclear, there was only cautious movement toward establishing new PACs. This situation changed in 1975. The FEC, in response to an inquiry from the Sun Oil Company, issued an advisory opinion in which it informed Sun

Oil that the corporation could legally establish a separate segregated fund for the purpose of contributing to political campaigns and that it could solicit voluntary contributions from its employees to support that fund. As a result of all these actions, many corporations decided to form PACs, and political action committees as a major force in funding congressional elections became a most visible aspect of electoral politics. Hundreds of other corporations eventually followed Sun Oil's lead (Epstein 1980).

Look back at table 4.2 (p. 126), which depicts the rapid growth of political action committees. The total number of PACs grew from slightly over six hundred, in 1974, to well over forty-two hundred, by 1988. While the number of active PACs has leveled off in the last two decades, PAC expenditures have continued to rise. From $12.5 million in 1974, PAC expenditures topped $100 million in 1984, $200 million in 1994, and reached $475 million in 2004.

It should be noted further that this growth has not been constant among the various types of PACs. On the one hand, organized labor was quick to see that PACs could increase their influence, and nearly all major labor unions organized political action committees. However, the number of labor PACs has never doubled the number that existed in 1974—and has declined in recent years. On the other hand, corporations were slower to realize the potential influence they could wield through PACs. But the number of corporate PACs eventually increased to far exceed that of labor unions, with major jumps coming after the **SUNPAC** opinion and again during the Reagan administration. (See Eismeier and Pollock 1985a, 1985b; Malbin 1984a, 1984b.) In the late 1980s growth was also seen in the nonconnected PACs, as more "political entrepreneurs" came to view this avenue as a viable way to increase political influence.

SUNPAC

The political action committee set up by the Sun Oil Corporation that tested the principle that corporations could establish PACs.

The growth in the number of PACs and the amount they contribute to political candidates, more specifically to congressional candidates, has led to a number of concerns: the necessity of PAC support to secure electoral victory, the link between PAC support and legislative behavior, the ideological imbalance of present and future PACs, and the responsibility of PAC leaders to contributors.

The influence of PACs on electoral outcomes. Some things are clear. Examining recent elections for the U.S. Congress shows that, by and large, winners spend more money than losers. Although it is appropriate to be concerned about who gets money from each source, attention has been focused on PACs because PACs are contributing an increasingly large amount of money.

Both the amount and the proportion of money contributed by PACs have been rising faster than the total amount spent on elections and the proportion coming from any other source.[11] Figures 5.4 and 5.5 show the patterns clearly. In more recent years, the

Figure 5.4 Growth of PAC Contributions to Congressional Elections, 1974–2004, in millions of dollars

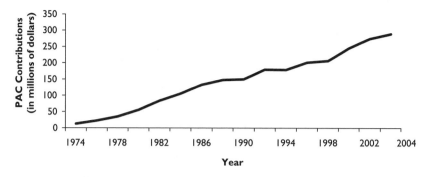

Source: Federal Election Commmission.

percentages of congressional expenditures from PACs have leveled off, as PACs have concentrated more of their spending on independent expenditures. But the total amount of money spent by PACs keeps rising and rising.

It is also clear from these data that virtually all successful candidates must raise a significant amount of money from political action committees; however, figure 5.6 shows that PACs do not distribute their money equally among all candidates. Incumbents are able to raise PAC money much more easily than their challengers. While PACs flirted with supporting more challengers in the early 1980s (see Eismeier and Pollock 1985b, 1986; Jacobson 1985–1986; Sabato 1985; Wright 1985), in the last decade PACs have typically given a minimum of 70 percent of their contributions to incumbents and less than 15 percent to challengers.[12] Ironically, money is more significant for challengers than it is for incumbents (Jacobson 1980,

Figure 5.5 Growth of PAC Contributions to Congressional Elections, by Chamber, 1974–2004, in percentages

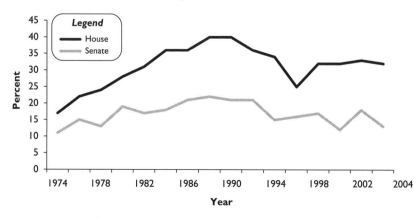

Source: Federal Election Commmission.

Figure 5.6. PAC Contributions to Congressional Candidates by Candidate Status, 2004

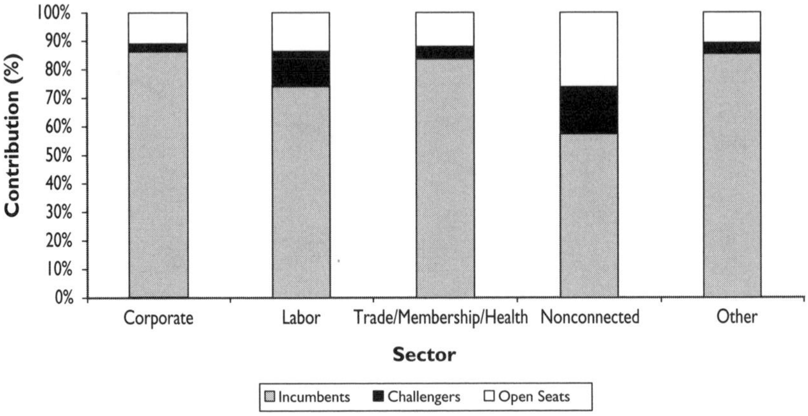

Source: Federal Election Commmission.

chap. 5) in terms of running a serious campaign. The key is whether challengers can attract enough money, including PAC money, to mount enough of a campaign to have a chance of victory. More and more, they do not seem to be able to do so.

The influence of PACs on legislative outcomes. PACs are connected to specific groups that have a direct interest in legislative decision making. The funds may be separate and segregated, but the connection is there in the minds of all involved. One does not have to stretch one's imagination too far to see that the directors of the Amoco political action committee have certain views on issues affecting the oil industry or that those deciding on the allocation of funds from the Machinists Nonpartisan Political League care greatly about the level of governmental support for the aerospace industry.

The PAC leaders know this, and the candidates know this. Former congresswoman Millicent Fenwick (R-N.J., 1975–1983) put it most succinctly: "That these groups influence voting is undeniable. 'I took $58,000. They want it,' was the explanation one colleague gave for his vote, bought by a number of donations from a number of groups of similar orientation" (quoted in Sorauf 1984, 90).

Note the figure $58,000. It could just as easily have been $100,000. Until the passage of the Bipartisan Campaign Reform Act, PACs were limited to contributions of $5,000 in a single campaign; that amount is now doubled. The sum of $5,000 (or $10,000) will not buy a great deal of influence in a campaign with a budget of $1.25 million; but if twenty groups with similar interests (e.g., oil or medical policy) each make maximum contributions, then the total impact may be significant—and that defines the concern. Many feel that PAC money does not directly buy influence; however, contributions do buy access, and access can lead indirectly to influence.

Another view notes that PACs contribute to individuals likely to support their cause in any case, and individual PAC contributions are not significant in terms of the total amounts spent on campaigns. Incumbents have tremendous electoral advantages, regardless of PAC actions or intentions, and they face an array of pressures; thus, they cannot listen to PAC leaders only.

Still, members of Congress do accept large amounts of money from groups with a direct stake in legislation. The total contributed by like-minded groups might well represent a sizable percentage of a candidate's campaign funds, and interest group representatives are often quite overt in exercising pressure when key decisions are pending. There is, in the words of the Supreme Court, "the appearance of impropriety," which may well be as detrimental to the system as the reality.

Alleged PAC influence on legislation tarnishes the reputation of political action committees (Common Cause 1986; Drew 1983; Jackson 1988; Stern 1988). PAC supporters argue persuasively that citizens should have a right to associate with others of similar views to maximize the likelihood of having their views heard. PAC detractors point to the number of cases in which large PAC contributions have been funneled to incumbents facing no challengers; they cite it as evidence that PACs are polluting the system by setting up an assumption that legislative behavior is for sale to the highest bidder. Political scientists have searched for evidence of PAC influence on legislative behavior, but their conclusion is that hard evidence of the corrupting influence of PACs is all but absent (Evans 1986; Frendeis and Waterman 1985; Grenzke 1989, 1990; Schroedel 1986; Wright 1985). In a very real sense, this debate has been the focus of reform efforts for more than a decade, and although the concerns surrounding 527 groups have taken some attention away from PAC influence, it is still a worry for many.

The ideological imbalance of present and future PACs. Labor leaders were among those most interested in writing legislation allowing for the formation of PACs in the early years of the 1970s reform movement. They saw tremendous advantages in trying to exert influence over the electoral process. However, these labor leaders were shortsighted, as the trends in the increases in PACs show. Labor PACs are as well organized and about as effective as they are likely to be, and, in terms of number and influence, corporate PACs and trade association PACs have far outstripped those formed by labor unions. Now, labor leaders, Democrats, and other liberals worry that PAC influence will increasingly become more conservative, business oriented, and Republican.

This argument can be dealt with on two levels. First, table 5.2 shows that PACs have not given significantly more to Republicans than to Democrats, but rather PACs have tended to support incumbents (figure 5.6). The Democrats controlled the House (and the Senate, except for the period between 1980 and 1986) for the first twenty years of the FECA. Since incumbents have received more PAC support, the Democrats benefited. When the Republicans regained control of Congress in 1994, PAC money has began to be split more evenly between the two parties, reflecting the fact that nearly equal numbers of incumbents of both parties have been seeking reelection and also that the Republicans were the new majority party.[13] The GOP exhibited its largest advantage in PAC money over the Democrats in 2004, a possible reflection of Tom DeLay's infamous

Table 5.2   PAC Contributions to Congressional Candidates by Party, 1998–2004

	Rep	Dem	Other	Total
1998				
Corporate	67.9%	32.1%	0.0%	$78.0 million
Labor	8.8	90.9	0.3	44.6
Trade/membership/health	62.3	37.6	0.1	62.3
Nonconnected	60.5	39.3	0.2	28.2
Other	54.3	45.6	0.1	6.8
Total	52.9	46.9	0.1	220.0
2000				
Corporate	67.4	32.5	0.2	91.5
Labor	8.0	91.6	0.3	51.6
Trade/membership/health	61.2	38.5	0.2	71.8
Nonconnected	59.3	40.5	0.2	37.3
Other	56.1	43.8	0.2	7.6
Total	52.4	47.4	0.2	259.8
2002				
Corporate	66.7	33.3	0.0	71.3
Labor	9.3	90.5	0.2	46.6
Trade/membership/health	60.9	39.1	0.0	56.5
Nonconnected	55.5	44.5	0.0	22.5
Other	58.7	41.3	0.0	6.9
Total	51.4	48.5	0.0	203.8
2004				
Corporate	67.7	32.3	0.0	104.3
Labor	12.2	87.6	0.2	50.3
Trade/membership/health	63.2	36.8	0.0	78.2
Nonconnected	64.5	35.5	0.0	49.8
Other	56.5	43.9	0.0	6.5
Total	56.0	43.9	0.0	289.1

Source: Federal Election Commission.

"K-Street Project." But now that the Democrats have retaken Congress, the split will once again likely return somewhere close to even.

At a more theoretical level, questions of the locus of power in the United States have long been debated. PAC influence is only one more manifestation of this question. Literally hundreds of PACs contribute to the most expensive campaigns for the House and Senate. Yet sheer numbers alone do not implicate influence. Our polity functioned under a system through which a few very wealthy individuals gave great sums to political campaigns in virtual anonymity. It is difficult to conclude that it cannot survive even a significant influx of PAC contributions made in the light of day.

The lack of accountability for PAC decision making. Even those who are not troubled by the supposed influence of political action committees have some concern over how decisions are made by PACs. Until recently, we knew little about how PACs function (Sabato 1985). The general assumption has been that, with the possible exception of labor union PACs, members have very little influence over how their money is spent. Former Iowa Republican congressman Jim Leach argues that

> groups seldom reflect the same collective judgment as all their members. More importantly, decisions for organizations frequently occur at the top not the bottom. . . . Individuals who control other people's money become power brokers in an elitist society. Their views, not the small contributors to their associations, become the views that carry influence. (quoted in Sorauf 1984, 96)

This concern is especially troublesome for nonconnected PACs, organizations that are often built around the reputation of one or two individuals and a mailing list. These PACs have been most active in influencing the electoral process through independent expenditures on behalf of, or in opposition to, a candidate. When only a few of these PACs spent significantly and when their influence seemed to be waning, decision making was not a major concern (Alexander and Bauer 1991, 84–86; Nelson 1990). However, the potential to use these instruments to affect specific elections—without adequate input from contributors—remains high.

Those who support the activity of political action groups most often argue that PAC activity is nothing more than constructive collective activity. If this is so, then collective decision making is a logical correlate. The lack of accountability of PAC leaders to their "followings" will be a pressing reform issue for the agenda of the future.

3. Political Parties

Perhaps the most underrated item on the agenda for reform in campaign financing is the changing role that the major political parties play in financing campaigns (Sorauf 1988, chap. 5; 1998).

The conventional wisdom in the 1970s was that parties did not play a major role in campaign finance. The Nixon campaigns of 1968 and 1972 raised substantial amounts of money independent of the Republican National Committee. The major financial effort on behalf of the Democrats was to retire the debts incurred by the Humphrey and Kennedy campaigns of 1968. In other words, the Democratic National Committee expended most of its fund-raising efforts in paying off debts, not in aiding candidates.

Congressional and senatorial campaigns did not cost the large amounts that are in evidence today. The national parties were not active in raising large sums for these campaigns, and the state and local parties did not have sufficient resources to make significant differences. However, as Gary Jacobson (1983, 49; 1985–1986), Frank Sorauf (1988, 127–49), Paul Herrnson (1995, 1998a, 1998b), and others have shown, the biggest change in campaign financing since the 1980s has been the significant role played by the political parties, particularly that of the Republican party, on behalf of congressional and senatorial candidates and of the efforts the Democrats made to match Republican efforts (Jackson 1988; Arterton 1982).

The difference between Republican and Democratic party efforts in this regard has been particularly troublesome for Democrats. The Republicans have had much more money to spend on campaign functions than the Democrats. This difference has been apparent at all electoral levels. The Republican National Committee spends money to provide in-kind services for candidates at reduced costs. They provide more funding so that, at the state and local levels, Republican organizations are stronger and better financed than their Democratic counterparts. The 1980s saw the emergence of the Hill committees—National Republican Senatorial Committee (NRSC), National Republican Congressional Committee (NRCC), Democratic Senatorial Campaign Committee (DSCC), and Democratic Congressional Campaign Committee (DCCC)—as important forces in congressional politics. Here too, the GOP had an edge over its Democratic counterparts. For many years, at each of these levels, the Republicans were much more active than Democrats and much more successful. Most discouraging for Democrats was the fact that, despite herculean efforts, the gap would not disappear. Over the last few years, however, Democrats have had reason to believe that perhaps things might be starting to look up in terms of their efforts to match the fund-raising capabilities of the GOP. As was noted previously, the Kerry campaign outspent the Bush campaign in the 2004 general election. This disparity came mostly from the fact that the Democratic party significantly outspent the GOP during the campaign. This is particularly important for the Democrats, given the important role the parties played in financing the campaigns of their respective presidential candidates in 2004, a trend that will likely continue in 2008 (Corrado 2006c, 2006d). According to the FEC, the totals raised by the two parties' Hill committees were very close in 2006, with the GOP committees outraising their Democratic counterparts by a smidge over $7 million. Finally, and perhaps most important, the Democratic party has exhibited a clear and relatively substantial edge over the Republicans in terms of raising money online (Vargas 2007).

The disparity between Republican and Democratic party funding (at least during the years of debate over McCain-Feingold) had clear implications for campaign finance reform, particularly for how long it took for reform to be enacted. While the Democrats held a comparative advantage in PAC funding, they were unwilling to look at reforms in that area so long as the Republicans retained their advantage in party funding. In a sense, reform was thwarted for many years because each party had a comparative advantage it was unwilling to concede.

4. Soft Money

This chapter has frequently referred to soft money, which in some ways became the tail that wagged the dog. So much soft money was spent in the last few campaigns pre-BCRA that all of the restrictions on existing campaign finance laws seemed useless. The authors of the McCain-Feingold bill were so obsessed with controlling soft money that they were willing to make a whole series of compromises to achieve that goal.

What exactly is the problem with soft money? Put in the most blunt terms, individuals and corporations could give as much as they wanted to campaigns through soft money. Even though these amounts were reported, the result was that influence could be purchased, or at least it seemed to be purchased, in much the same way as it was before the reforms of the 1970s. The soft money loophole eviscerated the effect of the restrictions on large contributions, thought by most to be the principal accomplishment of the FECA.

How serious was the problem? According to Public Disclosure, a watchdog group that monitors Federal Election Commission filings, the problem was exploding out of control. The amount raised and spent in the 2000 election year approached $500 million, nearly double the amount raised and spent in 1996. Stephen Weissman (2005) of the Campaign Finance Institute put the soft money figure for the 2002 election cycle—the last in which the national parties were allowed to accept soft money—at $556 million (remember, 2002 was a nonpresidential year). The money did not come equally from all rungs of American society. Businesses and trade associations gave more than ten times the amount contributed by labor unions. Extremely wealthy individual contributors reentered the system in significant numbers, contributing tens of millions of dollars. Think about who can give money in this way, in six- and seven-figure checks. Public Disclosure claimed that twenty-three of the twenty-five individuals who gave at least a quarter of a million dollars in 2000 were either chairpersons, or presidents, or CEOs of well-known corporations. Facts like these contributed to the drive to eliminate soft money.

Why did these individuals give, and why did they give to the extent that they did? Direct linkages between motivation for giving and legislation that is pending are difficult to confirm, but the appearance of impropriety is not hard to imagine. During a Congress in which tobacco regulation and telephone access legislation were high on the legislative agenda, Philip Morris contributed $2.1 million in soft money, and RJR Nabisco contributed $900,000; Bell Atlantic, MCI, and AT&T each contributed nearly $1 million. Cynical citizens were given a substantial amount of ammunition to fuel their concerns. Given this level of spending, and the lack of restrictions in the law and in FEC regulations, it is small wonder that reformers claimed that if Congress could only get a hold on soft money spending and fail to do anything else, that sole accomplishment would still represent significant progress. BCRA was their effort to do just that.

Of course, passage of BCRA did not end the soft money debate. In some ways, concerns about soft money and its impact have intensified post-McCain-Feingold. Even while the political community awaited the Supreme Court decision regarding the constitutionality of the law, many political players were already looking for ways around it. In September of 2003 (months before the Court would ultimately uphold the ban on national parties accepting soft money), hedge fund billionaire and philanthropist George Soros, whose foundation the Open Society Institute was among the leaders in pushing for campaign finance reform, announced that he would give $15 million to two liberal organizations—MoveOn.org and America Coming Together—whose primary goals in the 2004 election cycle were to advocate on behalf of liberal causes and register nonvoters and get them to vote—ideally, against incumbent president Bush. In announcing the gifts, Soros said that he was willing to do anything within the law to defeat George Bush in 2004 (for more on Soros see Carlisle 2004).

Even those who agree with Soros's goal fear that his methods undermine the campaign finance reforms about which he feels so strongly. The history of political money is that it finds a hole in the law and fills it, and with his large donation Soros pointed out for all to see the gaping hole in BCRA. America Coming Together and MoveOn.org are examples of what is known as a **527 group**, named after the provision of the tax code that governs the activities of these types of organizations (MoveOn.org also has a 501(c) component— see below). A 527 group is a political organization with a primary purpose of affecting elections. Such groups are tax exempt (except for investment income), and are not subject to any limits in terms of the amounts of money they raise or spend, or the size of donations they receive. Although 527 groups existed before BCRA, when the law banned soft money donations to parties but was silent on 527 groups, interest in and attention to the groups soared. Previously, wealthy individuals and interests who wanted to make large donations in the hope of affecting an election often gave soft money to the parties. With this door closed by BCRA, much (but not all) of these large soft money donations went to 527 groups. According to data reported by Patterson (2006), 527 groups spent $424 million in the 2003–2004 election cycle. The vast majority of the donations (over 80 percent) that generated this spending were $250,000 or more, including fifty-two individuals who gave over $1 million (Weissman and Hassan 2006). Soros himself eventually ending up donating almost $23.5 million to 527s in 2003–2004 (in support of Democratic efforts), while Texas billionaire Bob Perry (one of the primary donors to the infamous Swift Boat Veterans for Truth) was the top giver to Republican-supporting 527 groups at a little over $8 million (opensecrets.org). The high levels of spending by 527s continued in the off-year 2005–2006 election cycle, with Weissman and Ryan (2007) reporting that the groups spent $146 million in that round of contests.

Senators McCain and Feingold, and many other supporters of campaign finance reform, were aghast at the way in which 527 groups were able to take advantage of loopholes in election law and keep the massive amounts of soft money flowing. Congress considered new legislation to shut down 527s, but ultimately did nothing. Reform advocates urged the FEC through its rule-making process to force 527 groups to follow the same soft money guidelines that parties were forced to adhere to. The FEC refused to take this step, but it did issue some rulings that could potentially limit (but certainly not end) the attractiveness of 527 groups as destinations for soft money in some cases. But as is always the case with money and elections, where one door closes another one opens. In this case, that door is represented by **501(c) groups**, once again named after the provision of the IRS code that governs such groups. The 501(c) groups are social welfare organizations or labor unions or trade

527 GROUP

A political organization with a primary purpose of affecting elections, named after the provision of the tax code that governs the activities of these types of organizations. Such groups are tax exempt (except for investment income) and are not subject to any limits in terms of the amounts of money they raise or spend, or the size of donations they receive.

501(c) GROUP

A social welfare organization, labor union, or trade association that has tax exempt status, named after the provision of the tax code that governs the activities of these types or organizations. Under current tax and election law, these 501(c) groups can raise and spend soft money in virtually unlimited fashion, as long as campaign activity is not their "primary activity" or "major purpose."

associations that have tax-exempt status. Under current tax and election law, these 501(c) groups can raise and spend soft money in virtually unlimited fashion, as long as campaign activity is not their "primary activity" or "major purpose." In other words, as long as these groups keep their electioneering secondary to their social welfare or labor or business purposes, they can operate without soft money constraints. In fact, in one crucial way 501(c) groups are (to some) preferable to 527 groups. While each type of group can for the most part raise and spend soft money without restriction, 527 groups are required to disclose the identities of their donors; 501(c) groups are not. In many cases 501(c) groups are also not required to disclose expenditures. Given these facts, it is obviously difficult to know for sure how much 501(c) groups are actually raising and spending, but Weissman and Ryan (2007) put the figure for the 2006 election cycle at $90 million, at the same time stating that this figure is a dramatic underestimate of true spending (for more on 527 and 501(c) groups see Corrado 2006a; Corrado et al. 2005; Weissman and Hassan 2006; Weissman and Ryan 2007). The bottom line on soft money in federal elections is this—despite the McCain-Feingold, soft money is still very prevalent and very important in American elections.

5. Public Financing

The reformers of the 1970s proposed public financing as the way to take the taint of money out of politics. If political campaigns were funded by the mass public, politicians would not have to deal with those seeking to buy influence.

Since 1976, public financing has been an important part of presidential campaigns. During the prenomination phase of the presidential election, after reaching a qualifying plateau, candidates for the two parties' nominations can receive matching funds for all contributions of $250 or less received from individuals. Of course the number of active candidates for the nomination can affect the amount of public money spent on the campaigns, as can individual candidate decisions on whether or not to accept public money.[14]

Each major party is granted public funds to run its nominating convention. Each party's nominee is granted public funds for running a general election campaign; other candidates for the presidency qualify for public funding according to the success they achieve.[15] As shown in figure 5.7, the total cost to the public of running the 2004 presidential election was a bit over $207 million, and that is without George W. Bush, John Kerry, or Howard Dean accepting public money during the prenomination phase. The debate over public financing of congressional and senatorial elections is a heated one. Proponents say that public financing has worked for presidential elections and will do so at the congressional level as well. They hold that using public funds to finance elections is fairer; less susceptible to corruption; and, in the long run, the only way to reduce the costs of elections, especially given the Supreme Court ruling that only those who accept public financing can be restricted in the amounts they spend.

Opponents of public financing argue from a number of different points. Some argue that any public financing bill would automatically protect all incumbents because challengers must spend huge sums of money to overcome the advantages of incumbency. This argument is especially important in the House, as its incumbents are rarely defeated.

Others argue that public financing would be impossible to implement for congressional and senatorial elections because congressional districts (and even states) are so different that the amounts of money needed to campaign effectively in different districts would vary substantially. They are further concerned about candidates who receive public funds when no serious challenger exists.

Figure 5.7 Cost of Public Financing of the 2004 Presidential Election

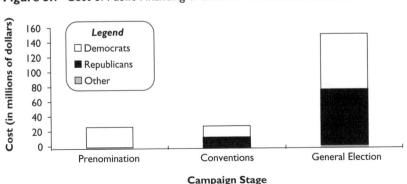

Source: Federal Election Commmission.

Still others argue that public funding would create opposition to popular incumbents where none currently exists. Some incumbents are forthright enough to state that they will not support public financing, because it is against their best interest. Others hedge this argument, stating that it is not in the interest of the nation to force people to pay for unwanted campaigns. Challengers and those eager to support competitive elections see this as an advantage of public financing because it encourages competition. But the level of public funding must be sufficient so that challengers can run credible campaigns. There is significant disagreement about what that level of funding is—and whether it is the same from district to district for House elections.

There are other points to consider as well. Should people be forced to pay for the campaigns of candidates they oppose? Can fair competition ever be imposed through law? Is there anything wrong with the current situation, and if not, why change it?

It should also be noted that twenty-four states have some form of public financing for political parties and some state offices; fifteen of those states fund candidates at some level (Common Cause). Some states allocate public funds to the political parties; other states allocate public funds directly to candidates for office; and some states, to both. State experiences vary widely in the amounts of money involved, in their methods of dispensing the funds, and in assessing the ways in which public financing has worked. The different public financing programs have provided interesting laboratories for those interested in public policy formation (for more information see www.commoncause.org).

Certainly public financing in some form has proven popular at the state level, and many would like to see public financing expand to additional states and even to all federal elections. Skeptics, however, wonder where the money will come from. If the goal is to have citizens voluntarily contribute the money through the tax system, the experience at the federal level is not promising. At its height in 1978, the tax form checkoff was only chosen by 29 percent of population. Since the mid-1990s the figure has hovered at slightly over 10 percent (Patterson 2006). Citizens might vote for public funding at the polling place, but they do not seem to do so on their tax forms. It is even more doubtful that they would support politicians who raise taxes to fund campaigns. The dilemma continues, although at least at the presidential level it may have been rendered irrelevant. Neither George W. Bush nor Steve Forbes took advantage of public financing at they pursued the 2000 Republican presidential nomination. Bush did the same thing in 2004, and was joined by Howard Dean and John Kerry on the Democratic side. In all instances, these candidates did very well raising money privately, and were subject to many fewer restrictions on what they could do with their money. However, both Bush (in 2000 and 2004) and Kerry did use public money to run their general election campaigns once they had secured the nomination. The 2008 party nominees most likely will not follow suit. Most experts widely believe that the 2008 presidential election will be the first since public financing was made available in 1976 where neither major party candidate will accept any public money. In all likelihood both the Republican and Democratic nominees will privately finance both their primary and general election campaigns (see Malbin 2006).

IV. POLITICIANS VIEW CAMPAIGN FINANCE POST-BCRA

Any elected official at the federal level, and increasingly at the state and sometimes even local level, will tell you that winning an election costs money, in many cases, a lot of money. This has been the case for some time now, and seemingly becomes more set in stone with every election cycle. But the campaign finance environment did change in some important ways with the passage of BCRA in 2002. At this point, with two full election cycles having taken place under the new rules, what can we say about how these reforms have affected campaign finance in the United States?

We can start by stating definitively that parties still play crucial roles in financing the campaigns of candidates for public office, especially at the federal level. Many experts warned that BCRA's ban on soft money for the national parties would significantly weaken the parties (see Polsby 2002 for an example). This has not happened. In fact, it appears that BCRA may have even strengthened the parties' role in bankrolling campaigns. Even without access to soft money, parties are raising more and spending more money than ever before (Corrado et al. 2005; Corrado 2006b, 2006c, 2006d; Kolodny and Dwyer 2006). One way the parties (and candidates as well) have been able to make up for the loss of soft money has been by dramatically increasing the amount of hard money they raise from small donors, defined as gifts of $200 or less. The number and importance of these small donors has increased substantially since BCRA went into effect (Corrado 2006c, 2006d, Graf et al. 2006; Magleby 2006; Malbin and Cain 2007). One of the goals of those looking to ban soft money was to force the parties to broaden their base of donors, and attract more small gifts. It would appear that BCRA has been successful here.

One of the ways the parties have attracted this growing number of small donors is by using the Internet. The web is fast becoming an essential tool in political fund-raising as the parties and their candidates continue to raise more and more money online (Corrado et al. 2005; Vargas 2007). It was John McCain in his 2000 presidential campaign who first demonstrated the fund-raising potential of the Internet, and Howard Dean significantly furthered the use of the web as cash cow in his 2004 presidential campaign. And no one is sure yet where the ceiling is for online fund-raising. As we write this a number of 2008 presidential hopefuls are raising sizable amounts of money online.

We can also say that the soft money that can no longer go to the national parties has found a home in the ever-expanding number of 527 and 501(c) groups that are active in federal elections. For many, this development has been one of the more troubling results of BCRA, and one that is certain to attract attention in the coming years. But under the current rules, 527s and some 501(c)s are important players in the electoral process (Weissman and Hassan 2006; Weissman and Ryan 2007).

Another hope of at least some BCRA supporters was that the legislation would reduce the importance of television advertising and force campaigns to return their attention to classic grassroots mobilization and get-out-the-vote (GOTV) efforts. While the former certainly has not occurred (TV advertising remains as important and costly as ever—see Franz et al. 2006), the latter definitely has. Over the last three election cycles, both parties have paid substantial attention and devoted significant resources to the ground war. Part of this renewed focus certainly has to do with the closeness of recent elections, but some of the restrictions that BCRA put on how and when money could be spent on television and radio ads are also relevant here. There are no such limits on spending on personal contact, telephone contact, mail, or web activities. Old-school grassroots mobilization—sometimes with new-school technology—has taken on increased importance in recent elections (Edsall and Grimaldi 2004; Magleby 2006).

Perhaps the final thing we can say about campaign finance post-BCRA is that for all the legislation has done and may yet do, it has not reduced the money spent on campaigns one bit. Inevitably, the 2008 presidential campaign will be the most expensive election campaign in American history, and this is without taking into account the rumors that New York City's billionaire mayor Michael Bloomberg might be willing to spend up to $1 billion of his own money on a third-party run for the presidency (Hallow 2007). Spending continues to rise, and there is no end in sight. In many ways this reflects the truth of the earlier statement on money always finding its way into elections. No matter how the rules are changed, it is likely impossible (short of amending the constitution) to keep money out of campaigns.

WEBSITES

www.fec.gov: This official website of the Federal Election Committee provides statistics and data analysis as well as information on campaign finance laws and guidelines. All candidate, party, and PAC filings are available online.

www.fecinfo.com: The PoliticalMoneyLine website breaks down FEC statistics into user-friendly information.

www.brook.edu/campaignfinance: The Brookings Institution's website aims to provide unbiased information on campaign-finance-related matters.

www.cfinst.org: The Campaign Finance Institute offers nonpartisan information, research, and policy recommendations regarding campaign finance.

www.opensecrets.org: This website for the Center for Responsive Politics, an advocacy group for campaign finance reform, tracks money in ongoing campaigns.

www.followthemoney.org: On this website the National Institute on Money in State Politics provides information to journalists, scholars, and citizens interested in campaign finance practices at the state level.

CHAPTER 6

State and Local Nominations

State Senator Rodney Ellis steps out of a meeting of Texas Democratic Senators in Albuquerque, New Mexico. In August 2003, the eleven Democrats in the Texas Senate—the "Texas Eleven"—crossed state lines into New Mexico in protest over the Republican-led congressional redistricting plan spearheaded by then-U.S. House Majority Leader and fellow Texan Tom DeLay. The Democrats were "holed up" in a hotel in Albuquerque to prevent lawmakers in Austin from achieving a quorum. Despite the best efforts of the Texas Democrats, the Republicans were eventually able to enact their redistricting plan. The Republicans' actions were ultimately upheld by the Supreme Court of the United States in a decision with potentially national implications.

W e elect one president of the United States. We elect 50 governors, 100 senators, 435 members of the House, 1,971 state senators, 5,441 state representatives, and literally thousands and thousands of mayors, city council members, county commissioners, judges of probate, clerks of court, water district commissioners, and other public officeholders. Although federal officeholders get most of the attention, state and local officials often make decisions that have more direct impact on our daily lives. It seems appropriate, therefore, to begin this discussion of nominations and elections with them.

We know a great deal about how presidents receive their party's nomination (chapter 8). For months on end we follow the candidate parade through the fields of Iowa and the snows of New Hampshire all the way to the national party **conventions** in late summer. We complain that the process is too long. But when the Democrats did not have an array of candidates on the hustings in the summer of 1991, political pundits wondered whether Democratic politicians were conceding the 1992 election. Of course, Democratic contenders did emerge before the winter **caucuses** and primaries; far from conceding the November election, the Democrats won it. As the year 2000 campaign approached, journalists seemed to worry that the Democratic nomination would go by default to Vice President Gore; then they trumpeted the chances of former New Jersey senator Bill Bradley. They speculated about the presence of a number of well-known candidates with large bankrolls vying for the Republican nomination (Shribman 1999). In 2007, speculation is focused on the presidential nomination contests in both parties, with no clear favorite in either party. By comparison, few stories appeared about possible nominating contests for governor, senator, U.S. representative, or state legislator.

The presidential nominating process is complex, but much of it is public and open. Anyone wanting to read about the presidential nomination contest for 2008 need only look at the front page of any major newspaper on almost any day from the spring of 2007 (if not earlier) through the conventions in summer of 2008. Readers interested in more analytical views can find magazine articles, journal essays, and a large number of books dedicated to the subject (e.g., Aldrich 1980; Buell and Sigelman 1991; Kessel 1992; Lengle and Shafer 1980; Orren and Polsby 1987; Polsby and Wildavsky 2000, 2004; Wayne 2000, 2004).

Still, what do we know about the ways in which the thousands of other elected public officials are nominated for office by their parties? Back in the days of party bosses and dominating political machines, Boss Tweed of Tammany Hall is reported to have claimed, "I don't care who does the electing, just so I do the nominating." When machines dominated American politics, one of the

CONVENTIONS

Meetings of party members to endorse or nominate candidates for office, adopt platforms, and establish party rules.

CAUCUSES

Local meetings of party members, often used to elect delegates to conventions; used to endorse or nominate candidates in some states.

most important aspects of their control was the ability to control political nominations. We know that machines no longer dominate our politics as they once did. But what has replaced them?

Ask yourself! What do you know about how your U.S. senators were nominated? Your representative in Congress? Your state representative (do you honestly even know who he or she is)? What about county commissioners? How do all these people receive their party's nod for the nomination? Where do they come from?

These questions are particularly important when we realize the significance of the decisions that many of these individuals make. They are also important when we remember that many holders of more prestigious positions have used lower offices as stepping-stones for higher, more visible public office. This chapter will look at the decision to run for office and how potential candidates view the political scene. It will then turn to the question of how state and local officials gain party nomination and thus access to the general election ballot. Finally, it will move to an examination of the politics of the nomination process.

I. POLITICAL CONTEXT AND POLITICIANS' DECISIONS TO RUN

Politicians often think in terms of career progression. Is this the time for me to move up? How one defines "up" in this context is not absolute, but some definitions are pretty well accepted. For instance, a seat in the House of Representatives is generally considered a step up from a seat in a state legislature. A seat in the U.S. Senate is a "promotion" from serving as a member of the House (Schlesinger 1966).[1]

How do politicians decide to risk seeking a higher office? Jacobson and Kernell (1983) have posited an important theory—that politicians weigh the value of the office for which they strive and the probability of winning against the risk involved in giving up the office they currently hold. Politicians weigh the public climate in determining whether or not they will run. The decisions made by **qualified candidates** (who for these purposes are defined as politicians already holding some elective office) about whether or not they will seek a higher office are very important (Maisel et al. 1999; Stone and Maisel 2003; Stone et al. 2004; Maestas et al. 2006).

One reason for incumbent reelection success, at least in House elections, is that qualified candidates, in the aggregate, decide that the political climate is not right for moving up. When candidates with the greatest likelihood of winning decide not to run, challengers of lesser quality frequently step up to fill the void (Abra-

QUALIFIED CANDIDATES

Candidates who are thought by experts to have the characteristics necessary to run a strong campaign.

mowitz 1981; Hinckley 1981; Jacobson 1981; Maisel and Cooper 1981).

Looking more deeply into the reasoning of individual candidates, Jacobson and Kernell review two competing sets of theories that are used to explain electoral results. One body of speculation stresses the impact of economic conditions on electoral outcome (most of this scholarship examines congressional campaigns because of the availability of data, but the conclusions can be generalized to other offices (Bloom and Price 1975; Kramer 1971; Tufte 1975, 1978). The other theory uses survey data to explain electoral results in terms of individual voter attitudes (Arsenau and Wolfinger 1973; Fiorina 1978, 1981; Kernell 1977; Kinder and Kiewiet 1979; Mann and Wolfinger 1980). In either case the operating assumption is that voters cast their votes for *some* offices based on their overall assessment of the political and economic situation in which they find themselves. Politicians certainly think in these terms, but they also think in terms of specific salient issues of the day, such as our military commitments in Iraq or the issue of immigration.

In making the decision about whether or not to run for higher office, politicians are very concerned about what else is going on at the time of that election. Potential candidates are aware that voters give most attention to the top of the ballot. In a presidential election year, electoral hopefuls must consider whether their party's presidential candidate is going to help or hurt them. Will they derive support from a popular candidate? Will they be able to separate themselves from an unpopular candidate? If it is an off-year election, one in which no presidential election is being held, what other elections are most likely to capture the voter interest (e.g., senator, governor)? Politicians are very concerned about insulating themselves from the fate of other politicians or taking advantage of the coattails of a popular candidate higher on the ballot.

Changes in state election laws demonstrate this trend. In the early 1950s, the governors of nineteen states were elected for two-year terms. As states have changed their two-year terms to four-year terms, virtually every one of them has decided to hold gubernatorial elections in nonpresidential election years, thus insulating state elections from national politics. Rhode Island was the most recent state to make this switch, leaving only New England neighbors New Hampshire and Vermont with governors serving two-year terms (see table 6.1). Candidates for office below governor are aware of this trend as well. In considering a run for the state senate, for instance, a political candidate is confronted with one political environment if the upcoming election year is a presidential election year in which there is also a gubernatorial and senatorial race in his or her state; that potential candidate faces a very different set of variables if it is

Table 6.1   Electoral Context of Gubernatorial Elections

	1951–1952	2007–2008
TWO-YEAR TERMS	19	2
FOUR-YEAR TERMS		
Elected with president	10	9
Elected in off year	14	34
Elected in odd year	5	5

Source: National Governors Association (www.nga.org).

a nonpresidential election year that features neither a senatorial nor a gubernatorial election.

Table 6.2 lists the various electoral environments that might confront potential candidates. These combinations are all possible because U.S. senators serve six-year terms and thus no senatorial seat is contested in any state in one out of three national elections (barring vacancies due to death, resignation, etc.).

These factors were not so important when all politicians for all offices campaigned in the same way. However, they become critically important when different types of campaigns are run for different offices. In this context politicians must evaluate how their careers are going to be affected, not only by the political climate of the times but also by their ability to campaign using different techniques.

II. COMMON VIEWS OF THE NOMINATING PROCESS

What is the conventional wisdom? How are nominations decided? One view is that a couple of guys (almost never women) sit in a smoke-filled back room and choose the nominee. They then anoint that person and dissuade other potential candidates. Who are these

Table 6.2   Offices at the Top of the Ballot

Offices	Number of States			
	2000	2002	2004	2006
P-G-S-R	9	—	8	—
P-G-R	2	—	3	—
P-S-R	25	—	26	—
P-R	14	—	13	—
G-S-R	—	24	—	22
G-R	—	12	—	17
S-R	—	10	—	8
R	—	4	—	3

Source: Compiled by the authors. 2006 data from the *Washington Post.*
Note: P = president; G = governor; S = senator; R = representative

people? They are the party leaders, not necessarily in a formal sense, but the people who make the party go. These kingmakers have at least three things in common: party loyalty, intense interest, and money.

Another view is that the nominating process represents the purest form of democracy. Candidates can present themselves to the people, and the people will choose. A person does not have to be tapped by anyone. Potential candidates declare their availability, and people choose from among those presenting themselves. No one is in control, and everyone is eligible.

A few hold yet a third view: the chairman of the local party organization meets with an official committee, and together they decide on the party nominees. This view suggests that the process is more open than the smoke-filled room but falls short of the purest democratic ideals. Curiously, all three views are accurate—in part.

As with so much in American politics, what one sees depends on where one looks. In the case of nominating politics, the factors to be examined include the locality and the office sought. How nominations are decided varies from state to state and from locality to locality within a given state. The process is also quite different for the most visible and hotly contested offices—governor, senator, congressman, state legislator in some states but not others, mayor in some cities but not others (one can see the variations by locality at work)—than it is for offices that are seemingly less important.

In the sections that follow, we will sort out some of the more important questions about our nominating process. Keeping in mind the differences among localities and offices, we will look at the variety of nominating systems, exploring the question of who participates in the process—as candidates and as voters—and the more general question of how an ideal nominating system for the American political system might be structured.

III. DEVELOPMENT OF THE DIRECT PRIMARY SYSTEM

The most common means of nomination in American politics today is the direct primary election. In a direct primary system, the citizens of a particular area who are permitted to vote in a party's primary election vote directly to choose the party's nominee. The direct primary is distinguished from any indirect means of nominating, the most notable example being the presidential nomination, which is decided upon in conventions by **delegates**—some chosen directly and some indirectly in caucuses, but delegates in either case.

DELEGATES

Party members who are elected to a convention to participate in doing the party's business.

Direct primaries were not always the most common means used for nominating in the American system. Chapter 2 traced the history of party systems in the United States and made the point that in the second party system the nominating system moved away from a legislative caucus system to a convention system; this move was seen as a democratizing reform. The further movement from the convention system to the direct primary system had two distinct impetuses.

A. Primaries as a Response to One-Party Domination

At the end of the Reconstruction era, following the Civil War, the Democratic party totally dominated Southern politics. The Republican party for all intents and purposes did not exist in the South. In an era of one-party politics, when nominations were determined only by party officials, no mass participatory democracy existed. Citizens were given the opportunity to vote for only one candidate nominated by an elite faction of the dominant party. The primary election was first used, in the Democratic party, as a means to extend some modicum of democracy into this heavily one-party system.

B. Primaries as an Item on the Progressive Agenda

For more philosophical and ideological reasons, the members of the Progressive party included the direct primary election as part of their party platform. Shortly after the turn of the century, primaries began to appear as part of the nominating process in states with Progressive party influence. Seen as a response to boss domination of the political process in many Northern cities and states, primaries spread rapidly; the direct primary was used to nominate candidates for at least some offices in all but a few states by the end of the second Wilson administration in 1920.

In contrast to the ebb and flow of the use of primaries in the presidential nominating process (see chapter 8), direct primaries as a means for choosing nominees for state and local office have had a more steady history of development and expansion. Few states that adopted direct primaries as the means for nominating candidates in the early years of this century have taken the nominating process out of the hands of the voter, even for short periods of time; today direct primaries are used as the means for nominating candidates for some offices in all states and for *all* offices in thirty-eight states, plus the District of Columbia.

It should be noted, however, that nominating conventions have not totally disappeared. A number of Southern states give party committees the option of having a primary or of nominating by convention. The Republican party in a number of states has used the convention option, since until recently the party nod was not valued enough to merit a primary contest (of course that justification has disappeared with the reemergence of the Republicans as viable contenders throughout the region).

In Virginia, both parties have used the means of nominating candidates as an instrument in guaranteeing the desired result. For instance, convention nominations have permitted "backroom" politicians to achieve geographically and racially balanced tickets. The Virginia law is indeed unique, allowing incumbent officeholders to choose the means through which they will be renominated. In 1996, Republican senator John Warner opted for a primary, rather than a convention, as was his right under the commonwealth's law. His opponent for the nomination, the much more conservative James C. Miller III, challenged the law but conceded after the commonwealth's attorney general ruled that the procedure should stand. Miller wanted a convention because his ideological supporters were more likely to dominate a convention than a primary, with its broader participation. Warner favored a primary, following the same logic but approaching it from a different perspective. This example shows how important the means of nominating can be in a particular case.[2] While nominating conventions are a rarer and rarer phenomenon, they remain among the most interesting aspects of politics for those able to participate in or observe them.

IV. VARIETIES OF PRIMARIES

Stating that the direct primary is the means used for nominating party candidates in most states is not the same as saying that an identical system is used in all states. Some state laws mandate that a primary will be used and set very specific rules for that primary. In other states the decision on how to nominate is left to the parties. Therefore, it is not really uncommon for a primary to be used in one party and not in the other; if a primary is used, the rules for that primary may be determined by the party, not by state law. As noted previously, in some states the primary is used for all offices; in others it is used for only the more prominent offices (see Epstein 1989, 1991).

A systematic examination of the state and local nominating process is difficult because of the variety of systems in place. The complexity is less troublesome for candidates for statewide office, however, than it is for candidates for the presidency for one very simple reason: whatever particular system is in place for a particular political party in any one state is the only system relevant for state and local candidates for that party's nomination. Candidates for the presidency and their strategists, by comparison, have to be aware of fifty separate and often different systems, which are given different weights both in the nominating process and in media coverage of that process (see chapter 8). Still, each candidate must be acutely aware of how his or her state's system works.

States using the direct primary differ in many ways. They differ in terms of who is eligible to vote in a particular primary, of whether parties can endorse—in an official way—in advance of the primary, of how such endorsements are made if they are permitted, and of whether a **plurality** or a **majority** is necessary to nominate. The variations among primary systems are explored in the following sections. (For further discussion of this material, see Jewell 1984; Jewell and Olson 1988; Jewell and Morehouse 2001.)

A. Who May Run

One would think that the question of who may run in a party's primary would be a simple one to answer. Democrats run in Democratic party primaries; Republicans run in Republican party primaries. If only it were that simple!

I. Party Membership and Petition Requirements

The most prevalent rules call for candidates to run in their party's primary if they meet certain fairly simple criteria. First, the prospective candidate must be a registered member of the political party whose nomination he or she seeks (or in some other way demonstrate allegiance to that party in states that do not have official party registration).

Second, candidates must meet some sort of "test" to gain access to the ballot. Often this test involves gathering a certain number of signatures on a petition, but the ease or difficulty candidates have in meeting this requirement is significant. The number of signatures necessary and who is eligible to sign are important factors. If the number is small and if anyone can sign any number of petitions, then access to the ballot is quite simple. For example, in Tennessee only twenty-five signatures are required for most offices. By contrast, if the number of signatures required is large and if some restrictions apply as to who may sign petitions, then access to the ballot is more restricted. In Maine, candidates must acquire a fairly large number of signatures (a percentage of those voting in the last election); only registered party members may sign petitions; and they must sign a petition that contains only the names of party members from the signers' hometown.

In states with easier requirements many more candidates frequently qualify for the primary ballot for the same office. Is this good or bad? "Good," one hears often, "because anyone can run." But what if one candidate appeals to a relatively small, but extremely dedicated, group of voters whose views are on the fringe of public opinion, and election law requires only a plurality to nomi-

PLURALITY

Receiving more votes than any other candidate.

MAJORITY

Receiving one-half plus at least one of the votes cast.

nate?[3] Would the extremist nominee represent the voters' opinions in these districts? Is democracy served?

If access to the ballot is relatively restricted, as when a large number of signatures is required, or when only certain voters can sign petitions (e.g., statewide office in New York requires signatures by 15,000, or 5 percent of, enrolled party registrants, of whom not less than 100, or 5 percent, whichever is less, must live in each of one-half of the state's congressional districts), then fields of candidates tend to be smaller. All the candidates tend to be serious contenders, but groups out of the mainstream have less influence. Moreover, lesser-known individuals are prevented from testing their views in primary campaigns. Is democracy better served?

2. The Role of Parties

Access to the ballot can be even more restricted in some states than it is in those states that require a large number of signatures from a select group of voters. Six states—Colorado, Connecticut, New Mexico, New York, North Dakota, and Utah—have party conventions that play a significant role in determining access to the primary ballot for at least some offices. The philosophy behind systems like these is that, while the party voters in the state should have the final say, those most involved with party affairs, that is, those willing to go through the process of selection as delegate to a convention, should have increased influence.

How do these systems work? In Utah, the top two finishers at the state convention are on the party's statewide primary ballot, unless one candidate wins 60 percent of the convention votes; in that case, he or she is declared the nominee without a primary. In Colorado, New Mexico, and New York anyone who receives a specified percentage of the votes at the state convention has his or her name placed on the primary ballot. In Delaware, North Dakota, and Rhode Island, the person endorsed at the state convention—or by local committees for local offices—automatically appears on the primary ballot, but others must follow the petition route.[4] **Preprimary conventions** tend to be used in competitive two-party states with relatively strong party systems.

Connecticut, which was the last state to adopt a direct primary, implemented a system called a **challenge primary** in 1955. New York State adopted a similar system, for statewide offices only, in 1967. In the challenge primary system, the convention nominee is automatically the party nominee unless he or she is challenged in a primary after the convention is over. The assumption that there has to be a primary election is reversed. Losers at the convention with a certain percentage of the delegate votes have an automatic right to challenge, but they have no obligation to do so. In Connecticut in

PREPRIMARY CONVENTIONS

Party conventions held in advance of a primary to endorse one of the candidates running in that primary.

CHALLENGE PRIMARY

Primary election held after a nominating convention at which the convention's nominee can be challenged by a defeated candidate who must meet some specified criteria.

2002, only one party endorsee for Congress was challenged in a primary. Those endorsed for governor were not challenged in either party, nor were most of the candidates for lesser statewide offices. However, the Connecticut law was challenged in court and found to be unduly restrictive. Today the challenge primary remains in place, but a new provision allows candidates to bypass the convention and go directly to a primary if they submit a petition signed by at least 2 percent of their fellow partisans in the state or district in which the candidate is running.

While party endorsement has official status in the eight states mentioned above and a "semiofficial" status in Massachusetts (where failure to obtain the minimum threshhold or even do well at the convention often leads candidates to drop out), in a number of other states (e.g., Illinois, Minnesota, and Wisconsin) party organization or other party groups endorse candidates and work for their election without that action having any official role in the primary process.

The quintessential example of this would be Cook County, Illinois, the Greater Chicago area. For many years the vaunted Cook County Democratic party machine was headed by "Hizzonah" the mayor, Richard J. Daley; today his son, also the mayor of the city, carries on that tradition, though to a much lesser degree. The first Mayor Daley's organization stands as the last of the classic urban machines (see Rakove 1975; Royko 1971; Tolchin and Tolchin 1971). When Daley endorsed a candidate, that candidate became a prohibitive favorite. The machine worked the streets. Few challenged the machine because a challenge was fruitless. However, reform clubs did eventually emerge in Chicago (Wilson 1962) to present an alternative to Daley. These clubs served as a base for political activists interested in a different type of politics in Chicago. Although they stood outside of the formal political system, these clubs helped structure politics in Chicago. They did not play an official role, but their influence was important nonetheless.

Can one generalize about how effective party endorsements have been? As is so often the case, the experience among the states varies widely. The ultimate statement of success is if the endorsed candidate is not challenged in a primary. In Connecticut the assumption has been that a challenge will not be held. Between 1956 and 2006 only 26 of 312 individuals nominated for the House of Representatives by congressional district conventions were forced to face challenge primaries. Challenges are more common for statewide offices, in both Connecticut and New York, two states with similar systems, but there the similarity ends. In Connecticut, the party endorsement is considered an important advantage, although Democratic candidates try to avoid being labeled as the candidate of the legendary party bosses.[5] In New York, to the contrary, many

Democratic candidates view the official party endorsement as the kiss of death.

Malcolm Jewell and Sarah Morehouse (2001, 109) have examined the history of party endorsements. Between 1960 and 1998, 57 percent of the endorsees in states with legal endorsement procedures were nominated without opposition; this figure compares with 26 percent in those states with informal endorsement procedures. Jewell and Morehouse note that some state parties are most effective, with endorsees rarely challenged (e.g., Connecticut and Delaware, Democrats and Republicans; Colorado, Democrats; New York, Republicans); other states' endorsees are sometimes challenged but rarely upset (e.g., North Dakota, Republicans; Utah, Democrats); and still other states' endorsees are usually challenged and sometimes upset (e.g., New York, Democrats; Utah, Republicans). The history of the party organizations helps explain this difference, as it does many such discrepancies among states.

3. Louisiana: An Exception

NONPARTISAN PRIMARY

Primary used only in Louisiana in which all of the candidates appear on one primary ballot and any candidate who polls a majority of the votes is declared the winner without competition in the general election.

Membership or allegiance to a political party has already been cited as one criterion for access to the ballot in almost all cases. Even that most basic rule has exceptions. In 1978 the State of Louisiana adopted a system called a **nonpartisan primary**, which sounds like a contradiction in terms. A primary, except when party labels are not used, is supposed to determine who a party's nominee will be. How can a "nonpartisan" primary determine a partisan nominee? In fact, Louisiana has changed the entire system around, and Republicans and Democrats appear on the same ballot. All candidates run on one ballot in the "primary" election, now held on the day of the general election in other states. Each citizen is allowed one vote. If any one candidate receives a majority of the votes cast, that person is declared elected. If no one receives a majority on the first ballot, a runoff election is held between the top two finishers, regardless of their party affiliation.

Obviously, party officials do not favor this system. Further, its implications for state politics are not at all clear. When Mississippi tried to adopt a similar system, the changes in the state's election laws were challenged under the provisions of the Voting Rights Act, and the proposed system was disallowed as being disadvantageous to black voters. One problem with assessing the impact of a change as fundamental as this one is that politicians need a certain amount of time to adjust to a new political reality.

In Louisiana the effect of the new system has been to protect incumbents. Of the ninety-two incumbents running for reelection to Congress from the time the system began through the 2006 election, eight-nine have been "reelected" at the primary election. Of the remaining three incumbents, all won the general election, with two of the three victories coming by substantial margins. Most of the **open seats** were also uncontested beyond the primary.

4. Cross-Filing: Another Exception to Party Allegiance

Cross-filing represents another exception to the rule that party nominees must be registered in or hold allegiance to the party whose nomination they seek. In New York State, a candidate may be the nominee of more than one party if the state party committee of the second party accepts that nominee. New York State has a tradition of strong third, fourth, and even fifth parties. While these parties do not win many offices on their own, they frequently hold the balance of power between the Democrats and Republicans.

One tactic used by the Conservative and Workers parties in New York is to endorse the candidate of one of the major parties. What is the strategy involved? What are the trade-offs? The minor parties know that they will not win office; however, they are very concerned about certain issues. Similarly, the candidates of the major parties know that minor party candidates will not win. However, they are concerned that these minor party candidates might draw votes from them and swing the election to their opponents. Thus the major party candidates are willing to accept certain issue positions of the minor parties in exchange for that party's nomination and another line—literally another listing—on the ballot and some advertising and organizational support from the minor party's followers.

Frequently the trade-offs are not as explicit as the scenario just outlined. However, the implicit understandings are clear. If a major party candidate in office offends a minor party, then the minor party will run its own candidate in the next election. Officeholders do not like to offend constituents who have that potential. Thus in congressional elections in New York in 2006, Democrats ran candidates in all twenty-nine districts; the Workers party endorsed twenty-six of these nominees. Eleven Democratic nominees also ran on an Independent line. Republicans ran candidates in twenty-five of the races; eighteen of those candidates had Conservative party backing and eight Republicans also ran on Independent lines. In 1996, one nominee, Michael P. Forbes (First Congressional District), was endorsed by five parties: Republican, Conservative, Independence, Right-to-Life, and the Property Tax Cut.

Because of the way in which the New York State law is written, a candidate may even be nominated by both the Republican and Democratic parties. All that candidates need is the approval of the appropriate party committees to run in their respective primaries. For example, Mayor Koch of New York City ran in the Republican as well as the Democratic party primary in 1981 and won both party

OPEN SEATS

Seats in which no incumbent is running for reelection.

CROSS-FILING

Nominating system that permits a candidate to seek the nomination of more than one political party.

nominations by enormous margins. Consequently, he faced only minor party opposition in the general election. When Republicans nominated Edward Adams to run against incumbent Democratic congressman Charles Rangel in 1996, Adams's candidacy broke a pattern in which, more often than not since his first election in 1970, Rangel's name appeared as the endorsee of both major parties. This kind of situation demonstrates the problems inherent in cross-filing. Popular incumbents can sew up the entire electoral process and eliminate any semblance of a competitive democratic election.

B. Who May Vote

Just as states and localities differ in who may run in partisan primaries, so too do they differ in who may vote in primary elections.

I. Closed, Open, and Blanket Primaries

CLOSED PRIMARIES

Primaries in which only voters enrolled in a particular party may participate.

Thirty-nine states use some form of **closed primaries**. Closed primaries are defined as primary elections in which only those who declare allegiance to a party in advance may vote. However, the manner in which citizens are required to declare allegiance is not uniform across states.

At one extreme are states that require citizens to enroll in a political party in a formal sense. Official lists of Democrats and Republicans (and members of minor parties) are maintained by the state. These lists are public information, and thus a registered voter's party affiliation can be found out by others.

States that fall into this category often have specific requirements for changing party affiliation from one party to another or from independent status to party membership. Six of these states prohibit voters from changing party identification after the date on which candidates must declare themselves for the upcoming primaries.[6] These and the other states that maintain formal party enrollment lists also differ in the length of time between when a voter must declare party affiliation and when the primary is held, time spans varying from approximately one year to primary day changes in Iowa, Ohio, Wyoming, and other states.[7] Further, we find variations in how state law applies to those previously unenrolled in a party—normally referred to as independents—as opposed to those who want to switch from one party to another.

At the other extreme among closed primary states are those in which citizens openly choose one party or another on primary day, but those choices are not formally recorded by state officials. In some states (e.g., Missouri) this choice involves nothing more than publicly selecting one party's ballot as the voter enters the voting booth. In other states (e.g., Illinois) it involves a public declaration of intent to support a party's nominees or of having supported them in the past. Records are not kept of these choices. Only those actually present at the time that the choice was made are aware of the partisan preference of the voter.[8]

A thin line separates closed primaries of this latter type from open primaries. In open primaries, those voting in the primary elections are not required to publicly choose one party or the other. Rather, they enter the voting booth and choose the party ballot on which they will vote in secret. Obviously, once again, no records are kept of these decisions.[9]

Washington and Alaska used a unique derivative of the **open primary,** called the **blanket primary,** for some time; California moved to this system beginning with the 1998 election, as a result of a citizen initiative.[10] The blanket primary ballot carries the theory of the open primary to its logical extreme. Citizens voting in a blanket primary can cast votes in the Republican primary for one office, the Democratic primary for a second and third office, the Republican primary for a fourth office, and so on. The only restriction is that they can only vote in one party's primary for each office. The winners of the primary are those affiliated with each party who draw the largest number of votes.

This type of primary is extremely detrimental to party organizations. A coalition of parties—the Democrats, Republicans, Libertarians, and Peace and Freedom party members—challenged the California law, claiming it violated their associational rights. This challenge was upheld, and the blanket primary was ruled unconstitutional in June 2000, in the case of *California Democratic Party v. Jones,* 530 U.S. 567. Washington pursued legal action to keep its blanket primary, but that state was ultimately denied in federal court as well (*Washington State Grange et al. v. Washington State Democratic Party,* 541 U.S. 957).

The rules governing state elections are generally specified in state law; those wanting to change the rules of the political game have to work through state legislatures (or in the case of California through a ballot initiative to impose the blanket primary and court action to eliminate it) to alter state law. However, in 1984, the Republican party of Connecticut challenged that norm, not for philosophical reasons but for purely political ones. For some time Connecticut has been a heavily Democratic state and has had a closed primary system. Independents, a large group in Connecticut, have not been permitted to participate in primaries. By allowing them to vote in Republican primaries, Republicans hoped to attract the allegiance of independents to Republican nominees. After unsuccessful attempts at changing state law, the state's Republican party challenged the closed primary law in the courts. In the case of *Tashjian v. Republican Party of Connecticut,* 479 U.S. 208 (1986),

OPEN PRIMARY

Primary in which each voter may choose one party's ballot or the other.

BLANKET PRIMARY

Primary election in which all names appear on one ballot, and each voter selects one candidate running for each race on the ballot; the candidates with the highest totals in each party qualify for the general election ballot.

the Supreme Court ruled that the Connecticut law failed to meet the First Amendment guarantee of freedom of association because it did not permit the Republican party to define its own membership. The law was thus ruled unconstitutional. Connecticut Republicans—and potentially other state parties—were permitted to define their own membership and have an open primary if they decided to do so (Epstein 1989; Maisel et al. 1990). The Court relied on the same reasoning as that of *California Democratic Party v. Jones*; the long-term implications of this remain unclear (Maisel and Bibby 2002). A conflict also exists between this precedent and the recent Connecticut case that ruled the state's means of achieving the primary ballot to be unduly restrictive.

Political scientists use the traditional categories—closed, open, or blanket—to distinguish among primaries. In truth, it is more meaningful to view the variety of primaries as constituting a continuum from those in which party affiliation is the most fixed to those in which it is the least fixed. These distinctions have important consequences, whether they are viewed in terms of the theory of how politics should work or in the most practical political terms, as the Connecticut example demonstrates (Carr and Scott 1984; Finkel and Scarrow 1985).

2. Theoretical Arguments regarding Primary Voter Eligibility

The question of who should be eligible to vote in a primary revolves around the theoretical debate over what role the political party should play in the electoral process. The more restrictive primary eligibility is, the greater the role that party plays.

If, on the one hand, the major political parties are viewed as distinct, as presenting differing philosophies from among which citizens should choose, then it follows that adherents of those philosophies should make the choice of who will carry their banner into the general election. Thus only those to whom the party is important and truly meaningful should decide the party's nominee. If, on the other hand, one feels that the parties are really two sides of the same philosophical coin, then the primary is merely a way to pare down the field of eligible candidates. In this case, voters should be able to support the candidate most closely linked with their views.

This assertion is an extension of the argument about who should be able to run. Those who favor stronger parties want more of a role for party organization in determining who can seek a party's nomination; they favor systems that call for preprimary conventions and endorsements of one sort or another. In contrast, those who view party as an unnecessary intermediary between citizens and their elected servants want anyone to be able to run; they favor no role for party regulars in determining primary contestants.

3. Pragmatic Considerations regarding Primary Voter Eligibility

The student of politics who looks at the systems in place in various states and then talks to politicians in those states is led to conclude that politicians generally feel that their state systems reflect the needs of their constituents quite well. Few call for change. Many, indeed, cannot understand why other states do not do things the way they do. Two conclusions follow from this observation: either state politicians have been incredibly astute in creating systems that correctly match the political culture of their state, or politicians are happy with a system they understand.

Very few politicians in the United States have expert knowledge of campaign laws beyond the boundary of the state in which they are working. Why should they? What they need to know is how to play the game in which they are currently involved. They approve of the rules that are in effect because they know how to play by and win under those rules. Reformers, conversely, tend to be those who are out of power, who have not managed to win with the rules in place. The efforts by Connecticut Republicans to open their primary stands as a case in point. More recently, both Democratic and Republican party leaders in California opposed the ballot initiative that led to the creation of that state's blanket primary; they led the court battle that overturned that initiative once it had passed. They knew how to play the political game under the old rules and were uncertain of the consequences of the new.

4. Strategic Consequences of Different Primary Rules

These comments about the views of working politicians point to the practical consequences of various primary systems. Regardless of how one evaluates a system, the details of that system determine how one will run a campaign.

Imagine the most basic problem facing a candidate in a primary: To whom must I appeal for votes? In a closed primary state, with recorded party enrollment, the constituency seems easy to determine. Candidates and their campaign managers simply obtain lists of potential voters, that is, lists of people who are enrolled in their party and are eligible to vote in their party's primary.

In a closed primary state without permanent enrollment, the only comparably available lists are rosters of those who voted in the party's last primary (if the party had workers collecting such a list at the poll in that last primary). Even where such lists are kept, they tend to be highly inaccurate, ignoring those who think of themselves as members of the party but did not vote in the last primary. And the lists have no way of accounting for new voters.

But those lists, as flawed as they are, are preferable to the lists that can be obtained in open primary states. The only official lists that candidates can collect in open primary states are lists of eligible voters and/or lists of those who did in fact vote in the last primary. Candidates have no way of knowing with certainty which ballot a particular voter marked.

Think of the consequences of these differences for campaign strategy. In the first case direct mail and/or door-to-door campaigning is possible and efficient. Campaigns can reach those who are eligible to vote. In the second case these techniques of contacting voters are much less efficient, though still possible. In the open primary scenario, if one does not want to contact all voters, it is necessary to rely on much less accurate methods of deciding on whom to concentrate, for example, targeting areas in which a high percentage of the voters seem to favor one's own party.

5. Crossover Voting

CROSSOVER VOTING

Practice of members of one political party voting in the other party's primary, presumably to nominate the weaker candidate.

Politicians are also very concerned about **crossover voting**; let us assume that a Democratic incumbent is running unopposed for his party's nomination in an open primary state. We further assume that there is a contested primary in the Republican party. No legal barrier prevents supporters of the Democratic incumbent from crossing over to the Republican primary and voting for the weaker of the two contestants in that primary, in an effort to nominate a weaker opponent for their favorite in the general election.

Hypothetically this scenario could happen easily enough. In practice, however, it is difficult to document instances of this kind of perfidy. First, an orchestrated campaign to nominate the weaker candidate in the other party would require a sophistication unknown to most American political organizations. Raiding the other party's primary could not happen without such orchestration because the American electorate is not sufficiently involved in the nuances of electoral politics to employ such a strategy.

Second, voters who participate in primaries most often are concerned about more than one race. Even if an incumbent lacked a Democratic opponent in one race, still other offices would very likely feature contested Democratic primaries. In open primary states, Democrats crossing over to influence the outcome of a Republican primary would forfeit their rights to vote in these Democratic races, which presumably would be of more interest to them than other Republican primaries (some of which might even be uncontested). However, it is important to note that this "problem" does not exist for voters in blanket primary states. For instance, in California in 1998, the Democratic gubernatorial primary featured three strong candidates thought to have realistic chances for the nomination, Lieutenant Governor Gray Davis, Congresswoman Jane Harman, and former airline executive Al Checchi; the Republican nomination was conceded to Attorney General Dan Lundgren. Citizens who were strong Republicans could vote for one of the Democratic candidates—either their personal favorite or the one they thought would fare least well against Lundgren—and still vote in other contests in which Republicans were competing against one another.[11]

Third, the American voting public believes in fair play. It is very unlikely that enough voters would engage in this type of behavior to have an impact on any particular election. A political party that openly promoted such a strategy would run the risk of a moral backlash and thus lose more than it hoped to gain.

The fact that behavior of this type is unlikely to happen does not diminish the paranoia of politicians who worry about perfidy. Be that as it may, the true importance of voter eligibility rules relates much more closely to impact on election strategy than it does to the loyalty of the voters to the party in whose primary they participate.

C. Who Wins

1. Plurality Rule

Despite the lip service given to our "basic principle" of **majority rule**, majority rule is the exception in American politics. Most elections in America—and certainly most primaries—are determined by **plurality rule**. That is, the person with the most votes (not necessarily 50 percent plus at least one) in the primary wins the nomination.

Plurality rule has important consequences, particularly in elections with large fields of candidates. For example, in 2002, in California's Thirty-ninth Congressional District, Linda Sanchez emerged victorious in a six-person primary, with only about one-third of the vote. The sister of Loretta Sanchez, already a House member from California, Linda Sanchez beat Hector de la Torre by only 4 percent of the vote, in a very negative campaign, to win the nomination in a new district, drawn to favor the Democrats. Many of the two-thirds of the Democrats who did not vote for Sanchez might well have been voting against her, preferring any of the other candidates, because her campaign drew a great deal of criticism. But the system does not recognize intensity of feeling behind a vote, nor does it allow voters to indicate a second choice. Sanchez won a narrow plurality and went on to win her seat in the 108th Congress.

2. Variations from Plurality Rule: Runoff Primaries

Plurality rule is not in effect in every electoral jurisdiction. The major exception to the plurality winner rule is in the South, where nine states require a majority vote to receive the nomination; if no

MAJORITY RULE

An election system in which a candidate must receive one-half plus at least one of the votes cast in order to be declared the victor.

PLURALITY RULE

An election system in which a candidate receiving a plurality of the votes is declared the winner.

candidate wins a majority, a runoff or second primary is held. During his 1984 presidential campaign, Jesse Jackson drew a great deal of attention to runoff primaries, claiming that they discriminated against black candidates.

Runoff primaries were instituted in the South shortly after the beginning of this century, during a period of Democratic dominance in the South. Party officials viewed the **runoff primary** as a means of guaranteeing continued party strength, of assuring that the party was united behind one candidate and could thwart any independent challengers.

Analysts differ over whether racial discrimination was a factor in creating runoff primaries. On the one hand, blacks were denied the right to vote through a whole series of Jim Crow laws and rules at this time; adding one more discriminatory obstacle to effective black participation would seem superfluous. On the other hand, almost all legislative action dealing with elections at the time was undertaken with an awareness of racial implications. It is difficult to imagine that those involved in establishing runoff primaries were incognizant of the fact that they could have an effect on the chances of blacks seeking office.

But let us put historical arguments aside and examine the effect that runoff primaries in fact have. Jesse Jackson's attention was directed to this issue by H. M. "Mickey" Michaux Jr., an African American who lost the Democratic party nomination in North Carolina's Second Congressional District in 1982 after having captured 44 percent of the vote against two white candidates in the first primary. In the runoff Michaux polled 46 percent and lost to Tim Valentine, who went on to capture the seat. Using the Michaux contest as an example, some have claimed that blacks and other minorities would have ten to fifteen more seats in the Congress if the runoff primary were eliminated. This claim is based on two premises. First is the assumption that whites vote for whites and blacks for blacks in primary elections. Thus in districts with large black populations but not black majorities, blacks can lead in the first primary but lose when the whites all vote together in the runoff. The second premise is that voters stick to party lines in the general election, regardless of the candidates. These two assumptions seem to be at odds with each other and with recent experience.

If the first assumption is accurate, then runoff primaries are discriminatory against minority groups only in those districts in which they constitute a large bloc but not a majority. In districts in which blacks or Hispanics constitute a majority, the runoff primary would seem to work in their favor. For instance, African American candidates can be helped in districts with African American majorities.[12] In neither case is it evident that the system is discriminatory, only that one electoral system out of several possible ones has been chosen.

Turning to the second assumption, would it help minority candidates to get the nomination if they were then to lose in the general election? If voters follow racial lines, wouldn't it be logical for white voters to desert the Democratic party in the general election and support white Republicans? As the South becomes more and more a two-party region, wouldn't the elimination of the runoff primary accelerate the growth of the Republicans and lead to victories by even fewer "progressive" candidates than is now the case (see Bullock and Johnson 1992; Lamis 1984; Stanley 1985)?

These issues have all come into play in more recent congressional elections in so-called **majority minority districts**, congressional districts in which a majority of the voters are members of a racial minority. A number of majority minority districts were drawn after the 1990 census in order to increase the likelihood of black representation from Southern states.

It is important to put this discussion into context, in this case the constitutionally mandated context of **redistricting** and **reapportionment**. Article 1, Section 2, of the Constitution says in part:

> Representatives shall be apportioned among the several States which may be included within this Union, according to their respective Numbers. . . . The actual Enumeration shall be made within three Years after the First Meeting of the Congress of the United States, and within every subsequent Term of ten Years, in such Manner as they shall by law direct.

Congress has ordered a census every ten years, as the Constitution stipulates. Actually, two processes are involved. Not only is the number of seats that each state is allocated in the House determined by the census (the process of reapportionment), but the boundaries of individual districts and of state legislative districts are also redrawn to reflect shifting population patterns (the process of legislative redistricting).

During much of the nation's history, the process of reapportionment was politically painless because Congress continuously voted to expand the size of the House of Representatives. Thus the House grew from its original 106 members to nearly 400 by 1900. In 1910, however, in part at least because of the size of the chamber, Congress voted to set the size of the House permanently at 435. Since that time this number has only been exceeded for the brief period of time between the admission of Alaska and Hawaii into the Union and the reapportionment following the 1960 census. As a result of the cap on the size of the House and of shifting population panels, reapportionment has become costly to some states after every cen-

MAJORITY MINORITY DISTRICTS

Districts in which a majority of the citizens or voters are members of a minority race.

REDISTRICTING

The redrawing of the lines for legislative districts that takes place after decennial censuses.

REAPPORTIONMENT

The reallocation of districts among the states after each census so that each state receives at least one representative in Congress and all other state delegation sizes reflect population.

sus, with some delegations shrinking to accommodate growth in others. Since the 1930 reapportionment, a formula has been used, which removes the politics from reapportioning decisions.

The same cannot be said for decisions regarding legislative redistricting once apportionment is known. Traditionally, district lines have been drawn to accomplish political purposes. **Gerrymandering** is a revered part of American political folklore. Gerrymandering involves drawing districts, often of strange shapes, to suit the drawer's particular purposes.

In the last forty years, judicial intervention has led to less blatant gerrymandering when district lines are redrawn. In *Colegrove v. Green*, 328 U.S. 549 (1946), the Supreme Court refused to intervene in a challenge that claimed that congressional districts in Illinois needed to be redrawn because they were of unusual size. The Court held that legislative apportionment was a political question and thus not justiciable. However, in *Baker v. Carr*, 369 U.S. 186 (1962), the Court decided that redistricting was not beyond its purview in all circumstances. The Court was responding to extreme cases of malapportionment; in Tennessee, for instance, state legislative district lines had not been redrawn in sixty years, despite massive population shifts that resulted in some legislators representing a hundred times as many citizens as others.

In subsequent rulings (especially *Gray v. Sanders*, 372 U.S. 368 [1963] and *Wesberry v. Sanders*, 376 U.S. 1 [1964]) the Court established a criterion of **one person–one vote** against which apportionment schemes would be measured (Butler and Cain 1991; Cain 1984; Cain and Butler 1991; Grofman 1990; Lowenstein l991b; Polsby 1971; Schuck 1987).

However, judicial regulation does not mean that reapportionment has become apolitical. Political scientists have spent a good deal of time and effort looking at the extent to which redistricting favors incumbents and impacts subsequent electoral chances (Abramowitz et al. 2006; Basehart and Comer 1991; Born 1985; Cain 1985; Forgette and Platt 2005; Forgette and Winkle 2006; Galderisi 2005; Gelman and King 1990; Glazer, Grofman, and Robbins 1987; King 1989; Niemi and Jackson 1991). The conclusions reached by these scholars convincingly demonstrate that redistricting does not affect one political party adversely and does not make the ultimate difference in reelection bids by incumbents. Yet there can be no doubt that politicians work very hard to be certain that district boundaries are redrawn in a way that meets the judicial criteria but also brings as much benefit as possible to those drawing the lines, and most (but not all) research indicates that incumbents do tend to benefit when politicians rather than the courts or an independent commission draw the district lines. The Court has moved cau-

GERRY-MANDERING

Drawing district lines to achieve certain political purposes.

ONE PERSON-ONE VOTE

Principle that reapportionment and redistricting must be accomplished in such a manner that each district has, to the extent possible, the same population and, therefore, each person's vote counts equally.

INCUMBENT ADVANTAGE

Advantages that current officeholders have in seeking reelection by virtue of the fact that they hold the office.

tiously into the area of reviewing partisan gerrymandering. In *Davis v. Bandemer*, 478 U.S. 109 (1986), the Court seemed to rule that partisan gerrymandering could be a violation of the equal protection clause of the Constitution but that the case before the Court did not appear sufficiently egregious to merit judicial intervention (Cain and Butler 1991, 32; Lowenstein 1991b; Schuck 1987).

Similarly, the Court has stepped gingerly into the area of racial vote dilution by gerrymandering. In these cases the Court was applying the criteria of the Voting Rights Act of 1965 as well as that of the equal protection clause of the Constitution. The Court has wavered between examining whether the *intent* of the redistricting was to dilute racial minorities' power (the standard before the 1982 amendments to the Voting Rights Act) and examining the *effect* of the redistricting, regardless of the intent. Since the Court laid out criteria for examination of unconstitutional dilution of racial minorities' voting power in *Thornburg v. Gingles*, 478 U.S. 30 (1986), state legislatures have looked very carefully at whether the courts might respond that any proposed legislative redistricting plan violated minority rights according to these criteria (Perry 1991).

The 1990 census seems to have caused particular problems. First, a number of states (and large cities) claimed that the census takers undercounted up to five million citizens, most of them minorities living in urban centers. If the Bush administration altered the census count in line with any of the proposed estimates of error, various states stood to gain or lose seats. In fact, the census count was accepted as originally tabulated (though various states challenged that count in court to no avail).

This controversy carried over to the 2000 census. The Census Bureau wanted to conduct the entire census using sampling techniques that they claimed would increase the accuracy of the count. Others disagreed, arguing that the Constitution called for an actual enumeration. The Supreme Court sided with the latter position and ruled that the 2000 census must be conducted using an actual count of citizens, for reapportionment, and using a sampling technique, for determining the population for other purposes—for example, the allocation of funds to states for various program-redistricting purposes. The decision did present the Census Bureau with the option of using a sampling technique for determining the population for other purposes, for example, the allocation of federal funds among the states.

The stakes were so high that lawmakers in state capitals, those charged with redrawing district lines, went about their work very slowly after each of the last two censuses. As late as August 1991, for example, less than seven months before the first congressional primaries, only seven of the forty-three states with more than one congressional district had drawn their district lines. *Congressional Quarterly*'s commentary on the politics of redistricting in 1991 used phrases like "both parties have enough power to gum up the redistricting process" in Louisiana, or Illinois Democrats "were ready to throw the politically sensitive chore to the courts" (Donovan 1991, 1776).

After the 2000 census some state legislatures were so slow in drawing districts that the parties could not recruit quality candidates to challenge incumbents, because the shape of the district was unknown. The 2002 congressional elections were even less competitive than usual because potential candidates deferred from running until it was too late to mount effective campaigns.

The chore was indeed sensitive and led to some bizarre results. Legislatures are charged with the task of redistricting, sometimes with governors having veto powers and sometimes not,[13] but the actual task of suggesting district lines falls to computer experts who have programmed their machines to draw maps according to certain agreed-upon criteria. Generally the computers have been fed information on the racial composition of each voting precinct, past electoral behavior, and party registration if available. With that information, the computers can draw districts to meet virtually any agreed-upon criteria (Monmonier 2001).

In North Carolina in 1991, the criteria included protecting the seat of each incumbent to the extent possible and creating a new black majority seat and a new Republican seat, as well as meeting the Court's criteria of populations in each district being as equal as possible (called for in the case of *Karcher v. Daggett*, 462 U.S. 725 [1983]). The resulting districts surely do not meet the criteria of being "compact and contiguous." In fact, the Second District looked remarkably like the very district after which gerrymandering was named.

That district, as well as other "majority minority districts," was challenged in the courts and found not to meet the judicial tests (see *Shaw v. Reno*, 509 U.S. 630 [1993]; *Miller v. Johnson*, 515 U.S. 900 [1995]; *Bush v. Vera*, 517 U.S. 952 [1996], *Abrams v. Johnson*, 117 S. Ct. 125 [1997], among other cases). The controversy lasted throughout the last decade of the twentieth century, with district lines in question right up to the elections of 1998. Some of these districts were challenged on the grounds that racial gerrymandering violated the equal protection clause of the Constitution. In other cases, the challenge was that the Voting Rights Act was being violated. In the cases in which the Supreme Court ruled the districts unacceptable, new lines were drawn, at times by courts because legislators were unable to reach agreement. In a number of cases the new plans created districts in which the black member of Congress who had been elected when the lines were first drawn now represented a district without a minority racial majority. And none of the incumbents so affected lost reelection bids.

The history of political fighting over the drawing of district lines in the United States is as old as the nation itself. However, battles over redistricting have likely entered a new phase as a result of recent events in Texas. In 2002 the Democrats and Republicans each controlled one house in the Texas legislature. But after the 2002 elections, the GOP held both houses, as well as the governorship. With newfound unified Republican control in his state, then U.S. House majority leader Tom DeLay came up with a plan. Under his leadership, the Republican governor and state legislators proposed drawing new Congressional districts in order to better take advantage of Texas's Republican majority, and to increase the number of Republicans in Texas's U.S. House delegation. Democrats were furious, saying that the redistricting that had been recently completed after the 2000 census (by a federal court) had to stay in effect until after the 2010 census. DeLay and Texas Republicans disagreed, and went forward with their plan.

The battle made for some very dramatic moments: First some House Democrats left Austin and crossed state lines into Oklahoma in order to prevent a quorum (the minimum number of members present in order for business to be conducted), and then some Senate Democrats did the same, choosing to head for New Mexico. But the GOP redistricting plan eventually passed, and was signed into law by Texas governor Rick Perry. Legal challenges immediately ensued, and the case eventually made it all the way to the Supreme Court. In a 2006 decision that surprised many observers, the Court ruled that the actions of the Texas Republicans were constitutional (*League of Latin American Citizens v. Perry*, 2006, 548 U.S.). Seven of the justices agreed that redrawing district lines for nothing more than partisan advantage was an acceptable practice. The Court also ruled that the Constitution only required states to redraw their election district boundaries once every ten years; it did not, the Court stated, prevent them from doing so more often if they chose to do so.

It is too early to know the full implications of this decision, but in all likelihood other states will try to follow in Texas's footsteps, and partisan redistricting battles will break out across the nation. As Congressman Rahm Emanuel (D-Ill.) said, "Every redistricting is a partisan political exercise, but this is to put it at a level we've never seen. That's the gift that the Supreme Court and Tom DeLay have given us" (Lane and Balz 2006, A1).

All of this is to say that redistricting may be a more exact art than it once was, and certain democratic principles must be considered. But in essence the act of redistricting today is just as political as it ever has been, if not more so. The stakes are high because the House of Representatives is so closely divided, and citizens do not seem to be well served by the machinations of their elected officials' seeking to gain or retain partisan advantage.

This discussion of alternatives to plurality rule—and drawing district lines as another means to affect outcomes—should be viewed from a broader perspective. Thus it could be argued that plurality elections are not a good mechanism for guaranteeing popular rule in the case of factionalized electorates. Both Iowa and South Dakota have provisions in their electoral laws that require a primary winner to receive at least 35 percent of the vote in order to be declared the nominee. If no candidate reaches that threshold in South Dakota, runoffs are held for the offices of governor, state senator, and state representative. For the other offices, as well as for all offices in Iowa, a state party convention meets to select the candidates.[14] Clearly, there are many distinctions among primaries. In the next section we will explore the ways in which the various primary systems shape the politics of the nominating process.

V. THE POLITICS OF NOMINATIONS

A. Uncontested Nominations

Recall the offices listed at the beginning of this chapter. How much competition is there for clerk of courts? For water district commissioner? Compare the interest in those offices with interest in U.S. senator or governor. Or compare the attractiveness of serving as a state legislator in Vermont, where the legislature sits for four to five months a year, there are 180 state legislators, and the annual salary in 2005 was $12,705, with the attractiveness of the same position in California, where serving in the state legislature is a full-time job and the base annual salary is $110,880 (Penchoff 2007).

These kinds of comparisons point to the difficulty in analyzing nominations at the state and local level. The situation varies from office to office and from state to state. Obviously, more seats are contested for the more prestigious offices. Nominations for the U.S. Senate are uncontested much less frequently than nominations for state assembly. Further, state offices in larger states are more likely to attract contested primaries than are similar offices in smaller states.[15] This thesis follows quite naturally from the fact that such offices are more likely to be full-time, highly paid, and prestigious in larger states.

Other conclusions about contested primaries have been found to be similarly predictable. Incumbents win nominations without the necessity of contesting a primary more often than do challengers. Contested primaries are more likely to occur for open seats, those without an incumbent running, particularly in the party of the retiring incumbent, than for seats in which incumbents are running. Primaries are always more likely to occur in dominant parties than in minority parties. One basic rule seems to apply: the more valuable the party nomination, the greater the likelihood of a contested primary. The value of the party nomination, in turn, relates to two variables—the prestige of the office sought and the likelihood that the party's nomination will result in victory in the general election.

How do candidates get nominated in situations in which there is no contested primary? No systematic research has addressed this question, and most students of politics would answer it based on their personal experiences. The process is seemingly simple. Each candidate follows whatever procedure is necessary to have his or her name placed on the primary ballot. No one else does so. The nomination then goes by default. But that analysis begs the question: Who is the individual who presents himself or herself as a candidate?

One working assumption is that incumbents normally want to

succeed themselves, even for the less-prestigious offices. Few people desire or are more qualified to serve as water district commissioner than the individual holding that position; more often than
not that individual will continue to hold the position.

If no incumbent is running, or if the incumbent is in the other
party, then party officials have the responsibility of finding candidates for office.[16] For prestigious offices this search is not difficult.
For less-prestigious offices, however, the role of the party official is
very different. In these cases, officials must identify potential candidates for office and convince them to run.

Party organization traditionally controlled access to the ballot.
This power was lost for prestigious offices with the advent of the
direct primary and with increased popular participation. However,
the party's role persists for lesser offices. Some party organizations
are quite successful in playing this role; others much less so.

In congressional elections in the 1980s, one major party or the
other did not field a candidate for the House of Representatives in
about one district in six. The parties each did somewhat better in
the early 1990s, but in 2006 111 House races offered no real choice
to voters. On the other hand, all eligible gubernatorial and all save
for a very few Senate seats have been contested by both parties in
all recent elections. Success in structuring the contest for office is
one measure of success of the ways that party organizations do their
jobs.

B. Contested Nominations

When most analysts talk about primary elections, they are actually
concerned with *contested* primary elections, a subgroup that is a
minority of all primaries.[17] Contested primaries receive the most
attention because they provide campaign watchers with something
to watch. They also play an important role in weeding out contestants for office. Any discussion of contested primaries needs to emphasize differences by office and locale.

1. Incumbent Advantage

Political observers have again been able to make some generalizations about these contested primaries. The first generalization is
that incumbents win a high proportion of the primaries in which
they are challenged (recall figures 3.6, 3.7, and 3.8). Second, incumbent victories are increasingly the rule for lesser or more local offices. Incumbents have an advantage over opponents in that they
have already built up support within the party (Fenno 1978). Unless
they have acted in a way that undercuts their own support, they are
rarely beaten in a primary.

Incumbent losers are so few that analysts can almost always explain each case as idiosyncratic. Only two U.S. senators have lost primaries since 1980. In 1992, Democratic senator Alan Dixon of Illinois lost to Carol Moseley-Braun, who went on to become the first black woman elected to the Senate. Dixon had no declared opposition until he cast one of the few Democratic votes in favor of confirming Clarence Thomas to the Supreme Court. That vote enraged feminists and liberals and led directly to Moseley-Braun's candidacy. A third candidate in the race attacked Dixon as representing an unresponsive Congress removed from the people and dominated by special interests. There is even some evidence that Dixon was tainted by the House bank scandal, not because he himself was involved in any way but more as guilt by association. The combination of these factors led to his unexpected defeat.

In 1996 Sheila Frahm (R-Kans.) was appointed to fill the Senate seat vacated when Majority Leader Robert Dole resigned to run for the presidency full-time. Frahm was beaten in a primary a few short months later; she had had little time to make a legislative or constituent service record for herself before she had to face the voters. Similarly, she had been unable to build a campaign organization or a financial war chest to hold off primary challenger Sam Brownback, a House member at the time.

Similarly, House defeats are few and far between, but the 1992 election stands as an exception as nineteen House members lost primaries. However, this exception can also be explained. As noted previously, every ten years House districts change. After reapportionment, which determines the size of each state's delegation, the states must undergo redistricting to account for added or subtracted seats when their relative population has changed significantly or to account for population shifts within the state, so that each district contains the same population, meeting the constitutional mandate of one person–one vote. As a result of reapportionment and redistricting, many House members faced substantially new districts in 1992; in fact, in a number of cases two members found themselves representing the same district. When this decennial phenomenon was combined with the House bank scandal, in which many members were tainted as frequent abusers of a congressional privilege, the result was an unusual number of incumbents defeated in primaries. Even in that record year, however, 95 percent of the incumbents seeking renomination to the House were chosen by their party.[18]

The experience of 1998 is more common. Only one House incumbent, first-term California Republican Jay C. Kim, lost a primary election. Kim had been convicted of campaign fund-raising abuses in his 1996 election and was forbidden by the courts from returning to his district to campaign for renomination. In 2006 only two House members lost primary elections; the most notable was Cynthia McKinney, who also lost a primary election in 2002. McKinney often seemed to attract attention for things other than her legislative performance, such as her altercation with a Capitol police officer in spring 2006.

2. Contests without Incumbents

What about races in which incumbents are not running? Conclusions in these cases are more tentative. Winners tend to be those who make best use of the resources necessary to win elections. Although the important resources may vary from race to race, key among them is name recognition. The candidate who is much more widely known than his or her opponent(s) is likely to win. How is such recognition achieved?

Some candidates have it when they enter a race. For instance, a state senator who is entering a congressional primary may have represented many of those who are eligible to vote in the primary, an eventuality likely to happen in large states with sizable state senate districts, such as California or Florida. Such a candidate would start with an advantage over a political neophyte.

Or a candidate may be known for other reasons. Two representatives to Congress from Oklahoma in the 1990s, Republicans Steve Largent and J. C. Watts, were extremely well known as football players before they became politicians. Athletes, actors, media personalities, astronauts, and others with similar fame start with a name recognition advantage when they enter the political arena (Canon 1990). They may even become president.

Yet many candidates do not start with these advantages, particularly candidates for local offices. How do they get known? Three key ingredients contribute to successful campaigns—candidate effort, campaign organization, and money. In smaller districts candidates themselves may well be able to "get around," to shake hands with a large portion of the potential electorate. Candidates for sheriff go into high schools and talk about drug and alcohol abuse. Candidates for state representative address the Rotary or the Lions in town after town. All candidates for these offices attend party meetings and picnics, town meetings, PTA meetings—any meeting at which they can be certain that they will be introduced. They go door-to-door and discuss mutual concerns with voters. Candidate after candidate will attest that there is no better campaign technique than actually talking to a potential voter. If a district is small enough and if a candidate can commit enough time, nothing is more effective.

Many districts (e.g., congressional districts, state senatorial districts) are too large, however, for a candidate to have any chance of meeting even a sizable proportion of the potential electorate.

Although candidates campaign personally to the extent possible, they must rely on an organization to extend their outreach. A candidate's campaign organization uses various techniques to serve as surrogates for personal contact. Workers go door-to-door seeking support for their candidate. They carry literature that describes the candidate's views and qualifications. They telephone potential voters and discuss why they favor the candidate for whom they are working. They put up lawn signs, hand out buttons and bumper stickers, speak on behalf of their candidate at functions she or he cannot attend. An effective organization reaches out for candidates further than they themselves can reach. Such organizations frequently give the appearance of widespread support, which itself leads to more recognition and eventually to more support.

Campaign organizations in smaller districts are frequently volunteer organizations. Friends and neighbors of a candidate will offer their assistance. But even these campaigns need some money in order to function effectively. Buttons and bumper stickers, brochures and balloons—all the paraphernalia of a campaign—cost money. As the size of the district expands, the cost of the campaign rises. In many of today's primaries money has become a sine qua non for success. As recently as 1974, when the FEC began keeping these records, only ten congressional campaigns spent $200,000 in the primary and general elections combined, and expenditures of $100,000 in primaries were all but unknown. A decade later a congressional primary that was won on a budget of $100,000 has been cited as evidence that "a congressional seat can still be won without spending a fortune" (*Congressional Quarterly Weekly Report* 1984, 1119). Since 2000, particularly in open seats in the party with a partisan electoral advantage, spending a million dollars in a primary is no longer considered unusual (see chapter 5).

The precise combination of candidate effort, organization, and money that is necessary to win any primary is difficult to ascertain with precision. The ability to arrive at that combination is what separates winners from losers. Still, the imprecision of the calculation is why politics remains more art than science. If one formula worked for every campaign, then every campaign manager and every candidate would do the same thing. Candidates and their campaign managers start with a certain amount of knowledge of how to campaign (most of it gained from experience), with an understanding of their districts, their candidacies, etc., and with a certain amount of resources. Working with these, they devise tactics and strategies. They play on their strengths and try to exploit the weaknesses of their opponents. They play down their weaknesses and try to undercut the strengths of their opponents. Politicians seek to find the formula that will give them the largest number of votes in the primary while doing the least harm to their chances in the general election, ultimately hoping to appear invincible and not worth challenging (Jacobson 1983). That, after all, is what the primary campaign is all about (Maisel 1982, 1986).

VI. POLITICIANS VIEW THE NOMINATING PROCESS

How do politicians view all of this? No surprises here: it all depends on their situation. The means through which a candidate achieves a party's nomination can either help or hurt that candidate's chances in the general election. The same route to nomination can have differing impact in different years. Contested primaries can be divisive or they can help winning candidates gain name recognition. Uncontested primaries can save candidate resources for a general election, but they can also leave a candidate virtually unknown when he or she runs against a well-established incumbent.

Politicians generally like to avoid hotly contested primaries. However, under certain circumstances, such as when a candidate is not well known and/or a candidate's organization has not been tested, "a little primary can be a good thing." Primaries can be seen as battles for the heart and soul of a party. Rather than look at individual experiences, some politicians view primaries from the "macro" level: What is happening to the party? Perhaps the 1998 Republican primaries as a whole are best viewed in this light.

In state after state, Republican primaries featured doctrinaire conservative Republicans against more mainstream office seekers. The argument of the more moderate candidates was that they could appeal to a wider range of voters in the general election and would thus be more likely to win in November. In the Illinois U.S. Senate primary to oppose Democrat Carol Moseley-Braun, for instance, candidate Loleta Didrickson claimed that she should be supported because "people know me," with reference to her statewide victory as comptroller. Her opponent, state senator Peter Fitzgerald, countered, "Stand up for your convictions. . . . Don't back down. Articulate our conservative principles as Ronald Reagan did, and you can win in Illinois" (Broder 1998, 3C).[19]

More conservative Republicans assert that their party has to stand on principles that many associate with Ronald Reagan. Battles along these lines were fought in statewide Republican primaries in states as widely separated as Alabama and Washington, Kansas and California.

The Republican party is divided in ways more typical of Democrats in years past. On the one hand, there is a split between moderates and ideological conservatives. On the other hand, avowed conservatives are not all of one mind. Some are deeply committed cultural or religious conservatives, many followers of the Christian

Coalition and related groups; others are more traditional economic conservatives. And intraparty primaries have been the scene of these battles as well. They cause real problems within the party. As former Representative Charles Bass (N.H.) has stated, "Their [Christian conservatives'] concerns and problems need to be taken very seriously and attended to with an open mind and open ears. . . . But there has to be a realization on their part that splitting from Republicans is basically the equivalent of political cannibalism. The result will be no winners at all" (Edsall and Connolly 1998, 14). In these cases politicians view the primaries as a means to power within the party, asserting the dominance of one wing over another. Or they view them as a chance that opportunities for victories will be lost in intraparty bickering.

How politicians view primaries depends very much on their political situation. They may view them from a personal point of view or from a broader perspective. But rarely do politicians lose sight of the ultimate goal—winning the general election in November.

WEBSITES

www.rollcall.com: *Roll Call* is one of two newspapers that specialize in covering Capitol Hill. During election years, its coverage of primaries and elections gives inside details.

www.hillnews.com: *The Hill* is the other Capitol Hill newspaper. Although somewhat less well known than *Roll Call*, *The Hill* provides excellent inside views.

www.cq.com: Congressional Quarterly Service's website follows congressional, senatorial, and presidential elections all the way through the process. Historical background is also available.

www.vote-smart.org: Project Vote Smart maintains an excellent website that highlights performance in office and election campaigns of candidates for president, governor, and other federal and state offices.

www.cnn.com/politics: This CNN political website does an excellent job of monitoring ongoing campaigns.

CHAPTER 7

State and Local Elections

California Governor Arnold Schwarzenegger campaigns for reelection in 2006. The Republican Schwarzenegger crushed his Democratic opponent in 2006 in a state where Democrat John Kerry easily defeated Republican President George W. Bush in 2004. While presidential elections routinely get the bulk of our attention, state and local elections are also important exercises in American representative democracy.

Compare the experiences of two politicians at the Washington County Fair. Thirty-one states in the Union have Washington counties. Their experiences could happen in any of them. The first politician is a candidate for the county board of supervisors. His district encompasses about one-fifteenth of the county. He has been active in county politics and county government for some years. The second candidate is a member of Congress running for U.S. senator. Washington County is one of over sixty counties in the state; she is from the other end of the state and has been in Washington County perhaps twice.

The candidate for board of supervisors has been looking forward to the county fair for months. The fair is one of the most important social events on his annual calendar. Since most of the people in the county attend the fair at least once during fair week, this is also an important political event. Our candidate is in charge of his party's voter registration booth at the fair, making sure that the decorations are in place and that the booth is always open. He sees to it that his signs are in evidence. He has set the entire week aside so that he can spend as much time at the fair as is possible. After all, what could be a better way to campaign among likely voters?

The Senate candidate will attend the fair too. She will put in one appearance, for about an hour, at a time that the local people tell her will be quite busy. She is not looking forward to the fair with eagerness. In fact, one day before, she is not even aware that she will be attending. Her staff arranged for the visit. Someone else will be certain that her signs are in place, that she is introduced to the right people, and, most importantly, that the media know she is there. She probably will attend every county fair in the state.

The board of supervisors candidate's fair visit is one of the truly major events of his entire campaign. He is filmed introducing the Senate candidate to some of the local folks; that scene is on television at eleven, and everyone sees it. He makes sure that someone takes candid pictures to use in his campaign flyer; maybe the photographer will even get the best one autographed.

The Senate candidate squeezed the visit to the fair into a busy day. She was up at dawn, shaking hands at a factory gate. She flew halfway across the state to have lunch with a union leader whose PAC had promised, but not delivered, financial support. After lunch she did a brief radio interview and stopped in at the local newspaper to talk with the editor. On the flight into Washington County Airport she conferred with her campaign manager and her pollster about the impact of her recent statements on dealing with the Iranian government. After the appearance at the fair, she was driven a hundred miles south for a fund-raising dinner. She did not even see the speech she was to give until an hour before the dinner. She did not know where she was staying that night but hoped she would have time to make some calls before she went to bed. One call would be to dictate some letters to her secretary; she would remember to tell her to write a note thanking that guy who introduced her at the fair. "Can't remember his name or where he's from. Find out from someone."

These two politicians seem to be engaged in the same enterprise—winning the votes of enough people to gain election. To win these votes, they must identify likely supporters and figure out some way to get those supporters to the polls. Both candidates have to set strategies aimed at accomplishing these goals. They must devise a strategy that involves identifying likely supporters and determining how they can structure a candidacy that will reach these voters. Each candidate must also come up with tactics aimed at carrying out the strategy.

But what do they do on a day-to-day basis? How do they structure an organization and what does that organization do? As the hypothetical scenario just depicted demonstrates, these two candidates on a day-to-day basis are actually involved in very different enterprises.

I. THE CONVENTIONAL WISDOM: OLD VERSUS NEW POLITICS

Under the old politics, campaigning was person-to-person and door-to-door; candidates were individuals representing the political parties that structured both the campaigns for office and the institutions of government. Supporters gave allegiance to the parties because they agreed with their stand on issues or because the parties' candidates would do certain things for voters if elected. The candidates of the party in control of government, as a group, were held accountable for the performance of the government.

New politics, however, is media and image oriented, not person-to-person. It is the politics of television and mass media (see chapter 10). Political party organization has been replaced in part by **candidate-centered** organization. Partisanship and party organization certainly still matter, but modern candidates, at least those for federal and in many cases state office, have assumed much more control over their own campaigns. Individual candidates call the shots, and they have much more (but not complete) freedom to do things without the consent of or that might be contrary to the interests of their party.

The reality of campaigning for office in the last decades of the twentieth century is, like so much else in this text, dependent on context. New politics has replaced old politics, in some areas, for

CANDIDATE-CENTERED

The focus of a campaign or an organization is on a particular candidate, not on a party or a group of candidates running together.

some offices. Often the change is more subtle than bold. Consider again the Washington County Fair. The Senate candidate was running a "new politics," candidate-centered campaign. She was concerned about the perception of *her* position on foreign policy, about raising money for *her* campaign from the union PAC, about the media coverage of *her* appearance at the Washington County Fair.

But the candidate for county supervisor was involved in an "old politics" campaign. The booth at the county fair was a party organization activity; it was part of a voter registration drive run by the party. All the party candidates together put up their posters. He took time out of his normal campaign pattern to "interact" with the senatorial campaign, to "use" it for party and personal publicity, but such events were not part of his overall tactics or strategy. He spent much of the week at the fair because that was where he could greet and talk to the greatest number of people. Even the Senate hopeful was engaging somewhat in "old politics" with her appearance at the fair. She was appearing as a partisan, at her party's booth, hoping to improve both her (primarily) and her fellow partisans (secondarily) election chances in a partisan context.

Old politics and new politics exist hand in hand in America today. New politics gets more attention because it is designed for getting attention—and because the bigger campaigns, for more visible offices, are often run using state-of-the-art new politics techniques. But that does not mean that all campaigning has changed. In this chapter we show how the two coexist—and how Tip O'Neill's famous adage that "all politics is local" continues to contain a good deal of truth.

II. THE NEW POLITICS: CAMPAIGNING IN A MEDIA AGE

Let us assume that a politician is making a fully rational decision about seeking office.[1] A politician considering stepping up to a larger constituency, a more prestigious office, will seek some information:

1. What voters am I going to need to appeal to?

2. What is the partisan distribution of voters within the new district?

3. What is the normal voting strength for candidates of my party in this district? Conversely, what are the strengths of the opposition candidate and his or her party?

4. What kinds of techniques will work in appealing to the voters whose support I will need?

This list could easily be expanded, but it serves as a starting point for the discussion of so-called new politics. Candidates for all offices ask the same questions about how to get the support of a plurality of all voters. They ask the same questions about their party and/or personal support and that of their opponents.

Based on an analysis of the district (often a very impressionistic analysis of the district), they decide if they can win the election they are considering. Rarely does victory seem certain. If victory were certain, others with similar qualifications would be seeking the office, thereby removing the apparent certainty because of a primary election. If a politician believes that victory in moving up to a higher elective office is indeed certain, the assumptions on which that prediction was made should be reexamined.

If preliminary analysis leads to a conclusion that victory is unlikely, experienced politicians, holding other elective office, generally stay put.[2] It is almost always easier to retain a seat than to move up the ladder (Jacobson and Kernell 1983, chap. 3).[3] If, however, they feel that victory is possible, that they have a legitimate chance, then they begin to analyze how to get the votes.

At this stage, they must look at party strength in detail, at the potential for a personal organization, and at the potential for a media campaign (Gibson et al. 1983, 1985). A candidate who is considering a campaign for Congress or for statewide office, or even for state senate in some of the larger states, must realize that he or she cannot personally reach all the voters. Also, voters no longer use party affiliation as the only cue in deciding how to vote. What techniques will be successful in convincing voters that they should cast their ballot for this particular candidate?

Let us now assume that the candidate, a nonincumbent, has decided to run.[4] Our candidate is either challenging an incumbent or running in an open seat. In either case the tactical problems are the same, though the difficulty of the task may be more exaggerated in the first instance (Maestas et al. 2006; Stone and Maisel 2003; Stone et al. 2004). The candidate has certain resources to utilize and certain tasks to accomplish. The problem is to match resources with tasks in the most effective way.

The first job is to identify likely supporters. The second is to ascertain what other voters are possible converts to the candidate's side. After identifying these two groups, the candidate must set a strategy for reaching both of these groups in a way that will solidify their support and increase the possibility that they will turn out to vote in droves. That might sound simple, but it certainly is not.

The most important resource that any candidate has is personal time (Mann and Wolfinger 1980). In some races nothing more is necessary. The candidate can identify supporters and potential supporters and go out and talk to them all. Many politicians started in that way for their first campaign. They are used to personal contact and have difficulty realizing that that will not work for all campaigns.

However, "pressing the flesh" of all the voters is not possible in a campaign for the House of Representatives, in which the average member represents almost seven hundred thousand people; nor is it possible in a campaign for statewide office, when over forty states have populations exceeding a million. Thus the candidate must learn how to use personal time in a new way, not merely contacting individual voters but maximizing the number of voters on whom that candidate can have an impact. Surrogates for the candidate are necessary in order to best use the results of time spent, essentially by "expanding" the amount of personal time (Morehouse and Jewell 2003).

A. The Role of Political Parties

Many candidates have experience in using party as a surrogate. Some voters will vote for a candidate because of party affiliation. For these voters, the candidate need only be certain that party affiliation is well known. Little candidate time is necessary to make this connection. Party, then, is one resource on which politicians are used to relying.

But political party is not a resource that is equally available to all candidates, nor is it a resource with which all candidates are equally comfortable. Candidates must weigh the impact of party in the new district. Is the organization efficient? Is the degree of partisan affiliation strong among voters? Is the candidate perceived to be in line with most of the others in the party? Or is the candidate an outsider to whom party people will not automatically flock? Is the candidate's party a majority or not? Is party strength spread equally throughout the district, or is it concentrated in some areas? What does the campaign do about the other areas? What is it that party organization can and cannot do in a particular campaign? How important is the campaign for the party organization? Are party activists likely to work hard for this campaign, or are they more concerned about another candidate or another race?

Merely posing these questions demonstrates how complex tactical campaign planning can be. Return for a moment to the question of what other offices are on the ballot. If John Doe is a candidate for Congress, in all likelihood his congressional district does not have the same boundaries that districts designed for other elective offices have. Most party organizations are structured around the county unit. In rural states, and in rural districts in some of the more urban states, congressional districts tend to encompass a large number of counties. For example, the First Congressional District in West Virginia includes all or part of twenty counties; the First Congressional District in California, in the northeastern corner of the state, includes all or part of seven counties. On the other hand, in urban areas many congressional districts fall into single counties. The five counties that compose New York City, as an extreme example, contain all or part of seventeen congressional districts; Harris County (Houston), Texas, contains all or part of eight congressional districts.

For all that, county organizations are often notoriously unconcerned about congressional politics. Members of Congress, and senators for that matter, deal with issues far away in Washington. Party people care more about issues closer to home because ultimately their concern involves those who can be counted on to do something tangible for them.

The local sheriff may have more immediate impact on these politicians than do their representatives in Washington. Consequently, local pols are more likely to work hard for local candidates. Similarly, they are more likely to work hard for candidates for executive office than they are for candidates for legislative office. All this theorizing assumes, of course, that the party organization exists and is capable of doing effective campaign work at all, an assumption that is far from clear in many areas of the country (Eldersveld 1982; Epstein 1986; for a more positive view of the role of county organizations, see Gibson 1991).

On the other hand, in recent years the national parties, particularly the Republican party, have become more active in local campaigns. Under the leadership of Bill Brock, who became Republican national chairman in 1977, and his successors, the Republicans have built a professional campaign organization at the national level. This organization concentrates on recruiting good candidates for office—at the congressional level and even at the level of state senator and state representative in some instances—training local candidates and their staffs in basic campaign techniques, and supplying certain technical support services, such as survey research, for their candidates. The Local Elections Division of the Republican National Committee has been active and effective for nearly twenty years. The Democrats, although behind the Republicans in this regard, have emulated their opponents' techniques. Current DNC chair Howard Dean is trying to bring his party up to speed here with his "50 state strategy," aiming to create a robust party organization at every precinct in the nation. Furthermore, both parties, again with the Republicans in the lead, are seeking means to persuade and mobilize voters, on a national or at least regional basis, to back party candidates (see Adamany 1984, 78–92; Bibby 1986, 1991; Herrnson 1988; Reichley 1985; Stewart 1991; and the discussion in chapter

2). Such "get out the vote" efforts have been critical in recent years given the closeness of the division between the two parties.

With all these caveats, what can be expected from party as a resource? First, in any geographic area some citizens will vote for a candidate because of party label. The number of die-hard party loyalists varies from area to area, but candidates should know the history of party loyalty in a district (Petrocik 2004). Similarly, some citizens use party label as a negative voting cue ("I could never vote for a Republican"). A candidate should know the history of antiparty voting as well (Sabato 1988, chap. 4).

Second, some jobs are better accomplished by party than by any other political organization. Some tasks benefit all candidates who are running under a party label. Thus candidates frequently call upon party organization to run voter registration drives, especially in areas or among groups that are likely to support candidates of that party. Party organizations can often be counted on to organize get-out-the-vote drives on election day, checking which of their regular supporters have voted and urging those who have not voted to do so. At the very least, the party can be counted on to monitor the polls on election day, to be certain that votes are not lost owing to error or fraud.

In 2002, President Bush made an intense effort for Republican candidates in the last weeks of the campaign. In fifteen states (almost every state with close elections for governor, House seats, or Senate seats), Bush campaigned hard to turn the election into a referendum on his national security policies in the wake of September 11 and to energize the Republican base. According to Bill Cobey, Republican party chair in North Carolina (where Elizabeth Dole beat President Clinton's former chief of staff Erskine Bowles for the Senate seat vacated by Strom Thurmond), "Bush was critical. Without his help, we couldn't have raised the kind of money we had for getting out the vote" (Purdum and Rosenbaum 2002, B4). The Democrats had been more successful in energizing their electorate in the 1998 and 2000 elections but could not compete with the sitting president on the campaign stump in 2002.

In sum, party is a resource that candidates have to be aware of but must also beware of. One cannot expect too much from an organization that might not be that strong and almost certainly will have at least some interests that differ from those of a single candidate. But candidates must use each resource for all that it has to offer, and party organizations often have much to offer.

B. The Role of Organized Groups

Organized groups often work hard in a particular candidate's campaign. Group involvement in political campaigns was discussed in chapter 4. From a candidate's perspective, questions involving organized groups are like those that must be asked of political parties. Which groups can provide active support? How can they help reach out to supporters or potential supporters? How effective are they going to be at that task? How concerned are they going to be about supporting this candidate as opposed to other candidates?

Groups can be very effective surrogates for candidates. The techniques that groups use in the political arena have already been noted (chapter 4). All of the techniques that attempt to influence the voting behavior of group members are important for candidates because the group replaces the candidate as the prime contact to the voter. Groups attempt to assure that the supporter remains a supporter and actually votes and that the potential supporter comes over to the candidate's side.

However, group support does not come automatically to a candidate. Our hypothetical candidate must expend blocks of time to garner group support and more time to assure that group support stays firm and is mobilized in the most effective way. Furthermore, candidates must recognize that groups have multiple interests that extend beyond any one campaign, and that, by definition, these groups are engaged in activities other than politics. Thus group activity can help in a campaign, but it too is a limited resource.[5]

Even more to the point, candidates must recognize that the very same groups that are most likely to generate a good deal of support for a candidacy from their followers are the ones that also alienate other voters. A candidate who is not firmly committed to the views of a particularly controversial group might view that group's support as something of a mixed blessing. For many years Democratic candidates worried whether vocal support for very liberal groups hurt their chances; of course, repudiating that support would have a deleterious impact as well. In recent campaigns, the Republicans have asked the same questions about vocal advocacy by culturally and religiously conservative groups.

In a special election in California in March 1998, the Family Research Council, then headed by the extremely conservative and extremely combative Gary Bauer, campaigned heavily for GOP candidate Tom Bordonaro. After he lost that election, a National Republican Congressional Committee poll showed a severe backlash against the campaigning and a perception that Bordonaro was an extremist as a result. Bordonaro is an extremely conservative candidate who shares the views of cultural conservatives like Bauer, but the focal support of those groups might well have hurt and not helped his chances for reelection (Edsall and Connolly 1998, 13). This example, which garnered a great deal of national attention, has had less-publicized parallels in almost every election.

Like political parties, special interest groups can be very effective at convincing their members to turn out to vote, when voting for a particular candidate is clearly perceived as in the members' interest.

C. Media Politics

The discussion to this point has purposefully avoided the major surrogate for personal contact by a candidate, media campaigning. A candidate who cannot reach the voters personally can surely reach them through the media. As the first decade of the twenty-first century draws to a close, media campaigning has become a way of life for all of us. Shouldn't that be obvious? Don't all successful candidates use television—and even radio—to reach voters?

Again, reality is not quite what it might appear. Certainly television and politics have blended in familiar ways in recent years. Using the media to carry political messages has become familiar to all viewers; a vast majority of Americans, moreover, receive most of their political information from television. But that does not end the discussion.

A number of different cases suggest themselves. First, look at a candidate for Congress from the Eighth Congressional District in Maryland. In 2002, incumbent Republican Constance Morella was challenged by state senator Christopher Van Hollen. Morella, a six-term incumbent, was representing a heavily Democratic district, and the Democrats saw this seat as one ripe for the plucking. But the voters in the district were also concerned about the gubernatorial race, with Republican Bob Ehrlich seeking to wrest partisan control from the Democrats, whose candidate was Kathleen Kennedy Townsend, the lieutenant governor on whom the spotlight attending all of the Kennedys shone. And more important than either race, in the last month or so of the campaign, the voters and the media gave most of their attention to the D.C. sniper, who was terrorizing the district. The media market for Maryland 8 includes the District of Columbia and the Virginia suburbs of Washington as well as the Maryland suburbs. The voters and the media follow national politics, not local. How can a candidate for Congress in this situation attract attention in the D.C. media market? Advertize effectively? Use the media as a surrogate for personal contact?

For a second scenario, imagine a candidate running for state senate from a district in Bangor, Maine, in 2002. Most voter attention was centered on the top of the ticket. Maine politics featured hotly contested races for governor in an open seat; for United States senator, in which incumbent Republican Susan Collins was challenged by former state senate majority leader Chellie Pingree in a race that set state records for media spending; and for an open seat race for the Second Congressional District that was viewed as one of the most competitive in the nation, with a pro-life Democrat running against a pro-choice Republican. The local media blankets the Bangor state senatorial districts, but over ninety cents of every television advertising dollar for state senate candidates is wasted because messages are also beamed to voters who reside in other districts. The same is true of radio and newspaper advertising. What role, then, should the media play in this state senate campaign?

Contrast these two cases with a third scenario, also from 2002. In North Dakota, Democratic incumbent Earl Pomeroy was challenged by Republican state tax commissioner Rick Clayburgh for the state's only seat in the U.S. House of Representatives. This race was on top of the ballot, as neither U.S. senator nor the governor was up for reelection. North Dakota is a sparsely populated state. Though the state has a population of less than 650,000, the voters are spread out, with an average citizen density of less than ten citizens per square mile. Although citizens expect to meet the candidates (as is custom in many smaller states), North Dakota is perfect for a media campaign because the state has only two dominant media markets—Fargo and Bismark, neither of which is an expensive market and neither of which beams to many voters out of the state. In this tightly contested race, both Pomeroy and Clayburgh blanketed the airwaves. These three examples point to the first conclusion about the role of media in general, and television in particular, in modern campaigns. (See chapter 10 for a more complete discussion of the role of the media in modern campaigning.) Media advertising as a surrogate for personal contact is very important in today's campaigns. However, the electoral context determines the extent to which media campaigning can replace personal campaigning as a way to reach the voters.

An increasing amount of money has been spent on television advertising in recent campaigns for the U.S. Senate and House of Representatives. Increasingly candidates go on television early, using the medium to attempt to define their image. Where successful, this can be a very important strategic move, especially for challengers or incumbents facing a tough race. The downside of this strategy is that much of the money spent in this way might be wasted because the voters are not yet paying attention. Moreover, ample television money is not a resource that is equally available to all candidates. Candidates must determine how much of their financial resources should be spent on media advertising and how much is better spent in other ways. Some districts will be dominated by television campaigns. In other congressional districts television advertising is all but unknown. Although media campaigns are more common in statewide races, here too analysts have noted a great variety (Goldenberg and Traugott 1984).

The second conclusion about the role of media in modern campaigning relates specifically to districts in which media advertising plays a dominant role. Only certain kinds of messages can be transmitted through thirty-second commercials. These messages can convey impressions and images, but they cannot present and analyze issue positions very well. Nonetheless, such advertisements play a crucial, perhaps even critical, role in many campaigns. Candidates who are virtually unknown become familiar household friends through repeated appearances on television. In districts and states in which media advertising is an expected part of campaigning, citizens use television and radio presentations as a prime means of evaluating candidates.

Since 1996, even more than in previous years, political parties and interest groups (through so-called issue advocacy advertisements [see chapter 4]) used the media to convey pointed messages to the electorate. These supplemented the candidates' own media campaigns but were often intense enough to overwhelm the candidates' own efforts. In 1996 organized labor targeted a group of Republican congressmen who had first been elected running on the Contract with America in 1994. In the race in Maine's first district, for example, Congressman James Longley was portrayed as anti–Social Security and anti–middle class. The accuracy of these advertisements is debatable, but their impact is not. Despite responses by Republican-supporting interest groups, like the National Federation of Independent Businessmen, the labor ads were successful in creating negative images that the Republican freshmen had to overcome. Maine analysts attribute Tom Allen's victory over Longley to the effectiveness of the independent attacks on his image. Across the nation, in districts in which Republican freshmen lost and in those in which they narrowly won, similar scenarios were repeated.

In the closing days of the 1998 midterm election, the Republican party launched a $10 million advertising blitz in selected congressional districts (many of which were in states holding U.S. Senate elections as well). This last-minute advertising campaign targeted President Clinton and asked whether he should be rewarded with more Democrats in Congress. The effort was to link the tarnished image of an embattled president to congressional candidates in his party. The effort apparently failed, as the Democrats won close races in many of the areas in which the advertisements were aired. But, again, there is no question that the campaign met its goal—keeping the president's problems in the forefront of voters' minds as they went to the polls for congressional elections. Their failure lay in interpreting how the voters would respond to this stimulus.

Since 2000, ample evidence leads to the conclusion that parties and interest groups have played a clearly defined role. They run the negative campaigns, attacking their candidates' opponents, leaving their own candidates to take the high road. Often, more media dollars are spent by these surrogate groups than by the candidates themselves. The Bipartisan Campaign Reform Act (BCRA) of 2002 was aimed, at least in part, at curtailing these roles, by limiting the amount of soft money that parties can raise and spend and by limiting others' independent expenditures. To this point however, any claims that BCRA has been successful here are at best dubious, and the Court's recent decision declaring limits on issue advocacy ads unconstitutional further reduces the likelihood of BCRA having any real impact (see chapter 5).

The charge is often made that the media consultant, the political equivalent of a Madison Avenue adman, makes or breaks a candidate. The implications of this charge for the role of campaigning in the political process are obvious and serious (cf. McGinniss 1969). Candidates must consider whether media advertising is appropriate for their particular campaign and must determine whether an impersonal message, often quick and slick, is the vehicle they want to use for presenting themselves to those whose support they seek.

D. The Candidate's Organization

Parties, groups, and media are frequently used as surrogates for personal campaigning in races for higher office. The fourth surrogate, the most common one, is the candidate's personal organization. When commentators speak of candidate organizations, they mean a number of different things. For the purposes of this discussion, they are volunteers who go out and campaign on behalf of a candidate. They function as the candidate's eyes, ears, and mouth. The candidate cannot personally contact every voter, but it is possible for others campaigning on the candidate's behalf to do so.

This type of campaigning is done in a number of different ways. Where possible, campaigners go door-to-door, talking to individual voters and seeking their support for a particular candidate. If an organization is sophisticated enough, these volunteers then compile lists of the voters they have visited, commenting on the likelihood that those voters will support the candidate. On election day the likely supporters are called again and urged to go to the polls. The voters who are likely to vote for another candidate are left alone. One congressional candidate claims to have contacted thirty-one thousand households in this way during the fifteen weeks before the 1998 election (Moberg 1998), but analysis and follow-up of this sort require a sophisticated organization with a large number of trained volunteers.

Other campaigns use volunteers in less complex ways. Some campaigns merely "drop" literature at every door, letting the brochures speak for themselves. Still other campaigns use volunteers, usually young volunteers, to distribute leaflets at shopping centers, malls, ball games, or other locations where large numbers of potential voters are to be found. Many areas have their own typical modes of reaching voters—"human billboards" along congested commuter routes, door holders at subway stations, refreshment providers at factory gates, and so on.

Still other campaigns employ telephone banks, phoning perspective voters with messages about the candidate. Telephone campaigns vary tremendously in sophistication, depending on how well trained the callers are and how organized the entire operation is. At one extreme these campaigns can be as effective as door-to-door campaigning, especially for rural districts; at the other extreme they resemble the scattershot technique of shopping mall leafleting.

One of the keys to establishing a volunteer organization is to have workers who will campaign for just one candidate. In some ways this service is inefficient. If a volunteer is to go door-to-door, why not carry propaganda for a group of candidates? Many volunteers will do this. The marginal difference in effort extended is minimal. However, from a candidate's perspective, the difference is important.

If a worker carries material or campaigns for more than one candidate, the potential effect of the volunteer contact on the voter is certainly diminished, and it might even be negated. What if the voter has not heard about one candidate but has a negative view of the other candidate, and, using only that opinion, discounts both candidates? The call has been dysfunctional. What if the voter has a negative view of politicians in general but might be persuaded because someone cares enough to go door-to-door on behalf of one very special politician in whom that volunteer truly believes? A New Hampshire candidate for state representative reported that one voter told her on election day 1998 that the only reason he bothered to vote at all was because of a call he received on the Sunday night before the election. He voted for one candidate on the whole ballot, the candidate from whose organization he received that call (Crosby 1998). Again, a positive response would be lost by combining campaign efforts.

Although scenarios can be imagined in which combined efforts would help a candidate, if they had their choice, most candidates would want volunteers to work for them and them alone, a far cry from the days when political parties did this kind of campaigning on behalf of an entire ticket.[6] Strong individual candidates who are supported by large numbers of dedicated volunteers eschew combined campaign efforts; weaker candidates with fewer supporters are the most eager to have a "team" approach to campaigning.

In the 1988 presidential election, a new twist emerged. Presidential campaigns are publicly financed; that is, the money to run these campaigns comes from a federal fund, and no more money can be spent if the federal grant is accepted (see chapters 5, 8, and 9). However, presidential campaigns also have the greatest ability to raise money. They developed the networks to do so during the primary, and the election stakes are highest for them. Campaign finance laws permit money to be raised at the national level and then spent locally, if it is spent in a coordinated manner on all the party's campaigns. Thus the Dukakis and Bush campaigns raised money during the general election phase of the 1988 presidential campaign and organized field campaigns for the entire ticket, as this was the only legal way in which they could raise and spend money on behalf of their candidates. The result was an interesting reversion to the days of party-centered field campaigns. (See Corrado 1992.) In the more recent presidential campaigns, this technique was repeated with greater sums of money, more of which was spent for coordinated advertising campaigns, but the coordinated field campaigns with staff from national party headquarters remained an important feature (see chapter 5).

The ability of candidates to form their own volunteer organization is another factor that varies with what other races are being held at the same time. However, once a winning candidate has a personal organization in place, maintaining it over a period of years is not difficult. Some supporters drop out; new supporters are recruited for each new campaign. But a core of candidate-inspired activists remains as a powerful resource (Fenno 1978).

E. The Structure of a Modern Campaign

Volunteer organizations such as the one just described have been an important part of American politics for some time, at least since the spread of direct primaries. In recent years, however, as campaigns have become more expensive and more complex, candidate organizations have taken on a different meaning.

Figure 7.1 depicts a possible organizational chart for a modern general election campaign. The coordination of various means of contacting voters, using traditional and modern techniques, defines the extent to which the new politics has come to dominate campaigns for many offices.

The candidate sits atop the organization. Or at least one hopes the candidate does. Too often campaigns run so efficiently that the candidates seem to be all but unimportant, merely the product to be packaged. However, in this case, let us assume that the candidate is in charge, selecting the campaign manager and coordinating strategy and tactics. (See Agranoff 1972, 1976; Hershey 1984; Johnson-Cartee and Copeland 1997; Kayden 1978; Luntz 1988; Maisel 1986; Rothenberg 1983; Salmore and Salmore 1985; and Shea 1996.)

Figure 7.1 Structure of a Modern Campaign

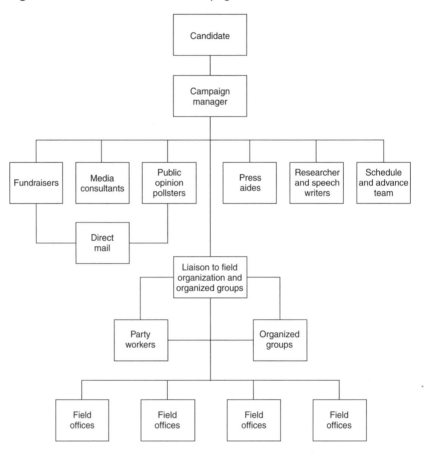

The campaign manager runs the day-to-day campaign. Campaigns for statewide office routinely require budgets in the millions of dollars. This is a major enterprise that requires professional management. In the last two decades a corps of "professional" campaign managers has emerged.

Some work as individual entrepreneurs, working one campaign at a time and then waiting for the next biennium to begin again. More and more, however, the pattern is for political managers to form companies that take over the management of a number of campaigns at the same time, handling many of the tasks from a central headquarters. Political campaign management is indeed a growth industry these days.[7]

Firms tend to specialize in either Republican or Democratic campaigns. Ralph Reed, former head of the Christian Coalition, opened his own consulting firm catering to Republican candidates who carry a message of social conservatism to the electorate. In 1998 he worked for candidates for governor in Alabama, lieutenant governor in Georgia, and Congress in Kentucky, among others. He then became chair of the Georgia Republican party and made an unsuccessful run for lieutenant governor in Georgia himself. The firm of Shrum, Devine, and Donilon only works for Democratic candidates, and lead partner Bob Shrum (now retired from consulting) worked on every Democratic presidential campaign since George McGovern's in 1972, with the exception of Jimmy Carter's 1980 campaign and Bill Clinton's two campaigns (he also resigned from Jimmy Carter's 1976 campaign after less than two weeks). Different firms have different expertise and/or are willing to handle different aspects of a campaign. But they all combine some of the functions we will now describe, with advice on how the campaign should proceed. (See Thurber and Nelson 2000; Luntz 1988; Sabato 1981.)

1. Public Opinion Polling

Modern campaigns do not rely on hunches to determine what the public is thinking or to evaluate how different approaches to campaigning are working. Public opinion polling has acquired a prominent role in modern campaigns. In some cases the campaign management firm handles the public opinion polling; in other cases a polling firm plays a major role in campaign management; in still other cases two firms work together. Prominent pollsters like Garin-Hart-Yang Strategic Research Group; the Tarrance Group; Penn, Schoen, and Berland; Fairbank, Maslin, Maullin, and Associates are sought after as key figures in major campaigns. Pollsters play major roles in ascertaining what issues concern the public, how the candidate is perceived, how the opponent is perceived, and what approaches will and will not work.

More elaborate campaigns do continuous polling during the campaign period. In lower-budget campaigns, a pollster takes a first poll, called a benchmark poll, to determine a candidate's position and the views of the public at the beginning of the campaign and then polls occasionally throughout the campaign, to measure attitudes and changes in opinions in response to specific events or to determine the impact of specific strategies. Professional pollsters working on major campaigns play a critical and central role in determining strategy to be followed. They not only provide and analyze the data, but they also interpret what those facts mean in light of other campaigns in which they have participated or are currently participating. (See Crespi 1988, 1989; Stonecash 2003.)

2. Media Consultants

The campaign manager and the pollster also work closely with the media expert on a campaign. Again, various patterns are possible. Some large management firms take care of designing media strategies, making commercials, and buying time for campaigns. Some firms, primarily advertising agencies, specialize in political advertising and take care of other aspects of campaign management as well. Because media expenditures constitute such a high percentage of total campaign expenditures, the role of the media consultant is central to most campaigns (Goldenberg and Traugott 1984, chap. 6; Pfau and Kenski 1990).

If the message of the campaign is to be carried by paid media, then the media consultant has to be involved not only in producing advertisements and commercials and buying time and space but also in setting strategies. Goldenberg and Traugott (1984, 86) found that congressional candidates in 1978 spent nearly 60 percent of their total campaign budgets on media expenditures and advertising; these expenses included consultant fees and production as well as sheer advertisement purchases. Undoubtedly, similar patterns would be found for campaigns for statewide office. The percentage of total budgets spent on this category probably increases with the total budget of the campaign and has undoubtedly continued to increase since the 1978 study was completed (see also Diamond and Bates 1984; Pfau and Kenski 1990).

3. Fund-Raisers

Polling and media advertising are expensive. Million-dollar campaigns were cause for concern in the late 1960s; multimillion-dollar campaigns are commonplace today. In order to run campaigns of this magnitude, candidates must spend a good deal of time and effort on fund-raising. (The complex topic of campaign financing is discussed in detail in chapter 5.) At this point it is sufficient to state that one important part of any campaign organization involves raising the money necessary to conduct the campaign and monitoring how that money is spent.

Many campaigns now hire professionals to handle these tasks. Professional fund-raisers set a strategy for raising money and follow through on that strategy (Cummings and Cummings 2004; Herrnson 1991). They must begin well in advance of the start of actual campaigning for two reasons. First, fund-raising requires a good deal of candidate time. It is difficult to convince a donor to make a major contribution if that donor cannot sit down and actually talk with the candidate. Second, most campaign expenditures require payment in advance. Few of those enterprises used to dealing with campaigns will do so on a credit basis; all too often campaigns end up with unpaid bills.

Therefore, candidates have to raise money in advance in order to start effective campaigning. A number of observers have commented that raising money early can have important strategic consequences for dissuading effective opposition (Goldenberg and

Traugott 1984; Green and Krasno 1988; Jacobson 1990b; Jacobson and Kernell 1983; Sorauf 1984). This lesson is not lost on politicians. One group interested in assisting more women who are running for office has based its entire strategy on this premise. Many think that EMILY's List is named for its founder, but in fact it is an acronym for EARLY MONEY IS LIKE YEAST. The group supports female candidates early in the process so that those candidates will be able to demonstrate viability to others who might give them money later on.

One important technique for raising money—as well as for communicating campaign messages—is **direct mail**, first employed on a national level by the Republican party under Chairman Ray Bliss and perfected by Richard Viguerie, a kind of direct mail guru who developed lists and raised money for a series of conservative candidates. Viguerie's success spurred others to copy his techniques, though none quite duplicated his early success in raising large sums of money from small donors. Today liberal and conservative candidates, as well as interest groups, use computer-generated lists of potential donors and/or potential voters. They appeal to these voters based on certain known characteristics or preferences. Although Viguerie's inflammatory techniques have not always been successful (in fact, declining response rates led him to cut back his efforts [Edsall 1986]), these techniques continue to reach many voters in each election cycle.

As a fund-raising tool, direct mail knows no political boundaries. Mailing firms appeal to potential donors throughout the country as they attempt to convince those who have donated to campaigns in the past that they should do so to similar campaigns now.

As a campaigning tool, direct mail is equally effective. Superstar GOP strategist Karl Rove got his start in electoral politics as a direct mail guru. Once lists have been developed, campaigns can direct "personalized" appeals to groups of voters who share certain characteristics. All environmentalists in a state might receive a mailing that stresses the candidate's record on environmental matters, and all members of the National Rifle Association might receive a mailing that describes the candidate's opposition to gun control legislation. The environmentalist mailing will not mention the candidate's position on gun control, and the NRA letter will not mention environmental issues, lest anyone be offended. However, voters who are on both lists will receive both mailings and will have two reasons to support the candidate.

If a sufficient number of lists can be developed and effective appeals drafted, direct mail can be a most effective way to reach voters with a particular campaign appeal. Because the letters can be personalized by computer, direct mail can be a perfect surrogate for

DIRECT MAIL
A campaign technique through which voters are contacted by mail because of a campaign's prior knowledge concerning those voters' views.

direct candidate contact. Direct mail approaches are so prevalent today that few voters actually believe that the candidate has written directly to them. Despite this cynicism, however, voters respond positively to letters from candidates who share their political views.

4. Scheduling and Advance Work, Press Relations, Field Organization, and Liaison to the Political Party and Organized Groups

Other parts of the campaign operation work to coordinate the use of candidate time and to link the candidate to various other actors involved in the electoral arena.

For instance, candidates for statewide offices, even in smaller states, frequently have more calls for personal time than they have time available. How to use the limited time of the candidate is not a trivial question. Every major campaign has one person—or even a staff of people—whose job it is to see that the candidate's time is used most effectively. Before a candidate arrives at a political event, someone has to be sure that the event will run efficiently; otherwise, the whole effort might be a waste of time. That is the role of the advance team (Bruno and Greenfield 1971).

Another important campaign function involves establishing ongoing relations with the working press. The extent of press coverage varies significantly from campaign to campaign. The key variable in this instance is how important the individual campaign is for the geographic area covered by the various media. Thus a congressional race in Nevada is important for the print and electronic media in Las Vegas and Reno, since Nevada has only two representatives in Congress. On the other hand, the *New York Times* and the electronic media in New York do not pay much attention to congressional races because more than two dozen members of Congress represent the metropolitan area served by the *Times*. The same is true for the electronic media in the New York area.

Press aides to candidates in major campaigns do not function alone. Their job is to deal with the press, but they do not do so in a vacuum. Their relationships with the press go a long way toward structuring how the candidate is perceived, indeed in some cases if the candidate is perceived at all. Thus press relations are part of an overall strategy. Press aides work with all of the major players in a campaign to coordinate the press strategy with the overall strategy of the campaign.

Field organization plays an essential role in almost any campaign organization. The campaign needs some way to reach out into the geographic area covered by the districts. Campaign managers talk about the need for a physical presence, a ground war; voters need to know that there are real people behind a campaign. This physical presence takes the form of district offices; of volunteers on the street; of leaflet drops and brochures; of bumper stickers, buttons, and lawn signs. Voters want to know that a candidate is well supported before they are willing to offer their support as well. The field organization gives supporters the feeling of joining an ongoing organization.

In any campaign, the campaign manager and the candidate must determine what effective role political party organization will play. However, even in those areas in which political party organization is not strong, someone in a campaign must have the responsibility of coordinating campaign efforts with those of the party leadership. Whatever party officials can do for a campaign to garner the support of their loyal followers is a plus. Whatever can be done to avoid alienating party regulars must be done. Whatever extra activities the party can undertake is a plus.

Another aspect of a large campaign organization coordinates the work of the organized groups that are supporting the candidate. This work involves a number of different problems. In some cases there must be coordination with the fund-raisers; in others, with direct mail; in others, with scheduling. At times it is appropriate to set up separate committees to demonstrate group support— Lawyers for Jones or Teachers for Miller. These efforts might require coordination with the press aide or with the media consultant. If organized groups aid a campaign by providing volunteers, their work should be coordinated with the field organization or with political party machinery. How each resource is used varies from situation to situation according to a number of intangibles, not the least of which is the strength of the candidate and the strategy and tactics that are to be employed.

III. OLD-STYLE POLITICS: A MORE PROMINENT ROLE FOR PARTIES

Look back at figure 7.1. The entire organization is directed toward getting in touch with as many voters as possible in as many effective and efficient ways as possible. Voters are informed about the candidate through the news media, through paid media, through sessions with the candidate, through mail, or through the campaign efforts of others. An efficient campaign organization will reach each prospective voter a number of times in a number of different ways; most of these appeals will be directed specifically at individual voters. Once voters have been informed about a candidate, they will be asked to support that candidate with their help, their money, and their votes. They will be asked, again and again, to help in whatever ways are possible. All the efforts of the campaign staff and organization, the professionals, the consultants, and the volunteers are aimed at this goal.

This campaign chart represents "new politics" because of the techniques used. Modern technology has, in fact, replaced older techniques that relied upon person-to-person contact and party allegiance. Now computers, not precinct committeemen, are used to identify and categorize voters, to analyze polling data, to monitor the progress toward reaching certain campaign goals, even to make telephone calls.

Television and radio are used to reach large numbers of voters with messages that were carried by volunteers on foot in an earlier time. Direct mail allows for "personal" contact with significant numbers of voters. Campaign budgets have multiplied to amounts beyond belief even twenty years ago. Professionals are called in to monitor these huge organizations. No candidate can personally manage a major campaign; the two functions (candidacy and management) are separate, and each needs full-time function fillers for a big campaign. However, it is important to keep in mind that the job of the campaign in the modern era is not fundamentally different from what it was in the days before modern techniques changed politics.

Politics has changed at all levels. Remember the candidate for county supervisor described at the beginning of this chapter? He staffed the voter registration booth; he put up posters; he scheduled his own time. He was the one shaking the hands of voters at the fair, creating the media event by introducing the Senate candidate, probably with remarks that he himself had labored over. Why was *he* doing all these things himself? Where was *his* organization?

The answer probably is that he doesn't really have one. How many people can he expect to get excited about working for a candidate for county supervisor? How many people are likely to contribute large sums of money to candidates who are running for county supervisor; for clerk of courts; for water district commissioner; for city council member or school board member; or even for state representative or state senator, in any of the smaller states?

Think about the people who hold these offices in any community. Who are they? What do they do? For such low-visibility offices, do most people really care enough to become involved with active campaigning?

The answer for most of us for most of these offices is a resounding, "Who cares?" When we do care, the reasons are quite obvious. Most often the "organization" of candidates for local offices is made up of friends and neighbors, who are friends and neighbors first and become involved in politics secondarily.

A personal connection is enough to get someone involved in a campaign. If a neighbor asks for help, a conscientious citizen will probably help in that campaign. She probably won't become totally engrossed in a campaign, and she is unlikely to make a large financial contribution. But she, like many people, will help.

Similarly, these campaigns often involve local issues. A parent who is concerned about a particular item on the school board's upcoming agenda, for instance, whether the junior high school should spend more money for football or start a girls' soccer program, might become involved in a campaign. Often local campaigns are the most intense because the issues strike closest to home. Issues and personalities are familiar. Neighbors work with and against neighbors.

But even when one is involved in these campaigns, the campaign is not of the same scale as a congressional or statewide campaign. With the exception of some of the very largest cities, candidates for city council or school board represent an approachable number of people. The candidate can personally touch those people. Large budgets are not necessary; surrogates are not necessary; complex organizations are not necessary. Furthermore, many of the important campaign functions that help one candidate help all candidates of the same party. Political parties play important roles.

A. Reexamination of the Role of Political Parties

This is not to say that local politics, campaigns for "less major" offices (*all* offices are major to the people seeking them), is a throwback to a time when political parties dominated our political scene. However, party plays a much more prominent role, and the style of campaigning is much more susceptible to party organizational efforts than is the case in larger campaigns.

Candidates for state and local offices face the same strategic questions that other candidates face. Who are one's likely supporters? Who are those who might be convinced to become supporters? How can these people be convinced? What will draw supporters to the polls? However, these candidates face these questions in an environment, in most cases, in which the public has little awareness or concern about either the candidates or the offices they seek.

Most campaigns for state and local office involve candidates seeking to represent districts that fall within one county, the most common party organizational unit (Eldersveld 1982). County party activists are familiar with the offices and the candidates; and candidates need only deal with one party committee. Consequently, political party organizations work best in campaigns in districts for which the boundaries coincide with existing party structures.

Furthermore, party organizations work best at stimulating activity by those who are affiliated with the party. When candidates are looking for likely supporters, all other things being equal, voters who share party affiliation with them stand out as an obvious target. Think about your own decisions on voting. You are probably saying, "I don't vote for the party! I vote for the best candidate." Okay, now that you feel good about that, consider specific examples. You vote for the presidential candidate you think is best, for the candidate for governor, for U.S. senator, maybe even for representative in the House. After all, you are a political science student; you care about these things. But what about the candidate for registrar of deeds, for probate judge, for clerk of courts? Do you honestly know who they are? Do you honestly know who you think is the "best" candidate? How do you judge that?

In a practical way, you need some other means to make a judgment. Party is often that voting cue. You might not be a "member" of one party or the other, but you probably have different feelings about the two major parties. And those feelings often determine votes for local office. Thus candidates are interested in party efforts to register copartisans and to get them out to vote on election day. Those are precisely the kinds of tasks that party organizations still perform quite well.

B. Local Campaigns in the Absence of Party

Campaigns using the party organization work well, if there is a party organization. How does a candidate run when the party organization is nonexistent or inactive, as is the case in many counties throughout the country? Or how does a candidate run if the opposition party is stronger in his or her district, making it necessary to appeal to those in the other party? In these cases it is necessary to return to the original form of "old politics," not party politics but person-to-person campaigning.

For some candidates, this is what politics is all about, getting to know those who live nearby. In city after city and town after town, evenings and weekends in the autumn see scores of candidates knocking on neighbors' doors. No kind of campaigning is more time consuming, but none bears greater fruit.

If candidates are willing to devote the time, frequently they can cover an entire district. An early morning breakfast in a country store is more important for a candidate for sheriff than any advertisement the party will take out. Five minutes over coffee in an elderly man's apartment pays more dividends than literature distributed in a shopping center. Politics at these levels is intensely personal, and often not very substantive. These kinds of politics also raise all sorts of questions about the functioning of our democracy. Why do we have such long ballots? Why are these kinds of positions filled by elections and not appointments? What does the electoral process mean in these cases?

IV. DO CAMPAIGNS DETERMINE
WHO WINS ELECTIONS?

Earlier in this chapter conflicting theories about what determines the results of elections were discussed. One theory accounted for election results on the basis of aggregate economic conditions in the country. The second theory related electoral results to individual citizens' opinions about conditions in the country. Although these theories were developed to explain the results of congressional elections, they should cause anyone reading a chapter on general election campaigns to pause for a moment. Do campaigns—at whatever level—matter?

A. Lack of Competition in American Elections

The answer, simply put, is that they do. Jacobson and Kernell (1983) take some pains to demonstrate that the quality of a candidate is an important factor in determining the results of an election. The better candidates, identified as those who have previously achieved electoral success, are more likely to run credible campaigns and, therefore, are more likely to win. (For additional discussions of the importance of candidate quality, see Fowler and McClure 1989; Jacobson 1987a, 1987b; Maisel 1989, 1990a; for a different perspective on candidate quality, see Maisel et al. 1999; Stone et al. 2004.) The problem analysts face is that there are not many of these better candidates running for office.

In the previous sections, in describing campaign structure, what we were really describing was how these things are done in well-run campaigns. For most campaigns, reality does not approximate this ideal. In district after district, in campaign after campaign, in year after year, candidates' names appear on ballots and then they are never heard from again. They lose. And they do not provide significant competition for the winner.

Most frequently they lose to incumbents. If no incumbent is running, they lose to the candidate of the dominant party in a particular locale. That they lose is less important than the fact that they never really run a campaign, that the voters are never really given a choice.

Simply put, without competitive campaigning by more than one candidate, the citizens of a district are denied the opportunity to choose. Even if two or more names appear on the ballot, electoral choice is effective only when the citizens are presented with candidates who appear serious to them. If this is not the case, the election goes by default.

B. Incumbent Advantage in U.S. House and State Legislative Races

For years political scientists have noted that incumbents running for reelection to the Congress have won in large numbers. Many

explanations have been offered for the observed phenomenon of incumbent advantage (Abramowitz 1975; Cover 1977; Ferejohn 1977; Fiorina 1977a, 1978; Herrnson 1998a, 2000; Mayhew 1974b). See Stonecash, forthcoming, for an different take on the incumbency advantage.

In 1978 it was possible, for the first time, to study this phenomenon in some depth, owing to the data provided by the National Election Study of that election. The analyses of that election were among the first to demonstrate what Jacobson (1981) has aptly called "the vanishing challengers" (see also Abramowitz 1981; Hinckley 1981; Maisel and Cooper 1981; Mann and Wolfinger 1980). Whether measured in terms of dollars spent, voter perception, even voter recognition, challengers were basically invisible; incumbents won because no one knew who was running against them.

The extent to which incumbents hold an advantage in races for the House of Representatives surprises many casual observers (see figure 3.6, p. 103). In only six elections since World War II have fewer than 90 percent of those seeking reelection been reelected. In nine of the last twelve congressional elections 95 percent or more of the incumbents seeking to return to the House did so.

Scholars who have studied this phenomenon have identified many causes that clearly contribute to the advantage, but no single cause—or even most prominent cause—has emerged. A current examination looks at the supply side of incumbent advantage, seeking to identify why stronger challengers do not run for office (Jewell and Whicker 1998; Maestas et al. 2006; Moncrief et al. 1998; Stone and Maisel 2003; Stone et al. 1998a; Stone et al. 1998b; Stone et al. 2004; Williamson 1999; see also Gaddie and Bullock 2000). One interesting finding that has resulted from this research is that to a certain degree strong challengers often choose not to challenge an incumbent because they think the incumbent is doing a good job and they value his or her public service (Stone et al. 2004). If this is the case, then perhaps we can worry less about the high rate at which incumbents get reelected.

State legislators seeking reelection also win virtually all of the time. Again, they do not seem to attract quality challengers (Jewell and Breaux 1988; see Calvert 1979, for an earlier but similar analysis of a group of twenty-nine states). Analysis by Ronald Weber, Harvey Tucker, and Paul Brace (1991) demonstrates that the number of **marginal seats** (i.e., seats in which contests are so close that either party has a legitimate chance of victory) and the number of contested seats in a group of twenty state lower houses declined between 1950 and 1986 (but see Garand 1991 and Jacobson 1987a). One further piece of data concerning House elections and elections to state legislatures merits our concern. Lack of quality challengers to incumbents is cause for worry, considering the importance of competition in elections. But lack of any challengers at all is more troublesome. In 2002, fifteen states had more than half their lower house seats go uncontested; nine had more than half the upper house seats decided without contest. As examples, 65 percent of the state legislative seats in Florida, 66 percent in Arkansas, and 68 percent in Massachusetts were decided without contest (Center for Voting and Democracy 2003). The trend was very similar for 2004 and 2006. In fifty-five races in the 2006 congressional elections, one or the other of the two major parties did not field a candidate. As third-party candidates are almost never serious contenders in these races, that lack of opposition meant that a little over one-eighth of the Congress knew that they would return for the 110th Congress while the 109th was still in session and dealing with important issues. On those issues, the members without any opposition were totally free to ignore their constituents' views. One should not jump to the conclusion that those members did ignore constituent opinion, but it is undeniable that they were free to do so without any fear of electoral retribution.

MARGINAL SEATS

Seats in which either major party has a legitimate chance of winning.

C. Competition in U.S. Senate and Gubernatorial Races

Researchers who hypothesize that incumbent advantage is due to lack of quality challengers point out that incumbent U.S. senators, although frequently reelected, are not sent back to the Senate in anywhere near the same proportion as are House members. Incumbent senators are often challenged by well-known politicians who run impressive campaigns. The challengers spend significant amounts of money, are visible throughout the state, are recognized by large percentages of the voters, and are perceived in ways that demonstrated that their campaigns were effective. These are not new phenomena but were recognized at the same time that the

advantages of House members were under exploration (Abramowitz 1975, 1981; Hinckley 1981; McAdams and Johannes 1981; see
also Mondak 1995; Zaller 1998). Figure 3.7 (p. 103) shows that
there has been tremendous variation in the percentage of incumbent senators winning reelection.[8] Even in the 2006 congressional
elections, regularly discussed as one of the most anti-incumbent in
recent years, 379 of the 402 House incumbents seeking reelection
were returned to office, as were twenty of the twenty-six Senators
wishing to return to Capitol Hill.

Data on gubernatorial elections are less easily obtained than
those on House and Senate elections (but see Jewell 1984). Figure
3.8 (p. 104) shows the success rates for gubernatorial challengers
in recent elections. Not all incumbent governors are eligible for reelection because of state laws restricting the number of consecutive
terms some governors may serve, and so the percentage of incumbents seeking reelection is not as large as it is for senators.[9] Nonetheless, the data still show that governors seeking reelection lose
more frequently than do members of Congress, seemingly in numbers more comparable to those for unsuccessful incumbent senators. In fact, the parallel to senators is quite close. Because of the
prominence of the office in most states, many incumbent governors
seeking reelection have attracted credible challengers. At times,
elections are quite competitive, and many incumbents lose; at other
times, this seems less so. The variables at play seem to be peculiar
to one election year and often to one election. Analysts were hard
put to explain, for instance, why an anti-incumbent mood in the
electorate in 1990 led to the defeat of more incumbent governors
than in any other election in two decades, while only one incumbent U.S. senator was defeated and more than 96 percent of the
House members seeking reelection were victorious.

D. Credible Competition in American Elections

What can be concluded from these facts? One obvious interpretation is that what has been happening at the congressional level has
been happening at other levels as well. Incumbents are winning
because challengers are poor campaigners (Jewell and Breaux 1988;
Holbrook and Tidmarch 1991; Weber, Tucker, and Brace 1991).
When challengers run good campaigns, demonstrated in exceptional case after exceptional case, in state after state, incumbents
can lose (Garand 1991). But good challengers appear too infre-
quently for too many important offices.

The lack of good challengers and good campaigns insulates incumbents in congressional races; in all probability, the same factors
insulate those incumbents seeking reelection to other less visible
and less attractive offices as well.

Campaigns do matter. The low number of credible campaigns for many offices, and the invulnerability of many incumbents because of the scarcity of these credible campaigns, points to a major flaw in the way in which our electoral system operates.

Is this flaw correctable? Some feel the system has failed and that the only way to remedy the flaw is to change the system in a fundamental way. The means most often suggested is **term limits**. Those who advocate term limits argue that because incumbents cannot be beaten it is necessary to remove them from office by law, by limiting the number of terms they are permitted to serve. The term limit movement spread widely in the country in the early 1990s; various term limitations for state legislators are now in effect in a number of states (recall table 1.3). Some states have attempted to impose term limits on members of their congressional delegation, though the constitutionality of such provisions has been challenged. A proposal for term limits for members of Congress was part of the Contract with America, though it did not achieve passage.

It is not our purpose here to debate the merits of the term limits movement. Arguments have been made on each side of the issue. The question for this discussion is whether or not term limits would increase electoral competition. To this question, the answer seems clear. When term limits are imposed, competition is increased in the years when seats become open. That is, when a legislator is forced out of office because he or she is not legally eligible to seek reelection, a high level of competition is likely in that district.[10] We know from long experience that competition in congressional elections is strongest when seats come open due to death, retirement, or an incumbent's leaving to seek another office. We would expect the same experience to follow if the seat became open when an incumbent was forced out by statute. And, in fact, early evidence from those states that have imposed term limitations on their state legislators seems to support this conclusion.

On the other hand, we also might expect *less* competition when a legislator is eligible to run for reelection. Here the reasoning of a potential candidate is quite different. Why should a potentially strong candidate run against an incumbent when he or she knows that that incumbent will shortly be forced to retire? The incentive to wait for an open seat is enhanced if it is known for certain when that seat will become open. Thus the effect of term limits on competition is most likely to be to increase competition in one election in every cycle (i.e., one in four if the limit is four terms; one in six if it is six terms, etc.), but to decrease competition or leave it unchanged in the other years. Whether this result is good or bad and (if it is judged to be beneficial) whether other results from the imposition of term limits merit such a change in the political system are value judgments, not matters that can be explored empirically.[11]

TERM LIMITS

Statutory limits on the number of successive terms an elected officeholder may serve.

BOX 7.1
THE CALIFORNIA RECALL

In 2003, the recall election of California governor Gray Davis captured the nation's attention, as 247 people filed candidacy papers
for the October 7 special election. An amendment to the California
constitution (article II, sections 13–20), adopted in 1911, provides
California voters with the ability to remove an elected state officer
before the end of his or her term in office; however, none of the
thirty-one previous attempts to recall a California governor reached
the voting stage.

The California recall process begins with an official "Notice of
Intention to Recall," signed by at least sixty-five voters, filed with
the California secretary of state's office. In 2003, there were ninety-
five official proponents of the recall drive against Governor Davis—
mostly Republican activists. Remember that proponents have 160
days to circulate the petition in a minimum of five California counties; the petition must be signed by electors equal in number to 12
percent of the last vote for the relevant office. In 2003, 897,156 signatures were required.

The first three months of the 2003 recall drive followed the
pattern of previously unsuccessful recall attempts. However, the
process changed when Congressman Darrell Issa (R-Calif.), whose
fortune is estimated at more than $100 million, joined the recall ef-
fort in June. Issa invested huge amounts of his own money, hiring
respected political consultants and paid petition gatherers. Issa, a
staunchly conservative junior member of the California house delegation, announced he would run to replace Davis while the petition
drive was under way.

As soon as the secretary of state certifies that the number of
required signatures has been collected—only those from registered
California voters count—the California constitution requires the
lieutenant governor to set the date of the recall election within the
next sixty to eighty days. Shortly after receiving notification that the
required signatures had indeed been collected within the permissible
period, Lieutenant Governor Cruz M. Bustamante, a Democrat,
called for the statewide special election to be held on October 7.

The recall ballot under the California constitution has two components: a *yes* or *no* vote for recall, and a separate vote for a replacement governor, should the recall be successful. The recall of a
governor requires a majority vote; a recalled governor is replaced
by the candidate who leads the second ballot; that is, only a plurality is required to win that election. If the recall measure fails, the
replacement candidate votes are ignored.

The California recall election in 2003 attracted a large field of candidates. The Democrats had to make a strategic choice. If any Democrats ran, they could be accused of supporting the recall. If none ran and if the recall were successful, then Democratic voters would have no copartisan to support. Democratic leaders urged popular senator Diane Feinstein to put her name forward, but she—and most other prominent Democrats—chose not to run. Lieutenant Governor Bustamante, who had frequently feuded with Davis, did run, claiming that Democratic voters needed a choice. His supporters urged a "No, Bustamante" vote—that is, *no* on the recall but *Bustamante* on the replacement governor, in the event that the recall was successful.

The Republicans had the opposite problem: they had many candidates who were interested in running and serving. If there were no Democrats on the ballot, this surplus of candidates would not be a strategic problem, as the election would resemble a Republican primary; but once Bustamante declared, the Republicans had to worry that they would divide the vote and that the lieutenant governor would win with a small plurality.

The most prominent Republicans in the field were Issa, Hollywood actor Arnold Schwarzenegger, state senator Tom McClintock, and former baseball commissioner and head of the Los Angeles Olympic Committee Peter Ueberroth. More than one hundred other candidates also registered for the ballot. After initial campaigning revealed they did not have enough support and that they were making a Bustamante victory more possible, Issa and Ueberroth withdrew. McClintock, who is much more conservative than the political neophyte Schwarzenegger seemed to be, stayed in the race, urging true Republicans to vote for him.

On October 7, more than 60 percent of California voters cast their ballots, a turnout higher than that by which Davis had been elected eleven months earlier. More than 55 percent supported the recall. Schwarzenegger received 48 percent of the votes on the second phase of the vote, easily besting Bustamante, who polled 31.5 percent, and McClintock, 13.5 percent. After the vote was officially certified, Schwarzenegger was sworn in as governor on November 17, 2003.

California is among eighteen states with recall provisions for elected state officials. The other seventeen states, most of whose recall statutes are more difficult than California's, are Alaska, Arizona, Colorado, Georgia, Idaho, Kansas, Louisiana, Michigan, Minnesota, Montana, Nevada, New Jersey, North Dakota, Oregon, Rhode Island, Washington, and Wisconsin.

Short of such a fundamental change in the political system, is it possible to find other ways to enhance competition? What is necessary to run good campaigns? In major elections, the answer that is most often given is money (e.g., Gierzynski and Breaux 1990, 1991; Jacobson 1981, 1985–1986). A good campaign could be run, an incumbent could be seriously challenged, if the opponent's campaign were adequately financed. But this explanation may well beg the question. A challenger's campaign *would* be adequately financed if the challenger were viewed as serious. Serious challengers always appear when the risk of running for office is offset by the attractiveness of the office and the perceived chances of winning.

Can this circle be broken? Two answers seem possible. The congressional elections of the 1990s and the relationship between those elections and the legislative sessions that followed them provide hints of one answer. If the electorate becomes dissatisfied with incumbents, and this dissatisfaction is widely perceived, then challengers will emerge to give voice to this dissatisfaction.

Dissatisfaction was evidenced in the 1990 congressional elections, but it became apparent well after challengers had been selected. Despite the fact that in House elections the average incumbent's vote total fell by nearly 5 percent, 96 percent of the incumbents won. Of the twenty-five incumbent representatives whose vote total fell most sharply, over 14 percent in each case, twenty won reelection. Thus, the 1990 election demonstrates the problem we are discussing. If quality challengers are not running, citizens cannot use the polls to express their views on the performance of those in power.

As the 1992 election approached, the public was voicing more dissatisfaction with members of Congress. The House bank scandal was in full bloom. Better challengers emerged; nineteen House members lost primaries and an additional twenty-four lost in the general election. In addition, sixty-five members did not seek reelection, the largest number in more than half a century. As a result, more than one in four members of the 103d Congress, sworn in January 1993, were new to the House.

The public expressed a different kind of dissatisfaction in 1994, clearly responding to the lack of progress on pressing problems, despite the fact that divided government had been ended with the Clinton victory and the return of a Democratic Congress two years earlier. The Republicans sought good candidates to challenge seemingly vulnerable Democrats. They ran as a team on the theme of implementing the Contract with America. And they won a major victory, gaining control of the House for the first time in four decades and regaining the majority status in the Senate that they had lost eight years earlier. Thirty-four incumbent House members and two incumbent senators were defeated in 1994—all Democrats defeated by Republicans. Republicans picked up eighteen House seats and six Senate seats because of partisan switches in open seats in that election as well. The Republicans in the House worked to pass the Contract, though they were thwarted on most items by a Democratic president and/or a Senate that was less enthralled with the items under discussion than were GOP House members.

In 1996 it was the Democrats' turn to field strong candidates. In the House particularly, they recruited and supported strong challengers to freshman Republicans. Although they did not win back majority control, despite retaining the White House, eighteen incumbent Republicans were defeated and many others had to fight off very serious challenges.

However, in the last two elections before redistricting (1998 and 2000) and in the first two elections after redistricting (2002 and 2004), incumbents emerged virtually unscathed. As noted previously, even in the 2006 elections, with an unhappy electorate in a relatively anti-incumbent mood, 95 percent of House incumbents and 79 percent of Senate incumbents won reelection. Why? The reason deals with strategic choices made by potential candidates once again. The most vulnerable Democrats had been defeated in 1994. The most vulnerable Republicans, especially of those first elected in 1994, had been defeated by Democrats in 1996. Most of those who remained were strong candidates for reelection. Most analysts viewed the 1998 election as a great victory for the Democrats because they held even in the Senate and picked up five seats in the House of Representatives, the first time a president's party had gained House seats since 1934 and only the second time since the Civil War. The correct interpretation is that these were victories for the incumbents: 98.5 percent of the incumbents who ran in November 1998 won reelection. As noted above, this trend continues today. Remember, 95 percent of House incumbents seeking reelection in 2006 saw their wishes granted by their constituents, and 75 percent of these incumbents won by at least twenty percentage points.

The second answer, clearly related to the first, may well be through a rejuvenation of political parties. Traditionally, as we have seen, political parties controlled access to the ballot. They controlled nominations. When they lost control over nominations, they also lost an important role in the recruiting process. In any case, we know very little about how individuals are recruited to run for office today (Canon 1990; Cotter et al. 1984; Eldersveld 1982; Gibson et al. 1985; Maisel 1991; Maisel et al. 1990; Seligman 1974; Snowiss 1966). We do know that many candidates are self-starters, that they themselves determine if and when they will seek office (Maisel 1986).

However, in the most recent elections, both national parties, through their congressional campaign committees, have begun to play a more active role in candidate recruitment at all levels (Adamany 1984; Bibby 1981, 1991; Bumiller and Sanger 2002). Jacobson and Kernell (1983) attribute unexpected Republican successes in the 1982 congressional elections to the fact that the Republicans ran a number of very attractive candidates. These candidates did not simply emerge; they were recruited and supported by the national party. The same was certainly true of Republican candidates in 1994 and Democratic candidates in 1996.

As has been typical of recent advances in party operations, Republicans have been way ahead of their Democratic counterparts in providing services for candidates for office. The Republicans have provided more money for their candidates, and they are able to help candidates raise money. In addition, they have been able to supply training and services to their candidates that the Democrats have not been able to match until most recently. This nationalization of congressional politics is an important trend to watch in the future (Herrnson 1988; Bumiller and Sanger 2002).

But more than that, the successful Republican (first) and Democratic (later) efforts on the national level have set a precedent for both parties' state-level organizations to follow (e.g., Cotter and Bibby 1980; Cotter et al. 1982, 1984; Gibson et al. 1983; Huckshorn et al. 1986). For some years parties have been looking for a role to play in the era of new politics; that role may now be emerging. Changes in campaign techniques and in what is expected of candidates, in what is necessary to run for office, have made electoral office less appealing to many prospective qualified candidates and officeholders. The role of the party may well be to recruit these candidates and support their efforts so that elections in America can become more competitive, with incumbents not being guaranteed victory in every election.

As the national party staffs have moved into fund-raising and polling, into issue research and speechwriting, into strategy setting and media advising, state party organizations have seen opportunities to provide services as well. It is becoming more and more clear that parties have an increasing role to play if our electoral system is to become competitive at all levels of government.

V. THIRD PARTIES IN STATE AND LOCAL ELECTIONS

What is the role of "third parties" in a two-party system? Would it surprise you to know that almost fifty different parties ran at least one candidate for federal office or for governor in the 2006 general election? (These parties are listed in table 7.1.)

The electoral system in the United States is described as a competitive two-party system because, all other things being equal

Table 7.1   "Third" Parties on the 2006 Congressional, Gubernatorial, or Presidential Ballot in at Least One State

A New Direction	Mountain
Alaskan Independence	Natural Law
American Constitution	Nebraska
American Independent	Pacific Green
American Party	Patriot Movement
An Independent Voice	Peace and Freedom
Anti-Bushist	Personal Choice
Concerned Citizens	Pirate
Connecticut for Lieberman	Politicians Are Crooks
Conservative	Preserve Green Space
Constitution	Progressive
Desert Greens	Pro-Life Conservative
Diversity Is Strength	Reform
Freedom	Socialist Equality
Green	Socialist Party USA
Impeach Bush Now	Socialist Workers Party
Impeach Now	United Party
Independence	Unity
Independent	U.S. Taxpayers
Independent American	Vermont Green
Independent Green	Vermont Localist
Legalize Marijuana	Wisconsin Greens
Libertarian	Withdraw Troops Now
Liberty Union	Working Families
Moderate Choice	

Source: CQ Weekly, November 13, 2006, and www.thegreenpapers.com.

(which in this case they usually are), only the Democratic or the Republican candidate for office in a partisan election anywhere in the United States has a realistic chance of winning. Ninety-eight of the one hundred U.S. senators are either Republicans or Democrats; all of the 435 representatives in the House of Representatives are affiliated with one of the two major parties; all fifty of the state governors and more than 7,350 of the approximately 7,400 state legislators elected in partisan elections[12] ran under major party labels. In plotting strategy, most major party candidates only need to consider the candidacy of the individual running on the other major party's ticket.

But this is not always the case. An examination of some of the exceptions is a good way to come to an understanding of the general rule. Bernie Sanders (I-Vt.) is one of two independents in the Senate. Senator Sanders, a former mayor of Burlington and a longtime member of the House of Representatives, has had a long and colorful career in Vermont politics. At one point he was the only avowed socialist mayor of any American city; his loyal band of followers was locally known as the Sandersistas, after the Nicaraguan socialist revolutionaries. When he ran for Congress, he drew support mostly from liberal Democrats; in both the House and the Senate he has caucused with Democratic members, who treat him as one of their own in awarding committee assignments. In fact, the Democrats have not run a candidate against Sanders, who has been reelected with relative ease since first winning his seat in 1990.

Angus King, who served two terms as the Independent governor of Maine (1995–2003), came to office in a very different way. King entered politics as a Democrat, serving on the staff of William Hathaway, who represented Maine in the House from 1965 until 1973 and in the Senate from 1973 until 1979. Leaving politics and government service, King followed two careers simultaneously, as a very successful owner of a small business and as the host of a statewide television program examining Maine politics on the state's public television network. In 1994 he decided to run for governor. He made two key decisions: that he would run as an independent and that his campaign would be largely self-funded. Maine has had a long history of supporting independent candidates. Since James Longley was elected governor in 1974, every gubernatorial election has seen a serious "third-party" candidate (Maisel and Ivry 1998). At the time King sought office, the Democrats and Republicans were engaged in a bitter feud in the legislature; at one point state government had been shut down over a budgetary impasse. Partisan animosity had turned many citizens (and public servants) sour on the two major parties. King narrowly defeated the Democratic candidate, former governor and former congressman Joseph Brennan, who had run for one office or another for more than twenty years; he was the very personification of a professional politician. The Republican candidate was Susan Collins, an untested former senatorial aide.[13] King did not run against the two major parties so much as he ran as a conciliator, one who would work with leaders from both parties. For four years, he governed in that manner, gaining credit for economic recovery in the state. In 1998, he won reelection with 60 percent of the vote. Neither the Republican nor the Democratic candidate polled even one-third of his total.

But then there was the candidacy of Jesse "The Body" Ventura, who surprised virtually everyone by winning Minnesota's gubernatorial election as the Reform party candidate in 1998. Some claim that Ventura's victory reflects a resurgence in the Reform party, the true emergence of a national third party that changed the shape of American politics. Evidence to support this conclusion was very thin. Ventura won, in many ways, for the same reasons, though in a very different manner, that King won in 1994. The public was dissatisfied with the major party candidates, who were rather colorless, traditional, career politicians. They had a well-publicized alternative. Ventura, a former professional wrestler and radio talk show host, was a character. His very physical presence drew attention. His name drew attention. His willingness to be outspoken, as he had demonstrated on his radio program, drew attention. His campaign gained momentum late; neither major party candidate was able to mount a significant reply to his advances.[14]

When King won in Maine and governed successfully for four years, he did so without forming a "third party." He dealt with the Democratic and Republican leadership in the Maine legislature and sought compromise. The citizens of Minnesota watched Ventura for four years. While he continued to gain a good deal of press attention, he did not build a new, third-party base and chose not to seek reelection in 2002 (see Bibby and Maisel 1998, 2003).

The exceptions are always interesting, but it is also important to look at the norm. By any measure, the impact of the overwhelming majority of third-party or independent candidates is limited. In only a few of the 435 races for Congress did the winner poll less than 50 percent of the vote. That means if all of those who voted for the "third-party" candidate had voted for the losing candidate, the losing candidate still would not have polled enough additional votes to win the election. And of course the assumption that all who voted for the minor party candidate would have voted at all, much less for one particular candidate, is difficult to justify.

But once again, it is valuable to look at cases in which the minor party candidate might have had an impact. Let's compare experiences in two congressional districts in New Mexico. Two special elections were held for congressional seats from New Mexico during the 105th Congress. In each case, the Green party ran a candidate in opposition to the Republican and Democratic nominees. The Green party, which appeals to environmentalists and generally those who might be described as "counterculturalists," is stronger in New Mexico than in any other state.

In a special election in the New Mexico Third Congressional District in 1997, Republican Bill Redmond won the seat by a margin of 3 percentage points. The Green party candidate in that special election, Carol Miller, polled 17 percent of the votes. It is logical to conclude that many of her votes would have gone to the Democratic candidate, who shared many of her views, had she not been in the race. A similar result occurred in the special election in New Mexico held in July 1998. Republican Heather Wilson won the election with 44 percent of the vote, beating Democrat Phillip Maloof by 5 percent; the Green candidate, Robert Anderson, polled 14 percent, again with most of those votes logically coming from the Democrat.

In the 1998 general election, the field was exactly the same in the First Congressional District. Once again Wilson, now the incumbent, beat Maloof, this time by only 3 percent of the votes. Again,

Anderson ran a strong third-party campaign, garnering 11 percent of the votes, more than enough to deny the Democratic candidate a chance for an upset. In the Third Congressional District, Miller also was the Green party candidate again in the 1998 election. In that election, however, there was a new Democratic candidate, Tom Udall, the state attorney general. The Udall name is well known in environmental circles in the Southwest; his father, Stewart, had been a congressman from Arizona before serving as President Kennedy's secretary of the interior; his uncle, Mo, was a leading environmentalist during his own long congressional career. Tom Udall drew on his reputation as a defender of the environment. He appealed directly to Green party leadership not to undermine his campaign against Congressman Redmond. Although Miller remained on the ballot, about six weeks before the election, nine leaders of the Green party sent out a letter to their supporters asking them to support Udall over Miller. Their argument was that support for Miller would virtually ensure a victory for Redmond, a conservative Republican whose environmental record was such that he was among the dirty dozen identified by the League of Conservation Voters (see chapter 4; Ayres 1998). In the November election Miller drew less than half of the support she had received only one year earlier; Udall was one of five Democrats to unseat incumbent Republicans in the off-year election.

Certainly, examples such as this are not common, but they are not all that uncommon either. In the 2006 gubernatorial elections, one could make the case that "third-party" votes, redistributed in what seems like the logical way, could have made the difference in at least five relatively close races—those in Alaska, Maine, Minnesota, Nevada, and Texas.

These examples demonstrate both the potential and the problem for third-party candidates. They have the potential to force the major party candidates to take a stand on issues that are most important to their followers. But they also have the potential to divide the vote in such a way that the candidate they least favor wins. And they rarely have the opportunity to win an election. Thus, as campaigns draw to a close, third-party candidates face the argument that a vote for them is at best a wasted vote and at worst counterproductive. As the case of New Mexico's Third Congressional District demonstrates, that is an argument that can be decisive even for leaders of a relatively strong third-party movement.[15] The effectiveness of this argument is likely to restrict the importance of third parties in state and local elections for the foreseeable future.

VI. POLITICIANS VIEW THE GENERAL ELECTION

Recall the two candidates with whom we began this chapter. The candidate for county supervisor rearranged other aspects of his life so that he could concentrate on the county fair. For the Senate candidate, the campaign was her life. That defines a critical difference not only between the two individuals but also between the two jobs.

Think about candidates for different offices. At the more local levels, candidates serve in part-time positions and run limited campaigns to get there. Many of these candidates like campaigning. It is a different experience for them. They have the opportunity to meet a variety of interesting people, to observe how people live and what they do for a living, to talk to them about their concerns and about their opinions of government. Even when the campaign is over, they have the opportunity to serve, to work on some of the problems they have learned about, to make their community a better place in which to live. And they also have the opportunity to go back to a more normal kind of existence. They can have dinners with their families, spend weekends in the backyard, shop for groceries without shaking hands. The campaign is what they did for a while to win office; it is not their life's work and certainly not their life itself.

Contrast this normality with the existence—and we have chosen that word carefully—of a member of Congress from a marginal district. Members of Congress in this situation start one campaign the minute the last one ends. Many of them are at the plant gates the morning after an election, thanking those who voted for them and hoping that they will remember how much the candidate cared when voting time comes around again. Even those who do not start campaigning for reelection on day one of the new term are constantly campaigning. They come back to the district every weekend, if travel times make it possible. They continue with the same kinds of activities they did in the campaign: speaking to anyone who will listen, attending countless suppers, judging at county fairs. During the week they work hard in Congress, spending much of their time ensuring that their constituents are happy and will vote for them (Cain, Ferejohn, and Fiorina 1987; Fiorina 1978; Mayhew 1974a). On weekends and during congressional recesses, they are back in the district. They know that if they work hard, they might be able to squeak out another term (Fenno 1978; Taggart and Durant 1985). But what about the rest of their lives—vacations, outings with their children or grandchildren, leisure reading?

Put simply, for many members of Congress, such things do not exist. They rarely see their children or spouses; there is no "rest of their lives." Their only enjoyment is politics. This picture should cause concern. Do we really want to be governed by a group of individuals who are willing to give up their lives to campaign full-time? Even if we are not concerned about the mental health of such individuals,[16] how much can they know about the problems facing their constituents, about the reality of ordinary day-to-day life for the majority of Americans?

Many have expressed concern that members of Congress represent a social and economic elite and cannot relate to the problems facing middle-class America. The problem may well be more serious than that. Many of today's politicians do not live a real life at all. Not only are they unrepresentative in terms of economic and social indicators, but they are even more unrepresentative in terms of their ability to understand the everyday problems Americans face.

Impressionistic evidence indicates that few members of Congress lead "normal" lives, even if normality is defined in as broad a way as is necessary, given today's heterogeneous world. Many are single and can imagine no time for a family; the divorce rate on Capitol Hill is very high. Few lead "normal" family lives. Competitive politics at this level has produced a group of officeholders unfamiliar with the daily experiences of most of the people they represent.

How do politicians react to this style of life? A number of responses are possible. Some politicians refuse to enter the arena. Every year political journalists speculate about likely candidates for office in a particular region. Every year some refuse to run; some say that they have enough to do where they are now; others are frank in saying that the sacrifices are not worth the honor.

Others immerse themselves in politics totally and then escape. In recent years many have been concerned about the number of members of Congress who are voluntarily retiring, a number that reached a modern record in 1992 (see, e.g., Cooper and West 1981). Many of these retirees state explicitly that they are leaving because the pressure to campaign is too heavy. Some of the best members of Congress have retired in recent years, often well before the age at which we might normally expect such officeholders to step down. Certainly we could list many reasons for such early retirements besides the exigencies of the two-year election cycle. However, as a matter of public policy, we must be concerned if some of the best officeholders feel that they cannot stay in office and serve because the electoral demands are too costly.

A third response is to avoid the pressure of constant election by seeking a different office. In 2006, eight members of Congress chose not to run for their old seats in order to seek seats in the Senate. One reason for taking this route is that senators face reelection every six years, not every other year. Senators campaign very hard in the two years before their term expires, but in the other four years they are able to concentrate on the policymaking aspects of their job (Fenno 1984). Another nine left the House to run for governor, again a position with a longer tenure and one that seems more likely to have policy impact.

Not all members of Congress face difficult elections every two years. Some of these members have reached accommodations with their jobs that are not unlike the positions of senators or others who do not feel they must campaign constantly. Consider the career choice that Congressman Barney Frank (D-Mass.), one of those who faced no opposition in his 2006 reelection bid, was confronted with some years ago.

In 1984, when Massachusetts senator Paul Tsongas (D) decided not to seek reelection in order to spend more time with his family (he was diagnosed as having a serious illness), many speculated that Frank would be among the first in the race for the Senate seat. Frank is one of the more outspoken members of Congress; he won his seat in a hotly contested race when Father Robert Drinan (D-Mass., 1971–1981) was forced not to seek reelection by the papal decree that forbids Catholic clergy from engaging actively in politics. After the 1980 census Frank had to win reelection against Margaret Heckler (R-Mass., 1967–1983) in one of those few races every ten years in which, because of redistricting in states that have lost seats in Congress, two incumbents must face each other. The 1982 Frank-Heckler race was the most expensive race in the country. Political journalists conjectured that Frank, fresh from two extremely difficult campaigns, would view the six-year term of a senator as a panacea for all his ills.

Frank saw it differently:

> I've got the best job in the world. Look, I can build up a relationship with this district. I won't have another tough campaign for ten years, when they might fool around with reapportionment again.
>
> I go back to the district every other weekend. I enjoy it. I enjoy what I do there. I can live a normal life here [in Washington]. How many Senators ever live a normal life? They are always in the spotlight. I don't need that. (Frank 1985)

Frank is satisfied with his life in the House. He, like others who have gained the spotlight in the House of Representatives—men like Minority Leader John Boehner (R-Ohio.) and John Dingell (D-Mich.), the senior member of the Democratic Caucus, or the leaders of the House Judiciary Committee, former chairman James Sensenbrenner (R-Wisc.) and Chairman John Conyers (D-Mich.)—have found the House to be a congenial home. In 1984 Frank had no desire to move on to the Senate. He was making the contributions he wanted to make in the House. He did not feel that the electoral pressure was burdensome because he had become comfortable with his district.

Frank's subsequent electoral experience demonstrates his point. In May 1987, Frank revealed that he is a homosexual, becoming only the second member of the Congress at that time to publicly announce that he is gay. After having won reelection without opposition in 1986, Frank faced a challenger in 1988 but won the election with over 70 percent of the vote. In August of 1989 the *Washington Times* revealed that Frank was involved with a male prostitute whom Frank had hired as a household assistant. The House Ethics Committee investigated to determine if Frank had violated any House rules, particularly in response to a charge that Frank had used his influence as a member of Congress to have parking tickets fixed. Even after cries for his resignation and weeks of bad publicity, Frank was easily able to weather another serious challenge, winning the 1990 election by nearly two to one. Massachusetts lost a seat in the House as a result of the 1990 census. But Frank was able to win easily in his reconfigured district and has had no difficulty since. His analysis of the difference between House and Senate seats, at least in his case, seems as prescient as it was nearly a decade and a half ago.

Thus politicians have a number of different ways of responding to general election pressures, from letting politics dominate their entire lives to opting out of the system. How they respond over a period of time is different, however, from how they view general elections in the short run.

The question of how politicians view elections can be approached in two ways. The first is affectively: What do politicians think about the prospect of campaigning? As was mentioned earlier in this section, this response varies from individual to individual and may vary as well from office to office and time to time. Many share the sentiments of an extremely successful politician who said, "I like lots of it, but not the door-to-door stuff. I feel I am imposing. People are awfully nice, but I feel their home should be their home, not a soapbox for my views." An opposite point of view is represented by former senator William Cohen (R-Maine; House, 1973–1979; Senate, 1979–1997), who routinely asked people if he could spend the night in their home while campaigning. Cohen figured that people really feel that they know you if they open their home to you and break bread with you in the morning.

Some politicians like talking to big contributors and impressing them with the importance of their being elected. Others, like the late senator (1949–1964; 1971–1978) and vice president (1965–1969) Hubert Humphrey (D-Minn.), found that asking someone for money was the most distasteful part of politics. Some enjoy appearing before large audiences and debating; others are more reticent and seek to have their records speak for themselves.

The list of variations could go on. All that can be said with certainty is that campaigning is a highly personal experience. Some find it totally rewarding in and of itself; others find it a necessary evil, withstood in order to attain or hold office.

The second way in which politicians view elections is in a strategic sense: What does this election mean to me? Can I win? What are the costs to me personally? Professionally? From this campaign? What are the costs if I win? What are the costs if I lose? What are the benefits if I win? What are the benefits if I lose?

Were politicians rational men and women in reaching these decisions, they would weigh the costs and benefits carefully and reach judgments based on that evidence. Jacobson and Kernell (1983) lay out this model of electoral decision making and defend it persuasively (see also Maisel et al. 1990; Brady, Maisel, and Warsh 1994). On the other hand, Maisel (1982, 1986) demonstrates that politicians do not always behave rationally in reaching decisions about their electoral future. Very often office seekers look at all the facts (e.g., the fact that over 90 percent of the incumbent members of Congress seeking reelection are successful) and make decisions.

Given this caveat, however, some strategies followed by candidates in the general election reflect their view of this process in the short run. The objective of the election is not merely to win, but to win by a wide margin. If a title can be given to this strategy, it would be a "run-scared" strategy. No matter what the evidence says, no matter what one's instincts are, "run scared." Do not appear to be complacent; do not take anything for granted. Build the margin. Assure a big victory; it might frighten away opponents the next time (Goldenberg, Traugott, and Baumgartner 1986; Jackson 1988; Krasno and Green 1988; Maisel 1990b).[17]

Analysts of elections and campaigns describe a rational process. They present a process in which politicians weigh alternatives, reach rational decisions, set appropriate strategies, allocate resources effectively, appeal to the voters persuasively, and evaluate their campaigns logically.

The difficulty with this description is that although the entire process viewed as a whole may be rational, individual politicians often act very irrationally. Two seemingly conflicting trends are in evidence. The first is represented by the incumbent member of Congress whose winning percentage has not fallen below 65 percent in ten years but is being confronted by one strongly organized group in his district on a particular issue. This politician "runs scared." All evidence from hundreds of campaigns for more than a decade indicates that as an incumbent he is safe. However, for a year he goes home every weekend, spending more time in the district than he has in years. He raises more money than has ever been spent on an election in his district. He employs a professional campaign staff and has it in place before any opposition has surfaced. He campaigns hard throughout the fall, despite the fact that his opponent is unknown and underfinanced.

The second trend could well be represented by his opponent.

She believes that the group supporting her has widespread support throughout the district that will carry her to victory. All the evidence about incumbent safety does not deter her. She views this campaign through rose-colored glasses. Objective views of her chances do not mute her optimism. Her efforts are undeterred by the fact that she has little money and is not well known beyond the members of her group. She campaigns hard right up until the election, convinced that the justice of her cause will be sufficient to guarantee victory in the end.

The incumbent wins big. The process is understandable and rational in the overall picture. These two candidates and literally thousands like them campaigning for all sorts of offices all over the country have been acting irrationally. They have been caught up in an amazing exercise in self-deception. Politicians invest so much of themselves in campaigns that they cannot believe that their experiences are not unique. The November campaigns are a critically important part of politicians' lives. For some, campaigns become too important. These politicians are not willing to put that much of themselves on the line and let others make a judgment about their merit. For others, the election is what their life is all about. Politics is not only a means to an end; it is an end in itself. Campaigning becomes not only their life's work but also their life. For all, it is a deeply personal experience. At whatever level the campaign, the candidate is aware that fellow citizens are making a judgment of him or her. Few can view that process in a detached way as objective analysts. Most are caught up in the election as one of life's crises, which can only be experienced in the most personal of ways.

WEBSITES

The websites noted in chapter 6 are pertinent for this discussion as well. In addition, most candidates launch their own websites during election campaigns but remove them shortly thereafter.

CHAPTER 8

Presidential Nominations

Democratic presidential candidates (from left) former senator Mike Gravel (Alaska), Senator Christopher Dodd (Conn.), former senator John Edwards (N.C.), Senator Hillary Rodham Clinton (N.Y.), Senator Barack Obama (Ill.), New Mexico governor Bill Richardson, Senator Joseph Biden (Del.), and Representative Dennis Kucinich (Ohio) stand together prior to the start of a debate jointly sponsored by CNN, YouTube, and Google at The Citadel in Charleston, South Carolina, July 23, 2007. The contests for the 2008 presidential nominations started earlier than ever before.

The political year 1968 must seem like ancient history, but it is the year you need to know about if you want to understand how Americans nominate their presidential candidates. That year, marred by the assassinations of Robert Kennedy and Martin Luther King Jr., saw President Lyndon Johnson challenged within his own party and eventually withdrawing from the presidential contest and Vice President Hubert Humphrey nominated while the American public watched frustration on the convention floor and violence on the streets of Chicago. Events were set into motion that could not be reversed and that would fundamentally change the way in which presidential nominees are chosen.

Each nomination since 1968 has been played out under its own unique circumstances. This chapter begins with a look back at some of the key presidential nomination battles fought over the last four decades. Emphasis will be given to changes in the process that have implications for the current circumstances. Following that review, we will turn to an examination of the strategic questions that face potential candidates for major party presidential nods. We will see that some of the important lessons from the past remained central for the candidates for the 2008 nomination.

I. THE POST-1968 REFORMS

PRESIDENTIAL PREFERENCE PRIMARIES

Primary elections in which voters cast their votes for presidential candidates or for delegates who will support specified presidential candidates.

Democrats competed in fifteen **presidential preference primaries** in 1968. Senator Robert Kennedy won eleven of the primaries; Senator Eugene McCarthy won the other four. Vice President Hubert Humphrey, the heir apparent after President Johnson announced that he would not seek reelection, followed a political strategy in which he avoided confrontation with McCarthy and Kennedy. He did not announce his candidacy until deadlines for filing intentions to run had passed in all states. Humphrey backers won just over 2 percent of the primary vote; but, in 1968, votes in primaries did not convert directly to convention votes. For example, Senator McCarthy won nearly three-quarters of the votes in the Pennsylvania primary; Vice President Humphrey garnered 80 percent of the Pennsylvania convention votes.

In 1968 primaries were seen as a tool used to influence party officials about electability; they were not a means to "win" a nomination. The conventional wisdom of party politicians was that the party bosses in the larger states had the power to control the nomination. They not only believed that this was true but also believed that this was as it should be. All of this was to change because of the 1968 Democratic Convention.[1] Needless to say, critics charged that the party was boss controlled and claimed that the selection process was undemocratic and unfair.

A. The McGovern-Fraser Commission

Party leaders responded to this criticism; they saw the frustration of those who worked within the system. They saw the damage done to the party and the nation by the 1968 nominating process, which so obviously did not reflect the will of those who participated.

Shortly after the 1968 elections, Democratic national chairman Fred Harris appointed a commission to examine the nominating process. The Commission on Party Structure and Delegate Selection was chaired by South Dakota senator George McGovern, who had taken up the mantle of Senator Kennedy after his assassination. The McGovern Commission (which became known as the **McGovern-Fraser Commission** after the chairman resigned to run for president and was replaced by Congressman Donald Fraser of Minnesota) began by assessing the situation that existed in 1968. Their general assessment can be summarized succinctly: the "system" was disjointed across geographic lines; the procedures were unfair to many and undemocratic in the broadest sense of that term; and the end result did not represent the views of many of those who participated.

Some of the procedures revealed by the McGovern-Fraser Commission seem unbelievable from today's perspective. In two states (Georgia and Louisiana) governors appointed all members of the delegation to the national convention. State committees appointed all or most of the national convention delegations in eight other states. So informal was the situation that no one really knew how the delegations were appointed in many other states. The usual explanation was that party officials met behind closed doors and reached secret accommodations. None of these revelations was surprising to the professionals in either the Democratic or Republican parties, however, for they made the decisions. From their point of view, that was how it should be done.

Research by the staff of the McGovern-Fraser Commission defined the philosophical issues that have structured the debate of the presidential nomination process since that time. On one side are party professionals who believe that the most important criterion for an effective process should be the selection of a nominee who can win the general election and govern the nation. They feel that those who have worked most closely with active politicians and know the political scene well can best make that judgment. On the other are those who believe that the process should be open and democratic and that the voters in a party should decide who their nominee will be. The debate has gone back and forth and is often the backdrop for arguments over obscure subissues. But the questions are fundamental: Should the process be elite dominated or popularly dominated? Should the outcome of the process be more important or the means by which that outcome was reached?

MCGOVERN-FRASER COMMISSION

The first of a series of reform commissions that have restructured the way in which the Democratic party nominates candidates for president and vice president.

The final report of the McGovern-Fraser Commission, entitled *Mandate for Reform*, specified that nominating procedures must be changed to make the process *open, timely, and representative.* To the members of the commission and those who were distressed by the events leading up to Humphrey's nomination in 1968, these goals appeared to be at the heart of a democratic process and thus noncontroversial. However, the specific reforms that were suggested (and then accepted as mandatory for state parties for the 1972 nominating process by the Democratic National Committee) rocked the existing system so fundamentally that the ground has yet to settle.

Perhaps the most important guideline promulgated by the McGovern-Fraser Commission was to require that all state parties adopt procedures consistent with the principles it outlined. This requirement led to the establishment of one nominating process, with the rules set at the national level by the national Democratic party and thus changed the power structure within the Democratic party in a way that has not since been altered.

Remember, in 1968 presidential preference primaries had been held in only fifteen states. In some of those states, such as Wisconsin, Oregon, and California, the primaries determined the delegations to the national convention. In many of the other states, such as New Jersey, Pennsylvania, and Illinois, the connection between primaries and convention delegations was less clear. And in thirty-five states, delegates were chosen through some appointive means with no voter input.

For 1972, two procedures were permissible. States could run primaries, under a variety of permissible rules, but in any case with the result determining at least 90 percent of the state's delegation. Or the states could continue to keep delegate selection a matter for party regulars, selecting delegations through series of meetings of party members and regulars in a series of local party **caucuses** and conventions organized under the new guidelines.

CAUCUSES

Meetings of party members at which presidential preferences are expressed and those representing preferred candidates are selected to reflect those views.

The differences between primary elections and a caucus/convention system are important and should be made explicit. In a presidential preference primary, party members go to their local polling place and cast a ballot for their preference much as they do in a general election. In a caucus/convention system, party members go to a meeting; they all must come at the same time and stay for the duration of the meeting. At the meeting or caucus, those in attendance elect representatives to attend another meeting—usually at the county, congressional district, or state level—in proportion to the presidential preferences of those at the caucus. Those at the subsequent meeting (or perhaps a third-level meeting) elect the delegates to the national convention, again in proportion to the presidential preferences of those in attendance.

Does it sound complicated? Party leaders thought so. Many had preferred the caucus/convention system in the past because they could control the results. No public notices; no rules; no stated preferences. Just party leaders selecting themselves and their friends as convention delegates, fully understanding that they would be told for whom to vote by those leaders, who really chose the nominees. But caucuses became more difficult to run under the new guidelines. Twenty-two states opted to hold presidential preference primaries in 1972; 65 percent of the delegates were chosen in these primaries.

B. The 1972 Nomination

Imagine that you wrote the rules for a very complicated card game. If hand A were dealt, one set of rules applied; if hand B were dealt, another set of rules came into play; hand C would be played in a different way. Don't you think you would have an advantage the first time you played the game?

George McGovern resigned the chairmanship of the Commission on Party Structure and Delegate Selection after most of the work of that group had been finished. He resigned to run for president—under the new rules, his rules. McGovern chose as his campaign manager and chief strategist a young fellow named Gary Hart, who had been a key staff member of the McGovern Commission. They knew the rules and played them to their advantage.

The front-runner in 1972 was Maine senator Ed Muskie, who had impressed the party leaders as Humphrey's vice presidential running mate four years earlier. Muskie followed the old conventional wisdom. He lined up all the party leaders, the opinion leaders in the big states, behind him. Then he lost because they could not deliver. Hubert Humphrey entered the race late, as he had done in 1968, but this time he was too late; party leaders could not deliver for him either. Delegates selected in primaries and caucuses remained loyal to George McGovern, not to local party leaders, and he won the nomination.

The openness of the process led to participation by activists interested in discussing controversial issues. The Democratic Convention showed the party for what it was, an amalgamation of differing and competing interests. All the warts were visible to the large national television audience. When McGovern lost the general election by a landslide to Richard Nixon, party leaders were quick to blame the new rules. McGovern had been an extremist; he was not the candidate of the traditional core of the party. He was not the candidate of the blue-collar, union, big-city Democrats. And he was not the candidate who would have been chosen by the party leaders who had dominated previous conventions.

In fact, the rules neither gave McGovern the nomination nor caused his defeat. But the rules did present something of a conflict between types of representation. As had always been the case, they called for **geographic representation**, specifying that states break delegations down to more local areas. They also called for **demographic representation**, at least of groups traditionally loyal to and underrepresented in the Democratic party—women, blacks, youth. And they called for representation by candidate preference. Individuals supported presidential candidates based on their views of critical issues; this last type of representation approximated, in the view of many, **ideological representation**.

Critics claimed that the mixing of three kinds of representation, rather than the traditional reliance on geographic representation and domination by party leaders, led to the replacement of delegates who were concerned with winning by issue-oriented delegates who cared more about specific matters of principle than electoral victory. This conclusion has been actively debated ever since (see Kirkpatrick 1976, 1978; Polsby 1983; Polsby and Wildavsky 1988, 2004; Ranney 1975; Sullivan et al. 1977–1978; Sullivan, Pressman, and Arterton 1976; Sullivan et al. 1977; Wayne 1988).

C. Continuing Reform of the Process

Between 1972 and 1988, the Democrats appointed a series of commissions that continually reexamined the nominating process. Each commission looked at the problems from the preceding election and sought to correct them.

After the 1972 election Democratic National Committee chairman Robert Strauss appointed a commission to reexamine the delegate selection process.[2] The Mikulski Commission made a number of concessions to party regulars, but the principles of reform were unchallenged. The major contributions of the Mikulski Commission were (1) the restriction of participation in the presidential nominating process to Democrats only, that is, outlawing the "open" primary and (2) the requirement that delegates be allocated proportionally among all contenders receiving at least 15 percent of the votes cast, that is, proportional representation according to candidate strength or, in the phrase employed by party rule makers, **fair reflection of presidential preference**. The legacy of these decisions persists in the nominating process today.

Most of the new rules were left intact, but state party leaders were given great leeway in interpreting them. The party and the press seemed tired of haggling and fighting over rules, and the 1976 nominating period proceeded without major incident.

While the 1976 nominating season was under way, Democratic National Committee chairman Strauss appointed Michigan Demo-

---

GEOGRAPHIC REPRESEN-TATION

Representation based on the geographic area in which a person resides.

DEMOGRAPHIC REPRESEN-TATION

Representation based on demographic characteristics such as gender, race, or age.

IDEOLOGICAL REPRESEN-TATION

Representation based on how individuals stand on the issues under debate.

FAIR REFLECTION OF PRESIDENTIAL PREFERENCE

Delegates are chosen to each subsequent level of the presidential nominating process in proportion to the level of support the candidates receive at a previous level.

cratic chair Morley Winograd as head of a new committee to look at the problem caused by the proliferation of primaries, an unintended consequence of the reforms. The regulars again wanted more control.

The 1976 convention called for another commission, in effect authorizing the extension of Winograd's group. However, the new commission was expanded to included representatives of the White House. The not-so-hidden agenda of the commissioners loyal to President Carter was to assure that the 1980 rules hindered a challenge to the incumbent president. The major contribution of the Winograd Commission was an attempt to shorten the "primary season" by restricting all primaries and first-round caucuses to a three-month period from early March to early June. This became known as the **window concept**, drawing an analogy from the space program in which a "window" of opportunity during which launches can be safely attempted is identified before each flight. Exceptions were allowed for those states that had held caucuses or primaries before the opening of the window in 1976, most notably the early Iowa caucuses and **New Hampshire's "first-in-the-nation" primary**, which had provided the twin launch pads for Jimmy Carter's drive to nomination.

Why restrict the time period? The stated rationale was to shorten the length of campaigns, but it was clear to all that candidates would still start campaigning years in advance of the first official event. The more logical reason was that it would be difficult for a challenger to gain the momentum needed to overcome an incumbent if all the events were closely packed.

Other proposals from the Winograd Commission also represented steps back from reform, designed instead to aid the president's drive for renomination and to increase the power of party regulars. The principle of fair reflection of presidential preference was not repealed, but it was diluted. The threshold of votes necessary in order to receive any representation was raised from 15 to 25 percent, as the campaign progressed.

As another step away from fair reflection, the Winograd Commission voted to allow **winner-take-all primaries**, if states created single-member districts. In a winner-take-all contest, the candidate with the most votes gets all of the delegates being contested. The winner-take-all primary at the state level had been eliminated by the McGovern-Fraser Commission; the justification was that such a system distorted the actual preference of those casting their votes. (See chapter 9 for a discussion of the winner-take-all aspect of the electoral college system.) In 1976 various states had exploited a **loophole** in the rules, running winner-take-all primaries at the congressional district level. The Winograd Commission legitimized that

WINDOW CONCEPT

Analogous to the space program, in which a launch is only possible during a specified period of time, the concept that primaries and caucuses selecting delegates to presidential nominating conventions must be held between certain dates on the calendar.

NEW HAMPSHIRE'S "FIRST-IN-THE-NATION" PRIMARY

The first primary held in every recent nominating season, so specified by New Hampshire state law that states that New Hampshire's primary is to be held at least a week in advance of that of any other state.

WINNER-TAKE-ALL PRIMARIES

Primary elections in which the plurality winner receives all of the delegates at stake.

LOOPHOLE

A way around the intent of a law or regulation.

loophole, since it appeared that most of the single-member districts to be created would favor Carter.

While the debates over the timing of the process, the cutoff level for fair reflection of candidate preference, and the prohibition or allowance of winner-take-all primaries seem esoteric at best, they consumed a great deal of energy because strategists saw clearly that changes in rules like these would impact the nominating process in important ways. These changes were victories for those who favored party elite domination of the nominating process over those who saw broad democratic participation as more important.

The relevant aspect of the 1980 nomination for the purpose of this review of procedural reforms is that Jimmy Carter won renomination despite the fact that by the time the Democratic National Convention ratified his renomination most party officials felt he was bound to lose the general election to Ronald Reagan. The response to this situation was predictable—another "reform" commission. The goals of this new commission, chaired by North Carolina governor James B. Hunt Jr., were simply to strengthen the party, increase the role of party regulars to help the party win elections, and ensure that the party could govern once in office (Crotty 1983, 88). What could be easier?

The Hunt Commission reaffirmed most of the positions taken by previous commissions, including the position that the Democratic party nominating process should be open only to Democrats.[3] However, in 1984 the commission adopted three policies that revamped the rules of 1980. First, it unbound the delegates, returning to a commitment of "good conscience" as the constraint for whether or not delegates could switch from the candidate to whom they had been pledged. The justification for this change was that the 1980 nominating contest had shown that commitments made early in the nominating season were often made before the true circumstances of an election were known.[4] Second, the commission relaxed the rules on proportional representation while maintaining that they were reaffirming the principle of fair reflection. The result was a reinstitution of "loophole" primaries at the congressional district level in a number of states.

Finally, and most importantly, the Hunt Commission offered a proposal to increase significantly the impact of elected officials at the national convention. The Winograd Commission had increased state delegation size by allowing certain party officials to be "added on" to the slate elected. The Hunt Commission accepted the concept of **"add-on" delegates** but supplemented them with a new category of delegates, quickly dubbed **superdelegates**. These individuals were to be prominent party and/or elected officials, for example, governors, senators, or members of Congress who had played key roles at conventions before the reforms but whose par-

"ADD-ON" DELEGATES

Convention delegates added to the total a state normally would be allocated in order to accommodate certain party and elected officials.

SUPERDELEGATES

Delegates to the Democratic National Convention who hold their seats by virtue of their office, for example, members of congress, senators, and governors.

ticipation levels had declined. The superdelegates were to come to the convention officially unpledged. The theory was that they would bring practical experience to the convention and help nominate a winning ticket should a situation such as the one that the Democrats faced in 1980 reemerge (Mann 1985).

The losing candidates at the 1984 convention—Senator Gary Hart and Reverend Jesse Jackson—were upset by the advantage that the rules had given to former vice president Walter Mondale and they called for a new reform commission, a so-called Fairness Commission, to examine what steps could be taken to respond to their complaints.[5] The Mondale forces, magnanimous in victory at the convention, acceded to their request for a new study but little came of it.

The Fairness Commission finished its work by November 1985. According to commission chairman Donald L. Fowler, a longtime party activist from South Carolina, "There was a recognition that the 1984 rules worked pretty well and there was no reason to change a lot" (Cook 1986, 2158). The commission did increase the number of party and elected officials who would be delegates to the 1988 Democratic National Convention, granting superdelegate status to all members of the Democratic National Committee and to 80 percent of the Democratic members of Congress. While the commission did lower the share of the vote that a candidate must receive in order to qualify for delegates to 15 percent from the 20 percent it had been in some states, none of its actions was the kind of fundamental change that the Hart and Jackson forces had originally sought.

In short, the commission adopted a strategic position, seeking to improve the chances that the 1988 Democratic nominee would emerge from the process of gaining the party's nod without hurting his chances of winning the general election. The goal for 1988 was to create a process that would bring more people into line behind the Democratic party candidate. No party obstacles were to stand in the way of Democrats being happy with the Democratic candidate.

However, while the party rules were not changed as a result of the 1984 nominating process, some states did alter their laws in ways that had a fundamental effect on the 1988 process. In 1984, the second Tuesday in March had been referred to in the press as **Super Tuesday**, because a large number of delegates were selected on that day; the general view was that those states had gained in their share of influence over the process.

In 1988 Southern politicians extended this strategy of concentrating their delegate selection processes early in the nominating season in order to maximize their influence. They felt that the voice of the South would be heard most loudly if the entire Southern chorus sang at the same time. Thus Southern state after Southern

SUPER TUESDAY
The Tuesday during the primary season on which the most delegates are chosen.

state took the steps necessary to move its delegate selection process up to the second week in March 1988. Eventually twenty-one states—including fourteen Southern or border states—chose convention delegates during this one-week period; more than a quarter of the delegates to the 1988 Democratic Convention and more than 35 percent of those elected to the Republican Convention were chosen during this single period.[6]

This change was as significant as any rule change. Candidates and their strategists had to rethink how the early stages of the nominating process were to be organized. As with many "reforms," unintended consequences are often as apparent as intended consequences. For Democrats, the "winners" of the Super Tuesday sweepstakes were Mike Dukakis and Jesse Jackson as well as Tennessee senator Al Gore, who took up the mantle of the Southern moderates. Clearly, devising a system to help Dukakis and Jackson was not what the Southern governors pushing this change had in mind. For Republicans the clear winner was George H. W. Bush, who had more than 60 percent of the delegates needed to be nominated by the end of balloting on Super Tuesday. Again, Bush was not the candidate most reformers thought would have benefited from this change.

However, the reforms can be looked at in another way. The 1984 process in the Democratic party had produced a candidate who represented the mainstream of the party. He might have lost badly in November, and he might not have achieved the nomination with the ease he desired, but the process had avoided nominating an extremist or nominating an outsider. The election of 1988 was the first in twenty years in which an incumbent president was not eligible for reelection. Each party sought to nominate a candidate who could bring the faithful together to achieve victory in November. And each aptly did that. The process worked as theorists of political parties would want it to work. As Gerald Pomper (1989b), has written:

> To achieve victory, they seek politically adept but inoffensive candidates and pursue party unity by conciliating diverse factions, promoting agreement on public policies, and focusing party members' efforts on effective campaigns. . . . In nominating Michael Dukakis and George Bush, they chose two men who were experienced politicians with extensive records of public service, men who, if not stirring, were at least acceptable to tens of millions of their party's voters. (33)

D. The Reform Movement: An Assessment

Compare the experience of the Democrats with that of the Republicans. We have just discussed a series of reform commissions within the Democratic party. The Republicans by contrast have been bliss-fully happy with their system. This is not to suggest that they have not had reform commissions. One was established at the behest of former president Eisenhower after the 1964 Republican Convention appeared on television. A second, the DO (Delegates and Organizations) Committee, established after the 1968 convention, was dominated by members of the Republican National Committee and dealt with no controversial matters. A third, the Rule 20 Committee, chaired by the late William R. Steiger, a moderate Republican congressman from Wisconsin (1967–1978), dealt with disclosing campaign expenditures by Republican candidates and with opening up the party to broader participation.

A number of factors distinguish Republican reform efforts from Democratic. First, Republicans, even when their nomination has been hotly contested, have not divided their party because of the nominating process. Each of the Republican nominees between 1968 and 1988 had a united party behind him once the convention had reached its decision.

Second, Republican "reforms" have been suggestions, not mandates. Philosophically the Republicans do not believe that the national party should dictate to the states. Certainly they do not believe that a committee of reformers should dictate procedures. The Republican party rules state clearly that the convention is the governing authority. Only the convention can change the rules. Thus any reform would have to be ratified by one convention to take effect in the process four years hence. As it is quite difficult to foresee the impact of some of these reforms, the lack of predictable detrimental political consequences has taken much of the sting out of Republican reform efforts.

However, the Republican process has changed significantly because some of the changes wrought by the Democrats have resulted in changes in state laws that also impact the Republicans. Look at table 8.1. In 1968, sixteen states chose delegates to the Republican National Convention through the primary process, making up 34 percent of the delegates. By 1988, these numbers had changed to thirty-five states holding primaries and 77 percent of the delegates being chosen in that manner. The Democrats instituted the changes and caused states to change their election laws accordingly. Therefore, the Republicans were forced to follow suit.

The reforms begun in 1968 have fundamentally changed the ways in which the two parties nominate their presidential candidates. The conventional wisdom before 1968 was that party leaders in large states had the most influence over the nominations. The conventional wisdom by 1988 was that the process is open and that demonstrated success in attracting voters will be necessary in order to win. The delegates to the national conventions are now represen-

Table 8.1 Number of Presidential Primaries and the Percentage of Delegates Selected in Them, 1968–2004

	Democrats		Republicans	
	Primaries (#)	Delegates (%)	Primaries (#)	Delegates (%)
1968	17	38	16	34
1972	23	61	22	53
1976	29	73	28	68
1980	31	75	35	74
1984	26	63	30	68
1988	34	67	35	77
1992	39	77	38	80
1996	34	63	43	90
2000	40	86	43	93
2004	34	56	32	72

Source: Data for 1968–2000 from Wayne (2000). Data for 2004 compiled by authors from RNC, DNC, and various state sources.

tatives of those who have participated in the process, not stand-ins for party bosses.

Party leaders and elected officeholders still retain influence, but the change in their role in the last forty years may provide a perfect example of the difference between influence and power. The strategic premises of presidential contenders in 1960 were not very different from those of 1948 nor for that matter from those of 1928. But since 1968, the situation has been one of continual flux. Winning in the reformed system involves mastering the rules, reading the political lay of the land, and learning the right lessons from the most recent contests, including lessons about the timing of primaries.

Critics claimed that the reforms after 1968 were harmful to the parties, particularly to the Democrats (Kirkpatrick 1976, 1978; Polsby 1983). By contrast, we would argue that the reform process, begun after 1968 but continuing for two decades, had a positive effect on the parties. Although party leaders can no longer dictate who the nominees will be, the process involves many more people in the work of the parties and gives them a stake in the nominees. The process has evolved in such a way that party leaders themselves are now comfortable that successful nominees will emerge strengthened as candidates, not weakened, by the road taken to their nomination.

II. NOMINATIONS UNDER THE CURRENT SYSTEM

A. The 1992, 1996, and 2000 Nominations

In 1988 the system had worked as it was designed. Party leaders looked at the results—and while the Democrats might have been dismayed by Dukakis's showing in the general election—they were satisfied with how he was nominated. So too were the Republicans. The only rule changes in party rules following the 1988 nominations involved guaranteeing proportional representation of presidential preference for all states' systems, removing the vestiges of loopholes. No major changes followed the next four nominating contests. The 2008 nominating process will thus be the seventh under essentially the same rules. Two factors have been altered, however. The timing of the contests has been even more **front-loaded,** and the ways in which candidates fund their campaigns have changed drastically—and those have made quite a difference.

Once again in 1992, various states, worrying that they did not have enough influence, sought to move earlier in the process. Because a number of states have moved earlier in the process, and because some Southern states have opted out of the early primary, the uniquely Southern flavor of Super Tuesday has been diluted. In 1992, candidates for nomination faced a three-week period in March in which twenty-three states chose a total of over seventeen hundred convention delegates, nearly 40 percent of the total. This concentration of delegate selection had an important impact on the Republicans' renomination of President George H. W. Bush and on the Democrats' selection of Arkansas governor Bill Clinton. President Bush was able to use a huge victory on Super Tuesday to thwart the insurgent campaign of conservative activist Patrick Buchanan; Governor Clinton, the candidate of the centrist **Democratic Leadership Council**, won seven of the twelve contests held that day and quickly emerged as the all but unassailable leader in a crowded field.

Again in 1996 the process had important consequences for the eventual choice of nominees. For President Bill Clinton, the nomination was assured when no prominent Democrats chose to oppose him. Early in 1995, on the heels of the Republican victory in the 1994 congressional elections and with investigations of potential scandals hounding his White House, it seemed likely that Clinton would be challenged within his own party. However, the president recovered in 1995, standing up to the Republicans over the government shutdown, defying conventional political judgment by sending American troops into action in Bosnia, and leading the nation in its response to the Oklahoma City bombing. Clinton appeared tough, seasoned, and "presidential." In addition he had accumulated a vast campaign war chest aimed toward dissuading any potential challengers. None emerged.

For the Republicans, Senator Robert Dole, the majority leader in the Senate, his party's nominee for the vice presidency in 1976, and an unsuccessful candidate for the presidential nomination in 1980 and 1988, organized early and raised a great deal of money.

FRONT-LOADING

The practice of holding primaries and caucuses near the beginning of the period in which such events are permitted.

DEMOCRATIC LEADERSHIP COUNCIL (DLC)

An organization of moderate Democrats formed in order to bring the party back from the liberal extreme toward the center.

He was the clear leader, representing the establishment, the core of the Republican party. But his candidacy would not go unchallenged as contenders such as Texas senator Phil Gramm, television commentator Pat Buchanan, former Tennessee governor Lamar Alexander, and millionaire magazine publisher Steve Forbes, each presented the voters with a claim that they would fare better against President Clinton than the seventy-two-year-old Dole—viewed as a symbol of the past, not the future.

However, only Buchanan did well in the early contests, and his chances of an upset evaporated on Super Tuesday and the days around it. Fourteen states held caucuses or primaries between March 3 and March 5; six others held their contests on March 12. Bob Dole won every one of those contests.[7] In the Republican party, states can still opt for winner-take-all systems. At the beginning of March, Bob Dole had only twenty-seven delegates pledged to his candidacy; the other candidates had a total of over a hundred. By the middle of the month, Dole had 710 delegates; the others, only 144. The nomination contest was over.

In 2000, as in 1988, no incumbent was seeking reelection. Both parties wanted a system that would permit their nominee to emerge without serious intraparty warfare, but despite efforts by the parties (and even by the Association of Secretaries of State) to rationalize the timing of the primaires and caucuses, no systematic changes occurred. Thus the calendar for the 2000 nominating process was decided by various state legislatures acting in their own interests, or in a way thought to improve the chances of candidates favored by those controlling the legislatures. California and New York moved their primaries to dates much earlier in the process than had been the case in the last.

For the Democrats, Vice President Al Gore entered the nominating race as the prohibitive favorite, the heir apparent to President Clinton, a man who had worked hard for the party for eight years, who twelve years earlier had sought his party's nomination, who was right on the issues and clearly the candidate of the party elite. Gore's only serious challenge came from former New Jersey senator Bill Bradley, who had retired from the Senate in 1998 and spent two years building an organization of young activists. Bradley stressed that he wanted to bring a new style to national politics. Somewhat wooden as a campaigner, the former Rhodes scholar and NBA star attracted a wide following of liberals and environmentalists who felt that the New Democrats had compromised too much on fundamental issues. The press was attracted to Bradley's campaign, and he was able to raise nearly as much money as the vice president, but Gore's superior name recognition and organizational support proved too much for the outsider, most notably because so many states held primaries and caucuses in such a condensed period of time, so no other candidate could use the process to become better known.

The Republican nominating process in 2000 was reminiscent in many ways of a prereform campaign. A large number of well-known Republicans were lining up to challenge Al Gore—former Tennessee governor and education secretary Lamar Alexander, Christian right leader Gary Bauer, Patrick Buchanan once again, twice cabinet secretary and wife of the 1996 nominee Elizabeth Dole, former candidate and magazine mogul Steve Forbes, Senate Judiciary Committee chair Orrin Hatch (Utah), House Budget Committee chair John Kasich (Ohio), former ambassador and conservative spokesman Alan Keyes, former POW and campaign finance reform advocate Senator John McCain (Ariz.), and former vice president Dan Quayle. But from the start, the Republican hierarchy, particularly the Republican governors and many large contributors, lined up behind Texas governor George W. Bush, the eldest son of the former president.

The key to Governor Bush's path to nomination was that early on he announced that he would not accept federal matching funds for the primary campaign; rather he would raise money from individual contributors. By refusing federal funds, Bush also freed himself from the state-by-state and overall spending limits that accompanied acceptance of those funds. And then the Bush campaign proceeded to raise more money than ever before thought possible. By the "first-in-the-nation" New Hampshire primary, he had raised more than $70 million and had spent more than $37 million. Most of the other candidates soon saw that they could not compete—Alexander, Bauer, Dole, Hatch, Kasich, and Quayle left the stage. Buchanan left the Republican party and decided to seek the Reform party nomination. Forbes, who was also funding his own campaign, remained slightly longer but attracted no widespread support. The field of challengers to the Bush ascendancy was left to the ideologically pure but noncompetitive conservative Keyes and more significantly to John McCain, he of the compelling personal story and the "Straight Talk Express," his campaign bus to which he gave virtually unlimited access to any journalist who would cover him.

McCain made the case that he was electable, that he was speaking to the issues that the American people wanted to hear. His strong showing in the New Hampshire primary led to an immediate infusion of campaign funds over the Internet, the first time the Internet had been used successfully to raise large amounts of money quickly. McCain appealed specifically to independents who could vote in open Republican primaries. And therein was both the strength and the weakness of his candidacy. He did in fact appeal to independents—and he did well in open primary states. But he was not acceptable to the Republican establishment. When the calendar turned from open primary states to closed primary states, the Mc-Cain threat to Bush dissipated. Like Bradley for Gore, McCain remained a nuisance for the Bush campaign, but little more. After Super Tuesday 2000, the inevitability of Bush's nomination, like that of Vice President Gore, demonstrated that the system had once again worked as party officials, if not the public, desired. Each party had settled on a nominee in the mainstream of the party followers early enough in the process to begin planning for the general election. Each had been briefly challenged—and the challenges each left some scars—but the party establishment had emerged victorious and ready to head for November before serious damage had been done.

B. The 2004 Nominating Process

Timing again was the major consideration as the 2004 process took shape. For the Republicans, the nomination was never in doubt, but timing was still important. President Bush, unopposed for renomination, once again declined public funding for the prenomination phase of the campaign. His goal was to raise as much money as possible; his campaign eventually raised over $250 million to spend before the fall campaign actually began. (See table 8.2.) Thus the Republicans scheduled their convention much later than normally the case, from August 30 until September 2, in New York City. Bush strategists hoped to be able to make the case for their candidate and against their opponent for as long a period as possible before they fell under the restrictions of the publicly funded fall campaign.[8]

For the Democrats, front-loading took on a whole new meaning in 2004. Iowa still held its caucus in January, and the New Hampshire primary was one week later. But then, twenty-one states scheduled primaries—and nine others, caucuses—before the middle of March. Five states held primaries and three caucuses on February 3. The conventional wisdom was that, to have any sort of chance, a candidate had to win something on or before that date. Nine states—including California, New York, and Ohio—held primaries on March 2, the date by which many pundits believed that the eventual nominee would be known. The rules for the nomination in 2004 might not have changed, but the calendar made a huge difference in candidate strategies—and it is to these strategies that we now turn.

III. STRATEGIC CONSIDERATIONS IN THE CONTESTS FOR NOMINATIONS

The nomination process is, by its very nature, complex. The goal for the two major parties at this stage is to winnow the field of potential

Table 8.2 Money Raised by Candidates for Presidential Nominations, 2004

	Federal Matching Funds	Indiv Contrib[a]	PAC Contrib[a]	Candidate Contrib[b]	Other Loans[b]	Previous-Campaign Transfers	Other Receipts	Adjusted Campaign Total
REPUBLICANS								
Bush	$0	$258,867,236	$2,647,900	$0	$0	$671,100	$7,392,959	$269,579,195
DEMOCRATS								
Clark	7,615,360	17,321,151	45,950	0	0	0	129,983	25,112,444
Dean	0	51,083,674	15,300	0	0	0	29,033	51,128,007
Edwards	6,647,851	21,640,719	2,000	0	0	962,908	0	29,253,478
Gephardt	4,104,320	14,263,715	406,462	0	0	2,403,521	25,120	21,203,138
Kerry	0	215,370,782	146,269	0	0	2,650,000	16,416,708	234,583,760
Kucinich	3,083,963	8,005,828	16,000	0	0	0	2,898	11,108,689
LaRouche	1,456,019	8,210,313	3,796	0	0	0	1,118	9,671,246
Lieberman	4,267,797	14,052,813	214,320	2,000	0	0	0	18,536,930
Moseley-Braun	0	537,807	39,273	14,848	0	0	0	591,928
Sharpton	0[c]	512,736	4,200	77,500	−4,569	0	0	589,867
OTHER PARTY								
Nader	865,425	1,527,944	0	40,544	0	98,078	159	2,532,150
REP SUBTOTAL	269,579,195							
DEM SUBTOTAL	401,779,487							
OTHER SUBTOTAL	2,532,150							
Total	673,890,832							

Source: Federal Election Commission.

[a]Minus refunds.

[b]Minus repayment.

[c]Sharpton initially received $100,000 in matching funds, but was forced to return the money after his campaign disclosed that he had spent more than $50,000 of his own money on his campaign.

presidents down from all those eligible to two—one Democrat and one Republican. What criteria are used? Obviously a principal concern is to find an individual qualified to hold the office, but that concern is for naught if the individual cannot win the general election. Thus the parties are looking for the individual who will be the best candidate and the best president. Those are separate jobs that call for different skills. Why would one think, for example, that the person who is best at campaigning on television or at raising money for a campaign would also have the skills necessary to negotiate with the leaders of other nations or to craft compromises that could be accepted by a Congress controlled by leaders of the other party? How should those skills be combined?

Perhaps a group of politicos reasoning together could arrive at the perfect mixture of skills and seek the best-qualified individual. But that is not the nature of our political system. The individuals selected are selected through a political process. More accurately, they are chosen through different political processes in each of the fifty states (and the District of Columbia and various other areas). And they are chosen by a large number of participants, each of whom is free to choose based on his or her own conception of how the choice should be made. It is a small wonder then that the process is characterized most by complexity.

Presidential contenders must face a complex process, with uncertain dynamics. They do not control the order of events, though they do have some say in the importance they attribute to different events. They do not control others' perceptions of events. To a large extent they proceed by instinct; success or failure is often a function of the acuity of their political instincts and those of their advisers. Politicians as a group are firm believers in learning the lessons of the past.

Given that, it is somewhat unbelievable how many politicians

have learned the wrong lessons from even very recent experiences. But others have clearly benefited from understanding what happened to others facing similar situations. In the following sections, we will examine some of the strategic considerations facing today's would-be candidates as they try to decipher the presidential nominating process.

A. The Political Calendar

Perhaps the most important lesson that candidates and their staff must learn is that the calendar of events is critical to success or failure. Past examples cannot be followed if those examples are drawn from contests run with different calendars. Three concepts dominate calendar considerations under the current system. Each must be understood if appropriate and effective strategies are to be adopted.

1. The Influence of Iowa and New Hampshire and Front-Loading the System

Front-loading refers to holding a large number of primaries and caucuses, contests in which a significant number of delegates are selected, early in the political year. Rules in both parties call for all contests to select delegates to the national conventions, to be held between the first Tuesday in February and the first Tuesday in June of the presidential election year. New Hampshire and Iowa have traditionally been given exemptions from these rules, but only by one and two weeks, respectively. Through 2004, all other states were restricted to holding their contests in the window provided by party rules.

A number of states—and some political reformers—have felt that Iowa and New Hampshire have more influence on the process than they should. After all, the citizens in these states are not representative of either party's voters, nor of the nation as a whole. However, because they have been permitted to hold their contests first, when no other states compete for attention, candidates have spent an inordinate amount of time there. The media has devoted a disproportionate amount of attention to the contests in these states (Orren and Polsby 1987).

Partially in response to the prominence of Iowa and New Hampshire, and certainly as a means to increase their influence, a number of states decided to hold their primaries early in the 1984 nominating season, and the move to advance the calendar accelerated after that. But front-loading, like so many reforms, has had unintended consequences. Candidates cannot enter the race late; in fact, because so many states have moved their process up, states holding later primaries and caucuses feel they have no influence. So more and more moved up. The process was certainly accelerated, but the influence of Iowa and New Hampshire was not diminished. As a result, for the 2008 nominating season, a limited number of caucus states have been permitted to begin their delegate selection process in the weeks immediately after the New Hampshire primary. In 2007, Florida's legislature voted to move its primary to late January, responding to the large number of states that had already moved their delegate selection process to February 5. The Democratic National Committee's dominance of the process is directly challenged by Florida's action—and the timing of the process remained in flux as the calendar year of the election approached. Candidate strategies had to be flexible as a result.

This change in the calendar might increase the influence of some more representative states, but no one sees it as a fundamental reform that will significantly improve the system. Front-loading remains a larger problem than ever; the calendar is determined by the whim of state legislators. And reformers remain uniquely unsuccessful in their efforts to rationalize the timing of the primary and caucus calendars.

2. Super Tuesday

Super Tuesday was originally invented to give more influence to the South. However, decisions on the timing of primaries and caucuses by various states have thwarted that goal. In 1992, March 10 was clearly Super Tuesday. Eight states held their primaries on that day—six Southern or border states, plus Massachusetts and Rhode Island. In 1996, eight states held primaries on March 5—five New England states plus Georgia, Maryland, and Colorado. Seven states, with more delegates among them, held their primaries one week later. In 2000 eleven states, including California, New York, and Ohio, as well as the New England states, held primaries on March 7; four other states had caucuses that week. The 2004 process followed a pattern similar to 2000, but five other states jumped ahead to February 3, reducing the influence of some of the bigger states that had selected their dates earlier.

REGIONAL PRIMARIES

Presidential primaries scheduled so that those in any one region of the country are held on the same day.

Thus the concept of Super Tuesday is an evolving one. It is now closely linked with the concept of **regional primaries**. Regional primaries represent efforts by state officials to enhance the influence of a region by holding all of that region's primaries on one day—or within a week, if one includes the caucus states. Because candidates want to appear in as many places holding primaries as possible, regional primaries advantage candidates by cutting down on travel time and costs. Also, because many media markets cross state lines, campaigns piggyback advertising budget for primaries in neighboring states, parts of which might well be in the same media market, when primaries are held on the same day. However, unless states out of the region defer the primaries to another day, the sheer number of states choosing to hold their contests on one day all but necessitates a national campaign—making the process extremely difficult for underfunded candidates. The advantages of a regional primary are lost.

For the 2008 nominating season approximately half of all states—including the very largest—moved their primaries to February 5. Candidates and their staffs had to determine how to marshall their financial resources and their staff and candidate time to compete in what was for all intents and purposes a national primary day. At the same time, they had to be sure to reserve enough money to be able to continue to compete if no nominee emerged from the most Super Tuesday in history.

3. Filing Deadlines

Each state specifies how a candidate wins a place on its primary ballot. In some cases the decision is made by a state official. In other cases the presidential candidates must file slates of proposed delegates. In still other cases the delegates themselves must file petitions to be on the ballot. The variety of requirements is almost endless. But each state, according to its own laws, specifies a certain date by which those who seek a place on the ballot must have fulfilled whatever requirements exist. **Filing deadlines** are a necessity so that ballots can be printed in advance of an election. But filing deadlines also have strategic implications. Anyone who does not meet a state's filing deadline cannot win delegates in that state. In 1984, for instance, Gary Hart was unable to gain the momentum he might have from his New Hampshire victory over front-runner Walter Mondale because Hart's campaign had failed to file delegate slates in many of the districts in Florida, a delegate-rich state whose primary followed shortly after New Hampshire's. A national campaign organization is important for a prospective presidential nominee in that someone can keep track of approaching deadlines and alert state campaigners, who are often rank amateurs, to their approach. For the 2004 nominating process, at least a half-dozen states had filing deadlines in late 2003, causing a logistical problem for the late entrant in the campaign, General Wesley Clark.

4. Strategic Implications of the Political Calendar

Recent campaign experience has demonstrated conclusively that the political calendar has serious implications for campaign strategy. In 1992, for example, many of the first tier of Democratic candidates held back because they feared President Bush's strength as a candidate. Bill Clinton stepped into that void and became the front-

FILING
DEADLINES

The dates by which candidates must fulfill whatever requirements exist to gain a place on a ballot.

runner. However, he looked like a flawed candidate, as his character and ethics were attacked during the New Hampshire primary. Many party leaders tried to urge one or more of those who had earlier decided not to run that it was time to step in. But it was too late to step in. By the time the New Hampshire primary was held, filing deadlines had passed in most of the states that would elect delegates in March and April. It was already too late to raise money and organize a campaign in those states that would hold primaries on the first two Tuesdays in March.

The concentration of many caucuses and primaries on the same day also has important implications. In the old system, when fewer states held primaries and they were spread out over the political calendar, it was possible for a candidate's organization to get by with a skeletal crew, moving key campaign operatives from one important primary state to another, after the first's contest had been held. However, to be successful under the new rules and calendar, a candidate must build a national organization from the start. If not, he will be overwhelmed by an opponent who has. Bill Bradley and John McCain each faced that reality in the 2000 contests, despite the encouraging starts that their campaigns achieved. This situation has only been exacerbated by changes in 2008.

B. The Rules of the Game

George McGovern's 1972 campaign will always stand as the example of a campaign that understood the rules and won because of how they were implemented. But in interesting ways that lesson has been repeated over and over again in the reform era. If there is a real lesson here, it is that campaign strategists ignore whatever rules are in effect at their peril. Although many rules were altered by state law changes in order to meet Democratic party mandates, there are still important areas in which the two parties' rules differ—with very significant consequences for the candidates.

I. Proportional Representation versus Winner-Take-All Systems

The Democratic party insists that delegates be apportioned according to the presidential preference of those voters participating in the process. While certain loopholes have been permitted, the basic concept of delegate strength reflecting proportional strength among the voters has been maintained. The Republicans have not followed the Democrats' lead. They have maintained a system that permits states to run winner-take-all primaries should they choose to do so. Each system has strengths and weaknesses; decidedly each has strategic implications.

Consider the Democrats. If one is on the ballot in a system that gives delegates proportionately to the strength at the ballot box, a candidate can "lose" an election but still pick up delegate support. As the nominee is the person with a majority of the delegates, close losses can be important "victories." In 1976, Jimmy Carter ran everywhere. He picked up some delegates everywhere. Even when Democrats seemed to be tiring of Carter, as the primaries drew to a close, he picked up delegates. Few recall that Carter lost five of the last seven primaries. What is remembered is that he had guaranteed himself a majority of the delegates at the convention on the day the primary process ended. He did so by winning delegates in primaries that he lost. Similarly, in 1992 Bill Clinton continued to gain strength when he lost primaries, with the result that unexpected victories by Jerry Brown as the process wore on did not encourage new opposition. Savvy politicians understood that Clinton would win the nomination by attrition, even if not by acclamation. Thus they joined his bandwagon.

But proportional representation could work in another way, one much less beneficial to the front-running candidate. In recent contests the Democrats have had one leader and other candidates trying to make themselves into the one principal opponent. The leader has prevailed by successfully playing off other candidates against each other and amassing delegate support. Imagine a scenario in which there are two or three equally well-positioned candidates contesting for the nomination in a front-loaded system. If two or even three candidates emerge from the early round of primaries in competitive positions, with enough money and organization to see themselves through the process, or if their resources are equally depleted (see section C, "Strategic Use of Campaign Resources"), then proportional representation might well mean that no one candidate can garner the support of a majority of the delegates before the convention. Serious strategists and analysts must consider the possibility as they plan a nominating campaign.

What about the Republicans? The winner-take-all system proved to be a huge advantage for George W. Bush. When there is a front-runner with a strong financial and organizational base, a winner-take-all system allows that front-runner to dispense with pesky challengers quite easily. George H. W. Bush did it in 1992; Bob Dole did it in 1996; by Super Tuesday 2000 George W. Bush had all but guaranteed himself the nomination. The system benefits the leaders. It allows the eventual nominee to have more time to bring the party together, united behind his candidacy.

But what if the leader is not likely to be a winner in November? What if the early primaries reveal hitherto unnoted weaknesses or a lack of voter appeal? The same system makes it difficult to change course in midstream. The Dole example is a good one. Bob Dole was the prohibitive favorite for the GOP nomination from early on in 1996, but the Dole candidacy looked weak at many points in the early caucuses and primaries. The political calendar worked in his favor; so too did the winner-take-all provisions in the rules of most states that held primaries in March of that year. In those primaries Dole never won more than two-thirds of the votes (albeit an impressive number) and on six occasions he won less than half of the votes, but in many states he won all of the delegates. The system exaggerated his strength and downplayed campaign weaknesses that would later become apparent.

2. Superdelegates versus Influential Party Leaders

Recall that the "add-on" delegates and the superdelegates were put back into the Democratic party process because influential party leaders and elected officials chose not to participate in the nominating process after the McGovern-Fraser reforms were implemented. These leaders refused to participate because they did not want their local reputations to be sullied by having backed a losing national candidate. Decisions not to back presidential candidates did not follow from lack of interest but rather from strategic considerations. Either an elected leader would beat some of his or her own constituents in a contest to be a convention delegate or he or she might lose. Neither was a good outcome. Thus many decided to opt out altogether; few party leaders were represented at the 1972, 1976, or even 1980 Democratic conventions.

The Republicans never faced the same problems. Because they allowed unpledged slates to run and because they did not require fair reflection of presidential preference, influential Republicans have continued to play a key role in their party's nominating process throughout the entire reform period. Most would argue that they have done so to the benefit of their party's candidates.

From the perspective of this discussion, what is important is the strategic differences that the two systems call for. The Republican process is not very different from what it has been in the past. Perspective candidates want party leaders and elected officials to support their candidacies. When all save one of the Republican governors came out for George W. Bush before the first primary vote had been cast, not only the national media but all of his opponents knew that he had a huge advantage. A Republican presidential candidate is wise to spend his time courting those who have influence in their own states because they can frequently turn that influence into delegate support.

Democratic party leaders tend to hold back support. Their role is supposed to be that of a broker, to be certain that popular participation in the convention does not run away with the party. Thus the superdelegates were extremely important in helping Walter Mondale secure the party nomination in 1984; those who had worked closely with Gary Hart did not see him as presidential material. Similarly, superdelegates worked against Jesse Jackson in his two bids for the Democratic nomination. He won support from the Congressional Black Caucus (though not from all of its members), but he was not able to attract a wider following among the party leadership. Democratic campaigns for party leader and elected official support are more subtle than those in the Republican party. Each individual is courted for his or her own support, not because he or she can necessarily translate that support to a wider following.

However, the support of the superdelegates viewed as a whole is an important element in the Democratic party process. When selected superdelegates declared for Bill Clinton in 1992, they were essentially conceding him the race. Their support said that they knew who the winner would be and that they wanted to be on his team. In 2004 observers watched to see whether superdelegates would desert John Kerry for the early front-runner, Howard Dean; when many stayed with Kerry, the signal was that his candidacy still had life.

The superdelegates and the party officials who have been added to state delegations have never played the brokering role that was intended for them. Again, however, that is not to say that a scenario could not eventuate that would necessitate that role. The brokered convention is a thing of the past according to most analysts. But if no nominee has a majority—or a near majority—of delegate support when a convention is called to order, no strategist and no contemporary analyst has a historical precedent to rely on to see what might happen. It seems very likely that the party elite would emerge as leaders in such a situation.

C. Strategic Use of Campaign Resources

Any serious candidate for president starts the campaign possessing certain resources. Others can be obtained. Still others must be done without. Campaign strategists are often in the business of resource management.

I. Office

The key resource to hold if one wants a presidential nomination seems to be the White House. Eligible incumbent presidents are normally renominated. Renomination may be semiautomatic, resembling coronations, as in the case of George W. Bush in 2004. Or renomination may require a battle, as was the case for the first President Bush in 1992.

These latter cases are particularly instructive.[9] As noted earlier, Bush I was challenged by Patrick Buchanan, who claimed that as president, Bush had not been a faithful successor in upholding Ronald Reagan's conservative agenda. Bush felt insecure about his own party base and was uncomfortable with the degree of strength Buchanan showed in some of the early primaries. Thus he responded to Buchanan, attacking him and positioning himself further toward the right on the political spectrum. Bush was able to use the power of his office to defeat Buchanan, but he was not secure enough in that power to dismiss him presumptively as others had done.

Other offices have also proved useful. The vice presidency seems to be something of a mixed blessing. Eight out of the last eleven vice presidents have either succeeded to the presidency or sought that office themselves.[10] For Vice President Mondale his service under Jimmy Carter clearly cut two ways. He was considered an excellent vice president, gained a good deal of national exposure, and built a wide range of political contacts during his four years in office. However, he was also saddled with the legacy of a failed presidency and with defending policies for which he was not, in fact, responsible.

On the other hand, Vice President Bush, in 1988, had a tremendous advantage. His only problem was to convince Reagan supporters that he was not only a loyal lieutenant but also a worthy heir. That problem continued to plague him as president.

Vice President Al Gore was able to draw on the allegiance of loyal Democrats who appreciated the hard work he had done for the party over an eight-year period, but he also had to deal with the legacy of Bill Clinton and the residual consequences of the scandals that plagued the Clinton presidency.

For some time the Senate was thought to be the incubator of presidential candidates. Thirty-three different senators have run for their party's presidential nomination since 1968 (see table 8.3); but as of June 2007 only three have been successful.

The Dole case may be most instructive. In 1988, when he ran for the nomination as a powerful senator and former vice presidential nominee, he was unable to get much traction. When he decided to seek his party's nomination again in 1996, Senator Dole was then the majority leader as Howard Baker had been when he ran unsuccessfully in 1980. Dole campaigned for a long period maintaining both positions. He hoped that the prominence of his role in the Senate would give him a public pulpit to compete with that of President Clinton. But when the Democrats in the Senate began to tie up his time with legislative haggling, Dole saw the Baker lesson, that you cannot hold a powerful job and run for president at the same time, more clearly. In May 1996 he resigned from the Senate to devote himself full-time to his presidential campaign. Dole's prominence in the Senate undoubtedly help him obtain the nomination, but it was impossible for him to continue to campaign and to hold his party's top Senate job as well. John Kerry was nominated

Table 8.3   Senators Seeking Their Party's Presidential Nomination, 1968–2008

1968	Robert F. Kennedy Eugene McCarthy	**1992**	Tom Harkin Bob Kerry
1972	Vance Hartke Hubert Humphrey Henry Jackson George McGovern Edmund S. Muskie	**1996**	Bob Dole Phil Gramm Richard Lugar Arlen Specter
1976	Birch Bayh Lloyd Bentsen Frank Church Fred Harris Hubert Humphrey Henry Jackson	**2000**	John McCain Orrin Hatch Bob Smith
		2004	John Edwards Bob Graham John Kerry Joseph Lieberman
1980	Howard Baker Robert Dole Edward M. Kennedy	**2008**	Joseph Biden Sam Brownback Hillary Clinton
1984	Alan Cranston John Glenn Gary Hart Ernest Hollings		Chris Dodd John McCain Barack Obama
1988	Joseph Biden Robert Dole Albert Gore Gary Hart Paul Simon		

Source: Compiled by authors. Senators seeking the 2008 nomination valid as of June 19, 2007.

as a sitting senator in 2004, but he was in the minority party and had plenty of time to spend on the campaign trail.

It is also important to note the experience of Jimmy Carter in 1976, Ronald Reagan in 1980, and Walter Mondale in 1984, all of whom won presidential nominations while not holding other elective offices, as these seem to confirm Dole's perception.

On the other hand, Michael Dukakis won nomination in 1988, Bill Clinton was nominated in 1992, and George W. Bush was nominated in 2000 while serving as state governors. Aren't the responsibilities of a sitting governor too burdensome to allow a race for the presidential nomination? Dukakis considered this question very seriously before deciding to enter the race. One key advantage he had was that Massachusetts is a heavily Democratic state; his party controlled the legislature, and his lieutenant governor was loyal to him. His top staff people could run the state government while he was campaigning (Black et al. 1988). Clinton and Bush were in similar situations, in Clinton's case because of Democratic control in Arkansas and in Bush's, in part at least because the Texas governor does not play as active a role as many other state governors, with many important duties falling to the lieutenant governor (Ceaser and Busch 1993).

The race would have been much harder for New York governor Mario Cuomo, who considered seeking the Democratic nomination in both 1988 and 1992. Cuomo was constantly bickering with his state's divided legislature over state policies. The Republicans in New York would have been anxious to argue over policies with an absent governor.

Context is thus crucially important. Dukakis, Clinton, and George W. Bush, like Bush's father in 1988 and Gore in 2000, could use their offices to their advantage, without worrying about constraints, but in today's complex world of governing, this situation may be more the exception than the rule.

2. Money

Running for a presidential nomination actually involves running more than fifty separate campaigns. In 2004 primary elections or caucuses were scheduled on twenty different days, obviously with a number of different events held on some of those days. Candidates had to monitor the selection of the individuals who would serve as convention delegates from the caucus states and many primary states as well as additional facets of the process. An enterprise this vast requires a complex organization, extensive travel by the candidate and staff, sophisticated information gathering and dissemination, and effective advertising. These require money.

Since the 1976 presidential nomination, all contenders for major party nomination have been eligible for federal matching funds. (See chapter 5 for a detailed discussion of campaign financing in all elections.) When Steve Forbes decided to forgo federal funding and finance his own campaign in 1996, he became only the second candidate in twenty years to do so.[11] In so doing, he launched a fundamental change in the way the nomination phase of the process is financed, a change that has yet to play out completely. Neither Forbes nor George W. Bush accepted federal funds in 2000, and Bush's huge war chest played a significant role in the outcome of the nominating contest.

As noted earlier, in 2004 President Bush again refused matching funds for the prenomination stage of the election; so, too, did Democrats Dean and Kerry. The Democrats understood that they would have to raise much more than the $19 million for which they would qualify in matching funds, if they were to compete at all with the president, once the nomination was secured. Table 8.2 shows their dramatic success in doing so. The table also reveals the distinct advantage that private fund-raising—much of it done through the Internet, emulating the strategy of John McCain from 2000—gave Kerry and Dean over the other Democrats seeking the nomination.

Whereas in the past a legitimate strategy was to concentrate on Iowa and New Hampshire and hope good showings there would lead to an infusion of the funds needed to contest later primaries, the front-loading of the calendar and the huge sums raised in recent years have made raising early money essential for viability. The withdrawal of Senator Bob Graham (D-Fla.) from the race for the 2004 Democratic nomination in the fall of 2003 was in recognition of the fact that he could not raise enough money to carry on an effective campaign.

Candidates other than those who have disdained federal matching funds have had to plan how to spend their money strategically because of the limitations to which they acquiesce when they accept public financing. Malbin (1985) has demonstrated that candidates spend a good deal of money before the year of the presidential nomination and that they spend a much higher percentage of the permitted limit in the early states than they do in later states. These decisions have consequences for later contests in a close race, since publicly funded candidates have accepted an overall limit in how much they will spend (Corrado and Maisel 1988; Maisel 1988). This problem did not exist for candidates like Bush II or Kerry, who, in 2004, did not accept public matching funds and thus were not required to limit their preconvention spending. Their experience may well have made the public funding route to the nomination unviable for future candidates. Budgetary planning by those who raise money without accepting matching federal dollars follow different strategic rules than do those by candidates who accept public funding. In the case of the self-financed candidates (like Steve Forbes), the key questions may well be, How much of their own wealth are they willing to invest in a campaign?—a question that must be reexamined as the fate of the campaign becomes clearer. How will the public view revelations about the amount of money the candidate has spent on his own behalf? In the case of a candidate like George W. Bush or John Kerry, the only questions are, How much money can be raised, and will the public react negatively to "buying" an election, particularly as the sources of that money are revealed? In 2004, the answer to the first question seemed to be "however much is needed" and to the second "apparently not." In the run-up a year before the 2008 nominating season, press reports speculated that the "buy-in" to a serious candidacy will be $100 million; four candidates shattered previous records in three reports filed after the first quarter of 2007. The current process is clearly a long way from the process envisioned when public funding was first proposed.

3. The Media

In many ways the press makes the presidential nominating process work. How many average citizens are thinking about presidential politics over a year before an election, when the contenders are courting delegate candidates in Florida, Iowa, and Maine? Has the public begun to focus on the next election when scores of candidates and their staffs are trooping through the snows of New Hampshire? The answer is a resounding "No!" But the working press is gearing up.

Initially one or two reporters will accompany a candidate on a campaign swing. If a candidate is lucky or if a press secretary is extremely good, a television crew may cover part of a campaign trip. Particularly at the beginning of the primary process, free publicity is the key. Odd as it seems, presidential contenders are not necessarily well known to the general public.[12]

In 2000 many people thought that the George Bush running for president was the same one who had been president before, until the media began to cover the Texas governor; John McCain was virtually unknown until the press began to cover his campaign. One "advantage" that the little-known Howard Dean had in the 2004 nominating process was that the other, better-known candidates, such as Senator Kerry, were not actually known by the public either.

The goal in the early stages of a campaign is to be mentioned. Television advertising cannot be effective without the public focusing on the campaign, and so candidates court press attention. They play to local media wherever they go; more important, they seek mention in the national press, some positive reference as a real contender.

Consider Bill Clinton in 1992. Clinton had a difficult press problem. In 1991 his candidacy began to be taken quite seriously by Washington insiders because most of the Democrats who were more prominently mentioned had decided not to seek the nomination. Washington journalists knew that Governor Clinton had a reputation in Little Rock as a womanizer. That reputation made the rounds of Washington cocktail parties, but it was never reported in nationally syndicated stories on the upcoming campaign. Then the accusations of Gennifer Flowers, first reported in a supermarket tabloid, hit the newsstands. The national press had to decide how to play the story. Media leaders decided that the story, once reported, had legitimacy; the pack of journalists on the presidential campaign trail followed. As the New Hampshire primary approached, the Clinton campaign was on the ropes. Clinton's response was again to use the media—this time an interview on *60 Minutes,* in which he and his wife talked about their marital difficulties and how they had worked them out. Clinton had gone around the intermediary of the journalists and used the media to communicate directly to the voters.[13] His strategy was successful. His campaign halted what could have been a fatal plunge in his support.

Or look back at the McCain campaign in 2000. John McCain was first elected to the House of Representatives in 1982; four years later he moved up to the Senate. McCain is the son and grandson of navy admirals. He is a decorated pilot who was shot down over Vietnam and spent five years in a prisoner-of-war camp; he refused to be given special treatment because of his family connections. But he was largely unknown when he announced what many thought was a quixotic campaign for the Republican nomination. McCain used the press masterfully. In a campaign in which the front-runners were staying away from the press in order to avoid making mistakes, McCain made himself available at every opportunity. And he labeled his campaign bus the "Straight Talk Express," to differentiate himself from politicians who did not give straight answers. While his fellow senators found McCain acerbic and difficult to work with, the press loved him. They told and retold his compelling personal story and drew parallels between his military career and his political career. In the end journalists had to report that McCain's campaign could not overcome Bush's advantages; but the campaign went as far as it did largely because of the media attention it drew.

We should return to the Clinton campaign for one more look, for it stands as an example of another aspect of media as a "resource" for a campaign. The media portrays images of candidates to the public—for good or for ill. At times, media delving into a candidate's personal life can have devastating effects. At other times, the portrait can be much more positive. Candidates certainly understand that they are perceived by the public largely as they are portrayed by the media; they go to great lengths to be sure that the image that comes across is one with which they are comfortable.

Recent experience leads to the conclusion that a key to gaining early press attention is to do better than is expected or to make a more positive showing than early reports would have predicted; but doing worse than expected can have a detrimental effect. In this regard the Iowa caucuses and the New Hampshire primary—and how candidates are presented as these events unfold—have been very important (Orren and Polsby 1987). The experience of Governor Dean in the 2004 Iowa caucuses, where he failed to meet expectations and then was pilloried for his emotional concession speech is an obvious case in point. In those same caucuses Senator John Edwards of North Carolina kept his candidacy viable by exceeding his anticipated vote total. Dean's momentum was stalled and Edwards's gained steam on the same night.

Surpassing expectations is not the only strategy for dealing with the media; demonstrating uniqueness—and thus newsworthiness—

certainly works as well. In 1984 Jesse Jackson demonstrated that the press can be a crucial resource when used in this way. Jackson was newsworthy. He ran an entire campaign based on free media exposure. The press did not dare ignore him because he was the first serious black contender for a major party nomination—that was news. He was articulate and controversial, and he was drawing large numbers of blacks to the polls—again, news. When he challenged his opponents, when he slept in the ghettos, when he traveled to Syria, when he did not disavow the support of the controversial Louis Farrakhan, when he ran well in the South, Jesse Jackson was news. He knew how to use the media. His rhetoric was made for television; his dynamism demanded action photos; his place in history commanded attention. Despite his total inability to draw financial support, despite the fact that his Rainbow Coalition never really materialized, Jesse Jackson stayed on page one. He stayed on the nightly news (Barker and Walter 1989).

In 1988, Jackson again built a campaign without a great deal of money, gaining attention from the media because of the symbolism of his campaign and its successes. Jackson won where the intensity of his supporters turned into electoral success. Thus he did better in caucus states than in primaries. His most noteworthy success was in the restricted primary in Michigan, a primary that functioned more like a caucus. But the press was notably unanalytical in examining the Jackson successes; Jackson was succeeding beyond everyone's expectation and that was all that the press noted (Black et al. 1988; Pomper 1989b; Runkel 1989).

In 2000 the press wanted a contest. If Governor Bush and Vice President Gore won their nominations without contests, what story would there be to cover? The press did not invent the competition, but media analysts certainly played up the contests—Bush versus McCain, Gore versus Bradley—at times when many outside the media thought it would only be a matter of time before these challenges to the front-runners evaporated.

The role of the press in the nominating process has received a great deal of critical attention. That attention has been deserved because the national media, print and electronic journalists alike, have not done a very good job of defining their role in this process. The nominating process itself has come under scrutiny because it is so easily manipulated by the press. (See Grassmuck 1985; Orren and Polsby 1987; Traugott 1985.) But reform is not the immediate province of candidates for party nominations. They are concerned with winning. In reaching for that goal, they must learn to use the press as a resource. Free media attention has made and broken many presidential campaigns.

D. Evaluating Nominating Campaigns

Nominating campaigns are difficult to assess. Viewed with twenty-twenty hindsight, one can easily see that the Muskie strategy in 1972 was flawed; that the Carter strategy in 1976 was brilliant; the Dole strategy in 1996, pragmatic and effective; and so on. The evidence again points strongly to the conclusion that politics is more art than science.

Some of the most effective members of Congress—Wilbur Mills of Arkansas, Fritz Hollings of South Carolina, Ed Muskie of Maine, Ted Kennedy of Massachusetts, Phil Gramm of Texas, and Orrin Hatch of Utah—proved to be poor presidential candidates. Skills are not always transferable. The corps of national campaign experts is very small, and these "experts" frequently learn the wrong lessons from their previous experience. New faces often have the clearest sense of how to attack the system—Hart as McGovern's strategist in 1972, Hamilton Jordan for Carter in 1976, Jim Baker for George Bush in a losing effort in 1980, John Sasso for Michael Dukakis in 1988, James Carville for Bill Clinton in 1992, Karl Rove for George W. Bush in 2000, and Joe Trippi for Howard Dean and Mary Beth Cahill for John Kerry in 2004.

All candidates show their strengths and weaknesses as they announce their candidacy. All understand the need for money, for an effective press strategy, for influential followers, for gaining and maintaining momentum, but few are successful in doing all these things. But the political terrain is difficult to read. In the preceding sections, many examples have been given that might seem to the reader in 2007 as if they are ancient history. Candidates have been mentioned of whom few reading these pages have heard. But presidential elections happen every four years. What happened in 1972 might be more than thirty years ago, but it is only ten elections ago. If one is going to understand a process, as a student, a researcher, or a practitioner, it is necessary to study what history there is. New situations have arisen in 2008, but they are not totally without precedent; the precedents need to be understood for that reason. The process is so interesting precisely because those of us who are political analysts and members of the interested public can sit back and watch the contenders compete and test their strategies. We can know nearly as much about the past as do the strategists themselves. And we can judge the ways in which the campaigns are contested. Monday morning quarterbacks have no better process to kibitz about.

IV. THE CONVENTIONS

The excitement was electric at the 1976 Republican National Convention in the Kemper Arena in Kansas City. Betty Ford came in from one end and the band struck up the University of Michigan fight song, "Hail to the Victors!" Nancy Reagan entered from the other end; the band responded with "California, Here I Come!" The crowds cheered loudly as Ford and Reagan supporters tried to drown each other out. Television commentators tried to gauge support for the two candidates by the intensity of the cheering. The convention was as thrilling as any college football game.

The excitement of conventions stirs the emotions in those of us who love politics. But the broader question to be addressed is whether or not national nominating conventions decide anything at all anymore. After all, no politican active today has ever participated in a convention whose nominee was not known before the opening gavel sounded.

The first party conventions were held in the Jacksonian period in the nineteenth century (recall chapter 2). Conventions were places to which delegates came in order to make decisions, to choose the presidential nominees. In fact, nine times delegates have had to cast ten or more ballots in order to choose their party's nominees. In 1924, the Democratic National Convention in Baltimore took 103 ballots before finally settling on the nomination of John W. Davis, the last true favorite son to gain a major party nomination. But since 1952, every presidential nominee has been chosen on the first ballot cast at his party's convention.

Many observers felt that the Democratic rule change that calls for "fair reflection of presidential preference" would return decision-making power to the conventions. The argument went that many candidates going through a system that called for proportional representation of their popular support as delegate support would guarantee a situation in which no one candidate achieved a majority. However, that has not been the case. While I have suggested a scenario in which conventions could once again become decision-making bodies, recent history suggests that they have become little more than rubber stamps for decisions reached by primary and caucus voters. Some claim that they are nothing but celebratory events, opportunities for the party faithful to unite behind their nominee (Nelson 1997). The television networks seem to reflect this view as they provide fewer and fewer hours of live coverage (Kerbel 1998). The delegate selection process has worked in such a way that one candidate has a guaranteed first-ballot majority by the time the convention opens. Little else remains to be decided.

As much of the nation's attention still focuses on the nominating conventions every fourth summer, it is appropriate for us to examine whether this attention is warranted. If the conventions do not decide the nominee, what about the other decisions made in these political arenas (Davis 1983; Parris 1972; Shafer 1988; Sullivan, Pressman, and Arterton 1976; Wayne 1996; Polsby and Wildavsky 1996, 2004)?

National nominating conventions make four different kinds of decisions. In addition to deciding on the nominees for president and vice president, they rule on credentials disputes, changes in the party rules, and platform language.

A. Credentials Challenges

Credentials disputes are the most easily understood. In party rules and in the call to the convention, each party establishes the procedures through which delegates are to be chosen. In most cases no one challenges the delegates presenting themselves as representing a certain state. However, the procedures are not always simple. The political situations are not always unbiased, and challenges result. Each party appoints a Credentials Committee that hears challenges to proposed delegations and rules on the disputes. The report of the Credentials Committee is the first order of official business before the nominating convention.

While most credentials challenges are disposed of without major controversy, those that do attract attention are often critically important. Among the most noteworthy challenges was that of the Mississippi Freedom Democratic party in 1964 (White 1965). The appeal by Mississippi black Democrats was instrumental in desegregating Democratic politics in the South.

The credentials battles at the 1972 Democratic Convention in Miami were more closely related to the impending presidential nominations and deserve a closer examination for what they say about the process. Recall that the 1972 nomination was the first conducted under the "reformed" rules. Many irregularities were in evidence. The results of a series of credentials challenges were to determine whether George McGovern, the clear front-runner, was going to be able to secure a first-ballot nomination or if the ABM forces (Anyone But McGovern) could derail his candidacy at the last moment.

The two most significant challenges dealt with Illinois (where McGovern forces charged that the Cook County organization of Mayor Richard Daley had not followed procedures for opening and publicizing caucuses) and California (where a winner-take-all primary had been given an exemption from the rules by the National Committee). On close votes, aided by an important procedural ruling from convention chair Lawrence O'Brien, McGovern delegates were allowed to replace anti-McGovern Daley delegates in Illinois and to hold all the delegates won in California. The result was that McGovern forces controlled enough votes to secure the first-ballot victory (White 1973). The decisions reflected the commitment of

McGovern delegates to their candidate, a commitment that was more important than any commitment to the new reform principles. Many delegates cast conflicting votes, supporting the reforms in the case of the Illinois challenge but opposing them in California; they were supporting the position needed to secure McGovern's nomination in both cases.

B. Rules Disputes

The National Convention of each party is the ultimate rule-making authority for the national party.[14] Each party appoints a Rules Committee that examines proposed changes in party rules. In most cases party rules are sufficiently obscure and esoteric that few notice the workings of the Rules Committee. Often the real impact of rules changes will not be felt for four years; in the heat of an ongoing campaign, few are looking that far ahead.

On occasion, however, the work of the convention Rules Committee is seen as having immediate impact. In 1976, candidate Ronald Reagan tried a desperate ploy to wrest the nomination from President Gerald Ford. In an unprecedented move, Reagan announced, in advance of the convention, that he would choose Pennsylvania senator Richard Schweiker as his running mate if he were nominated for the presidency. Reagan's bold move was a reaching out toward the liberal wing of his party, toward those who felt he was too conservative. The battle was very close. Reagan hoped the needed delegates would swing to his side, but few budged.

As a second step in his strategy, Reagan sought a change on rule 5 of the Republican Party Rules, requiring that prospective presidential candidates designate their choice for running mate in advance. Reagan hoped that this rule change would force President Ford into a choice that would cost him support from the followers of the hopefuls who were not chosen and give the nomination to Reagan. The ploy failed; the rule was not changed, although the vote on it was very close, and Ford secured the nomination (Pomper 1977, 18–27; Wayne 1988, chap. 5; Witcover 1977).

National political journalists have focused on disputes such as this one as pivotal events in nominating conventions. In some sense they were, but in a more realistic sense the results were very predictable. Delegates to conventions choose which candidate they will support early on, and then they work hard for that candidate. They are seeking two goals. Their principal goal is to help their candidate secure the nomination. Their secondary goal is to be a delegate for that candidate and share in the candidate's success.

These individuals are not fooled by the intricacies of credentials or rules fights. The questions may be worded differently, but delegates know that the real question is: Which candidate for the presidency do you favor? Female McGovern delegates in 1972 voted against the challenge by South Carolina women because it would have hurt McGovern's chances (Weil 1973; White 1973). Liberal Carter delegates voted against Kennedy's proposed rule change because it would hurt their candidate. The most important factor to note in convention votes on credentials or rules fights is how closely the votes in these battles parallel the first-ballot votes for the presidential nomination. Though roll calls by individual delegates are not available, delegates are very aware of the impact these votes have on their favorite candidate's chances for nomination and vote accordingly. Put simply, the Carter delegates in 1980 were not robots; they were dedicated supporters of Jimmy Carter voting their consciences (Pomper 1981b, 25–32). In that sense, to the extent that one candidate has been guaranteed the nomination before the convention opens, credentials and rules fights are much less likely to assume importance.

C. Party Platforms

The party platforms are statements of the direction in which the two parties want our country to go. Their significance is frequently disputed, though Gerald Pomper (1972) demonstrated that they show real differences between our parties and that much of them are implemented and not forgotten. It is clear that they receive a lot of press attention at the time they are adopted.

The Democrats use the platform-writing process as a means to reach out to grassroots activists around the country. In many years, their platform committee, the composition of which reflects candidates' strengths, has turned into a traveling road show, seeking advice from Democrats around the country. The Republican platform committee, on the other hand, normally only meets in the convention city on the weekend before the convention itself. It is not a road show, but perhaps a sideshow before the main event.

Platforms serve different purposes for different individuals. For activists and ideologues they are often a means to gain a foothold into party dogma. For interest groups, they represent one way to gain support for particular views. For candidates, the platform process has served as a way to reach out to those in the party who did not support them.

Each candidate at a national convention has an extensive organization. Since the 1960 nomination of John F. Kennedy in Los Angeles (White 1961), each convention has seen increasingly sophisticated communications networks so that candidate organizations can reach their supporters on the floor. Each candidate sets up a "whip" organization so that delegates are instantly informed how they must vote on matters coming to the floor for votes.

The whips inform the delegates, and the delegates fall in line. Thus, in 1988, the Dukakis campaign operatives allowed votes on the platform planks dealing with increasing taxes on upper-income families and pledging to forgo the first use of nuclear weapons, but they also assured that their candidate would not be saddled with a platform with which he was not comfortable (Pomper 1989b, 49–65). However, platform disputes are seen as matters of conscience more frequently than is the case of credentials or rules disputes. The delegates often are freed to vote as they choose. At times, winning candidates concede platform disputes to their vanquished foes so that the losers have some pride with which to return home and thus they retain some enthusiasm for the party.

That is not to say that the platform-writing and platform-adopting processes are not important. Never was this more clearly demonstrated than in 1992. The entire Democratic platform-writing process was controlled by the Clinton campaign. The platform was drafted by a Clinton loyalist. The drafting committee was chaired by Clinton supporter Bill Richardson, then a congressman from New Mexico and later Clinton cabinet appointee, the governor of New Mexico, and a candidate for his party's presidential nomination in 2008. The supporters of Paul Tsongas and Jerry Brown were allowed their say at platform hearings and were permitted to offer amendments on the convention floor, but the result was preordained. The Clinton campaign wanted to present the image of a new Democratic party; the platform was one vehicle for doing this. Controlling the process throughout assured this goal and was thus considered to be very important.

At the other extreme, George H. W. Bush's campaign lost control of the platform-writing process at the Republican Convention. The platform battle became a symbol of an intense ideological struggle being waged within the Republican party. To oversimplify, three camps, each claiming to be true conservatives, were in evidence. Bush represented the traditional conservatives in his party; these were fiscal conservatives, concerned with balancing the budget and deficit reduction. Buchanan fought for the soul of the Republican party on moral and value-related issues; his backers were engaged in a cultural war with those who had deserted traditional American values. Buchanan supporters controlled key positions on the platform subcommittees that dealt with values issues such as abortion. Finally, lurking in the background were economic conservatives represented by Jack Kemp; they favored opportunity and growth policies, but they also supported the Buchanan definition on family values. The platform that emerged reflected the most controversial statement of conservative views, particularly on social issues. Many Republicans, particularly moderate Republicans from the Northeast, felt that it was a divisive platform, one that divided them from their own party. It certainly was not a centrist platform that could help President Bush in the November election.

It would be too much to argue that the differences between the two parties' platforms in 1992 determined the result of that very complex election (see chapter 9). However, one can surely claim that the Republican platform in that year did go far toward defining the public's view of the GOP.

Platforms, which do distinguish the two parties, clearly can still play a role in uniting a party for the November showdown or preventing party activists from coming together behind the nominee. They are important statements about party philosophy. Writing the platform is an exercise in defining a party. Controversy may or may not be apparent at a convention, but this part of the process remains critically important and should not be underestimated.

D. Vice Presidential Nominations

Vice presidential running mates for major party candidates are officially nominated by the two parties' conventions. But the choices, of course, are made by the presidential candidate. The last presidential candidate to leave the choice of running mate to the convention was Adlai Stevenson, for whom the Democratic National Convention chose Tennessee's veteran senator Estes Kefauver over a young Massachusetts senator named John Fitzgerald Kennedy in 1956.

Today's presidential nominees know that the choice of vice president is a most serious undertaking. From a political standpoint, the vice presidential nominee can help or hurt the ticket. Certainly the nominee is evaluated in part on this choice, the first important decision he has to make after confirmation as his party's standard-bearer. In 1972, George McGovern's campaign suffered badly when it was revealed that his original choice, Thomas Eagleton, a senator from Missouri, had undergone shock treatment for mental depression. Under intense pressure, Eagleton eventually withdrew. McGovern faced the embarrassing situation of having to find a stand-in and of having a number of prominent Democrats turn him down before Sargent Shriver, President Kennedy's brother-in-law and the founding director of the Peace Corps, accepted McGovern's invitation.

But the choice is viewed as more than a political decision. The nominee is naming an individual who will be the proverbial "heartbeat away" from the presidency, should the ticket win. Since Harry S Truman succeeded to the presidency upon the death of Franklin Roosevelt in 1945, political leaders have been confronted with the seriousness of the vice presidential decision. Truman was picked for a variety of reasons, none of them clear at the time (Phillips 1966). What was clear was that he was not included in the Roosevelt inner circle as the president directed Allied efforts toward ending World War II. As an extreme example, Truman was only vaguely aware of the project to develop the atomic bomb when he became president. In a world in which the president of the United States is the most powerful single individual on earth, the choice of the person who is to succeed to the presidency should anything happen to the incumbent must be taken most seriously.

The process for choosing vice presidential candidates is not a formal one, but it has been a careful and organized one for each of the last eight elections. Candidate Jimmy Carter established a process that his successors as Democratic nominees have more or less followed since 1976. As it becomes clear that the nomination is in hand, each prospective nominee has asked a trusted adviser to begin to compile a list of possible running mates. These individuals are then screened in great detail, to make sure that none has any problems similar to that discovered with Senator Eagleton in 1972. The extent to which the names on the list have been public has varied from year to year. In part that is because being mentioned is a great political coup—and those seeking the nomination understand that they are involved in a political process. Eventually the list of many nominees is pared to a few, usually fewer than five. They are interviewed by the prospective nominee, again sometimes in secret and sometimes quite openly. The Republicans have not followed a process quite as formal as the Democrats, but their outline is basically the same.

The eventual decision rests with the nominee, but he consults widely, seeking opinions on the assets and liabilities of each of those under consideration. He wants to be certain that the nominee is someone with whom he is comfortable, personally, politically, and in terms of policy views. But he also wants to be certain that he chooses someone whom others respect—as a running mate, as a vice president, and potentially as a successor. When the choices have been announced, the nominee always hails his running mate as the person in the nation most qualified to assume the presidency should anything happen to the president.

And in fact, the nominees chosen in recent years have been quite competent. When Bob Dole was chosen as Gerald Ford's running mate in 1976, he had as much or more experience in government as did Ford. The same could be said of Walter Mondale (Jimmy Carter's choice in 1976), George Bush (Ronald Reagan's choice in 1980), Lloyd Bentsen (Michael Dukakis's running mate in 1988), Al Gore (Clinton's 1992 choice), and, of course, Dick Cheney and John Edwards in the case of the 2004 election.

Even the choices not on that list have been experienced public servants. When Geraldine Ferraro was chosen by Mondale in 1984 and Dan Quayle by Bush in 1988, each was criticized for lack of experience. While it is certainly true that these choices were made for obvious political reasons—Ferraro for the symbolism of choosing the first woman, and Quayle for his appeal to a younger generation of Republican voters—each nominee had experience in Congress and a record of competence. Jack Kemp, chosen in 1996, did not have as much experience as Bob Dole, but neither did anyone else, given the length of Dole's career. However, Kemp was a longtime member of Congress, a member of the first President Bush's cabinet, and a one-time contender for his party's presidential nomination—impressive credentials.

The vice presidential nominees are certainly chosen to aid the national ticket. In the past, they were often selected to balance the ticket—someone from a different wing of the party, from a different region of the country, with different types of experience. But the nomination of Al Gore by Bill Clinton in 1992 surprised many on that count. Gore was from the same Democratic Leadership Council, moderate wing of the party as was Clinton; he, like Clinton, is a Southerner; he is of the same generation, the same religion. The only way in which he "balanced" the ticket was that he had legislative experience in the national government, whereas Clinton had mainly executive experience in state government. Perhaps most important, Gore's life was very different from Clinton's, from his very traditional family to his service in Vietnam.

In 2000 George W. Bush, in choosing Cheney, opted for a veteran Washington hand, one who had the experience with national politics and with foreign affairs that Bush lacked. Cheney was not on the original list of names circulating as possible Bush choices. In fact, Cheney was chosen by Bush to vet possible running mates and to make a suggestion. When Bush selected Cheney, critics said that Cheney had not been put through the same vetting process as he had demanded of the possible candidates he had considered. But Bush had other goals in mind. He clearly wanted someone who had ties to his father's administration, who knew and could evaluate the Republicans who had been involved in governing before, who had worked in and with the Congress, who had organized a White House staff, and who had experience in the all-important national security area. While Cheney was criticized as a lackluster campaigner, Bush was praised for choosing a running mate who clearly was ready to step into the Oval Office at a moment's notice, in fact, someone more ready to do so than Bush himself.

Al Gore's choice of Connecticut senator Joseph Lieberman was made shortly after the Republican convention, in part at least to take the media spotlight away from Bush and Cheney. The choice was historic in that Lieberman is the first Jew to run for president or vice president. Not only is Lieberman a Jew, but he is an observant modern Orthodox Jew, a man whose religion clearly is a defining part of who he is. Gore was praised for his courage in breaking a religious barrier, and he deserves credit for taking that action. But the Lieberman nomination was strategic in other ways. Lieberman had been the first Democrat to criticize President Clinton for the Monica Lewinsky affair. He has developed a reputation for assuming and defending the high moral ground. With former Republican secretary of education Bill Bennett, he attacked Hollywood for not applying appropriate moral standards to mass entertainment. Lieberman is viewed in Washington as a man above reproach—and if he was willing to run with Al Gore, then he must view Gore that way as well.

Pundits questioned both nominations. Cheney may be long on experience, but is decidedly short on charisma. Critics claimed he brought nothing to the national ticket in terms of electoral strength. If Bush had nominated Pennsylvania governor Tom Ridge, for instance, a critical battleground state might have gone his way. In terms of strategic considerations, Cheney seemed to add little.

While Gore was praised for his courage in choosing a Jew, others questioned whether Lieberman's religion would hurt, not help, the ticket. After all, the criticism went, Jews are concentrated in a few states—New York and California, which already seemed safe for the Democrats—and Florida, which surely would fall into the Bush column because of the efforts of the candidate's brother, Jeb, the Florida governor. As it turned out, Lieberman brought much more to the Democratic ticket than did Cheney to the Republican. New York and California were, if anything, more safe for the Democrats, requiring less work, and Florida came into play. The point was not that Jews voted Democratic—they traditionally have—but rather that Jewish turnout was increased because of pride in the Lieberman candidacy.

E. An Evaluation of the Conventions

The national television networks have cut way back on their television coverage of the recent nominating conventions. They did this because the excitement was gone—because the ratings were not there. Obviously, they have every right to make that judgment.

But they are wrong. Conventions are important events. They are times for partisans to share and to celebrate. That is newsworthy. They are "comings together," which is what "convention" really means. Republicans and Democrats around the country can share this via television, if they are permitted to do so.

Television journalists define news as controversy. Surely the last seven conventions in each party lacked that. But the rhetoric of Mario Cuomo and Jesse Jackson and Pat Buchanan, the emotions caused by the nomination of Geraldine Ferraro and Joe Lieberman, the depth of feeling for Bob Dole and Fritz Mondale and Paul Tsongas, the humanness of photographer and outgoing Senate leader Howard Baker, the degree of unanimity behind and pride in Ronald Reagan and George Bush in 1984 and Bill Clinton and Al Gore in 1996—these too were important news events. So were the delegates' reactions to those individuals and their performances, but also their emotional reaction to the American flag and the National Anthem. Television misses a major opportunity for civic educaton by focusing on journalists' interviewing journalists when the public really wants to experience the thrill of a convention vicariously.

Conventions have not been forums for decision making in recent years. That is not to say they will not again become so. Delegates will continue to be pledged and bound (by conviction) to their favorite candidates. If one candidate has gained majority support before the opening gavel, the "competition" will be a charade. But if this does not eventuate, we may once again see real decisions made by conventions.

We can easily paint a scenario that would lead to the convention playing an important role in 2008 for each party if the large number of states holding early caucuses and primaries do not produce a clear leader. Others are free to hypothesize about how a convention faced with reaching important decisions would work, should the situation eventuate. The frank answer is that we do not know. Could candidates control their delegates? Would demographic representation—of women, blacks, Hispanics—become more potent? Would interest groups come to the fore? Would impressive rhetoric win the day? We just do not know. The old keys—domination by a few bosses—no longer fit, but it is unclear if anyone has yet cut the new ones.

In recent years Walter Cronkite, the very epitome of a network news anchor in the heyday of convention coverage, has nostalgically recalled conventions of another era, when the crowds and the demonstrations were important, when emotions swept the floor, when spontaneous excitement ruled the day. Conventions still have that potential. They are an important element of American politics and continue to deserve attention as potentially significant events, not as dinosaurs from another era. (See Polsby and Wildavsky 1988 [chap. 3], 2000, 2004; Shafer 1988; Wayne 1988 [chap. 5], 2000.)

V. POLITICIANS VIEW THE NOMINATING PROCESS

Frequently how one views a certain situation depends on whether or not one benefits from that situation. Junior members of congressional committees like the seniority system less than senior members do. Five-foot-eight-inch point guards favor a wider lane under the basket more than do seven-foot centers. Such is human nature.

The same holds for how politicians view the nominating process. At one extreme perhaps is Walter Mondale in 1976. After testing the presidential waters for a number of months, Mondale withdrew. The reason: "I simply do not want it enough. I cannot face a whole year of nights in Holiday Inns." The process was dehumanizing. It was too long and too boring, and, in Mondale's case that year, offered too little hope for success.

Sometimes the criticism of the process deals with the rules. Thus losing candidate Morris Udall in 1976 became an advocate for regional primaries, to restrict the amount of time and money spent traveling. Others have advocated a national primary. Of course that would favor well-known candidates and hurt those seeking to make a name for themselves. Obviously how one stands on a reform like that would depend on where one sits. What is progressive reform to some is unfair to others. Politicians' ultimate view of the nominating system—other than complaints about how arduous it is—relates to whether they are helped or hurt by it. Jesse Jackson was hurt by the rules so he cried for reform.

The process will always be long. But its length does not seem to bother the winning candidates. Bill Clinton thrived on it in 1992. Bob Dole had no complaints in 1996, even though he traveled the length and breadth of the North American continent over and over. Bush and Gore thought the process worked just fine in 2000; it invigorated them. The process will always be complex. It will always seem to favor some candidates over others. Some candidates will always be dissatisfied.

But the system can be viewed as successful if the citizens feel that the candidates have been tested fairly, in a variety of ways, under rules that were designed to be as fair as possible for all contenders. As the nation looks to the 2008 nominations, knowing that, as in 1988 and 2000, neither party will have an incumbent running for president, citizens want a system that tests if candidates can do the job. A candidate who is found wanting should not be chosen.

If Hillary Clinton or Barack Obama, or John McCain or Rudolph Guiliani, look less like presidential timber after they have been on the campaign trail for many months than they do as leading candidates, they should not be chosen. If one of the many others contemplating a race for the White House captures the public's fancy, they will win the nomination. Or one party or the other may turn back to a leader from the past. The system gives legitimacy to the nominees. The concessions of losing candidates confirm that legitimacy, and the process moves on from there.

CHAPTER 9

Presidential Elections

President George W. Bush and Democratic presidential nominee John Kerry shake hands at the end of their second presidential debate, October 8, 2004, at Washington University in St. Louis, Missouri. Millions of Americans watch the presidential debates in the weeks and months before Election Day.

John Kerry's campaign for the presidency hit its highest point at the Democratic National Convention in Boston. Kerry had overcome early troubles in his campaign and had put together a well-funded, superb organization that led him through the primaries as a popular conqueror. His choice of his closest rival, John Edwards, as his running mate was popular with party regulars and the media. The nominating campaign reached an incredible crescendo at his convention, when he stepped forward claiming his party's mantle, saluting the crowd and proclaiming he was "reporting for duty." In his acceptance speech, he made a strong case that he was ready to lead the nation.

And the campaign never reached to those heights again. Kerry, the decorated Vietnam veteran, was attacked on his military service by surrogates of President Bush, the candidate who had never served overseas. Kerry never found the voice with which to respond. He was attacked as being wishy-washy on the issues; he never found the voice with which to respond. His aloof persona contrasted with that of the folksy Bush; Kerry never found a way to dispel the image. His message in the general election was never as positive, never as forceful, never as successful as it had been in the primaries. The difference between the nominating campaign and the general election campaign could not have been more stark.

Well, yes, it could. If anything, the Mondale-Ferraro campaign of 1984 and the Dole-Kemp campaign of 1996 were even more disastrous than the Kerry-Edwards effort. The 1988 Dukakis general election campaign, in terms of strategy and execution, paled in comparison to the battle for the nomination; so too did the reelection campaign of George H. W. Bush in 1992 (though many claimed his drive to nomination led to the difficulties in the fall).

Why were such experienced, seasoned campaign organizations plagued by these problems? Why were they not solved during primary contests? After all, much more is known about the general election than about the contests for a party's nomination. At the most rudimentary level, strategy can target voters who use party affiliation as a cue to evaluating candidates; the campaign's plan of action can be formulated with a single opponent in mind. Shouldn't there be fewer problems instead of more problems? These are the issues we will address as we look at how presidential election campaigns are run.

I. FROM THE CONVENTION TO THE GENERAL ELECTION

Politicians at the national level spend a good deal of time complaining about the length of presidential campaigns. What they are really concerned with is the length of the campaign for nomination. For the candidates who win nomination, and for the advisers most closely involved with their campaigns, the break between the convention and the general election is almost seamless. They continue to campaign hard, to work on the same issues, to work at the same pace, with the same goal in mind. There is little time for relaxation or reflection.

What is lost in their fatigue is the realization that the general election is separate from the campaign for nomination. The opponent is different, the rules are different, the strategies are different, and the length of time one is campaigning is different. General election campaigns are in fact quite short. The party conventions are held in late summer. The general election is held on the first Tuesday after the first Monday in November. The general election campaign is over in about three months.

In this short period of time, the candidates and their staffs must run a truly national campaign. The battle for the nomination involves a separate campaign in each state. Different states have different rules, and the political calendar extends through five months. The general election campaign is different on all counts. Of the most significance is that the campaign must reach its peak in every state throughout the entire nation on the same date. Whereas during the preconvention period it was possible to run separate campaigns in each state and to reuse human resources by switching staff from one state in which the primary or caucus had been held to another state in which the contest was upcoming, in the general election the organization must cover the entire nation at one time. The logistics of an operation on this scale exceed anything that first-time campaign organizations have experienced.

Furthermore, the rules of the election contest make strategic planning intricate. The point in the general election is not simply to win a plurality of the votes. While vote maximization is desirable, in our presidential elections the winner is the candidate who is supported by a majority of the **electoral college**. Therefore, each state is a separate contest. Campaign strategists must determine into which states they should put how much effort. Because all states (except Maine and Nebraska) award the plurality winner of the popular vote all of that state's **electoral votes**, strategists not only focus on large states but also have to determine which states are lost (and therefore not worth additional effort), which states are safe (making further effort superfluous), and which states are competitive (and therefore worthy of increased effort).[1] These estimates must be evaluated and reevaluated as the campaign progresses.

Candidates for the presidency are interested first in winning, but they are also interested in winning with a large mandate. Therefore, even apparent winners cannot coast. They must be aware of their opponent's strategies and must counter them effectively. They

ELECTORAL COLLEGE

The indirect means through which U.S. presidents and vice presidents are chosen.

ELECTORAL VOTES

The actual votes cast for president and vice president by the electors, members of the electoral college, chosen for that purpose alone.

must take into account the mix of voters throughout the nation as they respond to the events of the day. They are uniquely aware of the complexity and the magnitude of the job that they are seeking. They have reached the point at which they are not just among those considered for the presidency, but are one of two individuals who will hold that job. They must be certain that the conduct of their campaign does not make governing more difficult.

In the remainder of this chapter, we will look at the campaigns for the presidency, from after the conventions to the November election. We will begin by examining campaign organization and planning and proceed to look at the strategies and **tactics** used in these most important contests. (On presidential elections generally, see Kessel 1988, 1992; Polsby and Wildavsky 1991, 1996, 2000, 2004; Wayne 1988, 1992, 1996, 2000, 2004. On specific campaigns see, e.g., Black and Oliphant 1989; Ceaser and Busch 1993, 1997; Drew 1981; Germond and Witcover 1985, 1989, 1993; Goldman and Fuller 1985; May and Fraser 1973; Moore 1981; Moore and Fraser 1977; Runkel 1989; Schram 1977; Simon 1998; White 1965, 1969, 1973, 1982; Witcover 1977.)

TACTICS

The specific techniques used to implement the overall strategic design.

II. ORGANIZING FOR THE GENERAL ELECTION

A presidential campaign must be run in each state at the same time. Some aspects of the campaign are controlled in a centralized manner, but others are decentralized. Further, the magnitude of the tasks that can be handled centrally call for significant and sophisticated staffing.

A. Structuring the Campaign Organization

1. The Campaign Headquarters

A number of questions must be faced when a nominee and his closest advisers reassess their campaign organization after their national convention. A very basic question involves the location of the campaign headquarters. Should there be one national headquarters for the campaign? Probably yes. Where should it be located? Washington is the logical choice, but it is not the only choice. In 1992, for example, candidate Bill Clinton decided that his national headquarters would remain in Little Rock, Arkansas. For Clinton, Little Rock was a strategic choice. Like Jimmy Carter, the last Democratic Southerner elected president, Clinton wanted to emphasize that he was not part of the old Washington crowd. While many "regular" Democrats and politicians who were old hands at presidential campaigns backed Clinton, they understood this decision. When Al Gore sought the presidency in 2000, he moved his headquarters from

Washington to Nashville, again to give the impression that he was not just a Washingtonian.

Most candidates have chosen Washington as their national headquarters, a decision dictated, in part at least, because Washington is the seat of government and also the home of the Democratic National Committee (DNC) and Republican National Committee (RNC). But merely mentioning these committees raises another set of questions.

2. The National Committee

What should be the relationship between the candidate's personal organization and the staff of the national committee? This is not an easy relationship to work out. Obviously the national committee staff is a resource that a candidate should use. Once the nominee has been chosen, the national committees are dedicated to helping their candidate win.

A number of patterns have become apparent. When an incumbent president is renominated, the national committee staff is often pretty much under his control before the nomination is secure. Thus throughout 2004 it is assumed that the staff of the Republican National Committee was committed to the reelection of President Bush. In 1992, on the other hand, while Republican National Committee members and staff generally favored the first President Bush over Pat Buchanan, they had to maintain a semblance of impartiality. That neutrality is the exception when a sitting president is seeking reelection, not the rule.

But what if no incumbent president has a nomination in hand or an out-party nominee begins to organize for the general election? The long-standing tradition was for the nominee to name his own people as officers of the national committee and for the national committee to get to work on the campaign, but that tradition has faded.

First, the two national committees are no longer the same. For some time the Republican National Committee has been better financed and more professionally run than its Democratic counterpart. The DNC has made significant inroads on the advantage that the Republicans gained in the late 1960s, but the gap between the two organizations remains appreciable. One aspect of this difference has been the extent to which the committees view themselves as independent. The RNC, more than the DNC, has been likely to retain its prenomination chair and its independent role.

But as the Democrats worked to rejuvenate their organization, their party leaders showed an independent streak as well. In 1984, Walter Mondale, assured of the Democratic nomination, sought to name Bert Lance, the chair of the Georgia State Democratic Committee and one of Mondale's most important Southern supporters, as chair of the Democratic National Committee. But many members of the DNC were not willing to see the chair, Chuck Manatt, who had been responsible for much of the party's rejuvenation, unceremoniously dumped in favor of a political crony. Vehement in their opposition to Lance, they forced Mondale to back down and announce that Manatt would stay on.

In 1992, the situation worked in the reverse fashion, although again the independence of the party organization was demonstrated. Ron Brown, DNC chair, decided that one of his priorities should be to help whoever gained the party's presidential nomination emerge from the convention with the greatest possible opportunity to win the general election in November. Brown thus used his position as DNC chair to negotiate with those whom Bill Clinton beat on his road to the nomination. While the DNC staff stayed separate from Clinton's, the Clinton operatives saw the utility of the role that Brown was playing and urged that he stay on as chair throughout the campaign. He did, and resigned only after the election, to accept a position in the Clinton cabinet.

Other factors further complicate the relationship between the national committee and the candidate. The **Federal Election Campaign Act of 1971** (FECA) mandated that each candidate have a separate central campaign committee that is responsible for all spending during the campaign. (This is discussed at length in chapter 5.) The roles played by the national committees have had to be pointedly separate from those played by candidates' central campaign committees.

One result in recent elections has been multiple campaign headquarters, a candidate's national headquarters and the national committee headquarters. The two national committees work for the presidential candidates as well as the entire ticket. However, since 1984 presidential campaigns for both parties have taken advantage of a loophole in the campaign finance legislation. Money raised by the national committees and spent on behalf of the entire ticket can be used in addition to the grants given the presidential campaigns from public financing. This money is the so-called **soft money**, meaning money outside of the limitations of the FECA, which has drawn so much attention in recent elections. While the use of soft money has been restricted by the Bipartisan Campaign Reform Act of 2002 (discussed in chapter 5), it is important to understand why reformers took the action they did.

How was this soft money raised? Really in two ways. First, the national committees have their own fund-raising operations. These groups work hard to raise money for the party, not only for party maintenance, but to use during the fall campaigns of the party's candidates. But, second, the presidential campaigns have extensive

FEDERAL ELECTION CAMPAIGN ACT OF 1971

Reform of the way in which the financing of elections is regulated that was the precursor to the current legislation.

SOFT MONEY

Campaign money raised and spent but not regulated by limitations of the FECA.

fund-raising operations in place during the primaries. Every winning nominee has a fund-raising organization in place with no candidate-related task, as the presidential campaigns are publicly funded. Thus, in each of the last four presidential elections, the nominees have essentially transferred their fund-raising operations to the national committees after the conventions, thus allowing the national committees to raise and spend more money on the fall campaign than they otherwise would have been able to do. As more and more soft money is raised by the parties by individuals loyal to the presidential nominee, the separation between party activities designed to help the entire ticket and those more helpful to the presidential nominee has blurred (chapter 5; Corrado et al. 1997, 2005; Magleby 2006; Magleby and Holt 1999; Alexander and Bauer 1991; Alexander 1986; Center for Responsive Politics 1985).[2]

However, during the second Clinton administration the DNC suffered because it did not maintain enough independence and distance from the Clinton reelection effort. The DNC was involved in and tainted by campaign-related fund-raising scandals that caused the Democrats to return vast sums of money raised in the 1996 campaign. One result of this scandal may well be a reseparation of the fund-raising and spending by the national committees and the presidential campaigns.

The rules of the game changed for the 2004 campaign, and the candidates' organizations altered tactics accordingly. President Bush did not accept public funding of his prenomination campaign in 2000; thus, he was able to raise and spend a good deal of money, above the limit set for publicly funded candidates, after he had secured the nomination. For the 2004 campaign he again refused public funds; his campaign set out to raise between $170 and $200 million prior to the Republican National Convention, which they scheduled as late as possible. Thus, the Bush campaign had a great deal of money to spend throughout 2004, with no in-party opposition.

Aware of this, two Democrats—former Vermont governor Howard Dean and Massachusetts senator John Kerry—announced in November 2003 that they too would not accept public funding for their primary campaigns. Both were criticized for violating the principles of campaign finance reform for which they have stood, but each understood that the general election campaign would be in full swing well before they receive the public money intended to fund that effort. These decisions by both parties show the degree to which presidential campaigns are now separated from party campaigns because of decisions made by individual candidates and changes in campaign finance laws.

Campaign headquarters are places in which decisions are made. Maintaining multiple headquarters makes some sense because different kinds of decisions can be made by national party committees, which are concerned with all candidates throughout the nation, and candidate organizations, which are only concerned about one office.

3. The Mobile Headquarters

But if the definition of campaign headquarters is where important decisions are made, then one must also consider the mobile nature of presidential campaigns in this era of crisscrossing the nation in a matter of hours. In a very real sense, the campaign headquarters is where the candidate is. Presidential campaigns travel in an airplane that is outfitted for the comfort of the candidate and the needs of his staff. In essence, the candidate's plane is a traveling office (Kessel 1984, 354; 1988, 131; 1992, 123–24). Those traveling with the candidate (not those in the permanent campaign headquarters) make many of the important strategic decisions, since decisions must often be made quickly. Thus candidates often insist that their most trusted advisers travel with them.[3] However, those on the plane can lose sight of the fact that many important decisions are not instantaneous, but rather require planning and staff work and must be made back in the more permanent headquarters.

Campaign managers face a dilemma. On the one hand they know that managing a national campaign with a multimillion-dollar budget represents a major administrative challenge. To handle this task requires time for planning, staff assistance, and a complete organization. On the other hand, they need access to the candidate, and he needs their counsel on the road. Most managers divide their time between the permanent headquarters and the plane—the traveling headquarters of the campaign.

In 1992 the Clinton campaign came up with a new headquarters concept. While some of Clinton's principal advisers traveled with him, others, including strategist James Carville, typically remained behind in the Little Rock "war room." Carville was convinced that the Dukakis campaign in 1988 suffered from an inability to respond to the actions of the campaign of George H. W. Bush. He did not want to repeat that error. Thus, taking a page from military strategists, he organized a rapid response team in the Little Rock headquarters. These strategists were constantly in touch with what was happening throughout the nation as well as with the candidate and his wife, vice presidential candidate Gore and his wife, and others on the campaign trail. The successful Clinton pattern has been followed by all campaigns since that time.[4]

4. Division and Integration of Authority and Responsibility

Since a presidential campaign requires a tremendous amount of work, a large number of people, all of whom are quite powerful politically, are involved in organization and management. Authority is divided among the chair of the national committee, the campaign manager, the chair of the candidate's campaign committee, and perhaps others with similar titles. Each of these has access to the candidate; each came to the campaign with a certain power base; each hopes to leave with more power. Each definitely has a personal stake not only in the outcome of the campaign but in his or her own role in reaching that outcome.

In addition, various individuals assume authority over functional aspects of the campaign. They carve out their own space and either apply existing expertise or quickly develop expertise, so that they know the area in which they are working better than anyone else. In short, they make themselves indispensable. These individuals must be made to fit into the campaign organization. On the one hand, they are important cogs in a wheel that needs to be complete in order to function efficiently. On the other hand, they demand (and often require) a certain amount of autonomy. The juggling act is often difficult.

One test of a campaign organization is how well it all works together. With the stakes so high, for the candidate and for the individuals involved, with the time so short, and with the task so formidable, it is possible that integration of the campaign organization is never accomplished. A fragmented campaign often is the result of frustration when strategies are not working; that kind of fragmentation only compounds the problems that created it. Observers of the Dukakis campaign in 1988 believed that his problems came from an inability to listen to what his advisers said (Black and Oliphant 1989). The losing efforts by President Bush in 1992 and Bob Dole in 1996 both showed signs of leadership difficulties.

Perhaps the most interesting contrast in recent years has been between the 1988 Bush campaign, which appeared to be a unified organization—a group working together for a common goal—and his 1992 effort, one that often seemed to be in total disarray. In 1988 Lee Atwater and James Baker, who later became RNC chair and secretary of state respectively, made public assurances that all staff rivalries and jealousies were put on the back burner. By 1992, Atwater had succumbed to brain cancer. Baker was reluctant to return to politics from his higher callings in government service. He was never able to control campaign rivalries nor to set **strategy** on a positive course. Of course, analysts can be guilty of exercising twenty-twenty hindsight. Winning campaigns always seem to have been well run and losing campaigns to have flailed about for direction. If things are going well, there is enough glory to share and enough spoils so that everyone can be rewarded. When things are going badly, the problems inherent in campaign organization are exacerbated as everyone looks for someone else to blame for the

STRATEGY

The overall design of a campaign.

deteriorating situation. But to a certain extent these characterizations do in fact reflect reality.

B. Functions of a Presidential Campaign Organization

In simplest terms, the function of a presidential campaign organization is to carry the candidate's campaign for the presidency the length and breadth of the country. The structures adopted by various campaigns over the years to achieve this goal have had a number of similarities.

1. Grassroots Politics

After securing a presidential nomination, candidates and their top aides do not take time to rest, but they are, in fact, engaged in a different type of activity that is, though less visible, no less important. They are engaged in the task of building and cementing an organization that spans the nation, that draws in as many different types of people from different locales as is possible, and that is ready to jump into action, to perform the tasks necessary to campaign nationally, as soon as it is called upon. Bill Clinton and Al Gore demonstrated this most conclusively in 1992 when they set off on a six-state bus tour right after the convention.

These tasks involve the grassroots approach to politics. Friends and neighbors must be convinced to support the candidate. A campaign must be visible in area after area. There must be a feeling that it is right to support a candidate actively because many others are doing so. When the candidate or his running mate appears in an area, enthusiastic crowds must be in evidence. This enthusiasm breeds more enthusiasm, but the initial response does not occur spontaneously; it results from continuous activity on the part of the most active on board.

Geographic organization. Basic to any presidential campaign organization is a national campaign committee that stands at the pinnacle of a pyramid of regional committees, state committees, and local committees. One test of the strength of an organization is its ability to find individuals willing to lead and serve on all these committees. During the prenomination phase of the campaign, it is not at all uncommon for a campaign to have spotty coverage, including some areas in which no coterie of supporters emerges to run the campaign for a candidate. After the nomination, the task is to fill these gaps and to augment previously existing committees with important individuals who may have previously supported other candidates. That is one of the first important tests for an organization after the nomination has been secured.

In establishing a national organization, a candidate and his campaign manager must remember a number of important factors.

First, they must be cognizant of the role of party and of the relationship of the candidate's supporters to local party officials in various areas. In some cases the local committee for a presidential campaign will be the same as the local party committee. In other areas, such an arrangement would be counterproductive. Detailed political knowledge is the only basis for making such decisions.

Demographic organization. Further, campaign organizers must beware of the trap of thinking only in geographic terms. An activist woman from Pittsburgh might well relate more closely to women's groups supporting a candidate than to the Pittsburgh party organization. Consequently, campaign organizers frequently set up a series of committees based on demographic characteristics that are parallel to those based on geographic location.

For these committees to work, a number of conditions must be met. Group members must have a sense of unity and a sense that there is a reason for them as a group, not just as individuals, to back one candidate. Second, a key leader of the group must be willing to take a visible position, heading that group's efforts on behalf of the candidate. The leader must be aware of the internal politics within the group and of the ways to unify that group behind one candidate. Finally, the communications network between the campaign organization and the group organization must be extremely sensitive.

Establishing parallel organizations with overlapping responsibilities always creates the possibility of conflict. Every woman, every black, every Hispanic, every Jew, every member of every group lives somewhere. Most of these individuals are members of more than one demographic group. Many are members of other self-defined groups, for example, labor unions, teachers, clergy. Their loyalty is often divided. They are undoubtedly part of a group for reasons other than electoral politics; members share a common interest but not necessarily a common political orientation. Group leaders in each group appeal for their support. These efforts, while all well intentioned, can work at cross-purposes. Gaining the benefits of group efforts without losing support because of intergroup conflict or conflict between group organizations and geographically defined committees defines another test of the strength of a candidate's overall campaign organization (Kessel 1984, 363; 1988, 131–36; 1992, 125–33).

2. Staffing the Candidate's Plane

As mentioned earlier, one of the key decisions faced early in a campaign is deciding who should travel with the candidate. Many of the functions that are performed at a campaign headquarters for a local campaign are service functions for the candidate. It only seems logical that those who perform these tasks need to be near the candidate wherever he happens to be campaigning.

Press aides must accompany a candidate, since the press is traveling with him. Speechwriters are similarly needed in a candidate's traveling entourage. For some time journalists have been aware that every candidate for national office develops a set speech that is given at virtually every campaign stop along the way. "The speech" is an important part of a candidate's campaign arsenal, but it is not the only public address given during a campaign.[5]

"The speech" is shaped and molded and improved along the way. Speechwriters come up with new lines for the candidate to try. If they receive a positive response, they are incorporated into the speech for future presentations. Some candidates work hard at the details of their set speech. Most leave that to the wordsmiths, staffers traveling with the candidate who are responsible for his spoken word.

"The speech" reflects the basic themes of a presidential campaign. A candidate must speak to a specialized audience or on a detailed or technical topic almost every day. The set speech is not appropriate for these occasions, and the speechwriter is called for. Many have marveled at the ability of candidates for national office to speak authoritatively on a wide range of subjects. Their real skill is to present the words of others as if they were their own.

When a speech to a group with a particular interest is called for or a new policy statement must be outlined or a candidate must respond to an important event during the campaign, the candidate and his top advisers go over the general topic, refining the positions to be taken. The speechwriters then take over, converting some vaguely stated ideas into smooth-flowing prose that echoes the cadences and images thought to be unique to their candidate. If the speech is of particular significance, the candidate and top staff might review draft after draft, suggesting changes and calling for the amplification of some points or the downplaying of others. The test for a good speechwriter is the ability to write in the voice of the candidate. The true test for a candidate comes when he is asked to clarify points he has made in a speech that he has hardly had time to read.

Advance men and women make certain that a candidate's day runs smoothly. The plane carries logistical staff of various types. Campaigns employ teams of young staff members, many right out of college, whose job is to go into an area ahead of a candidate, plan all the logistics of the visit, and then remain for the candidate's visit in order to ensure that all goes as planned. Advance work has become an art, the art of knowing where a candidate should appear and when, the art of knowing which politicians to consult and which not, the art of knowing how to bring out the biggest crowd (or the crowd that appears the biggest), the art of assuring good visuals for the nightly news. (See Bruno and Greenfield 1971 for a description of advance work by an acknowledged expert.)

Key political advisers and strategists are another element of the campaign plane staff. Everyone with important responsibilities on a campaign must decide whether those responsibilities can best be carried out on the road with the candidate or at the national headquarters. Access to the candidate means influence, and those who view themselves as important often want to be traveling with the candidate at all times. Senior campaign advisers, in consultation with the candidate, must determine who should have instant access to the candidate and on whose counsel the candidate wants to be most dependent when key strategic decisions are called for. These decisions often change as a campaign progresses.

3. Staffing the Campaign Headquarters

Two functions, research and public relations, are a part of every presidential campaign. Speechwriters, as mentioned earlier, perform one type of research necessary for a campaign to function smoothly. But more is expected of a presidential candidate than the ability to turn a quick phrase. Speechwriters draw on the research performed by an array of issue specialists.

Some of these people are paid staff, professionals who are working on detailed presentations of a candidate's views. Others are supporters of the candidate, or of his party, drawn into the campaign for a particular purpose. Recent campaigns have used task forces of experts drawn from universities, research think tanks, and the private sector to work on a candidate's position in a certain area. For instance, candidate George W. Bush tapped those who had worked in his father's administration and scholars like Condoleezza Rice for expert advice. Bill Clinton used many friends he had first met as a Rhodes scholar in England and contacts he had made through that most impressive network. Most often a staff member coordinates the work of these groups and presents the material in a coherent way, ready for review by the candidate and his top staff and for eventual presentation to the public.

The general public is not very concerned about the details of the wide range of proposals presented by presidential candidates. However, one of the means that the press uses to assess the effectiveness of a campaign and the quality of a candidate is to evaluate the specific proposals floated by that candidate to handle the nation's problems. The press (as well as the most interested segments of the public) is also concerned about the quality of the individuals who are working for a candidate. A candidate's campaign advisers give some idea of the kind of people who will staff an administration should that candidate be elected. The press and the attentive public view these matters seriously.

Public opinion pollsters do an entirely different kind of research for presidential campaigns. Though the tasks and the methods are different from those researching specific policy issues, the results are put to surprisingly similar use. Public opinion polling has played an important role in presidential campaign politics at least since John Kennedy's campaign in 1960. However, as pollsters have become more sophisticated and as campaigns have become more sophisticated, that role has been changing.

Today every major party candidate for the presidency employs a professional public opinion pollster or a team of pollsters throughout the campaign. Candidates vie for the best pollsters. Public opinion firms are engaged in many campaigns in any cycle, but securing a presidential campaign is their most important prize.

ROLLING SAMPLE

Technique used by pollsters to gauge public opinion by continuously replacing one portion of the group they are polling each night with a newly selected group.

FOCUS GROUPS

Technique used by pollsters to explore deeper aspects of public opinion.

Whereas pollsters once sampled public opinion a couple of times during a campaign, today that opinion is under scrutiny constantly. The latest polling technique involves a **rolling sample**: pollsters test public opinion continuously. They arrive at their latest judgments by replacing responses that are a couple of days old with ones coming in overnight, rolling over a third or a fourth of the sample each day. Thus the pollsters feel they can tell, on a day-to-day basis, how a campaign is moving, what appeals are working with what groups, and what ideas should be dropped.

In addition, public opinion experts rely on **focus groups** to supplement their polling data. Focus groups are smaller groups of citizens taken to be roughly representative of some subpopulation. Their views on a particular subject are probed in depth by a public opinion analyst. Focus groups are typically employed to see how people are likely to react to a new campaign initiative or to a proposed commercial.

The pollster of today is, almost by definition, a major adviser to a candidate. The pollster tests the political waters on new ideas, gauges how the public will respond to new issue positions or to the candidate's response to an emerging crisis, and advises how a campaign can present the best image to the public. Major party candidates for the presidency are too well known, and their positions are too well known, for any candidate to modify his or her views to fit the latest polling results. But that is not to say that these candidates are not capable of molding their views. A key factor in the Gore 2000 campaign was a debate among those polling for him as to whether he should stress those of his views perceived as centrist or those more appealing to the left.

The press aides who travel with the candidate are not the only ones on a campaign concerned with public relations. They are only part of a larger public relations team. The public relations team works on many different fronts.

Supplementing those traveling with the candidate are aides concerned with how the candidate is perceived by the press throughout the nation. The candidate on the road stimulates coverage in most of the nation's newspapers. The campaign headquarters staff concerned with press relations monitors this coverage and seeks means to assure that the campaign is perceived in the best light. Campaign managers are very concerned about the image a candidate portrays in the daily newspapers, on the nightly news shows on television, and in the weekly newsmagazines. A good deal of effort goes into working with those responsible for the media (Adams 1982; Crouse 1973; Patterson 1980; Patterson and McClure 1976; Robinson and Sheehan 1983; Wayne 2000, 2004; chapter 10 discusses the role of the media in greater detail).

However, to an uncomfortable extent, how a candidate and a campaign are portrayed in the press is beyond the control of the campaign staff. Hard as they may work, the final decisions are made by those observing and interpreting their actions, not by campaign staff. In contrast, the campaign organization has direct control over paid media. A crucial part of the public relations effort revolves around producing paid commercials for television and advertising for other media.

In modern presidential campaigns, the advertising executive is a key political adviser. This situation was apparent for everyone to see in the 1968 campaign, when Richard Nixon was presented to the public in a carefully packaged manner, as chronicled in Joe Mc-Ginniss's popular book, *The Selling of the President 1968* (1969). McGinniss presented a picture of a presidential candidate who was marketed to the American people just as any commercial product is marketed.

While the McGinniss book was clearly critical of the Nixon experience, more recent accounts have accepted the preeminence of media specialists as campaign advisers. Gerald Rafshoon set another precedent by accompanying Jimmy Carter to the White House in order to create the correct image for a president, just as he had for a presidential candidate. The transformation from media adviser for a candidate, creating paid commercials to garner necessary support, to media consultant for a president, staging walks down Pennsylvania Avenue on inauguration day or fireside chats in cardigan sweaters, seemed almost imperceptible as Rafshoon moved from a campaign payroll to a White House job.

In the most recent campaigns, the web has fostered a whole new breed of public relations experts on presidential campaigns, generally young politicos adept in designing websites and keeping them current and in blogging the candidates' messages. Some candidates have maintained their own blogs, some written personally and others ghosted. All candidates have bloggers writing on their behalf as twenty-first century campaigning attempts to keep up with twenty-first century information technology.

The public relations aspect of a campaign cannot be devised in a vacuum. What the candidate is saying on the road, what issues the candidate chooses to emphasize, how the candidate is perceived in the press, and the themes of paid media commercials and web-based information must all fit together in one harmonious package. In the 2000 election Vice President Gore was never able to define what he really stood for, to offset an image that he would say anything and do anything to become president. The job of coordinating and presenting a coherent message is the most important in the campaign. Its effectiveness is measured by public reaction, not by how critics respond to the way in which the message is portrayed (Buchanan 1991).

C. Directing the Campaign Organization

1. The Inner Core

In every modern presidential campaign, one individual has had the title campaign manager or perhaps campaign director; some campaigns include both. But it is essential to realize that the enterprise of running a national presidential campaign in such a short period of time is so monumental that no one person can have overall responsibility. In virtually every recent campaign the major party nominees have surrounded themselves with an inner core of dedicated and trusted advisers who collectively have made the major decisions for the campaign.

Who are the individuals who constitute this core group? Typically they are the advisers who have served the candidate throughout his political career—his personal friends and his most trusted confidantes.

In 2000 a clear contrast appeared. George W. Bush surrounded himself with those who had been with him during his rise to power in Texas, particularly his longtime friend Don Evans, his political strategist Karl Rove, his communications specialist Karen Hughes, and his campaign manager Joe Allbaugh. These four were at the center of a team that had worked together successfully and were ultimately loyal to their boss. By contrast, Vice President Gore changed his "core" group a number of times; he had developed so many contacts in the Democratic party that every political leader seemed to want to be part of his inner circle. He went so far as to change campaign managers twice, before settling on William Daley in the last months of his campaign. All of those involved were close to Gore, but none had been involved in building his political career.

The function of this core group, in any case, is to set the overall strategy and to coordinate all the aspects of the campaign in order to carry out that strategy. Typically members of this group who have specific areas of responsibility choose their own subordinates to monitor those areas. They in turn choose their own subordinates, and a network of campaign workers grows.

2. Expanding the Core

Expanding the campaign organization is a time-consuming task. Work in this area begins immediately after a nomination has been secured. Efforts are made to draw in party regulars who have worked for other candidates or remained neutral in the prenomination phase of the process. The party organization's role is defined, with an appropriate (but often second-level) loyalist in charge of that operation.

Once the vice presidential candidate has been named, his or her campaign staff must be melded with that of the presidential candidate. A number of different patterns have been seen. When candidate Clinton chose Al Gore in 1992 and when Bob Dole chose Jack Kemp in 1996, each was selecting an old hand at national political campaigns. Each had run unsuccessfully for his party's presidential nomination in the past. Although neither had a staff in place, each had contacts throughout the nation on which to draw. Governor Bush chose Dick Cheney in 2000 to tap into the reserve of Republican national leaders from the first President Bush's administration, to give a sense of gravitas to a campaign that seemed long on bravado but short on governing experience. Al Gore's choice of Senator Joe Lieberman in 2000 and John Kerry's selection of John Edwards in 2004 reflected efforts to expand the political base; neither had large established groups of national leaders who came to the campaign with them.

3. Co-opting the Losers

Finally, in working to establish a smoothly functioning organization for the general election campaign, strategists must find a way to bring into line key supporters of those who were defeated for the nomination. The ritualistic display of unity on the platform at the national convention must be converted into real support for the winning nominee. Unless one chooses an unsuccessful candidate for the nomination as a running mate, as Kerry did in 2004, this is not an easy task.

The efforts by the two winning candidates in 2000 to bring the losers on board were similar to each other, but unique in other ways. In each case the eventual nominee had one major opponent left as the nomination came into sight. In each case, that opponent—Arizona senator John McCain for George W. Bush and former New Jersey senator Bill Bradley for Al Gore—represented a minority view in the party, but a heartfelt minority. Bradley remained aloof from the campaign, but his supporters had nowhere to go other than to Gore. McCain, who had a somewhat bitter relationship with Bush during the primaries, campaigned hard for Republican candidates throughout the nation, but only on a few occasions with the head of the ticket. Neither was fully co-opted, but the followers of each seem to have come home to their parties' nominees.

Building an organization is not glamorous work, but some of that work is public in nature. As the organization takes shape, press aides to a candidate let the political world know who will be working for the candidate and what they will be doing. If these events are given the correct kind of press treatment, the act of building an organization can also be a demonstration of strength and competence. If supporters of vanquished opponents join a candidate's ranks, then the candidate is seen as having brought the party together.

D. Setting a Campaign Strategy

The enormity of postconvention work cannot be overestimated. Certainly much of the organization was in place during the nomination battle, and the key advisers were all known. But the game has changed: the organization has to be expanded, the prenomination opposition must be absorbed, and, most importantly, the new opposition has to be assessed.

Not only is setting a campaign strategy not glamorous work, but also it is not done in public. After the convention, candidates and their advisers are hard at work, devising a plan that will maximize chances of victory in November. The public is not privy to these plans, since their effectiveness would be limited if they were made known.

Chroniclers of recent campaigns have had access to some of these plans after the campaigns have ended (Caddell 1981; Drew 1981; Wirthlin 1981). Some are quite elaborate. The plan for Ronald Reagan's 1980 campaign filled two full volumes. Others have been little more than one-page outlines of what had to be accomplished. The sophistication of these plans says a good deal about the sophistication of the campaign organization. In fact, two sets of plans are put into motion. The first deals with the basic strategy of the campaign: What themes will be stressed? How will the candidate be portrayed? What issues will be spotlighted? Where will the necessary electoral votes be found? To whom will the candidate appeal? The second set of plans deals with tactics: How will the message be conveyed? What consideration will be given to **third-party candidates**,

THIRD-PARTY CANDIDATES

Candidates on the ballot representing any parties other than the two major parties.

if any are relevant? When and how will debates be structured? The tactical matters deal with how the strategic elements will be implemented.

III. STRATEGIES FOR THE GENERAL ELECTION

Every campaign must deal with various types of strategies, and these can be categorized in a variety of ways. We will look first at geographic determinations. In this section the basic questions deal with how the campaign views the country. Where are the necessary votes likely to be found? From there we move to considerations of group dynamics. Just as the campaign organization must be built geographically and demographically, so too must strategies be set to appeal to specific groups as well as to specific regions. Finally, we will look at the way in which the candidate is to be perceived. What is the basic theme of the campaign? Why should citizens support this candidate and not the other one? What kind of person is the candidate? How has he demonstrated the qualities that Americans look for in a president? What will the candidate do once in office? What concerns are highest on his priority list? How does he respond to the issues of the day?

A. Geographic Determinations

The basic goal of a presidential campaign is deceptively simple: garner 270 electoral college votes. Campaign strategists are all well aware that the **popular vote** is not the vote that counts in presidential elections. Each state has a number of electoral votes equal to the number of representatives plus the number of senators (always two) who represent that state in Congress. As mentioned earlier, in forty-eight states, plus the District of Columbia, the candidate who wins the plurality of the votes wins all of the electoral votes.[6] To win the presidential election, a candidate must win a majority of the electoral votes—270 electoral votes. If no one wins that number, the election is thrown into the House of Representatives for an election among the top three electoral vote recipients. Were such a contingency election to be held, each *state* would cast one vote—presumably cast according to the views of the majority of representatives from that state, though the procedures for such an election would be debated at the time. Again, a majority of the votes would be needed to win.[7]

In point of fact, the plurality winner in the popular vote normally wins a majority of the electoral votes. No election has been decided by the House of Representatives since that of 1824. But the results of the 2000 election demonstrate how important the rules

POPULAR VOTE

Direct vote for a candidate as opposed to an indirect method such as the electoral college.

of the presidential electoral game are. In the 2000 election Al Gore received more than half-a-million more votes than did George W. Bush. The outcome of the election was not determined, however, until the Supreme Court ruled that Governor Bush had won the disputed Florida electoral votes. Bush's slim margin in Florida gave him all 25 of Florida's electoral votes and put him over the magic number of 270. While the Democrats and the Gore campaign challenged the way in which votes were and were not counted in Florida, it is important to note that no one seriously challenged the legitimacy of the Bush victory because he had received fewer popular votes.

Different campaigns have used different techniques to determine which states are secure (won), which are hopeless (lost), and which are marginal (possible). Increasingly, the techniques used to devise campaign strategies are more and more sophisticated, but sophisticated scientific precision is not a substitute for political judgment. As has been oft repeated, politics remains more art than science. Strategies must reflect changing political times, multiple perceptions of the stakes involved, and the chemistry of certain candidacies as well as the more stark realities of political analysis.

Perhaps the best way to understand geographic strategies is to look at the Clinton campaign in 1992. By 1988 the concept of an electoral college "lock" was part of the everyday parlance of political analysts. The "lock" referred to states that seemed to be safe for Republican presidential candidates in recent elections. Twenty-three states (with over two hundred electoral votes) had voted for

the Republican candidate in every presidential election since 1968. If the states that supported only Jimmy Carter among the Democratic hopefuls in this period were added, considering them aberrations because of his Southern candidacy, the safe Republican states contained more electoral votes than the number needed for victory—the Republicans had a lock on the election. Despite losing the 1988 election to George H. W. Bush, Michael Dukakis demonstrated to some that the Republican lock might be "pickable." He came close to winning in a number of states that had gone to the Republicans for many years.

The 1992 Clinton strategy grew of what he considered a desperate situation—he was running third behind President Bush and Ross Perot in the early spring. In order to have any chance of winning, he needed to find a combination of states to give him an electoral majority. His strategists started with states that had gone consistently to the Democrats, added those in which Jimmy Carter had shown that a Southern Democrat (and eventually in this case, one with a Southern running mate) could do well, and finally tacked on those in which Dukakis had done better than expected. California and New York—the two biggest electoral prizes with eighty-seven electoral votes between them—were key to his strategy. By August both states appeared safe. The Clinton campaign could then put extra effort into other states—trying to secure what they thought were winnable states in the South, the Far West, and New England and then concentrating major efforts on the industrial heartland—states like Ohio, Pennsylvania, and Michigan. The results of the election show the extent to which the strategy succeeded. In addition to New York and California and the traditionally Democratic states, he won four Southern states, most of the Far West, all of New England, and the rust belt states of Pennsylvania, Ohio, Michigan, and Illinois (Ceaser and Busch 1993, 160–61; for discussions of geographic strategies in earlier campaigns, see Black and Oliphant 1989; Germond and Witcover 1985, 1989; Runkel 1989; Pomper 1985; Ranney 1985; Drew 1981; Jordan 1982; Moore 1981; White 1982; Schram 1977; Witcover 1977).

Of course, when an incumbent wins, he almost always follows his winning geographic strategy again in the next election. President Clinton did that in 1996, hoping to draw on the supporters he had attracted four years earlier. Figure 9.1 shows the extent to which his geographic winning coalition in 1996 paralleled that of 1992. Clinton lost only three states—Colorado, Georgia, and Montana, with a total of twenty-three electoral votes—that he had won in 1992; he picked up two states—Arizona and Florida with a total of thirty-three electoral votes—that he had not won in his first election.

However, Clinton's winning geographic coalition in 1992 and 1996 was not a portent of a new Democratic lock. Figures 9.2 and

Figure 9.1 Geographic Coalitions in Presidential Elections, 1992 and 1996

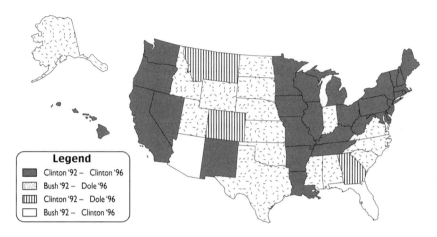

9.3 show the states won by George W. Bush and Al Gore in the 2000 election and by President Bush and John Kerry in 2004. The Democrats tried to capture the Clinton states. The Republicans tried to win back those carried by Reagan and George H. W. Bush. The results show that Bush recaptured the entire South; he was also successful in recapturing Ohio, Colorado, and Minnesota in both years, and New Hampshire in 2000 and New Mexico in 2004. These together were just enough to put him over the top. If Gore had been able to carry any one state that he lost, he would have won the electoral college majority as well as the popular vote plurality. Only three states switched between 2000 and 2004—New Hampshire from Bush to Kerry, and Iowa and New Mexico, from Gore to Bush.

What does it mean to follow a geographic strategy? Put simply, the question is one of campaign resources. A campaign has a limited

Figure 9.2 Breakdown of Geographic Coalitions in 2000

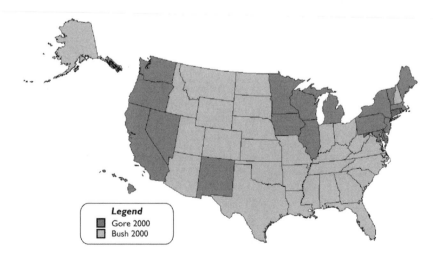

Figure 9.3 Breakdown of Geographic Coalitions in 2004

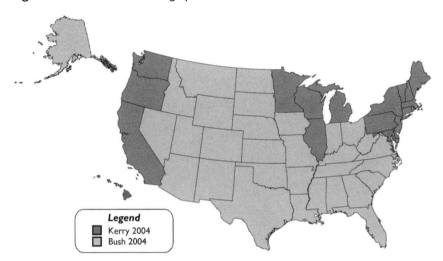

amount of resources, no matter how those are defined—candidate and surrogate time, money for television, staff. All votes across the country are not of equal value. A campaign puts more resources into states (and therefore looking for votes) that are more competitive but where it feels it has a chance. If a state is definitely won, then it will receive fewer resources—the candidate, the vice presidential candidate, and their wives will visit less often; less money will be spent on television. It does not matter by how much a state is won. There is no benefit in building up the margin of victory. What is important is that the state is in the win column and that its electoral votes are tallied. Conversely, if a state is lost, if there is no hope of winning the electoral votes, then it too receives fewer resources. It does not matter by how much it is lost, if it is lost. According to F. Christopher Arterton,

> The Clinton campaign [in 1992] used a sophisticated data-mapping operation to systematize its scheduling, media-buying, and get-out-the-vote operations. . . . Week by week, each media market was ranked in terms of the number of persuadable voters in the market weighted by the Electoral College votes and the perceived strategic importance of the states reached in that market. The resulting map . . . quickly revealed where the campaign needed to place its emphasis in travel, field operations, and media buys. (quoted in Pomper 1993, 87)

In 2000 and 2004 much of the talk by pundits dealt with the so-called battleground states, states that were too close to call and into which both campaigns poured enormous resources. The results of the election show that these resources were spent in the states that were in fact most closely contested—Florida, Oregon, Michigan, Pennsylvania, Wisconsin, and New Hampshire, among others. The goal is to concentrate efforts in winnable states in which the outcome is in doubt. Assessments of which states receive how much emphasis change over the course of a campaign. That is the nature of the dynamics of campaigning. And second-guessing is always possible—what if the Gore campaign had expended a little more effort in New Hampshire? If the Republicans had spent more time in Florida, would that race not have been so close? What if Kerry had concentrated more on Ohio? But the theory that campaigns seek electoral votes and emphasize states that are winnable but not assured never changes.

B. Coalition Strategies

The election is contested in the states, but voters do not see themselves merely as citizens of states, and they do not receive campaign stimuli as citizens of states only. Thus another approach that campaign advisers use is to look at voters as people who can be grouped according to their views on politics and may logically be expected to either favor or oppose a certain candidate. Strategies using this premise are less explicit than those based on geography, but they are nonetheless important in campaign planning.

Let's look back to the 1992 and 1996 appeals of Bill Clinton, as they serve as excellent examples. As mentioned earlier, Clinton's 1992 nomination marked a triumph for the Democratic Leadership Council, a group started by Southern Democrats who were convinced that their party needed a new, more centrist appeal. In their view, Democrats had based too much of their appeal on issues favored by relatively small minorities—blacks, gays, civil libertarians. While defending these groups involved important stands of principle, such actions also depicted the party as one defending the fringes and not concerned about the vast majority. Al From, the president of the DLC, argued that the Democrats could be true to their basic principles but still strive to appeal to a majority. He defined this group as suburban housewives, concerned with bread-and-butter issues, with the economy, with safety, with responsibility. The 1992 Democratic platform stressed these issues; candidate Clinton never strayed from them in the campaign. To a large part they made him President Clinton.

TRIANGULATION

The effort to position oneself between extreme positions so as to draw support from both sides.

In 1996 the term **triangulation** came into common parlance. Political consultant Richard Morris, an old friend of Bill Clinton who had worked for both Democratic and Republican candidates, was brought into the White House for advice after Democrats were badly beaten in the 1994 midterm election. Morris's advice was simple. If Clinton positioned himself between liberal Democrats and conservative Republicans in Congress, he would be able to form a winning coalition. By "capturing the center," he would take potential voters away from the Republicans while losing no Democrats, as they would have no viable alternative to whom they could turn. The strategy, exemplified by passage of a conservative welfare plan, worked admirably. The Republicans screamed because Clinton was usurping their issues. He did get credit for "Republican" programs passed on his watch. Liberal Democrats were distraught because they were forced to abandon some cherished programs, but they could not desert their president. And President Clinton was re-elected with relative ease.

Both Bush and Gore tried to capture the center in the 2000 campaign, but in this instance the coalitional strategy was compounded by the Clinton factor. Governor Bush appealed to those who liked Clinton's policies but not Clinton's morals, claiming that Gore was the heir to both. Vice President Gore had the difficult task of tying himself to the good aspects of the Clinton presidency without being tainted by the bad. In the final analysis, he distanced himself from the president to the extent possible. Thus he did not gain the benefit from the boom economy of the Clinton years. Some claim that Gore was put in a no-win situation because of President Clinton's personal problems; what is clearly shown is that the strategy he adopted did not succeed.

Polling and historical data can tell strategists how they are perceived by and have fared among groups of voters. Just as it is possible to set targets for states by analyzing election returns, so too is it possible to set targets for group support. It is also possible to base some parts of a candidate's appeal on group loyalties. However, with few exceptions, group members do not live in concentrated geographic areas. Most campaign appeals go out through the mass media, which is by and large geographically based. Therefore, appealing to group loyalties as separate from geographic location is a difficult task for a campaign to undertake and is, in fact, a tactical matter to which we will return.

C. Issue Strategies

In one sense, events define the issues of a campaign. President George W. Bush's 2004 reelection campaign centered on the war on terrorism, because he was in office when the 9/11 attacks occurred. But in a very important way, the candidate sets the tone for a campaign. He does so by the force of his personality, by his statements about why he wants to be president and what he would do if elected, and by the concerns that he chooses to emphasize as he campaigns throughout the nation.

I. Campaign Themes

In 1992, President George H. W. Bush was constantly criticized for not having "the vision thing." He never understood the term and never understood what was missing. In a very fundamental way, what was missing was any sense of why he should be reelected president of the United States. His campaign never had a theme. He never gave the citizens a sense of where he wanted to take the country.

Bush's two opponents in 1992, in very different ways, each adopted the same theme. Bill Clinton ran as an outsider, taking his cue from Jimmy Carter, who had run and won that way sixteen years earlier. He wanted to change the way things were done in Washington—to spark the economy, to end the gridlock of divided government and get things done, to rid Washington of those who had been there too long, personified by George Bush and his Republican colleagues who had run the executive branch for twelve years. He wanted to be the candidate for a new generation, the candidate who looked to make changes for the future. These variations on the change motif were symbolized by the theme song of the Clinton campaign, "Don't Stop Thinking about Tomorrow!"

H. Ross Perot was the ultimate outsider, stressing the change theme as no one had before. Perot wanted to "get under the hood and fix things." He wanted a whole different approach to government, his practical "down home" approach that had been so successful in business. There was nothing about Ross Perot, as a man, as a candidate, as a catalyst for new ideas, that did not say "change." He clearly struck a responsive chord with the American people. Before he dropped out of the campaign on the eve of the Democratic convention, his high poll showings suggested the extent to which his appeal was being heard. When he withdrew, those who had listened to his message turned toward Bill Clinton, the other change agent in the race. When Perot returned to the race, however, he was not able to recapture all of his former supporters. (See Ceaser and Busch 1993, 165.)

When a campaign begins, the opening theme needs to be presented often and forcefully. Candidates spend a great deal of time thinking about how to make their thematic statements most effectively. The messages conveyed in early speeches and television interviews, the ways in which those messages are delivered, the audiences to whom they are directed, the efforts made to disseminate them to the public. These are all part of a campaign's opening gambit. A candidate is most able to define his own message, to articulate his own theme, early in the campaign. After that, he often must respond to challenges from opponents and to events as they unfold.

Candidates must have a good deal of faith in their basic

theme—in the ways in which they are presenting that theme to the nation. Their campaign is built on that foundation. But what if it is not working? Campaign strategies are not static; they are not set in cement. Situations change and the candidate must react. Pollsters, journalists, strategists, and the candidate all make assessments about "how it is going." All these observers see what is working and what is not. They know when it is time for a change, when it is time for a "strategic adjustment" (Kessel 1984, 314; 1992, 75–76).

Changes in the basic theme of a campaign are not easy to make. First, it takes some time to realize that all is not going as planned. With modern polling and with candidates sensitive to the "pulse of the people," feedback is constant. Still it takes some time to realize that a pattern of failure is appearing, that the campaign is not having its desired impact. Second, those who have made the initial decision about a campaign's theme, by and large, are the same ones who are assessing this new information. The team consensus about what should work was not easily arrived at. Consequently, it is not easily disrupted either. The more a candidate is invested in the theme, the harder it is to shift.

Changes in general election campaigns are much more difficult than changes in primaries for a number of reasons. No events in a general election campaign are as decisive as a caucus or primary defeat to signal the need for change. The general election campaign team has experienced too much success together for the candidate to consider a change in senior advisers. The compressed fall campaign means that there will be little time remaining to articulate a new theme and to sell it to the American people. Doing so might appear hypocritical. Finally, the advisers on board have given the situation the benefit of their best analysis, and thus it is unlikely they will come up with anything different.

Thus despite the fact that campaigns are not static events, major thematic adjustments are most difficult to make. More frequently, concerns are expressed and minor adjustments are made. Tactical decisions, not strategic decisions, are the order of the day. And the days slip by while these assessments and adjustments are being made. Soon it is time for the final push to election day. And by that time, as political scientist John Kessel has so aptly put it, "time's up" (Kessel 1984, 316; 1992, 76). The push to election day might be very important in a close election, but what one does in those last days cannot represent a major change in the themes that have been set out in advance.

2. Character as a Campaign Issue

Americans hold their presidents to a high standard. The press examines candidates for party nominations in great detail, and those who are found wanting are often left by the wayside. But even among the survivors, character is an important issue. Americans vote for a party; they vote for a set of ideas; but they also vote for a person—someone they can trust to lead the nation.

To what kind of person do voters turn? George H. W. Bush had an idea. He had been "bred" to lead. He was the heir to a political family. He had the right pedigree. But more than that, he had the right résumé. He had volunteered for World War II at a very young age and his plane had been shot from the sky. He had started his own business and succeeded in rugged west Texas. He had served in Congress, as chair of the Republican National Committee, as director of the CIA, as ambassador to China and the United Nations, as vice president. He knew the government. He had experience. He was a leader.

Bush tried to make character a key campaign issue. And to a large extent he succeeded. Bill Clinton's character had been called into question during the 1992 primaries. His alleged marital infidelity was exposed to the nation, and his veracity was questioned as he responded to inquiries about his draft status during the Vietnam War and about his use of marijuana. Bush played on concerns raised by these issues throughout the 1992 campaign, trying to divert attention from the "change" theme to one of fitness for office.

Clinton's character was continuously assaulted throughout his first term in office. The Whitewater investigation, questions about firing workers in the White House travel office, the entire litany of charges that came under the purview of the Office of the Special Prosecutor, as well as the ways in which President Clinton responded to each allegation, caused people to remember his "Slick Willie" image. In the final hours of the 1996 campaign, Bob Dole, the wounded war veteran with a political pedigree nearly as long as President George H. W. Bush's, turned up the heat on the character issue. He did not believe that the American people would really choose someone with Clinton's character flaws over him.

Bush and Dole clearly won the "character wars" in their respective campaigns against Clinton, but that one issue was not enough to offset others. Clinton benefited from some aspects of the character issue, particularly his relative youth and his ability to appeal to minorities and others not from Main Street America. Clinton represented a new generation of American politician. That aspect of his character, while not offsetting the attacks leveled at him by his opponents—and the wounds he inflicted on himself—clearly aided his appeal in each election. His victories demonstrated that character has many dimensions in a campaign.

Oddly, the Clinton character issue might finally have come home to roost in the 2000 campaign. In that campaign Vice President Gore could not remove himself from the taint of the Clinton years. Governor Bush, subtly but firmly, stressed this issue. He said that he would return morality to the White House. He said that he wanted to be judged by the kind of person he was. The press—and the public—liked George W. Bush. He is a very likable man. He does not put on airs; what one sees is what one gets. There is no pretense. While Al Gore's friends like him and say that he is a funny man in private, in public he is stiff and seems calculating. During the campaign he kept changing his personality. During the three debates Gore seemed to switch persona, morphing to meet his handlers' suggestions. The overall impression was that he did not know who he really was. The late-night talk show hosts and *Saturday Night Live* had a field day imitating the changing character of Al Gore. In the final analysis, voters chose someone they liked—even if they were unsure of his positions and even of his abilities—over someone with whom they could not become comfortable, even though they liked the policies he stood for and knew he was very much up to the job.

3. The Issues Raised during a Campaign

Candidates for the presidency must be responsive to the issues of the day. They attempt to emphasize those issues that work to their advantage and downplay those that help their opponents. At times, events dictate how issues will affect a campaign. At other times, candidate strategy concerning issue emphasis has the most impact.

When the nation is involved in a foreign crisis, international concerns tend to dominate the issue discussion during a campaign. If America's sons and daughters are in harm's way, the citizenry focuses on these concerns.

However, in times of peace, domestic issues, particularly the bread-and-butter issues relating to the economy, are more salient. The electorate's attention to these issues is broader than it is deep. Citizens care how the economy is affecting them personally, and they credit or blame the incumbent president for these effects. They are not sophisticated critics of particular economic policies; rather they evaluate results. Views on controversial issues like affirmative action, abortion, or same sex marriage, are focused on an emotional level; citizens have general views on these policies but they do not want to examine programmatic details.

The 1992 and 1996 elections provide relevant examples of how issues play in presidential campaigns and of how they can be used for strategic purposes. The first President Bush was accorded record high poll ratings after the victory in the Persian Gulf War in 1991. However, when election time rolled around in 1992, the popular frenzy over the lightning-fast military victory had died down. The electorate was more concerned about the economy than what Bush had done more than a year earlier.

The Clinton campaign emphasized the economy. Recall the now famous sign on the desk of campaign press secretary George Stephanopoulos: "It's the economy, stupid!" Candidate Clinton stressed the economy at every opportunity. He talked about the problems caused by the expanding deficit; he talked about the need to create more jobs, "to grow the economy." He talked about the failures of the Bush administration to handle the perceived recession. Other issues also worked to Clinton's advantage. The Republican Convention had been dominated by those stressing "family values." But the stridency of the debate made many uncomfortable; it seemed as if the Republicans wanted to dictate what values should be important to all citizens. Clinton talked about health care, education, and the environment—noneconomic domestic issues about which the public clearly cared. Clinton came out ahead of Bush on the issues strategy. The one area in which Bush had an advantage—foreign and military policy—was the one about which the people cared least.

Fast-forward four years. By 1996 the recession had ended. The deficit was receding and the budget moving toward balance. More people had jobs, and they were more confident that they would retain jobs in the future. The voters credited Bill Clinton for these improving conditions. Many economists' belief that the seeds for the economy's improvement had been planted in the Bush administration was irrelevant. It was irrelevant that Clinton's policies at times were forced on him by the Republicans. What was relevant was that the public credited President Clinton with these improvements. The country was at peace, the economy was healthy, and people were optimistic. That left Dole with nothing to exploit but Bill Clinton's character flaws. Voters clearly demonstrated that they were more concerned with their quality of life and their economic future than they were with assessments of the moral rectitude of the man sitting in the Oval Office.

The 2004 campaign stands in stark contrast. President Bush had led the nation's response to the terrorist attacks of September 11, 2001. He had declared a "War on Terror" and was commander in chief of our troops battling in Afghanistan and Iraq. Senator Kerry's analysis of how the Bush leadership had made us more, not less, vulnerable did not persuade an electorate anxious to unite behind a leader who appeared decisive in time of war.

D. The Strategic Use of Incumbency

One would think that incumbent presidents would have enormous advantages in seeking reelection, as we have seen that members of the House do. Think about the advantages an incumbent president holds. First, he has the power and prestige of the office at his beck and call. No one speaks for the nation as does the president. Even the most cynical political observer realizes that "Hail to the Chief" quickens the heartbeat of many Americans. When the president travels, he travels in *Air Force One,* with "United States of America" proudly emblazoned on its side. When the president speaks, the presidential seal adorns the podium. The basic premise is that the incumbent is "our" president, and anyone else is a pretender to the throne.

Whatever the president says or does is news. Thus an incumbent president is guaranteed front-page stories in the nation's press every day. More than that, his views are considered important and legitimate merely because they are the views of the president. Few are willing to put presidential statements under the same scrutiny as those of a mere challenger to office.

Furthermore, presidential action shapes events. When a president travels overseas, he is the U.S. government negotiating with another power. When a challenger travels, he is gaining experience in foreign affairs. When a president signs a bill into law, the law goes on the books. When he vetoes legislation, Congress must address his veto. When a challenger says what he would do, there are no consequences. When a president says that he will not close an air force base or that he will push a public works project, the base remains open or the bridge is built. Citizens know too well the difference between wielding actual power and promising what might be done. Presidents for some time have used the advantages of their office to time grants, appointments, legislation, and travel for strategic political purposes.

Presidents do not have to prove that they are capable of handling the office or that they have the requisite background and experience; they have held the job for four years. What is better experience for being president than having been president?

Finally, incumbent presidents have a political organization in place. In most cases this is an organization that has already run and won a national election. But even in the case of incumbents who have succeeded to the presidency, the White House staff serves the president for political purposes as well as governmental purposes. Their job is to keep the president in a strong political position so that he can achieve his policy objectives (Neustadt 1976); one consequence of this job is to enhance his chances for reelection.

All these advantages would seem to make incumbent presidents seeking reelection invulnerable. But three of our last six presidents have lost bids for reelection. President Clinton was the first Democrat to be elected twice as president since Franklin Delano Roosevelt. Among Republicans, only Dwight Eisenhower, Richard Nixon, Ronald Reagan, and George W. Bush have achieved reelection in this century. The advantages in favor of incumbent presidents might appear to be strong, but their record of winning reelection is not unblemished.

President Truman won with great difficulty in 1948;[8] and Truman in 1952 and Johnson in 1968 each decided not to seek their party's nomination, in part at least because it seemed they would succeed in doing so only at great political cost. Presidents Ford, Carter, and Bush I have lost in recent years. How can their cases be distinguished from those of the presidents who sought and won reelection with relative ease—Wilson, Eisenhower, Nixon, Reagan, Clinton, and Bush II?

There are commonalities among Ford, Carter, and Bush I. For all the advantages of incumbency, one important consequence serves as a countervailing force. Incumbents are held accountable for what happens while they are in office, even if they do not cause those events. President Ford was an appointed vice president who succeeded to the Oval Office upon the resignation of his disgraced predecessor. His term was marked by continuing controversy over Watergate and his pardon of President Nixon and by a recession in 1975. President Carter presided when the nation's prestige was compromised as night after night the news programs emphasized that "America was held hostage" by a band of terrorists in Iran. The actions of terrorists in Iran and a continuing sluggish economy led voters to reject his leadership for that of the charismatic Ronald Reagan.

Similarly, despite his foreign policy successes, President Bush I was blamed for the recession that was being felt in 1992. His position was further hurt by the fact that he refused to recognize the recession and continued on a policy course that citizens felt was not working. The judgment of the voters can be cruel; their horizon is very short. That Bush's policies eventually proved effective did not counter the citizens' short-term view that their economic future was not bright.

The lessons for incumbents seeking reelection appear to be clear. The incumbency is a tremendous advantage in running for the White House if the first term has been a successful one and is perceived as such as it is ending. Only an incumbent can point to leadership ability, experience, and accomplishments in precisely the appropriate context. Only an incumbent can say to the American voting public, "Let's not rock the boat. Things are going well because of me. Why change?" Successful presidents can run a Rose Garden campaign in which the candidate is always seen as the president, not as a campaigner.

However, if the accomplishments are not there, if the country does not have a positive view of the way in which the incumbent has run the country, if the four years since the last election have been troubled ones, the president is likely to be blamed. If the difficulties outweigh the accomplishments, the election is just as likely to be a referendum on the last four years and the outcome is not so likely to be a happy one for the individual in the Oval Office.

IV. TACTICS FOR THE GENERAL ELECTION

The distinction between strategies and tactics is often a subtle one. The *strategy* that a campaign adopts is its overall plan to convince voters controlling a majority of the electoral college that a candidate deserves support. The *tactics* are the day-to-day means used to implement that strategy. A strategic decision involves identifying areas of the country to be emphasized; a tactical decision would be how to carry the message to the specified areas. This section will review four specific tactical considerations to which all campaigns must give attention—scheduling of the candidate and other campaign principles, the message that will be used in the paid media, the issues that will be emphasized, and the decisions concerning possible candidate debates.

A. Tactical Considerations of Where to Go

The most scarce resource in a presidential campaign, as with a campaign for state or local office, is the candidate's time. Strategic decisions about what areas of the country to stress dictate some tactical decisions about where the candidate should campaign.

But other factors must be taken into account as well. What image should be portrayed on the campaign trail? Thus, the Gore campaign in 2000 decided that Vice President Gore and Senator Lieberman should campaign together, particularly early in the campaign. The tactical consideration was that Lieberman, a person of irreproachable character, the first Democrat to be critical of President Clinton during the Lewinsky scandal, would symbolize that Gore had distanced himself from the president's moral problems. Similarly, the Mondale campaign in 1984 decided that Mondale and vice presidential nominee Ferraro, the first woman nominated for a national ticket, should campaign together for much of the early campaign, so that Mondale could draw on what some saw as Ferraro's charismatic appeal. This meant that the two of them could cover only half as many media markets in a day as would have been the case if they had traveled separately.

Other tactical decisions regarding candidate appearances deal with scheduling surrogates. Who should appear with the candidate? When? Who would be best for which areas? Or who would suffice in less important areas? The 2000 Bush campaign knew that it would only be able to use General Colin Powell on a limited number of occasions. How should this be done? Where should they campaign with John McCain? These tactical questions were aimed at implementing a strategy that determined where the candidate would have to do well in order to win.

Tactics, like strategies, can be changed over time. As some states become more marginal, as some campaigners gain in appeal or effectiveness, tactical decisions can be reviewed. It is difficult to make broad strategic adjustments, but it is much easier to refine the strategies by changing tactics. Candidate and surrogate schedules require some advanced planning. However, they require neither the lead time nor the fundamental rethinking that changes in strategy necessitate.

B. Tactical Considerations of Media Use

Today it is a given in planning a presidential campaign that a large percentage of a campaign's budget will be spent on paid media. With both presidential candidates in 2004 spending over $200 million on their campaigns and concentrating that spending in battleground states, it is no wonder that TiVo sales were way up in the regions overrun with political ads.

The general strategy of a campaign lays out how the campaign will appeal to the voters and how a candidate will be distinguished from his opponent. Tactical considerations include what specific messages will be emphasized on the media campaign at what times. Of particular importance is the opening message, for this sets the theme for a campaign. Just as important is the way in which candidates respond to changing situations.

In 2004 the Kerry campaign failed in part because its response to the attacks on the candidate's character by the Swift Boat Veterans for Truth was too slow. In 1992, James Carville, Bill Clinton's chief strategist, established the much publicized war room at the Little Rock campaign headquarters with the express purpose of being able to respond to anticipated negative campaign ads, gaining the tactical advantage of the ability to respond quickly with new, countering advertisements. Modern media technology allows campaigns to design, cut, and air commercials virtually overnight. But the Kerry campaign failed to benefit from the tactic Carville had pioneered.

C. Tactical Considerations of Which Issues to Discuss

The questions of what issues a candidate should discuss and what the emphasis of television ads should be are closely related. Right from the start, the content of the speech repeated at each stop by a candidate is a tactical expression of his basic strategy.

The tactical aspects of the 1980 Reagan campaign have been used as models by candidates in succeeding elections. The basic tactic was first to establish a positive image of the candidate and then to attack the opponent.

Reagan's campaign began by disabusing voters of the notion that his views were out of the mainstream and that electing him would be dangerous. His early speeches emphasized that his views were not set in ideological stone and that he was willing to change. When President Carter was unsuccessful in his attempt to convince Americans that they had to be afraid of a Reagan presidency, the Reagan strategists knew that their tactic had worked. Poll results confirmed this assessment.

At that point, Reagan's tactics changed. His image was secure, so he could begin to attack Carter's image. He could begin talking about the four-year Carter record. The tactical decision was to switch to issues that reflected badly on Carter once Reagan's own image was secure in the minds of the voters. The final weeks of the campaign saw Reagan repeatedly asking one question, "Are you better off now than you were four years ago?" The tactic was to change the focus of the debate from Reagan's image to Carter's record. It was a most successful switch.

The 1992 Clinton campaign portrayed an image of an outsider, "the man from Hope," someone who wanted to change the way things were done. Once he had set that basic picture in the electorate's eye, he turned to the message that the economy was in trouble, that Bush did not have the answer, and that he would "grow the economy" and provide jobs for the American people.

The same tactic was followed by George W. Bush in 2000, and it is an obvious ploy for any relatively unknown candidate. To pursue this tactic, the issues discussed by the candidate reflect the same concerns as those portrayed in television commercials. The basic strategy of theme and issues had been set; the tactic involved ways to portray that message forcefully and repeatedly to the voters.

D. The Tactics of Presidential Debates

Debates between (or among) presidential candidates have become a familiar part of the election process, but it was not always so. Until 1960 the television networks felt that they were restricted from presenting debates between the Republican and Democratic candidates for the presidency because of the **equal time provision**, which specified that if any candidate for an office was given free time on television, all candidates should be given equal time. The networks were concerned about how this applied to minor party candidates. In 1960 Congress suspended the equal time provision to allow for the famous Kennedy–Nixon debates (Kraus 1962; see also Ranney 1979). These set one agenda for campaign tacticians for the future. Should a candidate seek (or accept) a series of debates with his opponent(s)?

EQUAL TIME PROVISION

Regulation requiring that regulated media provide an equal amount of time to any candidate in an election in which they have given time to another candidate.

The legal questions about the viability of debates have been ironed out, and the debates have now become a much anticipated, institutionalized part of presidential campaigning. Since 1988, the debates have been sponsored by the Commission on Presidential Debates, a privately funded, bipartisan organization headed by the chairs of the two major political parties.[9] But every four years the candidates still face tactical decisions regarding the debates, in these cases questions of how many debates will be held, when, under what format, and with what participants. Candidates also must decide on the tactics they will use during the debates themselves. Let's look at two recent experiences.

Michael Dukakis felt that there was no way he could lose in debating George H. W. Bush in 1988. For a number of years Dukakis had hosted the PBS television show *The Advocates.* He felt totally comfortable on television and totally comfortable in the debate format.[10] The Democrats thus wanted as many debates as possible; the Republicans, as few. The Democrats also wanted to assure that the vice presidential candidates debated.

The presidential candidates debated twice in 1988; the vice presidential candidates, once. The presidential debates were another lost opportunity for Dukakis. He was given plenty of material by his staff, but he never went after Bush. Dukakis looked like the well-prepared, well-briefed technocrat; Bush looked human and funny. Dukakis won the debating points; Bush the hearts of the listeners. The most poignant moment came at the start of the second debate when Bernard Shaw of CNN asked Governor Dukakis, who opposed the death penalty, how he would respond if his wife Kitty were raped and killed. Dukakis responded mechanically, answering the question but never revealing any emotion. If Dukakis's goal was to connect with his audience, Shaw had flipped him a gopher ball, and he swung and missed. The debate came at a time when the Democratic campaign desperately needed a boost; instead it fell flat (Black and Oliphant 1989, 262–72, 282–96; Germond and Witcover 1989, 219, 251–54, 425–47).

The vice presidential debates, on the other hand, aided the Democrats and hurt the Republicans. Those who were preparing Senator Bentsen for this debate had noted that Dan Quayle frequently compared his background to President Kennedy's before he took office. When Quayle used the line in the debate, Bentsen pounced: "Senator, I served with Jack Kennedy. I knew Jack Kennedy. Jack Kennedy was a friend of mine. Senator, you're no Jack Kennedy." The lines were delivered so perfectly, so slowly, with such a measured rhythm that no one who heard them—least of all Dan Quayle—will ever forget them. Bentsen was the statesman who exuded confidence; Quayle was like a wounded puppy. The debate caused a momentary bump in the Dukakis-Bentsen polling numbers, but it had no lasting effect on the presidential election. It did, however, leave an indelible mark on Dan Quayle's reputation.

In 1992 the debates were held among three contenders—President Bush, Bill Clinton, and Ross Perot—and separately among their running mates. Perot's polling numbers were so high that there was no real question of excluding him from these nationally televised events.[11] One of the key questions in the "debates about the debates" dealt with format. President Bush was most comfortable with a formal arrangement, with set statements and responses, or with questions from journalists. Bill Clinton wanted a more open format. Perot seemed to be happy to be on the same stage, regardless of the format. In the debates that were held, Clinton's performance proved that his tactics were right. He excelled at the informal, town meeting debate in which citizens asked questions. He left his set position and walked out to the questioners. He communicated directly with his audience. President Bush seemed ill at ease and was caught checking his watch on camera at one point.

In that debate the moderator ruled out questions of character as matters not of concern to the citizens in the audience. Again, this decision played to Clinton's tactical advantage, allowing him to stress the economy question. Clinton was also aided by a Perot tactic, a decision to concentrate his fire on Bush and on the job he had not done on the economy. The debates drew huge audiences, with an estimated eighty million people watching the first debate (Nelson 1997, 67). They clearly helped candidate Clinton in that he appeared as "presidential" as the incumbent he sought to unseat.

More recent debates have also played key roles in presidential campaigns. In 1996 Senator Dole could not dent the presidential veneer of Bill Clinton. In 2000, Vice President Gore, like Dukakis before him, felt that his intellectual superiority would benefit him against George W. Bush, but Bush's team set the expectations for their candidate low, and he clearly exceeded them. Gore came across as a chameleon, someone so desperate to be president that he would change to appear as whatever the electorate wanted. Despite appearing more in command of his facts and better prepared than President Bush in the 2004 debates, John Kerry never showed the passion to convince wavering voters to get excited about his candidacy. And he failed to take advantage of yet another opportunity to respond to attacks on his character he felt were unfair.

The debates have become an accepted part of presidential campaigning. It is difficult to see how debates will not remain a permanent part of presidential campaigns. But they will also continue to raise tactical questions that all campaigns must address as they view ways to implement their strategies. And debates will have an impact, not necessarily a decisive impact, but surely one about which every campaign manager must be concerned.

V. THIRD-PARTY CANDIDATES IN PRESIDENTIAL ELECTIONS

The American party system has been described as a strong two-party system. Yet in six of the last fifteen presidential elections more than two parties have fielded candidates who have had a significant impact on the strategies of the major party nominees (and perhaps on the outcome of the elections themselves).[12]

DIXIECRATS

Southern Democrats who walked out of the 1948 Democratic National Convention in protest over the party's civil rights plank and ran Strom Thurmond as their candidate for president.

In 1948 the Democratic party was split from the left (by former vice president Henry Wallace) and from the right (by the **Dixiecrat** walkout and the candidacy of Strom Thurmond).[13] Wallace ran a national campaign that attracted over a million popular votes but no electoral college votes. Thurmond ran a regional campaign that attracted slightly fewer voters to his cause but, because they were regionally concentrated, garnered thirty-nine electoral votes.

The 1968 campaign of Alabama governor George Wallace and the 1980 campaign of Illinois congressman John Anderson provide examples of the potential impact of third-party efforts and how major party candidates must respond to them. Wallace left the Democratic party because he felt that the party was too liberal. Originally political analysts thought that he would only appeal to racist Southerners who remembered Wallace's defiance of Kennedy administration civil rights policies. However, during the course of the campaign it became clear that his appeal was to the more conservative elements of the Democratic party throughout the nation. Humphrey had to appeal to party loyalty in the North. Nixon had to be sure that Wallace was not gaining conservative votes that otherwise would have gone to him. As is always the case with third-party candidates, Wallace had to find a way to stay viable in all areas of the country, to convince followers that a vote for Wallace was not a wasted vote.

In 1980 the "Anderson difference" sought to set candidate John Anderson apart from the Democratic incumbent and his Republican challenger by finding a middle ground between the two major party candidates. In running an independent campaign in the general election, Anderson wanted to attract voters who combined the orthodox Republican party view on economic matters with the Democratic party view on social issues. He carved a nice niche and exploited his personal strengths—intelligence, charisma, and rhetorical skills—and policy positions to maximize his support among those who disliked each of the other two candidates.

The Carter campaign viewed Anderson as more of a threat than did the Reagan campaign. The strategy of Carter's staff members against Anderson was to belittle his campaign effort, to ignore him, and to convince the media to ignore him as well. The Reagan campaign understood that Anderson was taking votes from Carter, not from them. Thus they sought to boost his candidacy, agreeing to debate him. The Carter campaign responded not by attcking John Anderson the man, but by attacking the idea of a third-party candidacy. Their approach was to say, in essence, "John Anderson is a fine man with good ideas, but he is not going to win. If you really favor his ideas, vote for Carter, because his views are much closer to yours than are Reagan's."

Third-party candidates in American presidential elections frequently suffer a loss of support as election day approaches. Candidates win electoral votes only if they lead a state's ballot on election day, not if they do better than expected. Many voters realize that a protest vote for a third-party candidate is, in fact, a wasted vote, because that candidate will not win enough votes in their state to capture any electoral votes. Thus they are convinced that it serves their interest better to vote for whichever major party candidate more closely reflects their views. It is difficult to know the extent to which the Carter strategy of dealing with the Anderson candidacy worked. It is clear, however, that Anderson's vote total on election day was much less than the percentages he was drawing in the polls a month earlier in the campaign.

The Anderson campaign demonstrates the problem faced by third-party candidacies. Without the base of political party support, a non-major-party candidate has a difficult task demonstrating viability. To be viable, the candidate must remain visible throughout the campaign. The candidate must not fall too far behind in the polls. Television (both paid commercials and news broadcasts) must keep the candidate's name before the public, on a footing as nearly equal to those of the major party candidates as possible. Such a campaign requires a good deal of money. The major party candidates do not have to worry about having a critical mass of money with which to run their general election campaign. Their campaigns are funded out of the federal Treasury. But minor party candidates must raise their own money (which will be repaid from the Treasury if they poll a certain percentage of votes). The financial burden is a heavy one. Many thought that burden too heavy for any minor party candidate to overcome. However, H. Ross Perot gave lie to those sentiments in 1992.

Perot's 1992 campaign stands as the most successful challenge to major party dominance of presidential politics since former president Theodore Roosevelt ran on the Bull Moose party ticket in 1912. Perot's appeal was unique. Rather than splinter off from one of the two major parties, Perot denounced them both. He claimed that he stood as an alternative to business as usual in Washington. Using simple "down-home" language, Perot based his appeal on a simple premise: he had been fabulously successful in business and would do the same in running the government. He would not permit the kinds of sloppy business dealings that had been exhibited by the Democrats and the Republicans. He would butt heads and not permit partisan differences to obscure solutions to pressing problems. He was the pragmatist who could do it right.

His theme was clear and, despite its oversimplistic view of exceedingly complex problems with which the national government sought to deal, he struck a responsive chord. He also had one unique advantage over previous third-party candidates:[14] he was capable of and fully prepared to finance his own campaign. In fact, during the 1992 campaign Perot spent approximately the same amount of money as did the two major party candidates. Financing was not an issue in this case.

Perot crossed the first hurdle—viability—by gaining access to the ballot in every state. That alone is no mean feat. Every state has its own requirement. Some are quite onerous, though challenges by previous third-party candidates have eased the burden somewhat. Still, the logistical problem of exploring legal statutes and meeting petition requirements by the deadlines that are imposed is a major one. Previous candidates have had to rely on volunteers to cross this hurdle. Perot was able to hire "volunteers" whenever he needed to do so.

Viability also involves continuous exposure. In this case, while Perot's money certainly helped, his genius for gaining the spotlight was equally significant. He first announced that he would explore the possibility of running on Larry King's CNN television show. King is a flamboyant host with a large following. He is not known as a hard interviewer. Perot appeared on King's show over and over, garnering free publicity not only from his appearance but also from the news stories that reported on his appearance.

His genius for attracting attention carried over into the claim that he would only run if "the people" urged him to do so. They were to do this by calling his 800 line and volunteering to help in his campaign. He aptly named his organization United We Stand, clearly with the intent of implying a large following. And people did decide to follow him.

Perot pursued his campaign theme assiduously, never getting off message. His tactic was simple: to belittle his opposition and to pose solutions that everyone could understand. Whether or not those solutions were in fact practical, or if they were politically possible, mattered little to him or his followers. He implied that he would impose them on the system, seemingly ignoring the branches of government coequal to the one he sought to head. But again, none of this mattered. When Perot withdrew from the campaign in July, he was seen as running even with President Bush and Bill Clinton in most trial heat polls. When he reentered the campaign, he never quite achieved that position again, but he was always a strong contender.

Two other aspects of Perot's 1992 campaign should be noted. First, he was included in the presidential debates, and his running mate participated in the vice presidential debate. There is no question that his participation had an impact on how those debates were contested and on the election. His mere presence on the stage gave credibility to his campaign.

Second, Perot essentially invented a new form of political media advertising, the **infomercial**. Perot bought half-hour blocks of time and went before the cameras to explain his program. Political experts derided his effort when he announced his plans, arguing that no one would watch. They were wrong. The audience tuned in to see what this new phenomenon in American politics was all about. As Perot stood before the cameras with his charts and diagrams, millions watched. Many accepted his points—and many more understood that the complaints he had about the way the system was functioning were valid, even if his solutions might not be.

Perot did not crisscross the nation. He did not have an elaborate national campaign structure. He followed virtually none of the techniques we have laid out as typical of presidential campaigns. He had a dedicated corps of volunteers and enough paid staff to use them effectively. And he went his own way. He frustrated traditional politicians who simply did not know how to react to him. And in the end, he had an impact, forcing the two major parties and their candidates to pay attention to his message and his followers.

After the 1992 campaign, Perot remained on the national stage. As an example, he debated Vice President Gore on the issue of the North American Free Trade Agreement (NAFTA), arguing that it would send American jobs to Mexico. But the major decision that he made was to transform his movement, United We Stand, into a political party, the Reform party. In so doing, he signaled that a new force was on the political horizon, and he frightened the major parties. Both sought to appeal to his followers. When his organization had a meeting in Texas, virtually every potential Republican candidate sought to address them. The administration sent representatives as well. The goal was to stem the tide toward a new party and to bring Perot's followers back to the Republicans or the Democrats.

Perot persisted and claimed that he did not want to run for president; of course, he had said he did not want to run for president in 1992, but that he was forced into it. In 1996 he set up an elaborate apparatus to nominate a Reform party candidate for president. However, none of those he sought as his candidate chose to run, and when former Colorado governor Richard Lamm did decide to seek the Reform party nod, Perot reentered the arena. Lamm was

INFOMERCIAL

Long television commercials, exemplified by those used by H. Ross Perot, that purport to provide voters with enough information to make informed choices.

led to the slaughter. Perot had never relinquished control of the Reform party. It was too dependent on his financial largesse. He won the nomination at a convention that represented another first in American politics—a convention designed to meet in two different sites at two different times, again with the goal of gaining media exposure.

The 1996 Perot campaign never equaled the 1992 campaign. In many ways he seemed a caricature of himself, claiming that he did not want to run but showing every indication that he longed to have the attention once again. In 1996 Perot did not fund his own campaign; rather, he accepted the public funding that his effort in 1992 had earned. Accordingly, as his funding level was determined by the proportion of the major party vote that he received, Perot was outspent. When he did not seem to be attracting as many supporters as he had earlier, he was excluded from the presidential debates, thus further marginalizing his candidacy. In the end, the 1996 Perot campaign stands as a third-party effort that had the potential to impact the national race but never realized that potential.

If the potential for the Reform party was not realized in 1996, it was reduced to rubble in 2000. The party had one major victory in 1998, with Jesse "The Body" Ventura's upset gubernatorial victory in Minnesota. The party was to receive public funding for the 2000 presidential election, based on Perot's showing in 1996. But the party split over its candidate. Patrick Buchanan, thwarted in his effort to gain the Republican nomination, turned to the Reform party. Reform party members wanted a well-known candidate to take their banner and work for legitimacy as the alternative party. But the party could not settle on one nominee. Buchanan, much more conservative on social issues than most Reform party members, captured the party by taking advantage of its rules, which created an open, permeable party. When Reformers objected and encouraged the candidacy of alternatives to Buchanan, first Donald Trump and then Larry Hagelin, the Natural Law party nominee, the party was split. Buchanan eventually won the nomination and got the federal matching funds, but he ran a marginalized campaign, drew very few votes, and robbed the party of whatever legitimacy it had worked toward in 1992 and 1996.

By contrast, the Green party in 2000 had the most influence ever. While the party did not poll as many votes as its leaders hoped, candidate Ralph Nader was a force throughout the election and may well have been the factor that determined the eventual winner. The Greens hoped to poll 5 percent of the vote in order to qualify for public funding in the 2004 election. Nader fell far short of that goal. Nader did, however, raise the Green banner throughout the country; his candidacy was extremely influential in close states, especially those with strong environmental movements. Nader's candidacy affected the campaign in two ways. Before we look at these, however, it should be noted that Nader drew two types of voters—those who were disenchanted with both parties and excited by Nader and who turned out to vote for Nader as opposed to sitting at home; and those who were taken with Nader's positions on environmental and anticorporate policies and who voted for Nader for those reasons but who otherwise would have voted for Gore. Very few voters chose Nader over Bush; thus, the net effect of his candidacy was to take votes from the Democratic camp.

For some time the Gore camp chose to ignore Nader, but as the campaign reached its crescendo, it was clear that Nader was affecting Gore's chances in some states, especially those with strong environmental movements, like Oregon. Thus, the first effect of the Nader candidacy was to force Gore to put more resources into some states that he should have won easily, in order to avoid a loss. The second effect of the Nader candidacy was in holding the balance of power between the two major party candidates. In Florida, for instance, while Nader polled "only 96,000 votes," if one assumed that 50 percent of those would not have voted at all except for Nader and that Gore would have won 60 percent of the remaining votes (a very low estimate), Gore would have won Florida easily, with no worries about undervotes or hanging chads. The same could be argued about New Hampshire. The presence of this third-party candidate—and the ways in which the major party candidates responded to him—clearly had a determinative effect on the winner in 2000.

In presidential elections, third-party candidates have been of three types. First, the minor party candidates who run on ideologically pure platforms. Their goal is to express their views in the public forum. They expect to (and do) have little impact on the result of the election. But they play an important role by raising public debate on critical issues.

The second type of candidate represents a group that is splintering from one or the other of the major parties, or both. The 1948 Dixiecrats are a perfect example of this kind of third party. Generally, the major parties reabsorb these third-party candidacies after one election. But as demonstrated in chapter 2, other scenarios are possible. If the major parties do not respond, then a new party can come into existence, replacing one or both of the major parties.

Perot represents a third type of third-party candidate—one based on the individual. As individuals frequently act as catalysts for a split from the major parties, it is difficult to be certain that this category is in fact distinct. Was George Wallace's campaign a split within the party or the effort of one man? Perot's case can be differentiated in two ways, however. First, he had no previous allegiance to either of the major parties; nor did many of his followers. He was appealing to those who were disaffected with politics as usual. Second, he institutionalized what had been personal by establishing the Reform party. But the institution was not able to outlast the candidate. (For further discussions of the significance of the Perot campaigns, see Black and Black 1993; Abramson et al. 1995; see also Aldrich 1995; Abramson, Aldrich, and Rohde 1995; Bibby and Maisel 2003; and Rosenstone, Behr, and Lazarus 1984.) The unsuccessful 2004 Green party campaign raises doubts if it can grow institutionally into a continuing force. The stated goal for the Green party has been to build its institutional base at the grass roots, but its success has most definitely been limited.

VI. POLITICIANS VIEW THE CAMPAIGNS

From a candidate's perspective, the key aspect of a presidential campaign is that it is totally consuming. If the incumbent president is running, he certainly has other duties to perform. But the emphasis is on winning reelection. The duties of the presidency are performed around the exigencies of the campaign. For the challenger (or if no incumbent is running), the campaign is everything. The race for the White House is the peak of any candidate's political career. There is no higher prize in the American system; no higher stakes exist.

Once the strategy is set and the active phase of the fall campaign begins, the two presidential candidates and their chief surrogates are on the road constantly. If the campaign is going well, then they continue what they are doing. If it is not going well, then they must figure out what to do with the feeling that they are not accomplishing their goals. But they cannot sit down and think about a new strategy. They must leave that to someone else. They simply do not have time. The candidate and his entourage can have input, but their fate is in the hands of the organization they have carefully molded over an extended period of time. And they must live with the results.

Think back on the career of Al Gore. Son of a senator, Gore first rejected politics for a career in journalism. However, clearly affected by his father's career, including the loss of his Senate seat in a bitter campaign, Gore turned to politics himself. He was elected to the House in 1976 and reelected three times. He was elected to the Senate in 1984. In 1988, he sought the Democratic nomination for president but was rejected by the voters. He was the first candidate to try the Democratic Leadership Council strategy of appealing to more moderate Democrats, not to the liberal wing of the party. Reelected to the Senate in 1990, Gore was tapped by Bill Clinton to run for vice president in 1992. For the next eight years, he was the hardworking number two. He did what he was asked. He was Clinton's partner in the White House. He was the loyal party man. And he waited his turn.

Gore was Clinton's heir apparent, and he was ready. He had served his apprenticeship. He had served the party. He won the nomination, beating a stubborn Bill Bradley, demonstrating he could take on a fight. But during the general election, he never could resolve the Clinton problem. How did he accept credit for the accomplishments of the Clinton administration in which he had played such a key role without being tainted by the scandal mentality that pervaded Washington for eight years?

Gore struggled with this issue. How could he be his own man? How could he show the nation that he deserved to be president? To the end there were those in his campaign who urged him to let Clinton loose, to let Clinton save the Gore campaign. But Gore stuck with his own sense that he had to do it on his own. And then he and his family faced election night—and the night after, and the night after, and more than a month of counting in Florida. In the end, while a plurality of those who voted chose Gore, the electoral college majority went to George W. Bush. And Al Gore, as the sitting vice president, faced the unenviable task of announcing his opponent's victory before a joint session of Congress.

How did Gore react to this devastating defeat? He had put himself before the American public, asked the voters to weigh his lifelong commitment to service, and was rejected. And to many observers it was a rejection of Gore the man, not the policies he favored. Al Gore's reaction seemingly was one of equanimity. He had done the best he could. He would move on to something else—but he would decide later if he would run again. By 2006 Gore had reemerged as an important figure in the environmental movement, winning rave reviews and an Oscar for his film, *An Inconvenient Truth*, focusing attention on the earth's climate crisis. Followers have urged him to run for president again. He has had to think long and hard on that course of action. All potential presidential candidates must focus on the personal costs that they will bear—and that their families will bear.

As you think about Al Gore considering another presidential race, consider the amazing tenacity of Thomas Dewey, of Adlai Stevenson, of Richard Nixon, and of Hubert Humphrey. If you do not know about their careers, you should look them up. Their lives speak volumes about this nation's call to public service. How these men could receive the verdict of a nation regarding their candidacy and then come back to run again is difficult to comprehend. Each must have had a great sense of his own worth, of his ability to convince the nation that its decision had been in error, or of the inability of his strategists to convey the correct image and message. Nixon went on to victory and then to disgrace. Humphrey died as the Happy Warrior, seemingly always ready to have another go at the nation's highest office. We still do not know Al Gore's fate, but he is a relatively young man who has many years ahead for potential campaigns.

For most, however, one unsuccessful campaign for the presidency is enough. A number of candidates have tried in the prenomination phase more than once, but few have come back from a losing general election campaign to try again. Why? Because of the effort involved, because of the finality of the decision, because once one has campaigned throughout the entire nation, once one has presented his best effort to the electorate, and once one has been rejected, that verdict is enough.

In contrast, victorious presidential candidates want to have that experience again. Harsh personal attacks did not deter Bill Clinton from seeking reelection; George H. W. Bush's health did not deter him; Ronald Reagan's age did not deter him; Jimmy Carter's lack of popularity did not deter him. In the last seventy-five years, only Lyndon Johnson, saddled with an unpopular war and dissent within his own party, and Harry Truman, in much the same situation, did not run for reelection when they were eligible (and each of these had served more than one full term, having first succeeded to the presidency). Victory in a national election seems to have nearly aphrodisiac qualities. "If the public loved me once, they will love me again. And I owe it to them to give them the chance." That very personal reaction is the essence of a candidate's evaluation of a presidential campaign.

WEBSITES

These websites are relevant to both chapter 8 and chapter 9.

www.democrats.org and **www.rnc.org**: The websites of the two national committees have a good deal of information about their respective candidates, party rules, nominating calendars, party platforms, and similar matters. Various candidates for party nominations also maintain their own websites.

www.cq.com and **www.cnn.com/politics**: These sites, mentioned in chapter 6, are also excellent for getting information on the presidential nominating process.

www.fec.gov: The Federal Election Commission maintains up-to-date records of all candidate fund-raising and spending during the nominating phase of the electoral process.

CHAPTER 10

The Media and the Electoral Process

President George W. Bush declares the end of major combat in Iraq as he speaks aboard the aircraft carrier USS Abraham Lincoln *off the California coast, May 1, 2003. The Bush administration's carefully staged event, including Bush's arrival by harrier jet in combat fatigues, was deemed by critics and supporters alike as the "mother of all photo opportunities." While the event was viewed as a positive for Bush at the time, it has since come to serve as an emblem of his administration's arrogance and ineptitude in the eyes of his critics, and even Bush's supporters admit that the "mission" is far from "accomplished." Attempting to use the media for political gain is a high-risk game, with the potential for both large rewards and steep penalties.*

How many of the candidates for president in 2008 did you see? We do not mean "see" as in seeing on television or the web. We mean "see" as in seeing face-to-face in person, whether across a room, in an auditorium, or even at a football stadium. We do not want to be too restrictive in our definition.

Let's go back a step. How many of the candidates for governor, U.S. senator, or even member of the House of Representatives in 2008 in your state did you see (same sense of the word)? One? Well, if you didn't see these people often enough to form an opinion about them and their views, then how did you learn about them? Where did your political information come from?

A century ago the answer to that question would have been easy. Citizens did not know much about candidates for office. But they did know about political parties. And candidates were candidates of political parties. Today, candidates have greater control over their campaigns, and in many instances greater freedom from their parties. Citizens proudly claim (somewhat inaccurately) that they vote for the candidate, not the party. How do they find out about the candidate?

The short answer is that they find out from "the media." But that very answer begs the question. What do we mean by "the media"? How are political messages communicated through the media? How effectively does this institution serve our democracy?

I. THE MEDIA IN THE CONTEMPORARY CONTEXT

Sixty years ago, newspapers dominated the mass media that affected American politics. Citizens learned the news of the day through their daily papers; in major cities multiple newspapers competed for the public's attention, and both a morning and evening newspaper were standard. Newspapers lost their primacy with the emergence of television. By the late 1950s television sets had saturated the American landscape. Today 99 percent of American homes have at least one television, and two-thirds have three or more.

Twenty years ago, three major networks—ABC, CBS, and NBC—dominated television broadcasting. According to Nielsen Media Research ratings, nearly three out of every five homes watched one of the major networks during prime viewing hours in 1979 (Samuelson 1999, A23). In mid-2007, the three major networks captured only about one-quarter of the market. Even if newer networks are added in, the number does not reach a third. Citizens are turning to cable or satellite outlets, means of viewing that were available to only a small minority at the time of the ratings first cited.

It is becoming increasingly evident that we are currently at the dawn of yet another evolutionary period in the relationship between politics and the media. While television undoubtedly remains the most important media source in the political world, it is also true that the Internet is assuming a greater role in American politics, a role that seemingly grows exponentially by the day. In 2006 31 percent of Americans went online for news three or more times a week; that compares with less than 2 percent in 1996. For 15 percent of Americans in 2006 the Internet was a primary source for news, compared with only 3 percent in 1996 (Pew Research Center 2007a, 2007b). The number of weblogs, or blogs as they are called, where anyone who wishes to can post political commentary increases every day, as does their readership. With some relatively inexpensive equipment, relatively little technical expertise, and a broadband connection, any individual can produce and disseminate video across the web. Seemingly everyone has a cell phone with a digital camera, and politicians now realize that today they are never truly off the record or safe from public view. We will have much more to say later in the chapter about the rise of the Internet. But at the outset we want to make two things clear: First, there is no doubt that the Internet has changed politics in important and sometimes dramatic ways. Second, no one knows where this development will end or where it will take us next.

What has been the effect of these changes on the impact of the mass media on politics? Put simply, it is more difficult to cut through the noise and also to control the message and content. Twenty years ago, politicians had a pretty good idea of what sources their constituents would turn to for news. National politicians were concerned about the major networks. Statewide, politicians tried to garner national media attention, but they concentrated on local outlets, television stations, and major newspapers. Local politicians lowered their sights again, hoping for some television coverage but trying to ensure that the local press covered them adequately.[1]

Today's politicians try to find an audience wherever it might appear. Table 10.1 presents the percentages of Americans who regularly use various media outlets for news. The diversity in this list is impressive, and gives an idea as to how difficult it is for politicians to get their messages across. The political elite might tune in to the *News Hour with Jim Lehrer* or spend time watching C-SPAN or Fox News or listening to NPR or Rush Limbaugh. Certainly many still watch the network newscasts and read the major newspapers. But others pay less attention to the news or get their news from unconventional sources—and politicians must find their targets "where they live." Presidential candidate Bill Clinton was one of the first national politicians to recognize this when he appeared on MTV in 1992, and again as President Clinton in 1994 (where he famously informed viewers that he wore briefs rather than boxer shorts). Today all serious presidential candidates, and many congressional

Table 10.1   Percentage of Americans Who Regularly Watch/Read/Listen to News via Various Outlets, February 2007

Source	Percentage Who Regularly Watch/Read/Listen
Local Television News	71
Local Daily Newspaper	54
Network Evening News	46
Fox News Channel	43
CNN	39
Network Morning Shows	34
National Public Radio	28
News from Google, Yahoo, etc.	25
Newsmagazines	23
Television News Websites	22
The O'Reilly Factor	17
The Daily Show and/or The Colbert Report	16
Newshour with Jim Lehrer	14
Major Newspaper Websites	12
Online Blogs	11
Rush Limbaugh Radio Show	8

Source: "What Americans Know: 1989–2007." Pew Research Center for the People and the Press, Washington, D.C. Study released April 15, 2007. Study conducted February 1–13, 2007.

Note: The question asked respondents, "Now I'd like to know how often you watch, listen to, or read some different news sources. Do you [read or watch or listen to as appropriate, plus the source] regularly, or not?"

and state candidates have followed Clinton's lead (in terms of where they appear, not necessarily underwear preference). Candidates appear on *The Daily Show* and *The Colbert Report* on Comedy Central; they have elaborate websites (often more than one) and produce video and other content specifically for websites like YouTube, MySpace, and Facebook; they participate in conference calls with popular bloggers. And this only scratches the surface of what campaigns do today in the attempt to communicate their message. In today's fragmented media environment, political consultants worry about where to communicate a message just as much as they worry about what message to communicate.

Thirty years ago—the date is arbitrary, for the process has been changing over time—reporters covered the news. Increasingly today, candidates for office take actions in order to be covered by the media, and preferably covered on their own terms. No clearer example can be found of this phenomenon than the national nominating conventions.

In the 1960s, presidential nominating conventions were major events on television. The networks competed with each other to provide the best "gavel-to-gavel" coverage. They were concerned about what was going on at the podium, what decisions were being made in the hall, and who was having what influence.

At the 1964 Republican National Convention, when nominee Barry Goldwater chided his vanquished moderate opponents that "extremism in the defense of liberty is no vice," the networks reported that his selection marked a defining moment for his party. The drama at the site of the convention, San Francisco's Cow Palace, was presented "live" for the entire nation to watch. Few who watched would forget the late John Chancellor's exit line as he was forcibly removed from the convention floor: "This is John Chancellor, NBC News, somewhere in custody!"

When the Democratic National Convention in Chicago broke into chaos in 1968, the networks covered the disorder as a major news event. Again, few who watched would soon forget the delegates barred from the floor, the protestors beaten outside delegate hotels, or the religious slur shouted by Chicago mayor Richard Daley at Connecticut senator Abraham Ribicoff, who was decrying the violent tactics of the Chicago police. The events were real; the reporting was real; the news was real.

But the parties could not stand the criticism. Internal schism, they felt, should not be viewed by potential voters. Not atypically, the Republicans learned this lesson before the Democrats. In 1972, Democratic nominee George McGovern accepted his party's nomination with a truly great speech, which was heard by nearly no one because it was delivered long after most people had gone to bed. Convention business had dragged on—viewed in all of its untidiness by a large television audience—and McGovern was not afforded his finest hour until well past midnight. By contrast, the Republican convention of that year was scripted down to the minute to guarantee that the viewing audience saw only what the party officials wanted them to see and saw it when they wanted it to be seen. President Nixon's renomination was as carefully orchestrated as a royal coronation, down to the minutest detail (Davis 1996, chap. 13).

It didn't take the Democrats long to learn the lesson of careful planning from the Republicans; their conventions came to be as carefully scripted as their opponent's. Once, national nominating conventions were widely anticipated events with huge television audiences, but by the time George H. W. Bush and Michael Dukakis were nominated in 1988, fewer than one in five households bothered to watch. The major networks abandoned the gavel-to-gavel coverage of which they had been so proud only a few short years earlier, leaving such coverage to C-SPAN, CNN, and PBS.[2] Even when the networks were on the air, they covered the podium only selectively, preferring to air their own versions of what was going on.

Network disenchantment with the extent to which the conventions had become a showcase for the parties as opposed to news reached a new height in 1996. Ted Koppel had moved his *Nightline* television show to California, the site of the Republican National Convention. After one night, he pulled up stakes and returned to New York with the disclaimer, "There is no news here." Little changed for the staged shows in the summer of 2004, and likely little will change for the 2008 conventions.

Recent national conventions demonstrate two points regarding the relationship between the media and politics in the United States. First, politicians try to use the media to "make the news" they want. Second, media coverage is no longer cast broadly; it is now cast narrowly. Each media outlet is aware of its audience, and programs accordingly. Thus the major networks reduced their coverage of the conventions, but the more news-oriented cable networks continued theirs. The media context for politics as we enter the twenty-first century is an extremely complex one. Politicians try to structure the ways in which they appear on **free media** (also called earned media) outlets; they continue to use **paid media** in ways to present their message as they define it in a way most likely to impact the intended audience. The distinction between free media and paid media continues to be important. And both types of media have changed as a result of the Internet.

II. FREE MEDIA: JOURNALISTS' PRESENTATIONS OF CANDIDATES AND CAMPAIGNS

A. The Varieties of Free Media

There was a time when anyone who heard the phrase "free media" would have a pretty good sense of what was meant. In the early days of the republic, free media referred to pamphlets and early newspapers, the so-called **penny press**, that printed news for all to read. Frequently the news was slanted in one political direction or another because many of the early presses were controlled by persons having specific political agendas.

As the country grew and as technology advanced, free media came to mean newspapers, many of which were parts of national or regional chains, and eventually newsmagazines. In the first half of the twentieth century radio and television—network and local— were added to the media mix. When free media was discussed in the context of political parties and elections, it meant news as covered in the free media.

In the contemporary context both the media and the ways in which political messages are communicated have changed. To be

---

FREE MEDIA

Media exposure that a candidate receives without having to pay for it, for example, coverage in newspapers or on television news shows.

PAID MEDIA

Media exposure that a candidate's campaign pays for and thus controls.

PENNY PRESS

Newspapers and leaflets in the early years of the republic, so named because they sold for a penny.

sure, the media still include newspapers and magazines, radio, and television. But none of these is the same as it was even a few decades ago. For instance, the number of newspapers—and the number of communities served by more than one major paper—has shrunk dramatically. In addition, the instant newspaper, *USA Today*, serves a national audience in a way vastly different from that done by any competitor. News is condensed and homogenized in a way that makes many more traditional newspaper professionals uncomfortable.

More and more specialized magazines are filling part of the news picture. Whereas once "newsmagazine" meant *Time, Newsweek, U.S. News & World Report*, and a couple of opinion monthlies, today the number of magazines has expanded greatly. Many aim at a narrow readership and are not at all hesitant to voice their views. *Modern Maturity*, the magazine for members of the American Association of Retired Persons, reaches millions with each issue. Although the readership of magazines put out by other groups tends to be smaller, their influence on public policy matters may well be greater.

Changes in television have already been noted. The trend is clear. Major network audiences are falling and cable audiences are growing. Cable networks aim at particular audiences. The news that they provide, if any, is also aimed at those audiences—youth, women, religious people, sports enthusiasts, and so on.

As a result, how citizens receive their news has changed. As recently as a decade ago, news was conveyed mainly on news shows, nightly news broadcasts, and the occasional television magazine, such as *60 Minutes*. The nightly news broadcast continues and the number of newsmagazines has greatly increased. News stations now dot the dial. There is more news available than any one person can digest. But many people choose not to avail themselves of these sources.

For what news they get, they turn to other sources. **Talk shows**, on radio as well as on television, provide much of the political information that reaches many people. These shows provide a forum for citizens (and often opinionated hosts) to inform and misinform each other. Opinion replaces action as the message communicated. Balance is almost never a goal and is rarely achieved. The majority of radio talk shows are hosted by conservatives. Liberals (and Democrats) felt so disadvantaged that they eventually started their own liberal talk network, Air America Radio, in spring 2004. Air America, however, has struggled to attract listeners, and conservative voices still dominate the radio dial.

Entertainment programming informs the public as well. How many of you have seen the footage of President Clinton playing his saxophone on the *Arsenio Hall Show*? Clinton as musician is one

TALK SHOWS

Radio (and occasionally television) broadcasts in which the format consists of a host, often with guests, interacting with the audience either in person or via telephone and expressing views on the issues of the day.

way the politics and entertainment shows mingle, but political humor has long been one of the most common ways that politics and entertainment meet on television. For many years this meant programs like *Saturday Night Live, Politically Incorrect*, or the Leno and Letterman shows. In recent years, however, the Comedy Central programs *The Daily Show* and its spinoff *The Colbert Report* have taken political humor to a different level, mixing real news and commentary with humor and sarcasm. These shows are important; as noted in table 10.1, 16 percent of Americans regularly get news from *The Daily Show* or *The Colbert Report*, and this figure is much higher among young Americans. Each show has affected both politics itself and how the rest of the media covers politics (de Morales 2006; Smolkin 2007).

Politicians covet appearances on these types of shows, but as with any free media interaction there is a certain amount of risk that goes with the reward of coverage and exposure. For example, Representative Robert Wexler (D-Fla.) appeared on *The Colbert Report* during the 2006 campaign. As he was interviewing Wexler, Colbert asked the congressman to complete the following sentence: "I enjoy cocaine because . . ." Wexler looked directly into the camera and said: "I enjoy cocaine because it's a fun thing to do." Wexler also stated that he enjoyed prostitutes during the interview. The next day Wexler was forced repeatedly to assert that his comments had been in jest as a number of media outlets reported the story.

The biggest change in the free media in recent years is of course the rise of the Internet. As noted in the introduction to this chapter, almost one-third of Americans regularly get news from the web. A majority of these online Americans get their news from the websites of traditional media outlets such as the three broadcast networks, Fox News and CNN, and major daily newspapers. But people are increasingly seeking out news from web-only sources such as *Slate Magazine, Salon.com*, and *The Drudge Report*. A rising number of Americans are also getting at least some of their news from blogs—of the 31 percent who got news regularly online in 2006, 20 percent frequented at least one blog (Pew Research Center 2007b). As of summer 2005 there were over fourteen million blogs out there (Bowers and Stoller 2005), and the most popular blog—the liberal *Daily Kos*—gets over five hundred thousand distinct hits a day (Myers 2007). Politicians recognize the importance of blogs, and now regularly hold conference calls with popular bloggers in the hopes of getting their message out.

But blogs are just one example of what some are calling the democratization of the news. Supporters and opponents alike of various candidates now regularly post commentary and other materials on popular websites such as YouTube, MySpace, and Facebook. Some go so far as to create flashy, professional-looking videos either for or against candidates and post them on the web. Some, such as the famous "Hillary 1984," which parodied Senator Clinton as Big Brother from George Orwell's *1984*, and "Crush on Obama," where a sometimes scantily clad woman sung about how much she loved Senator Obama, become what has been termed "viral video," meaning that they spread around the Internet like a virus as discussions about and links to the video spread from user to user (Marinucci 2007; Parsons and McCormick 2007; Sender 2007).

While the two videos mentioned above generated mostly laughs, viral video can sometimes be very damaging. During his reelection campaign in 2006, Senator George Allen (R-Va.) was captured on video calling a volunteer of Indian descent working for his opponent's campaign a "macaca," which is a type of monkey and is also used as a racial slur (Craig and Shear 2006). As the video spread across the web, Allen repeatedly denied that there was any racist intent behind his comments, but to little avail. Allen, who until that point had been widely expected to win reelection easily and was seen as one of the top candidates for the 2008 GOP presidential nomination, lost in November 2006. As Mark McKinnon, chief media adviser for the 2000 and 2004 Bush campaigns, stated, in many ways today anyone with a camera can in fact be in control of the message, and to a certain extent the news.

B. The Role of the Free Media

Perhaps there is another way to view the role of the free media in political contexts. Rather than look at the number of media and the ways in which they communicate information, perhaps we can concentrate on the role that they should be playing in electoral theory. That is, what is it we hope free media do in order to make our political processes function more effectively?

1. Informed Consent of the Governed

A representative democracy rests not just on the consent of the governed but on the **informed consent of the governed**. The role that the media should play in our political system is to permit those who choose our elected officials to do so in an informed way. That answer, however, oversimplifies a complex situation. As noted earlier, one important question deals with how much information citizens need to make an informed judgment. That obviously reflects on what kind of information we should expect the media to provide.

Let's look at the question from a slightly different perspective. The media are an intermediary institution in our system. That is, they link other important actors; in the case we are interested in, they link those seeking elective office (including those currently holding office) with those who will make the electoral choice. In an

INFORMED CONSENT OF THE GOVERNED

A minimal requirement for an effectively functioning representative democracy.

earlier era, political parties performed this role for almost all offices. Today, many citizens reject the automatic link between themselves and political parties, even if they assume the link between parties and candidates. The media fill that void.

But we still need to explore what kinds of information should be provided. Should citizens only be concerned about candidates' policy positions? Should they be concerned about personalities? Should they be concerned about personal lifestyle, about "youthful indiscretions," and about families? Do the media have an obligation to provide all of this information? In what form? The briefest answer is that the media can be expected to provide the information that citizens seek.

How that definition is reached still poses difficult questions. For instance, we claimed earlier that the media today do provide virtually any information that a citizen could want about officeholders and candidates for office. But the citizen must play an active role in finding that information. On the other hand, information that may not be relevant to citizens' needs reaches many "automatically." Certainly in recent years the media have delved more deeply into highly personal aspects of candidates' lives than was true in the past. Many complain that they are learning things that they do not need to know, that candidates' private lives should remain just that, private. Some claim that this kind of intrusive media information changes the political scene by discouraging strong candidates.

Speaking before an informal meeting of senators during the heat of the Senate trial on the impeachment of President Clinton, former president George Bush echoed this view: "I worry too about sleaze, about excessive intrusion into private lives. I worry about once great news organizations that seem to resort to tabloid journalism, giving us sensationalism at best and smut at worst" (Dewar 1999, A16).

On that very same day, the former president's daughter-in-law Laura told a group of journalists in Austin that she was very reticent to have her husband seek the presidency, owing to the loss of privacy such a campaign would entail (Neal and Duggan 1999, A8). Of course, she overcame that reticence as her husband began his successful campaign.

Why do the media insist on presenting stories that cause these concerns? Simply put, because the public buys them. They sell newspapers and magazines; they increase Nielsen ratings. The public expresses its desires in a number of ways. The media react to the cash register, to the public's demonstrating its real desire by what it purchases.

2. Window on the Candidates

The media should play other roles as well—and these too may be controversial. As noted already, it is impossible for every citizen to see every candidate. But many voters want to "experience" the candidates they are supporting or opposing. The media should let them have this experience. These windows should be free from outside manipulation; they should be free from candidate manipulation. And in searching for this lack of interference, controversy arises. It is clear that candidates know when the media are covering them—and they act accordingly. It is thus difficult for the media to provide a clear picture. In the most recent electoral cycles, C-SPAN has played this role probably as well as it can be played, following candidates for various offices for extended periods of time, making it more difficult for candidates to perform for the camera in ways different from how they act when not under such scrutiny.

3. Referee between Candidates

We have all seen campaigns in which candidates get involved in a "'He said . . .,' 'No, I didn't'" kind of dispute. In recent years these battles have often been fought through competing television advertisements. A relatively new role for the media is serving as a referee in these battles and thus raising the chances that candidate advertisements will be honest. During the 1988 presidential campaign, the record of Democratic candidate Michael Dukakis as governor of Massachusetts was attacked in a series of negative ads that many observers felt unfair. Following suggestions by veteran campaign watchers David Broder of the *Washington Post* and Ken Bode, host of Public Television's *Washington Week in Review,* largely as a result of this experience, many newspapers and television stations took on the role of monitoring political advertisements for truthfulness, so-called **adwatch campaigns**. "For the first time in most places, a referee in the form of political reporters showing up in the campaign arena with the savvy to call fouls and a voice that's being heard [is present]. A game with a referee is a different kind of game" (Monroe 1990, 6).

Adwatches "force campaigns to issue extensive documentation *before* the ad is aired—instead of waiting until the other side has complained" (Alter 1992, 37). Adwatches have even spread to small-town newspapers. Most feel that their impact has been positive, reducing the likelihood of campaign ads being false or misleading (Milburn and Brown 1997). However, some scholars argue that adwatches have not had the desired effect of making voters less favorably disposed toward those whose advertisements are most severely criticized (Ansolabehere and Iyengar 1995). That the referee's role in the rough-and-tumble of political campaigns is an appropriate one for the media, however, is now well accepted.

ADWATCH CAMPAIGNS

Efforts by newspapers and some television stations to monitor political advertising for accuracy.

C. The Actual Role That the Media Play

It should come as little surprise that analysis of the role that the media actually do play in the political process differs significantly from the role observers theoretically feel that they should play. Much of the work on this topic has looked at presidential campaigns and the role that the media have played in them, but the findings apply almost as directly to campaigns for other offices in which candidates must rely on the media to communicate with potential voters (see Iyengar and Reeves 1997; Norris 1997; Davis 1996; Seib 1994). Based on this work, it is possible to characterize the role actually played by the media in modern campaigns according to a number of different categories.[3]

1. The Great Mentioner

How did George W. Bush become the front-runner for the 2000 Republican presidential nomination so early in the preprimary process? Bush became a front-runner before he announced his candidacy for the White House or even formed an exploratory committee. How did he get to be a front-runner? The press dubbed him one. To be sure, Bush had enormous political assets—his name and family connections, his ability to raise money, and his popularity in a large state. But he was not the only Republican governor reelected in 1998, and many of the others were not "mentioned" as leading contenders for their party's nomination.

Thus one role that the press has come to play is to raise some potential candidates above others in the months before a campaign really starts. This kind of mention can give momentum to a nascent campaign, whereas the lack of such recognition can stop a campaign in its tracks. One key to a candidate's being taken seriously is having his or her name recognized by large numbers of citizens. Early preference polls are often nothing more than name recognition polls. Candidates who do not do well in them are not taken seriously by influential politicians. Thus the media role at this early stage is a most critical one.

2. Image Creator

Think for a moment about what you know about any major political figure, other than those of whom you have some detailed knowledge. How did you acquire that image? Where did it come from? The simple answer is that most images of that type are media created.

In 1988, when no major Democratic candidates came forward to seek their party's presidential nomination, the candidates who did run were dubbed the "seven dwarves" by the media. That image—lack of stature—stuck, despite the fact that the field included men who were prominent in their states and in Congress. In 1984, Walter Mondale was characterized as the candidate of big labor and other Democratic-leaning interest groups; Gary Hart was the candidate of new ideas. Each picture was oversimplified but widely accepted.

The press has the ability to portray such an image because members of the press tend to read each other's writing, talk with each other, and follow each other's lead. The concept of **pack journalism**, in which "one reporter's story becomes every reporter's story" (Seib 1994, 60–61), has been expounded for more than twenty years (see Sabato 1991; Crouse 1973; Thompson 1973). Although reporters strive for independence, the news of the day is often dictated by the schedules set by the campaigns themselves. Events are planned in order to create good visual effects for television and to meet deadlines for the print media. Candidates rush from event to event; so too must those covering them. As a result there is little time for reflection, and stories tend to be similar from one reporter to the next. When one reporter comes up with a new, apt way of describing a candidate, with a new image, it is not long before others adopt it. And those images tend to stick. Do you think this is an exaggeration? Which presidential candidate was so challenged he could not even spell "potato"?

3. Expectation Setter

Commentator after commentator, as well as media critic after media critic, has pointed to the role that the media play in setting expectations for candidates at various early stages in campaigns.

When looking at presidential campaigns, the media note how much money each candidate raises at the times of various Federal Election Commission reports. They comment on candidate performance in debates vis-à-vis their opponents. They examine poll results, noting who is doing better than predicted and whose ratings are not so high. And, most importantly, they lay out in advance how each candidate is likely to do in an upcoming primary and weigh that candidate's performance and standing in the polls in terms of how well he or she fared in comparison to those expectations. State and local media play similar roles in the campaigns they cover. And evaluations of expectation meeting are important as a campaign progresses.

Merely look at the **expectation game** and the New Hampshire primary. In each of the last nine presidential nomination races, in one party or the other, expectations of who would win New Hampshire were as important, if not more important, than the actual results. To cite some examples, in 1968, President Johnson won that primary, but he did not do nearly as well as he had been expected to do; shortly thereafter he withdrew from the race. In 1972, Maine Democratic senator Edmund S. Muskie won the primary, but his margin was low; his campaign never recovered. In 1976, former

PACK JOURNALISM

The phenomenon of all journalists covering an event following the lead of one of their colleagues instead of pursuing their own angles on the story.

EXPECTATION GAME

The strategy of setting expectations of performance low so that results will be viewed in a favorable light.

Georgia governor Jimmy Carter won the Democratic primary, exceeding expectations; his campaign took off. In 1980, former California governor Ronald Reagan met expectations for a victory in the Republican primary, after having done poorly in the Iowa caucuses; the serious challengers to his nomination lost their momentum. In 1984, Colorado senator Gary Hart upset front-runner Walter Mondale, who had been Carter's vice president; a tight campaign followed for many months because Hart had exceeded expectations and Mondale had failed to reach them. In 1988, Kansas senator Bob Dole failed to do as well as had been predicted; his campaign never seriously challenged that of Vice President George Bush again. In 1992, Patrick Buchanan exceeded expectations, and President Bush did not meet them in the Republican primary; Buchanan gained the momentum needed to carry his campaign to his party's convention. In 2000, Senator John McCain exceeded expectations and became the only serious challenger in the way of George W. Bush's march to the Republican nomination. When Senator John Kerry followed up his win in Iowa with a victory in New Hampshire, the race for the 2004 Democratic presidential nomination was over. The expectations game is already well under way for the 2008 presidential election, and it will be interesting to see which candidates can measure up.

Where did the expectations come from? From the media—often prodded by candidates who tried to set low standards for themselves so that they could exceed these standards. But in each case, the popular view of the expectations—and of whether they were met or not—was put forth by the media covering the campaign.

4. Issue Identifier

The media determine what is important in a campaign. That is, they determine which of the items that candidates mention are transmitted to the public. Every candidate for a major office discusses a large number of issues during a campaign. All develop position papers. All give speeches on many topics. All make a sincere attempt to tell the public what they stand for.

However, detailed issue discussion is not "good news." The media determine what the agenda for the public will be. The agenda might well be the personal characteristics of a candidate. It might be how competing candidates stand on contentious issues. It might be which candidate in a primary election is likely to poll better in the general election.

In primary elections the agenda is very frequently related to the game of politics, not to the business of governing. That is, the journalists covering a campaign are concerned about who is likely to win, what techniques are in use to push a campaign forward, what groups or key individuals favor which candidates. Even in general elections, the media frequently concentrate more on the nuts and bolts of the campaign than they do on differences among candidates. Consequently, that is what the public knows about the campaign. That is what is discussed over the watercooler, at the mall, on the subway, at the dinner table. Citizens are more likely to view campaigns in terms of the latest poll results, debate strategy, or advertising gambits than they are to know about substantive differences in candidates' stands on key issues, since citizen knowledge reflects media presentation.

5. Field Narrower

When all of these roles are combined, one result is that the press plays an important role in narrowing multicandidate fields. This role, also known as **field winnower**, has long been recognized in presidential primaries (Barber 1978) and is just as apparent in statewide and other highly visible primaries.

FIELD WINNOWER
Playing the role of eliminating some candidates from a multicandidate competition.

When the media stop mentioning a candidate, when the image associated with a candidate is an unflattering one, when a candidate does not meet expectations, or when the agenda discussed in the media excludes issues raised by a candidate or his or her role in a campaign, a signal goes out that that candidacy has lost viability. This role is an important one in primary campaigns, particularly in presidential primary campaigns, in which it is necessary to present the public with a set of choices with which it can cope. But this role is not necessarily one that the media are best suited to play.

In primaries below the level of the presidency, this role is often played either by political parties in a formal way (when state laws or party rules permit it; chapter 6) or by party leaders in an informal way. Some candidates are supported by party regulars; others are not. Some find encouragement from those who typically fund campaigns; others cannot raise money. While these "winnowers" are not always part of the formal process, they have a certain legitimacy within the process. Below the presidential level, the extent to which the media have assumed this role varies from state to state. As at the level of presidential nominations, the extent to which the media's playing such an important role is accepted often depends on the perspective of the person evaluating the process. Not surprisingly, those who are "winnowed out" tend to be less satisfied than those who are "winnowed in."

6. Campaign Critic

The media have also assumed the role of critic, judging the performance of those seeking office. Some patterns have become clear in recent elections.

First, the media tend to view themselves as watchdogs of the public good. Thus they are particularly vigilant in observing and commenting on the character and performance of individuals who are likely to be elected, or who are serious contenders to be elected. Much of what is reported is negative. Rarely does one read a story that is full of praise for all aspects of a front-running candidate's qualities (Davis 1996, 187–89). On the other hand, underdog candidates are often afforded much kinder treatment. In 1992, when Texas billionaire H. Ross Perot was seeking the presidency, the press treated him as something of a darling early in the campaign season. He was photogenic, funny, willing to take controversial stands, and he was polling better than was expected. However, once Perot started to receive serious consideration from voters, the press turned more critical, raising questions about his electability and the extent to which his solutions were more simplistic than the problems they addressed (Germond and Witcover 1993).

Of course, the result of this kind of treatment has a certain impact not only on the campaigns but also on the public officials subsequently elected. Winners appear in a less-favorable light than do losers, who frequently emerge from elections as sympathetic figures. Certainly this kind of media treatment contributes to public cynicism.

7. Documentor of Elections

It is also true that the media play the role of documenting elections for the public. That is, we know what happens in an election because the media tell us.

In some instances, this role is played because the election events themselves take place on or in front of the media. Thus debates among or between candidates for many offices are aired on and closely covered by the various media. The public has the opportunity to observe these events as they happen, to read transcripts, to absorb analysis, or to follow others' reactions.

In other instances, the role involves media documentation of what is happening. Media polls tell the public how the various campaigns are doing. Whereas media polls were intermittent during the elections of the 1960s, by the 1990s national and statewide polls were so frequent that individual voters began to wonder how so many polls could be published without their opinions having been sought.[4] These polls have proven accurate as predictors of outcomes to be sure, but they are also important to provide an understanding of which voters are supporting which candidate and for what reasons.

These polls have also been criticized. In most recent presidential elections, pollsters have known the results well in advance of the actual voting; for instance, President Clinton's lead over Senator Dole was so large in 1996—and his lead in so many states was so overwhelming—that his reelection was assured well before election day. Critics claim not only that these polls remove the drama from a campaign but also that they deflate turnout and may impact elections lower on the ballot. Although they may be documenting one election, they can alter the results of another. The media have been sensitive to this charge—changing the ways in which they use exit polls on election night, as one example—but they also feel an obligation to provide such information about a campaign as they are able to garner.

Analyses by political journalists document campaigns in other ways as well. As controversy has swirled around political advertisements, the media have begun to monitor these attempts to influence the public. Adwatch campaigns seek to ensure that advertisements are accurate and not deceptive. Other journalists have also begun to report on strategy used in designing advertisements.

In the 1998 midterm elections, newspaper after newspaper and television special after television special commented on what various campaigns were doing and why they were doing it. In the closing days of that campaign, the Republicans launched a $10 million ad blitz in selective districts, seeking to link Democratic candidates to President Clinton and the scandal surrounding him. As soon as the ad campaign began, journalists wrote about what the Republicans were trying to do, where they were doing it, and what the Democrats' likely reaction was going to be (Associated Press 1998; Berke 1998; Connolly 1998). In the 2000 presidential election this kind of analysis followed every change in media strategy by each campaign.

In these and other ways, the media ensure that the public knows what is happening in an election. But the line between "news" and "analysis" can blur in these circumstances. The media are certainly a documentor of what is happening during an election; but in playing that role, they become a participant as well.

8. Purveyor of Results

Many of us stay up late on election night, our eyes glued to our favorite analysts as they give us the results of the elections. The networks are our respected source—fast and accurate, up to the minute. And then there was Election Night 2000, the night that would never end.

But first let's take a step back, for giving results on election night has been controversial for some time. For years networks predicted winners based on results in sample precincts. They were conservative in their estimates, but they were often very early in giving results. The controversy arose when networks gave "results" before the polls were all closed. They were able to do so, with great accuracy, based on exit polls, surveys taken of voters as they were leaving the poll booths. The problem was that many politicians felt that early predictions affected races lower down on the ballot, because voters who had not gone to their polling places might be dissuaded from doing so if they knew the results of the top-of-the-ticket races.

The situation was exacerbated in 1980 when President Carter conceded to his challenger, Ronald Reagan, well before the polls closed on the West Coast. To be fair to the networks, Carter did so based on the advice of his own pollster, Patrick Caddell, not based on nework predictions, though those predictions were in place. Many observers felt that the results of congressional and senatorial races—as well as state and local races—on the West Coast were affected; there was anecdotal evidence of citizens getting out of voting lines when they heard that Carter had conceded the race to Reagan.

As a result, the networks decided to police themselves, not to release predictions based on exit polls until all polls in a jurisdiction have closed. But they still do exit polling, and they still race to be first with their predictions. And thus arose the problem on Election Night 2000. The networks, rushing to be first and then not to fall behind the opposition, declared Florida for Vice President Gore early in the evening. The Bush campaign, confident that the candidate's brother, Florida governor Jeb Bush, would carry the state for the Republicans and in possession of data running counter to the exit polls, cried foul, noting that some polling places in western Florida had yet to close. As more results came in, the networks first withdrew their prediction of a Gore victory, calling the state too close to call, then gave it to Bush, and then withdrew that prediction as the contentiousness of the vote tallying became apparent.

It is difficult to imagine network news executives more chagrined. The purveyors of truth had missed badly and given false information not once, but twice, to the public. In a rush to be first, they had failed in their most important task—to be accurate. The major news organizations have undertaken internal analyses of how they went so badly wrong; they have pledged to avoid such disasters in the future. But they have not escaped becoming the butts of late-night talk show hosts' jokes, and they have lost the respect of parts of their audience.

Their failing, of course, was a result of the closeness of the race in Florida and the confusion concerning how voters cast their ballots in relation to how they meant to cast those votes. The exit polls might well have reflected how voters intended to vote, but the actual vote count was something else. Think of the words used by post-election-night analysts—overvote (a person casting votes for more than one candidate for the same office), undervote (a person not voting for a candidate at the top of the ticket but voting for those further down the ballot), and, of course, chads of all sorts (hanging, dimpled, pregnant). None of these was part of the vocabulary of even the most avid political junkie before Election Night 2000. They undoubtedly account for the errors made by the networks in reporting the Florida results. They also account for why we, as a nation, can never and will never know what the voters of Florida intended to do in casting their votes. In 2000 Florida as a state—and we as a nation, and the networks as news gatherers—did not have a means sufficiently sophisticated to know the result in a timely and accurate manner. The networks' failure was not that they did not give us an accurate count; it was that they purported to do so when subsequent events proved that to be impossible.

D. An Assessment of the Role of Free Media

Leaving aside the delicious controversy caused by election night reporting, it is clear that the role that the free media play in the electoral process itself differs from theories propounded about that role by political scientists. Two questions remain: Why is it different? Is this good or bad?

1. Why Do the Media Play the Roles They Do?

No journalist feels compelled to play a role dictated by electoral theories. That should go without saying. Journalists follow the dictates of their profession. They cover stories. They write about events in what they perceive to be an evenhanded way.

But their efforts are by necessity constrained. They must meet deadlines. They can only cover so many campaigns in so much detail. They have limited access to some sources. They must be aware of the costs to their owners of their efforts. Publishers and editors, and executives in electronic media outlets, are concerned about audience share.

Many journalists would like to cover every aspect of a certain campaign in great depth. But they must also cover other campaigns. They must compete for space in their newspaper or time on the air. They must be certain that their stories are accurate and fair, that one candidate is not advantaged over another. Thus they follow certain patterns. Their access is dictated largely by campaign staff. Their ability to file complete stories is compromised at times by deadlines. They compete with fellow journalists covering a campaign, but they also do not want to be too far away from what most of their colleagues are saying, for fear that they will be proven wrong or that they will have missed the "real story."

In short, media coverage of campaigns evolves the way it does because of the norms of the journalists' profession, the demands of their employers, and the constraints on their efforts. Just as all candidates do not run their campaigns as they would were there no limits on what they could do, so too are journalists limited. And the cumulating of this limitation is the role that the media as a whole play. It is not a designed role; it is an evolved role. And thus it is one that must be accepted as part of the system. Marginal changes can be wrought. Individual journalists can do their job well or less well. Innovations such as adwatch campaigns can alter the performance in sometimes significant ways. But fundamental change is not likely to be forthcoming in a system whose parameters are so clearly set by a variety of forces over which they have little control.

2. How Should We Evaluate That Role?

In a sense, it does not matter how the role is evaluated because it is largely inevitable. But the media do have an impact on campaigns. Is it good or bad? By what standards should that impact be judged?

In general, the answer is that the media role contributes positively to the electoral process as long as that role is played openly, honestly, and fairly. But that final caveat is not an empty one. One important factor to note concerning the media's coverage of elections is the number of media markets that are dominated by one particular provider of information.

One example should suffice to demonstrate how this can be a problem. For years, the *Manchester Union Leader* has dominated media coverage of campaigns in New Hampshire. The paper, which circulated statewide, is unabashedly conservative, not just Republican but ultraconservative Republican. The editor of the paper frequently writes front-page editorials trumpeting personal views. The paper treats politicians with whom it does not agree with disdain, often preventing them from getting their message through to the public. In that case, the media does not serve the public and the electoral process. Certainly, on a statewide basis, the influence of the *Union Leader* has been unusual, but even its influence in New Hampshire has diminished. However, in local communities, many of which are served by only one newspaper and for which television is not really a viable source of local election news, the problem persists. And that problem is often exacerbated when the single source of news decides that political coverage should be limited; then the effect is not negative—it is all but nonexistent.

With that exception noted, however, the electoral process is quite well served by the free media. Given constraints, the media cover campaigns quite well. Citizens can get what information they need. Journalists look carefully at how they practice their own craft and seek to correct obvious flaws. Thus, for instance, the major networks now routinely rotate reporters among various campaign assignments so that no reporter becomes too close to one campaign and loses objectivity. Campaigns attempt to get the best publicity that they can—for that is the nature of their enterprise—but they also permit journalists to do their job. And the public picks and chooses what it watches and reads, as another example of citizens participating in the process to the extent that they desire to be involved.

III. Paid Media: The Candidate Provides the Message

The difference between free media and paid media could not be more stark. With free media, candidates put their best face forward, but someone else communicates the message to the public. There is an intermediary—the journalists who determine how the message will reach the public. With paid media, candidates determine their message and pay to communicate it directly to potential voters. No intermediary. Straight shot. In this section, we will explore who produces paid advertisements for political campaigns (and what types of advertisements they produce); we will then look at controversies surrounding the ways in which paid media impact political campaigns. We will conclude by looking at the impact of paid media on the electoral process.

A. Types of Paid Media

Paid commercials for political campaigns in this country come from three sources—candidates and their campaigns, the political parties, and interest groups. In fact, the producers of these advertisements are frequently paid consultants to the candidates, parties, or groups; but the message is determined in conjunction with strategies set by campaign committees.

Broadly speaking, political advertisements on television fall into two categories—**spot advertisements** and longer advertisements. Radio advertisements and print media advertisements frequently follow the same themes as do the television ads we discuss here. The spots are equivalent to the ads used by commercial enterprises to sell their products or services (Diamond and Bates 1984). They tend to be short—always under one minute in length—colorful, and polished. The longer commercials, most recently known as infomercials, are often thirty minutes in length or even longer. Some believe that H. Ross Perot invented infomercials for his presidential campaigns, but in fact their history is much longer. Many of the original television commercials were longer attempts by candidates to explain their campaigns to the citizens. These messages were short-

SPOT ADVERTISE- MENTS

Short paid political advertisements that must simplify a message to conform to a ten-, twenty-, or thirty-second time frame.

ened because consultants felt that viewer attention span was too short, that citizens turned off longer commercials and sought entertainment television. Perot resurrected the genre to great effect, as Nielsen ratings demonstrated that citizens were willing to spend the time to become informed.

What purposes are served by political advertisements? The purpose clearly depends on the candidate—and the state of his or her candidacy (Seib 1994). For candidates who are not well known to the public, early in a campaign the purpose of ads is to improve name recognition, essentially to prove that a candidacy is viable. For statewide campaigns and even for congressional campaigns, this kind of advertising can be quite expensive. Quality ads must be produced and repeated over and over in order to make an impression on prospective voters. Of course, incumbents, who have by definition run in the past, do not need to spend money in this way. However, incumbents often run biographical ads early in a campaign to cement a positive image in the public's mind.

Once a candidacy has achieved viability, advertisements are used for one of two purposes. Either they are intended to convince citizens to vote for the candidate or they are designed to denigrate an opponent.[5] These ads have been characterized as **positive ads** or **negative ads**, though there is a great deal of disagreement about how these terms should be defined.

Positive ads state the case for a candidate. The goal is to convince the public that the candidate is the right person for the job, that he has the right qualities to do the job effectively, that he is on the right side of the crucial issues. Negative ads try to convince voters that they should vote against the sponsoring candidate's opponent. Some feel that all negative ads have a deleterious effect on the system; this view will be discussed later. At this point, let it suffice to state that all negative ads are not alike. Most analysts would claim that it is perfectly legitimate for a challenger to point to his or her opponent's record in office and to question whether citizens approve of that record. Most would also agree that it is inappropriate to distort that record or to present it in a confusing manner. The first of these ads are often called **contrast ads,** and they make up an important part of legitimate campaign discourse. But truly negative ads, ads aimed solely at destroying an opponent's image, are another matter. Furthermore, the appropriateness of other ads raises questions. What about ads discussing a candidate's moral fitness for office? Some claim that such personal matters should not be part of the political discourse. Others claim that they are at the heart of a candidate's qualifications for office. No consensus exists on this point. In addition, disagreement exists on how all of these points can or should be made.

The purpose of ads that are run during the heat of a campaign

POSITIVE ADS

Political advertising that stresses the record of the sponsoring candidate, not that of his or her opponent.

NEGATIVE ADS

Political advertising that points to perceived flaws in the record of the sponsoring candidate's opponent.

CONTRAST ADS

Campaign advertisements that offer both an attack and a defense of a candidate's position; more than 30 percent but less than 70 percent attack.

is to ensure that the voters consider the views of the candidate sponsoring the ads. In so doing, paid commercials create an impression of the candidate and go a long way toward setting the agenda for a campaign. As was pointed out in chapter 7, candidates coordinate their media message with the message they are transmitting throughout the campaign.

Infomercials, such as those sponsored by Ross Perot, are a special case of political advertising. Their strength is that they give a candidate sufficient time to explain his or her position on often complex matters. By necessity viewers gain a different kind of impression of a candidate than they would from a thirty-second spot. It is difficult to maintain a false image when speaking to a television audience for half an hour or more.[6]

A number of candidates have seen the advantage of longer presentations, but they do not want to spend the money that such exposure on television costs. They have found a solution to this dilemma through the production of campaign videos. Through this medium they can discuss their issues in great detail; campaign videos also have the advantage that they can be targeted to specific audiences. Generally a campaign will mail or distribute videos to those with interests in certain topics; thus, they can avoid fallout from those not interested in one issue or another. While videos distributed in this way do not reach an audience as large as that reached by television infomercials, they have proven to be a successful technique and will be used more and more as Internet technology makes widespread distribution more feasible.

Much like free media, paid media are also evolving due to the Internet. All serious candidates for federal office, and many state and even local candidates as well, now have websites, sometimes more than one. Many of these websites are elaborate productions that cost a good deal of money to create and maintain. But the payoff can be well worth the effort; as John McCain (in the 2000 campaign) and Howard Dean (in 2004) demonstrated, serious money can be raised on the web, and the Internet can also be a valuable tool in informing and rallying supporters. And it is no longer just websites. All three of the top-tier candidates for the 2008 Democratic presidential nomination—Hillary Clinton, Barack Obama, and John Edwards—have Facebook and MySpace profiles, as do three of the four top GOP hopefuls—John McCain, Mitt Romney, and Fred Thompson. (For some reason, Rudy Giuliani has opted not to create such profiles.) Campaigns now routinely use the web to get information of all kinds out to the public. As we put the finishing touches on this edition, McCain and Romney are trading attack videos on YouTube (which has over twenty million visitors a month), and Hillary Clinton has just unveiled "HillaryHub," a new web portal for

all (presumably good) things Hillary, modeled after the wildly successful Drudge Report site.

Paid political advertisements have become the principal means through which candidates for national and statewide office, and those for other offices with large constituencies, communicate with the voters. They are used because candidates have found them to be effective. There is no more effective means of creating name recognition. Once a campaign is under way, advertisements have been shown to work most effectively at reinforcing existing loyalties (Ansolabehere and Iyengar 1995, 64ff.). They help candidates focus a campaign on the issues they want to discuss. And they allow candidates to raise questions about their opponents, questions that often impact undecided voters. But, as noted earlier, paid media raise a number of questions concerning how the American political process functions. We turn to them next.

B. Controversies Caused by the Use of Paid Media

At least three separate controversies are connected with the use of paid media in political campaigns. The first involves the question of balance—of whether it is fair if one candidate dominates the political discussion because his or her campaign has been able to raise much more money than opponents' campaigns. That question was considered in chapter 5. But two important controversies remain to be explored. In the following sections we will examine the questions surrounding negative advertising and those raised by so-called issue advocacy advertisements.

1. Negative Advertising

As noted earlier, no consensus exists on the question of negative advertising. While most agree that it is appropriate to raise questions about an opponent's record and to contrast one candidate's record with another, most also agree that the practice of attacking an opponent can, at times, go too far. The controversy in the use of paid advertising relates to negative **attack ads** that are either personal in nature or presented in a way that invites criticism as unfair, deceptive, or in other ways inappropriate in political discourse.

Washington Post media commentator Howard Kurtz examined this issue in an analysis of advertising in a series of statewide campaigns during the 1998 election cycle. Kurtz's article appeared under the headline, "Attack Ads Carpet TV, Spinning the Issues; Distortions Rule the Airwaves; Attack Ads Carpet TV as Issues Are Swept Away."[7] In that article, which focused on campaigns in California, Florida, Georgia, New York, and Texas, Kurtz concluded that

> America is again being carpet-bombed by political ads, many of them fiercely negative. . . . The themes vary from race to race, from education to the environment to health care to gun control, but many of [them] oversimplify and distort the opponent's record. (Kurtz 1998, A1)

In Maryland in 1998, "voters [witnessed] the most sustained assault of negative political advertising in state history" (Wilson 1998, A1), with several hundred ads appearing on Baltimore and Washington television stations each week.

Why do candidates engage in negative advertising? The answer is quite simple. They believe—and they have evidence from recent electoral experience—that such techniques are effective. They work. The point is to win, not to be a nice guy. Thus Mary Crawford, communications director of the National Republican Congressional Committee, justified her party's $10 million advertising blitz linking votes for Democratic candidates to the scandals surrounding President Clinton in 1998: "The challenge in this environment is to acknowledge [the scandal's] existence and to pivot the issues that we want to focus on" (Berke 1998, A1). "The president's scandal is on the very top of the minds of the public, particularly as it turns its attention to the election. . . . To ignore it is as if you're ignoring a dead horse in the middle of the table" (Connolly 1998, A5).

But there is also counterevidence, and a clear recognition that relying on negative advertising can backfire. "Political analysts say hostile advertising can be risky in Maryland, where political debate is generally restrained compared with the shrill name-calling of New York or the racial overtones of North Carolina campaigns" (Wilson 1998, A1).

Similarly, in Michigan, the concern was that negative ads had gone too far: "They can make a heroine out of [the attacked candidate]. Whenever a negative ad pushes the line too far, a negative ad can backfire and make the victim the hero" (Hoffman 1998).

ATTACK ADS

Political advertisements that attack the sponsoring candidate's opponent, often on personal and not political grounds; viewed by many as contributing to citizen cynicism.

Some Republicans considered the 1998 attack ads aimed at the president during the last week of the congressional elections unnecessarily risky. Ralph Reed, then a conservative Republican consultant and current chair of the Georgia Republican party, expressed the view that "people who are going to vote Republican because of their distaste for the personal conduct of the president made that decision some time ago" (Associated Press 1998).

Those sharing this view feared that voters would react negatively to the advertising campaign and stay home or, alternatively, that it would invigorate Democrats, who were ignoring the election because they were angry at the president, to turn out to vote because of their equal revulsion toward the Republican campaign. The results of the 1998 midterm elections, in which hotly contested districts targeted for the Republican attack ads broke in favor of the Democrats, seemed to confirm the accuracy of these fears.

Strategists have debated the efficacy of negative attack ads in terms of their contribution to electoral outcomes, but others are concerned about their broader impact on the electoral process. One line of argument holds that the negativity of campaigns has kept qualified citizens from seeking elective office (Maisel, Stone, and Maestas 1999). Another concern is that citizens have turned off to political process because they view it as unnecessarily negative. Ansolabehere and Iyengar (1995, 101, 107–10) have demonstrated that positive political advertisements encourage people to vote, whereas negative advertisements reduce voter turnout. According to their analysis, citizens exposed to relentless negative advertising aimed at candidates they favor find that "dropping out may be easier than switching to the attacker" (Ansolabehere and Iyengar 1995, 109–10). On the other hand, Geer (2006) presents compelling evidence that negative advertising actually presents meaningful information to voters, and thus represents a positive contribution to representative democracy.

Whether viewed in a favorable or unfavorable light, negative advertising is not likely to go away. The right of candidates to press their political cause as they see fit is a fundamental aspect of freedom of speech; it is unimaginable that the content of political advertising would be restricted in a way that would survive a legal challenge on constitutional grounds.

That certainty has not deterred reformers from seeking a means of ameliorating the impact of negative attack ads. One proposal that has been seriously floated requires candidates who name their opponents in a political advertisement to do so themselves; that is, any negative attack on an opponent must come from the attacking candidate in his or her own words. The theory behind this reform is that it is more difficult to make outlandish statements personally than it is to do so through a third party, or through clever media presentations.

Whether this or any similar reform effort could pass either Congress or a state legislature, and whether it would pass a constitutional challenge, is highly debatable. However, the mere existence of proposals such as this one suggests that the issue of negative advertising is of enough concern to keep efforts to restrain such practices high on reformers' agendas.

2. Issue Advocacy Advertisements

Political groups have used a variety of means to further their policy agendas (chapter 4). One technique used by wealthier groups on critical issues has been to advertise to the public, seeking to gain popular support for their positions. In 1994 opponents of President Clinton's health care reform package ran a very successful set of commercials—the "Harry and Louise" commercials, named after the characters portrayed in the ads—that were given credit for turning public opinion against the president's plan.

Noting the success of the "Harry and Louise" commercials, a number of interest groups decided to tie their issue concerns to particular candidacies in the 1996 election. In so doing, they were taking advantage of a judicial interpretation that the right of groups to advertise on behalf of issues with which they were concerned was constitutionally protected, and could not be restricted by campaign finance regulations as long as the advertisements did not explicitly call for the election or defeat of a particular candidate.

Organized labor was the first to exploit this interpretation of the law. In 1996 they ran a $35 million campaign targeting particular Republican candidates running for reelection to the House of Representatives. Entering the relevant media markets very early in these campaigns, the labor advertisements were successful in raising doubts in voters' minds about their representatives in Congress. Later in the campaign, a coalition of business groups including the National Federation of Independent Businesses and the National Association of Manufacturers countered the labor campaign with a multimillion-dollar effort of their own, targeted at the same contested districts.

The Annenberg Public Policy Center studied these 1996 advertisements. They noted that 87 percent of these "issue" ads mentioned an individual candidate by name and that the tone of these ads was significantly more negative than the tone of candidate ads in the same districts (Broder and Marcus 1997, 6). They also noted that between $130 million and $150 million was spent on such ads during the 1996 congressional elections. Supporters of the McCain-Feingold campaign finance reform hoped that the elimination of soft money for parties at the federal level and scheduling limitations would reduce the number of issue advocacy advertisements, but this has not happened. The 2004 presidential election saw these ads play a prominent role, and more money was spent on them than ever before. And since the Supreme Court has removed the scheduling limitations by recently declaring them unconstitutional, it is likely issue advocacy ads will once again be prominent in 2008 (for more on this see chapter 5).

C. Impact of Paid Media on Election Campaigns

Obviously, modern campaigns have spent such a high percentage of their resources on paid media advertising because candidates, campaign managers, and consultants feel that such expenditures pay electoral dividends. At the most basic level, campaigning through the media allows a candidacy to reach the largest possible audience with a message that is designed by the campaign strategists, not interpreted by journalists. But it is possible to be slightly more explicit, to be clear about what effects campaign commercials are designed to produce.

1. Intended Consequences of Paid Media Campaigns

Campaign strategists have at least four separate goals for paid media campaigns. The first goal is to establish a positive image for the candidate. If the candidate is an incumbent, that image is of a hardworking, effective public servant. If the candidate is a challenger, the goal is to depict the candidate as one who can do the job well. If the candidate is not well known, the first aspect of this strategy is merely to create name recognition. Tactics vary. Some candidacies stress personal characteristics: he is a family man who is loyal to his friends. Others emphasize connections between the candidate and the electorate: she went to high school here and has always lived here; she knows our people. Still others might talk about job qualifications: she has been successful on the city council and will be a great representative in Sacramento. But whatever the tactic, the strategic premise is to build a positive image. Typically commercials of this type run early in a campaign.

The second goal is to set the agenda for the campaign. Through saturating the airwaves with commercials, campaigns hope to affect how the potential voters see the entire campaign. If all commercials talk about local issues, voters are likely to think of the candidate and the campaign in those terms. If the paid media stress a candidate's work in Washington or in a state capital, those issues are likely to be at the forefront. The discussions may be very concrete (i.e., about specific legislation) or diffuse (i.e., about the state of the local economy), but the goal is the same—to concentrate public attention on items that play well for the candidate sponsoring the ads and put his or her candidacy in the most positive light.

The third goal of a campaign is to reinforce the loyalties of party members and others who should logically support a candidate. These ads often link the candidate to popular figures in the same party; congressional candidates appear with the governor or senator of their party to remind voters where their loyalty should lie. One strategy in any campaign is to protect one's base, to be sure that those who are your most likely supporters turn out to vote. Paid media is used to further this effort.

Finally, some (many observers would say most) campaigns use paid media to attack their opponents. Even critics of negative advertising admit that it is appropriate for a candidate to point to flaws in the record of his or her opponent. A challenger has to provide a reason for replacing the incumbent. As discussed above, the question here revolves around the specific points that are attacked and the way in which the message is presented. From a strategic point of view, the goal is clear—to convince voters that there are reasons not to vote for one candidate—and presumably therefore to vote for the other candidate.

IV. POLITICIANS VIEW THE MEDIA

Without meaning to belittle politicians, one could say that their relationship to the media resembles that familiar lament of Kermit D. Frog: "You can't live with 'em; you can't live without 'em." Politicians complain frequently about how unfairly they are treated in the media, about how difficult it is to talk about issues, about how paid advertising presents distorted images, about how they wish they could talk about issues at length, not in sound bites.

But their actions tell another story. Virtually every politician in Washington has a press secretary whose job is to guarantee that the politician is seen frequently in the media, particularly in the media that serves the elected official's constituents. Every campaign has a press secretary who is charged with the care and feeding (in two senses of that word) of journalists covering the campaign. Candidates treat the press well so that journalists are inclined to treat them favorably; and they want to influence the substance of the stories that are reported. Every campaign for a major office hires political consultants to design and place advertisements. Few candidates fret about the length of the ads, only about their effectiveness. None of the examples described herein sound like politicians who cannot stand the media.

And, of course, the reason is the other side of the equation. They cannot live without them. And this is not all bad. After all, elected officials and candidates for office need to communicate with large numbers of citizens. Mass media—free and paid—are the only effective means of doing this. Journalists, in legitimately and professionally pursuing their craft, cover politicians. Politicians have a clear stake in trying to influence what is said so that their message is heard as they intend it to be delivered. Advertisements do not produce themselves. Candidates, if they want to win, have an obligation to work with professional media consultants who can produce effective ads. There is nothing evil in any of this.

The problem that thoughtful politicians really worry about is balance. What happens when the press reaction to one set of circumstances impacts another? Examples abound. Potential candidates worry about private matters from their past being raised during campaigns. Some even decide not to run for office, based on such worries (Maisel, Stone, and Maestas 1999). Officeholders worry that principled positions taken forcibly on one set of salient issues might well define their image for some time to come.

The media is an important part of politics, but it is one only partially controlled by politicians themselves. They must accept that constraint if they are going to enter the public arena. The positive contributions of the media to our polity were considered so important that the press was given a uniquely privileged position in the Constitution. Nothing in our political experience since the founding has led even the harshest critic of the media to think that the judgment of the founders regarding the sanctity of a free press should be questioned.

WEBSITES

Most media outlets have their own websites. Among those of prominent national media include the following:

www.nytimes.com: *New York Times*
www.washingtonpost.com: *Washington Post*
http://wsj.com: *Wall Street Journal*
www.abcnews.go.com: ABC News
www.cbsnews.com: CBS News
www.cnn.com: CNN
www.msnbc.msn.com: NBC and MSNBC News
www.foxnews.com: Fox News
http://appcpenn.org: The Annenberg Public Policy Center, at the University of Pennsylvania, analyzes media usage during election campaigns. It maintains an ongoing study of issue advocacy advertising as purchased by more than seventy organizations.

CHAPTER 11

Party in Government

House Minority Leader John Boehner (R-Ohio), right, hands the gavel to newly elected Speaker of the House Nancy Pelosi (D-Calif.) on the floor of the House at the start of the 110th Congress, January 4, 2007. The Democrats won back control of the House of Representatives (and the Senate too) for the first time since 1994, and Pelosi became the first female Speaker of the House in the history of the United States.

Whoever said C-SPAN wasn't exciting wasn't watching television in the early hours of June 27, 2003. After six years of stalled legislation, weeks of intense debates, and two days of visits by members of the Bush administration to the House floor, the vote on the Republican-sponsored bill to add prescription drug benefits to Medicare was finally called. At 2:00 AM, the fifteen minutes allocated for the vote had run out, and it was clear that the Bush-supported plan was doomed, with the roll call standing at 210–214. Instead of succumbing to the Democrats' calls for "regular order," which would close the vote, the GOP leadership kept the clock ticking. The vote would stay open through the night if necessary while Speaker of the House Dennis Hastert (R-Ill.), Majority Leader Tom DeLay (R-Tex.), and Majority Whip Roy Blunt (R-Mo.) worked over any wavering Republicans.

By 2:30 AM, the vote was tied. The leadership team, aided by Energy and Commerce Committee chair Billy Tauzin (R-La.) and by Ways and Means Committee chair Bill Thomas (R-Calif.), circled in on Representative Jo Ann Emerson (R-Mo.). After heated conversation with the powerful Republicans, Emerson switched her nay to aye but not before securing a promise from the Speaker. In exchange for her vote, Hastert would bring to the House floor Emerson's cosponsored bill on the importation of less-expensive prescription drugs from Canada and Europe. Leadership was against the bill, but Majority Whip Blunt vowed not to rally the troops in opposition. With the GOP leadership promise secured, a visibly shaken Emerson cast the deciding green ballot, after which the audible disappointment of Democrats followed her back to her desk. With the House scoreboard showing a one-vote advantage to the GOP, the Speaker banged the gavel and the vote closed. Final tally: 216–215. Bush's Medicare reform bill had made it through the House, but barely (Allen and Graham-Silverman 2003, 1614–15).

The dramatic GOP victory is less a demonstration of the power of parties in American government than it is of the constraints on that power. The toughest battles for the passage of Medicare reform in the House were not waged across party lines but within them. Emerson was not the only Republican to extract a promise in exchange for supporting the party. Her conservative GOP colleagues cast their votes only after Hastert guaranteed that changes would be made in the **conference committee** with the Senate. Republican fiscal conservatives insisted that the final conference report contain more structural change to Medicare—such as privatization and market competition—before they would sign off on the most expensive expansion of an entitlement program in U.S. history.

A closer look at the down-to-the-wire vote reveals not a strong majority party organization whipping its members into line but a majority party leadership constrained in its ability to exert its will

CONFERENCE COMMITTEE

An ad hoc committee comprised of senators and representatives called together to resolve differences between Senate and House versions of the same bill.

over members. In the American political system, members of Congress are hired and fired by their constituents, not by the national parties. Representative Emerson owes her seat to the Eighth District of Missouri, not to the Republican National Committee. She would not support her party's position unless it reflected the interests of her constituents, specifically the seniors in her district who make weekly bus trips from Missouri to Canada just to purchase their prescription drugs at affordable prices. Similarly, conservative Republicans were willing to defer to party leadership only if the final bill would appease their "anti–big government" bases back home that turn out to vote in primary elections. Without a hold on the electoral careers of its members, the majority party in Congress derives its power less from coercion than from persuasion and the wishes of its members. Parties in Congress are only as strong—or weak—as their members want them to be.

Although parties are not mentioned in the Constitution, they are certainly constrained by the governmental structure established by it. Federalism ensures that ideological, social, and economic differences are built into the two-party system from the local level up; that is, the two major parties in the United States can look significantly different from state to state. A Massachusetts Democrat may find little in common with a Georgian Democrat; Republicans from Maine and Texas may vary greatly on legislative priorities. Because members of Congress are elected by local parties (or groups) on the basis of local issues, these regional, state, and local interests are reflected at the national level. Members responsible to, and punishable only by, local electorates tend to be responsive to constituents, not necessarily to party leadership. Thus, the American federal system and an electoral system of single-member districts with plurality winners (first-past-the-post) work against strong parties in Congress (Brady and Buckley 2002).

Furthermore, unlike their European counterparts in parliamentary democracies, American parties operate in a context of the separation of powers and of checks and balances, or "separate institutions sharing powers" (Neustadt 1960). The legislative process is shared by both the House and the Senate, with the Constitution requiring the two to forge a final agreement on policy; yet these institutions differ in their organization, procedures, rules, and norms. As established at the founding, majority rule governs the House, while minority rights are protected in the Senate. Partisanship and disciplined leadership are trademarks of the House as the majority party works to bring together what a fragmented, decentralized committee system pulls apart. In the more individualized Senate, majority party leadership cannot push the party position through the chamber but must forge unanimous consent agreements, always aware of obstructionist tools available to the opposi-

FILIBUSTER

Exercising the right to un-limited debate in the Sen-ate; used literally "to talk a bill to death."

SENATORIAL HOLDS

The practice through which a United States Sena-tor keeps a nomination from coming to a vote by asking for it to be held up until he or she is ready to vote.

tion, such as the **filibuster** and **senatorial holds**. These differences across governmental institutions make coordination, organization, and "responsible party" governance all the more difficult for Ameri-can parties.

Thus, we are faced with a dilemma. Political parties are the most important, dominating element in organizing the government of the United States, but they do not control legislative outcomes. Even with the White House and Congress firmly unified under Republi-can control after the 2002 midterm elections, the GOP Medicare bill, the centerpiece of Bush's domestic agenda, barely made it through the Republican-dominated House. The closeness of the Medicare vote and the closeness of votes on other key domestic priorities for the Bush administration illustrate the intense partisan divide in the 108th Congress and the consequent challenges to party leadership within and across the institutions of governance. More than a half century ago, E. E. Schattschneider (1942, 1), a pre-eminent theorist of political parties asked, "What kind of party is it that, having won control of the government, is unable to govern?" That question remains as relevant now as it was at the beginning of World War II. It is the question to which we turn in this chapter.

I. THEORETICAL AND HISTORICAL CONTEXT: IS STRONG PARTY GOVERNMENT POSSIBLE IN THE UNITED STATES?

In his classic text *Politics, Parties, and Pressure Groups* (1964), V. O. Key Jr., his generation's most prominent analyst of American politics, divides his discussion of party into the party organization, the party in the electorate, and the party in government. The basis for that division is the classic notion that partisans, once elected to office, should be able to implement the programs on which they ran. This normative "responsible party" idea is an old and revered one in the study of the American polity. In fact, as far back as 1885, Woodrow Wilson (1885) (in his prepresidential days as a political scientist) lamented what he viewed as "committee government"—strong committees, weak parties, and no effective party leaders in Congress. Impressed by the strength of parties in the electorate at the time, Wilson wished for the same in Congress. His solution: "The great need is, not to get rid of parties, but to find and use some expedient by which they can be managed and made amenable from day to day to public opinion" (79–80). In his view, strong parties were the best mechanism through which a democracy could convert public opinion into policy alternatives. Congressional par-ties must be strong to govern.

Sixty-five years after Wilson's *Congressional Government*, the

Committee on Political Parties of the American Political Science Association prescribed stronger parties in its influential report "Toward a More Responsible Two-Party System" (1950), a report frequently referred to as the "Schattschneider report" (after the committee's chair). Again the complaint was familiar. American parties were too weak to form a link between the electorate and the elected. Parties did not stand firmly on issues; candidates did not feel bound to implement party programs once in office. Essentially the norm espoused in the report was a parliamentary system, that is, a government specifically structured to enact the majority party's agenda. In the parliamentary model, implicit in responsible party arguments, the individual who leads a party in the election (e.g., the British prime minister) is the same person who leads that party in government. Programmatic parties stand for opposing policies, enabling voters to cast ballots for or against a distinct party platform. In the legislature, party leaders are strong; party members are loyal; and party unity is high. Certainly, there was little evidence of responsible congressional parties by this definition at the time of the Schattschneider report.

So under what circumstances can we expect party leaders to exert control over the legislative process in the American system? Joseph Cooper and David Brady (1981a), in their seminal article on congressional leadership, noted the importance of context in examining the ways in which Speakers of the House have led their body. More specifically, they delineate the circumstances under which Speakers have led disciplined, hierarchical, strong party organizations, much like those in parliamentary systems. They point to the turn of the century, not long after Wilson wrote *Congressional Government*, when the two major parties stood for opposing policies and represented distinct electoral bases. During this period of relative homogeneity within each congressional party, Speakers ruled—in particular, two powerful Republican Speakers, Thomas Brackett Reed (1889–1890; 1895–1899) and Joseph G. Cannon (1903–1911). The tenures of "Boss" Reed and "Czar" Cannon marked the transformation from the committee government of Wilson's observations to the party government characterized by centralized leadership, hierarchal party organization, and strict party line voting (Brady 1973). The party and committee systems were essentially fused to maintain party discipline. Committee seats and chair positions were doled out by the Speaker according to party loyalty, while the top echelon of the party leadership—the Speaker, the majority leader, and the majority whip—chaired the Rules Committee, the Appropriations Committee, and the Ways and Means Committee, respectively.

But division within the Republican party began to surface. With the rise of the Progressive movement in the electorate, preferences within the majority party in the House shifted from homogeneous to heterogeneous. Speaker Cannon, however, refused to acknowledge the new wing within his party. He wielded his exclusive power to appoint committee seats and chair positions (power granted to the Speaker under the "Reed rules"), and he exercised his power as the chair of the Rules Committee to reward loyalists and punish traitors. Cannon denied the Progressive Republicans chairmanships and committee seats, and he refused to recognize them on the floor. Under the "Czar" system, the Speaker effectively controlled the policy process in the House—if he opposed legislation, such as any Progressive policy, he would not let it reach the floor. To the Progressives and Democrats, it was tyrannical rule; to Cannon, it was responsible party government:

> This is a government by the people acting through the representatives of a majority of the people. Results can not be had except by a majority, and in the House of Representatives a majority, being responsible, should have full power and should exercise that power; otherwise the majority is inefficient and does not perform its function. (Speaker Cannon, *Congressional Record*, March 19, 1910, 3436)

In March 1910, Progressive Republicans joined forces with Democrats to strip the Republican Speaker Joe Cannon of his position on the Rules Committee, to expand the committee, and to vote for its members on the floor. The following year, the Democrats took over the House, voting to turn the committee appointment process over to the House as a whole, further decentralizing party control and weakening the Speaker's hold over members' careers (Galloway 1961; Peters 1990; Brady, Buckley, and Rivers 2000; Sinclair 1998).

What can explain this shift away from strong party government? Cooper and Brady (1981) argue that parties and party leadership are strong (and active) only when their members' policy preferences are relatively homogeneous—for example, the Republicans at the turn of the century. Rising heterogeneity in the party in the electorate (such as the impact of the Progressive movement) is reflected in rising heterogenity in the party in government (such as the election of Progressive Republicans to the U.S. House of Representatives). The more diverse the member preferences are within a party, the tougher it is to lead it, and the stronger the incentives are for members to build cross-party coalitions—such as Progressive Republicans and Democrats—and decentralize party organization (see also Brady and Epstein 1997; Brady and Buckley 2002).

The rise of heterogeneity within the congressional parties and the resulting institutional reforms that decentralized power in the

House both contributed to the long-term decline in party voting after 1910 (Brady, Cooper, and Hurley 1977, 1979; Collie and Brady 1985; Brady and Sinclair 1984). After the revolt against the Speaker, the strong, centralized, hierarchical party government evident at the turn of the century was replaced with a committee government much like the one Woodrow Wilson complained about. Committee chairs rivaled party leadership in power, rendering the Speaker's job one of coalition building from policy to policy, to get legislation passed. In each instance—pre- and postrevolt—the parties in Congress were what their members wanted them to be: strong in prerevolt period and weak thereafter. As we will see in this chapter, this relationship remains in place today.

By the 1960s, these party chairs were predominantly Southern Democrats, many of whom were members of the Conservative Coalition, a dominant force of Democrats and Republicans who voted together, forming a conservative majority from 1938 to 1965. With the elections of 1958 and 1964, an influx of liberal Democrats from the Northeast infused the House Democratic majority with greater heterogeneity, specifically on social policy. Much like the Progressives at the turn of the century, the liberal Democrats found senior committee chairs in their own party unwilling to support the majority-preferred position on such issues as civil rights (Rohde 1991). Frustrated at powerful (often patronizing) committee chairs' boxing them out of the legislative process, junior Democratic members joined with Republicans to pass institutional reforms in the 1970s. The House reforms shifted power from the committee chairs to the subcommittee chairs, while granting additional, albeit nominal, powers to the Speaker. The adoption of the "subcommittee bill of rights" essentially transformed an already decentralized system of "committee government" to an even more decentralized system of "subcommittee government" (Davidson 1981).

The House reforms of the 1970s essentially shifted the balance of power to the Speaker and to the rank and file at the expense of the committee chairs and thus contributed to the strengthening of the congressional parties in the long run (Rohde 1991); yet the conventional wisdom in the literature claims just the opposite: the decentralizing reforms of the 1970s in combination with the electoral changes evident by the 1960s stripped the parties of their ability to influence the behavior of legislators and, consequently, their ability to shape policy.

Outside Congress, the hold of parties over their members' careers was clearly diminishing. As of the mid-1960s, members of Congress began winning reelection by larger margins, reducing the number of competitive districts across the United States. But the rising incumbency advantage was based less on members' party affiliation and more on their **personal vote**—that is, the voters' sup-

PERSONAL VOTE

Vote cast for a candidate based on his or her personal relationship with voters as opposed to partisan ties.

port of individual candidates (Alford and Brady 1989). Clearly, holding a congressional seat and engaging in constituency service gave members greater electoral advantages over their challengers outside Congress. The rising importance of electronic media in congressional campaigns also benefited incumbents at the expense of challengers; electronic campaigning costs money, and incumbents are much better positioned to raise the necessary funds than are challengers.

In a somewhat ironic development, at the same time that members of Congress were assuming greater control over their own campaigns, partisanship within Congress began to rise. What could explain reduced party control over members' campaigns *and* a surge in partisan voting? In an attempt to explain this rise in partisanship (and the rise in party bickering, as highlighted in the media), scholars first turned their attention to the rise of **divided government**. Perhaps partisanship and "deadlocked democracy" (Burns 1963) were being promoted by the American constitutional system, which allows for separate election of the president and Congress and thus permits split party control of the government.[1]

From 1900 to 1952, only four elections resulted in split party control of the government; but since 1952, seventeen elections have brought divided government to power, and only ten have resulted in **unified control**. Between 1953 and 2007, the same party has controlled the presidency and both houses of Congress for only twenty-one years, about one-third of the time. Less often recognized is the extent to which divided government has existed in the states as well. Figure 11.1 shows the extent to which the situation in the states has come to parallel the one in Washington. (See Fiorina 1996 and Jacobson 1990c on the causes and consequences of divided government at the national and state levels.)

Political scientists and pundits alike complained that divided party control of Congress and the White House was creating gridlock, or stalemates and a lack of significant policy change. James Sundquist (1988, 1993) decries divided party control as lacking in party responsibility and effective policymaking. Split party control of the government, he argues, puts parties head-to-head, inevitably resulting in policy impasse, legislative paralysis, and irresponsible parties. Unified control, however, enables the majority leadership to rally the party around the president's policy proposals; unified party government is strong, responsible party government.

Inherent in the debate over unified government versus divided is the assumption that party matters. In a party-oriented interpretation of gridlock, the president bargains with the median of the majority party in Congress; when the two are of different parties, it is difficult to pass legislation to move policy away from the status quo (see Fiorina 1996; Jacobson 1990a; Mayhew 1991; Cox and Kernell

DIVIDED GOVERNMENT

The situation in which one elected branch of government is under the partisan control of one party and the other branch of the other party.

UNIFIED CONTROL

The situation in which one political party controls both elected branches of government.

Figure 11.1 Partisan Division of State Governments, 1954–2006

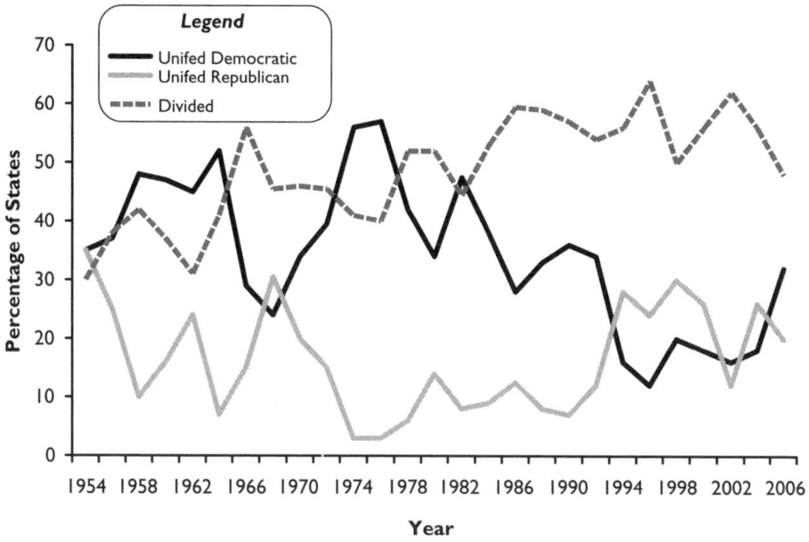

Source: Council of State Governments (www.csg.org).

1991; Brady and Volden 1998). In such a scenario, unified party control would result in inherently less gridlock and more party-sponsored legislation, a sure positive for advocates of responsible party government.

But what if legislative impasses are not solely party-driven phenomena? The heterogeneity of preferences in the electorate and in Congress, and the complexity of policy areas, may be the sources of legislative stalemates, regardless of divided or unified control. In *Divided We Govern*, David Mayhew (1991, 2005) compares periods of divided and unified party government in terms of the amount of legislation passed, vetoes sustained, congressional hearings held, presidential treaties signed, and judicial appointments approved. Excluding the number of vetoes, he concludes that there is no significant difference in these variables under divided versus unified control. In fact, "the number of laws per Congress varies more *within* universes of unified or divided times than it does between them" (Mayhew 1991, 76; emphasis added). Clearly more is at work than two parties butting heads over policy across institutions.

In sum, when they exist, heterogeneous policy preferences within the parties create barriers to legislation in times of both unified and divided party control. For example, consider the 103d Congress, when Democrats controlled Congress and the White House for the first time in twelve years. At the start of Bill Clinton's first term, it looked like unified Democratic government had cleared the way for legislation previously vetoed by President George H. W. Bush, such as the Family and Medical Leave Act. But Clinton soon faced divisions within his own party over health care reform, budget resolutions, trade policy, and even gun control. Unified Democratic government did not yield unified Democratic legislation on many fronts. The defeat of Clinton's 1994 crime bill came at the hands of his own party, and health care reform died without even a floor vote in either of the Democrat-dominated chambers. Conservative Democrats would not agree to his budget reconciliation without caps to entitlement programs. The Democratic president actually had to rely on moderate Republicans to get Congressional support for NAFTA, as he was unable to shift a traditional Democratic anti-free-trade bias (Nather 2003, 1309). Clinton's tactic of triangulation—positioning himself between liberal Democrats and conservative Republicans to gain support of moderates—was a more successful route to pass legislation than relying on the unified support of his party.

Republicans in the 108th Congress faced divisions within their unified government as well. Even on the two most important components of their president's domestic agenda—tax cuts and Medicare reform—the party remains divided. Yet the heterogeneity of preferences within the party vary according to policy arena, with tax cuts being the less controversial of the two: Republicans may disagree on how deep to cut taxes, but they do agree to cut them. The more difficult policy proposals are those that require a shift in traditional party policy, such as Clinton's asking Democrats to embrace free trade or Bush's trying to convince Republicans to expand an entitlement program such as Medicare. John D. Rockefeller IV (D-W.Va.) describes the difficulties members have compromising on policies such as Medicare reform: "People say 'Just split the difference.' You can't. You've got to be one way or the other. . . . It's not like, you know, water and sewer. There are principles involved" (quoted in Carey and Adams 2003, 1971). Even traditional policy arenas, such as those that determine the role and size of the federal government, create rifts not just between the major parties but within them as well. Many of the battles within the parties are waged across the institutions—White House versus Senate versus House of Representatives; thus, unified control may actually expose more intraparty heterogeneity than times of divided control, when policy impasses are merely blamed on the other party.

So if there are legislative roadblocks under unified control, do parties *not* matter? No. If we think of parties as aggregates of their members' preferences and if these preferences are heterogeneous within a party on a particular policy, then unified party control of the government does not guarantee legislative harmony. Stalemates may simply be the result of legislation proposed that is too far from the median members in Congress, regardless of their party. On the other hand, when preferences within the respective parties are relatively homogeneous on a specific issue, then parties and divided or unified partisan control of government will matter a great deal. Given the constitutional and institutional constraints on party in government, electoral majorities in the United States do not always translate into policy majorities (Brady and Buckley 2002).

II. Measuring Party Strength in Congress

So how do we measure party strength in government? One method is to look at patterns of party voting in Congress. Political scientists use three measures to do so. First, **party unity votes** are votes in which a majority of the Democrats voting cast their votes on one side of an issue and the majority of Republicans on the other side. **Party unity scores** are the percentage of times that an individual legislator votes with his or her party on party unity votes. Thus, if every Democrat voted aye on a particular vote while 75 percent of the Republicans voted nay and 25 percent voted aye, that would be a party unity vote (a majority of Democrats voting on one side and a majority of Republicans on the other). That vote would be included in a computation of the legislators' party unity score. Political systems in which parties structure legislative decisions tend to have more party unity votes and higher party unity scores.

Figure 11.2 depicts the percentage of party unity votes in the House and Senate since 1954. Even from these rudimentary data, a number of conclusions follow. First, the number of party unity votes fell during the middle years of this period, but just as significant, partisan voting has made a comeback in more recent years. The percentage of party unity votes has been at or near a majority of all votes in both houses of Congress since the beginning of the second

PARTY UNITY VOTES

Votes on which a majority of one party votes against a majority of the other party.

PARTY UNITY SCORES

The percentage of times that an individual legislator votes with his or her party on those votes in which a majority of one party votes against a majority of the other party (party unity votes).

Figure 11.2 Party Unity Votes in Congress, 1954–2006

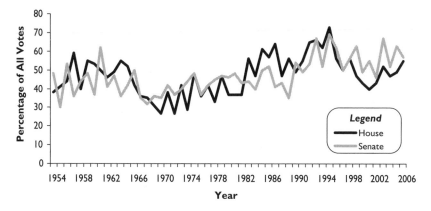

Source: CQ Almanac.

Reagan term, with the sole exception of the Senate in 1989. The extent to which voting in Congress was on a partisan basis was most notable in the first year after the Republicans regained majority status in 1994. The extent of partisanship in 1998 reverses a noticeable downward trend that began after the extremely contentious first session of the 104th Congress. More recently, the relatively even partisan split in the nation after the 2000 election and the slim margins held by majorities in Congress have promoted even greater partisanship in House and Senate votes.

Figures 11.3 and 11.4 reveal the truly remarkable extent to which party voting has again become an important factor in Congress, and they give some clues to the reasons. First, claiming that party voting is not important is difficult when the average party unity scores of Democrats and Republicans in both houses of Congress have been above 80 percent for the last decade. The Republican party, always assumed to be the more ideologically homogeneous, has shown remarkable unity throughout the period under study, but most particularly in the most recent years.

Democratic party scores declined in the mid-1960s and into the 1970s, particularly in the House of Representatives. However, David Rohde (1991, 50–58) has demonstrated that much of the decline in the Democratic party scores was in fact a decline in the party unity scores of *Southern* Democrats. The Democratic scores rebounded—to astoundingly high levels—during the Reagan administration, and have stayed very high ever since.

Party unity scores are clearly much higher today than they were thirty years ago, yet that leaves us with some important questions: Does greater party unity in Congress reflect effective party leadership or greater homogeneity within the parties? Do party unity

Figure 11.3 Party Unity Scores in the House, 1954–2006

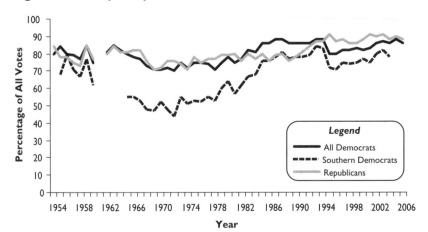

Source: CQ Almanac.

Figure 11.4 Party Unity Scores in the Senate, 1954–2006

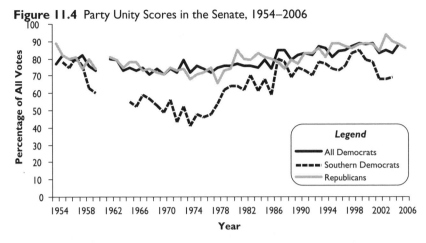

Source: CQ Almanac.

scores increase as a result of strong whip organizations, or would members have voted this way regardless of party pressure? The difficulty is in determining the motivation behind the voting patterns: Did some legislators vote against their own ideology or interests (as established by the electoral connection) because an organized and disciplined party organization pressured them to do so, or did the party position happen to coincide with the members' personal interests (Krehbiel 1993, 1998, 1999)?

There is a major dispute in the literature over how to answer these questions, or, in other words, how to understand the significance of parties in Congress. Krehbiel's (1993, 1998, 1999) view, in extreme form, is that party is the mere aggregation of induced preferences. Thus, on any given policy, when legislators' preferences within the parties are separate or distinct, we call the parties *strong*; when they overlap, we call the parties *weak*. For Aldrich (1995), Aldrich and Rohde (1997), Cox and McCubbins (1993, 2005), Rohde (1991), and Stonecash and colleagues (2003), parties are, roughly speaking, more than aggregations of preferences (Brady and Buckley 2002). The parties tie together voters, elections, institutions, and strategy. For example, Cox and McCubbins describe the congressional parties as "legislative cartels," far more powerful than others would surmise. With the structural deck stacked in its favor, the majority party can dole out leadership positions in exchange for loyalty (see also Kolodny 1999).

But Rohde (1991) does not expect party leaders to dominate on all issues; rather, they are expected to utilize the institutional tools available to them if and only if there is widespread agreement within the party caucus or conference on the policy. Rohde has developed this concept of "conditional party government" to explain the higher levels of party cohesion found in the House in the late 1980s.

He explains that parties are conditionally active coalitions: if there is preference homogeneity within the party on an issue, then leaders take action.

All would agree that homogeneity within the parties certainly facilitates strong party leadership. When members of the same party share similar views, they are more likely to give more power to their congressional leaders because the party position does not conflict with their electoral interests. Conversely, members of heterogeneous parties have less incentive to follow the party leaders' agenda, especially when it could be electorally damaging (Sinclair 1995). Yet, as Rohde (1991) points out, the power of party leaders can vary from issue to issue, depending on the distribution of its members' preferences on a given piece of legislation. Taking this argument one step further, in policy arenas with more-heterogeneous preference distributions, we would then expect votes cast with members' respective parties to be indicative of strong party leadership.

The June 2003 House vote on Medicare demonstrates the difficulties facing party leadership, even within the relatively homogeneous GOP. Conservative Republicans who traditionally oppose the expansion of entitlement programs had to go against their ideological preferences to vote for the bill. This would suggest strong party cohesion and effective leadership within the GOP. But we know that the conservative members that did vote the party position only did so when promised by leadership that their demands (for greater privatization and structural reform) would be met in the final conference report. Representative Emerson was only willing to defer to the GOP leadership and support the Republican-sponsored plan if and only if the Speaker promised to schedule a vote on a bill that the GOP leadership opposed—not exactly examples of coercive party pressure by any definition.

In a political system in which constituents, not the parties, hire and fire members, party leadership must offer incentives to members in exchange for their loyalty. Leadership can schedule (or block) a vote important to the member, designate (or deny) committee seats and chair positions, and dole out (or withhold) contributions to reelection campaigns from their own PACs. Thus, the party hierarchy can influence the effectiveness of a member's legislative capabilities, but it has limited ability to cajole, and practically no ability to force, members to vote with the party. The reality is that members of Congress who are elected on their own owe little to the party leaders on the Hill. As long as members can please their constituents, neither the national party nor the congressional party can affect members' electoral careers. At best, the leadership can coordinate the preferences of its party members—a job made more difficult when these preferences are diverse.

But preference distributions can sometimes be difficult to predict, especially before a vote. The party leadership must know where any given member's constituent and ideology-driven preferences lie across policy areas, a complicated and at times unpredictable endeavor. Many variables can come into play once a bill is on the floor, exposing even greater heterogeneity than the leadership banked on. Such was the situation with the July 2003 vote on drug importation, one month after the slim GOP Medicare victory in the House.

Jo Ann Emerson's savvy vote exchange with Speaker Hastert enabled HR 2427 to reach the House floor without the party's blessing (HR 2427 is legislation to allow the import of FDA-approved drugs from FDA-approved sites in twenty-five industrialized countries, a bill Emerson cosponsored with fellow Republican Gil Gutknecht [Minn.]). In the past, a low-cost drug importation bill was signed into law by Democrats and Republicans alike, but it was never implemented. The law contained a "poison pill" that ensured its demise—a requirement that the secretary of health and human services certify all prescription drug imports as safe, a risk members voting for the bill knew neither the Clinton nor the Bush administration was willing to take. Thus members of Congress from both parties could stand for the importation of cheaper prescription drugs without attracting the wrath of the pharmaceutical industry, which was among the biggest of contributors to their congressional campaigns (in 2002, they donated $27 million to candidates). Drug companies are firmly against any importation of price-controlled drugs from other countries because it would force them to lower their prices in the United States (Stolberg and Harris 2003; Stolberg 2003a).

The Emerson-Gutknecht bill, however, bypassed the controversial certification process altogether, requiring FDA approval of all imported drugs and their manufacturing sites but not requiring the blessing of the health and human services secretary. Once the barrier to implementation was eliminated, drug companies went into overdrive to defeat the bill, as over six hundred of their lobbyists descended on Capitol Hill. Given its teeth back, the drug importation bill was given a low survival rate against the onslaught of attacks by the pharmaceutical industry. Even the cosponsors tried to convince leadership to limit imports to just Canada in the hopes of gaining some support from members of the caucus. The GOP leadership, of course, refused the request in the hopes of killing the bill.

Once it hit the floor, however, HR 2427 received far greater bipartisan support than expected. The bill struck a chord with both Republicans and Democrats, many of whom had constituents traveling abroad for less-expensive medications or purchasing prescription drugs on the Internet to save costs on drugs needed to treat a gamut of heath concerns, from allergies to cancer.

The unsavory tactics of the opposition only seemed to garner more attention and support for HR 2427. Many members of Congress were disturbed by the pharmaceutical industries' connection to a mailing sent by an anti-abortion group to social conservatives—a flyer that claimed the bill would make RU 486 as available as aspirin (RU 486 induces abortion in early pregnancy by blocking the body's use of progesterone). Another tactic that concerned members of Congress involved the FDA. Given the illegality of a federal agency to lobby Congress, many members were surprised when FDA bureaucrats called to "inform their votes." The FDA joined the debate on the side of the pharmaceutical companies, which it regulates, asserting that imported drugs could not be guaranteed as safe for consumers. And lastly, when the bill seemed to be gaining ground in the House among the rank-and-file Republicans, the GOP leadership reneged on their promise to Emerson and fought to defeat the bill.

The final vote on the measure took House leadership and even the bill's cosponsors by surprise—the drug importation bill not only passed, but it passed overwhelmingly, 243–186. Money pumped into drug ads seemed to have backfired. The lobbying tactics of the pharmaceutical companies, in addition to the FDA's appearance of lobbying, shifted the vote for many a member. What started in the House as a policy debate about the role and size of the federal government (such as in the previous vote on Medicare) turned into a David-and-Goliath showdown between average Americans and the drug companies.

The wild card may be how the new campaign finance law affected the outcome. One could argue that the new campaign finance law helped to decrease the dependence of members on the pharmaceutical industry. Under the new law, the drug companies could no longer contribute the large sums of soft money to the parties for congressional campaigns. House members may have factored this into their vote calculation and found that the benefits of supporting the drug companies no longer outweighed the costs. The extent to which this occurred may never be known.[2]

Regardless of the motivations, the success of HR 2427 meant that GOP leadership would head into Medicare negotiations with the Senate with a new (and unexpected) position. Needless to say, neither Representative Emerson nor Representative Gutknecht was selected as a conferee to the Medicare conference committee. Clearly, preference heterogeneity within the GOP across policy areas created a formidable barrier to strong party leadership in the House. The conference committee, composed of delegates handpicked by the GOP leadership to work out differences in the House and Senate versions of the Medicare bill, would provide greater homogeneity; all but two Democrats (both conservative) were effectively shut out of the process.

When the Medicare bill finally did emerge from conference, after much stalled negotiations throughout the summer and into the fall of 2003, the Emerson-Gutknecht drug import provisions had essentially been dropped (not surprisingly, as fifty-three senators had signed a letter in opposition to HR 2427 immediately after the House vote). The final bill would allow for drug imports under the condition that then health and human services secretary Tommy Thompson guarantee their safety (which he said he could not)—thus including the same "poison pill" that eviscerated drug import legislation in the past.

Under mounting pressure to get the Medicare bill through Congress before the Thanksgiving recess, GOP leadership finally called for a vote on November 22, another all-night squeaker of a vote, with Speaker Hastert predicting its chance of passage as "tenuous" at best. When the fifteen-minute vote was called at 3:00 AM, the initial tally clearly favored the Democrats. Instead of admitting defeat, Republican leadership pulled out all the stops, keeping the vote open for an unprecedented three hours to persuade at least five members to change their position. Secretary Thompson and GOP party leaders honed in on potential switchers on the House floor while Bush called them by cell phone. (Representative Emerson wisely left the chamber this time, after casting her "nay" vote.) By 6:00 AM the Republicans had managed to persuade three of their own and three Democrats to switch their votes. The vote was closed, and the GOP Medicare bill headed for the Senate. After withstanding filibuster attempts by Minority Leader Daschle and Senator Ted Kennedy (D-Mass.), both of whom were opposed to changes made in the conference committee, the GOP Medicare prescription drug coverage bill finally made it to the president's desk and was signed into law on December 8, 2003 (Cranford 2004).

Down-to-the-wire, contentious party line votes have become business as usual in recent Congresses. As the party unity scores illustrate, the divisive politics of the Medicare bill are less of an outlier than a recent norm. The congressional wings of both parties have grown further apart in the past thirty years, reflecting greater homogeneity within their rank and file. Congressional Republicans have grown more conservative and Democrats more liberal—as many of the conservative Southern Democrats have been replaced by Republican members of Congress. The shift is even evident in the Americans for Democratic Action (ADA) scores of the House leadership: Speaker Nancy Pelosi had an ADA score of ninety-five in 2006, while Minority Leader John Boehner had a score of five. Neither are outliers in their respective party conference or caucus. Rising homogeneity within the parties clearly facilitates strong party leadership.

But as the House votes on Medicare reform indicate, there is only so much leadership can do to rein in the troops and influence the final tally. To complicate matters, preferences within the party can shift according to policy area; thus, we are left with the conclusion that party leaders in the American political system can only lead as far and as fast as their followers want them to. Leadership has its privileges to be sure, but rank-and-file members still exert those independent judgments that constrain leadership prerogatives. In the next section, we see how the unique history, rules, norms, and traditions in each chamber of Congress place further constraints on party leadership.

III. Party Organization in Congress: The Leadership Hierarchy in the House and Senate

The major political parties are quite elaborately organized to coordinate their work in Congress. They have to be. Given the enormous workload confronting members and given the complicated committee system developed to tackle that workload, parties must be the integrative mechanisms that bring together what the division of labor pulls apart; yet the ability of House and Senate leaders to coordinate party positions and legislate party policies is constrained by the two very different institutions in which they serve.

Leadership positions in Congress are partisan positions. Although party positions are not mentioned in the Constitution (the document is in fact silent on parties), Article 2, Section 2, does mandate an institutional leader for the House of Representatives. Members must elect their own **Speaker**, and since the earliest days of the Republic, the Speaker has always been partisan, the highest-ranking party leader of the House (Peters 1990). In fact, in the period from Reconstruction to the turn of the century, Speakers were recognized more than presidents as the leaders of their party, rivaling presidential power to set and execute the party agenda and even rivaling the president in recognition among the electorate. At this time the party organization became more structured. The party leadership roles of **majority leader** and **minority leader** (and **majority whip** and **minority whip**, their assistants) developed out of the intense partisan conflict of the period, appearing in the House in the late nineteenth century and in the Senate in the first decade of the twentieth century. The institutional development of the organizational support for these leaders followed slowly (Sinclair 1983).

SPEAKER

The leader of the House of Representatives, who, in addition to being the leader of the majority party, also has administrative duties.

MAJORITY LEADER

The floor leader for the majority party in a legislature.

MINORITY LEADER

The floor leader for the minority party in a legislature.

MAJORITY WHIP

The majority party official in a legislature charged with aiding the floor leader, informing members of party positions, tracking the intentions of individual members, and attempting to persuade reluctant members to follow the party stance (when appropriate).

MINORITY WHIP

The minority party official in a legislature charged with aiding the floor leader, informing members of party positions, tracking the intentions of individual members, and attempting to persuade reluctant members to follow the party stance (when appropriate).

A. House Leadership

Although Speakers are officially elected by the entire House, the vote to elect them is essentially party line. Each party's caucus (i.e., a meeting of all party members) nominates a candidate for Speaker. All the Republicans vote for their candidate; all the Democrats for their candidate. Because the Democrats regained the majority in the 2006 elections, Nancy Pelosi's nomination at the start of the 110th Congress by the Democratic Caucus (the name of all the Democrats in the House; the Republicans use the term "Conference") effectively guaranteed that she would become the first female Speaker in the history of the United States.

The Speaker's "right hand" is the majority leader. Elected by members of his or her own party to handle the day-to-day leadership of the party, the majority leader schedules legislation; coordinates committee work; and negotiates with the president, the House minority leader, and the Senate leadership. The goal of a majority leader is to build and maintain voting coalitions and essentially to keep peace in the family (Sinclair 1983).

Next in line in the party hierarchy are the whips—named after the "whippers-in" of the hounds, in the traditional English fox hunt. Their job is to link the rank and file to the party leadership. They are the information disseminators, in-house pollsters, and vote counters. They make the party position known to all members of the party caucus; assess who is for, against, or on the fence on any given piece of legislation; try to persuade reluctant members to follow the party line; and report back to the Speaker and the majority and minority leaders with the expected vote tallies. Consequently, the whip organization for both parties is extensive, comprising a chief deputy whip and the deputy whips, assistant whips, regional whips, and zone whips. Such a large whip organization allows for many members to participate in party leadership. In addition, members can also serve on the party committees—the Democratic and Republican Steering and Policy Committees— which establish each party's legislative priorities, develop tactical strategies for passage of the party agenda, and nominate members for committees.

How exactly do members obtain seats on the party hierarchy? Races for seats in the U.S. House are, for the majority of incumbents, uncompetitive; races for seats in the U.S. House leadership, however, remain contentious.[3] As all members geared up for their reelection bids in November 2002, Democratic House members in particular were conscious of their party's leadership elections, which were to take place shortly after the congressional midterm elections. No matter which party controlled the chamber after the elections, the 108th House would have an entirely new set of Democratic leaders, as almost every seat of the Democratic party hierarchy was up for grabs. Many of those running for leadership positions spent time in other members districts, by helping their colleagues raise money and by showing support (especially for endangered incumbents), hoping their help would pay off when their fellow Democrats cast secret ballots for party leaders for the next Congress.[4] So, in addition to running *for* Congress in 2002, many House Democrats ran *in* Congress.

As a consequence of the failure of the Democrats to regain the House (and a generally poor showing by the party), Majority Leader Richard Gephardt chose to step down from his leadership post, thus producing a chain reaction in the party hierarchy. As others in the party leadership vied for his spot, their positions opened up. Term limits also created open slots for caucus chair and vice chair (Foerstel 2002b, 1449).[5] Gephardt's exit and Nancy Pelosi's election speak to the caucus-driven preference for new leadership. The Democratic party had been the majority party in the House for forty years, assuming the majority in 1954 and relinquishing control in 1994. With the election of Speaker Newt Gingrich in 1995, the Democrats stood a shocked but chastened party, having lost majority status and their leader, Speaker Tom Foley (D-Wash.), to boot. The Democrats of course reversed this situation in 2006.

Newt Gingrich's attempt to centralize power and strengthen the majority congressional party under the Speaker had much to do with the development of party organization in the House under the long tenure of Democratic leadership. Changes in the structure of the Democratic party leadership in the House have reflected changes in the role of the party in the government. It was this organization that the Republicans adopted once they took over the House in 1995, as Gingrich further centralized power to get his party's legislative agenda, dubbed the Contract with America, through the House.

I. Democratic Hegemony

Democratic leadership before 1994 had much to do with decentralization of power since the days of the revolt of Speaker Cannon (1910) and the desire to strip the Speaker of authoritarian power. During the first half of Democratic hegemony in the House—not just the unbroken forty-year period of rule but the period from the election of 1932 on—party leaders shared power with, and often were at the mercy of, committee leaders in the House. Speakers had to rely heavily on their relationships with powerful and independent committee chairs to pass legislation—that is, they relied on those who owed their positions to the safety of their seats and to their seniority on their committees, not to the party or to the

Speaker. Committee chairs were chosen strictly by their seniority, not by party loyalty; the Democratic member who had served longest on a committee was the chair (Hinckley 1971).

Recall our discussion on institutional changes in the House in the 1970s. A group of new Democratic members, frustrated by the seniority system and their inability to pass legislation important to them and their constituents, initiated a period of reform aimed at restructuring power in the House. The reform movement took power away from the committee chairs and spread it more evenly among the members. For a time, power was seemingly fragmented, and no one appeared to be able to formulate a party position in the House (Oleszek 1989; Ornstein 1975; Sheppard 1985; Smith and Deering 1990). Yet the decentralization of power to subcommittees and their leaders, and the empowerment of rank-and-file (and thus junior) members of Congress, would eventually strengthen the party; in fact, in the long run, the movement would reinvigorate the caucus and empower party leadership (Rohde 1974, 1991).

Although the committee system became more decentralized, the party leadership became more centralized. Part of 1970s reforms saw the first efforts aimed at centralizing party leadership, as party leaders were seen as more likely to be responsive to rank-and-file members than committee chairs protective of their legislative turf. More power was given to the Democratic Steering and Policy Committee (which has recently been divided into two committees), and the Speaker was given more control over that committee. Thus, Steering and Policy became the committee that recommends committee assignments for all House Democrats and subcommittee chairs for the important Appropriations Committee. Composed of the key members of the party hierarchy—the party leader is the chair, the whip is vice chair, and caucus chair is second vice chair—the Steering and Policy Committee sets the party priorities and strategy.[6]

Due to these centralizing reforms, during the last years of Democratic rule the Speaker stood atop a party hierarchy that had the potential not only to present party positions effectively but also to induce allegiance from rank-and-file members.[7] During the last years of Democratic party rule in the House, Speakers Tip O'Neill (D-Mass.) and Jim Wright (D-Tex.) claimed more power than their predecessors. For example, they had the power to appoint (with caucus approval) the Democratic members of the powerful Rules Committee. They had also been given the power to refer bills to more than one committee, either simultaneously or sequentially, and to control other aspects of the flow of legislation (Bach and Smith 1988; Collie and Cooper 1989). Thus, the clear trend was for the Speaker to become more of a true party leader, and party and House rules were shifting to give him the potential to exercise leadership powers in an effective way. Gingrich's changes at the beginning of the 104th Congress can therefore be seen as long steps in a progression but steps that clearly had precedents in the actions of his Democratic predecessors.

2. Republican Revolution

Many of Gingrich's Republican predecessors, the former minority leaders during the period of Democratic hegemony, had a strategy of attacking the opposing party publicly while working with Democratic leaders cooperatively in private. This style rankled a group of younger, more ideologically conservative Republicans at the time that Ronald Reagan assumed the presidency. Robert Michel (R-Ill., minority leader, 1983–1995), for example, would castigate the vociferous Speaker Wright for overt partisanship, yet he would temper his actions and forge compromises within and across parties to achieve some (albeit limited) legislative goals. His increasingly conservative troops wanted more forceful leadership.

As Michel's whip, Trent Lott (R-Miss.) became the first of this new breed of Southern conservative Republicans to step into a party hierarchy position. After giving up his safe seat in 1988 to run successfully for the Senate, Lott was followed briefly by Richard Cheney (R-Wyom.). Rising rapidly in the party leadership hierarchy, Cheney was considered by many to be the "future" of the House Republican party, perhaps as a future Republican Speaker. But just as suddenly as he had switched from service in the Ford White House (as chief of staff) to running for Congress, Cheney switched branches again in 1989, resigning his seat and minority whip position to accept the nomination of the first President Bush to serve as secretary of defense.

Minority Leader Michel endorsed the candidacy of his friend and fellow Illinoisan Edward Madigan (R-Ill.) to succeed Cheney as minority whip. The House GOP caucus, however, had other ideas. Despite Michel's popularity as a leader, the Republican membership chose Newt Gingrich, an outspoken conservative and the leading critic of deposed Speaker Wright. Pressure from the conservative wing of the GOP under the leadership of Gingrich led Michel to announce his retirement, after the 103d Congress.

CONTRACT WITH AMERICA

Campaign pledges made by Republican candidates for the House of Representatives prior to the 1994 election.

a. Gingrich and the 104th House Gingrich's ascent from party whip to party leader can be attributable to his leadership in the 1994 campaign. It was Gingrich who is credited with formulating the idea of a **Contract with America**, a pact on which all Republican candidates would stand as they fought to take over the House. It was Gingrich who gathered all of the Republican candidates for the House on the steps of the Capitol, had them sign the contract, and proclaimed that they would guarantee a vote on the issues in the contract within the first hundred days of the 104th Congress. And it was Gingrich to whom the new members of that Congress, in the Republican majority for the first time in forty years, looked for continued leadership (Kolodny 1996).

Not only did Gingrich become the Speaker of the House at the beginning of the 104th Congress, but he also brought with him an entire leadership team. Dick Armey of Texas became the new majority leader; if Gingrich conceived the Contract with America, Armey was its primary draftsman, a true doctrinaire, conservative on the issues that defined the Republican party in the 1994 election. Armey was one of those least happy about compromises that House Republicans had wrought with those in the White House of President George H. W. Bush, much less with conservative Democrats. The rest of the leadership team—including Majority Whip Tom DeLay (Tex.)—were all Gingrich loyalists. No room was left for dissenters within the party hierarchy.

Gingrich clearly understood the need to solidify his organizational power base if he wanted to implement the Contract with America. Thus, he moved quickly to consolidate his power through the whip organization, which comprised members appointed by DeLay (but all acceptable to Gingrich). Built on the model developed by the Democrats some years earlier, the Republican whip organization consisted of a chief deputy whip (considered part of the leadership's inner circle), thirteen deputy whips, and forty assistant whips—the most extensive in the history of the House. Using sophisticated computer and communications technology, the whip organization can contact every Republican member in a matter of minutes, guaranteeing efficient scheduling and the maximization of Republican support for party proposals.

The Steering Committee, headed by the Speaker and comprised of members of the leadership team plus seven selected committee chairs, was given the power to make all committee assignments—a critical change from how Republicans secured their committee seats prior to the 104th Congress. No aspect of the organization of the House is more important to members than the committee appointment process. Members' prestige within the institution, their ability to pass legislation that is most important to them, and their opportunities to serve their constituents are all determined by the standing legislative committees to which they are assigned (Fenno 1973). Prior to the 1994 election, Republican assignments were made by a Committee on Committees composed of the senior GOP member of each state's delegation. Most of the work was done by an executive committee—senior members of the Committee on Committees— with each region of the nation guaranteed representation. Votes for the committee seats were allotted according to the number of Republican members elected from each region. During the forty-year period in the minority, the GOP-ranking minority members of each standing committee were those with the longest service on the committees; seniority was not violated.

Led and dominated by Gingrich, the Steering Committee made the committee assignments. Furthermore, the Steering Committee recommended committee chairs to the Republican Conference. In 1995, seniority was violated in three instances to guarantee that Gingrich loyalists, members well versed in the party agenda and in fund-raising, were in key committee positions. The result was not only a leadership team but also a cadre of committee chairs who were loyal to Gingrich and dedicated to the same conservative cause.

To demonstrate that he was true to the principle of rotating those in power as stated in the Contract with America, Gingrich insisted that committee chairs serve only three terms in office. He also limited the term of the Speaker, but his limit was to be four terms, not three, to have a major influence on the next set of committee chairs as well as on those whose initial appointment he oversaw. Gingrich also stripped committee chairs of some of their powers—control over their own budgets, staff allocations, and scheduling of events—assuming those powers for himself and his lieutenants, in an effort to get the Contract with America through the House. He instituted the use of leadership task forces to draft some of the GOP-sponsored bills and to move legislation through committees that might be recalcitrant, essentially bypassing committee chair jurisdiction. Gingrich supervised aggressive use of the House rules to ensure the timing of legislation that came to the floor.

The picture was a clear one—a dominating Speaker and a loyal party. Gingrich assumed powers that were more evident than those of any Speaker of the House since "Czar" Joe Cannon (deposed in the famous Revolt of 1910). Under Gingrich's leadership, at the beginning of the 104th Congress, party rule dominated once again. In fact, every item on the Contract with America did come out of committee and was voted on by the House within the promised one hundred days. If the contract items did not all become law, it had to do with a less-committed group of Republicans in the Senate, not because of any lack of effective leadership by Speaker Gingrich and his allies.

b. The Abortive Revolt of 1997 To be sure, Gingrich's power did not remain absolute. In July 1997, a mere two and a half years after the Republicans returned to power (after forty years in the wilderness), a group of dissidents plotted against the leader who had brought them to the promised land of majority status.

The first hundred days of the 104th Congress marked the high point of Gingrich's party leadership. From that point on, the reality set in regarding how difficult it is to institute party government. In the winter of 1995 to 1996, the public blamed Gingrich and the House Republicans, not President Clinton, for the seven-day shutdown of the federal government. The standoff between the Congress and the executive branch was over the Republican-endorsed budget resolution that included cuts to domestic spending to balance the budget. Clinton vetoed the legislation, criticizing the cuts as too severe. House Republicans, led by Gingrich, then refused to pass continuing resolutions to allow the government to function until a new budget was signed. The government shutdown essentially shifted the debate: what began as congressional Republicans following through on their promise to balance the budget became conservatives pushing through yet another agenda item from the Contract with America at the expense of the greater good. Clinton emerged as a hero—a president willing to stand up to the conservative troops in the House to save important domestic programs for the greater populace.

Needless to say, the results of the conflict were evident later that year, in the 1996 elections; not only was President Clinton reelected, but the Republican majority in the House was pared to a mere eleven seats. Talk of an emerging Republican hegemony was silenced. Shortly after the new Congress convened, the House reprimanded Gingrich for ethics violations and forced him to pay a $300,000 fine. His poll ratings continued to decline, no longer the invulnerable foe of a weakened president. According to press reports, there was dissatisfaction among the conservative ideologues, as Gingrich sought compromises with President Clinton on a number of important items.

Gingrich was able to fight off what nearly developed into a full-blown coup attempt. In part, he was successful, it seems, because those plotting against him could not agree on who should replace him as Speaker. Those interested in the job fought one another, and Gingrich was the beneficiary. In the end Gingrich met with the conference and noted that he had heard the voices of dissent and would respond. Congressman Bill Paxon (N.Y.), chair of the National Republican Congressional Committee, a person once high on the list of Gingrich loyalists but actively courted by the dissidents as a potential successor to Gingrich, was removed from the leadership team (and eventually decided not to seek reelection). He was the only victim of the movement against the Speaker. The other leaders remained on board, but they were certainly viewed with less of an unwavering eye than in the past.

c. The End of the Gingrich Speakership   Speaker Gingrich was successful in fighting off earlier challenges to his leadership, but he was not able to survive the Republican electoral debacle in 1998. Gingrich was blamed for setting the strategy that led to the Republican party's loss of seats in the midterm election—a rare occurrence given that conventional wisdom has it that the party of the president—especially a president in his sixth year in office—is expected to lose seats in a midterm election. Instead, Democrats actually gained seats in November 1996. After the election debacle, Appropriations Committee chair Robert Livingston announced that he was considering a challenge to Gingrich. The Speaker saw the handwriting on the wall and announced that he would not seek reelection.

For a brief period, congressional Republicans were in disarray when Speaker designate Livingston resigned as well, but they quickly came together behind the candidacy of Dennis Hastert, who was elected Speaker without opposition from any other Republican and assumed the gavel at the beginning of the 106th Congress. Hopes were high that the conservative, low-profile, ex-high-school wrestling coach could lead the party and the House without attracting the controversy that plagued the Gingrich speakership. The leadership did not back away from its conservative ideals, as the caucus reelected Majority Leader Armey after some opposition—and after he had to give up his own ambition to succeed Gingrich—and reelected Majority Whip DeLay, the leader of the most conservative faction within the party.

d. The Post-Gingrich Years of GOP Majority Power: Hastert, the "Hammer," and Party Discipline   Although Hastert returned jurisdictional control of legislation to the standing committees (a power Gingrich had stripped away from the committees and given to leadership task forces), many of the changes instituted under Gingrich's tenure remained as the GOP leadership continued to achieve and maintain centralized command. Even the subcommittee chairs of the House Appropriations Committee, often referred to as the "College of Cardinals," were reviewed at the start of the 108th Congress. Many of the cardinals, residing in safe districts, had little problem defying leadership. The House voted to curb their power by giving the GOP Steering Committee, not the Appropriations chair, the power to appoint the cardinals—a move made to rein in in spending and ensure greater party loyalty. Seniority no longer protected their positions.

Although powerful party leadership has been a trademark of Republican House rule since 1994, the GOP leadership team of the 108th and 109th Houses was arguably the most cohesive (and centralized) of any in recent memory. Political scientist Ronald Peters goes even further, arguing that Hastert and his associates were perhaps the strongest House leadership team in *seventy-five* years (Allen 2003b, 746–47). Whereas Gingrich's tenure conjured up images of Joseph Cannon, Peters compares Hastert's speakership to that of Nicholas Longworth (R-Ohio), the House Speaker from 1925 to 1931. Longworth garnered a close-knit group of "trusted associates" to help him lead the House, unlike Cannon and his individualistic rule.

Whereas Gingrich suffered from fragmented leadership exemplified by the abortive coup in 1997, Hastert's team in the 108th and 109th Congresses offered little sibling rivalry. Even when Gingrich left, there were turf wars and conflicts between Majority Leader Armey, Majority Whip DeLay, and Conference Chair J. C. Watts (R-Okla.). Not so in the 108th and 109th Houses. The retirements of Armey and Watts and the election of DeLay as majority leader left the key players in the GOP leadership team essentially trained in the same "school"—both Speaker Hastert and Majority Whip Roy Blunt (R.-Mo.) had served as chief deputy whips under DeLay during the Gingrich years, and it was DeLay who supported his chief deputy Hastert to replace the resigning Speaker (Allen 2003b, 746–47).

Before ascending to majority leader, DeLay served eight years as the majority whip, where he earned the nickname "the Hammer"—party loyalty votes were not to be defied without repercussions under his leadership. Christopher Shays (R-Conn.) learned this the hard way when he was denied chair of the Government Reform and Oversight Committee, after defying leadership and forcing a vote on his campaign finance overhaul bill. With the election of the conservative Texan as majority leader came the expectation of strict party discipline: the GOP position would be clear; the floor debate would be controlled; the flow of legislation would be managed by the party hierarchy; and the membership would be expected to stick with intended votes, no surprises.

But as we have discussed, such deference to party is rational behavior for members when they share the same preferences on legislation. Deference to leadership must be at little cost to members' careers and, in the best case, beneficial to members' careers. Even though the GOP Conference in the 108th and 109th Houses was relatively homogeneous (thus amenable to strict party discipline), DeLay solidified party loyalty from both conservatives *and* moderates through member services, from raising campaign money to securing funds for projects back home. Through his Strategic Task Force for Organizing and Mobilizing People (STOMP), he brought out the vote for many a GOP incumbent in 2002, sending busloads of volunteers to help Republican House members in competitive districts. Seventeen out of twenty of the candidates he assisted won in the 2002 midterm elections, and not all were conservatives: DeLay even supported the campaigns of GOP moderates Jim Leach, in Iowa, and Constance Morella, in Maryland. The majority leader may have been the ardent leader of the right wing of his party, but he was also well aware that the GOP could not retain control of Congress with support of conservatives alone.

3. The Democrats Bounce Back: The 2006 Elections and the 110th House

The strong majority party organization of the Hastert/DeLay years necessitated minority party cohesion, a difficult task for the Democrats given the wide spectrum of ideological, geographical, and ethnic constituencies in their caucus. Much of the blame for the Democrats' losses in the 2002 midterms was directed at the minority party's leaders for their failure to build consensus in the heterogeneous caucus and to put forth a clear, united, and coherent party platform. The question after the 2002 election was, What exactly do the House Democrats stand for? not, What do they stand against? One reaction to this question was replacing outgoing majority leader Richard Gephardt with Nancy Pelosi, the party whip who had represented San Francisco, one of the most liberal districts in the country, since 1987.

When Pelosi won election to what was then the highest leadership position held by a woman in Congress, defeating centrists Martin Frost (D-Tex.) and Harold Ford (D-Tenn.), political pundits and the media portrayed her as the "liberal's liberal," an easy target for conservative critics and the Bush White House—Karl Rove's dream come true. Yet the new minority leader's liberalness was not nearly as much of an outlier in her party as some made it out to be. In addition, Pelosi made it clear that she understood that as minority leader she must appeal not only to her liberal base but to Democratic centrists as well.

Pelosi and the Democrats illustrated how well they understood this need to go beyond the liberal base in the 2006 election cycle. Pelosi, along with DCCC chair Rahm Emanuel (Ill.), actively sought out and gave strong support to more centrist Democratic candidates in districts where it would have been very difficult, if not impossible, for a liberal Democrat to win (Dewan and Kornblut 2006). This move paid handsome dividends as the party took back the House for the first time since 1995. What remains to be seen, however, is how the Democrats will perform with their newfound control. Early results indicate more of the same high levels of party unity, but with a different majority party.

4. The Backbone of House Leadership: The Whip Systems

Both the majority and minority leaders rely heavily on their respective whips to garner support for party policies. As Minority Whip Roy Blunt explains, "The whip should know the members better than anybody else in the leadership and know the whole conference better than anybody else in the building" (Allen 2003a, 750). Whips build majorities by knowing each and every district and by understanding the needs of members—a seat on a specific committee, a project of importance back home, or even a spot in the whip organization. Whips can come under fire, as Blunt well knows. Fingers pointed at him when a GOP-sponsored bill that allowed companies to offer workers compensatory time off instead of extra pay had to be pulled from its floor debut for lack of votes. Unions had lobbied heavily against the bill. Misjudgment on where Republican members stood on the issue (the job of the whip) led to an embarrassing defeat for GOP leaders (Martinez 2003b).[8]

The responsibilities of this demanding job—from polling to persuasion—necessitate an extensive organization, the development of which is only recent. Although the majority and minority whips have been in operation since the late nineteenth century (having emerged out of the intense partisanship of the era), the whip organization has not been an integral part of the leadership structure until recent times. (This section draws on Rohde 1991, 82–93; Ripley 1964, 1967; Sinclair 1983.) During the New Deal period, the sectional and ideological conflicts within the Democratic party necessitated the addition of a phalanx of regional whips to assist the majority whip. Yet Speaker Sam Rayburn rarely relied on the new whips, instead relying on his personal relationships with the rank and file to rally support for legislation. Either appointed or elected by the members from their area, the regional whips owed little loyalty to the Speaker and the majority leader. In fact, during the Kennedy and Johnson administrations (when New Frontier and Great Society programs split the party, on both ideological and regional grounds), these whips often went against the party leader's policy preferences.

Much of this rebellious individualism changed during the Nixon administration, when the majority Democrats saw the need to organize in opposition to Republican policy initiatives. They enlarged their whip organization to include a chief deputy; three deputies; and at-large whips representing the Women's Caucus, the Black Caucus, and the first-year members. The whip and the chief deputy whip were given ex officio seats on the Steering and Policy Committee. With increased numbers, status, and visibility, the whip organization began to play both the role of persuading members to support the party and the traditional role of informing members of the party position, counting votes, and reporting back to leadership. With continued expansion throughout the 1980s, the majority whip organization at the end of the Democratic period of hegemonic rule in the House included 40 percent of the members of the caucus.[9]

When the Republicans rose to majority status in 1994, they based their leadership structure on this Democratic model.

The greatest challenge to party leadership for both Democrats and Republicans in the House remains the electoral connection—given that members owe their seats to constituents back home, they are inevitably more loyal to their districts than to their parties when conflicting interests arise. Thus, the leadership structure, in particular the whip system, has developed over time to accommodate the electoral, constituent-driven needs of members. Remember, the extent of party control in the House is contingent upon the value members place on participation in the party hierarchy and in deference to its leadership.

The constraints on strong party leadership in the House are even greater in the more heterogeneous, individualized Senate. The Senate's norms, traditions, and unique historical development preclude strong party control. Thus, the institutional differences between the House and Senate limit the cohesiveness of party leadership across the two chambers.

B. Senate Leadership

"The purpose of the Senate is entirely different from the purpose of the House of Representatives. From the beginning it was intended to be a deliberative body where the expenditure of time and the exchange of views should determine judgment in any pending

Table 11.1   Party Leadership in the House, June 2007

Democrats

Speaker of the House	Nancy Pelosi (Calif.)
Majority Leader	Steny Hoyer (Md.)
Majority Whip	James E. Clyburn (S.C.)
Caucus Chair	Rahm Emanuel (Ill.)
Vice Chair	John Larson (Conn.)
Democratic Congressional Campaign Committee Chair	Chris Van Hollen (Md.)
Steering and Policy Committee Chair	Nancy Pelosi (Calif.)

Republicans

Minority Leader	John Boehner (Ohio)
Minority Whip	Roy Blunt (Mo.)
Conference Chair	Adam Putnam (Fla.)
Vice Chair	Kay Granger (Tex.)
National Republican Congressional Committee Chair	Tom Cole (Okla.)
Policy Committee Chair	Thaddeus McCotter (Mich.)

Source: www.house.gov.

Table 11.2   Party Leadership in the Senate, June 2007

Democrats

President Pro Tempore	Robert C. Byrd (W. Va.)
Majority Leader	Harry Reid (Nev.)
Assistant Majority Leader (Democratic Whip)	Richard Durbin (Ill.)
Caucus Chair	Harry Reid (Nev.)
Vice Chair	Charles Schumer (N.Y.)
Policy Committee Chair	Byron Dorgan (N. Dak.)
Democratic Senatorial Campaign Committee Chair	Charles Schumer (N.Y.)

Republicans

President	Richard Cheney (Wyom.)
Minority Leader	Mitch McConnell (Ky.)
Assistant Minority Leader (Republican Whip)	Trent Lott (Miss.)
Conference Chair	Jon Kyl (Ariz.)
Vice Chair	John Cornyn (Tex.)
Policy Committee Chair	Kay Bailey Hutchison (Tex.)
National Republican Senatorial Committee Chair	John Ensign (Nev.)

Source: www.senate.gov.

matter" (quoted in Binder and Smith, 1997, 29). Senator Royal Copeland's 1926 analysis of the founders' intent dovetails well with George Washington's classic analogy that the Senate was to be the "saucer" to cool the passions of the more popular House. A slow, deliberative body created to temper majority rule, characterized by consensus and compromise—not exactly the makings for strong party government.

While majorities work their will in the House, minorities wield far greater power in the Senate.[10] For example, in the 108th Congress, a small group of senators blocked drilling in the Arctic National Wildlife Refuge (ANWR) even though the House already passed the legislation in its energy bill. A single senator blocked the promotions of more than 850 air force officers in an effort to secure four cargo planes for the National Guard back home.[11] Such obstructionist and dilatory tactics available to individual senators are unheard of in the majority-minded House.

Perhaps the most important constraint on strong party governance in the Senate is the tradition of unlimited debate—the filibuster. Any single senator can prevent a vote on a bill or a resolution by speaking indefinitely or by offering amendments or motions to delay. According to Senate Rule 22 (the rule on the cloture vote), sixty members are needed to break a filibuster, end debate, and bring the bill up for consideration. Thus, the Senate majority leader cannot move any controversial legislation through the chamber if a mere forty-one senators oppose it.[12]

Traditionally, the filibuster is employed to prevent the majority party from enacting their preferred legislation without accounting for the preferences of the minority. But in the 108th Senate, Democrats employed the filibuster for a new purpose: to prevent conservative judicial nominees from being voted on. Battles over controversial judicial nominees are intensely partisan, namely, because the ideological makeup of the courts can affect such hot-button policy issues as abortion, gun control, and states' rights. For this reason, the partisan core of a member's constituency pays close attention to judicial nominations, and it is this core that consistently turns up to vote in primary elections. Thus, partisan confirmation hearings in the Senate translate into vote mobilization on election day (Dlouhy 2002).

Historically, however, no nominee approved by the Senate Judiciary Committee had ever been prevented from a floor vote by the minority party (Dlouhy 2003, 1078). Senate Republicans did put holds on some of Clinton's lower-court nominees to prevent them from advancing out of the Judicial Committee, but no filibusters were employed to block a vote on their confirmation. Thus, the Democratic filibusters of Bush's appeals court nominees, Priscilla Owen, Miguel Estrada (who eventually rescinded his name), and William Pryor, infuriated the Republicans. GOP senators argued that the constitutional duty of the Senate to advise and give consent to the president on nominations implied a vote to approve or reject a nominee—the filibuster should not be used to block judicial nominations. In fact, in February 2004, President Bush used his recess appointment power to place Pryor on the bench without Senate confirmation. Though the appointment circumvented the Democratic filibuster, recess appointees can serve only until the beginning of the next Congress, in this case about nine months.

Not able to garner enough support to end the Democratic filibusters, then majority leader Frist in spring 2005 moved to change the rules and employee the so-called nuclear option—amend the Senate rules to allow a filibuster on a judicial nominee to be ended by a simple majority, rather than a sixty-vote supermajority. This option was averted when a bipartisan group of Senators—termed "The Gang of 14"—worked out a compromise in which they agreed to allow a vote on three of President Bush's nominees, effectively agreed to allow votes to be blocked on two others, and agreed to limit the use of the filibuster on future judicial nominees to "extraordinary circumstances." But this compromise is tenuous at best, and only applies to judicial nominees. Because of the ever-present threat of filibusters and the fact that one senator can place a hold on legislation, nominations, and even promotions, the primary job of the senate majority leader is that of chief negotiator. As the Senate does not have a powerful Rules Committee to schedule floor debate, the flow of legislation onto the floor is arranged through unanimous consent agreements. These decrees are hammered out by the majority leader and negotiated by the party leadership in consultation with committee leaders and other concerned senators. Unanimous consent agreements outline the terms of debate and the amendments to be offered, their order, and even how long to debate each one. The majority leader must constantly confer with allies, to be certain that they are all on board; and, at the same time, the majority leader must work closely with the minority leader, to be certain the other party will not disrupt agreed-upon arrangements. The legislative schedule is even changed to accommodate, say, an individual senator who cares about a particular vote but cannot attend the Senate session on a certain day. Individual egos must be stroked, with individual personalities taken into account and individual agendas accommodated. Senate party leaders must be managers and persuaders—they must cajole and coax, negotiate and compromise. (On these aspects of the role of the majority leader, see Sinclair 1990.)

Gone are the days when the Senate was an intimate club with its own social hierarchy and culture, characterized by unequal power distribution; gone are the days when a freshman was "expected to keep his mouth shut, not to take the lead in floor fights, to listen and learn" (Matthews 1960, 93; Sinclair 1989, 18). The transformation of the Senate from an institution dominated by powerful senior committee chairs and deferential junior members resulted much in part from the similar pressures that prompted institutional change in the House. An influx of newly elected Northern liberal Democratic senators in the 1958 and 1964 elections infused the Senate with more heterogeneous policy preferences. Conservative chairs and apprentice norms presented formidable barriers to the advancement of the more liberal newcomers and the more liberal majority policy preferences. In addition, the rise in complex issue areas from the 1970s on meant senators could no longer afford to specialize. Committees and subcommittee positions expanded, staff resources increased, and there was greater access to media. The result was a Senate where everyone was influential (Sinclair 1989). Harry Reid is no Lyndon Baines Johnson, the intimidating Texan Democratic majority leader from 1955 to 1961, but in the modern Senate, LBJ's tactics would not necessarily work. Senators are more autonomous and difficult to control; modern senate leadership is about management, not strong-arm tactics.

Parties do "organize" the Senate (e.g., make committee assignments), but their leaders are not given the powers and resources held by their counterparts in the House. The majority leader is responsible for scheduling floor debate and for providing leadership for the majority party's positions, but that person is not given the tools to do so without significant cooperation from colleagues. To contrast the constraints to party leadership across the House and the Senate, we turn to the battle to get the Bush 2003 tax cut package through the GOP-controlled Congress. In many ways the tax battle represented not a clash between parties but a clash between institutions: the majoritarian, partisan House, with its strictly disciplined leadership team and strong whip organization, versus the individualized Senate, where bipartisan agreement on legislation is paramount and where unanimous consent agreements are the norm. Constraints faced by the GOP leadership in coordinating the party's position on the tax cut legislation across the House and Senate speak to the difficulty of "responsible," strong party governance in the American political system.

IV. Institutional Constraints on Strong Party Government: The 2003 Tax Cut Package

The Republicans had a fleeting hold on unified government in 2001. At the start of the 107th Congress, majority status in the fifty-fifty-split Senate went to the Republicans only because of Vice President Dick Cheney's constitutionally granted role as tiebreaker;[13] the GOP held the House by only six votes; and Republican president George W. Bush won election to the White House with fewer popular votes than his opponent. But Republicans would see their unified government, the first since the Eisenhower administration in 1954, slip from their hands in a matter of months. In May 2001, Senator James Jeffords (R-Vt.) abandoned the GOP and declared himself an independent who would caucus with the Democrats. The balance of power in the Senate shifted to the Democrats, and the government was yet again under divided control.

Bush campaigned hard in 2002 to regain unified Republican control, getting personally involved in fund-raising and even candidate selection in Senate and House races. Bush's top adviser, Karl Rove, sent the president to districts and states where GOP candidates faced tough elections—a risky strategy that put the president's reputation on the line, but it paid off. Republican congressional victories solidified the party's hold on the House and shifted control of the Senate back to the GOP. With the Congress and the White House back under Republican control, the party was under pressure to produce before the 2004 elections. First priority: tax cuts. Bush considered it a political imperative to demonstrate to voters that he not only cared about the economy but was actively doing something about it—something his father failed to do and some-thing his father ultimately paid for, in his loss to Clinton, in 1992.

On May 23, 2003, President Bush won a substantial political victory, with the passage in the House and Senate of the $350 billion economic stimulus package, including tax cuts, state aid, and child tax credits—twenty-five million checks of up to $400 per child would be sent to families in the summer of 2003. The final bill, the third largest tax cut in American history, was less than one-half of what Bush had initially demanded, but, given the rancor within the Republican party over what the tax cuts would look like, Bush found himself less concerned with the details of the legislation and more concerned with just getting the legislation passed.

Although Bush's original proposal to Congress demanded $726 billion in tax cuts, the House GOP leaders proposed a $550 billion package—as deep as they believed they could cut without alienating the moderates needed for a majority vote passage. On the morning of April 10, Speaker of the House Dennis Hastert made a handshake deal with Senate majority leader Bill Frist in their budget negotia-tions—the two agreed to hold the line at the House number.

But hours later, the rookie Senate majority leader made a criti-cal blunder. To secure votes for the stimulus package in the Senate, Frist promised GOP moderates Olympia Snowe (R-Maine) and George Voinovich (R-Ohio) that tax cuts would not exceed $350 billion. Neither senator would vote for any bill containing deeper cuts, and without their support Frist could not get the tax cut through the closely divided Senate. Although senators can not fili-buster budget resolutions, the slim 51–49 GOP majority in the Sen-ate demanded Frist's leadership to keep Republican moderates from bolting. When Charles Grassley, the chair of the Finance Com-mittee, came up with the deal amenable to moderate Republicans, Frist and Budget Committee chair Don Nickles (R-Okla.) signed on.

Frist, however, failed to inform Speaker Hastert of the behind-closed-doors deal with the two moderate senators, a deal that would ultimately cut the president's tax cut plan in half. Word leaked out that Frist had reneged on his handshake deal with the Speaker. Naturally, Hastert, DeLay, and the GOP House leadership were furious. But having made a public promise on the floor of the Senate, Frist could not back down. His reputation as majority leader meant standing behind the Grassley deal. Ninety-six days into his new job, he had just placed himself at odds with party leadership in the House and the president.

Tensions within the Republican party were at an all-time high after Frist's breach of the unwritten House-Senate GOP leadership rule of "no surprises" (Stevens and Taylor 2003, 932). It was clear that neither side would budge, with the Republican Senate standing firm at $350 billion and the Republican House at $550 billion. Focused on getting tax cut legislation to his desk, Bush dispatched Vice President Dick Cheney to Congress to negotiate a deal within his party, between House conservatives and moderate senators. Instead of having to go to a divisive conference committee, where chances for an expedient resolution would be low, Cheney met with House Ways and Means chair Bill Thomas (R-Calif.) and Senator Voinovich. Cheney proposed early expiration dates for tax cuts demanded by the House, to reach the Senate-imposed cost ceiling. For example, "sunset" clauses essentially moved the expiration date of capital gains and dividend taxes to 2008 (back from 2009), to save $29 billion (Cochran 2003, 3076). With conservative House Republicans (represented by Thomas) and moderate senators (represented by Voinovich) on board, Cheney then sealed the deal with Senate majority leader Frist.

Cheney brokered the deal and broke the tie—the final vote in the Senate was 51–50. Snowe and two other Senate GOP moderates, John McCain (Ariz.) and Lincoln Chafee (R.I.), voted against their party, unconvinced that sunset clauses would keep costs down in the long run—members know full well that reinstating an already cut tax can be political suicide. Two Democrats, Zell Miller (Ga.) and Ben Nelson (Neb.), voted with the GOP when the final plan included aid to states, a priority for these two former governors. With the package then passing in the House 231–200, Bush could finally sign a tax cut into law.

Frist's breach did serious damage to relations between House and Senate Republicans, a stumble due much in part to his inexperience. Frist's predecessor, Trent Lott, the Senate GOP party leader for six and a half years, was forced to step down after making public comments supportive of Strom Thurmond's 1948 segregationist presidential campaign. At the start of the 108th Congress, the Senate GOP elected a conservative, inexperienced senator, Bill Frist, to take his place as majority leader. Having been a cardiac surgeon before being elected in 1994—that is, having no prior service in public office—Frist certainly lacked an understanding of the institutional norms and constraints on majority party leadership in the Senate. As Senate Democratic leader Tom Daschle (S.Dak.) explains, "Bill Frist is learning what it is to be the leader of a majority with 51 votes. You have to earn that majority every day with every bill and every amendment and every vote. That learning process can be excruciating" (Hulse 2003, A18).

But the conflicts across the institutions and within the GOP ranks did not stop at passage of the new tax law. When Democratic senator Blanche Lincoln (Ark.) made it clear to the American public that the children of 6.5 million low-income families were left out of the new tax credit, the Senate GOP leaders moved quickly to mitigate political damage. In a practically unanimous vote, senators passed an extension of the child tax credit to the excluded families, a reluctant vote by many Republicans (exemplified by Senator Lott's finger-down-the-throat, gagging gesture, to signal his disgust at his own aye vote). Even though conservative senators are ideologically opposed to extending benefits to millions of families who pay little or no federal income tax, all senators are elected statewide and have thousands of low-income constituents that would benefit from the tax credit extension. With the 2004 election looming, the White House wanted to neutralize attacks by Democrats who claimed that the Bush tax cut was unfair to the working poor. Thus, the administration urged the House GOP leadership to follow the lead of the Senate GOP leadership and pass the extension.

The president's demand was met by defiance in the House. Still fuming over the Senate majority leader's breach and the Senate-imposed ceiling on tax cuts, House majority leader DeLay outrightly rejected the Senate's bill to extend the child tax credit. House conservatives railed that the tax package was to stimulate the economy, not redistribute wealth; if the Senate and the White House wanted to give tax relief to people who don't pay federal income tax, then they would have to give more relief to those that do. By adding the "poison pill" of more benefits to middle- and upper-class families to the Senate's child tax credit to low-income families, the House leadership essentially killed the bill, knowing the deficit-averse Senate would consider the added benefits too costly (Firestone 2003a).

These institutional clashes have less to do with clashes between the parties than clashes within the GOP across the governing institutions. Speaking to this very point, Republican House member Jennifer Dunn (Wash.) explains, "We call the Democrats our opponents and the Senate our enemy" (Martinez 2003a, 1733). Representative Bill Thomas, the House Ways and Means chair, is often overtly contemptuous of bills sent over by the Senate: "Sounds like a Senate product" (Firestone 2003b). Often heard in the 108th House were the voices of frustration directed toward fellow Republicans in the Senate who were not acting like Republicans. "Someone's slipped something into the water over there" (Foley, quoted by Hulse 2003, A18). Truth be told, the GOP in the Senate were acting like senators, well aware that the "Senate is a 60-vote marathon, not a 50-vote sprint" (Korologos, quoted by Stevens and Taylor 2003, 934). House members have a tough time accepting the Senate reality that one lone senator can hold up legislation, while forty-one can block most legislation indefinitely.

The tax cut and child tax credit extension battles also highlight the fact that House members, senators, and the president are beholden to different constituencies—district, statewide, and national. The president must appeal to the nation as a whole—a constraint that pulled Clinton's policy positions from left to center and pulls Bush's from right to center. House members—the majority of whom hold relatively safe seats, on account of the incumbency advantage, redistricting, and rising homogeneity within their districts—can take more-extreme views (and often have more incentives to advocate extreme positions, to secure their electoral base at home). With six-year terms and more heterogeneous constituencies, senators are less persuaded by party positions than their House colleagues. Thus, the president, as party leader, can put only so much pressure on his party's congressional leaders, and party leaders can only put so much pressure on their copartisans.

Pressure from party leadership can backfire with great ramifications. As previously noted, in spring 2001, James Jeffords, frustrated over Republican leadership tactics in the Senate, stunned his party by leaving the GOP to become an independent and caucus with the Democrats. His switch shifted the balance of power in the Senate to the Democrats. The Republicans lost their majority status and all of the powers that come with it, from agenda setting to committee chairs. Senate leadership is well aware of the price of defection.

Given the relatively close divisions between the parties in recent Senates, moderates of both parties have arguably gained more leverage and bargaining power. Their votes are often crucial to success or failure, and in some cases they can force action on their own (recall "The Gang of 14" from earlier in this chapter). Republican moderates such as Susan Collins and Olympia Snowe (both from Maine) and Arlen Specter (Pa.) and Democratic moderates like Ben Nelson (Neb.) and Ken Salazar (Colo.) and independent (and former Democrat) Joe Lieberman (Conn.) often play key roles in policymaking in the Senate (Smith 2006).

The moderates also incur costs associated with bucking the party line outside of Congress. The goal of the Conservative Club for Growth, for example, funded conservative challengers to the GOP moderates in the 2004 primaries. The club's primary targets—legislators who resisted deeper tax cuts and who chiseled away at the Bush tax plan—were members of the centrist Republican Main Street Partnership, which includes the Senate "mod squad." Senator Arlen Specter is one such target, having voted against Bush's full tax cut proposal in 2001. The club contributed generously to Specter's primary challenger, Representative Patrick Toomey (R-Penn.), a die-hard supporter in the House of larger tax cuts (Firestone 2003c). Specter barely survived the challenge.

V. THE PRESIDENT AS LEADER OF PARTY IN GOVERNMENT

In such a political system where party leadership is constrained by the institutions in which it operates, what role exactly does the president play as the leader of his party in government? Political analysts are virtually unanimous in agreeing that presidents play the primary role in setting the congressional agenda (Fishel 1985; Jones 1988b, 1988c; Kingdon 1984; Light 1983). It is the president's program that is presented to Congress, the president's budget to which Congress responds, and even the president's cabinet that defends his proposals in hearings on Capitol Hill. The tax cut signed into law in 2003 was the Bush tax cut, not the Bush-Frist-Grassley-DeLay-Thomas (among others) tax cut or even the GOP tax cut. The president clearly serves as the leader of his party in government, by setting the agenda and defining the issues—a process that begins as early as the presidential campaigns, when candidates make promises and set goals for their administrations.

In 2000 candidate Bush made such an agenda-setting campaign promise to seniors: as president, he would see to it that prescription drug benefits for Medicare recipients were signed into law. Once in office, the message from the president to his party in Congress was clear: do whatever it takes to get a Medicare drug bill to his desk before the 2004 election. His motivations were twofold. As president of a nation with more and more citizens voicing concerns about their health care coverage in a time of stock market declines and economic uncertainty, Bush vowed to overhaul the financially troubled entitlement program before the upcoming baby boomer generation retires. As party leader, Bush aimed to take the expansion of Medicare, an entitlement program long associated with the Democratic party, and make it a Republican priority. In the process he would not only neutralize a volatile issue for the GOP in the 2004 election, but he would secure the votes of seniors, a critical voting bloc, especially in such swing states as Florida (the pivotal state in 2000). Similarly, Bill Clinton, as leader of the Democratic party, took a traditionally Republican issue—getting welfare recipients to seek work—and saw to it that it was signed into law, thereby neutralizing GOP criticism of his party in the 1996 presidential and congressional elections.

As much as agenda setting is important, getting that agenda from the White House through the House and Senate and back is the president's greatest challenge. Thus, a president leads his party in government by convincing legislators that following the chief executive's lead is in their best interest. For this reason, Richard Neustadt describes presidential power as essentially the "power to persuade" (Neustadt 1960, 1976), a description as accurate at the dawn of the twenty-first century as when Neustadt wrote his seminal book on the presidency four decades prior.

But, as demonstrated by the difficulties faced by Bush on his top domestic priorities—tax cuts and Medicare drug benefits— persuasion is a formidable and complicated task in a political system where members of Congress are more beholden to their constituencies than to their president. To convince his party's conservative lawmakers to expand Medicare, Bush employed the full force of his leadership team in the House, with the addition of Vice President Cheney and Health and Human Services Secretary Tommy Thompson. The office of Majority Whip Blunt served as the "war room," for briefing lawmakers on the details of the 692-page bill to add prescription drug benefits to Medicare (Allen and Graham-Silverman 2003). But many were not persuaded. Although a Rose Garden ceremony with President Bush and Senator Ted Kennedy (D-Mass.) cosigning a Medicare benefit bill might enhance the reelectability of Bush, a bipartisan signing of a "prescription drug giveaway" would not play well to conservatives back home.

Uncertainty also works against the presidential ability to persuade members. With the major changes to Medicare not in effect until 2006, GOP House members in particular were concerned about political backlash when the reforms kicked in. Facing reelection every two years, they would be more susceptible to criticism of any new Medicare law in 2006 than a second-term president or, in the case of a failed reelection bid by Bush, more susceptible than a Democratic president not responsible for the reform. Because of uncertainty about the outcome of legislation and how it would affect their constituents, members were far more cautious than the president is on this issue. It is uncertainty like this that often makes it difficult for the president to court members, even those of his own party. As Representative Jim McCrery (R-La.) explained, "Social security is number crunching, but Medicare is health care and harder to predict" (Rogers 2003). Members are looking not just for any legislation but for the right legislation.

VI. POLITICIANS VIEW PARTY IN GOVERNMENT

Hesitant legislators, weighing out the costs to their own careers of supporting controversial presidential proposals, require a president who is willing to go the extra mile for them. President Bush made enormous efforts in the 2002 midterm elections to do just that, becoming personally involved in the reelection campaigns of his fellow Republicans, even traveling to fifteen states in the last five days before the election, to support GOP candidates in tough races. Bush's goal, as party leader, was to get as many Republicans in Congress as possible to support his agenda while demonstrating his commitment to campaign for members in their districts and states if position taking on presidential priorities had placed them at odds with their constituents. This paid off well for President Bush, as his party gained seats in a midterm election (a rarity) and many members were beholden to the president for his efforts. He was obviously not in such an advantageous position during the 2006 elections, when many GOP members were not eager to have the increasingly unpopular President Bush in their states or districts. The GOP lost control of Congress, and many members laid the blame for this development, rightly or wrongly, at the feet of the president. This failure, combined with his lame-duck status and his lack of popularity, have emboldened an increasing number of Republicans in both Houses to publicly oppose the president. Consider this comment from Senator Jeff Sessions (R-Ala.) on CNN's *American Morning* regarding President Bush's lobbying efforts for his immigration reform plan, which ultimately died in the Senate on June 28, 2007:

> I think the president is wrong to push this piece of legislation so hard after we've demonstrated the flaws that are in it. He needs to back off. He needs to help us write a better bill and not push a bill that so many of us can't support (June 12, 2007).

America is not a parliamentary democracy. We do not elect presidents and give them a mandate to push their policy alternatives through Congress. Congress is a separate branch of the government: representatives and senators have separate electoral bases from the president. Therefore, the ability of the president to lead his party in Congress will depend on two criteria: first, institutional constraints, where his agenda falls relative to the preferences of his party's majority in the House and of the moderates who can uphold or defeat a filibuster in the Senate; and, second, external factors—from scandal to war to the economy—all of which affect the ability of a president to persuade even members of his own party to follow

www.CoxAndForkum.com

his lead. A president can be a party leader, but nothing in our system guarantees that he will play that role, much less that he will play it effectively.

WEBSITES

www.house.gov and **www.senate.gov**: Each house of the Congress maintains a website with links to member offices, committee offices, leadership offices; the sites also provide references to pending House and Senate business.

www.cq.com: The *Congressional Quarterly* website provides up-to-date information on legislation pending before the Congress and on breaking political events.

www.hillnews.com and **www.rollcall.com**: These websites for the two newspapers devoted to coverage of Capitol Hill provide behind-the-scenes stories of congressional policymaking and politics.

www.gpoaccess.gov/crecord/index.html: The main page of the *Congressional Record*, the official record of the proceedings and debates of the U.S. Congress.

www.c-span.org/: The main page of C-SPAN, the family of cable channels that covers Congress and other government-related events.

CHAPTER 12

The Role of Political Parties at the Dawn of the Twenty-first Century

The CNN/YouTube/Google Democratic presidential debate at The Citadel in Charleston, S.C., July 23, 2007. The rise of the Internet is one of the most important developments for political parties and elections as we move through the early years of the twenty-first century.

Modern political parties were in their infancy at the dawn of the nineteenth century. They were dominating the American political landscape at the dawn of the twentieth century. What can be said of them in these, the early years of the new century?

To this point, we have examined the historical development of political parties and the electoral process, and the context in which they currently exist, from an empirical point of view. That is, we have analyzed the role played by parties in nominations and elections, explored why elections have been decided as they were, described the processes, and explained how variations in processes influence results. Then we looked at the implications of some of the aspects of those processes and of institutional linkages for politics and for governance.

In this final chapter, we move from empirical analysis to evaluation. Specifically, we look at how well the electoral process and political parties within that process play the roles that have been assigned to them in the American system of government.

I. THE ROLE OF ELECTIONS

Recall Professor Finer's definition of the role that elections must play if a democracy is to function effectively:

> The real question . . . is not whether the government deigns to take notice of popular criticisms and votes, but whether it can be voted out of office or forced by some machinery or procedures to change its policy, above all against its own will. (Finer 1949, 219)

In the most theoretical terms, the answer to Professor Finer's question with regard to the American system is that the government can be forced to change its policies against its own will; the government can be voted out of office. But in an empirical sense, is that what elections mean in the United States? Do elections today give the citizenry a chance to decide on the course of action that their government will take? These questions are more easily posed than answered.

A. The Context of Federalism

It should come as no surprise that the answer to the basic question will vary depending upon whether one is analyzing federal, state, or local elections. Once again we must be alert not to generalize about the electoral process in the United States, when the process at the federal level is different from that at the state level (and states differ significantly from each other), and the processes in the various states are different from those in localities throughout the country.

I. Presidential Elections

Presidential elections have come closest to meeting the criterion set forth here. The American public has shown that it is willing and able to remove presidents when the policies of the government have consequences that displease the citizenry. And, of course, it has shown that it will retain presidents and policies with which it is in agreement. A number of linkages are implied in that conclusion.

First, we assume that the policies of the president and those of the government are the same. We know this assumption to be false in part because separation of powers necessitates that nearly all policies are the result of compromise. But we also know that the public makes this linkage even if it is not in fact accurate.

Second, we assume that the consequences of governmental policies were the ones desired or at least foreseen when those policies were implemented. Again, we know that this linkage is partial at best. For example, the success or failure of an administration's agricultural policies is dependent on the weather, advances in technology, and the actions of other nations as well as on the wisdom of the policies put forth. Again, however, we know that the public holds the president accountable for the consequences of his (and often others') actions, not for the intentions of those actions, and so the assumed linkage has the effect hypothesized.

Third, we assume that all citizens view all policies in the same way and vote accordingly. Again, we know that this linkage is not complete. From the time of Madison, American politicians have recognized and dealt with the diversity of interests throughout this land. Even in landslide presidential elections approximately two out of every five voters support the losing candidate. In any election those supporting any candidate do not all do so for the same reasons. But, once again, a perfect linkage is not necessary. What is necessary is for a critical mass of citizens to express dissatisfaction with the policies and performance (either general or specific) of an administration and to translate those feelings into support for another candidate.

Given the standard stipulated here, a number of the presidential elections discussed in chapter 9 meet the criterion of serving as an appropriate expression of the views of the citizenry in opposition to the actions of the government. In the election of 1992, as the most recent example, the Clinton campaign emphasized "the economy, stupid." The voters agreed with the Democratic candidate that the Republican incumbent had not been successful in economic terms. Candidate Clinton portrayed himself as an agent of change; the public chose him on that basis.

The elections of 1932, 1952, 1960, 1968, 1976, and 1980 all can also be interpreted as examples of elections in which citizens chose to change the direction of policy. Obvious differences exist among these examples. The election of 1932 is described as a critical election in which public attachment to the major political parties underwent major changes. In 1952 and 1968, dissatisfaction with the policies of incumbent administrations was strong enough to convince Presidents Truman and Johnson not to seek reelection. The nominees of their parties were unable to dissociate themselves sufficiently to avoid defeat. In 1976 and again in 1980 sitting presidents lost to challengers whose campaigns emphasized the policies that were in place. In each case, the public chose to replace a government holding policies of which it disapproved.

The elections of 1964, 1972, 1984, 1996, and 2004—elections in which incumbents were reelected—can be seen as cases in which the public said, in effect, that it preferred policies enacted by the sitting president to those proposed by the challenger.[1] In the first three elections, in 1964, 1972, and 1984, challengers proposed truly radical changes in the policies in place—and those radical changes were rousingly rejected (Converse, Clausen, and Miller 1965; Miller et al. 1976; Wayne 1984; Shanks and Miller 1990). In the 1996 election, as we have already seen, Republican candidate Dole attacked President Clinton on issues of character as much as policy; the public voted to stay the course with a president whose policies had proven to be popular. Multiple interpretations of the 2004 presidential election have been offered, but the most plausible seems to be that George W. Bush made the election primarily about terrorism and security, and was able to convince a majority of voters that based on past performance he was better equipped to handle those issues than was Senator Kerry.

In each of these cases, the claim that the electorate expressed its views on the policies of the day through the ballot box can be supported. Presidential elections are highly salient. Although incumbents have some advantages and it can be argued that the "right" issues are not discussed and that the electorate lacks requisite sophistication, the argument can also be sustained that presidential elections fulfill the role they were designed to play in American politics. Despite relatively common complaints to the contrary, presidential elections in the United States offer Americans a real, meaningful choice on election day. And at least on the high salience issues of the day, Americans appear to be relatively well equipped to make that choice.

2. Congressional Elections

What about elections to other federal offices—to the Senate and the House of Representatives—when the campaigns, the candidates, and the issues are not as visible to the public as they are in presidential elections?

In these cases, the findings are mixed, as are the views of political scientists. In chapters 6 and 7 we presented a good deal of evidence demonstrating incumbent advantages in House elections (but see Stonecash, forthcoming, for a different view of incumbency). Senate incumbents have fewer advantages—and challengers have greater assets—but recent Senate elections suggest that incumbents in those races are not without strengths. Do these elections serve to link the views of the public with the policies of the government? Or are incumbents so protected as to erase the connection between elections and outcomes that Professor Finer defines as necessary?

On their face, elections in many individual districts and/or states do not seem to demonstrate the prescribed connection. Yet there are a few cases in which key issues have led to the defeat of an incumbent and thus indirectly to a representative's reflecting the views of constituents in a different manner. For instance, the defeat of Congresswoman Marjorie Margolies-Mezvinsky (D-Pa., 1993–1995), who cast the deciding vote in favor of President Clinton's budget and tax package in 1993, is generally attributed to that vote. She had barely won election in 1992 in wealthy Montgomery County. In 1994 she lost to the same Republican candidate, John Fox, who used the vote over and over in the campaign to show that Margolies-Mevzinsky opposed tax cuts, an unpopular position among voters.

But more frequently incumbents seeking reelection are sent back to Washington. Over 90 percent of House incumbents seeking to return are successful in election after election. Even the 2006 House elections, with all of the discontent over the war in Iraq and attention to a number of high-profile scandals involving former or current House members such as Randy "Duke" Cunningham, Tom DeLay, William Jefferson, Bob Ney, and Mark Foley (among others), saw 94.5 percent of all House incumbents who sought reelection returned to office. Senators too are rarely defeated, although they are at higher risk than House members. And when incumbents do lose, more frequently personal scandals, not stands on policies, play a key role in those defeats. There is ample evidence, from a recent study conducted for the Pew Charitable Trusts, that campaign discourse in House and Senate elections does not effectively present citizens with informed presentations on the differences between candidates on the issues of the day (Maisel and West 2004).

However, the case that elections allow the electorate to hold its representatives accountable can still be made in a number of less direct ways. First, one could simply talk to incumbent members of Congress. As anyone who has ever worked with an elected official can tell you, the majority of incumbents are genuinely concerned about their reelection. Certainly some are more concerned than others, but the majority of members do not believe they are safe from defeat on election day. They worry about how the media or a future opponent will portray a policy stand or specific vote, and they act accordingly. If an incumbent behaves in such a fashion accountability can be reasonably assumed to exist, regardless of the fact that the congressman or senator gets 65 percent of the vote in election after election.

Second, high reelection rates for incumbents could simply be due to the fact that constituents are happy with what their members of Congress are doing. Under this scenario, reelection is simply a reward for and recognition of good and faithful public service. There is a reason, after all, why one regularly hears that Americans hate Congress as a whole, but love their individual members of Congress.

A third reason for the high rate of incumbency reelection could have nothing to do with candidate-centered politics and the personal vote, but rather be all about partisanship. At least in the House of Representatives, the majority of districts are reliably Democrat or reliably Republican (Bishop 2004; Stonecash et al. 2003). In such districts, one could argue that it doesn't really matter who the specific candidate in question is; as long as the dominant party in the district manages to put forward a reasonably qualified, reasonably competent, scandal-free candidate, that candidate will win, and will keep on winning as long as she or he remains reasonably competent and scandal free and generally follows the party line. This scenario too presents a picture of accountability, although here it is accountability rooted mostly in partisanship rather than individual behavior.

Fourth, look at the role of interest groups and their use of soft money (chapter 5; Cigler 2006; Magleby and Holt 1999). Groups tend to invest heavily in campaigns in competitive congressional districts when the major party candidates differ on the issues that the groups feel are most critical. Organized labor, business and industry groups, environmentalists, those on both sides of the abortion issue, and those favoring term limits are all obvious examples of groups that strive to hold representatives accountable for their actions in Washington. Even when these groups are not successful in defeating incumbents, they often define the issue agenda for a campaign, with two consequences: (1) voters do in fact have an opportunity to focus on key issues and to express their preference and (2) representatives often moderate positions in order to accommodate the views of more of their constituents. Whatever one concludes about the role of money in campaigns—an issue of never-ending controversy—it is difficult not to see that campaign spending often raises the issue content of certain campaigns, allowing for better informed voters (Geer 2006).

A fifth argument in favor of the proposition that congressional elections serve the purpose of holding representatives accountable for their actions rests on observing the results of these elections at the macro level, that is, looking at all elections held in one year together rather than at individual elections separately. There is a good deal of evidence that these elections reflect the views of the voters, at least on the major economic issues of the day (Jacobson and Kernell 1983; Tufte 1975, 1978). At times when there has been massive public discontent with governmental policies, changes wrought on the composition of the legislature as a result of congressional elections have been sufficient to lead to changes in those policies (Brady, Bullock, and Maisel 1988). The election of 1966, generally interpreted as a reaction to excesses in social welfare policies passed by the so-called Great Society Democrat–dominated Eighty-ninth Congress, is one clear example of this linkage. Certainly it could be argued that the election of 1994, in which Republicans regained control of both houses of Congress for the first time since 1954, had the same impact. It is also possible that the 2006 election, which returned Democrats to power after twelve years of minority status, will be another example of this dynamic, although it is too early to say at this point.

3. State and Local Elections

While most states now see some level of two-party competition for at least some offices (Bibby et al. 1983; Brown and Bruce 2002; Jewell and Olson 1982, 1988; Holbrook and Van Dunk 1993), one party or the other still has a decided advantage in statewide elections in many states. Moreover, in legislative districts in virtually every state, true two-party competition remains the exception, not the rule (Crotty 1985; Jewell and Morehouse 2001). The difficulty here is the same in some ways as it is for finding competition in congressional elections. When districts are redrawn after each ten-year census, it seems clear that one criterion used by mapmakers is protection of incumbents. Districts dominated by one party are the norm for state legislative races to an even greater extent than is the case for congressional races. How can citizens effect policy change if the result of the election is known in advance and will have virtually no impact on who governs? Under such a scenario, citizens would have to rely on competition in the primary election.

Local elections have the same types of problems that state elections have, only even more so. Many localities are now and have been for some time dominated by one political party or the other. We read often about the strength of the Democratic party organization in Cook County, Illinois, the area including and surrounding Chicago. In the city of Chicago, Democratic party nomination is all but tantamount to election. Other organizations are not as strong as that in Cook County, but one-party rule in local elections remains very common (see Gibson et al. 1985; Schlesinger 1985).

4. Nonpartisan Politics

Even more common than one-party rule in local governing units is nonpartisan government. This text has dealt only with partisan elections because those are the elections that see the most competition in the American system. Yet nonpartisan elections merit comment.

Approximately two-thirds to three-fourths of U.S. municipalities hold nonpartisan elections to determine who will hold local offices (Crotty 1985; Schaffner et al. 2001). The movement toward nonpartisan government was part of Progressive Era reforms; advocates of nonpartisan local government feel that running a local government should be more like administering a business than playing partisan politics. Frequently they cite the corruption and the inefficiency of partisan politics. "There is no Republican and no Democratic way to clean a street."

On the other hand, those concerned with democratic control over the means of governing have not been overly impressed with the experience of nonpartisan elections. Critics contend that nonpartisan elections tend to draw fewer voters because citizens do not care who wins these elections and because elections without the cue of party often confuse voters. The voters are less informed about the issues than is the case in partisan elections. Fewer races are competitive in the sense of close elections; in fact, in many races only one candidate runs. The advantages of incumbency are increased over those in even heavily one-party areas with partisan elections, since the opposition is deprived of its chance to organize.

The end result is less serious, less issue-oriented campaigning, more domination by those with well-recognized names, an increase in domination by single-issue groups that have the ability to mobilize their supporters, and generally less representative and less accountable government.

If the goal of reformers was to establish a system in which democracy functions more effectively, and if democracy for this purpose is defined as a system in which the views of the voters on policy matters are converted into government policy, then nonpartisan elections represent a regressive step. Only someone who believes that local government involves only administration, with no policy implications, can view the results of the nonpartisan movement as a movement toward more democracy. Given the nature of citizen concerns about local issues, about education and crime and growth policies, as well as about street repair and garbage collection, that argument is difficult to sustain, if not downright irresponsible to make.

II. Voters, Parties, and Elections

In evaluating the effectiveness of elections, it is also important to look at how voters are deciding for whom they will vote. The *American Voter* model (focused on the electoral politics of 1950s America) stipulated that most voters used political party as a cue in determining their electoral choices during the decade of the 1950s. The *Changing American Voter* analysis (examining the 1960s–mid-1970s) revealed that issue orientation was more important in determining vote than had been the case when the earlier study was undertaken. The *New American Voter* (analysis through 1992) argued that the importance of the concept of party identification should not be underestimated, even as we enter the twenty-first century and many voters view politics cynically. Much recent work supports this latter view, presenting evidence that partisanship is once again strongly affecting electoral behavior (Bartels 2000; Green et al. 2002; Hetherington 2001; Stonecash 2006).

So where does this leave us? Clearly the world has changed since the era of the 1950s described by *The American Voter*. While the sources of this change are numerous, perhaps none has been larger or more important than the changes in communications technology and the media. As discussed in chapter 10, the media plays a central role in American electoral politics, and both this role and the media have changed radically over the past five decades.

A. The Rise of Television

When discussing the media and politics, one must begin with television. Television is the news source most relied on by the American voting public. For more than three decades approximately two-thirds of those responding to the National Election Studies surveys conducted by the Center for Political Studies of the Survey Research Center at the University of Michigan have responded that television is their most important source for political information. Nearly 90 percent rely on television to some extent. Although newspapers are listed as one source by approximately 75 percent of respondents, for a majority of citizens they are a secondary source, at best. (See, e.g., Adams 1982; Patterson 1980; Ranney 1990; Robinson and Sheehan 1983.) Even with the rise of the Internet as option for political news, television is still dominant. According to the Pew Research Center Internet and American Life Project, in 2004, television was the primary source of news for 78 percent of Americans. Newspapers were second with 39 percent, followed by the Internet at 18 percent and radio at 17 percent (Pew Research Center 2007b).

What are the implications of this reliance on television? Television is a visual medium and emphasizes stories that can be presented visually. A number of earlier chapters discussed the media's emphasis on campaign-oriented stories: Who is gaining? Who is losing? What are the various strategies, and how are they working?

Doris Graber has studied television coverage of presidential elections for some years. Her conclusions support the commonly held view that television presents the news and covers campaigns in a simplified manner. In every election that she studied, save that of 1968, the media in general and television journalists in particular presented stories on campaign events more than analyses of domestic politics, foreign affairs, economic policy, or social problems (Graber 1980, 1982, 1984a, 1984b, 1989, 1990, 2005, 2006; see also Buchanan 1991; Crouse 1973; Patterson 1980, 1993; Robinson and Sheehan 1983).

During the election of 1968 the war in Vietnam as a news event and as an issue received more coverage than did campaign events. However, this may well be the exception that proves the rule. Vietnam was a news issue that could be covered visually. That was the first war that was telecast live into America's living rooms. As a news story, it had the ability to capture the attention of the viewing audience.

But compare the coverage of the war in Vietnam with television coverage of the major economic policy crises that have dominated the governmental agenda in recent years. How many times can the network news anchors show bar graphs that describe the growth of the federal debt? How many times can they depict the federal budget with pie charts? How can a two-minute story adequately explain the complicated issues of Social Security and Medicare solvency? These economic issues—and the important issues of domestic politics, foreign affairs, and social problems—are complex problems that do not translate easily into two-minute spots on the network news (Graber 1980; see also Kerbel 1998; Buchanan 1991; Gans 1979). Yet these are undoubtedly the important issues of the day. And television, which cannot and does not cover these issues very well, is the medium most relied on by the voting public for its political information. Even the Iraq war, far and away the most important issue to American citizens as we write this book, has been far too complex for television to cover at anything more than the most rudimentary level. The necessary conclusion is that voters are making decisions based on a grossly oversimplified view of the important issues of the day.

The above discussion focused on national news events and presidential elections because that is the only context that has been studied in depth by social scientists. It does not take much intuition, however, to extend this discussion to the state and local contexts. Think for a moment about the quality of news coverage in local newspapers and on local television news broadcasts. Let us assume for the moment that most citizens gain their political information about events at the state and local level from television, just as they do for events at the national level.[2]

The average local news program spends nearly as much time on weather and sports as it does on all news. The news segment frequently carries one story about national news and at least one human interest story. Then, of course, there is the obligatory story about the latest local disaster—fire, murder, automobile accident. But how often is there in-depth coverage of a state house hearing on workers' compensation, of a city council debate on zoning ordinances, of a school board discussion on resource allocation? When state and local elections are held, how often are the candidates seen on local television?

Example after example could be mounted, but the point would remain the same. It should be emphasized, however, that all the blame does not rest with television journalists (nor with newspaper reporters, for much the same argument would apply to most local papers). In point of fact, they are faced with a nearly impossible task. Local journalists for all media have very few resources with which to cover a vast amount of material. They do not have large staffs or large budgets; they have limited space and/or time; they have many localities and issues to cover.

And they are under tremendous pressure to draw an audience. It is difficult to imagine how most issues that face state and local governments—or most issues that distinguish candidates for state and local offices—could be covered in a way that would excite the public. Yet if newspapers do not sell and if television broadcasts do not achieve high ratings, the business end of these enterprises fails and the public is even less well served (Kerbel 1998; Berkman and Kitch 1986; Gans 1979). As a consequence, local journalists do what they can to cover state and local government and politics; in most instances what they can do is very little. And again, very little is what the public is left to rely on in making its decisions.

Thus far we have devoted our attention to the media's performance in providing citizens with information about politics, and for good reason. Representative democracy is only possible with a citizenry that is at least minimally informed about civic affairs, and in a nation of over 300 million people the media is the only way for us to get such a citizenry. But this is only part of the story of the media and politics. At a number of points in this book we have examined the ways in which various political actors use communications technology and the media in the attempt to affect electoral outcomes. In the pretelevision era, campaigns tended to be labor-intensive affairs, where armies of volunteers were crucial to spreading the word and mobilizing the electorate on behalf of candidates for public office. Most of the time, these armies were provided by and under the direction of political parties. With the dawn of television, campaigns gradually became more capital intensive. As discussed earlier, campaigns increasingly came to rely on television (and radio too) advertising to get their message out to voters and to get these voters to the polls on election day. Television advertising time costs money, and thus money became a more important weapon in election wars. This development also allowed individual candidates to assume greater responsibility for and direction of their own campaigns. If a candidate could raise the money, she or he could largely call the shots.

B. The Parties in the Modern Election

Today one regularly is told that contemporary American elections are "candidate centered." Let's be certain we understand what that term means. Candidate-centered campaigns are to be distinguished from party-centered campaigns. A candidate-centered campaign is directed by the candidate and his or her staff. They are in control. A party-centered campaign is directed by the party organization and its leaders. They dictate to the candidate how to run the campaign. Saying that American elections are now candidate centered is to say that the political parties have lost control of their own candidates.

To a large degree this is true. Why? Two reasons stand out. First, parties lost control of the nominating process. The major cause for this change was the advent of the direct primary system. Although state law and state party rules vary, the norm is that party organization cannot be involved in determining who will be the party's nominees. In a sense, that is ludicrous on its face. A well-meaning reform, aimed at restoring intraparty democracy and lessening the influence of party bosses making decisions out of public view, essentially removed political parties' raison d'être. Parties exist to run candidates who will carry forth the programs supported by party adherents into government. The primary system removed from party control the selection of candidates whom party officials feel could carry out that task. From a practical point of view, the imposition of primary elections as the principal way of nominating candidates meant that those candidates had to set up their own organizations, separate from the party organization, in order to run a primary campaign. This requirement went a long way toward focusing campaigns on candidates and not parties.

Obviously the impact of this reform was not felt everywhere in the nation at the same time. Some states adopted the primary system essentially as a means of weakening political parties—and that effect was felt. In other states, party organizations resisted and developed coping mechanisms, preprimary endorsements as one example. At the national level, party organizations remained important in determining presidential nominees until after the 1968 reforms. But certainly by the end of the century, the role of party in the nominating process had been reduced from a once prominent position to a much lesser one, everywhere in the nation. Variation still exists, but a pattern is clear.

The second reason for the replacement of party-centered campaigns with candidate-centered campaigns relates to campaign techniques, particularly the revolution in communications avenues discussed earlier in this chapter. Parties were strongest when the most valuable resource in a campaign was manpower. Party organizations, often building on material incentives, could command the troops who would go door-to-door and bring the voters to the polls. Men and women literally worked hour upon hour to turn out the loyal voters, many of whom were also committed to the party because of material benefits that they had received.

With the advent of television advertising and of computer-generated, targeted direct mail, the role of dedicated, loyal campaign workers diminished. These techniques required skilled professionals to design campaigns and raise money to pay for them. Political party organizations responded to this changing environment, but they did so in competition with others who could also provide these resources. Candidates could hire their own consultants and raise their own money. Party organization became one of many players in a game orchestrated by candidate organizations (Kolodny 2000).

As critical as these changes are, it is important not to push the candidate-centered argument too far. It is true that because parties no longer control nominations for office and because candidates can now speak to voters without the assistance of parties individual candidates now control the direction of their campaigns. The candidate for office is now at the center of the campaign. But it is also true that the candidate is not able to do whatever he or she wants. Candidates must run for office in an environment that for the most part is beyond their control, and they must deal with reality (or at least the perception of reality) as they find it. In many ways that environment and that reality are both partisan in nature. Almost all candidates with a legitimate shot at winning office, at least at the federal and state level, run under a partisan banner. These banners are meaningful to voters, and conjure up certain mental images of the candidates regardless of the candidates' individual characteristics (Brewer 2008). The vast majority of Americans identify with or at least lean toward the Democrats or the Republicans, and no other factor even comes close to party identification in determining individual vote choice. Candidates today are indeed at the center of their own campaigns for public office, but their success or failure in these campaigns more often than not still comes down to partisan factors.

The common description of elections as candidate centered to a certain extent also ignores how successfully parties have adapted to the changes that American electoral politics have seen since the 1950s (Aldrich 1995). Today both national party organizations are staffed with campaign professionals, skilled at aiding their copartisans with all aspects of electioneering (Herrnson 1998b, 2002). This is increasingly true at the state level as well (Bibby 1998, 2002). Parties are now crucial service providers, and as is the case with any service, the individual or organization doing the providing retains a certain degree of control over the service. In addition, over the past few election cycles we have increasingly seen parties turn to the past in a search for future success. As we've discussed in this book, party organizations at all levels are returning to traditional roles, though implementing them in new ways. Both the state and national parties have rediscovered the value in mobilizing their supporters and turning them out on election day. Some of these efforts are almost traditional registration and "get out the vote" drives, similar to those run in the heyday of party organizations. But much more frequently they are sophisticated targeting and get-out-the-vote drives using modern techniques to identify and increase turnout among specific segments of the population thought to favor their candidates. The "microtargeting" and "seventy-two-hour task force" used by Karl Rove and the Republican party in recent years is currently the state of the art here. It is important to note that it would be virtually impossible for all but the wealthiest of candidates to carry out these types of activities on her or his own.

C. Parties' Appeal to the Electorate

The most interesting debate about the role of political parties in the twenty-first century may not be the debate about how parties try to influence elections but rather the debate about how the two parties define themselves.

For much of the last half of the twentieth century this debate was fought within the Democratic party. The Democrats had two wings—a conservative wing and a liberal wing. The conservative wing was largely Southern; the liberal wing was largely Northern. The liberals were dominant nationally, but the conservatives controlled Southern states; the liberals needed their support to win presidential elections and to pass legislation in Congress. Frequently, that support was not forthcoming and Democrats lost.

Late in the 1980s, Democrats began to move away from the two extremes toward the center. Philosophically, this movement was defined as "the third way," not all government and not all private sector, but a third way, a partnership, a sense that government largesse came with personal responsibility. These views were voiced by the Democratic Leadership Council and served as the basis for President Clinton's successful campaign for election in 1992 and reelection in 1996 and for Al Gore's unsuccessful race in 2000. Liberals complained that the DLC was throwing away fundamental Democratic principles in order to win elections. "New" Democrats countered that they were true to those principles and voicing them in a way that resonated with the American electorate. As the Clinton administration drew to a close, some still complained that he ran as a Democrat but governed like a Republican. But more Democrats accepted his successes in electoral terms and in policy terms. The positive side of the Clinton legacy may well be defined as his ability to unite his party around an agenda that appealed to most voters.[3]

However, the Gore defeat reopened some of the wounds that the Clinton victories seemed to mask. Liberals within the party grew increasingly restless. This restlessness was visible for all to see in the contest for the 2004 Democratic presidential nomination. Former Vermont governor and current DNC chair Howard Dean clearly appealed to the more liberal elements of the Democratic coalition. He staked out this claim with early and vocal opposition to the war in Iraq, lambasting the more centrist Democrats for remaining quiet. This largely explains his sudden and surprising rise to front-runner status in the early period of the contest. After Dean's implosion in Iowa, the Democrats settled relatively quickly on John Kerry, Massachusetts's junior senator. While a good deal of Kerry's appeal to the party faithful was that he could beat President Bush in the general election, he also possessed a liberal track record that the more left-leaning members of the party could feel comfortable with. In the early stages of the 2008 presidential nomination process we can see that this tension remains within the Democratic party. Among the front-runners, Illinois senator Barack Obama is directing his appeals to the more liberal elements within the party, while New York senator Hillary Clinton is attempting to follow the moderate approach utilized so successfully by her husband. And John Edwards, former North Carolina senator, is attempting to position himself somewhere between the two. But even with all this talk of tension, we should not lose sight of one crucially important matter. For just about all Democrats here in mid-2007, *any* Democratic option would be preferable to whatever the Republicans offer up in November 2008.

For most of the twentieth century, the Republican party was widely seen as more unified (although less successful) than the Democrats. Even the slight rift in the 1960s between social and economic conservatives within the party seemed to be fully repaired with the victories first of Richard Nixon in 1968 and 1972, and especially of Ronald Reagan in 1980. However, during the 1990s some cracks began to show among Republicans. A party that had been united under Ronald Reagan as the conservative alternative to radical Democrats, a party that had brought blue-collar Democrats into its fold, split over the definition of true conservatism. Never was this more clear than during the 1998 elections and the debate over the impeachment of President Clinton. Essentially the Republican party was divided into three camps, each fighting for control (chapter 8).

The social conservatives feel that the party should define its principles clearly and stick to them. That group pushed hard for impeaching President Clinton. They thought that the election of 1998 should be fought over the issue of the president's character and were responsible for the last-minute Republican campaign blitz aimed at the president. Despite the fact that that blitz did not result in electoral success and was viewed as a failure by many, they remained committed. According to Gary Bauer, former head of the Family Research Council and a candidate for the Republican presidential nomination in 2000, Republican candidates "bailed out on social issues. . . . We just ran one of the least ideological campaigns in years and none of us feel [*sic*] very good" (Balz and Broder 1998, A1). His views were echoed by Randy Tate, executive director of the Christian Coalition:

> If the 106th Congress does not immediately take up pro-family, conservative issues and talk about them, not just for one day, but day in and day out, if they don't do these things, things will get worse before they get better for them [GOP congressional leaders]. (Balz and Broder 1998, A1)

These views were also reflected in the words of the House managers of the impeachment trial and in the actions of those Republicans who prolonged that trial, to the detriment of their party's standing with the public, long after the eventual outcome was apparent. When one Democratic leader was asked why the Republicans were acting in a manner that seemed certain to hurt them at the polls, he replied, "Tom DeLay would rather be the Minority Leader of 190 committed Republicans than Whip for a majority that is not ideologically pure."

Congressman Chris Shays (R-Conn.) has a very different view. According to Shays, the disproportionate influence of the religious and social conservatives is causing serious problems for the party. "As soon as my leaders started to jump when the Christian Coalition and Gary Bauer and others said jump, we lost a lot of voters" (Mitchell 1998).

Economic conservatives, by contrast, are concerned that the conservative Christian agenda not dominate party thinking in terms of the issues about which they care most. Congressman Rick Lazio (R-N.Y.), in reviewing the 1998 election, concluded, "I think the party has the best cohesion when it talks about fiscal issues" (Mitchell 1998).

The third wing of the party might be called pragmatic conservatives. Looking at the electoral debacle of 1998, former congressman Steve Gunderson (R-Wisc.) concluded, "I really see this as a clarion call from the nation to bring the political parties back to the pragmatic governing center. . . . It's a wonderful warning to my party between now and the year 2000" (Balz and Broder 1998, A1). Marshall Wittman of the Heritage Foundation discussed the victories of Republican governors in key states in 1998 in the same terms. "I think that the lesson of the election is that sharp-elbowed conservatism doesn't work and what they offer is a new paradigm of compassionate conservatism" (Balz 1998, A4).

An airplane with three wings cannot fly. A political party with three wings, struggling against itself, will have difficulty defining an electorate to which it can appeal. The Republicans seemed to recognize this in their choice of a 2000 presidential nominee. George W. Bush presented himself and ran as a "compassionate conservative," seemingly in-line with the pragmatic conservatives described above, and obviously appealing enough to win office. But President Bush's actions in office, especially post-9/11, have once again exposed tensions within the GOP. At various points during his presidency he has managed to anger each of the three elements within his party. Social conservatives have perhaps been the happiest with Bush's performance as president, but they were angered by his nomination of former White House counsel Harriet Miers to the Supreme Court (she eventually withdrew) and by his plan for immigration reform. Economic conservatives are in many cases appalled by what they see as the profligate spending of the Bush administration. Pragmatic conservatives disapprove of the rigid and unyielding nature of the administration overall. In these ways President Bush has presented something to dislike for everyone in the party. The jousting among 2008 Republican nomination hopefuls John McCain, Mitt Romney, and Rudy Giuliani, combined with the unhappiness of many social conservatives with any of these options, illustrates these tensions to perfection.

D. The Tone of Twenty-first-Century Politics

One further question about the future of American politics in the decade ahead remains to be discussed. It is directly related to the positions the two parties are taking. Citizens and politicians alike have become increasingly distressed about the tone of the political debate. Politicians who are frustrated by a lack of effective compromising have taken to personal attacks on one another. Comity, even in the Senate once known for just such an atmosphere, seems to have disappeared, and the public does not like what it sees.

Evidence of this dissatisfaction is rampant. Citizens respond to poll questions that they are cynical, that they do not like the tone of campaigns, that they will not vote because of how candidates come across. Potential candidates decide not to run, in part at least because they do not want to face the negativity of a campaign and because they do not want to be associated with that negativity. Those in office decry the lack of civility among officeholders as they go about the nation's business. When those in the media discuss or write about current American politics, the only thing more frequent than statements about political polarization are condemnations of this polarized state.

The Annenberg Public Policy Center Issue Advocacy Advertising Reports conclude that express advocacy advertisements are distinctly more negative than candidate advertisements—and their role in competitive campaigns is on the rise (Magleby and Holt 1999, 27). The Pew Study of campaign discourse in 2002 reached the same conclusion about party advertising in congressional campaigns (cited in Maisel and West 2004). All of these factors point in one direction, a negative one. The health of the polity and the efficacy of the roles played by the electoral process and political parties within that process depend on citizen commitment to America's democracy. Alienation from politics has the potential to reduce participation and trust in government, which could raise issues about government's legitimacy. Cynical reactions to negative campaigns that depress turnout and lower the probability that those who might best lead the nation will even enter political life are a cancer on the body politic.

On the other hand, these type of reactions could be somewhat overheated. Politics, after all, is conflict. The stakes are high. High-stakes conflict almost by necessity results in certain levels of negativity and animosity. American politics has never been a pursuit for those whose sensibilities are easily offended, and much of the tenor and tone of contemporary American politics can be found in the politics of nineteenth-century America as well. Conflict and tension can promote alienation and withdrawal, but they can also promote engagement and participation. We will see what the years ahead hold.

III. CONCLUDING REMARKS

It is of more than passing interest to some that the political scientists who are vocal advocates for stronger political party organizations have themselves been active in politics (Bill Crotty, David Price, Tom Cronin, Bob Huckshorn, John Bibby, Kay Lawson, the late Larry Longley, Paul Herrnson, and the senior author of this text, to name a few). That link is not coincidental. Those who become involved in the political process are acutely aware that many citizens simply do not care. They are also aware that policies pursued by government officials often have direct and immediate impact on those citizens. Further, it is difficult to know how the people feel on lots of issues, certainly in advance of the time at which decisions must be made. Politicians hear from the citizens who are most concerned, but not from a wide variety of citizens.

So the search begins for a mechanism to involve more people in the political process, particularly in the electoral process because it is the vital link between the citizens and their government. And the institution of party readily stands out. For all its imperfections, so vividly described by political analysts and journalists of all types, party remains the vital linking institution. When parties are weak, the linkage role of the electoral process is not played well. When they are strong, a possibility exists that representation and accountability will follow. Other institutions—the media, interest groups— have tried to pick up the slack, but they have done so without notable success. And thus we are drawn back to the conclusion that if political parties did not exist, someone would have to invent them. Our parties are critical to our system of government, like them or not. They are not going anywhere. So the key would seem to be to try and get America's political parties to play their optimum role in our system of representative democracy.

Notes

CHAPTER 1

1. The Seventeenth Amendment to the Constitution was ratified in 1913. Prior to that time, U.S. senators were elected to the Senate by members of the state legislatures.

2. Feinstein's decision may well have been prescient. Checchi, the former chairman of Northwest Airlines, spent approximately $40 million of his own money in the Democratic gubernatorial primary. Congresswoman Jane Harman, who was encouraged to enter the race by Feinstein after she demurred, spent nearly half that much, again most of it family money. They finished second and third respectively to Lieutenant Governor Gray Davis, who himself spent nearly $10 million, an amount that would have been a record in a primary election had it not been so far exceeded by his two opponents.

3. As each state has two U.S. senators, this provision means that senatorial elections are held in roughly two-thirds of the states and not in the other states during each national election.

4. In *Baker v. Carr*, 369 U.S. 186 (1962), the Court ruled that Tennessee's legislative districts, which had not been redrawn since 1901, despite major demographic changes in the state, violated the constitutionally guaranteed rights of those citizens living in highly populated areas because they were less well represented than those living in less densely populated areas. This ruling set a precedent for changes in districts throughout the country and led to a series of rulings on how districts could legitimately be drawn (Perry 1991).

5. Some states have also attempted to impose limitations on the number of terms their representatives and senators can serve in Congress, but these efforts have been deemed unconstitutional.

6. This "double election" was permissible only because of the precedent set when Lyndon Johnson ran for vice president under John F. Kennedy in 1960 and simultaneously sought reelection to the Senate. The state legislature passed a special law in 1960 to permit Johnson to seek both offices and it applied to Bentsen as well. The law has since been repealed.

7. Most of the prominent elections in the United States are partisan elec-

tions, that is, contests between nominees of political parties. However, when all contests for office are considered, including local contests for positions such as city council, selectman, and even less-prominent positions, such as trustee of the local library, nonpartisan elections outnumber those in which party is involved. This text will only deal with partisan elections, though a wide variety of those will be mentioned.

8. The distinction between *independent candidacies* and *third-party candidacies* is an important one and will be discussed in chapters 8, 10, and 11. In Anderson's case the situation was further complicated because his designation on the ballot differed from state to state. See Bibby and Maisel (1998, 2002).

9. Anderson eventually decided that he would not run in 1984, preferring to build the organizational base for his "party," a task that proved fruitless.

10. Party systems are described, classified, and criticized in many scholars' works, for example, Chambers and Burnham (1975), Sartori (1976), and Sundquist (1983).

11. Silbey (1990, 1991, 1998, 2002) applies a very different definition of party system, emphasizing the centrality of parties to the electoral process. See chapter 2.

12. Richard Fenno (1978, chap. 1) writes at length of how politicians judge public opinion and about the ways in which they reach their judgments. Jacobson (1980, 108) suggests that this process might well be a natural act, even for seemingly safe incumbents.

13. And even the necessity of party nomination does not apply in some states for some offices. Although Nebraska's state legislature is the only such body with nonpartisan elections, Louisiana has a "nonpartisan" primary for Congress and statewide offices. See chapter 6.

14. Some state party organizations have on occasion been so opposed to the national candidate that they have denied him a place on the ballot. This happened throughout the South to Harry Truman in 1948 and in two states to John Kennedy in 1960. State party organizations placed the names of Strom Thurmond (1948) and Harry Byrd (1960) on the ballot instead of those of the national standard-bearers. The problems of ballot access for even these nominees pales in comparison to those faced by "independent" candidates such as George Wallace in 1968 or John Anderson and Barry Commoner in 1980. However, ballot access rules for independent and minor party candidates were changed considerably as a result of the legal as well as political battle fought by Ross Perot in 1992.

CHAPTER 2

1. Using Key's concepts, political scientists have been able to refine their classifications of various presidential elections. Angus Campbell and his associates classified elections according to whether the majority party won the election and whether the existing line of cleavage prevailed or was changed (Campbell et al. 1960, 531–38). They identified

three types of elections—**maintaining elections**, **deviating elections**, and **realigning elections**. Seeing a logical gap in this reasoning and referring particularly to the election of 1896, Gerald Pomper (1973, 104) added a fourth category, the **converting election**.

2. James Sundquist (1983, 41–47) maintains that the interaction of five variables determines when and in what ways established patterns of political behavior will change. The five variables are (1) how strongly a new issue divides the nation; (2) the capacity of those supporting the status quo to resist change; (3) the skill of the political leaders; (4) whether the new cleavage cuts across existing differences or mirrors them; and (5) the strength of existing party attachments in the electorate.

3. Recall William N. Chambers's (1975) definition of a competitive party system: "A pattern of interaction in which two or more political parties compete for office or power in government and for the support of the electorate, and must therefore take one another into account in their behavior in government and in election contests" (6).

4. The two parties in this period also developed clearly distinguishable national ideologies. As early as 1792, a noticeably partisan James Madison wrote of these differences in the Philadelphia *National Gazette*:

> One of the divisions consists of those, who from particular interest, from natural temper, or from the habits of life, are more partial to the opulent than to the other classes of society; and having debauched themselves into a persuasion that mankind are incapable of governing themselves, it follows with them, of course, that government can be carried on only by the pageantry of rank, the influence of money and emoluments, and the terror of military force. Men of those sentiments must naturally wish to point the measures of government less to the interest of the many than of a few. . . . The other division consists of those believing in the doctrine that mankind are capable of governing themselves, and hating hereditary power as an insult to the reason and an outrage to the rights of man, are naturally offended at any public measure that does not appeal to the understanding and to the general interest of the community, or that is not strictly conformable to the principles, and conducive to the preservation of republican government. (Cunningham 1965, 11)

Not only were the ideologies clear, but politicians were already beginning to bring the American art form of rhetorical overstatement into the public eye.

5. William E. Gienapp (1987, 1991) provides a detailed analysis of the formation of the Republican party. His account makes note of the importance of temperance and of nativism as well as of the antislavery movement in describing, as opposed to other anti-Democratic parties, the demise of the Whigs and their replacement by the Republicans. While his discussion of realignment and of the decomposition of the Whig coalition is consistent with that provided here, he gives a much more detailed, state-by-state account of the strategies followed by Republican politicians and of the role of pragmatic politics and ideology in the decisions they made.

6. The New Deal coalition has been defined in many ways—see, for ex-

MAINTAINING ELECTIONS

Elections whose outcomes result in the preservation of power by the majority party and a maintenance of the existing lines of cleavage.

DEVIATING ELECTIONS

Elections in which the majority party is defeated in a temporary reversal of fortunes, but the existing lines of cleavage remain intact.

REALIGNING ELECTIONS

Elections in which the lines of cleavage on which the electorate is divided shift, resulting often, but not always, in a new majority party. See CONVERTING ELECTIONS.

CONVERTING ELECTIONS

A election during which the same party retains control on the basis of different issues and coalitions. Also, see REALIGNING ELECTIONS.

ample, Erikson, Lancaster, and Romero (1989); Ladd and Hadley (1975); and Stanley, Bianco, and Niemi (1986).

7. Southern voters, nearly all of whom were white, were Democrats for a variety of reasons; but it is not too much of a stretch to say that this allegiance dated back to the Civil War and to Reconstruction and was unaffected by the issues that lead to realignments in the rest of the nation in the 1890s and again in the 1930s. It is also accurate to say that the Republican party, as an ongoing organization that ran candidates and claimed the allegiance of a significant number of voters, did not exist in much of the South during the first decades of the New Deal party system.

8. As David Mayhew (1986) has observed, machine politics was much more likely to exist in those states that had been settled by the beginning of the second party system, the Jacksonian party system, when the spoils system came into existence. Although the spoils system established a base and gave rise to a political culture that persisted for some time, the other areas never followed suit.

9. Robert Huckshorn (1976, chap. 4) has developed a now familiar categorization of the types of party leadership exercised by party chairs, regardless of the formal means by which those leaders were selected (roughly three-quarters were chosen by state party committees, the rest at state conventions). Most state party chairs serving while their party is in control of the governorship are classified as political agents of the governor—often the favored choice of the chief executive. Power and influence flow to the state chair as a result of close ties to the governor; the role of the political-agent state chair is to mold the party machinery to meet the governor's best interest. Sharing a party label, however, does not ensure coordination between the state party and the governorship. **In-party independent** state chairs may well be in office before the governor is elected, perhaps even as a supporter of someone who has opposed the winning governor for nomination. Party rules do not require state chairs to resign if the candidate they support loses; norms for remaining in this position vary from state to state. More frequently in this age of personalized campaigning, governors have shown little interest in the state party chair (thus permitting state committees to select their own leaders) because the governor has his or her own totally independent campaign organization. In still other cases, state party chairs serve for longer periods of time, remaining in office even though the governorship changes hands and, more seriously, even though the other party takes control (shifting the chair's role to **out-party independent**). In any of these instances, the state party chair and the committee work separately from the governor. The strength of the leader depends on his or her ability to run an organization that has a significant impact on the electoral process.

IN-PARTY INDEPENDENT

State party chairs who act without regard to the views of the governor, even though the governor is a member of their own party.

OUT-PARTY INDEPENDENT

Chair of a state party committee whose party does not control the governorship and who therefore can act as a free agent.

10. In 1990, Massachusetts Republicans pointed with pride to the fact that they competed for over three-quarters of the seats in the lower house of the state legislature and all but two state senate seats. That would not seem noteworthy except for the fact that only four years earlier 103 (of 160) Democratic candidates for state representative and 25 (of

42) Democratic candidates for state senate had faced no Republican opposition.

11. The addition of representatives from American Samoa, the District of Columbia, Guam, Puerto Rico, and the Virgin Islands brings the total membership of the RNC to 165.

12. The RNC's executive council includes eleven members, three appointed by the chair and eight elected from regional caucuses; in addition, it has a number of ex officio members—the RNC officers and chairs of the various committees. The DNC's executive committee is chosen in a way that reflects the constituent groups that constitute the full committee.

13. Joel Silbey (1990, 1991, 1998) claims that American political history can be divided into four periods, distinguished by the importance of the role of political parties and the different kinds of political institutions, norms, and behavior that have predominated in each era. The period from the 1790s to the 1830s—the preparty period (Formisano 1974)—was a period of party development, not electoral prominence, as parties were resisted by many in politics. The only time in American political history when parties totally dominated the political landscape (Silbey 1990, 4) was from 1838 to 1893—the Gilded Age, or the party period. From the 1890s until the 1950s—the postparty period— parties were on the decline. And, according to Silbey, from the latter half of the twentieth century to today, the American political system has been dominated by candidates, not their parties; thus, he characterizes the present period as the nonparty period.

CHAPTER 3

1. To understand just how close elections can be, consider the New Hampshire election for the U.S. Senate in 1974. In the race between Congressman Louis Wyman, the Republican nominee, and John Durkin, the Democrat, Wyman was first thought to be the winner, by 355 votes. After a recount, Durkin was declared the winner by *ten votes* out of nearly 300,000 cast. Many ballots were challenged by both sides as having been improperly cast. After seven months of dispute, the decision was made to have a new election, as no fair way could be determined to ascertain who had really won. Durkin won the special election but served only one term before losing to Warren Rudman by the "overwhelming" margin of 17,000 votes.

   Those interested in other close elections might examine the congressional race in Indiana's Eighth District in 1984 between incumbent Democrat Frank McCloskey and Republican challenger Richard McIntyre; that race was determined by four votes out of nearly a quarter of a million cast. Because of a number of irregularities that occurred as the vote was counted, the election was disputed and eventually decided on a party line vote in the House.

2. This debate also points to the cumulative way in which a discipline informs itself. A careful review of this literature reveals concern with normative questions, with pragmatic consequences of those normative

questions, and with methodological controversies over how to answer the important questions posed.

3. Some claimed that people would take advantage of a holiday to travel or vacation and that the effect would therefore be the exact opposite of that desired.

4. A few states still hold statewide elections in odd-numbered years that do not include either presidential or congressional elections. Many cities hold municipal elections in those years as well. Turnouts for them are typically lower than that for congressional elections—though highly salient state or local issues can stimulate larger turnout from time to time. Primary elections see the lowest turnouts of all. For example, although Maine typically comes close to leading the nation in turnout in presidential and off-year general elections, fewer than 12 percent of the electorate turned out to vote in the Maine primary elections in 1998.

5. We also know that there is a problem in distinguishing voters from nonvoters in surveys. Typically survey data overrepresent actual voters by as much as 20 percent. Citizens are not anxious to admit they do not vote. (See Gant and Luttbeg 1991, 84–86; Hill and Luttbeg 1980, 79–80; Sigelman 1982.)

6. Verba and Nie do not ask similar questions and thus do not identify this group.

7. Milbrath (Milbrath and Goel 1977, 15) made distinctions among protesters by race and other factors; however, this is not a major part of his finding and might well be peculiar to the situation in Buffalo in the late 1960s.

CHAPTER 4

1. This information is available at www.fec.gov.

CHAPTER 5

1. Those who have come of political age in the last four decades might think that the problems of campaign finance are new and associated with the advent of television as a means for communicating campaign messages. Nothing could be further from the truth, and there is a vast literature of previous reform efforts. For more than four decades the research into campaign finance practices and reform has been dominated by a small group of political scientists. Alexander Heard of Vanderbilt University set the agenda for much of the work in this area (see Heard 1960). Since 1960 Herbert Alexander, director of the Citizens' Research Foundation, has gathered and analyzed more data on the financing of federal elections than anyone would have thought possible (see Alexander 1976a, 1976b, 1979a, 1979b, 1980, 1983, 1991; Alexander and Bauer 1991; Alexander and Corrado 1995; Alexander and Haggerty 1987; Citizens' Research Foundation 1997). Since the Federal Election Commission has been gathering data, more political scientists have begun to look systematically at the ways in which

American elections are financed (see particularly Corrado et al. 1997, 2005; 1995; Jacobson 1980, 1991; Magleby and Nelson 1990; Malbin 1984b; Mutch 1988; Sabato 1989; Sorauf 1988). Relatively little work has been done on elections at the state or local level, largely because the experiences differ so widely from state to state and data are difficult to gather (but see Gierzynski and Breaux 1991; Gierzynski 1992; Jones 1984, 1991; Malbin and Gais 1998).

2. The recent history of campaign finance reform can be traced through many of the sources mentioned in this chapter (see Mutch 1988; Corrado et al. 1997; Corrado et al. 2005). The first congressional response to pressure to reform campaign finance laws was the passage of an act regulating political broadcasts; however, this bill, which passed Congress in 1970, was vetoed by President Nixon.

3. The congressional response dealt only with candidates for federal office (and thus would not have impacted the Shapp or Rockefeller campaign discussed previously) because of perceived limitations of congressional jurisdiction. Various states responded in different ways at different times (Alexander 1976a; Jones 1984, 1991).

4. It should also be noted that this law did have a significant impact on campaign finance practice. Despite the fact that the Government Accounting Office, which was assigned enforcement responsibilities for presidential campaign compliance with this law, had very little time to gear up for its new role, that office did investigate and prosecute some major violations of the law, including the "laundering" of campaign funds by President Nixon's Committee to Reelect the President during the 1972 campaign.

5. It should be noted that the public financing of presidential elections, called for in the 1971 act, was not to go into effect until the 1976 election; this provision was part of the agreement necessary to prevent a veto of the legislation by Richard Nixon, who was, of course, a candidate for reelection in 1972.

6. These data do not deflate the averages by including uncontested seats. The data used in this discussion are drawn from FEC reports on the elections over this period. These data, for the period from 1974 to 1990, have been summarized in various sources, including Malbin (1984b) and Ornstein, Mann, and Malbin (1998).

7. It should be noted that total spending for Senate campaigns in 1990 and 1996 was less than those in 1988 and 1994, respectively. These figures clearly reflect the fact that elections in some states are more expensive than those in others and that different states had open seats in each of those years.

8. Ruth Jones, an expert on the cost of state and local campaigns, feels that Alexander's estimate is low; on this topic scholars must speculate because of the lack of systematic data. Election officials in a majority of states do not publish aggregate figures on receipts and expenditures for those offices (Sorauf 1988, 288).

9. This rosy conclusion should not be accepted casually. In point of fact, a small number of individuals still manage to give large sums of money,

much of it to the political parties in soft money. In addition, wealthy individuals often play the role of broker, bringing their wealthy friends in contact with candidates they support in order to add significantly to those candidates' war chests.

10. It also lists cooperative PACs and PACs for corporations without stock, but these two categories together constitute fewer than 5 percent of all political action committees, in terms of number of committees and/ or amounts contributed.

11. The one apparent exception is in 1990, but the total spending went down slightly because of the particular mix of Senate seats contested in that year, as compared with those in 1988.

12. The remaining money, of course, went to candidates in open seats.

13. When the Republicans controlled the Senate, between 1980 and 1986, there was some evidence that PACs were giving more to the Republicans than to the Democrats. Upon careful scrutiny, it was revealed that this finding reflected the larger number of incumbent Republicans than Democrats whose seats happened to be contested in the years studied (Magleby and Nelson 1990, 82, table 5-3).

14. In 1988, neither party had an incumbent running, so both parties had spirited primary campaigns. In 1992, President Bush was challenged by Patrick Buchanan, but the campaign was not one in which large sums were spent. In 1996, though he was without a challenger in his own party, President Clinton spent extensively to jump-start his reelection effort. The Republicans also had a spirited campaign in that race.

15. For example, H. Ross Perot received $29 million in 1996, which is just under half of what the major party nominees received; the amount was determined because he had received just under half of the average major party vote in 1992.

CHAPTER 6

1. Certainly, how politicians view career progression can change during an individual's career as a result of political decisions or personal decisions. See Stone, Maisel, and Maestas (1998) and the work evolving from the Candidate Emergence Study.

2. We are indebted to Larry Sabato and Ron Rapoport for information on Virginia politics. It should also be noted that a number of states use party conventions either for endorsing purposes or for building solidarity within the party.

3. When a majority is required to win a nomination or an election, the winner must poll one-half plus at least one of the votes cast. When a plurality is required, the winner is the candidate who polls more votes than any other candidate, even if that number is considerably less than half. Some systems require that a plurality winner must have received a certain percentage of the total votes cast or a runoff between the top two (or perhaps among the top three) finishers is held to determine the winner. See section IV.C. "Who Wins."

4. To further demonstrate the variety of state experiences, the Democratic party charter in Massachusetts requires that a candidate receive

15 percent of the vote at the convention to appear on the primary ballot; despite the fact that this provision is *not* in state law, the Massachusetts courts have upheld the provision, so that it has the same impact as if it were law. (See Jewell and Olson 1988, 97.)

5. For some endorsed candidates, avoiding the label as the candidate of the party "bosses" is more difficult than it is for others. The 1998 Democratic candidate for governor of Connecticut was Barbara Kennelly, who was the candidate of the party leaders. She is also the daughter of the most well-known Connecticut Democratic leader of the immediate past, John Bailey, who served not only as Connecticut party chair but also as chair of the Democratic National Committee during the Kennedy administration.

6. These states are Connecticut, Kentucky, Maryland, New Hampshire, New Jersey, and New York.

7. These other states are Alaska, California, Arizona, Colorado, Delaware, Florida, Kansas, Massachusetts, North Carolina, Oregon, Pennsylvania, Rhode Island, South Dakota, and West Virginia.

8. These states show the difficulty and futility of attempting to classify the wide variety of state systems into a small number of categories. Carr and Scott (1984) and Jewell and Olson (1988) classify these states as having open primaries because of the ease with which one can vote in either party's primary. However, Carr and Scott (but not Jewell and Olson) place Rhode Island in the category of open primary state, despite the fact that the state maintains party enrollment lists and prospective primary voters must change three months before a primary if they wish to participate in a primary of a party other than the one in which they last voted. This is clearly more restrictive than the rules in some of the other states Carr and Scott classified as closed. The states that require party registration of this type are Alabama, Arkansas, Georgia, Illinois, Indiana, Mississippi, Missouri, South Carolina, Tennessee, Texas, and Virginia.

9. The open primary states are Hawaii, Idaho, Michigan, Minnesota, Montana, North Dakota, Vermont, and Wisconsin.

10. The Louisiana primary, in which all candidates appear on one ballot, is a variation of the blanket primary. It differs in that the result carries over to the general election if any candidate polls a majority of the primary votes. See section IV.A.

11. Orchestration of a concerted effort to nominate the weakest opponent for Lundgren would still be very difficult.

12. In 1989 North Carolina amended its runoff primary law to lower the threshold to 40 percent. Furthermore, the second-place finisher must request a runoff. In 1992, in the newly created majority minority First District, Walter Jones, the only white candidate in a six-person field, led the primary field with 38 percent of the vote. The runner-up, Eva M. Clayton, won the primary runoff with 55 percent of the vote, beating Jones by eight thousand votes. Three of the primary candidates openly endorsed Clayton. Jones was on the defensive for most of the campaign, accused of trying to thwart black political aspirations. He denied this and yet tried to get on the ballot the following November as an independent, an action deemed illegal under North Carolina law.

13. The means of redistricting is set by state law. Some states have special commissions for the purpose. Often the courts are a last resort if the political institutions cannot resolve conflicts.

14. Provision calling for a runoff election if no nominee polls 40 percent of the primary vote. This provision was struck down by a federal court that accepted the argument that the runoff provision unfairly discriminated against minorities and thus violated the Constitution and the Voting Rights Act. However, that decision was reversed by the circuit court of appeals. Similarly, the Arkansas runoff primary provision was struck down by a three-judge panel of the court of appeals but reinstated by the entire court sitting en banc. I am indebted to Charles Bullock for these examples.

15. It should also be noted that there are fewer Republican primaries than Democratic primaries for similar offices in similar states. This phenomenon deserves further study.

16. Party officials—county chairs, state and county committee members, ward and precinct leaders, and the like—are frequently not well known. Why they seek and accept such positions is a most interesting question, the answer to which varies significantly from locale to locale and individual to individual. In any case, one of the principal responsibilities they undertake is to assure that their party is represented on the general election ballot.

17. One could make the subgroup smaller still. Primary contests could be divided into those involving serious opposition and those in which the opposition is marginal or frivolous. Candidates have a sense of this distinction in advance, but analysts have trouble determining who is serious and who is frivolous until some additional information is added, e.g., how much money a candidate can raise, what kind of organizations or endorsements a candidate can attract, etc. Because these judgments are essentially subjective, this differentiation will not be pursued in this discussion.

18. It should be noted that ten or more incumbents were defeated in primaries in 1982, 1972, and 1962 as well.

19. Fitzgerald won the Republican primary and went on to beat Senator Moseley-Braun in the general election, the only senatorial challenger to beat an incumbent Democrat. However, most analysts feel that Senator Moseley-Braun's performance in office and a scandal from which she had to defend herself in the campaign's closing days had more to do with her defeat than did Fitzgerald's ideological purity.

CHAPTER 7

1. Before we proceed any further, we should recognize that this assumption is, in all likelihood, not supportable. Few politicians really understand the process into which they are entering; even experienced politicians make decisions about campaigns in spite of information that would lead a rational person to another conclusion (Hershey 1984; Maisel 1982, 1986).

2. Exceptions to this generalization include a politician's race for office

in order to increase name recognition and visibility for a future race, politicians who might be "term limited" out of a seat in another two years and see the chance now, no matter how slim, as better than it will be in the future, and/or a politician's willingness to run a seemingly futile race in order to assure that a respectable candidate is fielded. The candidate in the latter instance earns many IOUs from the party.

3. Obviously one key factor is whether one must give up a current office to run for another office. In most cases this is so, but exceptions exist. For example, as noted earlier, five states hold state elections in odd-numbered years and thus terms for state legislature do not expire when congressional elections are held.

4. The candidate is not an incumbent. Incumbents have all faced this problem at some point—when they first sought the office. They are now in the position of a candidate seeking to stay in the same office. By and large, their campaign tactics were dictated by what worked well the last time.

5. This discussion does not deal with financial contributions by organized groups. These contributions are often critical for campaigns. However, they are used to pay for campaign techniques that in turn substitute for candidate time or otherwise transmit the candidate's message. These techniques and the entire question of campaign financing were discussed briefly in chapter 3 and in depth in chapter 5.

6. In areas with strong party organizations, party volunteers still carry "sample ballots," urging supporters to vote for all candidates in their party. This technique is particularly effective in areas dominated by one party or the other, or in areas in which the organization can effectively target households in which their supporters live (Hicks 1998).

7. There is a growing literature on campaign consultants. See, as examples, Thurber and Nelson 2000; Johnson-Cartee and Copeland (1997); Medvic and Lenart (1997); Petracca (1989); Shea (1996); Sabato (1981).

8. As is always the case with data concerning U.S. Senate elections, it is necessary to interpret percentages with great caution. Although percentaging among 435 House elections makes good sense, presenting percentage data when the total number involved is generally less than thirty can lead to misinterpretation. The number of incumbent senators seeking reelection in any campaign is small enough that analysis of individual races is often most appropriate.

9. The very small numbers involved in some years is the reason that we have presented raw numbers rather than percentages. Following the logic in note 8, above, percentaging would be even more likely to lead to misinterpretation because of the very few cases examined.

10. The caveat that increased competition is not likely in strong one-party areas needs to be added, though it is rarely raised by those arguing for term limits.

11. It is worth noting that the momentum for term limits seems to have abated. After they captured majority status in the Congress in 1994, the Republicans attempted to pass a constitutional amendment mandating

term limits, as they had promised in the Contract with America. That amendment did not pass; it was opposed by a significant number of Republicans. As the 2000 congressional elections approached, Republican representatives first elected on the Contract faced the inevitability of the self-imposed three-term limit on which they originally campaigned. Many had second thoughts but were faced with a dilemma—to leave the House or to risk giving an opponent a campaign issue, the broken term limit promise. None of those who "broke the pledge" was punished by the electorate to the extent of losing his or her seat.

12. Nebraska's state legislature differs from those in all of the other states in two regards. First, legislators are elected on nonpartisan ballots, i.e., they do not run under a party label. Second, the legislature has only one house; it is unicameral, not bicameral, as are the other state legislatures as well as Congress.

13. As noted earlier, in 1996 Collins and Brennan again faced each other, in a race to succeed retiring senator William Cohen. Collins won that race, perhaps finally ending Joseph Brennan's long, and at times illustrious, career in Maine electoral politics.

14. In Ventura's case, the Minnesota campaign finance law, which restricted the amounts the major party candidates could spend, worked in the Reform party candidate's favor. He was unable to secure loans to spend money until late in the campaign. By the time Ventura was viewed as a serious candidate and had money to advertise, his opponents had already committed most of their money. Thus the playing field tilted to his advantage. We are indebted to former Congressman Bill Frenzel of Minnesota for this insight into his home state's politics.

15. State law can make a difference in the impact of third-party candidacies. In New York State, as discussed in chapter 6, candidates can run on more than one party label at the same time. If that is the case, their *total* vote is the one that is counted, i.e., their votes on different labels are added together. In that situation, third parties use the leverage of either giving or refraining from giving an extra line on the ballot as a means to convince candidates to adopt certain policy positions. To counter the influence of third parties, or in some cases to supplement that influence, many candidates run as "independents" as well as on party lines, in the same election. Although the "independent" label might appear oxymoronic, candidates believe that some voters will support them on that label, rather than as a candidate of a party, in order to show lack of support for the parties themselves.

16. One defeated congressional challenger has concluded, "No one can win a congressional seat unless he is willing to campaign full-time twice, knowing that he will lose the first time. Anyone who is willing to do that must be crazy." The reader can draw his or her own conclusion about what that statement says about successful congressional candidates.

17. A corollary of this strategy is that a candidate whose chances do not appear strong must look for how events could break so that he or she would have a chance. He or she seeks the positive interpretation. More

votes mean a "symbolic" (if not an actual) triumph, and enhanced credibility for future campaigns.

CHAPTER 8

1. Much of this discussion focuses on the Democratic party because most recent reform efforts have been made by Democrats. Republicans have been more satisfied with their procedures but have had to change as well because many of the reforms implemented by the Democrats involved changes in state laws affecting both parties.

2. The post-1972 commission was originally an effort to bring labor back into the fold of the Democratic party. Leonard Woodcock, president of the United Auto Workers, was originally named as the commission chair; Barbara Mikulski, a little-known Baltimore city council member, was named as vice chair. Woodcock resigned, and the leadership role fell to Mikulski. As she has subsequently demonstrated in her congressional career, the fiery Mikulski proved an able and independent leader, not at all what Democratic National chairman Robert Strauss had in mind when he named her.

3. As a result of this decision, ratified by the Supreme Court in *Democratic Party of the United States v. Wisconsin*, 450 U.S. 107 (1980), Wisconsin and other states hold "beauty contest" open primaries that have no role in determining the composition of the state's delegation to the national convention; the delegations are chosen through a caucus/convention system.

4. When Senator Kennedy challenged President Carter in 1980, he claimed that delegates pledged early in the process to Carter were nothing but "robots" by the time of the convention, unable to exercise independent judgment. The Kennedy campaign forced a vote on a rules change that would have freed the delegates to vote their conscience. However, on that vote the Carter delegates held firm, demonstrating that they were not mere robots but rather true Carter loyalists. The reform freeing bound delegates turned out to be more symbolic than effective.

5. The ingenuity of state party officials to devise rules and systems to their benefit seems unbounded. In 1984 some states used a system in which the plurality winner of a primary was given a bonus delegate (or more) for winning the primary while the remaining delegates were allocated in accord with the presidential preference of those voting. These primaries were thus dubbed "winner take more."

6. Once again this change wrought by Democratic party officials in the various states had an impact on the Republican nominating process, even though the Republicans played little role in its implementation. Changes in state law, even if pushed by only one party, affect both.

7. Missouri held its caucuses on March 9; Buchanan in fact edged Dole in those caucuses, though the estimated turnout was only ten thousand (Stanley, in Nelson 1997, 22).

8. Partially in recognition of the Bush strategy, two candidates for the Democratic nomination, former Vermont governor Howard Dean and

Massachusetts senator John Kerry, announced in November 2003 that they too would not take public money during the nominating phase of the campaign. Dean justified his decision as a necessary step to counter Bush after the nomination was won. Kerry said that he would not "unilaterally disarm," blaming Dean for forcing his decision. It should be noted that candidates who do not accept public funds can spend more in the early primary states than those who abide by the restrictions that are imposed on publicly funded candidates (see chapter 5).

9. Of the others, one resigned in disgrace (Agnew), one was an appointed vice president who had earlier sought the presidential nomination of his party (Rockefeller), and one ran in 2000 (Quayle).

10. John Connally, former governor of Texas who became famous when he was shot in the motorcade with President Kennedy and later switched to the Republican party (serving as President Nixon's secretary of the treasury), did so in 1976. Connally felt that his only chance for success was to outspend and thus outadvertise all his opponents. He felt, correctly, that he could raise a good deal of money from his Texas oil friends and the big business connections he had cemented during his tenure as treasury secretary. He was wrong in believing that he could parlay that money into a successful campaign. When Connally withdrew from the race, he had won only one delegate who, when interviewed on television at the Republican National Convention, was kiddingly referred to as the "$6,000,000 delegate."

11. Many candidates in recent years have campaigned extensively before the time when they announced their candidacy and/or federal funds have become available. The money that some candidates have used has been raised by independent candidate-sponsored political action committees. These PACs have raised and spent significant amounts of money, giving a platform to the candidate, staffing a nascent organization, and preparing for a major campaign. For example, Walter Mondale's PAC was called the Committee for the Future of America; Ronald Reagan's, Citizens for the Republic; Howard Baker's, the Republican Majority Fund; and Ted Kennedy's, the Fund for a Democratic Majority. See Corrado (1992). Virtually all of those who considered a campaign for the presidency in the year 2000 had established leadership PACs in 1998 or early 1999. For example, Vice President Gore's PAC was called Leadership '98; former New Jersey senator Bill Bradley's, Time Future Inc.; former vice president Dan Quayle's, Campaign America; and former Tennessee governor and secretary of education Lamar Alexander's, Campaign for a New American Century.

12. Early poll results also have an impact on the ability to raise money. When Michael Dukakis approached his principal fund-raiser, Robert Farmer, to ask if enough money could be raised to wage a viable campaign in 1988, Farmer first assured the governor that it could be done—he added the caveat that he had never raised money for someone who stood at 1 percent in the polls before (Black et al. 1988).

13. The Clinton campaign used another extremely effective technique in the 1992 primary campaign, again seeking to communicate directly

with the voters. The campaign mailed approximately thirty thousand campaign-produced videotapes to potential undecided voters in order to rebut personal attacks on the candidate. Polling results showed that those who in fact viewed these positive biographical tapes voted overwhelmingly for Clinton (Arterton 1993).

14. By any definition this is true in the Republican party. As mentioned earlier, in recent years the Democrats have permitted the National Committee and/or specially appointed commissions to change rules between national conventions. Whether these commissions in the DNC can overrule specific votes at a national convention is still in question.

CHAPTER 9

1. In Maine the winner of the First Congressional District's popular vote receives one electoral vote, the winner of the Second Congressional District's popular vote receives one electoral vote, and the winner of the entire state receives two electoral votes. Since this provision has been in effect (1976), Maine has delivered all of its electoral votes to the same candidate every time. Nebraska switched to a similar system for 1992, with the similar result of no splits in electoral vote allocation through 2004.

2. The amounts raised and spent in this manner are discussed in chapter 5.

3. Even in an age of virtually instantaneous communication, candidates want the physical proximity of their closest advisers. Bill Clinton and Al Gore have been the exceptions among presidential candidates in that they have been comfortable with the technological innovations in telecommunications and computers that many feel will lessen the need for advisers to travel with candidates.

4. The drama of the 1992 Clinton campaign experience was captured in the film *The War Room*, released in 1994.

5. "The speech" is as much a part of the arsenal of candidates when they are seeking the nomination as it is after they are nominated. In January 1988, the *New York Times* ran a series in which the set speeches of those seeking the nomination were reprinted. Similar series have appeared in various newspapers across the nation in each subsequent campaign.

6. Recall note 1 in this chapter.

7. The general procedure for the contingency election is spelled out in the Constitution, in Article 2 and in the Twelfth and Twenty-second Amendments. The specific procedures to be used in the House would be determined by the rules adopted by the House at that time. In a curiosity that has given pause to many analysts, the president would be elected by the House, but the vice president would be chosen by the Senate. In this age of divided government, it would theoretically be possible for the two individuals so chosen to be from different political parties.

8. The 1948 election was the first time Truman had run for president on his own, but he had served all but a few months of the fourth term to which President Roosevelt had been elected in 1944.

9. The Commission on Presidential Debates took over this role from the League of Women Voters, which had sponsored presidential debates in 1976, 1980, and 1984. The commission itself is somewhat controversial because it is made up of Democrats and Republicans and they are making decisions about whether or not third-party candidates should be involved in the debates.

10. All of the presidential contenders in 1988—and all of those since then—have become debate veterans. During the primary campaign seasons all of the candidates of the two parties have participated in a large number of debates, with the exception of President Clinton, who was unopposed for his party's renomination.

11. In 1980, one of the key questions was whether third-party contender John Anderson should be included in the debates. The sponsoring organization, the League of Women Voters, ruled that if he were above 15 percent in the polls, he would be included. President Carter refused to participate in one debate in which Anderson took part, feeling that allowing Anderson to appear with the other candidates would give his campaign a legitimacy that would hurt Carter in the long run. Although the audience for the Reagan-Anderson debate was small, the two took turns attacking the absent Carter and essentially forced him to reverse tactics and participate in later debates.

12. In addition, a series of minor party candidates have qualified for the ballot in some states in virtually every modern presidential election. The role of minor party candidates in American politics is an interesting one, particularly in historical perspective, but these candidates do not have significant impact on either the strategies of the major party candidates or the outcome of the general election. For those reasons only, they are not dealt with in greater length in this text. (See Bibby and Maisel 1998; Mazmanian 1974.)

13. Students should note that Strom Thurmond, who ran as the Dixiecrat candidate for president from his position as Democratic governor of South Carolina, was the same Strom Thurmond who, more than half a century later, represented South Carolina in the Senate, as a Republican. He was one of the few American politicians who successfully switched parties and continued in office.

14. We have been using the term "third-party candidate" to refer to any candidate other than one of the two major party candidates. In fact, the individuals under consideration have been, more often than not, independent candidates, not third-party candidates, because the labels under which they ran were not those of political parties that meet the definition used throughout this text.

CHAPTER 10

1. Radio has never had the same impact on politics that newspapers and television have had, though local politicians do spend a good deal of

time trying to be certain that their views are aired on that medium as well and recent GOP success is due in no small part to talk radio.

2. In fairness, it should be noted that the two parties' nominees were known well in advance of these conventions. Thus, even in the absence of party orchestration, there would have been very little drama.

3. What follows draws heavily on Davis (1996), though similar categories have been used in other earlier works. See, for example, Barber (1978).

4. In fact this very question has been asked of many pollsters. Sampling techniques allow pollsters to obtain accurate assessments of the mood of the nation (always within a specified margin of error) by asking questions to relatively few citizens (under fifteen hundred). The same is true for polling within the various states.

5. The discussion to this point deals with candidate advertisements. Party advertisements have similar goals, either for one candidate or for a group of candidates running under the party label. Interest group advertisements are somewhat more complex and are discussed in section III.B.

6. A variation on paid advertising is the use of advertising that is paid for by the public. Proposals to restrict campaign spending using publicly provided advertising have been around for some time, but none has been implemented in the United States. It is unclear how the form of these ads would or would not vary from those currently in use.

7. The cited headlines reflect both the initial appearance of the article and its continuation inside the newspaper.

CHAPTER 11

1. Political historian James MacGregor Burns, writing in the early 1960s, noted with alarm that our political parties were causing a *Deadlock of Democracy* (1963). Burns claimed that the inability of those in government to address pressing problems was due to the four "political parties" constantly struggling with each other—the congressional Democratic party, the congressional Republican party, the presidential Democratic party, and the presidential Republican party. He felt that each of these stood for different policies and represented a different base of constituent support. The deadlock in policymaking followed from these factions, each with its own power base in the government, and all struggling with one another.

2. The Center for Responsive Politics did report, however, that House members who voted against the drug importation bill received, on average, three times more in campaign contributions from drug makers than did those members who voted for the measure (Stolberg 2003b).

3. According to political analyst Charles Cook (2006), only sixty-two House seats were competitive in 2006, a number that is actually quite a bit higher than in the recent past. Protected by redistricting, most House seats are safe for either one party or the other, with incumbents facing any serious challenge to their seat in the primary elections.

4. By the summer of 2002, Robert Menendez (D-N.J.)—who was seeking the caucus chair against Rosa DeLauro (Conn.), House assistant to the

Democratic leader—had already contributed $200,000 to his Democratic colleagues, with over $300,000 more left in his political action committee, New Millennium. He had also contributed $150,000 to the Democratic Congressional Campaign Committee (DCCC) from his personal campaign funds. Menendez was successful in his bid, elected Democratic Caucus chair. DeLauro, who contributed almost $1 million to her colleagues and to Democratic candidates in the two elections preceding 2002, was appointed Steering Policy cochair, with Pelosi (Foerstel 2002b, 1451).

5. Democrats, however, do not have term limits on their positions as committee chair or subcommittee chair.

6. Other party leaders have seats on this committee because of the offices they hold—the chief deputy, the chair of the DCCC, the vice chair of the caucus. Based on their region of the country, twelve rank-and-file members are elected to the committee by fellow Democrats. The minority leader appoints nine additional members; these members, with the members of the leadership team, ensure dominance over the committee. It is equally important to note that the ranking members of the four most powerful committees in the House—Appropriations, Budget, Rules, and Ways and Means—are also members of the committee.

7. The Democrats have developed a fairly routine path of succession. Richard Gephardt, first elected to the House in 1976, worked his way up the party hierarchy before becoming minority leader in 1995. His predecessor, Thomas S. Foley from Washington, had served in the House for a quarter century before his election as Speaker, in 1989; he had served as chair of the Agriculture Committee (1975–1981), majority whip (1981–1987), and majority leader (1987–1989). His predecessors, Jim Wright (Tex., 1954–1989; Speaker 1987–1989) and Thomas P. (Tip) O'Neill Jr. (Mass., 1952–1987; Speaker 1977–1987), had served thirty-three and twenty-five years, respectively, before their elections as Speaker.

8. In July 2003, the bill passed in the House by a narrow margin but was blocked in September by Senate Democrats and six Senate Republicans. In an amendment to a spending bill, the Senate voted 54–45 to oppose the new overtime revision. Bush threatened to veto the final appropriations package if it included the amendment.

9. The first elected whip was Tony Coehlo (D-Calif., 1978–1989). Coehlo's election says a good deal about the connections among party in government, party organization, and party in the electorate. Coehlo had sought and received appointment as chairman of the Democratic Congressional Campaign Committee (DCCC) in 1980. The DCCC had never been a base of power in the House; indeed, it seemed only a poor imitation of its Republican counterpart. But Coehlo saw potential and grabbed it. He raised unprecedented sums of money by emulating the methods of the National Republican Congressional Committee (NRCC) and reminding political action committees of which party controlled the House. He won the DCCC chair (and thus himself) a position in the House leadership hierarchy by virtue of the increasingly important role that the DCCC played in maintaining majority status.

Although he could not match the NRCC's dollar totals, he built a first-class operation and earned the admiration of (and accumulated political IOUs from) those whose campaigns he supported (Jackson 1988). When the whip's seat opened with Foley's ascent on the leadership ladder, Coehlo was ready. He drew on his reputation, called in his chits, and won the election.

10. For an analysis of the differences between the House and Senate—in terms of the size of the two bodies, the electoral environments, the prominence of the members, and the partisan contexts—see Baker (1989).

11. In the 108th Congress, the practice of holds made front page when Larry Craig (R-Idaho) blocked the promotions of more than 850 air force officers, many of whom served in Iraq, until the air force agreed to assign four additional C-130 cargo planes to the Idaho National Guard. (He had been promised eight planes seven years earlier but only received four to date.) Craig's GOP colleagues pressured him to back down, fearing alienation of some of their ardent supporters: young military officers. (See Schmitt 2003.)

12. Members who choose to employ the filibuster must weigh the benefits of their opposition against the costs of appearing too obstructionist. In 2002, Senate Democrats filibustered the GOP version of the Homeland Security Department Act, on the principle that it infringed upon employees' civil service protections (organized labor opposed the Senate bill). After the November midterm elections, the Democrats backed down: it was evident that the filibuster had little effect on the Republicans; in fact, it had negative repercussions on one of their own. Senator Max Cleland (D-Ga.), a decorated Vietnam vet, was defeated in his reelection bid, much in part for his opposition to the act and regardless of his military service.

13. Given the Senate's membership of one hundred, the Constitution assigns the job as tiebreaker, "if necessary," to the vice president. From its first session, the Senate has chosen a president pro tempore to serve in the chair in the absence of the vice president (whom the Constitution designates as the president of the Senate); the sheer numbers that have served in that position (twenty-four senators served as president pro tem in the first ten Congresses) speaks more to its position of honor than power.

Chapter 12

1. It could be argued that the election of 1988 is another example of this kind of election. In that election, the voters elected a president of the same party as a retiring incumbent. This election is generally interpreted as a reaffirmation of the Reagan legacy, though definitions of that legacy vary. Even with that caveat accepted, the election of George H. W. Bush, Ronald Reagan's vice president and designated heir, as Reagan's successor reinforces the point that presidential elections can serve as an effective means to allow citizens to express their view of the policies of the day (Jones 1988a; Pomper 1989a; Shanks and Miller 1989).

2. Although this assumption is untested in the professional literature, it seems reasonable. One piece of evidence comes from a Pew Research Center Poll conducted right after the 1998 election in which voters responded that they had obtained much more of their information about the election from local news broadcasts than had been the case in 1992 or 1996, when presidential elections were being held.

3. In 1972 Democratic nominee George McGovern's nomination represented the victory of the liberal wing of the party; his overwhelming defeat in the general election led to a reaction against extreme candidates. McGovern had been dubbed the candidate of "amnesty, acid, and abortion," and the Democratic party was associated with social extremism. The other way to view the Clinton legacy is that he converted the image of the party to a more centrist one, often adapting policy positions previously held by Republicans and making them his own.

References

Abramowitz, Alan I. 1975. "Name Familiarity, Reputation, and the Incumbency Effect in a Congressional Election." *Western Political Quarterly* 28:668–84.

———. 1981. "Party and Individual Accountability in the 1978 Congressional Election." In *Congressional Elections*, edited by L. Sandy Maisel and Joseph Cooper. Beverly Hills, Calif.: Sage.

Abramowitz, Alan I., Brad Alexander, and Matthew Gunning. 2006. "Incumbency, Redistricting, and the Decline of Competition in U.S. House Elections." *Journal of Politics* 68:75–88.

Abramowitz, Alan I., and Kyle L. Saunders. 1998. "Ideological Realignment in the U.S. Electorate." *Journal of Politics* 6:634–53.

———. 2005. "Why Can't We All Just Get Along? The Reality of a Polarized America." *The Forum* 3:1–19.

Abramson, Paul R., John H. Aldrich, Phil Paolino, and David W. Rohde. 1995. "Third Party and Independent Candidates in American Politics: Wallace, Anderson, and Perot." *Political Science Quarterly* 110:347–67.

Abramson, Paul R., John H. Aldrich, and David W. Rohde. 1995. *Change and Continuity in the 1992 Elections*. Rev. ed. Washington, D.C.: Congressional Quarterly Press.

———. 1998. *Change and Continuity in the 1996 Elections*. Washington, D.C.: Congressional Quarterly Press.

———. 2005. *Change and Continuity in the 2004 Elections*. Washington, D.C.: Congressional Quarterly Press.

———. 2007. *Change and Continuity in the 2004 and 2006 Elections*. Washington, D.C.: Congressional Quarterly Press.

Adamany, David. 1984. "Political Parties in the 1980s." In *Money and Politics in the United States*, edited by Michael J. Malbin. Washington, D.C.: American Enterprise Institute/Chatham House.

Adams, William C. 1982. "Media Power in Presidential Elections: An Exploratory Analysis, 1960–1980." In *The President and the Public*, edited by Doris A. Graber. Philadelphia: Institute for the Study of Human Issues.

Agranoff, Robert. 1972. *The Management of Election Campaigns*. Boston: Holbrook.

———. 1976. *The New Style in Election Campaigns*. Boston: Holbrook.

Aistrup, Joseph D. 1996. *The Southern Strategy Revisited*. Lexington: University of Kentucky Press.

Aldrich, John. 1980. *Before the Convention: Strategies and Choices in Presidential Nomination Campaigns*. Chicago: University of Chicago Press.

———. 1995. *Why Parties? The Origin and Transformation of Political Parties in America*. Chicago: University of Chicago Press.

Aldrich, John, and Richard G. Niemi. 1990. "The Sixth American Party System: The 1960s Realignment and Candidate-Centered Parties." Unpublished manuscript, University of Rochester, New York.

Aldrich, John H., and David W. Rohde. 1997. "The Transition to Republican Rule in the House: Implications for Theories of Congressional Politics." *Political Science Quarterly* 112:541–67.

Alexander, Herbert E. 1976a. *Financing Politics: Money, Elections, and Political Reform*. Washington, D.C.: Congressional Quarterly Press.

———. 1976b. *Financing the 1972 Election*. Lexington, Mass.: Lexington Books.

———. 1979a. *Financing the 1976 Election*. Washington, D.C.: Congressional Quarterly Press.

———. 1979b. *Political Finance*. Beverly Hills, Calif.: Sage.

———. 1980. "The Impact of the Federal Election Campaign Act on the 1976 Presidential Campaign: The Complexities of Compliance." *Emory Law Review* 29:315.

———. 1983. *Financing the 1980 Election*. Lexington, Mass.: D. C. Heath.

———. 1984. "Making Sense about Dollars in the 1980 Presidential Campaigns." In *Money and Politics in the United States: Financing Elections in the 1980s*, edited by Michael J. Malbin. Washington, D.C.: American Enterprise Institute/Chatham House.

———. 1986. *"Soft Money" and Campaign Financing*. Washington, D.C.: Public Affairs Council.

———. 1991. "Financing Presidential Campaigns." In *Political Parties and Elections in the United States: An Encyclopedia*, edited by L. Sandy Maisel. New York: Garland.

Alexander, Herbert E., and Monica Bauer. 1991. *Financing the 1988 Election*. Boulder, Colo.: Westview.

Alexander, Herbert E., and Anthony Corrado. 1995. *Financing the 1992 Elections*. New York: Sharpe.

Alexander, Herbert E., and Brian A. Haggerty. 1981. *The Federal Election Campaign Act: After a Decade of Political Reform*. Washington, D.C.: Citizens' Research Foundation.

———. 1987. *Financing the 1984 Election*. Lexington, Mass.: Lexington Books.

Alford, John R., and David W. Brady. 1989. "Personal and Partisan Advantage in U.S. Congressional Elections, 1846–1990." In *Congress Reconsidered*, edited by Lawrence C. Dodd and Bruce I. Oppenheimer. 4th ed. Washington, D.C.: Congressional Quarterly Press.

Allen, Jonathan. 2003a. "House GOP's 'Stealth Whip' Knows the Power of Listening." *Congressional Quarterly Weekly*, March 29, 750.

———. 2003b. "Effective House Leadership Makes the Most of Majority." *Congressional Quarterly Weekly*, March 29, 746–50.

Allen, Jonathan, and Adam Graham-Silverman. 2003. "Hour by Hour, Vote by Vote, GOP Breaks Tense Tie." *Congressional Quarterly Weekly*, June 28, 1614–15.

Almond, Gabriel A., and Sidney Verba. 1965. *The Civic Culture*. Boston: Little, Brown.

Alt, James E. 1994. *The Impact of the Voting Rights Act on Black and White Voter Registration in the South*. Princeton, N.J.: Princeton University Press.

Alter, Jonathan. 1992. "The Media Mud Squad." *Newsweek*, October 29, 37.

American Political Science Association. Committee on Political Parties. 1950. "Toward a More Responsible Two-Party System." *American Political Science Review* 64. (Volume 44, No. 3, Part 2, Supplement – p. v–ix, 1–96)

Ansolabehere, Stephen, and Shanto Iyengar. 1995. *Going Negative: How Political Advertisements Shrink and Polarize the Electorate*. New York: Free Press.

Aoki, Andrew L., and Mark Rom. 1985. "Financing a Comeback: Campaign Finance Laws and Prospects for Political Party Resurgence." Paper presented at the annual meeting of the American Political Science Association, New Orleans, La.

Appleton, Andrew M., and Daniel S. Ward. 1997. *State Party Profits: A Fifty-State Guide to Development, Organization, and Resources*. Washington, D.C.: Congressional Quarterly Press.

Arsenau, Robert B., and Raymond E. Wolfinger. 1973. "Voting Behavior in Congressional Elections." Paper presented at the annual meeting of the American Political Science Association, New Orleans, La.

Arterton, F. Christopher. 1982. "Political Money and Party Strength." In *The Future of American Political Parties*, edited by Joel L. Fleishman. Englewood Cliffs, N.J.: Prentice-Hall.

———. 1993. "Campaign '92: Strategies and Tactics of the Candidates." In *The Election of 1992: Reports and Interpretation*, edited by Gerald M. Pomper. Chatham, N.J.: Chatham House.

Associated Press. 1998. "Democrats Assail Republicans for Attack Ads." October 28.

Axelrod, Robert. 1972. "Where the Votes Come From: An Analysis of Electoral Coalitions, 1952–1968." *American Political Science Review* 66:11–20.

Ayres, Drummond. 1998. "Political Briefing: Greens Abandon One of Their Own." *New York Times*, September 29, online edition.

Bach, Stanley, and Steven S. Smith. 1988. *Managing Uncertainty in the House of Representatives: Adaption and Innovation in Special Rules*. Washington, D.C.: Brookings Institution.

Baker, Ross K. 1989. *House and Senate*. New York: Norton.

Balz, Dan. 1998. "GOP Governors Look to Wield Stronger Hand in Party Affairs." *Washington Post*, November 16, A4.

Balz, Dan, and David Broder. 1998. "Shaken Republicans Count Losses, Debate Blame." *Washington Post*, November 5, A1.

Balz, Dan, and Jim VandeHei. 2006. "Amid the Last-Minute Blitz, Some Polls Hold Positive Signs for Republicans." *Washington Post*, November 6, A1.

Banfield, Edward C., and James Q. Wilson. 1963. *City Politics*. Cambridge, Mass.: Harvard University Press.

Barber, Denise Roth. 2005. *Declining Fortunes: State Party Finances, 2004*. Helena, Mont.: The Institute on Money in State Politics.

Barber, James David. 1978. *The Race for the Presidency: The Media and the Nominating Process*. Englewood Cliffs, N.J.: Prentice-Hall.

Barker, Lucius J., and Ronald Walter, eds. 1989. *Jesse Jackson and the 1984 Presidential Campaign*. Urbana: University of Illinois Press.

Bartels, Larry M. 2000. "Partisanship and Voting Behavior, 1952-1996." *American Journal of Political Science* 44 (January):35–50.

Basehart, Harry, and John Comer. 1991. "Partisan and Incumbent Effects in State Legislative Redistricting." *Legislative Studies Quarterly* 16:65–79.

Beck, Paul Allen. 1984. "The Dealignment Era in America." In *Electoral Change in Advanced Industrial Democracies*, edited by Russell J. Dalton, Scott C. Flanagan, and Paul Allen Beck. Princeton, N.J.: Princeton University Press.

Bennett, Stephen E. 1990. "The Uses and Abuses of Registration and Turnout Data." *PS: Political Science and Politics* 23:166–71.

Bennett, Stephen E., and David Resnick. 1991. "The Implications for Nonvoting for Democracy in the United States." *American Journal of Political Science* 34:771–803.

Berelson, Bernard, Paul F. Lazarsfeld, and William N. McPhee. 1954. *Voting*. Chicago: University of Chicago Press.

Berke, Richard L. 1998. "New Republican Advertising Blitz Centers on President's Sex Scandal." *New York Times*, October 28, A1.

Berkman, Ronald, and Laura Kitch. 1986. *Politics in the Media Age*. New York: McGraw-Hill.

Berry, Jeffrey M. 1997. *The Interest Group Society*. New York: Longman.

Berry, Jeffrey M., and Clyde Wilcox. 2007. *The Interest Group Society*. 4th ed. New York: Pearson/Longman.

Bibby, John F. 1981. "Party Renewal in the National Republican Party." In *Party Renewal in America*, edited by Gerald Pomper. New York: Praeger.

———. 1986. "Party Trends in 1985: Constrained Advance of the National Party." *Publius* 16:79–91.

———. 1990. "Party Organization at the State Level." In *The Parties Respond: Changes in the American Party System*, edited by L. Sandy Maisel. Boulder, Colo.: Westview.

———. 1991. "Republican National Committee." In *Political Parties and Elections in the United States: An Encyclopedia*, edited by L. Sandy Maisel. New York: Garland.

———. 1998. "State Party Organizations: Coping and Adapting to Candidate-Centered Politics and Nationalization." In *The Parties Respond*, edited by L. Sandy Maisel. 3d ed. Boulder, Colo.: Westview.

———. 2002. "State Party Organizations: Strengthened and Adapting to

Candidate-Centered Politics and Nationalization." In *The Parties Respond*, edited by L. Sandy Maisel. 4th ed. Boulder, Colo.: Westview.

Bibby, John F., Cornelius P. Cotter, James L. Gibson, and Robert J. Huckshorn. 1983. "Political Parties." In *Politics in the American States*, edited by Virginia Gray, Herbert Jacob, and Kenneth N. Vines. 4th ed. Boston: Little, Brown.

Bibby, John F., and Thomas M. Holbrook. 1996. "Parties and Elections." In *Politics in the American States: A Comparative Analysis*, edited by Virginia Gray and Herbert Jacob. 6th ed. Washington, D.C.: Congressional Quarterly Press.

Bibby, John F., and L. Sandy Maisel. 1998. *Two Parties or More?* Boulder, Colo.: Westview.

———. 2002. *Two Parties or More?* 2d ed. Boulder, Colo.: Westview.

Binder, Sarah, and Steven Smith. 1997. *Politics or Principle? Filibustering in the U.S. Senate*. Washington, D.C.: Brookings Institution.

Binkley, Wilfred. 1963. *American Political Parties*. 4th ed. New York: Knopf.

Bishop, Bill. 2004 "The Great Divide." Series in *Austin American-Statesman*.

Black, Christine, Andrew Blake, John Aloysius Farrell, Thomas Oliphant, and Joan Vennochi. 1988. "The Road to Nomination." *Boston Globe*, May 8–11, 1.

Black, Christine M., and Thomas Oliphant. 1989. *All by Myself: The Unmaking of a Presidential Campaign*. Chester, Conn.: Globe Pequot Press.

Black, Earl, and Merle Black. 1987. *Politics and Society in the South*. Cambridge, Mass.: Harvard University Press.

———. 2002. *The Rise of Southern Republicans*. Cambridge, Mass.: Harvard University Press.

Black, Gordon S., and Benjamin D. Black. 1993. "Perot Wins: The Election That Could Have Been." *Public Perspective* 4:15–16.

Bloom, Howard S., and H. Douglas Price. 1975. "Voter Response to Short-Run Economic Conditions: The Asymmetric Effect of Prosperity and Recession." *American Political Science Review* 69:1240–54.

Blum, John M., William McFeely, Edmund Morgan, Arthur Schlesinger Jr., Kenneth Stampp, and C. Vann Woodward. 1993. *The National Experience: A History of the United States*. 8th ed. New York: Harcourt.

Bolingbroke, Lord. [1841] 1976. *The Works of Lord Bolingbroke*. Philadelphia: Carey and Hart. Cited in Giovanni Sartori, *Parties and Party Systems: A Framework for Analysis*. New York: Cambridge University Press.

Bone, Hugh A., and Austin Ranney. 1976. *Politics and Voters*. 4th ed. New York: McGraw-Hill.

Born, Richard. 1985. "Partisan Intentions and Election Day Realities in the Congressional Redistricting Process." *American Political Science Review* 79:305–19.

Bowers, Chris, and Matthew Stoller. 2005. "Emergence of the Progressive Blogosphere: A New Force in American Politics." Washington, D.C.: New Politics Institute.

Brady, David W. 1973. *Congressional Voting in a Partisan Era*. Lawrence: University Press of Kansas.

Brady, David W., and Kara Z. Buckley. 2002. "Governing by Coalition: Policymaking in the U.S. Congress." In *The Parties Respond*, edited by L. Sandy Maisel. 4th ed. Boulder, Colo.: Westview.

Brady, David, Kara Buckley, and Doug Rivers. 2000. "Elections and Insurance Incentives: Parties at the Turn of the Century." Paper presented at the annual meeting of the Midwest Political Science Association, Chicago.

Brady, David W., Charles S. Bullock III, and L. Sandy Maisel. 1988. "The Electoral Antecedents of Policy Innovations: A Comparative Analysis." *Comparative Political Studies* 20:395–422.

Brady, David W., Joseph Cooper, and Patricia A. Hurley. 1977. "The Electoral Basis of Party Voting: Patterns and Trends in the U.S. House of Representatives 1887–1969." In *The Impact of the Electoral Process*, edited by Louis Maisel and Joseph Cooper. Beverly Hills, Calif.: Sage Publications.

———. 1979. "The Decline of Party in the U.S. House of Representatives, 1887–1968." *Legislative Studies Quarterly* 4:381–407.

Brady, David W., and David Epstein. 1997. "Intra-party Preferences, Heterogeneity, and the Origins of the Modern Congress: Progressive Reformers in the House and Senate, 1890–1970." *Journal of Law, Economics, and Organization* 13:26–49.

Brady, David W., L. Sandy Maisel, and Kevin M. Warsh. 1994. "An Opportunity Cost Model of the Decision to Run for Congress: Another Contributor to Democratic Hegemony." Paper presented at the annual meeting of the American Political Science Association, New York.

Brady, David W., and Barbara Sinclair. 1984. "Building Majorities for Policy Change in the House of Representatives." *Journal of Politics* 46:1033–60.

Brady, David W., and Joseph Stewart Jr. 1986. "When Elections Really Matter: Realignment and Changes in Public Policy." In *Do Elections Matter?* edited by Benjamin Ginsberg and Alan Stone. Armonk, N.Y.: Sharpe.

Brady, David W., and Craig Volden. 1998. *Revolving Gridlock: Politics and Policy from Carter to Clinton*. Boulder, Colo.: Westview.

Brewer, Mark D. 2005. "The Rise of Partisanship and the Expansion of Partisan Conflict within the American Electorate." *Political Research Quarterly* 58:219–29.

———. 2008. *Party Images in the American Electorate*. New York: Routledge.

Brewer, Mark D., and Jeffrey M. Stonecash. 2007. *Split: Class and Cultural Divides in American Politics*. Washington, D.C.: CQ Press.

Bridges, Amy. 1984. *A City in the Republic: Antebellum New York and the Origins of Machine Politics*. New York: Cambridge University Press.

Broder, David S. 1971. *The Party's Over*. New York: Harper and Row.

———. 1998. "Key Republican Primaries to Focus on Right's Appeal." *Maine Sunday Telegram*, March 8, 3C.

Broder, David, and Ruth Marcus. 1997. "The Debate Over 'Issue Ads.'" *Washington Post National Weekly Edition*, September 29, 6.

Brody, Richard A., and Benjamin I. Page. 1972. "Policy Voting and the Electoral Process: The Vietnam War Issue." *American Political Science Review* 66:979–95.

Brown, Robert D., and John M. Bruce. 2002. "Political Parties in State and Nation: Party Advantage and Party Competition in a Federal Setting." *Party Politics* 8:635–56.

Brunell, Thomas L., and Bernard Grofman. 1998. "Explaining Divided U.S. Senate Delegations, 1788–1996: A Realignment Approach." *American Political Science Review* 92:391–99.

Bruno, Jerry, and Jeff Greenfield. 1971. *The Advance Man*. New York: Morrow.

Buchanan, Bruce. 1991. *Electing a President: The Markle Commission Research on Campaign '88*. Austin: University of Texas Press.

Buell, Emmett H., Jr., and Lee Sigelman. 1991. *Nominating the President*. Knoxville: University of Tennessee Press.

Bullock, Charles S., III. 1988. "Regional Realignment from an Officeholding Perspective." *Journal of Politics* 50:553–74.

Bullock, Charles S., III, and David W. Brady. 1983. "Party, Constituency, and Roll-Call Voting in the U. S. Senate." *Legislative Studies Quarterly* 8:29–43.

Bullock, Charles S., and Loch K. Johnson. 1992. *Runoff Elections in the United States*. Chapel Hill: University of North Carolina Press.

Bumiller, Elisabeth, and David E. Sanger. 2002. "Republicans Say Rove Was Mastermind of Big Victory." *New York Times*, November 7, B1.

Burke, Edmund. 1976. "Thoughts on the Cause of the Present Discontents." In *The Works of Edmund Burke. Vol. 3*. Boston: Little, Brown. Cited in *Parties and Party Systems: A Framework for Analysis*, edited by Giovanni Sartori. New York: Cambridge University Press.

Burnham, Walter Dean. 1965. "The Changing Shape of the American Political Universe." *American Political Science Review* 59:7–28.

———. 1970. *Critical Elections and the Mainsprings of American Democracy*. New York: Norton.

———. 1991. "Critical Realignment: Dead or Alive?" In *The End of Realignment*, edited by Byron E. Shafer. Madison: University of Wisconsin Press.

Burns, James MacGregor. 1963. *The Deadlock of Democracy: Four-Party Politics in America*. Englewood Cliffs, N.J.: Prentice-Hall.

Butler, David, and Bruce E. Cain. 1991. *Congressional Redistricting: Comparative and Theoretical Perspectives*. New York: Macmillan.

Caddell, Patrick H. 1981. "The Democratic Strategy and Its Electoral Consequences." In *Party Coalitions in the 1980s*, edited by Seymour Martin Lipset. San Francisco: Institute for Contemporary Studies.

Cain, Bruce E. 1984. *The Reapportionment Puzzle*. Berkeley: University of California Press.

———. 1985. "Assessing the Partisan Effects of Redistricting." *American Political Science Review* 79:320–33.

Cain, Bruce E., and David Butler. 1991. "Redrawing District Lines: What's Going On and What's at Stake?" *American Enterprise* 2 (July/August): 28–39.

Cain, Bruce E., John Ferejohn, and Morris Fiorina. 1987. *The Personal Vote: Constituency Service and Electoral Independence*. Cambridge, Mass.: Harvard University Press.

Calvert, Jerry W. 1979. "Revolving Doors: Volunteerism in State Legislatures." *State Government* 52:174.

Campbell, Angus, Philip E. Converse, Warren E. Miller, and Donald A. Stokes. 1960. *The American Voter*. New York: Wiley.

Canon, David T. 1990. *Actors, Athletes, and Astronauts: Political Amateurs in the United States Congress*. Chicago: University of Chicago Press.

Carey, Mary Agnes, and Rebecca Adams. 2003. "Constituents Will Determine if Recess Helps or Hinders Medicare Conference." *Congressional Quarterly Weekly Report*, 1971.

Carlisle, John K. 2004. "George Soros: His Plan to Defeat George Bush, Part I." Foundation Watch, Capital Research Center, February.

Carmines, Edward G., John P. McIver, and James A. Stimson. 1987. "Unrealized Partisanship: A Theory of Dealignment." *Journal of Politics* 49:376–400.

Carmines, Edward G., and James A. Stimson. 1989. *Issue Evolution: Race and the Transformation of American Politics*. Princeton, N.J.: Princeton University Press.

Carr, Craig L., and Gary L. Scott. 1984. "The Logic of State Primary Classification Schemes." *American Politics Quarterly* 12:465–76.

Carter, Jimmy. 1982. *Public Papers of the President*. Washington, D.C.: U.S. Government Printing Office.

Cassel, Carol A., and Robert C. Luskin. 1988. "Simple Explanations of Voter Turnout." *American Political Science Review* 82:1321–30.

Catt, Carrie C., and Nettie R. Shuler. 1969. *Woman Suffrage and Politics*. Seattle: University of Washington Press.

Ceaser, James, and Andrew Busch. 1993. *Upside-Down and Inside-Out: The 1992 Elections and American Politics*. Lanham, Md.: Rowman and Littlefield.

———. 1997. *Losing to Win: The 1996 Election and American Politics*. Lanham, Md.: Rowman and Littlefield.

Center for Responsive Politics. 1985. *Soft Money: A Loophole for the '80s*. Washington, D.C.: Center for Responsive Politics.

Center for Voting and Democracy. 2003. "Uncontested State Legislative Races 2002." http://fairvote.org/reports/uncontestedraces.htm (accessed August 5, 2003).

Chambers, William N. 1963. *Political Parties in a New Nation: The American Experience, 1776–1809*. New York: Oxford University Press.

———. 1975. "Party Development in the American Mainstream." In *The American Party Systems: Stages of Political Development*, edited by William N. Chambers and Walter D. Burnham. 2d ed. New York: Oxford University Press.

Chambers, Willliam N., and Walter D. Burnham, eds. 1975. *The American Party Systems: Stages of Political Development*. 2d ed. New York: Oxford University Press.

Cigler, Allan J. 2006. "Interest Groups and Financing the 2004 Elections."

In *Financing the 2004 Election*, edited by David B. Magleby, Anthony J. Corrado, and Kelly D. Patterson. Washington, D.C.: Brookings Institution.

Cigler, Allan J., and Burdett A. Loomis, eds. 1995. Interest Group Politics. 4th ed. Washington, D.C.: Congressional Quarterly Press.

———. 2007. Interest Group Politics. 7th ed. Washington, D.C.: Congressional Quarterly Press.

Citizens' Research Foundation. 1997. *New Realities, New Thinking: Report of the Task Force on Campaign Finance Reform*. Los Angeles: Citizens' Research Foundation, University of Southern California.

Clymer, Adam. 2003a. "Buoyed by Resurgence, GOP Strives for an Era of Dominance," *New York Times*, May 25. (Section 1, page 1)

———. 2003b. "Washington Talk: Campaign Finance Muddle Recalls Election of '76." *New York Times*, May 6, A28.

Clymer, Adam, and David E. Rosenbaum. 2002. "Republicans Hold the House." *New York Times*, November 6, B5.

Cochran, John. 2003. "Supreme Court Narrowly Upholds Core Campaign Finance Provisions," *Congressional Quarterly Weekly*, December 13, 3076–3079.

Collie, Melissa P., and David W. Brady. 1985. "The Decline of Partisan Voting Coalitions in the House of Representatives." In *Congress Reconsidered*, edited by Lawrence C. Dodd and Bruce I. Oppenheimer. 3d ed. Washington, D.C.: Congressional Quarterly Press.

Collie, Melissa P., and Joseph Cooper. 1989. "Multiple Referral and the 'New' Committee System in the House of Representatives." In *Congress Reconsidered*, edited by Lawrence C. Dodd and Bruce I. Oppenheimer. 4th ed. Washington, D.C.: Congressional Quarterly Press.

Common Cause. 1986. *Financing the Finance Committee*. Washington, D.C.: Common Cause.

Congressional Quarterly Almanac. 1971–2003. Washington, D.C.: Congressional Quarterly.

Congressional Quarterly Weekly. 2003. "Sharp Divide on Highest Court Revealed in Disparate Opinions," December 13, 3078.

Connolly, Ceci. 1998. "GOP Spends Millions on TV Ads Attacking President's Conduct." *Washington Post*, October 28, A5.

Converse, Philip E., Aage R. Clausen, and Warren E. Miller. 1965. "Electoral Myth and Reality: The 1964 Election." *American Political Science Review* 59:321–36.

Converse, Philip E., and Richard G. Niemi. 1971. "Nonvoting among Young Adults in the United States." In *Political Parties and Political Behavior*, edited by William J. Crotty, Donald M. Freeman, and Douglas S. Gatlin. 2d ed. Boston: Allyn and Bacon.

Converse, Philip E., and Roy Pierce. 1987. "Measuring Partisanship." *Political Methodology* 11:143.

Cook, Charles. 2006. *The Cook Political Report*, November 6, 1–2.

Cook, Rhodes. 1986. "Democrats Alter Rules Slightly in Effort to Broaden Party Base." *Congressional Quarterly* 44:2158.

Cooper, Joseph, and David W. Brady. 1981. "Institutional Context and Leadership Style: The House from Cannon to Rayburn." *American Political Science Review* 75:411-25.

Cooper, Joseph, and William West. 1981. "The Congressional Career in the '70's." In *Congress Reconsidered*, edited by Lawrence Dodd and Bruce I. Oppenheimer. 2d ed. Washington, D.C.: Congressional Quarterly Press.

Corrado, Anthony J. 1991a. "Federal Election Campaign Act of 1971." In *Political Parties and Elections in the United States: An Encyclopedia*, edited by L. Sandy Maisel. New York: Garland.

———. 1991b. "Federal Election Campaign Act Amendments of 1974." In *Political Parties and Elections in the United States: An Encyclopedia*, edited by L. Sandy Maisel. New York: Garland.

———. 1992. *Creative Campaigning: PACs and the Presidential Selection Process*. Boulder, Colo.: Westview.

———. 1993. *Paying for Presidents: Public Financing in National Elections*. New York: Twentieth Century Fund Press.

———. 2006a. "The Regulatory Environment: Uncertainty in the Wake of Change." In *Financing the 2004 Election*, edited by David B. Magleby, Anthony J. Corrado, and Kelly D. Patterson. Washington, D.C.: Brookings Institution.

———. 2006b. "Financing the 2004 Presidential General Election." In *Financing the 2004 Election*, edited by David B. Magleby, Anthony J. Corrado, and Kelly D. Patterson. Washington, D.C.: Brookings Institution.

———. 2006c. *Parties Playing a Major Role in Election '06*. CFI Working Paper on the Political Parties. Campaign Finance Institute.

———. 2006d. "Party Finance in the Wake of BCRA: An Overview." In *The Election after Reform*, edited by Michael J. Malbin. Lanham, Md.: Rowman and Littlefield.

Corrado, Anthony J., and L. Sandy Maisel. 1988. "Campaigning for Presidential Nominations: The Experience with State Spending Ceilings, 1976–1984." Paper presented at the annual meeting of the Western Political Science Association, San Francisco. Occasional Paper nos. 88–84, Center for American Political Studies Harvard University, Cambridge, Mass.

Corrado, Anthony J., Thomas E. Mann, Daniel R. Ortiz, Trevor Potter, and Frank J. Sorauf, eds. 1997. *Campaign Finance Reform: A Sourcebook*. Washington, D.C.: Brookings Institution.

Corrado, Anthony J., Thomas E. Mann, Daniel R. Ortiz, and Trevor Potter. 2005. *The New Campaign Finance Sourcebook*. Washington, D.C.: Brookings Institution.

Cotter, Cornelius P., and John F. Bibby. 1980. "Institutional Developments of Parties and the Thesis of Party Decline." *Political Science Quarterly* 1:95.

Cotter, Cornelius P., James L. Gibson, John F. Bibby, and Robert J. Huckshorn. 1982. "Party–Government Linkages in the States." Paper delivered at the annual meeting of the American Political Science Association, Washington, D.C.

———. 1984. *Party Organization in American Politics*. New York: Praeger.

———. 1989. *Party Organization in American Politics*. 2d ed. New York: Praeger.

Cotter, Cornelius P., and Bernard C. Hennessy. 1964. *Politics without Power: The National Party Committees*. New York: Atherton.

Courser, Zachary. 2007. "Mugwumps and Goo-Goos: American Democracy and Nineteenth Century Anti-Partisanship." Paper presented at the annual meeting of the Midwest Political Science Association, Chicago, Ill.

Coval, Michael. 1984. "The Impact of the 1980 Election on Liberal Political Organization." Honors project presented at Colby College, Waterville, Maine.

Cover, Albert D. 1977. "One Good Term Deserves Another: The Advantages of Incumbency in Congressional Elections." *American Journal of Political Science* 21:523–41.

Cox, Gary, and Samuel Kernell, eds. 1991. *The Politics of Divided Government*. Boulder, Colo.: Westview.

Cox, Gary, and Mathew D. McCubbins. 1993. *Legislative Leviathan: Party Government in the House*. Berkeley: University of California Press.

———. 2005. *Setting the Agenda: Responsible Party Government in the U.S. House of Representatives*. New York: Cambridge University Press.

Cox, Gary W., and Scott Morgenstern. 1993. "The Increasing Advantage of Incumbency in the U.S. States." *Legislative Studies Quarterly* 18:495–514.

———. 1995. "The Incumbency Advantage in Multimember Districts: Evidence from the U.S. States." *Legislative Studies Quarterly* 20:329–49.

Craig, Tim, and Michael D. Shear. 2006. "Allen Quip Provokes Outrage, Apology." *Washington Post*. August 15, A01.

Cranford, John. 2004. "'Key Votes' Highly Partisan." *Congressional Quarterly Weekly*, January 3.

Crespi, Irving. 1988. *Pre-election Polling: Sources of Accuracy and Error*. New York: Russell Sage Foundation.

———. 1989. *Public Opinion, Polls, and Democracy*. Boulder, Colo.: Westview.

Crosby, Stephen. 1998. Correspondence, September 2.

Crotty, William J. 1983. *Party Reform*. New York: Longman.

———. 1984. *American Political Parties in Decline*, 2d edition. Boston: Little Brown.

———. 1985. *The Party Game*. New York: Freeman.

Crouse, Timothy. 1973. *The Boys on the Bus*. New York: Ballantine.

Cummings, Norman, and Grace Cummings. 2004. "Strategy and Tactics for Campaign Fundraising." In *Campaigns and Elections American Style*, 2d ed., edited by James A. Thurber and Candice J. Nelson. Boulder, Colo.: Westview.

Cunningham, Noble E. 1965. *The Making of the American Party System, 1789 to 1809*. Englewood Cliffs, N.J.: Prentice-Hall.

Dahl, Robert. 1961. *Who Governs? Democracy and Power in an American City*. New Haven, Conn.: Yale University Press.

Daley, Steve, and Roger Worthington. 1989. "Senior's Wrath Stings Lobby Protests over Catastrophic Care Law Targets AARP." *Chicago Tribune*, September 3, 1.

Davidson, Roger H. 1981. "Subcommittee Government: New Channels for Policy Making." In *The New Congress*, edited by Thomas E. Mann and

Norman J. Ornstein. Washington, D.C.: American Enterprise Institute for Public Policy Research.

Davis, James W. 1983. *National Conventions in an Age of Party Reform*. Westport, Conn.: Greenwood.

Davis, Richard. 1996. *The Press and American Politics: The New Mediator*. 2d ed. Upper Saddle River, N.J.: Prentice-Hall.

de Morales, Lisa. 2006. "Colbert, Still Digesting His Correspondents' Dinner Reception." *Washington Post*. May 2, C07.

Dewan, Shaila, and Anne E. Kornblut. 2006. "In Key House Races, Democrats Run to the Right." *New York Times*, October 30, A1.

Dewar, Helen. 1999. "Senate Democrats Seek an Early Vote on Articles." *Washington Post*, January 21, A1, A16.

Diamond, Edwin, and Stephen Bates. 1984. *The Spot: The Rise of Political Advertising on Television*. Cambridge, Mass.: MIT Press.

Dlouhy, Jennifer A. 2002. "Parties Use Judicial Standoff to Play to Core Constituents." *Congressional Quarterly Weekly*, October 19, 2722–27.

———. 2003. "A New Level of Acrimony in Parties' War of Procedure." *Congressional Quarterly Weekly*, May 10, 1078–84.

Dobson, John M. 1972. *Politics in the Gilded Age*. New York: Praeger.

Donovan, Beth. 1991. "Deadlines Not Always Met When Stakes Are High." *Congressional Quarterly Weekly Report* 49:1776.

Downs, Anthony. 1957. *An Economic Theory of Democracy*. New York: Harper and Row.

Drew, Elizabeth. 1981. *Portrait of an Election: The 1980 Presidential Campaign*. New York: Simon and Schuster.

———. 1983. *Politics and Money: The New Road to Corruption*. New York: Macmillan.

Duverger, Maurice. 1951. *Political Parties*. New York: Wiley.

Dwyer, Diana, and Robin Kolodny. 2006. "The Parties' Congressional Campaign Committees in 2004." In *The Election after Reform*, edited by Michael J. Malbin. Lanham, Md.: Rowman and Littlefield.

Edsall, Thomas B. 1986. "Conservative Fund-Raisers Hit Hard Times." *Washington Post*.

———. 2006. *Building Red America*. New York: Basic Books.

Edsall, Thomas B., and Ceci Connolly. 1998. "The GOP Is Coming Apart at the Seams." *Washington Post National Weekly Edition*, April 6, 13–14.

Edsall, Thomas B., and James V. Grimaldi. 2004. "How the Two Parties Split Their Millions." *Washington Post*, December 30, A7.

Eismeier, Theodore J., and Philip H. Pollock III. 1984. "Political Action Committees: Varieties of Organization and Strategy." In *Money and Politics in the United States*, edited by Michael J. Malbin. Washington, D.C.: American Enterprise Institute/Chatham House.

———. 1985a. "The Microeconomy of PACs." Paper delivered at the annual meeting of the American Political Science Association, Washington, D.C.

———. 1985b. "An Organizational Analysis of Political Action Committees." *Political Behavior* 7:192–216.

———. 1986. "Strategy and Choice in Congressional Elections: The Role of Political Action Committees." *American Journal of Political Science* 30:197–213.

Eldersveld, Samuel J. 1982. *Political Parties in American Society*. New York: Basic Books.

Elshtain, Jean Bethke, and Christopher Beem. 1997. "Issues and Themes: Economics, Culture, and 'Small-Party' Politics." In *The Elections of 1996*, edited by Michael Nelson. Washington, D.C.: CQ Press.

Epstein, Edwin M. 1980. "Business and Labor under the Federal Election Campaign Act of 1971." In *Parties, Interest Groups, and Campaign Finance Laws*, edited by Michael J. Malbin. Washington, D.C.: American Enterprise Institute for Public Policy Research.

Epstein, Leon D. 1967. *Political Parties in Western Democracies*. New York: Praeger.

———. 1986. *Political Parties in the American Mold*. Madison: University of Wisconsin Press.

———. 1989. "Will American Political Parties Be Privatized?" *Journal of Law and Politics* 5:239.

———. 1991. "The Regulation of State Political Parties." In *Political Parties and Elections in the United States: An Encyclopedia*, edited by L. Sandy Maisel. New York: Garland.

Erie, Steven. 1988. *Rainbow's End: Irish-Americans and the Dilemmas of Urban Machine Politics, 1840–1985*. Berkeley: University of California Press.

Erikson, Robert S. 1981. "Why Do People Vote? Because They Are Registered." *American Politics Quarterly* 9:259.

Erikson, Robert S., Thomas D. Lancaster, and David W. Romero. 1989. "Group Components of the Presidential Vote, 1952–1984." *Journal of Politics* 51:337–46.

Evans, Diana. 1986. "PAC Contributions and Roll-Call Voting." In *Interest Groups and Politics*, edited by Allan Cigler and Burdett A. Loomis. Washington, D.C.: Congressional Quarterly Press.

Fenno, Richard F., Jr. 1972. "If, As Ralph Nader Says, Congress Is 'the Broken Branch,' How Come We Love Our Congressmen So Much?" Paper presented for discussion at the Harvard Club, Boston.

———. 1973. *Congressmen in Committees*. Boston: Little, Brown.

———. 1978. *Home Style: House Members in Their Own Districts*. Boston: Little, Brown.

———. 1984. *The United States Senate: A Bicameral Perspective*. Washington, D.C.: American Enterprise Institute for Public Policy Research.

Ferejohn, John A. 1977. "On the Decline of Competition in Congressional Elections." *American Political Science Review* 71:166–76.

Finer, Herman. 1949. *The Theory and Practice of Modern Government*. New York: Holt.

Fink, Leon. 1983. *Workingmen's Democracy: The Knights of Labor and American Politics*. Urbana: University of Illinois Press.

Finkel, Steven E., and Howard A. Scarrow. 1985. "Party Identification and Party Enrollment: The Difference and the Consequence." *Journal of Politics* 47:620–42.

Fiorina, Morris P. 1977a. "The Case of the Vanishing Marginals: The Bureaucracy Did It." *American Political Science Review* 71:177–81.

———. 1977b. "An Outline for a Model of Party Choice." *American Journal of Political Science* 21:601–25.

————. 1978. *Congress: Keystone of the Washington Establishment*. 4th ed. New Haven, Conn.: Yale University Press.

————. 1981. *Retrospective Voting in American National Elections*. New Haven, Conn.: Yale University Press.

————. 1996. *Divided Government*. 2d ed. Boston: Allyn and Bacon.

Fiorina, Morris P, with Samuel J. Abrams and Jeremy C. Pope. 2006. *Culture War? The Myth of a Polarized America*. 2d ed. New York: Pearson/Longman.

Firestone, David. 2003a. "Fate of Tax Credits Rests with Houses Divided." *New York Times*, June 16, A16.

————. 2003b. "GOP Moderates Show Signs of Strength." *New York Times*, March 31, A11.

————. 2003c. "Deal Offered on Child Tax Credit." *New York Times*, July, 23, A12.

Fishel, Jeff. 1977. "Agenda Building in Presidential Campaigns: The Case of Jimmy Carter." Paper presented at the annual meeting of the American Political Science Association, Washington, D.C.

————. 1985. *Presidents and Promises*. Washington, D.C.: Congressional Quarterly Press.

Foerstel, Karen. 2002a. "Campaign Finance Passage Ends a Political Odyssey." *Congressional Quarterly Weekly*, March 23, 799–803.

————. 2002b. "House Democratic Leadership to Undergo Complete Overhaul." *Congressional Quarterly Weekly*, June 1, 1449–52.

Forgette, Richard, and Glenn Platt. 2005. "Redistricting Principles and Incumbency Protection in the U.S. Congress." *Political Geography* 24: 934–51.

Forgette, Richard, and John W. Winkle III. 2006. "Partisan Gerrymandering and the Voting Rights Act." *Social Science Quarterly* 87:155–73.

Formisano, Ronald P. 1974. "Deferential-Participant Politics: The Early Republic's Political Culture, 1789–1890." *American Political Science Review* 68:473–87.

Fowler, Linda L. 1982. "How Interest Groups Select Issues for Rating Voting Records of Members of the U.S. Congress." *Legislative Studies Quarterly* 7:401–13.

Fowler, Linda L., and Robert McClure. 1989. *Political Ambition: Who Decides to Run for Congress*. New Haven, Conn.: Yale University Press.

Francia, Peter L., John C. Green, Paul S. Herrnson, Lynda W. Powell, and Clyde Wilcox. 2003. *The Financiers of Congressional Elections*. New York: Columbia University Press.

Frank, Barney. 1985. Personal Interview.

Frank, Thomas. 2004. *What's the Matter with Kansas?* New York: Metropolitan Books.

Franklin, Charles H. 1984. "Issues, Preferences, Socialization, and the Evolution of Party Identification." *American Journal of Political Science* 28:459–78.

Franklin, Charles H., and John E. Jackson. 1983. "The Dynamics of Party Identification." *American Political Science Review* 77:957–73.

Franz, Michael M., Joel Rivlin, and Kenneth Goldstein. 2006. "Much More of the Same: Television Advertising Pre- and Post-BCRA." In *The Elec-

tion after Reform, edited by Michael J. Malbin. Lanham, Md.: Rowman and Littlefield.

Frendeis, John P., James L. Gibson, and Laura L. Vertz. 1990. "The Electoral Relevance of Local Party Organization." *American Political Science Review* 84:225–35.

Frendeis, John P., and Richard Waterman. 1985. "PAC Contributions and Legislative Behavior: Senate Voting on Trucking Deregulation." *Social Science Quarterly* 66:401–12.

Frymer, Paul. 1994. "Ideological Consensus within Divided Government." *Political Science Quarterly* 109:287–312.

Gaddie, Robert Keith, and Charles S. Bullock III. 2000. *Elections to Open Seats in the U.S. House: Where the Action Is*. Lanham, Md.: Rowman & Littlefield.

Galderisi, Peter F., ed. 2005. *Redistricting in the New Millennium*. Lanham, Md.: Lexington Books.

Galloway, George B. 1961. *A History of the House of Representatives*. New York: Crowell.

Gans, Curtis B. 1990. "A Rejoinder to Piven and Cloward." *PS: Political Science and Politics* 23:175–78.

Gans, Herbert J. 1979. *Deciding What's News*. New York: Random House.

Gant, Michael M., and Norman R. Luttbeg. 1991. *American Electoral Behavior*. Itasca, Ill.: F. E. Peacock.

Garand, James C. 1991. "Electoral Marginality in State Legislative Elections, 1968–86." *Legislative Studies Quarterly* 16:7–28.

Geer, John G. 2006. *In Defense of Negativity*. Chicago: University of Chicago Press.

Gelman, Andrew, and Gary King. 1990. "Estimating the Electoral Consequences of Legislative Redistricting." *Journal of the American Statistical Politics* 85:274. (I found this in the *Journal of the American Statistical Association*, 85:274–82)

Germond, Jack, and Jules Witcover. 1985. *Wake Us When It's Over: Presidential Politics of 1984*. New York: Macmillan.

———. 1989. *Whose Broad Stripes and Bright Stars? The Trivial Pursuit of the Presidency, 1988*. New York: Warner Books.

———. 1993. *Mad as Hell: Revolt at the Ballot Box, 1992*. New York: Warner Books.

Gibson, James L. 1991. "County Party Organizations." In *Political Parties and Elections in the United States: An Encyclopedia*, edited by L. Sandy Maisel. New York: Garland.

Gibson, James L., Cornelius P. Cotter, John F. Bibby, and Robert J. Huckshorn. 1983. "Assessing Party Organizational Strength." *American Journal of Political Science* 27:193–222.

———. 1985. "Whither the Local Parties? A Cross-sectional Analysis and Longitudinal Analysis of the Strength of Party Organizations." *American Journal of Political Science* 29:139–60.

Gienapp, William E. 1987. *The Origins of the Republican Party, 1852–1856*. New York: Oxford University Press.

———. 1991. "The Formation of the Republican Party." In *The Encyclopedia of American Political Parties and Elections*, edited by L. Sandy Maisel. New York: Garland.

Gierzynski, Anthony. 1992. *Legislative Party Campaign Committees in the American States*. Lexington: University of Kentucky Press.

Gierzynski, Anthony, and David Breaux. 1990. "It's Money That Matters: The Role of Campaign Expenditures in State Legislative Primaries." Paper presented at the annual meeting of the American Political Science Association, San Francisco.

———. 1991. "Money and Votes in State Legislative Elections." *Legislative Studies Quarterly* 16:203–17.

Glaser, James. 1996. *Race, Campaign Politics in Realignment in the South*. New Haven, Conn.: Yale University Press.

Glazer, Amihai, Bernard Grofman, and Marc Robbins. 1987. "Partisan and Incumbency Effects of the 1970s Congressional Redistricting." *American Journal of Political Science* 31:680–707.

Goldenberg, Edie N., and Michael W. Traugott. 1984. *Campaigning for Congress*. Washington, D.C.: Congressional Quarterly Press.

Goldenberg, Edie N., Michael W. Traugott, and Frank R. Baumgartner. 1986. "Preemptive and Reactive Spending in U.S. House Races." *Political Behavior* 8:3–20.

Goldman, Peter, and Tony Fuller. 1985. *The Quest for the Presidency, 1984*. New York: Bantam.

Goldman, Ralph M. 1990. *The National Party Chairmen and Committees: Factionalism at the Top*. Armonk, N.Y.: Sharpe.

Gosnell, Harold. 1939. *Machine Politics: Chicago Model*. Chicago: University of Chicago Press.

Gottlieb, Stephen E. 1985. "Fleshing Out the Right of Association: The Problem of the Contribution Limits of the Federal Election Campaign Act." *Albany Law Review* 49:825.

———. 1991. "Buckley v. Valeo." In *Political Parties and Elections in the United States: An Encyclopedia*, edited by L. Sandy Maisel. New York: Garland.

Graber, Doris A. 1980. *Mass Media in American Politics*. Washington, D.C.: Congressional Quarterly Press.

———. 1982. *The President and the Public*. Philadelphia: Institute for the Study of Human Issues.

———. 1984a. *Mass Media and American Elections*. Washington, D.C.: Congressional Quarterly Press.

———. 1984b. *Media Power in Politics*. Washington, D.C.: Congressional Quarterly Press.

———. 1989. *Mass Media in American Politics*. 3d ed. Washington, D.C.: Congressional Quarterly Press.

———. 1990. *Media Power in Politics*. 2d ed. Washington, D.C.: Congressional Quarterly Press.

———. 2005. *Mass Media in American Politics*. 7th ed. Washington, D.C.: Congressional Quarterly Press.

———. 2006. *Media Power in Politics*. 5th ed. Washington, D.C.: Congressional Quarterly Press.

Graf, Joseph, Grant Reeher, Michael J. Malbin, and Costas Panagopoulos. 2006. *Small Donors and Online Giving*. Institute for Politics, Democracy, and the Internet and Campaign Finance Institute.

Grassmuck, George, ed. 1985. *Before Nomination: Our Primary Problem*. Washington, D.C.: American Enterprise Institute for Public Policy Research.

Green, Donald, and Jonathan Krasno. 1988. "Salvation for the Spendthrift Incumbent: Reestimating the Effects of Campaign Spending in House Elections." *American Journal of Political Science* 32:884–907.

Green, Donald, Bradley Palmquist, and Eric Schickler. 2002. *Partisan Hearts and Minds*. New Haven, Conn.: Yale University Press.

Green, John C., Mark J. Rozell, and Clyde Wilcox. 2006. *The Values Campaign?: The Christian Right and the 2004 Elections*. Washington, D.C.: Georgetown University Press.

Greenhouse, Linda. 2003. "Ban on Corporate Contributions Is Upheld." *New York Times*, June 17, online edition.

Greenhouse, Steven. 2006. "Labor Movement Dusts Off Agenda as Power Shifts in Congress." *New York Times*, November 11, A13.

Grenzke, Janet. 1989. "PACs in the Congressional Supermarket: The Currency Is Complex." *American Journal of Political Science* 33:1–24.

———. 1990. "Money and Congressional Behavior." In *Money, Elections, and Democracy: Reforming Congressional Campaign Finance*, edited by Margaret Latus Nugent and John R. Johannes. Boulder, Colo.: Westview.

Grofman, Bernard, ed. 1990. Political *Gerrymandering and the Courts*. New York: Agathon.

Gugliotta, Guy. 1998. "Going Where the Money Is." *Washington Post National Weekly Edition*, July 6, 12.

Hadley, Charles D. 1985. "Dual Partisan Identification in the South." *Journal of Politics* 47:254–68.

Halbfinger, David M. 2002. "Bush's Push, Volunteers and Big Turnout Led to Georgia Sweep." *New York Times*, November 10. (Section 1, p. 28)

Hallow, Ralph Z. 2007. "Bloomberg Poised for Third-Party Run." *Washington Times*, May 15, A01.

Handlin, Oscar. 1951. *The Uprooted*. New York: Grosset & Dunlap.

Heard, Alexander. 1960. *The Costs of Democracy*. Chapel Hill: University of North Carolina Press.

Herrnson, Paul S. 1988. *Party Campaigning in the 1980s*. Cambridge, Mass.: Harvard University Press.

———. 1990. "Reemergent National Party Organizations." In *The Parties Respond: Changes in the American Party System*, edited by L. Sandy Maisel. Boulder, Colo.: Westview.

———. 1991. "Campaign Professionalism and Fundraising in Congressional Elections." Unpublished manuscript, University of Maryland.

———. 1995. "Potential Research Policies for Political Science." *PS: Political Science and Politics* 28:492–94.

———. 1998a. *Congressional Elections: Campaigning at Home and in Washington*. 2d ed. Washington, D.C.: Congressional Quarterly Press.

———. 1998b. "National Party Organizations at the Century's End." In *The Parties Respond*, edited by L. Sandy Maisel. 3d ed. Boulder, Colo.: Westview.

———. 2000. *Congressional Elections: Campaigning at Home and in Washington*. 3d ed. Washington, D.C.: Congressional Quarterly Press.

———. 2002. "National Party Organizations at the Dawn of the 21st Century." In *The Parties Respond*, edited by L. Sandy Maisel. 4th ed. Boulder, Colo.: Westview.

Herrnson, Paul S., Ronald G. Shaiko, and Clyde Wilcox. 1998. *The Interest Group Connection: Engineering, Lobbying, and Policymaking in Washington*. Chatham, N.J.: Chatham House.

———. 2005. *The Interest Group Connection: Engineering, Lobbying, and Policymaking in Washington*, 2d ed. Washington, D.C.: CQ Press.

Hershey, Marjorie R. 1984. *Running for Office: The Political Education of Campaigners*. Chatham, N.J.: Chatham House.

Hetherington, Marc J. 2001. "Resurgent Mass Partisanship: The Role of Elite Polarization." *American Political Science Review* 95:619–31.

Hicks, Jonathan P. 1998. "Efforts to Get Voters to the Polls Are Feverish for Both Sides." *New York Times*, November 2, online edition.

Hill, David. 2006. *American Voter Turnout: An Institutional Perspective*. Boulder, Colo.: Westview.

Hill, David B., and Norman R. Luttbeg. 1980. *Trends in American Electoral Behavior*. Itasca, Ill.: F. E. Peacock.

Hinckley, Barbara. 1971. *The Seniority System in Congress*. Bloomington: Indiana University Press.

———. 1981. *Congressional Elections*. Washington, D.C.: Congressional Quarterly Press.

Hoffman, Kathy Barks. 1998. "Negative Ads Hurt Turnout—Or Increase It." *Detroit News*, October 17, online edition.

Hofstadter, Richard. 1955. *The Age of Reform: From Bryan to F.D.R.* New York: Knopf.

Holbrook, Thomas, and Charles Tidmarch. 1991. "Sophomore Surge in State Legislative Elections." *Legislative Studies Quarterly* 16:49–63.

Holbrook, Thomas, and Emily Van Dunk. 1993. "Electoral Competition in the American States." *American Political Science Review* 87 (December):955–63.

Huckshorn, Robert J. 1976. *Party Leadership in the States*. Amherst: University of Massachusetts Press.

———. 1991. "State Party Leaders." In *Political Parties and Elections in the United States: An Encyclopedia*, edited by L. Sandy Maisel. New York: Garland.

Huckshorn, Robert J., James L. Gibson, Cornelius P. Cotter, and John F. Bibby. 1986. "Party Integration and Party Organizational Strength." *Journal of Politics* 48:976–91.

Hulse, Carl. 2003. "Behind Clashes, Two Chambers That Don't Understand Each Other." *New York Times*, May 12, A18.

Hume, David. 1976. "The Philosophical Works of David Hume." In *Parties and Party Systems: A Framework for Analysis*, edited by Giovanni Sartori. New York: Cambridge University Press.

Hunter, James Davison. 1991. *Culture Wars: The Struggle to Define America*. New York: Basic Books.

Institute on Money in State Politics. 2004. *State Elections Overview 2002*. Helena, Mont.: Institute on Money in State Politics.

———. 2005. *State Elections Overview 2004*. Helena, Mont.: Institute on Money in State Politics.

Iyengar, Shanto, and Richard Reeves. 1997. *Do the Media Govern? Politicians, Voters, and Reporters in America*. Thousand Oaks, Calif.: Sage.

Jackman, Robert W. 1987. "Political Institutions and Voter Turnout in Industrial Democracies." *American Political Science Review* 81:405–24.

Jackson, Brooks. 1988. *Honest Graft*. New York: Knopf.

Jackson, John E. 1975. "Issues, Party Choices, and Presidential Votes." *American Journal of Political Science* 19:161–85.

Jacobson, Gary C. 1980. *Money in Congressional Elections*. New Haven, Conn.: Yale University Press.

———. 1981. "Congressional Elections, 1978: The Case of the Vanishing Challengers." In *Congressional Elections*, edited by L. Sandy Maisel and Joseph Cooper. Beverly Hills, Calif.: Sage.

———. 1983. *The Politics of Congressional Elections*. Boston: Little, Brown.

———. 1985a. "Congress: Politics after a Landslide without Coattails." In *The Elections of 1984*, edited by Michael Nelson. Washington, D.C.: Congressional Quarterly Press.

———. 1985b. "Parties and PACs in Congressional Elections." In *Congress Reconsidered*, edited by Lawrence D. Dodd and Bruce I. Oppenheimer. 3d ed. Washington, D.C.: Congressional Quarterly Press.

———. 1985–1986. "Party Organization and Distribution of Campaign Resources, Republicans and Democrats in 1982." *Political Science Quarterly* 100:603–25.

———. 1987a. "The Marginals Never Vanished: Incumbency and Competition in Elections to the U.S. House of Representatives, 1952–1982." *American Journal of Political Science* 31:126–41.

———. 1987b. *The Politics of Congressional Elections*. 2d ed. Boston: Little, Brown.

———. 1990a. "Divided Government, Strategic Politicians, and the 1990 Congressional Elections." Paper presented at the annual meeting of the Midwest Political Science Association, Chicago.

———. 1990b. "The Effects of Campaign Spending in House Elections: New Evidence for Old Arguments." *American Journal of Political Science* 34:334–62.

———. 1990c. *The Electoral Origins of Divided Government: Competition in U.S. House Elections, 1946–1988*. Boulder, Colo.: Westview.

———. 1991. "Financing Congressional Campaigns." In *Political Parties and Elections in the United States: An Encyclopedia*, edited by L. Sandy Maisel. New York: Garland.

———. 1992. *The Politics of Congressional Elections*, 3d ed. Boston: Little, Brown.

———. 1996. *The Politics of Congressional Elections*. 4th ed. New York: Longman.

———. 2001. *The Politics of Congressional Elections*. 5th ed. New York: Longman.

Jacobson, Gary C., and Samuel Kernell. 1983. *Strategy and Choice in Congressional Elections*. New Haven, Conn.: Yale University Press.

Jensen, Richard J. 1971. *The Winning of the Midwest: Social and Political Conflict, 1888–1896*. Chicago: University of Chicago Press.

Jewell, Malcolm E. 1984. *Parties and Primaries*. New York: Praeger.

Jewell, Malcolm E., and David Breaux. 1988. "The Effect of Incumbency on State Legislative Elections." *Legislative Studies Quarterly* 13:495–514.

———. 1991. "Southern Primary and Electoral Competition and Incumbent Success." *Legislative Studies Quarterly* 16:129–43.

Jewell, Malcolm E., and Sarah M. Morehouse. 2001. *Political Parties and Elections in American States*. Washington, D.C.: CQ Press.

Jewell, Malcolm E., and David M. Olson. 1982. *American State Political Parties and Elections*. Homewood, Ill.: Dorsey.

———. 1988. *Political Parties and Elections in American States*. 3d ed. Chicago: Dorsey.

Jewell, Malcolm E., and Marcia Lynn Whicker. 1998. *Legislative Leadership in the American States*. Ann Arbor: University of Michigan Press.

Johnson-Cartee, Karen S., and Gary W. Copeland. 1997. *Inside Political Campaigns: Theory and Practice*. Westport, Conn.: Praeger.

Jones, Charles O. 1988a. "Ronald Reagan and the U.S. Congress: Visible-Hand Politics." In *The Reagan Legacy*, edited by Charles O. Jones. Chatham, N.J.: Chatham House.

———. 1988b. *The Trusteeship Presidency: Jimmy Carter and the United States Congress*. Baton Rouge: Louisiana State University Press.

———, ed. 1988c. *The Reagan Legacy*. Chatham, N.J.: Chatham House.

Jones, Ruth S. 1980. "State Public Financing and the State Parties." In *Parties, Interest Groups, and Campaign Finance Laws*, edited by Michael J. Malbin. Washington, D.C.: American Enterprise Institute for Public Policy Research.

———. 1984. "Financing State Elections." In *Money and Politics in the United States: Financing Elections in the 1980s*, edited by Michael J. Malbin. Washington, D.C.: American Enterprise Institute for Public Policy Research.

———. 1991. "Financing State Campaigns." In *Political Parties and Elections in the United States: An Encyclopedia*, edited by L. Sandy Maisel. New York: Garland.

Jordan, Hamilton. 1982. *Crisis: The Last Year of Carter's Presidency*. New York: Putnam.

Kayden, Xandra. 1978. *Campaign Organization*. Lexington, Mass.: D. C. Heath.

Keller, Morton 1977. *Affairs of State: Public Life in Late Nineteenth Century America*. Cambridge, Mass.: Belknap Press.

———. 2003. "Money and Politics: The Long View." Forum 1, no. 1. Berkeley: Berkeley Electronic Press of the University of California.

Kerbel, Matthew Robert. 1998. *Remote and Controlled: Media Politics in a Cynical Age*. 2d ed. Boulder, Colo.: Westview.

Kernell, Samuel. 1977. "Presidential Popularity and Negative Voting: An Alternative Explanation of Midterm Congressional Decline of the President's Party." *American Political Science Review* 71:44–66.

Kessel, John H. 1984. *Presidential Campaign Politics: Coalition Strategies and Citizen Response*. 2d ed. Homewood, Ill.: Dorsey.

———. 1988. *Presidential Campaign Politics: Coalition Strategies and Citizen Response*. 3d ed. Homewood, Ill.: Dorsey.

———. 1992. *Presidential Campaign Politics: Coalition Strategies and Citizen Response*. 4th ed. Homewood, Ill.: Dorsey.

Key, V. O., Jr. 1949. *Southern Politics in State and Nation*. New York: Knopf.

———. 1955. "A Theory of Critical Elections." *Journal of Politics* 17:3–18.

———. 1956. *American State Politics*. New York: Knopf.

———. 1959. "Secular Realignment and the Party System." *Journal of Politics* 21:198–210.

———. 1964. *Politics, Parties, and Pressure Groups*. New York: Crowell.

———. 1966. *The Responsible Electorate*. Cambridge, Mass.: Harvard University Press.

Kinder, Donald R., and P. Roderick Kiewiet. 1979. "Economic Discontent and Political Behavior: The Role of Personal Grievances and Collective Economic Judgments in Congressional Voting." *American Journal of Political Science* 23:495–527.

King, Gary. 1989. "Representation through Legislative Redistricting: A Stochastic Model." *American Journal of Political Science* 33:787–824.

Kingdon, John W. 1984. *Agendas, Alternatives, and Public Policies*. Boston: Little, Brown.

Kirkpatrick, Jeane Jordan. 1976. *The New Presidential Elite: Men and Women in National Politics*. New York: Russell Sage Foundation.

———. 1978. *Dismantling the Parties*. Washington, D.C.: American Enterprise Institute for Public Policy Research.

Knack, Stephen. 1995. "Does 'Motor Voter' Work? Evidence from State-Level Data." *Journal of Politics* 57:796–812.

Kolodny, Robin. 1996. "The Contract with America in the 104th Congress." In *The State of the Parties*, edited by John C. Green and Daniel M. Shea. 2d ed. Lanham, Md.: Rowman & Littlefield.

———. 1998. *Pursuing Majorities: Congressional Campaign Committees in American Politics*. Norman: University of Oklahoma Press.

———. 1999. "Moderate Party Factions in the U.S. House of Representatives." In *The State of the Parties*, edited by John C. Green and Daniel M. Shea. 3d ed. Lanham, Md.: Rowman & Littlefield.

———. 2000. "Electoral Partnerships: Political Consultants and Political Parties." In *Campaign Warriors: Political Consultants in Elections*, edited by James A. Thurber and Candice J. Nelson. Washington, D.C.: Brookings Institution.

Kolodny, Robin, and Diana Dwyer. 2006. "A New Rule Book: Party Money after BCRA." In *Financing the 2004 Election*, edited by David B. Magleby, Anthony J. Corrado, and Kelly D. Patterson. Washington, D.C.: Brookings Institution.

Kramer, Gerald L. 1971. "Short-Term Fluctuations in U.S. Voting Behavior, 1896–1964." *American Political Science Review* 65:131–43.

Krasno, Jonathon S., and Donald Philip Green. 1988. "Pre-empting Quality Challengers in House Elections." *Journal of Politics* 50:920–36.

Kraus, Sidney. 1962. *The Great Debates: Kennedy vs. Nixon, 1960*. Bloomington: Indiana University Press.

Krehbiel, Keith. 1993. "Where's the Party?" *British Journal of Political Science* 23:235.

———. 1998. *Pivotal Politics: A Theory of U.S. Lawmaking*. Chicago: University of Chicago Press.

———. 1999. "The Party Effect from A to Z and Beyond." *Journal of Politics* 61:832–40.

Kurtz, Howard. 1998. "Attack Ads Carpet TV, Spinning the Issues." *Washington Post*, October 20, A1.

Ladd, Everett Carll, Jr. 1978. "The Shifting Party Coalitions: 1932–1976." In *Emerging Coalitions in American Politics*, edited by Seymour M. Lipset. San Francisco: Institute for Contemporary Studies.

———. 1991. *The American Polity: The People and Their Government*. New York: Norton.

Ladd, Everett Carll, Jr., and Charles D. Hadley. 1975. *Transformations of the American Party System*. Rev. ed. New York: Norton.

Lamis, Alexander. 1984. "The Runoff Primary Controversy: Implications for Southern Politics." *PS: Political Science and Politics* 17:782–87.

Lane, Charles, and Dan Balz. 2006. "Justices Affirm GOP Map for Texas." *Washington Post*, June 29, A1.

Lane, Robert E. 1959. *Political Life*. New York: Free Press.

Layman, Geoffrey. 2001. *The Great Divide: Religious and Cultural Conflict in American Party Politics*. New York: Columbia University Press.

Layman, Geoffrey C., and Thomas M. Carsey. 2002a. "Party Polarization and Party Structuring of Policy Attitudes: A Comparison of Three NES Panel Studies." *Political Behavior* 24:199–236.

———. 2002b. "Party Polarization and 'Conflict Extension' in the American Electorate." *American Journal of Political Science* 46:786–802.

Lazarsfeld, Paul F., Barnard Berelson, and Hazel Gaudet. 1944. *The People's Choice: How the Voter Makes Up His Mind in a Presidential Campaign*. New York: Columbia University Press.

Leege, David C., Kenneth D. Wald, Brian S. Krueger, and Paul D. Mueller. 2002. *The Politics of Cultural Differences*. Princeton, N.J.: Princeton University Press.

Lengle, James I., and Byron E. Shafer. 1980. *Presidential Politics*. New York: St. Martin's.

Light, Paul C. 1983. *The President's Agenda*. Baltimore, Md.: Johns Hopkins University Press.

Lowenstein, Daniel Hays. 1991a. "Campaign Finance and the Constitution." In *Political Parties and Elections in the United States: An Encyclopedia*, edited by L. Sandy Maisel. New York: Garland.

———. 1991b. "Legislative Districting." In *Political Parties and Elections in the United States: An Encyclopedia*, edited by L. Sandy Maisel. New York: Garland.

Luntz, Frank I. 1988. *Candidates, Consultants, and Campaigns*. Oxford, England: Blackwell.

Mackenzie, G. Calvin. 1990. "Partisan Presidential Leadership: The President's Appointees." In *The Parties Respond: Changes in the American Party System*, edited by L. Sandy Maisel. Boulder, Colo.: Westview.

———. 1998. "Partisan Presidential Leadership: The Presidents' Appointees." In *The Parties Respond: Changes in American Parties and Campaigns*, edited by L. Sandy Maisel. 3d ed. Boulder, Colo.: Westview.

———. 2002. "Partisan Presidential Leadership: The Presidents' Appointees." In *The Parties Respond: Changes in American Parties and Campaigns*, edited by L. Sandy Maisel. 4th ed. Boulder, Colo.: Westview.

Maestas, Cherie D., Sarah Fulton, L. Sandy Maisel, and Walter J. Stone. 2006. "When to Risk It? Institutions, Ambitions, and the Decision to Run for the U.S. House." *American Political Science Review* 100: 195–208.

Magleby, David B. 2006. "Change and Continuity in the Financing of Federal Elections." In *Financing the 2004 Election*, edited by David B. Magleby, Anthony J. Corrado, and Kelly D. Patterson. Washington, D.C.: Brookings Institution.

Magleby, David B., and Marjorie Holt, eds. 1999. *Outside Money: Soft Money and Issue Ads in Competitive 1998 Congressional Elections*. Provo, Utah: Brigham Young University.

Magleby, David B., and Candice J. Nelson. 1990. *The Money Chase*. Washington, D.C.: Brookings Institution.

Maisel, L. Sandy. 1982. *From Obscurity to Oblivion: Running in the Congressional Primary*. Knoxville: University of Tennessee Press.

———. 1986. *From Obscurity to Oblivion: Running in the Congressional Primary*. 2d ed. Knoxville: University of Tennessee Press.

———. 1988. "Spending Patterns in Presidential Nominating Campaigns, 1976–1988." Paper presented at the annual meeting of the American Political Science Association, Washington, D.C. Occasional Paper no. 88, Center for American Political Studies, Harvard University, Cambridge, Mass.

———. 1989. "Challenger Quality and the Outcome of the 1988 Congressional Elections." Paper presented at the annual meeting of the Midwest Political Science Association, Chicago.

———. 1990a. "Congressional Elections: Quality Candidates in House and Senate Elections, 1982–1988." Paper presented at the Back to the Future: The United States Congress at the Bicentennial Conference at the Carl Albert Congressional Research and Studies Center, University of Oklahoma, Norman.

———. 1990b. "The Incumbency Advantage." In *Money, Elections, and Democracy: Reforming Congressional Campaign Finance*, edited by Margaret Latus Nugent and John R. Johannes. Boulder, Colo.: Westview.

———. 1990c. *The Parties Respond: Changes in the American Party System*. Boulder, Colo.: Westview.

———. 1991. *Political Parties and Elections in the United States: An Encyclopedia*. New York: Garland.

———, ed. 1998. *The Parties Respond*. 3d ed. Boulder, Colo.: Westview.

———, ed. 2002. *The Parties Respond*. 4th ed. Boulder, Colo.: Westview.

Maisel, L. Sandy, and John F. Bibby. 2002. "Election Laws, Court Rulings, Party Rules and Practices: Steps Toward and Away From a Stronger Party Role." In *Responsible Partisanship? The Evolution of American Political Parties since 1950*, edited by John C. Green and Paul S. Herrnson. Lawrence: University Press of Kansas.

Maisel, L. Sandy, and Joseph Cooper. 1981. *Congressional Elections*. Beverly Hills, Calif.: Sage.

Maisel, L. Sandy, Linda L. Fowler, Ruth S. Jones, and Walter J. Stone. 1990. "The Naming of Candidates: Recruitment or Emergence." In *The Parties Respond: Changes in the American Party System*, edited by L. Sandy Maisel. Boulder, Colo.: Westview.

Maisel, L. Sandy, and Elizabeth J. Ivry. 1998. "If You Don't Like Our Politics, Wait a Minute: Party Politics in Maine at the Century's End." *Polity*. Supplement to the winter issue.

Maisel, L. Sandy, Walter J. Stone, and Cherie Maestas. 1999. "Re-evaluating the Definition of Quality Candidates: Evidence from the Candidate Emergence Study." Paper presented at the annual meeting of the Midwest Political Science Association, Chicago.

Maisel, L. Sandy, and Darrell West. 2004. *Running on Empty? Political Discourse in Congressional Elections*. Lanham, Md.: Rowman & Littlefield.

Malbin, Michael J. 1981. "The Conventions, Platforms, and Issue Activists." In *The American Elections of 1980*, edited by Austin Ranney. Washington, D.C.: American Enterprise Institute for Public Policy Research.

———. 1984a. "Looking Back at the Future of Campaign Finance Reform: Interest Groups and American Elections." In *Money and Politics in the United States: Financing Elections in the 1980s*, edited by Michael J. Malbin. Washington, D.C.: American Enterprise Institute for Public Policy Research.

———, ed. 1984b. *Money and Politics in the United States: Financing Elections in the 1980s*. Washington, D.C.: American Enterprise Institute for Public Policy Research.

———. 1985. "You Get What You Pay For, but Is That What You Want?" In *Before Nomination: Our Primary Problem*, edited by George Grassmuck. Washington, D.C.: American Enterprise Institute for Public Policy Research.

———. 2006. "A Public Funding System in Jeopardy: Lessons from the Presidential Nomination Contest of 2004." In *The Election after Reform*, edited by Michael J. Malbin. Lanham, Md.: Rowman and Littlefield.

Malbin, Michael J., and Sean Cain. 2007. "The Ups and Downs of Small Donors and Large." Washington, D.C.: Campaign Finance Institute.

Malbin, Michael J., and Thomas L. Gais. 1998. *The Day after Reform: Sobering Campaign Finance Lessons from the American States*. Albany, N.Y.: Rockefeller Institute Press.

Mann, Thomas E. 1985. "Elected Officials and the Politics of Presidential Selection." In *The American Elections of 1984*, edited by Austin Ranney. Durham, N.C.: Duke University Press.

Mann, Thomas E., and Raymond E. Wolfinger. 1980. "Candidates and Parties in Congressional Elections." *American Political Science Review* 74:617–32.

Marinucci, Carla. 2007. "Political Video Smackdown." *San Francisco Chronicle*. March 18, A-1.

Martinez, Gebe. 2003a. "Delay's Conservativism Solidifies GOP Base for Bush." *Congressional Quarterly Weekly*, July 12, 1726–33.

———. 2003b. "Despite Missteps, DeLay and Blunt Close Ranks, Stay Unified." *Congressional Quarterly Weekly*, July 12, 1731.

Mattei, Franco, and Richard G. Niemi. 1991. "Unrealized Partisans, Realized Independents, and the Intergenerational Transmission of Partisan Identification." *Journal of Politics* 53:161–74.

Matthews, Donald. 1960. *U.S. Senators & Their World*. New York: Vintage Books.

May, Ernest R., and Janet Fraser. 1973. *Campaign '72: The Managers Speak*. Cambridge, Mass.: Harvard University Press.

Mayhew, David R. 1974a. *Congress: The Electoral Connection*. New Haven, Conn.: Yale University Press.

———. 1974b. "Congressional Elections: The Case of the Vanishing Marginals." *Polity* 6:295–317.

———. 1986. *Placing Parties in American Politics*. Princeton, N.J.: Princeton University Press.

———. 1991. *Divided We Govern: Party Control, Lawmaking, and Investigations, 1946–1990*. New Haven, Conn.: Yale University Press.

———. 2005. *Divided We Govern*. 2d ed. New Haven, Conn.: Yale University Press.

Mazmanian, Daniel A. 1974. *Third Parties in Presidential Elections*. Washington, D.C.: Brookings Institution.

McAdams, John C., and John R. Johannes. 1981. "Does Casework Matter? A Reply to Professor Fiorina." *American Journal of Political Science* 25:581–604.

McClain, Paula D., and Joseph Stewart Jr. 1995. *Can We All Get Along? Racial and Ethnic Minorities in American Politics*. Boulder, Colo.: Westview.

———. 1999. *Can We All Get Along? Racial and Ethnic Minorities in American Politics*. 2d ed. Boulder, Colo.: Westview.

———. 2002. *Can We All Get Along? Racial and Ethnic Minorities in American Politics*. 3d ed. Boulder, Colo.: Westview.

———. 2006. *"Can We All Get Along?" Racial and Ethnic Minorities in American Politics*. 4th ed. Boulder, Colo.: Westview Press.

McCormick, Richard L. 1986. *The Party Period and Public Policy: American Politics from the Age of Jackson to the Progressive Era*. New York: Oxford University Press.

McDonald, Michael P., and Samuel L. Popkin. 2001. "The Myth of the Vanishing Voter." *American Political Science Review* 95:963–74.

McFarland, Andrew S. 1984. *Common Cause*. Chatham, N.J.: Chatham House.

McGinniss, Joe. 1969. *The Selling of the President 1968*. New York: Trident.

McKibben, Gordon. 1989. "AARP Takes One in the Chin in Congress." *Boston Globe*, October 15, A1.

Medvic, Stephen K., and Silvio Lenart. 1997. "The Influence of Political Consultants in the 1992 Congressional Elections." *Legislative Studies Quarterly* 22:61–77.

Merton, Robert K. 1957. *Social Theory and Social Structure*. New York: The Free Press.

Milbrath, Lester W., and M. L. Goel. 1977. *Political Participation: How and Why Do People Get Involved in Politics?* Chicago: Rand McNally.

Milburn, Michael, and Justin Brown. 1997. "Adwatch: Covering Campaign Ads." In *Politics and the Press: The News Media and Their Influence*, edited by Pippa Norris. Boulder, Colo.: Lynne Rienner.

Mileur, Jerome. 1991. "Party Renewal." In *Political Parties and Elections in the United States: An Encyclopedia*, edited by L. Sandy Maisel. New York: Garland.

Miller, Arthur H. 1978. "The Majority Party Reunited? A Comparison of the 1972 and 1976 Elections." In *Parties and Elections in an Anti-party Age*, edited by Jeff Fishel. Bloomington: Indiana University Press.

Miller, Arthur H., and Warren E. Miller. 1977. "Partisanship and Performance: 'Rational' Choice in the 1976 Presidential Elections." Paper presented at the annual meeting of the American Political Science Association, Washington, D.C.

Miller, Arthur H., Warren E. Miller, Aldern S. Raine, and Thad E. Brown. 1976. "A Majority Party in Disarray: Policy Polarization in the 1972 Election." *American Political Science Review* 70:753–78.

Miller, Arthur H., and Martin P. Wattenberg. 1985. "Throwing the Rascals Out: Policy and Performance Evaluations of Presidential Candidates, 1952–1980." *American Political Science Review* 79:359–72.

Miller, Warren E. 1990. "The Electorate's View of the Parties." In *The Parties Respond: Changes in the American Party System*, edited by L. Sandy Maisel. Boulder, Colo.: Westview.

———. 1991. "Party Identification, Realignment, and Party Voting: Back to Basics." *American Political Science Review* 85:557–68.

———. 1992. "The Puzzle Transformed: Explaining Declining Turnout." *Political Behavior* 14:1–43.

———. 1998. "Party Identification and the Electorate of the 1990s." In *The Parties Respond*, edited by L. Sandy Maisel. 3d ed. Boulder, Colo.: Westview.

Miller, Warren E., and J. Merrill Shanks. 1996. *The New American Voter*. Cambridge, Mass.: Harvard University Press.

Miller, Warren E., and Donald S. Stokes. 1963. "Constituency Influence in Congress." *American Political Science Review* 57:45–56.

Mitchell, Alison. 1998. "Just Whose Party Is It? A G.O.P. House Divided." *New York Times*, November 12, online edition.

Moberg, David. 1998. "Grass-Roots Politics in Comeback—With Winning Results." *Boston Sunday Globe*, June 14, A11.

Moncrief, Gary F., Peverill Squire, and Karl Kurtz. 1998. "Gateways to the Statehouse: Recruitment Patterns among State Legislative Candidates." Paper presented at the annual meeting of the American Political Science Association, Boston.

Mondak, Jeffrey J. 1995. "Competence, Integrity, and the Electoral Success of Congressional Incumbents." *Journal of Politics* 57:1043–69.

Monmonier, Mark. 2001. *Bushmanders and Bullwinkles*. Chicago: University of Chicago Press.

Monroe, Bill. 1990. "Covering the Real Campaign: TV Sports." *Washington Journalism Review*, October 6, 6.

Moore, Jonathan. 1981. *The Campaign for President: 1980 in Retrospect*. Cambridge, Mass.: Ballinger.

Moore, Jonathan, and Janet Fraser, eds. 1977. *Campaign for President: The Managers Look at 1976*. Cambridge, Mass.: Ballinger.

Morehouse, Sarah McCally, and Malcolm E. Jewell. 2003. *State Politics, Parties, and Policy*. 2d ed. Lanham, Md.: Rowman & Littlefield.

Mutch, Robert E. 1988. *Campaigns, Congress, and Courts: The Making of Federal Campaign Finance Laws*. New York: Praeger.

Myers, Randy. 2007. "Bloggers' Rants Draw Masses." *Contra Costa Times*, June 10.

Nader, Ralph. 1965. *Unsafe at Any Speed: The Designed-In Dangers of the American Automobile*. New York: Grossman.

Nather, David. 2003. "GOP Infighting: Not Fatal." *Congressional Quarterly Weekly*, May 31, 1309–10.

Neal, Terry M., and Paul Duggan. 1999. "Concerns in Bush Household." *Washington Post*, January 21, A8.

Nelson, Candice J. 1990. "Loose Cannons: Independent Expenditures." In *Money, Elections, and Democracy: Reforming Congressional Campaign Finance*, edited by Margaret Latus Nugent and John R. Johannes. Boulder, Colo.: Westview.

Nelson, Michael, ed. 1997. *The Elections of 1996*. Washington, D.C.: Congressional Quarterly Press.

———. 2005. *The Elections of 2004*. Washington, D.C.: Congressional Quarterly Press.

Neumann, Sigmund, ed. 1956. *Modern Political Parties: Approaches to Comparative Politics*. Chicago: University of Chicago Press.

Neustadt, Richard E. 1960. *Presidential Power: The Politics of Leadership*. New York: Wiley.

———. 1976. *Presidential Power: The Politics of Leadership with Reflections on Johnson and Nixon*. New York: Wiley.

Nie, Norman H., Sidney Verba, and John R. Petrocik. 1979. *The Changing American Voter*. Enl. ed. Cambridge, Mass.: Harvard University Press.

Niemi, Richard G., and Simon Jackson. 1991. "Bias and Responsiveness in State Legislative Districting." *Legislative Studies Quarterly* 16:183–202.

Niemi, Richard G., and Herbert F. Weisberg, eds. 1993. *Controversies in Voting Behavior*. 3d ed. Washington, D.C.: Congressional Quarterly Press.

———. 2001. *Controversies in Voting Behavior*. 4th ed. Washington, D.C.: Congressional Quarterly Press.

Niemi, Richard G., Stephen Wright, and Linda W. Powell. 1987. "Multiple Party Identifiers and the Measurement of Party Identification." *Journal of Politics* 49:1093–103.

Norris, Pippa, ed. 1997. *Politics and the Press: The News Media and Their Influence*. Boulder, Colo.: Lynne Rienner.

Oleszek, Walter J. 1989. *Congressional Procedures and the Policy Process*. 3d ed. Washington, D.C.: Congressional Quarterly Press.

Ornstein, Norman J. 1975. "Causes and Consequences of Congressional Change: Subcommittee Reforms in the House of Representatives." In *Congress in Change*, edited by Norman J. Ornstein. New York: Praeger.

Ornstein, Norman J., Thomas E. Mann, and Michael J. Malbin. 1998. *Vital Statistics on Congress*. Washington, D.C.: Congressional Quarterly.

———. 2002. *Vital Statistics on Congress*. Washington, D.C.: Congressional Quarterly.

Ornstein, Norman J., Thomas E. Mann, Michael J. Malbin, and John F. Bibby. 1982. *Vital Statistics on Congress*. Washington, D.C.: American Enterprise Institute.

Orren, Gary R., and Nelson W. Polsby. 1987. *Media and Momentum: The New Hampshire Primary and Nomination Politics*. Chatham, N.J.: Chatham House.

Overacker, Louise. 1932. *Money in Elections*. New York: Macmillan.

Parris, Judith. 1972. *The Convention Problem*. Washington, D.C.: Brookings Institution.

Parsons, Christi, and John McCormick. 2007. "'Crush on Obama' Is You-Tube Hit." *Chicago Tribune*, June 14, 1.

Patterson, Kelly D. 2006. "Spending in the 2004 Election." In *Financing the 2004 Election*, edited by David B. Magleby, Anthony J. Corrado, and Kelly D. Patterson. Washington, D.C.: Brookings Institution.

Patterson, Thomas E. 1980. *The Mass Media Election: How Americans Choose Their President*. New York: Praeger.

———. 1990. *The American Democracy*. New York: McGraw-Hill.

———. 1993. *Out of Order*. New York: Alfred A. Knopf.

Patterson, Thomas E., and Robert D. McClure. 1976. *The Unseeing Eye: The Myth of Television Power in National Politics*. New York: Putnam.

Penchoff, Jack. 2007. *Legislative Pay Daze*. Lexington, Ky.: Council of State Governments.

Perry, H. W., Jr. 1991. "Racial Vote Dilution Cases." In *Political Parties and Elections in the United States: An Encyclopedia*, edited by L. Sandy Maisel. New York: Garland.

Peters, Ronald M., Jr. 1990. *The American Speakership: The Office in Historical Perspective*. Baltimore, Md.: Johns Hopkins University Press.

Petracca, Mark P. 1989. "Political Consultants and Democratic Governance." *PS: Political Science and Politics* 22:11–14.

Petrocik, John R. 2004. "Hard Facts: The Media and Elections with a Look at 2000 and 2002." In *Campaigns and Elections American Style*, 2d ed., edited by James A. Thurber and Candice J. Nelson. Boulder, Colo.: Westview.

Pew Research Center. 2007a. "Election 2006 Online." Pew Internet and American Life Project, Washington, D.C.

Pew Research Center. 2007b. "What Americans Know: 1989-2007." Washington, D.C., April 15.

Pfau, Michael, and Henry C. Kenski. 1990. *Attack Politics: Strategy and Defense*. New York: Praeger.

Phillips, Cabell B. H. 1966. *The Truman Presidency: The History of a Triumphant Succession*. New York: Macmillan.

Piven, Frances Fox, and Richard A. Cloward. 1988. *Why Americans Don't Vote*. New York: Pantheon.

———. 1989. "Governmental Statistics and Conflicting Explanations of Nonvoting." *PS: Political Science and Politics* 22:580–88.

———. 1990. "A Reply to Bennett." *PS: Political Science and Politics* 23:172–73.

———. 2000. *Why Americans Still Don't Vote*. Boston: Beacon Press.

Polsby, Nelson W., ed. 1971. *Reapportionment in the 1970s*. Berkeley: University of California Press.

————. 1983. *Consequences of Party Reform*. New York: Oxford University Press.

————. 2002. "American Presidential Elections: The Last One and the Next One." *Forum* 1, no. 1. Berkeley: Berkeley Electronic Press, University of California, Berkeley.

Polsby, Nelson W., and Aaron Wildavsky. 1988. *Presidential Elections*. 7th ed. New York: Scribner.

————. 1991. *Presidential Elections*. 8th ed. New York: Scribner.

————. 1996. *Presidential Elections*. 9th ed. New York: Scribner.

————. 2000. *Presidential Elections*. 10th ed. Chatham, N.J.: Chatham House.

————. 2004. *Presidential Elections*. 11th ed. Lanham, Md.: Rowman and Littlefield.

Pomper, Gerald M. 1972. "From Confusion to Clarity: Issues and American Voters, 1952–1968." *American Political Science Review* 66:415–28.

————. 1973. *Elections in America*. New York: Dodd, Mead.

————. 1975. *Voter's Choice: Varieties of American Electoral Behavior*. New York: Dodd, Mead.

————. 1977. "The Nominating Contests and Conventions." In *The Election of 1976: Reports and Interpretations*, edited by Gerald M. Pomper. New York: McKay.

————, ed. 1981a. *The Election of 1980: Reports and Interpretations*. Chatham, N.J.: Chatham House.

————. 1981b. "The Nominating Contests." In *The Election of 1980: Reports and Interpretations*, edited by Gerald M. Pomper. Chatham, N.J.: Chatham House.

————, ed. 1985. *The Elections of 1984: Reports and Interpretations*. Chatham, N.J.: Chatham House.

————, ed. 1989a. *The Election of 1988: Reports and Interpretations*. Chatham, N.J.: Chatham House.

————. 1989b. "The Presidential Nominations." In *The Election of 1988: Reports and Interpretations*, edited by Gerald M. Pomper. Chatham, N.J.: Chatham House.

————, ed. 1993. *The Election of 1992*. Chatham, N.J.: Chatham House.

Pomper, Gerald M., with Susan S. Lederman. 1980. *Elections in America*. 2d ed. New York: Longman.

Powell, G. Bingham. 1986. "American Voter Turnout in Comparative Perspective." *American Political Science Review* 80:17–43.

President's Commission on Campaign Costs. 1962. *Financing Presidential Campaigns*. Washington, D.C.: Government Printing Office.

Price, David E. 1984. *Bringing Back the Parties*. Washington, D.C.: Congressional Quarterly Press.

Price, H. Douglas. 1971. "Congressional Careers—Then and Now." In *Congressional Behavior*, edited by Nelson W. Polsby. New York: Random House.

Purdum, Todd S., and David E. Rosenbaum. 2002. "Bush's Stumping for Candidates Is Seen as a Critical Factor in Republican Victories." *New York Times*, November 7, B4.

Putnam, Robert D. 2000. *Bowling Alone: The Collapse and Revival of American Community*. New York: Simon and Schuster.

Quirk, Paul J., and Jon K. Dalager. 1993. "The Election: A 'New Democrat' and a New Kind of Presidential Campaign." In *The Elections of 1996*, edited by Michael Nelson. Washington, D.C.: CQ Press.

Rakove, Milton L. 1975. *Don't Make No Waves . . . Don't Back No Losers*. Bloomington: Indiana University Press.

Ranney, Austin. 1975. *Curing the Mischiefs of Faction: Party Reform in America*. Berkeley: University of California Press.

———. 1979. *The Past and Future of Presidential Debates*. Washington, D.C.: American Enterprise Institute for Public Policy Research.

———, ed. 1985. *The American Elections of 1984*. Durham, N.C.: Duke University Press.

———. 1990. "Broadcasting, Narrowcasting, and Politics." In *The New American Political System*, edited by Anthony King. 2d ed. Washington, D.C.: American Enterprise Institute Press.

Rapoport, Ronald B., and Walter J. Stone. 2005. *Three's a Crowd: The Dynamic of Third Parties, Ross Perot, and Republican Resurgence*. Ann Arbor: University of Michigan Press.

Reichley, James. 1985. "The Rise of the National Parties." In *The New Directions in American Politics*, edited by John E. Clubb and Paul E. Peterson. Washington, D.C.: Brookings Institution.

———. 1992. *The Life of the Parties*. New York: Free Press.

Riordan, William L., ed. 1963. *Plunkitt of Tammany Hall*. New York: Dutton.

———. 1995. *Plunkitt of Tammany Hall: A Series of Very Plain Talks on Very Practical Politics*. New York: Signet.

Ripley, Randall B. 1964. "The Whip Organizations in the United States House of Representatives." *American Political Science Review* 58:561–76.

———. 1967. *Party Leaders in the House of Representatives*. Washington, D.C.: Brookings Institution.

Robinson, Michael, and Margaret Sheehan. 1983. *Over the Wire and on TV*. New York: Russell Sage Foundation.

Rogers, David. 2003. "Medicare Proposal Yields an Odd Couple." *Wall Street Journal*, June 16, A4.

Rohde, David W. 1974. "Committee Reform in the House of Representatives and the 'Subcommittee Bill of Rights.'" *Annals* 411:39–47.

———. 1991. *Parties and Leaders in the Post-reform House*. Chicago: University of Chicago Press.

Rosenbaum, David E. 2003. "Washington Talk: In a Test of Lobbying Muscle, Realtors Prevail." *New York Times*, July 13, online edition.

Rosenstone, Steven J., Roy L. Behr, and Edward H. Lazarus. 1984. *Third Parties in America: Citizen Response to Major Party Failure*. Princeton, N.J.: Princeton University Press.

Rosenstone, Steven J., and Raymond E. Wolfinger. 1978. "The Effect of Registration Laws on Voter Turnout." *American Political Science Review* 72:22–45.

Rothenberg, Stuart. 1983. *Winners and Losers: Campaigns, Candidates, and Congressional Elections*. Washington, D.C.: Free Congress Research and Education Foundation.

Royko, Mike. 1971. *Boss: Richard J. Daley of Chicago*. New York: Dutton.

Rozell, Mark J., and Clyde Wilcox, eds. 1995. *God at the Grass Roots: The Christian Right in the 1994 Elections*. Lanham, Md.: Rowman & Littlefield.

Runkel, David B., ed. 1989. *Campaign for President: The Managers Look at '88*. Dover, Mass.: Auburn House.

Rusk, Jerrold G. 1970. "The Effect of the Australian Ballot Reform on Split Ticket Voting: 1876-1908." *American Political Science Review* 64:1220–38.

———. 1974. "The American Electoral Universe: Speculation and Evidence." *American Political Science Review* 68:1028–49.

Sabato, Larry J. 1981. *The Rise of Political Consultants: New Ways of Winning Campaigns*. New York: Basic Books.

———. 1985. *PAC Power: Inside the World of Political Action Committees*. New York: Norton.

———. 1988. *The Party's Just Begun: Shaping Political Parties for America's Future*. Glenview, Ill.: Scott Foresman.

———. 1989. *Paying for Elections: The Campaign Finance Thicket*. New York: Priority Press Publications/Twentieth Century Fund.

———. 1991. *Feeding Frenzy: How Attack Journalism Has Transformed American Politics*. New York: Free Press.

Salmore, Stephen A., and Barbara G. Salmore. 1985. *Candidates, Parties, and Campaigns*. Washington, D.C.: Congressional Quarterly Press.

Samuelson, Robert J. 1999. "Network Fadeout." *Washington Post*, January 13, A23.

Sartori, Giovanni. 1976. *Parties and Party Systems: A Framework for Analysis*. Cambridge, Mass.: Cambridge University Press.

Schaffner, Brian F., Matthew Streb, and Gerald Wright. 2001. "Teams without Uniforms: The Nonpartisan Ballot in State and Local Elections." *Political Research Quarterly* 54:7–30.

Schattschneider, E. E. 1942. *Party Government*. New York: Holt, Rinehart, and Winston.

———. 1956. "United States: The Functional Approach to Party Government." In *Modern Political Parties*, edited by Sigmund Neumann. Chicago: University of Chicago Press.

———. 1960. *The Semisovereign People*. Hinsdale, Ill.: Dryden.

Schlesinger, Joseph A. 1966. *Ambition and Politics: Political Careers in the United States*. Chicago: Rand McNally.

———. 1985. "The New American Political Party." *American Political Science Review* 79:1152–69.

Schlozman, Kay L., and John T. Tierney. 1986. *Organized Interests and American Democracy*. New York: Harper and Row.

Schmitt, Eric. 2003. "Pressure on Senator for Blocking Promotions." *New York Times*, June 10, A23.

Schrag, Peter. 2003. "California Revolts, Again." *New York Times*, June 15. (Section 4, p. 6)

Schram, Martin. 1977. *Running for President, 1976: The Carter Campaign*. New York: Stein and Day.

Schroedel, Jean Reith. 1986. "Campaign Contributions and Legislative Outcomes." *Western Political Quarterly* 39:371–89.

Schuck, Peter H. 1987. "The Thickest Thicket: Partisan Gerrymandering and Judicial Regulation of Politics." *Columbia Law Review* 87:1325–84.

Seelye, Katharine, and Alison Mitchell. 2002. "Pocketing Soft Money Before the Pockets Are Sewn Up." *New York Times*, March 4, A1.

Seib, Philip. 1994. *Campaigns and Conscience: The Ethics of Political Journalism*. Westport, Conn.: Praeger.

Seligman, Lester. 1974. *Patterns of Recruitment: A State Chooses Its Lawmakers*. Chicago: Rand McNally.

Sender, Julie Bergman. 2007. *Viral Video in Politics*. Washington, D.C.: New Politics Institute

Shafer, Byron E. 1988. *Bifurcated Politics: Evolution and Reform in the National Nominating Convention*. Cambridge, Mass.: Harvard University Press.

Shafer, Byron E., and Richard Johnston. 2006. *The End of Southern Exceptionalism*. Cambridge, Mass.: 2006.

Shanks, J. Merrill, and Warren E. Miller. 1989. "Alternative Interpretations of the 1988 Election: Policy Direction, Current Conditions, Presidential Performance, and Candidate Traits." Paper presented at the annual meeting of the American Political Science Association, Atlanta, Ga.

———. 1990. "Policy Direction and Performance Evaluation: Contemporary Explanations of the Reagan Elections." *British Journal of Political Science* 20:143–235.

Shea, Daniel M. 1996. *Campaign Craft: The Strategies, Tactics, and Art of Campaign Management*. Westport, Conn.: Praeger.

———. 1999. "The Passing of Realignment and the Advent of the 'Base-Less' Party System." *American Politics Quarterly* 27:33–57.

Sheppard, Burton D. 1985. *Rethinking Congressional Reform*. Cambridge, Mass.: Schenkman.

Shribman, David. 1999. "National Perspective." *Boston Globe*, February 16, A3.

Sigelman, Lee. 1982. "The Nonvoting Voter in Voting Research." *American Journal of Political Science* 26:47–56.

Silbey, Joel H. 1990. "The Rise and Fall of American Political Parties." In *The Parties Respond: Changes in the American Party System*, edited by L. Sandy Maisel. Boulder, Colo.: Westview.

———. 1991. *The American Political Nation, 1838–1893*. Stanford, Calif.: Stanford University Press.

———. 1994. *Encyclopedia of the American Legislative System: Studies of the Principal Structures, Processes, and Policies of Congress and the State Legislatures since the Colonial Era*. New York: Scribner's.

———. 1998. "From 'Essential to the Existence of Our Institutions' to 'Rapacious Enemies of Honest and Responsible Government': The Rise and Fall of American Parties, 1790–2000." In *The Parties Respond*, edited by L. Sandy Maisel. 3d ed. Boulder, Colo.: Westview.

———. 2002. "From 'Essential to the Existence of Our Institutions' to 'Rapacious Enemies of Honest and Responsible Government': The Rise and Fall of American Parties, 1790–2000." In *The Parties Respond*, edited by L. Sandy Maisel. 4th ed. Boulder, Colo.: Westview.

Simon, Roger. 1998. *Show Time: The American Presidential Circus and the Race for the White House*. New York: Times Books.

Sinclair, Barbara. 1983. *Majority Party Leadership in the U.S. House*. Baltimore, Md.: Johns Hopkins University Press.

———. 1989. *The Transformation of the U.S. Senate*. Baltimore, Md.: Johns Hopkins University Press.

———. 1990. "The Congressional Party: Evolving Organizational, Agenda Setting, and Policy Roles." In *The Parties Respond: Changes in the American Party System*, edited by L. Sandy Maisel. Boulder, Colo.: Westview.

———. 1995. *Legislators, Leaders, and Lawmaking: The U.S. House of Representatives in the Postreform Era*. Baltimore, Md.: Johns Hopkins University Press.

———. 1998. "Evolution or Revolution? Policy-Oriented Congressional Parties in the 1990s." In *The Parties Respond*, edited by L. Sandy Maisel. 3d ed. Boulder, Colo.: Westview.

———. 2006. *Party Wars: Polarization and the Politics of National Policy Making*. Norman: University of Oklahoma Press.

Smith, Lauren. 2006. "Moderates Still Wield Power in Congress." *Bangor Daily News*, November 30.

Smith, Steven S., and Christopher J. Deering. 1990. *Committees in Congress*. 2d ed. Washington, D.C.: Congressional Quarterly Press.

Smolkin, Rachel. 2007. "What the Mainstream Media Can Learn from Jon Stewart." *American Journalism Review*, June/July.

Snowiss, Leo M. 1966. "Congressional Recruitment and Representation." *American Political Science Review* 60:627–39.

Sorauf, Frank J. 1980. *Party Politics in America*. Boston: Little, Brown.

———. 1984. "Political Action Committees in American Politics: An Overview." In *What Price PACs?* New York: Twentieth Century Fund.

———. 1988. *Money in American Elections*. Glenview, Ill.: Scott, Foresman.

———. 1991. "Political Action Committees." In *Political Parties and Elections in the United States: An Encyclopedia*, edited by L. Sandy Maisel. New York: Garland.

———. 1998. "Political Parties and the New World of Campaign Finance." In *The Parties Respond*, edited by L. Sandy Maisel. 3d ed. Boulder, Colo.: Westview.

Southwell, Priscilla, and Justin Burchett. 1997. "Survey of Vote-by-Mail Senate Election in the State of Oregon." *PS: Political Science and Politics* 30 (March):53–58.

Sparks, Jared, ed. 1840. *The Writings of George Washington*. Boston: F. Andrews.

Squire, Peverill, Raymond E. Wolfinger, and David P. Glass. 1987. "Residential Mobility and Voter Turnout." *American Political Science Review* 81:45–66.

Stanley, Harold W. 1985. "The Runoff: The Case for Retention." *PS: Political Science and Politics* 18:231–36.

Stanley, Harold W., William T. Bianco, and Richard G. Niemi. 1986. "Partisanship and Group Support over Time: A Multivariate Analysis." *American Political Science Review* 80:969–76.

Stanley, Harold W., and Richard G. Niemi. 2006a. *Vital Statistics on American Politics*. Washington, D.C.: Congressional Quarterly Press.

———. 2006b. "Partisanship, Party Coalitions, and Group Support, 1952-2004," *Presidential Studies Quarterly* 36:172–88.

Stein, Robert M., and Patricia Garcia-Monet. 1997. "Voting Early but Not Often." *Social Science Quarterly* 78 (September):657–72.

Steinberg, Alfred. 1972. *The Bosses*. New York: Macmillan.

Stern, Philip M. 1988. *The Best Congress Money Can Buy*. New York: Pantheon Books.

Stevens, Allison, and Andrew Taylor. 2003. "Frist Faced with Deep Party Rift after Charge of Double Dealing." *Congressional Quarterly Weekly*, April 19, 931–34.

Stewart, John G. 1991. "Democratic National Committee." In *Political Parties and Elections in the United States: An Encyclopedia*, edited by L. Sandy Maisel. New York: Garland.

Stokes, Donald E., and Warren E. Miller. 1962. "Party Government and the Saliency of Congress." *Public Opinion Quarterly* 26:531–46.

Stolberg, Sheryl Gay. 2003a. "House Approves Bill Easing Imports of Less Expensive Drugs." *New York Times*, July 25.

———. 2003b. "House Passes Drug Measure, but Faces Fight with Senate." *New York Times*, July 26.

Stolberg, Sheryl Gay, and Gardiner Harris. 2003. "Bill to Ease Imports of Less Expensive Drugs Gains in House." *New York Times*, July 22.

Stone, Walter J., and L. Sandy Maisel. 2003. "The Not-So-Simple Calculus of Winning: Potential U.S. House Candidates' Nomination and General Election Prospects." *Journal of Politics* 65:951–77.

Stone, Walter J., L. Sandy Maisel, and Cherie Maestas. 1998. "Candidate Emergence in U.S. House Elections." Paper presented at the annual meeting of the American Political Science Association, Boston.

———. 2004. "Quality Counts: Extending the Strategic Politician Model of Incumbent Deterrence." *American Journal of Political Science* 48: 479–95.

Stone, Walter J., L. Sandy Maisel, Cherie Maestas, and Sean Evans. 1998. "Candidate Quality in U.S. House Elections: Candidate Emergence in the 1998 Elections." Paper presented at the annual meeting of the Midwest Political Science Association, Chicago.

Stonecash, Jeffrey M. 2000. *Class and Party in American Politics*. Boulder, Colo.: Westview.

———. 2003. *Political Polling: Strategic Information in Campaigns*. Lanham, MD: Rowman and Littlefield.

———. 2006. *Political Parties Matter: Realignment and the Return of Partisan Voting*. Boulder, Colo.: Lynne Rienner.

———. Forthcoming. *The Incumbency Effect?*

Stonecash, Jeffrey M., Mark D. Brewer, and Mack D. Mariani. 2003. *Diverging Parties*. Boulder, Colo.: Westview.

Sullivan, Denis G., Robert T. Nakamura, Martha Wagner Weinberg, F. Christopher Arterton, and Jeffrey L. Pressman. 1977–1978. "Exploring the 1976 Republican Convention." *Political Science Quarterly* 92:633–34.

Sullivan, Denis G., Jeffrey L. Pressman, and F. Christopher Arterton. 1976.

Explorations in Convention Decision Making: The Democratic Party in the 1970s. San Francisco: Freeman.

Sullivan, Denis G., Jeffrey L. Pressman, F. Christopher Arterton, Robert T. Nakamura, and Martha Wagner Weinberg. 1977. "Candidates, Caucuses, and Issues: The Democratic Convention, 1976." In *The Impact of the Electoral Process*, edited by Louis Maisel and Joseph Cooper. Beverly Hills, Calif.: Sage.

Sundquist, James L. 1983. *Dynamics of the Party System: Alignment and Realignment of Political Parties in the United States.* Rev. ed. Washington, D.C.: Brookings Institution.

———. 1988. "Needed: A Political Theory for the New Era of Coalition Government in the United States." *Political Science Quarterly* 103:613–35.

———. 1993. *Beyond Gridlock? Prospects for Governance in the Clinton Years—and After.* Rev. ed. Washington, D.C.: Brookings Institution

Taggart, William A., and Robert F. Durant. 1985. "Home Style of a U.S. Senator: A Longitudinal Study." *Legislative Studies Quarterly* 10:489–504.

Tarrance, V. Lance. 1978. "Suffrage and Voter Turnout in the United States: The Vanishing Voter." In *Parties and Elections in an Anti-party Age*, edited by Jeff Fishel. Bloomington: Indiana University Press.

Teixeira, Ruy. 1987. *Why Americans Don't Vote.* New York: Greenwood.

———. 1992. *The Disappearing American Voter.* Washington, D.C.: Brookings Institution.

Thayer, George. 1973. *Who Shakes the Money Tree?* New York: Simon and Schuster.

Thompson, Hunter. 1973. *Fear and Loathing: On the Campaign Trail '72.* New York: Quick Fox.

Thurber, James A., and Candice J. Nelson. 2000. *Campaign Warriors: Political Consultants in Elections.* Washington, D.C.: Brookings Institution.

Timpone, Richard. 1998. "Structure, Behavior, and Voter Turnout in the United States." *American Political Science Review* 92:145–58.

Tolchin, Martin, and Susan Tolchin. 1971. *To the Victor . . . Political Patronage from the Clubhouse to the White House.* New York: Vintage Books.

Tolchin, Susan J. 1999. *The Angry American: How Voter Rage Is Changing the Nation.* 2d ed. Boulder, Colo.: Westview.

Traugott, Michael W. 1985. "The Media and the Nominating Process." In *Before Nomination: Our Primary Problem*, edited by George Grassmuck. Washington, D.C.: American Enterprise Institute for Public Policy Research.

Truman, David B. 1951. *The Governmental Process.* New York: Knopf.

Tufte, Edward E. 1975. "Determinants of the Outcomes of Midterm Congressional Elections." *American Political Science Review* 69:812–26.

———. 1978. *Political Control of the Economy.* Princeton, N.J.: Princeton University Press.

Usher, Douglas L. 1998. "Party Institutions and Issue Activist Strength." Unpublished manuscript, Cornell University.

Vargas, Jose Antonio. 2007. "Online, GOP Is Playing Catch-up." *Washington Post*, May 21.

Verba, Sidney, and Norman H. Nie. 1972. *Participation in America: Political Democracy and Social Equality*. New York: Harper and Row.

Verba, Sidney, Kay Lehman Schlozman, and Henry Brady. 1995. *Voice and Equality: Civic Voluntarism in American Politics*. Cambridge, Mass.: Harvard University Press.

Walker, Jack L. 1983. "The Origins and Maintenance of Interest Groups in America." *American Political Science Review* 77:390–406.

Wattenberg, Martin P. 1984. *The Decline of American Political Parties, 1952–1980*. Cambridge, Mass.: Harvard University Press.

———. 1986. *The Decline of American Political Parties, 1952–1984*. Cambridge, Mass.: Harvard University Press.

———. 1990. *The Decline of American Political Parties, 1952–1988*. Cambridge, Mass.: Harvard University Press.

———. 1994. *The Decline of American Political Parties, 1952–1992*. Cambridge, Mass.: Harvard University Press.

———. 1996. *The Decline of American Political Parties, 1952–1994*. Cambridge, Mass.: Harvard University Press.

———. 1998. *The Decline of American Political Parties, 1952–1996*. Cambridge, Mass.: Harvard University Press.

Waxman, Seth. 2002. "Free Speech and Campaign Finance Reform Don't Conflict." *New York Times*, July 10, online edition.

Wayne, Stephen J. 1984. *The Road to the White House: The Politics of Presidential Elections*. 2d ed. New York: St. Martin's.

———. 1988. *The Road to the White House: The Politics of Presidential Elections*. 3d ed. New York: St. Martin's.

———. 1992. *The Road to the White House: The Politics of Presidential Elections*. 4th ed. New York: St. Martin's.

———. 1996. *The Road to the White House, 1996*. New York: St. Martin's.

———. 2000. *The Road to the White House, 2000*. New York: St. Martin's.

———. 2004. *The Road to the White House, 2004*. Belmont, Calif.: Wadsworth/Thomson.

Weber, Ronald, Harvey Tucker, and Paul Brace. 1991. "Vanishing Marginals in State Legislative Elections." *Legislative Studies Quarterly* 16:29–47.

Weil, Gordon L. 1973. *The Long Shot*. New York: Norton.

Weisbrot, Robert S. 1990. *Freedom Bound*. New York: Norton.

Weissman, Stephen R. 2005. Remarks at the Campaign Finance Institute Campaign Finance Reform Forum, National Press Club, Washington, D.C., January 14.

Weissman, Stephen R., and Ruth Hassan. 2006. "BCRA and the 527 Groups." In *The Election after Reform*, edited by Michael J. Malbin. Lanham, Md.: Rowman and Littlefield.

Weissman, Stephen R., and Kara D. Ryan. 2007. "Soft Money in the 2006 Election and the Outlook for 2008." Washington, D.C.: Campaign Finance Institute.

White, Theodore H. 1961. *The Making of the President, 1960*. New York: Atheneum.

———. 1965. *The Making of the President, 1964*. New York: Atheneum.

———. 1969. *The Making of the President, 1968*. New York: Atheneum.

———. 1973. *The Making of the President, 1972*. New York: Atheneum.

———. 1982. *America in Search of Itself: The Making of the President, 1956–1980*. New York: Harper and Row.

Wilcox, Clyde. 1988. "I Owe It All to Me: Candidates' Investments in Their Own Campaigns." *American Politics Quarterly* 16:266–79.

———. 1996. *Onward Christian Soldiers? The Religious Right in American Politics*. Boulder, Colo.: Westview

———. 2000. *Onward Christian Soldiers*. 2d ed. Boulder, Colo.: Westview Press.

Williamson, Jonathan. 1999. "Supply-Side of Southern Politics: Candidate Quality and Candidate Emergence in House Elections." Paper presented at the annual meeting of the Midwest Political Science Association, Chicago.

Wilson, James Q. 1962. *The Amateur Democrat*. Chicago: University of Chicago Press.

———. 1973. *Political Organizations*. New York: Basic Books.

Wilson, Scott. 1998. "Negative Ads Fill the Air in Maryland; Unprecedented Hostility Marks the Governor's Race." *Washington Post*, October 27, A1.

Wilson, Woodrow. 1885. *Congressional Government*. Boston: Houghton Mifflin.

Wirthlin, Richard B. 1981. "The Republican Strategy and Its Electoral Consequences." In *Party Coalitions in the 1980s*, edited by Seymour Martin Lipset. San Francisco: Institute for Contemporary Studies.

Witcover, James. 1977. *Marathon: The Pursuit of the Presidency, 1972–1976*. New York: Viking.

Wolfinger, Raymond E., and Jonathon Hoffman. 2001. "Registering and Voting with Motor Voter." *PS: Political Science and Politics* 34:85–92.

Wolfinger, Raymond E., and Steven J. Rosenstone. 1980. *Who Votes?* New Haven, Conn.: Yale University Press.

Wolpe, Bruce C., and Bertram J. Levine. 1996. *Lobbying Cogress: How the System Works*. 2d edition. Washington, D.C.: Congressional Quarterly.

Wright, John R. 1985. "PACs, Contributions, and Roll Calls: An Organizational Perspective." *American Political Science Review* 79:400–14.

———. 1996. *Interest Groups and Congress: Lobbying, Contributions, and Influence*. Needham Heights, Mass.: Simon and Schuster.

Young, James. 1966. *The Washington Community*. New York: Harcourt, Brace and World.

Zaller, John. 1998. "Politicians as Prize Fighters: Electoral Selection and Incumbency Advantage." In *Politicians and Party Politics*, edited by John G. Gear. Baltimore, Md.: Johns Hopkins University Press.

Credits

Chapter 1: 1 Balloons and confetti fall from the ceiling of the United Center in Chicago as Bill Clinton completes his speech accepting the Democratic Party's nomination to run for reelection as president of the United States, August 29, 1996. AP Photo/Robert F. Bukaty.

Chapter 2: 27 A classic New England fall setting marks Election Day in Hopkinton, New Hampshire, November 2, 2004. AP Photo/Lee Marriner. **44** "That's What's the Matter." 1871. Thomas Nast, *Harper's Weekly*.

Chapter 3: 71 Young people demonstrate at a Republican rally featuring Vice President Dick Cheney at Allegheny College in Meadville, Pennsylvania, in 2004. Photo: Bill Owen. **87** "I don't know and I don't care." © Gary Markstein, *Milwaukee Journal Sentinel*. Reprinted with permission of Copley News Service.

Chapter 4: 119 AFL-CIO member and election volunteer John Michalec mans a phone bank at the AFL-CIO's Michigan headquarters in Lansing, Michigan, November 2, 2006. AP Photo/Al Goldis. **147** "Go ahead, bite the hand that feeds us!" M. Wuerker, Politico.com.

Chapter 5: 149 Rep. Marty Meehan, D-Mass. (left), Sen. John McCain, R-Ariz., and Sen. Russ Feingold, D-Wis. (right), descend the Supreme Court steps, September 8, 2003, following special arguments in a challenge to campaign finance reform legislation. AP Photo/Dennis Cook. **188** "I swear . . . if I see one more 527 ad . . ." 2004. Mike Keefe, *The Denver Post*.

Chapter 6: 195 State Senator Rodney Ellis steps out of a meeting of Texas Democratic Senators, August 1, 2003, in Albuquerque,

Index

Note: Page numbers in bold type indicate that the term is defined in a sidebar. Figures, illustrations, and tables are denoted by *f*, *i*, or *t*, respectively, following page numbers.

About the Authors

L. Sandy Maisel is the William R. Kenan, Jr., Professor of Government, chair of the Department of Government, and director of the Goldfarb Center for Public Affairs and Civic Engagement at Colby College.

Mark D. Brewer is assistant professor of political science at the University of Maine.